D1093851

CULTURGRAMS:

The Nations around Us

Produced by the
David M. Kennedy Center
for International Studies

Brigham Young University

Volume I

The Americas and Europe

About the Culturgram Series...

This book (Volume I) includes *Culturgrams* for the Americas and Europe.

A related volume (Volume II) includes *Culturgrams* for Africa, Asia, and Oceania.

Bound volumes of *Culturgrams* may be ordered from Ferguson Publishing Company, 200 West Madison Street, Suite 300, Chicago, IL 60606; phone (800) 306–9941; fax (800) 306–9942, or Brigham Young University, David M. Kennedy Center for International Studies, PO Box 24538, Provo, UT 84602–4538; phones (800) 528–6279 and (801) 378–6528; fax (801) 378–5882. The internet address is: http://www.byu.edu/culturgrams. The prices for Volume I are $35.00 for education and nonprofit groups, $50.00 retail for profit-making organizations. The prices for Volume II are $40.00 for education and nonprofit groups, $65.00 retail for profit-making organizations.

Because the reproduction of the *Culturgrams* in this volume is strictly prohibited, copies should be ordered directly from Kennedy Center Publications. *Culturgrams* are currently available as a complete set (both bound and loose-leaf), as area and language sets, and individually. To order, contact Kennedy Center Publications at the address above.

Library of Congress Cataloging-in-Publication Data

Culturgrams : the nations around us /
developed by the David M. Kennedy Center for International Studies, Brigham Young University. 2 v. : maps : 28 cm.

ISBN 0-89434-191-X (set)

Contents: v. 1. The Americas and Europe — v. 2. Africa, Asia, and Oceania.

1. Manners and customs. 2. Intercultural communication. I. David M. Kennedy Center for International Studies.

GT150.C85 1993
390—dc20   93-29643

David M. Kennedy Center for International Studies,
Grant P. Skabelund, Managing Editor; Susan M. Sims, Editor; Lisa M. Ralph and Amy L. Andrus, Associate Editors.

ISBN 0-89434-189-8

Library of Congress Card 93-29643 (for set)

Contents

Foreword iv

Introduction v

Culturgram Glossary vii

Culturgrams:

Albania 1

Antigua and Barbuda 5

Argentina 9

Austria 13

Barbados 17

Belgium 21

Belize 25

Bolivia 29

Brazil 33

Bulgaria 37

Canada (Atlantic) 41

Canada (Ontario & West) 45

Canada (Québec) 49

Chile 53

Colombia 57

Costa Rica 61

Croatia 65

Cuba 69

Czech Republic 73

Denmark 77

Dominican Republic 81

Ecuador 85

El Salvador 89

England 93

Estonia 97

Finland 101

France 105

Georgia 109

Germany 113

Greece 117

Grenada 121

Guatemala 125

Guyana 129

Honduras 133

Hungary 137

Iceland 141

Ireland 145

Ireland, Northern 149

Italy 153

Jamaica 157

Liechtenstein 161

Lithuania 165

Luxembourg 169

Mexico 173

Moldova 177

Montserrat 181

Netherlands 185

Nicaragua 189

Norway 193

Panama 197

Paraguay 201

Peru 205

Poland 209

Portugal 213

Puerto Rico 217

Romania 221

Russia 225

Saint Kitts and Nevis 229

Saint Lucia 233

Scotland 237

Serbia and Montenegro 241

Slovakia 245

Slovenia 249

Spain 253

Sweden 257

Switzerland 261

Turkey 265

Ukraine 269

United States of America 273

Uruguay 277

Venezuela 281

Wales 285

Foreword

For years the best-known introduction of many Americans to many foreign countries has come by way of the four-page *Culturgrams* prepared and distributed by the David M. Kennedy Center for International Studies at Brigham Young University in Provo, Utah. Millions of these simple, straightforward handouts have been distributed to Americans in all levels of our society and by all types of organizations.

Culturgrams are particularly useful because they put so much emphasis on the unique values, customs, and cultural assumptions of the people they describe. One can find the population statistics or the square mileage of the country from many other standard sources, but the "people maps" are much more difficult to locate. I believe this is why *Culturgrams* remain at the top of the list in people's minds, and this is what justifies their continuing success as the most widely distributed publications explaining the customs and traditions of the world's peoples.

With a high concern for accuracy and current validity of the data *Culturgrams* contain, Kennedy Center Publications keeps the reports up-to-date and continues to add more countries to their expanding coverage.

The inclusion of the set in two bound volumes (*Culturgrams: The Nations around Us*, Volumes I and II) places a wealth of information about more than 150 countries in a single repository, so that those who need handy access to such data will be able to keep the book within reach of their desk.

I sincerely hope new editions of *Culturgrams: The Nations around Us* will continue to be forthcoming well into the 21st century.

L. Robert Kohls
Scholar in Residence
Institute for Intercultural Leadership

Introduction

In 1974, President Spencer W. Kimball of the Church of Jesus Christ of Latter-day Saints issued a challenge to Mormons to build more effective bridges of understanding and friendship with people all over the world. Brigham Young University contributed to the effort by inviting people from about 50 countries to share what they thought was essential information about their country and its people. These interviews laid the foundation for *Culturgrams*, which were first published by BYU's Language and Intercultural Research Center and were later transferred to the David M. Kennedy Center for International Studies (1981).

The 1996–97 edition consists of 154 *Culturgrams*. Included in both volumes is a glossary; it contains some of the concepts used throughout *Culturgrams*. Also part of this edition are 11 new *Culturgrams*. Volume I of *The Nations around Us* now includes Albania, Guyana, Saint Kitts and Nevis, and Slovenia. Volume II now contains Burkina Faso, Kyrgyzstan, Mauritania, Namibia, Swaziland, Tajikistan, and United Arab Emirates. In addition, for the first time, Turkey is included in Volume I and Russia in Volume II. Our readers suggested these two countries, which straddle Asia and Europe geographically and culturally, be included in both volumes. We concurred with their feedback by instituting the change.

Each four-page *Culturgram* introduces the reader to the daily customs and lifestyle of a society, as well as its political and economic structure. Each text represents the efforts of individuals from all over the world who have lived and worked in that country. Kennedy Center Publications requests and receives input from scholars within the target culture, U.S. and European academics, volunteers from organizations such as the Peace Corps and International Red Cross, expatriate diplomats and businesspeople, educators, and many others.

This approach allows the Center to take advantage of a wide variety of perspectives and professional backgrounds to bring our readers a unique look at daily life around the globe. It also means that *Culturgrams* contain information based as much on opinion as fact. *Culturgrams* do not focus on statistical data. Other resources present country statistics, but none tells a reader about people on a personal level. Our goal is to present the people of a culture to the reader, thus encouraging understanding and appreciation between people of different nationalities.

Each new *Culturgram* is written by someone who meets certain residence, educational, and professional criteria. The draft is reviewed by a panel of individuals with similar qualifications but usually different backgrounds. This panel is asked to correct errors, comment on accuracy, and generally help us determine whether the expressed opinions and facts form a fair and broad description of the culture. A *Culturgram* cannot describe every aspect of a culture or ethnic group in a particular country, but it does paint a broad picture about life for the majority of people there. All project participants are asked to be as fair and up-to-date as possible. Once a new *Culturgram* has been published (after six to twelve months of work), it is reviewed periodically by qualified reviewers and annually by our professional staff of editors trained in international studies. When necessary, our editors revise the text to keep it current. This helps ensure that each *Culturgram* is a timely source of information about people's lives, society, and culture.

The list of contributors to and supporters of *Culturgrams* is long and irretrievable. We thank the hundreds of individuals who have shared their valuable expertise to make *Culturgrams* a beneficial intercultural learning tool. We also acknowledge the enthusiastic support of the current university leadership. Specific to this volume, we thank Matt Scherer (designer) and John Rees (photographer), whose talents are so beautifully displayed on the cover.

Students, teachers, resource librarians, international student advisors, business travelers, health-care workers, government and military personnel, tourists, missionaries, international development workers, and many others benefit from *Culturgrams*. With your purchase of *Culturgrams*, you join the millions who have come to count on the accurate, up-to-date information that continues to build bridges of understanding between Earth's peoples. Enjoy.

Grant Paul Skabelund
Managing Editor
Kennedy Center Publications

CULTURGRAM '97 ™

Aa Glossary Zz

The following is a list of some common concepts found in Culturgrams. *These are not definitions; they are explanations of how the terms are used in the series, what significance they hold in regard to understanding cultures, and often how they are calculated. For explanations of international organizations (United Nations, European Union, and so forth), please refer to reference sources in a library.*

Cash Crops

A cash crop is an agricultural product that is grown for sale, not for the farmer's consumption. It is often a crop (coffee, cotton, sugarcane, rice and other grains) that requires manufacturing or processing. It may also be a crop (oranges, potatoes, bananas) that can be consumed upon harvest but is cultivated primarily to be sold. Cash crops are most effectively produced on a large scale, but they can be grown on small plots of land. When grown on a large scale, the crops are more likely to be exported than consumed locally, although small growers in developing countries may sell to a local buyer who then sells larger quantities domestically and abroad. The economies of many countries depend heavily on the sale of cash crops.

Diversified Economy

An economy is considered diversified if its stability relies on a variety of industries rather than one or two commodities. For example, oil-rich countries that rely almost solely on the petroleum industry for their income are vulnerable to changes in the price of oil on the world market. When the price drops significantly, the countries are suddenly unable to pay debts or finance social development projects. The same is true for countries that rely on agricultural products such as coffee or on minerals such as copper for their income. Countries whose economies are based not only on agricultural products but also on manufacturing, services, technology, and so forth are better able to withstand global price changes. Thus, the more diversified a country's economic base, the better.

What is a *Culturgram*?

Each four-page *Culturgram* is designed to introduce readers to the daily customs and lifestyles, as well as the political and economic structure, of a nation. *Culturgrams* represent the contributions of individuals worldwide who have experienced living and working in each country. BYU's David M. Kennedy Center for International Studies requests and receives input from scholars within each target culture, U.S. and European academics, volunteers from organizations such as the Peace Corps and International Red Cross, expatriate diplomats and businesspeople, educators, and others.

This approach allows us to draw from a wide variety of perspectives and professional backgrounds in bringing our readers a unique look at culture. It also means that *Culturgrams* contain information based as much on opinion as on fact; however, we consult a wide variety of perspectives before publishing any information. A *Culturgram* cannot describe every ethnic group or cultural aspect of a given country, but it does paint a broad picture about life for the majority of people there.

Culturgrams do not focus on statistical data. A number of other fine resources present national statistics, but none really informs readers about people on a personal level. Our goal is to give readers an accurate view of a culture in order to encourage understanding and appreciation between people of different nationalities.

Each new *Culturgram* is written by someone who meets certain residency, educational, and professional criteria.

Drafts are reviewed by panels of individuals with similar qualifications but differing backgrounds. Panels are asked to correct errors and generally comment on whether the expressed opinions and facts form a broad, fair description of the culture. All project participants are asked to be as fair and up-to-date as possible.

Once a new *Culturgram* has been published (after six to twelve months of work), it is reviewed periodically by qualified reviewers and annually by our professional staff of editors trained in international relations. When necessary, the editors revise and update the text to reflect current events. This helps ensure that each text is a timely source of information about people's lives, their society, and the cultural environment in which they live.

Extended Family

As used in *Culturgrams*, this term refers to a family unit that includes parents, their children, and one or more relatives. The relatives most often include grandparents and sometimes cousins, aunts, and uncles. Some extended family units are organized with older parents, their married sons (occasionally daughters) and their families, and all unmarried sons and daughters. Extended families may share a single household or live in a compound that includes living structures for each nuclear unit, in which case families share work and other responsibilities. When a *Culturgram* states the extended family is the basic unit of society, it means households generally are composed of the extended family or the extended family network, both of which are essential to personal and social security.

Foreign Language Phrases

Most *Culturgrams* contain phrases and words in the target culture's official or common language. In general, a *Culturgram* does not provide a pronunciation guide for these phrases due to limited space. Also, including pronunciation and a translation tends to interrupt the flow of the text. A *Culturgram* is not designed to teach foreign languages. Rather, the phrases contained in a *Culturgram* are there to facilitate the description of how people interact with one another. Their translation often provides insights about the culture, but pronunciation is not necessary to gain that insight. In the few cases where pronunciation hints are provided, they are necessary for English-speakers to properly pronounce a word. For instance, the country Lesotho is not pronounced as it would seem. Instead of saying "le-SEW-tho," one should say "le-SUE-too."

Free and Compulsory Education

Most countries provide free education to their citizens, meaning the government operates a public school system open to all children who fall into a certain age group. It does not necessarily mean there are no costs involved in attending school. Students may be required to wear uniforms (which must be purchased), might live far from the nearest school (and parents must pay for transportation), or may need to supply their own paper, pencils, and other basic items. In addition, having a child in school can cost a rural family one laborer on the family farm. This can become such a burden to poorer families that free education is still not accessible to them.

Compulsory education refers to the fact that the law requires children to attend school for a certain number of years. In many countries this rule is seldom enforced. Therefore, it may reflect the government's target for how long children should remain in school to obtain a basic education, rather than how long they are actually required to attend. Compulsory education usually encompasses six to nine years, and optional schooling usually continues for three or more years.

Gross Domestic Product (GDP) Per Capita

This economic statistic refers to the value of all goods and services produced annually in an economy per person. Naturally, not every person produces goods and services, but the total is averaged for the entire population. If the term is expressed as "gross national product" (GNP), it is essentially the same statistic except for the addition of income earned abroad, minus the income earned in the country by noncitizens. This is significant when part of the population works in other countries and sends back money to their families. It is also significant for countries that have substantial investments abroad. For most countries, the two statistics, GDP and GNP, are almost interchangeable.

In the past, GDP was calculated in terms of the U.S. dollar after conversion from the local currency at official exchange rates. This caused accuracy problems because of artificially set exchange rates and because a dollar may not buy the same amount of goods in the United States as it does in another country. Social scientists have recently developed the concept of Purchasing Power Parity (PPP), a measurement that tries to account for the inconsistencies of the past. When GDP is figured in terms of PPP, an *international dollar* not affected by exchange rates is used. Likewise, PPP attempts to express the relative ability of a person to purchase goods with the local currency. Therefore, measured with PPP, $500 will buy essentially the same things in the United States as it will in Brazil or Japan. For many countries, PPP data does not yet exist and only estimates are available for others. Most *Culturgrams* use PPP with GDP, as expressed with the phrase "real gross domestic product." When the word "real" is absent, only the GDP has been calculated. The real GDPs in *Culturgrams* are usually taken from the *Human Development Report 1995* (New York: Oxford University Press for the United Nations Development Program, 1995). In cases where the real GDP is low (less than $1,000, for example), one can assume that people have very little disposable income. But one should also remember that rural families may grow their own food and, therefore, need less disposable income to meet basic needs. In other cases, such a low figure indicates people may indeed be without food, shelter, clothing, or other necessities.

Human Development and Gender-related Development Indexes

Originating with the United Nations's Development Program, the Human Development Index (HDI) and Gender-related Development Index (GDI) attempt to compensate for the inability of traditional economic indicators to accurately portray the environment in which people live—whether that environment nurtures personal development or hinders it. The project functions under the assumption that human development is "a process of enlarging people's choices" (UNDP 1995, 11). The three essential choices that people must have in order to access others include the ability to "lead a long and healthy life, to acquire knowledge and to have access to the resources needed for a decent standard of living" (UNDP, 11). Accordingly, the basis of the HDI and GDI are statistics related to literacy, infant mortality, life expectancy, and real GDP. If people have access to a useful education, adequate health care, and a decent wage, they are more likely to be involved in community affairs, join the middle class, and contribute skills and time to society. Such societies are more often democratic and respecting of human rights.

Each country is ranked in relation to the others according to its index rating, which falls between 0 and 1. The HDI "shows how far a country has to travel to provide . . . essential choices to all its people. It is not a measure of well-being. Nor is it a measure of happiness. Instead, it is a measure of empowerment" (UNDP, p. 12). The GDI looks at the same data as the HDI but is restricted to women. It is common for women to lag behind men in having access to the same basic resources and choices. Only 130 nations have been ranked for the GDI, whereas 174 have been listed for the HDI. Each *Culturgram* for which HDI and GDI data are available lists the country's index and rank. Some interpretation is also given. For more detailed analysis and additional data, refer to the entire *Human Development Report*, which is revised and updated each year.

Income Distribution

This phrase is generally used in connection with the gap between what the poorest people in a country earn and what the richest earn. If income distribution is highly unequal, a small wealthy class generally controls the economy (and often the government) and owns most property. The much larger poor class is often landless, which is significant since the people are probably farmers who must rent property and receive only a small share of the benefits from their labor. An unequal, but not highly unequal, income distribution often indicates that a middle class is beginning to grow. When the distribution is fairly equal, as is the case in a minority of countries, it is due mostly to a large and prosperous middle class. However, it can also indicate the presence of a broad poor class and absence of a wealthy elite. Generally, having a highly unequal income distribution means the economy is unhealthy, whereas the existence of a strong middle (consumer) class is good for an economy.

Infant Mortality Rate

This statistic is expressed as the number of children per 1,000 live births who die before their first birthday. It is an important indicator of the overall health of a population, since infants who die at this age usually are subject to preventable diseases or birth defects related to the mother's health. Those who die at birth often do so because of a lack of prenatal care and medical attention at birth. People who have access to health care, clean water, nutritious food, and education are more likely to have a low infant mortality rate than people who lack such access. Industrialized countries generally have a low rate (fewer than 10 per 1,000), while developing countries usually have a higher rate (averaging more than 30). The poorest countries may have rates exceeding 100.

Life Expectancy

This measurement refers to how long a person can expect to live from birth if mortality patterns remain unchanged. Someone born today may be expected to live 80 years if living in some European countries but only 58 years if living in parts of Africa. However, since mortality patterns do change throughout a person's lifetime, the statistic is really a better reflection of how long an adult who is currently living can expect to live. So a person who is 50 today can expect to live until 80 in some countries or only a few more years in others. Women live longer than men in most countries, and people in industrialized countries live longer than those in developing countries. People in countries with high pollution have lower rates of life expectancy.

Culturgrams usually express this statistic as a range of years, which most often corresponds to an average for women at the longer-living end and men at the shorter-living end. This statistic, like infant mortality, helps the reader understand the overall health of a population and whether the people have access to nutritious food, clean water, health care, and proper sanitation.

Literacy Rate

Most countries and international organizations define literacy in terms of those older than 15 years of age who can read and write. Sometimes that only means they can read and write their names or perform other basic tasks. In a few cases, literacy is defined as having attended school, even if only for a short time. Most educational experts agree that current definitions fall short of actually measuring whether the population is literate, since being able to write one's name does not mean one can read a newspaper or understand a bus schedule or work instructions.

Literacy may also be defined in terms of an official language not spoken on a daily basis by a majority of the population, which can make the definition even more irrelevant. However, since world organizations cannot agree on how to measure literacy, and since collecting such data is difficult, the current definitions remain in force. Researchers try to add to the statistic by looking at other factors, such as how many years of schooling the average person completes, whether the labor force is skilled or unskilled, and so forth. *Culturgrams* usually list the official literacy rate or an expert estimate and often contain other relevant information.

Nuclear Family

 As used in *Culturgrams*, this term refers to a family unit that includes one or two parents and their children. The nuclear family usually lives in a single-family dwelling. When a *Culturgram* states the nuclear family is the basic social unit, it means the average household is composed of a nuclear family.

Population and Population Growth Rate

The population listed for each country in the *Culturgram* series is an estimate for the year previous to publication (i.e., 1995 population for text published in 1996). The estimate is based on the actual population at the last census multiplied by an annual growth rate. The estimate may seem to conflict with other sources, since other sources often only print the population as of the latest census (whenever it may have been taken) or an estimate made in a base year (i.e., 1990). *Culturgram* estimates are in keeping with figures in

U.S. government publications, but they are sometimes modified by information from the target culture's government. Each population estimate is revised on an annual basis; it is rounded to the nearest 100,000 or 10,000, depending on the size of the population.

The population growth rate is an estimate, rounded to the nearest tenth of a percent, based on the previous year's difference between births and deaths and the net number of migrants leaving or entering the country. The growth rate may change substantially in a single year if there is a large influx of immigrants, a massive emigration, a natural disaster, or an epidemic. Growth rates tend to be low in industrialized countries because families are small, averaging one or two children. Growth rates are generally high in developing countries, especially in areas where subsistence farming is the primary economic activity. These cultures require large families to help farm the land, but they often have a high infant mortality rate; many children are conceived to ensure that enough will survive into adulthood. In small nations, the growth rate may be low due to emigration, as people must go elsewhere to find work.

Staple Food

Staple foods are those foods that supply the majority of the average person's calories and nutrition. A culture's primary staple food is usually starchy, such as cassava (manioc), corn, rice, millet, or wheat. Staple foods also include any meats, fruits, and vegetables eaten in large quantities or on a frequent basis.

Subsistence Farming

Subsistence farming refers to farming as the main source of a family's livelihood. That is, a family will grow its own food, raise its own livestock, build its own home, and often make its own clothing. Members of such a family generally do not earn a wage by working at a job, but they usually are not entirely without a cash income. Family members might sell surplus produce or livestock, or make crafts or other items (blankets, baskets, etc.), in order to buy things they cannot provide for themselves. These usually include items such as sugar, cooking oil, clothing, rice or another staple food, and so forth. Subsistence farmers may also set aside part of their land to grow cash crops in order to earn money. Subsistence farmers generally do not grow an abundance of anything. They often live on small owned or rented plots of land, and they seldom enjoy the luxuries of running water or electricity.

Underemployment

Underemployment refers to the case when workers are not officially unemployed but either are not able to find enough work in their profession or are working in jobs below their skill level. For example, if a country's universities graduate many people in engineering or other professional fields but the economy is not diversified or well developed, those people may find themselves unemployed, working in jobs that do not take advantage of their skills, or only working part-time in their fields. In the latter case, they may return to farming or local retailing. In too many cases, the most educated people simply emigrate to another country to find work, resulting in what is called a "brain drain."

Government unemployment figures generally do not include underemployment; it must be estimated. However, when unemployment is high (more than 10 percent), one usually can assume that underemployment affects at least as many or more workers. This condition reflects an economy that is not growing, and it can lead to social unrest. High underemployment (more than 40 percent) often leads to political turmoil and violence. Employing and paying people according to their skill level helps secure social stability and encourage economic growth.

Western/Western-style

This term usually refers to the dress and eating customs, culture, and traditions of Western Europe, the United States, and Canada. This culture is often referred to as Western because of its common ancient (primarily Greek and Roman) philosophical, legal, political, and social heritage. The term *Western* can also refer to cultures that have a Judeo-Christian value system and religious orientation.

Metric Conversions

Celsius	Fahrenheit	Kilometers	Miles	Meters	Inches/Feet
0°	32°	1	.62	1mm	.039"
4°	39°	10	6.2	50mm	1.95"
8°	46°	50	31	100mm	3.9"
12°	54°	100	62	1m	39.37"
16°	61°	250	155	50m	164'
20°	68°	500	311	100m	328'
24°	75°	750	465	500m	1,640'
28°	82°	1,000	621	1,000m	3,280'
32°	90°	2,000	1,242	1,609m	5,280'
36°	97°	3,000	1,860	5,000m	16,400'
40°	104°	5,000	3,100	10,000m	22,960'

Republic of
Albania

Boundary representations not necessarily authoritative.

E
U
R
O
P
E

BACKGROUND

Land and Climate

Albania, covering 11,100 square miles (28,750 square kilometers), is one of the smallest countries in Europe. The terrain is mostly mountainous, with narrow coastal lowlands along the Adriatic and Ionian Seas. Coastal soils are fertile but not well drained for agriculture. Instead, the rocks, forested mountains, and sandy beaches are considered a treasure by Albanians for their tourism potential.

Several river valleys carve their way through Albania's mountains, providing spring water and room for towns and cities. The largest rivers include the Drin, Vjosa, Mati, Semani, and Shkumbini. Mountain lakes also dot the landscape. Albania's northern Alps feature the nation's highest peak, Korabi (9,026 feet or 2,751 meters), but other ranges also have peaks above 8,000 feet (2,400 meters).

Summers along the Adriatic are hot and dry, while winters are mild and wet. A continental climate prevails inland, with more marked seasonal temperature extremes. Summer readings may reach 95°F (35°C), and winter lows may fall to 0°F (-18°C), especially in the north and southeast.

History

Descended from the ancient Illyrians, Albanians are considered one of the oldest native Balkan peoples. Illyria covered a wide portion of the southern Balkans. It was invaded by the Romans in the second century B.C., and when the Roman Empire divided in the fourth century A.D., Illyria remained with the eastern portion. Many of Rome's emperors—including Claudius II and Justinian—had Illyrian ancestry.

A fifth century Bulgar invasion was followed by the Slavs in the sixth and seventh centuries. Slavic attempts to impose their culture and religion on the native population forced Albanians south and into the mountains. A native prince, Progon, established an independent state in 1190 that lasted less than a century, and Albania was conquered in the 14th century by Serbs. Their empire fell in 1355 and Albania was divided under local feudal lords: the Dukagjinis and Topias ruled in the north, and the Muzakas and Shpatas in the south.

Turkish incursions began in the late 1300s, but Albanian resistance was organized by Gjergj Kastrioti (known as Skanderbeg) in 1444. Skanderbeg was revered by Albanians as a national hero, and even respected by the Ottomans who could not conquer him until the 1470s. By 1500, the Turks had complete control, thousands of Albanians had fled, and the nation entered a long period under Ottoman rule. A renaissance in the 1870s eventually contributed to a 1911 uprising against the Turks.

In the 1912 London Conference on the Balkans, an independent Albanian state was created. Its disputed borders, finalized in 1913 after the First Balkan War, left some 40 percent of ethnic Albanians outside of Albania. World War I soon engulfed Albania, leading to grinding poverty in the 1920s. Archbishop Fan Noli failed in 1924 to create a Western-style democracy, and he was ousted from power by his rival, Ahmed Bey Zogu. Zogu declared himself King Zog in 1928 and ruled repressively until 1939; he fled when Italy occupied Albania. Italy's rule was followed by a German invasion in 1943. Liberation came in 1944.

After a short civil war, the National Liberation Movement formed a provisional government and named Communist leader Enver Hoxha as president in 1945. Hoxha eventually led Albania down the path of oppression, poverty, and isolation until his death in 1985.

Albanians responded to democratization in Eastern Europe after 1989 by seeking greater freedoms at home or by trying to leave the impoverished country in 1991. Communist leaders won elections in 1991 but soon met with food riots and other turmoil. A second election in 1992 brought the Democratic Party to power with Sali Berisha as president. He began working with international organizations to build a viable economy. Parliamentary elections in May 1996 returned the Democrats to power, although opposition leaders and outside observers reported serious flaws in the voting process. Post-election protests were quickly quelled. Berisha faces reelection in 1997.

PEOPLE

Population

Albania's population of 3.4 million is not growing, as people continue to emigrate. Another three to four million Albanians live in neighboring countries, but they have lived in those regions for generations. Albania's desire to seek protection of these people's rights is a source of some tension between the governments involved. Albania itself is about 98 percent ethnic Albanian. Small groups of Greeks, Serbs, Romany (Gypsies), and Bulgarians live in the country. Only about 40 percent of the population resides in urban areas. The country's Human Development Index (0.739) ranks it 82d out of 174 nations. This rank reflects an educated populace more than a society in which people enjoy prosperity or personal advancement opportunities.

Language

Albanians speak *Shqip* (Albanian), an Indo-European language directly descended from Illyrian. In 1908, Albania adopted a Latin script. The alphabet has 36 letters (7 are vowels). Two dialects, Gheg and Tosk, were historically spoken in Albania, but a national language based on Tosk was adopted after 1945. This Tosk-based Albanian is the official language.

Religion

Prior to the Ottoman era, Albanians were mostly Christian. Under the Turks, however, a large percentage of the population converted to Islam and accordingly changed their names. Albanians could practice religion freely until the Communist era, when the country's many mosques, monasteries, and churches suffered damage and destruction under the government's antireligion policy. In 1965, religious practices were outlawed altogether.

Religious freedom was restored in 1990 and religion is again becoming important in people's daily lives. Although official figures are lacking, it is estimated that 70 percent of the population is Muslim (Sunni and Bektashi), 20 percent Orthodox Christian, and 10 percent Catholic. Protestant Christian churches and other denominations are beginning to establish a presence in Albania.

General Attitudes

Albanians view themselves as an optimistic, hospitable, and patient people with the ability to think clearly and understand quickly. They value their families and their ethnic heritage. Personal honor is important.

Northern Albanians, particularly the mountaineers, are known to be courageous, resourceful, courteous, and hardy. They honor a traditional institution called the *besa* (sworn truce). Adherence to the *besa*, family honor, hospitality, and a patriarchal order are considered to be the basis for successful relationships. Otherwise, northerners tend to engage in blood feuds, resist governance by others, and distrust outsiders. Southern Albanians are known to be openly emotional and socially more liberal. Albanians resist appealing to the wisdom and advice of others.

Unfortunately, Albanians are more accustomed to force and autocracy than to democracy and the rule of law. Adjusting to a Western system of competition, free speech, capitalism, and materialism has been difficult. People are frustrated by economic difficulties, conflicts between political parties, corruption, crime, and widening gaps between rich and poor. Still, most are confident that Albania's future is one of freedom and democracy.

Personal Appearance

Before 1991, clothing was often homemade, but now it is mostly purchased. Urban professional men wear business suits and ties. Urban women wear dresses and skirts more than pants. They wear Western tops and colorful blouses. The youth like jeans, T-shirts, and sneakers.

Villagers wear traditional outfits, which vary by region. In the north, women wear a head scarf and a *fustanelle* (full, colorful wool skirt) over tights. Men wear cotton or wool pants, heavy cotton shirts, a *xhamadan* (wool vest), and a *qeleshe* (white cap). In the south, such traditional attire is used mainly in ceremonies. For all Albanians, it is important that clothing be neat and clean. In fact, they consider cleanliness a personal duty. People prefer natural fabrics (cotton, wool) over synthetic fibers.

CUSTOMS AND COURTESIES

Greetings

Albanians greet with a handshake and add a hug for friends. Between women, a greeting may also include a kiss to each cheek. Typical phrases include *Si jeni?* (How are you?), *Si keni kaluar?* (How are you doing?), *Ç' kemi?* (What's up?), or *Njatjeta* (Hello). Friends may also greet by saying *Miremengjes* (Good morning). When parting, they say *Mir u pafshim* (Good-bye), *Do te shihemi* (See you later), *Shendet!* (Stay healthy!), or *Gjithe te mirat* (All the best). Northern male villagers greet by lifting their cap and saying *Tungjat jeta* (Have a long life). Albanians smile or nod when passing strangers on the street.

Close friends address each other by first name, but Albanians otherwise use *Zonja* (Mrs.), *Zonjushe* (Miss), or *Zoteri* (Mr.) with first or last names. Before 1990, *Shok* (Comrade) was used for introducing someone. Specific kinship terms are important when addressing family members. For instance, an uncle may be called *xhaxha* (father's brother) or *daje* (mother's brother). Likewise, an aunt is either *halle* or *teto* (father's sister) or *teze* (mother's sister). It is common to call an older man *xhaxha* or older woman *nene* (a term for mother), whether they are related or not.

Gestures

Albanians often move their hands and heads when conversing, although they maintain as much eye contact as possible. To indicate "yes," one shakes the head slowly from left to right. A person indicates "no" either by nodding briefly up and down or by clicking the tongue and nodding the head down once. A "thumbs-up" gesture is impolite, meaning "You'll get nothing from me." Placing the left hand over the chest and moving the head slighty shows appreciation.

Albanians use the index finger when they want to make a point, whether expressing an opinion or pointing at another person. Showing both hands with open fingers, palms up, means "our conversation is over." To pat another person's shoulder means "I am proud of you." Young people might show strong approval by quickly moving the hand horizontally, while at the same time bringing the thumb and index finger together and clicking the tongue.

Visiting

Visiting is considered a joyful event, and Albanian hospitality is a cultural hallmark. Unplanned visits are common. Guests usually are greeted with the phrase *Mire se vini* or *Mire se erdhet* (Welcome). Guests bring gifts for birthdays or special occasions, but not if they are invited for a meal or are just visiting. Gifts, even birthday presents, are opened only after the guests are gone.

In northern villages, people commonly socialize while sitting cross-legged on the floor near the fireplace, a custom that stems from an old tradition of sitting around a low table (*sofra*). Otherwise, people sit on chairs.

After seating guests, the hostess offers the men strong alcoholic drinks such as *raki* or *konjak* and sweet liquors to the women, even during the day. These drinks are accompanied by homemade jam, candies, and Turkish coffee, which is served with biscuits, cookies, or cake.

Before drinking, visitors politely say *Gezuar* (Cheers) and *Mire se ju gjeta* (I am glad I find you all well). The host and hostess reply *Mire se erdhet*. Evening visits occur between 4:00 and 8:30 P.M. They do not necessarily include a meal, but hosts may extend such an invitation. Albanian hosts traditionally walk their guests a little way down the street when they leave.

Eating

An Albanian breakfast (6:30–7:00 A.M.) usually consists of milk, eggs, bread and butter, jam, cheese, and Turkish or espresso coffee. A traditional restaurant breakfast is *paçe*, a creamy soup made with a cow or calf head, tomato sauce, garlic, flour, butter, and seasonings. Lunch (3:00–4:00 P.M.), usually the main meal, begins with vegetables, rice soup flavored with chicken or veal, and fresh green or tomato salad, followed by the main course of *gjelle* (boiled beans or vegetables with meat) or baked, stuffed eggplants or peppers. Cakes, fresh fruits, and coffee follow the meal.

Dinner (7:30–9:30 P.M.) consists of light soup or pasta, plain yogurt, bread, and dessert. The mother usually prepares each plate before serving it. For holidays or when guests are present, serving dishes are put on the table and each person chooses his or her portion. When guests are present, hosts serve *meze* (antipasto with boiled eggs, feta and *kackavall* cheese, cold cuts or sausage, onions, tomatoes, and olives) accompanied

by *raki*. In the north, *meze* is prepared with cottage cheese and *turshi* (vegetables preserved in saltwater).

Private restaurants reopened after 1990. Albanians eat in the continental style, with the fork in the left hand and the knife in the right. Toasting is common, with the first toast made to everyone's health and friendship. Bills are presented on request and are paid at the table. Tipping is customary.

LIFESTYLE

Family

Urban families generally have one or two children, while rural families have three or four. For the most part, the father heads the family, and women are responsible for cooking, cleaning, and caring for the children. Male children are seen as the future backbone of the family and protectors of the family name. Both parents usually work and send their children to day care. Men and women have equal social rights.

Village homes, shared by two or three generations, usually are built of stone or brick and have two to three bedrooms. City dwellers most often live in apartments with one to three rooms. Due to a housing shortage, unmarried adults often live with their parents, as do married children, usually on the groom's side. These children are expected to take care of their aging parents.

Dating and Marriage

Prior to 1945, most marriages were arranged. This custom came from an early era when northern tribes would announce a girl's engagement at birth. Today, young people make their own choices regarding a spouse, but rural families are still heavily involved in the selection process. Urban youth begin dating around age 16; they go to movies or small café bars to socialize. Men generally marry after they are 26 and women marry in their early twenties.

There are usually two wedding celebrations: one on Saturday for the bride and one on Sunday for the groom. At the first party, given by the bride's parents, the groom and his family representatives only appear after 10:00 P.M., and the bride changes from a white dress to a more colorful one after midnight. The party continues until 3:00 A.M. The next day around noon, the groom goes with a few relatives to the bride's house to take her to his parents' home. There they receive the congratulations of visitors before having the second dinner party, sponsored by the groom's parents.

A civil ceremony is required for a marriage to be legal, but since 1991 many couples are having a church ceremony in addition to the civil one.

Diet

The Albanian diet is influenced by Greek, Turkish, and Italian cuisine. Traditional specialties include *fasule* (boiled dried beans) cooked with onions and tomatoes and flavored with *pasterma* (dried salt mutton); *turshi* salads; *byrek* (a pastry) with vegetables, cottage cheese, or minced meat; and *tave kosi* (meat or liver baked in yogurt). Lamb, veal, and chicken are the most popular meats. Albanians also enjoy pork and seafood. Meat often is boiled together with vegetables such as potatoes, onions, okra, peas, beans, leeks, spinach, or cabbage. In the south, roasted lamb served with fresh vegetables and baked potatoes is considered traditional. Typical dairy products include homemade yogurt, cottage cheese, and feta and *kackavall* cheeses. Locally grown fruits include apples, pears, peaches, watermelons, plums, oranges, figs, and grapes. *Raki* is often served before the main meal, while wine is served during or after the meal.

Recreation

Albanians enjoy visiting friends and family, taking a stroll, and meeting in coffee bars. They like to talk about everyday life and be informed about politics and other social matters. Families gather for religious, historical, and cultural events. Urban families like to picnic or go to the beach in the summer. Most people have a two-week summer vacation. Travel outside Albania was banned until 1987, but many people are now visiting other countries.

Men play basketball or soccer. People like to watch television or attend movies. Western music, especially from the United States, is popular. Albania also has indigenous music played on unique instruments: a *çiftelia* (type of mandolin with two strings) or *lahuta* (one-stringed instrument played with a bow) in the north, a *gajde* (type of bagpipe) in the central region, and a kind of wailing clarinet in the south.

Holidays

Official public holidays include New Year's (1–2 January), Easter (Friday–Monday), May Day (1 May), Independence Day and Liberation Day (28 November for both holidays), and Christmas (25–26 December). Muslims celebrate *Ramasan Bairam* (feast at the end of the holy month of *Ramadan*) and *Kurban Bairam* (Feast of Sacrifice). On Memorial Day (5 May), people place flowers on graves and honor fallen warriors. The most popular holiday is New Year's Eve, which Albanians celebrate with big meals (usually a turkey dinner with special desserts in syrup, like *baklava* or *kadaif*), dancing, joking, and singing. They spend the following day visiting and sharing holiday sweets.

Commerce

Businesses are open Monday through Friday, 7:00 A.M. to 3:00 P.M., but shops, open-air markets, and private grocery stores are open 12 hours a day. Factories and other industrial places operate weekdays from 6:00 A.M. to 3:30 P.M.

SOCIETY

Government

Albania has yet to ratify a new constitution to replace Communist-era codes, but an interim basic law established in 1991 functions as a constitution. Executive power rests with the president. The head of government is Prime Minister Aleksander Gabriel Meksi. The Democratic Party dominates the 140-seat People's Assembly (*Kuvendi Popullor*). Primary opposition is provided by the Socialist Party (former Communists), but other parties also have representation. Democracy is not yet strong, and inexperience is a key stumbling block. The voting age is 18.

Economy

Until 1990, the economy was centralized and heavily controlled, but free-market principles have since been introduced and the number of small businesses is increasing. Land was privatized in 1992. Economic growth in 1995 was more than 10 percent. Unfortunately, the infrastructure is weak, factories remain idle, and unemployment is at 20 percent. Real gross domestic product per capita is estimated at $3,500, although most people earn only about $600 per year. International investment is vital to success, and the government has established liberal standards to attract foreign funds. For now, Albania relies on foreign aid, remittances from Albanians working abroad, and revenues from contraband smuggling. Plans to revive certain industries and create a tourism sector face the challenges of a poor supply network, a small domestic market, and outdated equipment. Albania's greatest asset is a skilled and educated workforce. Albania exports asphalt, iron ore, chromium ore, copper, and agricultural produce. The currency is the *lek* (L).

Transportation and Communication

Urban transportation is operated by the state, but private lines provide intercity transport. The number of automobiles (used cars from Europe) is increasing rapidly. Bicycles are popular for getting around, as are motorcycles. Albania has a small railway system and one airport at Tirana.

With the end of communism, private newspapers were established. The country's one television station is joined by several radio stations. Phones are not readily available, but televisions and radios are found in most homes.

Education

Education is provided free to all citizens. Children begin school at age six and are required to attend for ten years (up from eight before 1994). Parents are fined if they do not send their children to school for the full period. Education is extremely important to Albanians, and the literacy rate among young people approaches 100 percent. The adult rate is 85 percent. At age 16, students can obtain secondary education at vocational and other schools. After four years, qualified students may attend college at state expense. Albania's first university was founded in Tirana in 1957. Other institutions exist, and some students study in other countries.

Health

The government provides free health care at clinics and hospitals, and private clinics are available to those who can afford them. Most medicine is either imported or donated. Facilities are poorly equipped and reliant on international aid. Child and maternal care is a high priority. The infant mortality rate is 28 per 1,000. The life expectancy rate is 74 years.

FOR THE TRAVELER

A passport is required of U.S. citizens visiting Albania, but a visa is not necessary for stays of less than three months. Tourist facilities are lacking, and travelers should expect to pay cash for most things. Avoid being out late at night, and protect your passport at all times. The spring water flowing through the pipes is clean, but the pipes themselves render tap water unsafe. Sites of interest include Dajti Mountain in Tirana, the old castle ruins in Kruja, the Adriatic coast, and the seven Lura lakes in the north. For more information, contact the Embassy of the Republic of Albania, 1150 18th Street NW, Washington, DC 20036; phone (202) 223–4942.

CULTURGRAM ™ '97

Antigua and Barbuda

Codrington

BARBUDA

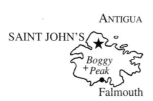

ANTIGUA

SAINT JOHN'S

Boggy Peak

Falmouth

Boundary representations not necessarily authoritative.

THE AMERICAS

BACKGROUND

Land and Climate

Located 250 miles (400 kilometers) southeast of Puerto Rico, Antigua is relatively low and flat and has a dry, sunny, desert-like climate most months of the year. Boggy Peak, the island's highest elevation at 1,319 feet (402 meters), is located near a small tropical rain forest.

Barbuda, located across shallow water 30 miles north of Antigua, is even flatter, with its highest elevation being only 207 feet (63 meters). Sparsely populated, with most people living in Codrington, it is covered by shrubs and brush. It features soft pink sand beaches, a frigate bird sanctuary, abundant wild deer, and lobster. Including small uninhabited islands, the country covers 170 square miles (440 square kilometers).

In September 1995, Hurricane Luis hammered Antigua and Barbuda, destroying nearly three-fourths of the islands' buildings. Efforts to rebuild continue with assistance from the international community.

History

Called *Wadadli* by the Amerindians who maintained a lively culture through the 17th century, the island was renamed by Christopher Columbus in 1493 for the Santa Maria de la Antigua cathedral in Spain. (Antigua is pronounced without the *u*.) A lack of water and a thriving indigenous population discouraged European settlement for many years, but English settlers crossed over from Saint Kitts in 1632. Despite attempts to dislodge them, the settlers persisted, cultivating tobacco, indigo, and ginger. The two islands eventually became part of the British Leeward Islands Colony in 1666.

In 1674, Christopher Codrington came from Barbados and established the first large sugar plantation, called "Betty's Hope." His success prompted other settlers to turn to sugar, and during the next one hundred years the landscape was cleared of all vegetation to grow this highly demanded cash crop. More than 150 wind-powered sugar mills (the ruins of many are still standing) soon dotted the island. Antigua was divided into parishes, the boundaries of which remain.

The plantation economy thrived on slave labor, the British having imported thousands of Africans to Antigua. Colonists even used Barbuda as a slave-breeding center. When emancipation finally came in 1834, many of the newly freed African people began new lives in villages that bear such names as Freetown, Liberta, and Freeman's Village. But landowners continued exploitation by charging former slaves for hoe rentals and other services; this kept them working for minimal compensation into the 1930s. Reduced profitability of sugar and growing labor unrest led to the demise in the 1940s of the island's sugar industry, and by 1970 the last sugar refinery on the island had closed. Most light industries were replaced by the steadily growing tourism industry.

When Britain began granting greater autonomy to its colonies following World War II, Antigua's Vere Cornwall Bird was named chief minister. Antigua joined the West Indies Federation in 1958, but that body dissolved in 1962. In 1967, Antigua and Barbuda became a West Indies Associated State. This status granted internal autonomy, with Bird as premier. In 1981, Antigua, with Barbuda as a dependency, achieved full independence under the leadership of Bird's Antigua Labour Party (ALP). Barbuda attempted to remain a British colony, but the request was denied. The ALP consistently won elections, and Bird remained prime minister until he retired in 1994. His son, Lester Bird, became prime minister when the ALP won elections in March 1994.

THE PEOPLE

Population

The country's population is about 65,000 (1,600 living on Barbuda). Nearly half of all Antiguans live in the area surrounding the capital, Saint John's. Despite its size, Antigua's various regions are identified with distinct population groups. For example, Old Road prides itself on connections to certain family and West African lines that Freetown may not share.

Barbuda's population consists almost entirely of African descendants. Most Barbudans go to Antigua to shop, work, or live, but many Antiguans have never been to Barbuda. Antigua's population is 96 percent Black African and 3 percent white. One percent is a mixture of Syrian, Lebanese, Asians, and other immigrants. Most whites are foreigners engaged in business and tourism.

A crossroads in the Caribbean, Antigua historically has attracted seafaring peoples, so there are both Spanish and French elements mixed with the African people. The island is also home to more recent immigrants from countries in the region. Although racial disputes are virtually unheard of, the different racial groups do not mix socially. Likewise, while tourism brings thousands of people to the island (especially in winter), contact between tourists and locals is mostly limited to professional services.

Language

Most Antiguans speak English. But they also speak a dialect similar to others in the region; it is a mixture of English, various African tongues, and some European languages. Commonly used words such as *nyam* (to eat) have African origins. Forms of speech vary between areas and classes. Many upper-class Antiguans look down on those who speak the dialect, but most people appreciate it for its color and expressiveness. Traditional sayings are still popular, such as *No tro way you belly and tek trash tuff um* (Don't lose the substance for the shadow) and *Wah eye no see heart no grieve* (What you don't know won't hurt you). The dialect is used in casual, friendly situations. *T'all* means "Not at all," and *How!* means "But of course!" *You lie* can mean "You're kidding." Barbudans have their own accent.

Religion

Antiguans are religious people. Women and children attend church regularly, while men go less frequently. Most people belong to various Protestant groups. The Anglican Church, with the island's largest cathedral (St. John's), is the nation's state religion. The Methodist Church has a long tradition in the country as well. A significant Catholic population (mostly non-Africans) also exists. Various other Christian groups have facilities and churches on the island, and there are some followers of Islam, Baha'i, and Rastafarianism.

General Attitudes

The people of Antigua and Barbuda are relaxed, friendly, and warm. They take a casual approach to life, sometimes expressed in the phrase *Soon come*. This is related to the general feeling that life presents or takes care of itself—that it is in God's hands and not necessarily in mankind's. Time is also viewed on a more casual basis. People are more important than schedules. They may have things to do along the way to an event or appointment, so it is rarely a problem for them to be late.

Antiguans have a great deal of pride in their families, homes, and nation. This is manifest by the community spirit that surrounds school and church events and displays of local talent. People are especially proud of their international cricket reputation. A number of star players for championship West Indies teams are from Antigua. National pride also emerges during the annual Carnival arts festival, when performers compete in various events.

Personal Appearance

Public dress is neat, sharply pressed, and stylish. Funerals, weddings, and other special events bring out the most elegant and formal clothes in one's wardrobe. Sunday, particularly, is a day for dressing up. At parties or recreational events, Antiguans combine vivid Caribbean colors with international fashions.

On a daily basis, men do not wear shorts. Lightweight trousers and pressed shirts with colorful designs are popular. Some men wear ties and a few wear suits. The combination *shirt-jacket* (formal, embroidered, cotton shirt cut square and worn like a jacket) is common in offices. Laborers wear work pants or uniforms.

Women wear stylish dresses, high-heeled shoes, and jewelry in offices; for some occupations, they wear dress uniforms. Around the home, men and women dress in shorts, T-shirts, and athletic shoes or sandals. Women also wear comfortable dresses. In this modest society, people wear bathing suits at the beach, not in town.

CUSTOMS AND COURTESIES

Greetings

Antiguans and Barbudans generally are informal in greeting one another. *How are you?* or *Hi* is common, but friends also use variations like *What's up?* or *How you do?* or *Alright?* The response to *Alright?* is *Okay, Okay*. The general *Good morning*, *Good day*, *Good evening*, and *Good night* are spoken at specific times of the day, with *Good evening* being inappropriate, for example, after dark.

Most Antiguans address friends by first names, but they address a boss by a title (*Mr., Mrs., Miss*), and professional exchanges between people (such as between a customer and a shopkeeper) are kept on this level. Children and young people address their elders and relatives with *Aunt, Uncle*, or an appropriate familial title.

Male friends use various hand-slapping, fist-touching, and thumb-locking handshakes as well as long handshakes. An entire brief conversation might be conducted with hands together. A man waits for a woman to extend her hand before shaking it.

Gestures

Although modest and reserved in appropriate circumstances, Antiguans are generally lively and expressive among friends. A conversation can include a person "acting out" or "demonstrating" something with body gestures. People usually point with the index finger, but some situations call for the use of hands, arms, or even the head, eyes, or shoulders. Hand and facial gestures punctuate conversation and often express something better than words. Raising the hand, palm out, and wagging an extended index finger from side to side indicates disagreement. It is usually accompanied with "No, no, no." A hearty "thumbs-up" means things are going well. Sucking air through the teeth (called *chups* or *choops*), expresses exasperation or annoyance (at a flat tire or the store being out of bread, for example). Often, a mild *chups* provokes laughter and is a good release of tension. However, when directed at an individual, the noise is very rude.

People do not like to hear their names called out in public, so a discreet "psssst" is often used to get someone's attention. A quick *Hey* or *Yo* is also common between friends.

Visiting

Antiguans enjoy socializing with relatives, neighbors, and friends. They use the term *lime* or *liming* for the time spent relaxing and chatting with each other. Most visits occur on weekends or after work. Appointments or plans are rarely made; people sitting in the yard or on the porch usually are willing to chat. Friendly encounters elsewhere can turn into a social visit. For example, much socializing occurs in public, whether among men meeting to repair a fishing net or among women who are washing or shopping in public areas. Neighbors socialize while preparing meals.

When visiting someone who is inside a home, a person often approaches the gate and shouts *"Inside."* The occupant then comes out to greet the person, and the two may spend the entire visit on the porch. Friends or relatives will often be invited inside. It is polite to offer light refreshments, such as fruit juice or herbal tea. Visitors often *walk with* (carry) fresh fruit from trees in their yards to share with hosts. Visits can be of any length, and hosts rarely ask guests to leave. Whole families may visit, especially among relatives. Conversation is seasonal, with cricket or calypso dominating, but people might also sit for extended periods without talking. At more formal, invitation events (birthdays, graduations, and holidays), hosts provide food and drink, and guests bring appropriate gifts.

Eating

During the workweek, people start the day with a simple breakfast of fruit, porridge, or eggs. Most workers stop for a full meal at midday, either in the workplace, at restaurants, or at home. Boys and girls usually help with cooking at home. *Coal pots* (clay ovens) are often used to cook food; they are placed outside the kitchen. Saturday is a busy day for chores and errands, so people might buy barbecued chicken or fried fish at the market for the main meal. Evening meals are light if the main meal is eaten at midday.

On Sundays, the family has a large breakfast. Later, grand preparations precede an extended family evening meal featuring roast pork, leg of lamb, or beef. So much food is served that plates generally are sent home with relatives for those who could not come. When fishermen bring in a good catch, a pot of *fish water* (fish stew) is usually cooked up and shared. Church picnics or celebrations bring many cooks out cooperating on a large scale, serving such dishes as *goat water*, a spicy stew made with goat meat.

LIFESTYLE
Family

The extended family forms the heart of Antiguan society. Grandparents, aunts, and uncles often raise children for parents who live out of the country for economic reasons. Families are large and living space is often shared between nuclear units. No matter what the living arrangements, family ties are strong and there are frequent gatherings. In Antigua, people like to joke that everybody is really related to each other if one traces the line back far enough.

Children are highly prized and bearing or fathering them is valued by all. The traditional two-parent family is the norm, but it is not uncommon for a young unmarried woman to have children and live with her parents. In such cases, the baby's father provides financial support and is encouraged by both families to be involved in the child's life. Half siblings live with their mother, and women are not uncommon as heads of households. Men may have children with different women and never marry, and some women choose to remain single parents.

Dating and Marriage

Boys and girls have many opportunities to socialize and interact, including school parties and dances, church functions, and holiday events. Couples are affectionate, but not in public. At some point in a courtship, the young man is brought home for the approval of the young woman's family. Parents and churches encourage marriage over other types of relationships. Weddings are lavish, with a decorated church service, formal attire, and plenty of food and dance music.

Diet

People keep small gardens in their yards, but most food is imported. Antigua is subject to drought and supports little agriculture or livestock raising. Tropical fruits (coconuts and mangoes) and vegetables (pumpkins, yams, and potatoes) grow well. There is some fishing, but hotels are increasingly expanding into spawning areas of the mangrove wetlands, threatening future catches.

The basic diet revolves around rice, beans (*peas*, usually red beans or white pigeon peas), and meat (chicken, pork, beef, goat) and fish, plus fruits and vegetables in season. During mango season, when mangoes ripen on trees literally by the thousands, people commonly *turn their pots down* (cook less) and eat large amounts of the fruit. At Christmastime, the bright red sorrel fruit is mixed with sugar and spices in a delicious tea. Antiguans boast that their local pineapple (Antigua Black) is the sweetest in the world.

A popular dish is seasoned rice (rice, peas, vegetables, and meat chunks with seasonings). *Fungee* is a spoon bread made with cornmeal and okra. *Doucana* is coconut, sweet potatoes, flour, sugar and spices, served with spicy *saltfish* (dried cod). *Pepperpot*, a spicy vegetable stew, is different from home to home. Specialties include *Johnny Cakes* (sweet fried dumplings), *souse* (pickled pigs' feet), and blood sausage (called *rice pudding* or *black pudding*). Fast-food is making its way into the national diet, and sidewalk vendors sell roasted corn or peanuts as snacks.

Recreation

Antiguans are passionate about sports. Cricket is most popular, with formal and casual games played during a

November-to-May season. Soccer dominates the rest of the year, and basketball is almost as popular. Girls are less involved with athletics than boys, but they compete in *netball* (similar to basketball) leagues. Water sports remain the domain of tourists and some in the upper class. Most Antiguans do not swim; at beach parties, they *sea bathe* in shallow water.

Antiguans also love music and dancing; anyone with the right speaker system can get a party going at a restaurant or picnic. Church choirs (with mostly women as members) are numerous and practice regularly. Other social activities for women usually center around household duties or their children's activities.

Dominoes and draughts (a form of checkers) are popular with men and boys, who play on tables set up under trees or on porches. A direct link to the nation's African heritage is the strategy game *Warri*. Complicated stratagems are required to capture the opponent's 24 seeds (four each in six cups) and win.

Holidays

Old Year's Night (31 December) and New Year's Day (1 January) cap off the important Christmas season that is marked by religious and secular celebrations. Easter (Friday–Monday) is as significant as Christmas. Labour Day (1 May, observed the first Monday in May) is important because of the role labor unions had in gaining independence. Pentecost (50 days after Easter) is a time of spiritual renewal and also coincides with Barbuda's *Caribana* (Carnival). CARICOM Day (4 July) celebrates Caribbean unity.

During Antigua's Carnival and national arts festival, emancipation from slavery (1 August) is celebrated. This is an important time for Antiguans and Barbudans living abroad to return home. Parades, dancing, and music fill the streets for a week. Calypso music competitions are especially prominent and are long anticipated. Aspiring "Calypsonians" perform all-new original songs. Calypsos can be comical, political, or whatever. The climax of Carnival is the Calypso King show, where a winner is crowned. Street dancing at dawn the next day celebrates the first morning of freedom from slavery.

Christmas is celebrated on 25 and 26 December. The 26th is Boxing Day, which comes from the old British tradition of giving servants a holiday and boxed gifts. It is now a day to relax and visit. The prime minister can also call for holidays, such as the case in 1994 during an important cricket match in Antigua between the West Indies and England.

Commerce

Major shops and businesses are located in St. John's. Most are open between 8:00 A.M. and 5:00 P.M. St. John's also has a large open-air market featuring fresh produce. Large supermarkets offer a full variety of food.

SOCIETY

Government

As a parliamentary democracy within the Commonwealth, Antigua recognizes Britain's Queen Elizabeth II as head of state. She is represented by a governor general, who is also head of government after elections before a prime minister is named. Parliament has two houses, a Senate and a House of Representatives, each with 17 seats. The voting age is 18. The United Progressive Party (UPP) opposes the ALP.

Economy

Tourism is the primary industry. St. John's is also home to a commercial deep-water harbor. While most revenues from tourism belong to foreign developers, Antiguans benefit from jobs and taxes on the industry. The Human Development Index (0.840) ranks Antigua and Barbuda 55th out of 174 countries. Real gross domestic product per capita is $4,436.

The government employs one-third of the labor force and tourism employs most of the rest. Some manufacturing exists, most often to supply the tourist industry (beds, towels, etc.). A member of the Caribbean Community (CARICOM) and the Organization of Eastern Caribbean States (OECS), Antigua uses the East Caribbean dollar (EC$) as its currency.

Transportation and Communication

Plentiful buses serve the island, although private cars are common and a fleet of taxis caters to tourists. Following the British tradition, traffic moves on the left. Buses leave the station when full and do not follow written schedules; they stop on request. Locations in St. John's are accessible by foot, but people avoid long walks in the hot afternoon. Telecommunications systems are modern and extensive. One broadcast television station is supplemented by satellite and cable services. There are two radio stations.

Education

The adult literacy rate is 89 percent, although actual figures may be closer to 60 percent. Most Antiguans have had some secondary schooling. The system is modeled after Britain's. Public schools are free; more expensive private schools exist and are often church-affiliated. Children are required to wear uniforms; parents purchase their textbooks. Mandatory schooling lasts to age 16. Antigua State College provides post-secondary vocational training and college preparatory classes. Qualified students attend universities in other countries. Many of these never return home due to the lack of advanced career opportunities.

Health

The country's one hospital is adequate for minor treatment and surgeries, but serious cases may be flown to Puerto Rico. Most people have health insurance, and the government provides medical benefits. A clinic and doctor serve most parishes and provide basic care free of charge. Nurse practitioners and nurse midwives play an important role. The infant mortality rate is 18 per 1,000; life expectancy is 73 years.

FOR THE TRAVELER

Proof of citizenship (a passport is best) and a return ticket are required for U.S. citizens to visit Antigua and Barbuda. There is a $10 departure tax. For travel information, contact the Antigua and Barbuda Department of Tourism, 610 Fifth Avenue, Suite 311, New York, NY 10020; phone (212) 541–4117. You may also contact the Embassy of Antigua and Barbuda, 3216 New Mexico Avenue NW, Washington, DC 20016; phone (202) 362–5122.

Argentina

(Argentine Republic)

Boundary representations not necessarily authoritative.

BACKGROUND

Land and Climate

With an area of 1,068,296 square miles (2,766,890 square kilometers), Argentina is the eighth largest country in the world; it is one-third the size of the United States. Laced with rivers, Argentina, which literally means "silver," is a large plain rising from the Atlantic Ocean in the east to the towering Andes Mountains in the west, along the Chilean border. The Chaco region in the northeast is dry except during the summer rainy season. *Las Pampas*, the central plains, is famous for wheat and cattle production. Patagonia, to the south, consists of flat to rolling hills that are known for sheep raising. Approximately 60 percent of the land is used for agriculture; another 22 percent is covered by forests.

The nation's landscape varies, containing such wonders as the Iguazú Falls (1.5 times higher than the Niagara Falls) in the north and the Perito Moreno Glacier of Santa Cruz to the south. The Moreno Glacier is one of the few glaciers in the world that is still advancing. Argentina's climate is generally temperate, though hot in the subtropical north and cold in the subantarctic region of southern Patagonia. Cool ocean breezes help keep Buenos Aires relatively smog free. The seasons are opposite of those in the Northern Hemisphere: the warmest month is January, the coolest is July.

History

Before the Spanish began to colonize Argentina in the 1500s, the area was populated by various indigenous groups, some of whom (in the north) belonged to the Incan Empire. However, most groups were nomadic or autonomous. Colonization got off to a slow start, but it increased in the 1700s as more indigenous peoples became marginalized and the Spanish established more cities. The British tried to capture Buenos Aires in 1806, but they were defeated. This, and friction with Spain, led to calls for independence. At the time, the colony included not only Argentina, but Paraguay and Uruguay as well.

A revolution erupted in 1810 and lasted six years before independence was finally declared. *Porteños* (coastal inhabitants favoring a centrist government based in Buenos Aires) then fought with those who favored a federal form of government. The actual fighting did not last long, but tensions remained and Argentina finally became a unified nation in 1862. (Paraguay and Uruguay had long since become independent.) Civilian rule was generally peaceful and stable until a military coup of 1930. Another coup occurred in 1943, after which Juan Domingo Perón (a key figure in the coup) emerged as the country's leader. He was elected president in 1946 and ruled until 1955, when he was overthrown. After a series of military governments, Perón returned to power in 1973 but died in 1974, leaving his wife, Isabel, as the first woman to head a national government in the Western Hemisphere. She was ousted in 1976 by the military, which then waged a "Dirty War" against civilians to maintain power; thousands died or disappeared.

In 1982, Argentina went to war with Great Britain over the *Islas Malvinas* (Falkland Islands). The military's defeat in the war led to 1983 elections that broke military rule and brought Raúl Alfonsín to power. In May 1989, he became the first leader in nearly half a century to be replaced through peaceful elections, when Carlos Saúl Menem, the son of Syrian immigrants, was elected president. Menem promised to improve the economy by introducing free-market principles. Although initially unpopular, Menem's economic policies lowered inflation, produced growth, and opened the market to freer trade. By 1993, the economy was stable and Menem's popularity had risen significantly.

Menem had also stabilized democratic institutions in the country, paving the way for a future of peaceful transfers of power. Congressional elections in 1993 gave a strong victory to Menem's party (*Partido Justicialista*, also known as the Perónist Party) over the other major party, the Radical Civic Union. The strong victory enabled Menem and his supporters to call for a constitutional assembly to rewrite the constitution allowing a sitting president to run for reelection. The assembly was elected in 1994, but a third party, the Broad Front, made a strong showing and became an important part of the process. The new constitution, unveiled in 1995, lifted the ban on reelections, reduced the presidential term to four years, and changed how senators are elected, among other things. Menem was reelected in 1995 with his Perónist Party, which won a majority in both legislative houses. During his second term, Menem has continued to implement plans for economic reform.

THE PEOPLE

Population

The population of Argentina is about 33.9 million (the second largest in South America) and is growing yearly by 1.1 percent. At least 85 percent of the people live in urban areas. With more than 12 million people, the capital of Buenos Aires is one of the most populated metropolitan areas in the world. Approximately 85 percent of the people are descendants of European immigrants (Italian, Spanish, German, Welsh, English, French, and Russian). *Mestizos* (Spanish and Indian mix), Indians, and others make up the remaining 15 percent. More than 45 percent of the population is under age 15.

Argentina's Human Development Index (0.882) ranks it 30th out of 174 countries. This reflects the availability of choices needed to enjoy a decent standard of living. Adjusted for women, the index (0.768) ranks it 39th out of 130 countries.

Language

While Spanish is the official language of Argentina, many people speak some English. Argentine Spanish contains many distinct phrases and terms not used in other Spanish-speaking countries. German, French, and Italian are spoken by members of the older generation and by some of their descendants. Aboriginals speak several indigenous languages, the most common of which are Quichua, Guaraní, and Mapuche.

Religion

Roughly 90 percent of the people belong to the Roman Catholic Church, which exercises great influence over many social customs and celebrations. Most weddings and funerals follow traditional Catholic norms. Despite this, a majority of Catholics are not actively involved with their church, and Argentine society is somewhat more secularized than other Latin American countries.

Non-Catholic Christian churches are gaining popularity. Approximately 2 percent of the people are members of various Protestant churches, another 2 percent are Jewish, and the remaining 6 percent belong to other religious organizations. Religious freedom is guaranteed, as church and state are officially separate.

General Attitudes

Argentines are proud of their nation, which has risen above difficult times to become a modern, thriving, democratic, and economically sound state. Political problems are solved through democratic institutions rather than coups, and the days of the "Dirty War" are past. People now look forward to improving their economic and social status, providing a better future for their children, and improving the country's image in the world. Prosperity, home ownership, strong personal and family relationships, education, and holding or being near someone who holds political or social power are important to Argentines.

Urban Argentines tend to be cosmopolitan, progressive, and outgoing. They consider themselves somewhat superior to their rural countrymen and even others in Latin America. Rural Argentines are more conservative and traditional. Latin American *machismo* (macho man image) is still admired in Argentina, although by a shrinking number of people.

Personal Appearance

While dress may differ considerably from region to region, it is generally conservative. Also universal is the desire to be well dressed in public. In Buenos Aires, European and North American fashions are popular and readily available. European designs are considered more fashionable by Argentine women than styles from North America. Older women seldom wear pants but the younger generation prefers dressing more casually. In other areas, dress may reflect regional culture, such as among the *gauchos* (cowboys) of the Pampa region, who wear traditional clothing.

CUSTOMS AND COURTESIES

Greetings

When greeting formally or for the first time, Argentines use a handshake and a slight nod to show respect. In places such as Buenos Aires, a brief embrace with a kiss on the cheek is also common. Women are most likely to kiss each other, but a man and woman may greet in this manner if well acquainted. A person might wave and smile at an acquaintance who is too distant to greet verbally; it is not polite to call out a greeting. The Spanish *¡Buenos días!* (Good morning—*¡Buen día!* in Buenos Aires) or *¡Buenas tardes!* (Good afternoon) are commonly used when people pass on the street or greet friends and acquaintances. When one approaches a stranger or an official for information, it is polite to greet the person before asking any questions.

Argentines customarily address people by a title (*Señor, Señora,* or *Doctor,* among others) when first introduced or in formal situations. Friends and relatives use given names. Older, respected persons are addressed by first name, preceded by the title *Don* (for men) or *Doña* (for women).

Gestures

Hand gestures are often used in daily conversation to supplement verbal communication. People also use certain gestures to communicate with others from a distance. For example, to order a cup of coffee from a distant bartender or waiter, Argentines hold up their extended thumb and index finger separated slightly (by less than a centimeter), with the other fingers folded in a fist.

It is improper for a man and woman to show affection in public. During conversation, personal space tends to be small, and conversants might touch each other or stand close when speaking. Yawning without covering the mouth, as well as placing one's hands on the hips, is impolite. Eye contact is considered important in conversation. Hats are removed in buildings, houses, elevators, and in the presence of women.

Visiting

Argentines often visit friends and relatives without prior arrangement. People enjoy having guests in the home and usually offer them refreshments. Espresso-style coffee is typical. Invited guests are not expected to arrive on time, as punctuality is not as important as the individual person. Guests will not offend hosts by arriving up to 30 minutes or more late. Visitors greet each person of the group individually; a group greeting is inappropriate. Dinner guests often bring a small gift such as flowers, candy, or pastries to their hosts. Guests do not take a seat until the host directs them to do so. Compliments about the home, meal, or hosts' family are appreciated. When leaving, a guest again addresses every person present, using such common phrases for good-bye as *¡Cíao!* or *Hasta luego.* The host usually opens the door for guests when they leave.

Eating

Three meals are eaten each day. The main meal is traditionally served at midday, although urban work schedules have affected many families. That is, while rural people can usually eat most meals together, urban families may only be able to come together for supper, which is often served after 9:00 P.M. Argentines use the continental style of eating, with the fork in the left hand and the knife remaining in the right. Hands (but not elbows) should always be above the table, not in the lap. Using a toothpick in public is considered bad manners, as is blowing one's nose, talking with the mouth full, or clearing one's throat at the table. Eating in the street or on public transportation is inappropriate. Restaurant waiters may be summoned by raising the hand with the index finger extended. Tipping is not required, but it is becoming customary

in many restaurants. Porters and other individuals providing personal services are tipped about 10 percent.

LIFESTYLE

Family

Urban families tend to be rather small, averaging two children, but rural families are larger. The responsibility of raising children and managing household finances falls heavily on the mother, and she, in turn, exerts great influence on family decisions. More women are working outside the home, but they presently comprise less than 30 percent of the work force. Men tend to be more occupied with their work, often not coming home before 9:00 P.M. Children are central to the family and receive a great deal of attention. Families will sacrifice much to give their children a good education. Until 1987, divorce was illegal in Argentina, but it is now increasing.

Dating and Marriage

Group activities between boys and girls begin at about age 15, when girls have their most important birthday (*cumpleaños de quince*) that ends their childhood. A favorite activity of young couples is dancing. The youth also play sports, eat out, or go to movies. Serious relationships develop slowly over several years; most couples marry between 23 and 27 years of age. Weddings are very elaborate, containing three different events: the civil ceremony, the church wedding (no bridesmaids or groomsmen; instead, the parents stand with the couple), and a large reception (dinner and dancing). Gifts are not brought to the reception but are purchased at and delivered by a gift shop where the couple has registered.

Diet

Beef is the staple of the Argentine diet; in fact, Argentines eat more beef per capita than any other people in the world, including citizens of the United States. Because Argentina is a major beef producer, domestic prices are low enough for most people to eat beef every day. Road and construction companies are known to provide workers access to portable grills for use at lunchtime. A favorite way to entertain is the *asado* (barbecue) on weekends. Other foods include baked, stuffed beef and *empanadas* (meat or vegetable pies). A preferred winter stew is *locro* (made of meat, corn, and potatoes). Argentines also eat chicken and pork. A wide variety of fruits and vegetables are included in the average diet. *Mate* is a popular hot tea. Italian and French foods are widely available.

Recreation

Soccer is the national sport and is enjoyed by children and adults alike. Argentina's national soccer team reached the quarterfinals of the 1994 World Cup. Other popular sports include horse racing, rugby, field hockey, tennis, polo, and basketball.

A fine opera house (the *Colón)* is located in Buenos Aires, as are many excellent movie theaters that receive regular attendance. Buenos Aires has many late-night theaters, restaurants, and clubs. The popular tango dance originated in Argentina. For years it has been more popular outside of Argentina than among Argentines, who prefer heavy rock or Central American music like salsa. Some effort is being made to revive the tango's popularity with the younger generation.

In their leisure time, Argentines also enjoy watching television, reading, relaxing with friends, or going to movies.

Holidays

Argentines celebrate religious holidays more festively than national ones, using the latter ones for leisure time or to catch up on household repairs. Christmas and New Year's Day are usually marked with fireworks. Other holidays include Good Friday and Easter; Labor Day (1 May); Anniversary of the May Revolution (25 May); Malvinas Day (10 June); Flag Day (20 June); Independence Day (9 July); Death of General José de San Martín, who is known as the "Liberator" of Peru, Chile, and Argentina for his defeat of the Spanish in 1812 (17 August); Student Day (21 September); and Columbus Day (12 October).

Commerce

In Buenos Aires, stores generally open at 9:00 A.M. and close at 8:00 P.M. In other cities, they open at 8:00 A.M., close for lunch between noon and 3:00 or 4:00 P.M., and remain open until 8:00 P.M., Monday through Friday. On Saturday, stores close around 1:00 P.M. for the day. Professional and government offices have variable hours depending on their function, but most government offices are open weekdays between 9:00 A.M. and 5:00 P.M. Any shopping items, including groceries, are wrapped or placed in shopping bags before being taken from the store. Workers in Argentina enjoy an *aguinaldo* (13th-month bonus) equal to one month's pay; it is often paid in two semiannual installments.

SOCIETY

Government

The Argentine Republic has 23 provinces and one federal district. The executive branch consists of a president, a vice president, and a cabinet. The president is both chief of state and head of government. The National Congress has two houses, a 72-seat Senate and a 257-seat Chamber of Deputies. Members of the independent Supreme Court are appointed by the president. The voting age is 18.

Economy

Agriculture, which currently employs about 12 percent of the people, has always been the mainstay of the Argentine economy, although industry is also vital. Argentina is famous for its livestock and is a major exporter of beef, hides, and wool. The country also exports large amounts of wheat, corn, and flaxseed, as well as soybean and cotton. Important industries include food processing, meat packing, motor vehicles, consumer goods, textiles, chemicals, printing, and metallurgy.

Argentina's economic progress has benefitted a broad portion of the population. Due to President Menem's reforms, economic growth averaged 7 percent between 1991 and 1994. Inflation was less than 10 percent and unemployment was low. Foreign investment increased substantially to stimulate growth. Growth slowed in 1995 due to low investor confidence, but the economy is expected to recover in 1996. Real gross domestic product per capita is $8,860, which has improved steadily in the last generation. Although economic opportunities are available to a majority of the people, unemployment has recently doubled and now affects nearly one in five people. Inflation is the lowest in the world at 0.2 percent. The currency is the *peso*.

Transportation and Communication

Transportation and communication systems are well developed. Argentines have access to private cars, taxis, buses, subways, and trains. A few people ride motorcycles, but bicycles are reserved for recreation. Airlines link major cities in Argentina and neighboring countries. Buenos Aires is the most important seaport. Televisions and telephones are increasingly common and service is likewise improving. Postal service is extensive but not always reliable. The Cable News Network (CNN) broadcasts 24 hours a day in Argentina. Newspapers are widely available, including an English-speaking daily, the *Buenos Aires Herald*.

Education

Argentina's adult literacy rate is 96 percent, one of the highest in Latin America. School is compulsory and free from ages six through fourteen. Secondary and higher education are also free but must be entered by examination. Nearly three-fourths of all eligible students are enrolled in secondary schools. Argentines may seek higher education at 26 national and 24 private universities, as well as at teacher-training colleges, vocational schools, and other institutions.

Health

Argentines enjoy relatively good health and have access to both public and private health-care facilities. Public hospitals provide care for citizens free of charge. The most modern facilities are found in Buenos Aires. Care is less reliable and less available in rural areas. Trade unions often provide health services to their members. The average life expectancy is 68 to 75 years. The infant mortality rate is 29 per 1,000.

FOR THE TRAVELER

U.S. citizens need a valid passport to enter Argentina; a visa is only required for stays of more than 90 days. One's passport is often required to register at a hotel and should be carried at all times. No immunizations are required, but yellow fever vaccinations may be recommended for visits to the northeastern forests. Protection against malaria is sometimes advisable for travel to outlying areas. Water is generally safe to drink.

Argentina offers a great deal to the traveler, from the European-style city of Buenos Aires and large beach resorts to virgin forests and breathtaking waterfalls (such as Iguazú Falls). For more information, contact the Argentina Tourist Information Office, 12 West 56th Street, New York, NY 10019; phone (212) 603–0443. You may also wish to contact the Embassy of Argentina, 1600 New Hampshire Avenue NW, Washington, DC 20009; phone (202) 939–6400. Consulates, which provide the same services as embassies, are located in several U.S. cities.

CULTURGRAM ™ '97

Republic of

Austria

Boundary representations not necessarily authoritative.

BACKGROUND

Land and Climate

A landlocked country in central Europe, Austria covers 32,375 square miles (83,850 square kilometers) and is slightly smaller than Maine. Spectacular mountains, clear lakes, beautiful scenery, and green valleys all comprise Austria's grandeur. The famous Alps cover much of the west and south, while flatlands dominate in the east and northeast. The country generally enjoys a mild climate. Spring and summer are temperate. However, winters in some mountain areas can be very cold. In Vienna, the average temperature in winter is 32°F (0°C) and in summer is 67°F (20°C).

History

Despite its present size, Austria has had a significant impact on European history and world culture. Present-day Austria was once part of both the Roman and Charlemagne's Empires. Otto I, who later became emperor of the Holy Roman Empire, began his rule in 955. He is often considered the real founder of Austria because of the borders he established. "Austria" is the Latin equivalent of the German *Österreich* (realm of the east).

In 1156, with Vienna as its capital, Austria became an autonomous duchy under the Babenburgs. The Hapsburg Dynasty came to power in 1273. For six hundred years, the Hapsburgs gradually spread their Austro-Hungarian Empire over central Europe through marriages and other strategies. They helped push the Ottoman Turks out of Europe after the 18th century. Their power was greatest in the early 19th century, after they helped defeat Napoleon.

By 1914, the empire covered present-day Austria, Hungary, the Czech Republic, Slovakia, Slovenia, Croatia, Bosnia-Herzegovina, and parts of Poland and Romania. Still, it was in decline due to growing nationalism among its various peoples. In 1914, when the Archduke Franz Ferdinand, heir to the Hapsburg throne, was assassinated in Sarajevo, what should have been a local civil conflict quickly mushroomed into World War I, as most European nations became involved. "The Great War," as it was called, led to the empire's destruction. Yugoslavia and Czechoslovakia were created from parts of the old empire; both countries have since divided.

The first Austrian republic (1918–38) struggled to survive and was swallowed up by Hitler's Germany before the start of World War II. After 1945, Austria was divided into four zones, each governed by one of the four Allied powers (Great Britain, France, the United States, and the Soviet Union). Ten years later, Austria was reborn as an independent and permanently neutral democratic republic, with strong ties to Western Europe. The republic has since been a model of political, economic, and social stability.

Because of Austria's political neutrality, Vienna has become a key United Nations city where nations meet to discuss problems or negotiate treaties. Austria's trade ties with Hungary prompted the Hungarian government to tear down the barbed-wire fence along the Austrian-Hungarian border in 1989. This action is recognized as a significant event that encouraged the 1990 political reforms in Eastern Europe.

With voters supporting European economic integration by an almost two-to-one margin in 1994, Austria joined the

EUROPE

European Union (EU) in January 1995. Budget disputes led to early elections in December 1995, but Austria's ruling coalition returned to power and has approved austere economic reforms in preparation for joining the EU monetary union.

PEOPLE

Population

Austria's population of almost eight million is growing at 0.4 percent annually. At least 99 percent of the people are Germanic, while minorities include Croatians, Slovenes, and various other groups. In addition, approximately 200,000 foreign workers—mainly from Turkey and the former Yugoslavia—live and work in Austria, but they are not counted as part of the population. About 58 percent of the people live in urban areas. Austria's Human Development Index (0.925) ranks it 14th out of 174 nations. Adjusted for women, the index (0.882) ranks Austria 10th out of 130 countries.

Language

The official language is High German, but each area has its own dialect. Dialects are more pronounced in rural areas. A minority in southern Austria speaks Croatian. English is a required language in high schools and is spoken by many people.

Religion

Some 85 percent of all Austrians are Roman Catholic, while 6 percent are Protestant. The other 9 percent belong to various other Christian churches, some non-Christian religions, or no denomination. Younger people are generally less devout than the older generation; many young people have withdrawn their membership from the Catholic Church. At the same time, Austrians are generally more religious than people in many other western European countries, and Catholic traditions, shrines, and churches are still treasured. The Jewish community has about 10,000 members, down from 200,000 before World War II.

General Attitudes

Austrians are known for their *Gemütlichkeit*, a relaxed and happy approach to life. A good-natured sense of frustration and bittersweet attitude toward reality are considered unique national traits. Although a relaxed people, Austrians are hardworking. They value cleanliness, neatness, and order. Litter is rare. People love to learn and engage in conversation. Austrians have a deep regard for the environment and take pride in their country's beautiful landscape. Austrian society values its professionals, academics, and artists. Cultural arts are important to all segments of society, as Austrians are extremely proud of their culture's contributions to Western civilization.

Austrians are not Germans and should not be referred to as such; some Austrians may consider it an insult. While the two peoples speak the same basic language (with important differences in dialect), Austrians and Germans have a different historical and political heritage; they also differ in some customs, values, and attitudes.

Personal Appearance

Austrians generally wear European clothing fashions, but they often add a distinctive Austrian touch to their wardrobes. They take pride in dressing well, even if they are only going grocery shopping. It is important to dress properly for all events. While older people might mix traditional Austrian clothing with conservative European fashions, young people prefer modern European attire. Folk costumes (*Trachten*) are often worn on formal occasions and for celebrations. Each area has its own particular costume. This traditional clothing includes *Lederhosen* (leather knee pants) and *Trachtenjacken* (woolen jackets) for men and a *Dirndl* (dress with an apron) or *Trachtenanzug* (suit) for women. Both may have intricate designs and are usually prized items in a person's wardrobe. Those who have more than one traditional outfit will reserve an especially nice one for special occasions.

CUSTOMS AND COURTESIES

Greetings

Austrians shake hands when greeting and parting. Even children shake hands with adults when greeting, as this is an important social courtesy. In Vienna, a man may still kiss the hand of a woman when introduced to her. Common greetings in Austria include *Grüß Gott* (May God greet you), *Guten Morgen* (Good morning), *Guten Tag* (Good day), and *Guten Abend* (Good evening). Popular casual greetings include *Servus* (used as "Hi") and *Grüß Dich!* (Greetings to you!). Austrians do not ask "How are you?" (*Wie geht es Ihnen?*) unless they wish to hear a detailed account.

Professional titles are important among the adult population and are used whenever known. Otherwise, people combine titles such as *Herr* (Mr.), *Fräulein* (Miss), and *Frau* (Mrs. or Ms.) with family names when addressing acquaintances and strangers. Close friends and the youth use first names.

Gestures

Hand gestures are used conservatively in polite company, as verbal communication is preferred. It is impolite for adults to chew gum in public. Motioning with the entire hand is more polite than using the index finger. Touching the index finger to one's forehead or temple is an insult. Yawns and coughs are covered when they cannot be avoided.

Visiting

Austrians enjoy entertaining in their homes and having guests. Dropping by unannounced is impolite. It is better to make arrangements in advance or telephone ahead of an impromptu visit. Invited guests should arrive on time. Punctuality is important to Austrians. Customarily, guests remove their shoes when entering a home. This tradition is not practiced in many homes today, however, and guests who reach for their shoes might be told by the hostess that it is all right to leave them on. In homes where the hosts expect guests to remove shoes, guest slippers are usually visible near the door.

Guests remain standing until invited to sit down; they often remain standing until told just where to sit. Hosts customarily offer the best seats to their guests. If the host must leave the room for a moment, the guest is offered something to read or occupy the time until the host returns. Men stand when a woman enters the room or when talking to a woman who is standing.

While guests usually are offered a drink (tea, coffee, mineral water, juice, or soda), further refreshments depend on the hosts. Invited guests bring flowers, candy, or a small gift (such as a handcrafted item or something appropriate for the occasion). Even married children often bring such a gift when visiting their parents. Gifts are given to the wife, or perhaps the children, but not the husband—even if the gift is for the family. People only give flowers in odd numbers (even numbers are bad luck) and they unwrap them in the presence of the hostess. A gift of red roses is a sign of romantic love. Giving purchased flowers is more polite than flowers from one's own garden.

To show courtesy to the hosts, guests do not ask to use the telephone (all calls are billed, even local ones, and the cost is high). In addition, guests do not offer to help make any preparations if they are not well acquainted with the hosts or if the hostess does not seem to have everything under control. When guests leave, the hosts accompany them outside to the gate, where the hosts remain until the guests are out of sight. It is polite and generally expected for guests on foot to turn once or twice while walking away and wave to the hosts.

While most Austrians prefer to entertain in the home, they also socialize in restaurants and other public places. For many people, especially in small villages, it is a custom on Sunday after church services (usually Catholic) for women to go home and fix dinner and men to go to a *Gasthaus* (pub) to do business, exchange ideas, and drink. This socializing is less about drinking and much more about networking and socializing with male friends.

Eating

Eating habits are changing in Austria. For example, the main meal was once eaten at midday but is now eaten more commonly in the evening. This is necessary when both the husband and wife work outside of the home. Likewise, afternoon "tea" is now less common among working Austrians. At the same time, certain traditions remain strong, such as keeping hands above the table during the meal, not gesturing with utensils, and not placing elbows on the table while eating. It is impolite to begin eating until all persons at the table are served. Austrians eat in the continental style, with the fork in the left hand and the knife remaining in the right. When guests are present, the hostess will nearly always offer second helpings but will gracefully accept a polite *Danke, nein* (Thank you, no).

Restaurants serve tap water rather than mineral water. (Generally, tap water is drunk only in the home.) The bill, which usually includes a service charge, is paid at the table to the server. Most people round the bill up to the nearest *schilling* (Austrian) as a tip.

LIFESTYLE
Family

Austrian families usually are small, with one or two children. However, rural families are often a bit larger. Most Austrians expect to marry and have a family. Both parents generally work outside the home, with women comprising nearly 40 percent of the labor force. In such cases, married couples tend to share duties related to the household and children. Some homes, especially in rural areas, maintain a more strict patriarchal family structure. The government gives families financial allowances for each child. Children who are not in school and whose parents both work are cared for privately or in day care centers. Most urban Austrians live in apartments; sometimes extended families will share one large house

that contains several apartments. About one-fifth of all housing is publicly owned. Rural families generally live in single-family homes.

Dating and Marriage

Austrian youth begin associating in groups. When they start getting together as couples, they usually date only one person at a time and the relationship generally is considered serious. Actual dates are rather casual affairs, as people often just agree to meet somewhere. Boys and girls pay their own expenses, with one or the other offering to pay for both only on special occasions. Eating out, going to movies, and dancing are favorite activities.

Couples often decide to live together before or instead of marrying. The typical age for marriage is between 25 and 28 years. A civil ceremony must be performed for the marriage to be legal; church weddings are optional.

Diet

Austrians love good food and have a rich and varied cuisine drawn from the various cultures that once comprised the Austro-Hungarian Empire. Specialties vary by region but include such favorites as *Wienerschnitzel* (breaded veal cutlet), *Sachertorte* (a rich chocolate cake with apricot jam and chocolate icing), *Knödel* (moist potato dumplings), and goulash.

A typical day begins early with a light breakfast of coffee or hot chocolate, rolls, bread, and jam or marmalade. Later in the morning, some eat a second, heartier breakfast, including goulash or hot sausages. The main meal, whether at midday or in the evening, may include soup, meat (often pork) with potatoes or pasta, vegetables, a salad, and often dessert (such as a homemade pastry). Afternoon tea (*Jause*) may include sandwiches, pastries, and coffee. If the main meal is eaten at midday, families have *Abendbrot* (evening bread) in the evening. It generally includes cold cuts, eggs, cheese, rye and other breads, and a salad. After a visit to the theater or other evening activity, a light supper might end the day. Austrians enjoy beer, wine, herbal teas, apple juice with sparkling mineral water, fruit juices, and soft drinks.

Recreation

Austrians love the outdoors. Taking a walk (*ein Spaziergang*) is a national pastime. Hiking, skiing, boating, and swimming are all popular activities. Soccer is a favorite sport, but Austrians are better known for their excellence in winter sports. They are consistent medalists in Winter Olympic events. Gardening is popular, even when space is limited. Window boxes full of flowers are favorites throughout the country.

Cultural arts play a key role in Austrian society. People enjoy modern art and music, but they also treasure more traditional music. Even large numbers of the youth attend opera performances and orchestral concerts. The names Haydn, Mozart, Schubert, Strauss, Beethoven, and Brahms (who all worked in Vienna), as well as Wolf, Mahler, Bruckner, and others, attest to Austria's traditional musical splendor. The Vienna State Opera, the Vienna Philharmonic, the Vienna Boys Choir, and the Salzburg Festival are four of many music institutions that enjoy worldwide fame. Austria is also noted for its writers (Franz Kafka, Hofmansthal, Karl Kraus). Painters and architects have also flourished in Austria in the 20th century, especially since World War II. With Vienna as its center, Austria continues to give strong support to the development and performance of cultural arts.

Folk music is important in Austria. Common folk instruments include the *hackbrett* (hammered dulcimer) and *zither* (a stringed instrument). Guitars and harps are also prevalent in folk music. In addition, nearly every village has a band (usually brass), any town of size has a professional orchestra, and there are many local theaters.

Holidays

Austrians celebrate New Year's Day, *Heilige Drei Könige* (Three Kings, 6 January), Easter (Saturday–Monday), Labor Day (1 May), Flag Day (26 October, the national holiday), All Saints' Day (1 November), and Christmas (25–26 December), as well as various religious holidays throughout the year. Christmas Eve (*Heiliger Abend* or Holy Evening) is the most important part of Christmas. Families gather to share a meal and sing Christmas carols. Children receive their presents, which are customarily put under the tree by the Christ child when they are out of the room. There is little tradition of Santa Claus, although it is making its way into the commercial aspect of Christmas. Christmas Day is reserved for visiting family. In the summer, most families vacation in August. Small, family-owned shops might be closed the entire month while the family is away.

Commerce

Large stores are open from 8:00 A.M. until 6:00 P.M. on weekdays and from 8:00 A.M. until noon on Saturdays. Large chain stores remain open on Saturday until evening. Small open-air markets often open at 6:00 A.M. Banks close at 4:30 P.M. An increasing number of stores are open on Sunday. Small, private shops might still close for the traditional *Mittagspause* (midday break), which was once universal as the two- or three-hour break for the main meal.

SOCIETY

Government

The Republic of Austria has nine states. The government's executive branch consists of a federal president, a federal chancellor, and the chancellor's cabinet. The president, Thomas Klestil, was elected in 1992. The Federal Assembly (*Bundesversammlung*) has a 63-member upper house, called a Federal Council (*Bundesrat*), and a 183-seat lower house, called a National Council (*Nationalrat*). Austria's various political parties have a tradition of cooperation, which has promoted political stability. The strongest parties include the Social Democratic Party of Austria (SPOE), Austrian People's Party (OEVP), and Freedom Party of Austria (FPOE). The voting age is 19. For presidential elections, voting is mandatory. There are three types of high courts, each one having jurisdiction over either justice, administration, or the constitution.

Economy

Austria is an industrialized nation with a mixed free-market/social-welfare economy. Social-welfare programs are fairly extensive and provide support for the unemployed. Agriculture plays only a minor role in the economy, although the country is mostly self-sufficient in food. Important resources include iron ore, timber, tungsten, coal, and other minerals. Austria exports machinery, lumber, textiles, iron, steel, chemicals, and paper products. Tourism is also an important industry.

The economy is generally strong and stable, a result of a unique system of social partnerships in which unions and owners or employers cooperate to exercise restraint on prices and wages. They also try to reach a consensus on managing the national economy. Real gross domestic product per capita is $18,710, about four times higher than it was in 1960. This figure reflects the economy's expansion in the last generation. Most people have access to economic opportunities and prosperity. The currency is the Austrian *schilling* (S).

Transportation and Communication

Most families own at least one car, and private cars are important for daily transportation. The public system of trains, buses, and streetcars is also heavily used, especially in large urban areas. Buses reach even the remotest areas, and a good system of trains crisscrosses the country. On the expressway, there is a speed limit of 80 miles per hour (120 kilometers per hour); seat belt laws are strictly enforced. Children under age 12 must ride in the back seat.

The communications system is efficient and extensive. Most homes have televisions and phones. Daily newspapers are available throughout the country.

Education

Each state is responsible for public schooling, which is free and compulsory for children ages six to fifteen. Most Austrians complete this amount of schooling and also gain other training or higher education. Education traditionally has been important in Austria, which is home to many Nobel Prize winners and noted scholars such as Sigmund Freud. Austrian universities offer a high-quality education; they attract many students from abroad. The adult literacy rate is 99 percent.

Health

Health care is provided for retired persons and those in need. Working persons have private health insurance. Austrians enjoy good health and have access to adequate care. The infant mortality rate is 7 per 1,000. Adults generally can expect to live an average of 74 to 80 years.

FOR THE TRAVELER

No visa is required of U.S. travelers staying up to three months, although a passport is necessary. Most hotels reserve the right to bill those who do not keep their reservations. There are countless things to do in Austria: shopping, eating, visiting the many folk museums, attending concerts, hiking around a lake or in the mountains, or just taking in the scenic beauty. For more information, contact the Austrian National Tourist Office, 500 Fifth Avenue, Suite 800, New York, NY 10110; phone (212) 944–6880. You may also wish to contact the Embassy of Austria, 3524 International Court NW, Washington, DC 20008–3035; phone (202) 895–6767. Consulate offices are located in Chicago, Los Angeles, and New York.

Barbados

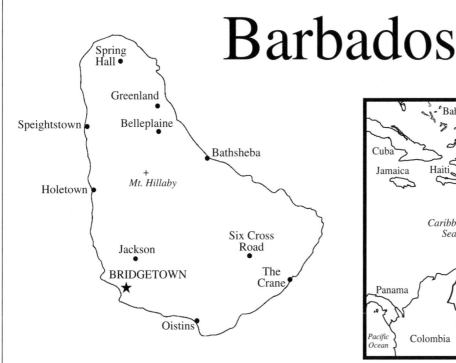

Boundary representations not necessarily authoritative.

THE AMERICAS

BACKGROUND

Land and Climate

Barbados lies farthest east in the Caribbean Archipelago. The island is 166 square miles (430 square kilometers) in size—just smaller than 2.5 times the size of Washington, D.C.—and is mostly flat. The tropical climate provides an average temperature of 85°F (29°C). The rainy season is from June to October. Between 43 and 80 inches of rain falls each year. A thin layer of topsoil covers the thick layer of coral that forms the island. The soil is very fertile, making the island lush with flowering trees, shrubs, and tropical flowers. Three-fourths of the island is suitable for cultivation. Natural resources include crude oil, fish, and natural gas.

History

The original inhabitants of Barbados were Arawak and Carib Indians. However, they disappeared before British settlers arrived—maybe even by 1536—but the reason is uncertain. The British came to the island in 1625, when Captain John Powell claimed it in the name of King James I. In 1627, Powell brought the first colonists (80 of them) and settled Holetown. As the population grew, sugarcane was introduced, and slave labor was brought in from Africa. Independence-minded colonists were forced to surrender to England’s forces

in 1652 by signing the Articles of Capitulation, which became the Charter of Barbados.

Barbados later moved toward independence by emancipating its slaves between 1834 and 1838, enfranchising women in 1944, and providing universal suffrage in 1951. A leader of the independence movement, Sir Grantley Adams, became the first premier under home rule in 1954. Barbados became part of the West Indies Federation in 1958, but the federation dissolved in 1962. Barbados thereafter sought full independence from Great Britain, which was granted on 30 November 1966. The first prime minister of an independent Barbados was Errol Barrow. The country remains a member of the Commonwealth of Nations. Since independence, Barbados has enjoyed a high degree of political stability. The island capitalized on its natural strengths and, by the 1980s, had developed a successful tourist industry. With economic and political stability, the nation was able to provide a high standard of living for its inhabitants.

During the global recession of the early 1990s, however, the economy suffered various setbacks. After his election in 1991, Prime Minister Lloyd Sandiford introduced an austerity package to improve economic conditions. However, Sandiford lost a vote of no confidence and was forced to call elections in 1994. A strong voter turnout brought economist Owen Arthur to power as the new prime minister.

THE PEOPLE

Population

The population of Barbados is approximately 256,000 and is growing at 0.24 percent annually. The birthrate is actually higher than that, but emigration holds net growth to nearly zero. The island has a high population density: 1,533 persons per square mile (592 per square kilometer). About 60 percent of the population lives in urban centers stretching along the western side of the island, which is more sheltered from storms. The capital city of Bridgetown is the largest urban area. Actually, the island is almost a city-country, with Bridgetown serving as "downtown" for the whole island. Only 4 percent of the people have a European heritage, while 16 percent are of mixed descent, and 80 percent have African origins. The people of Barbados are called Barbadians, but they are often referred to as *Bajans*.

Barbados has one of the highest levels of human development among developing nations. Its Human Develoment Index (0.900) ranks Barbados 25th out of 174 nations. Good access to health care, education, and economic prosperity provides Bajans many opportunities and choices in their lives. Adjusted for women, the index (0.878) ranks Barbados 11th out of 130 countries, indicating that women earn a comparable share of the nation's income.

Language

The official language is English. *Bajans* also speak a dialect that can be understood by other English speakers if they listen carefully. German, Spanish, French, and Italian are taught in the schools and in Board of Tourism classes.

Religion

The majority (67 percent) of Barbadians are Protestant Christians, with about 40 percent belonging to the Anglican Church and 7 percent to the Methodist Church. A number of Christian organizations are active on the island, including the Roman Catholic Church (4 percent). Nearly 30 percent of all people belong to either no church at all or smaller Christian and non-Christian organizations. There is a small Jewish community. A Jewish synagogue was first built on the island in 1654. Regardless of one's religious affiliation, funeral attendance is considered important. *Bajans* make a special effort to go to services and offer condolences to the family.

General Attitudes

Bajans are warm, happy, and friendly, although they may act reserved around strangers. They are hospitable to visitors and will welcome them to their homes. They take pride in their nation, their cultural heritage, and their people's accomplishments. A generally peaceful atmosphere allows the police to patrol unarmed. Social unity is important to Barbadians. Their view of life is evident in the carefully kept homes, beautiful pastels used to paint houses, and lively festivals that represent past and present culture. They love music and dancing.

Personal Appearance

Women usually wear tailored dresses or blouses and skirts to work, but they get very dressed up for parties and other social events. They wear their finest dresses and hats to church meetings. For casual events, women usually dress in colorful, long skirts with open-type sandals. Sometimes they wear their hair in small braids with colorful beads at the ends. Men usually wear lightweight pants with a casual shirt of white, pastel, or flowered fabric (usually locally made). This "shirt-jac" suit is generally accepted everywhere (parties, offices, and churches), but a more formal suit is normally required for certain party functions and formal events. Swimwear is limited to the beach and is not worn in the city or other public places.

CUSTOMS AND COURTESIES

Greetings

Bajans generally greet each other with a handshake and a smile. Acquaintances often embrace upon meeting. A common greeting is "How do you do?" An answer such as "Not bad" does not carry any negative feeling but is a friendly response. An evening telephone call begins with "Hello, good night. . . ."

Gestures

Barbadians call taxis and buses by waving the hand. They often use their hands when conversing as well. In passing, people wave the hand to say hello. They often express disgust by making a sound with puckered lips (sounding something like CHUPSE) and show defiance by standing *akimbo* (placing their hands on their hips) while arguing a point. *Bajans* frequently will fold their arms as a sign that they are paying complete attention to what is going on.

Visiting

Bajans usually visit one another on weekends. A favorite time for men to get together is Sunday morning, when topics of conversation range from politics to cricket. Hosts usually serve drinks to guests in the home. Other significant visiting occurs at cricket and other sporting events when old friends see each other. Shops in the country districts and barber salons in the city are important places for lively discussion, especially around election time. As in English households, guests are often invited to afternoon tea.

Eating

Barbadians eat in the continental style, with the fork in the left hand and the knife remaining in the right. *Bajan* food is unique, a combination of African and English traditions, and can be found in most restaurants. Fast-food is also becoming popular, as is pizza. A 5 percent tax is applied to all meals, and a 10 percent service charge is added to the bill or included in menu prices. International cuisine is available in resort areas.

LIFESTYLE

Family

The extended family is important in Barbados, and parents, children, grandparents, and cousins enjoy substantial interaction. This pattern is changing somewhat with modernization, but it is still important. Extended families may live together or near one another. Single-parent (usually the mother) families are common. In homes where the father is present, he is the leader. Economic circumstances have caused many women to seek employment outside the home, leaving the care of children to grandparents. Nearly half of the workforce is female. Some people have emigrated to the United States, Canada, or the United Kingdom for work, but they still maintain extended family ties through monetary support and visits.

Many families live in traditional *chattel houses*. These look like mobile wooden homes, set on coral stone three or four feet above ground for better air circulation. *Chattel houses* are designed for easy assembly and disassembly, as plantation workers in the past were often required to move from one working area to another. They are so well built that they may be passed from one generation to the next. Other permanent homes exist, of course. They are made of concrete and painted with pastel colors.

Dating and Marriage

Dating usually begins in the early teens. Many young people marry after they have established themselves financially or have begun their careers. Marriage is an important event in the life of a *Bajan*. Weddings are traditionally held in churches, followed by a gala reception in a local hall, hotel, or restaurant. *Bajan* steel bands perform local or English music. Bridal dresses are similar to those in North America, and brides wear long veils. Elaborate wedding cakes are provided by the family or are purchased.

Diet

Barbados offers a wide variety of foods in plentiful supply. The national dish is flying fish and *cou cou* (made of okra and cornmeal). Also popular are lobster, shrimp, dorado, red snapper, turtle, tuna, kingfish, and the Crane Chubb fish. White sea urchin eggs are a delicacy. The tropical soil yields mangoes, papayas, bananas, cucumbers, tomatoes, guavas, avocados, and coconuts, as well as squash, eggplant, breadfruit, and numerous other vegetables. Popular local dishes include *jug-jug* (Guinea corn and green peas), *pepperpot* (a spicy stew), and *conkies* (cornmeal, coconut, pumpkin, raisins, sweet potatoes, and spices steamed in a banana leaf). Black-bellied sheep and goats provide meat. Both cow and goat milk are popular.

Recreation

Cricket is the national sport. With excellent wind and water conditions, wind surfing and surfing are favorites, as are yachting, waterskiing, sailing, scuba diving, and skin diving. Diving is popular because of the extensive coral reefs and three sunken ships. People enjoy swimming on the south and west coast beaches. Other sporting activities include polo, horse racing, golf, squash, and tennis. The national table game is dominoes. *Bajans* also enjoy soccer, bridge, chess, cycling, basketball, rugby, and volleyball. Sunday and holiday picnics at the beach are popular. When vacationing, Barbadians may visit another part of the island, another English-speaking island, or relatives in the United States, Canada, or England. The people often relax with *Bajan* folk songs, calypso songs, and dancing. Many of these date back to slave songs brought by West Africans to the West Indies in the 1600s.

Holidays

Four annual festivals celebrate important events in Barbados. The Holetown Festival (three days in February) celebrates the arrival of the first settlers; the Oistins Fish Festival is held on Easter weekend as a tribute to the fishing industry; the Crop Over Festival (mid-July–early August) celebrates the end of the sugarcane harvest; and the National Independence Festival of the Creative Arts (November) allows people to display talents in various fields. Other holidays include New Year's Day, Errol Barrow Day (21 January), Good Friday, Easter Monday, May Day (1 May), Whitmonday, *Kadooment* Day (first Monday in July), United Nations Day (first Monday in October), Independence Day (30 November), Christmas, and Boxing Day (26 December). Boxing Day was originally set aside for the British tradition of giving small boxed gifts to servants and tradesmen the day after Christmas; it is now a day to visit friends and family.

Commerce

Most businesses are open from 8:00 A.M. to 4:00 P.M., Monday through Friday, and until noon on Saturday. Grocery stores are open somewhat later, closing either at 6:00 or 7:00 P.M. on weekdays and at 1:00 P.M. on Saturdays. Some convenience stores are open until 9:00 P.M. Most businesses close on Sunday, although large stores remain open on Sunday when cruise ships are in port. Banking hours are generally shorter. Banks are open from 9:00 A.M. until 3:00 P.M., Monday through Thursday, and from 9:00 A.M. to 1:00 P.M. and 3:00 to 5:00 P.M. on Friday. The average workweek is 40 hours.

SOCIETY

Government

Barbados is a parliamentary democracy. As a sovereign member of the Commonwealth of Nations, it recognizes Queen Elizabeth II as head of state. She is represented by a governor general, who was Dame Nita Barrow until her death in December 1995. Sir Denys Williams currently serves as acting governor general. The prime minister is the leader of the majority party in the National Assembly, which has 28 seats. Parliament also has a senate, whose members are appointed. Barbados is divided into 11 parishes. National elections are held at least every five years. If necessary, the prime minister may call elections earlier, as Sandiford did in 1994.

Prime Minister Owen Arthur heads the Barbados Labour Party. Sandiford remains head of the Democratic Labour Party. The National Democratic Party also has representation in Parliament. All citizens may vote at age 18.

Economy

Despite recent economic troubles, Barbados has one of the highest standards of living in the Caribbean. Real gross domestic product per capita is $9,667. This figure reflects the fact that 85 percent of the people can meet basic needs and enjoy economic opportunities. Tourism, light manufacturing, and the sugar industry are primary sources of foreign exchange. Tourism has expanded in importance in recent years, and it provides much of the country's employment. Barbados exports sugar, rum, electrical equipment, and textiles. It trades with the United States, other Caribbean nations, the United Kingdom, and Canada. One of the greatest problems in Barbados is a high unemployment rate of 20 percent. The economy grew in 1994 at an annual rate of 3.7 percent after three years of decline. Diversified agriculture provides the people with an adequate food supply. The currency is the Barbadian dollar (Bds$).

Transportation and Communication

Barbados has one international airport. Exports and imports are served by the Bridgetown Harbor or the Air Freight Terminal Airport. A central paved highway serves Barbadians, and the island is covered by an adequate network of roads. Following the British tradition, cars travel on the left side of the road. Public transportation consists of buses and taxis, which are readily available. Barbados has one government-owned television station and a satellite subscription television service; there are many radio stations. In addition to two daily newspapers, foreign-language papers are also available. Telecommunication links to other nations are well established.

Education

With an adult literacy rate of 97 percent, the public education system in Barbados is one of the finest in the Caribbean. Actual literacy rates may be somewhat lower due to differences in reporting. Still, more than 85 percent of all pupils complete primary schooling and attend secondary school. Attendance is compulsory to age 16. Private schools have less than 5 percent of the total enrollment. The government sponsors qualified students to study at the University of the West Indies in Jamaica and Trinidad, but the university also has a campus in Barbados that offers a college-level education. Technical-training schools are available in Barbados. Schools for physically and mentally handicapped children are also provided. Primary and secondary schools generally require school uniforms.

Health

Bajans are a relatively healthy people. The infant mortality rate has improved to the level of an industrial nation: 9 per 1,000. Barbadian water is some of the purest in the world. Tap water is safe to drink and most homes have running water. Medical care, including maternity and dental care, is provided free to all Barbadians at local *polyclinics*. Care is also offered in private offices and in the Queen Elizabeth Hospital. Preschool immunization is mandatory, and fluoride mouth-rinse programs are improving dental health. Health inspectors monitor meat and poultry production; garbage collection is well organized. Life expectancy ranges from 71 to 77 years.

FOR THE TRAVELER

Although U.S. citizens do not need a visa for visits of up to three months, a passport is necessary. Light clothing is best for the tropical climate. Barbados is known for its good food and excellent beaches, which provide a variety of activities. Also of interest is a wide variety of animal and plant life. No immunizations are required. For information regarding travel opportunities, contact the Barbados Board of Tourism, 800 Second Avenue, New York, NY 10017; phone (800) 221–9831; or 3440 Wilshire Boulevard, Suite 1215, Los Angeles, CA 90010. You may also wish to contact the Embassy of Barbados, 2144 Wyoming Avenue NW, Washington, DC 20008; phone (202) 939–9200.

Kingdom of
Belgium

Boundary representations not necessarily authoritative.

BACKGROUND

Land and Climate

With an area of 11,780 square miles (30,510 square kilometers), Belgium is slightly larger than Maryland. It is generally flat, with increasingly hilly terrain near the southeast Ardennes forests. The highest elevation is only 2,275 feet (693 meters). Like the Netherlands, Belgium has a system of dikes and seawalls along the coast to prevent tidal flooding. The climate is mild, damp, and temperate. Summer temperatures range from 54°F to 72°F (12–22°C); winter temperatures generally do not go below 32°F (0°C). Belgium's maritime climate is heavily influenced by the sea. Hence, fog and rain are common and there is little snow in winter. June through September are the most pleasant months.

History

The history of Belgium is one of great achievement in art and commerce, as well as heavy conflict. Before the area was known as Belgium, dukes and counts ruled four basic regions. As the 15th century approached, the French dukes of Burgundy began to consolidate territory and eventually gained all of what is now Belgium, reigning over several decades of prosperity and progress. Belgians were the first to land on the island of Manhattan in 1623 and later founded New York at Albany, calling it *Novum Belgii*. A Belgian named Minuit purchased Manhattan Island from the local Indians for goods worth only $24.

From the 1600s to 1830, Belgium was a battleground for France, the Netherlands, Austria, Germany, Spain, the Protestant-Catholic wars, and Napoleon (Waterloo is south of Brussels). The territories of Belgium gained independence from the Netherlands in 1830 and became a constitutional monarchy. Although the monarchy united several regions, divisions existed based on linguistic patterns. Celtic tribes had settled in the south and spoke what later became French. Germanic Franks, speaking low German (basically Dutch), settled in the north. The two groups developed separate cultural and linguistic traditions but remained together politically.

Because of Belgium's location and topography, it was often subject to battle, as evident in the period preceding independence and again in the 20th century. Despite its claims to neutrality during both World Wars, Belgium was overrun by conquering German armies in 1914 and again in 1940. Some of World War I's fiercest battles were fought in Flanders (northern Belgium). In World War II, the famous "Battle of the Bulge" was fought in Bastogne, where the American 101st Airborne division held off a massive assault by German troops that were attempting to reach the Allied port at Antwerp. This pivotal battle helped secure an Allied victory in the war.

As a consequence of its vulnerability and size, Belgium has had a strong inclination toward European cooperation and integration since the 1940s. It was a founding member of the North Atlantic Treaty Organization (NATO) and serves as that alliance's headquarters. Brussels is home to the European Union (EU) headquarters as well, making it an important city for business and diplomacy. Belgium has also devoted attention to internal cultural conflicts, creating a system to meet

EUROPE

the needs of both major linguistic groups and various minorities. In 1960, Belgium granted independence to its African colony called the Belgian Congo (now Zaire).

After World War II, Belgium remained a constitutional monarchy. From 1951 to 1993, King Baudouin I ruled as head of state. Upon his death, he was succeeded by King Albert II.

THE PEOPLE
Population

The population of Belgium is slightly more than ten million and is growing at 0.2 percent. Nearly 97 percent of the people live in cities or towns. Walloons occupy the south (Wallonia) and comprise 33 percent of Belgium's population. The Flemish (55 percent) live in the northern half (Flanders), and the remaining 12 percent are of various mixed groups. The German-speaking minority (1 percent) lives east of Wallonia. Many Italians, Spaniards, and North Africans (mainly Moroccans) work in Belgian industry. Due to Brussels's international importance, nearly 25 percent of its inhabitants are foreigners. In all, almost 10 percent of the population is non-Belgian.

Belgium's Human Development Index (0.926) ranks it 12th out of 174 countries. Adequate access to health care, education, and the resources needed for a decent standard of living affords Belgians many choices and opportunities in their lives. Adjusted for women, the index (0.852) ranks Belgium 18th out of 130 countries.

Language

French and Dutch (Flemish) are the primary official languages of Belgium. French dominates in southern areas and the capital, and Dutch is more prominent in the north. Most Belgians also speak English. Although bilingual Brussels is in Flanders, visitors should speak French or English, as 85 percent of its people speak French. Some towns in Wallonia have retained Latin dialects for festivals and folklore. Eleven percent of the Belgian population is officially bilingual and 1 percent speaks German (also an official language). Because of the two distinct languages, French and Dutch names for the same city are often quite different. For example, the Wallonian city of Mons is referred to in Flanders as Bergen (both names mean "mountains"). Generally, road signs are not bilingual; they are written in the principal language of the region in which they stand.

Religion

Although Belgium is a secular society, it is also traditionally Roman Catholic, and 75 percent of the population belongs to the church. In fact, most cultural festivals have their origin in, or have been strongly influenced by, Catholicism. Religion plays a role in people's personal lives mostly in connection with such major events as birth, marriage, and death.

The Walloons have a history of being less devoted to the Catholic faith than the Flemish. Most other major world religions can also be found in Belgium. All Catholic, Protestant, Jewish, and Islamic clergy that have official recognition from the government receive their salaries from the state. Private religious schools are also subsidized with government funding.

General Attitudes

A strong work ethic and an appreciation of culture are important to Belgians. The people tend to have tight regional and family ties, holding to the traditions of both. Nevertheless, Belgium's geographical position in Europe also makes the people cosmopolitan and open to outside interaction. Both the Walloons and the Flemish have a love for life and live it to the fullest, working and playing hard. The Flemish are considered somewhat more reserved and conservative than the Walloons.

A mixture of material wealth, good living, and family values is the lifestyle most Belgians hope for. Individuals generally like being regarded for their social achievements, having good housing, and enjoying pleasant living conditions.

Like those in other European countries, Belgians are struggling with their feelings toward immigrants. Most people accept them and would like to see their living conditions improved. Yet very little is done to integrate some immigrant groups into mainstream society. This tends to alienate immigrants, especially their children born in Belgium. Therefore, violence sometimes erupts in immigrant sections of large cities. Adding to the tensions is a small but vocal segment of the population that would like to end immigration from certain countries.

Personal Appearance

Belgians follow European fashions and tend to dress well in public. Tattered or extremely casual attire is reserved for the privacy of the home. Men who wear hats remove them in the building. Suits and dresses are standard in offices.

CUSTOMS AND COURTESIES
Greetings

Belgians greet each other with a handshake, which is often quick with light pressure; people in some areas give firmer handshakes. The phrases used for greeting depend on the region. The most typical Flemish greetings are *Hallo* (Hello) and a more formal *Goedendag* (Good day). The French equivalents are *Salut* (Hello) and *Bonjour* (Good day). English and German greetings would not be out of place in Brussels and some other cities. Close friends, even younger people, greet each other with three light kisses on the cheek. This gesture is actually more like "kissing the air" while touching cheeks. Belgians greet only friends and relatives by first name; otherwise, they address people by last name. When leaving a group, they usually shake hands with and bid farewell to each person in the group.

Gestures

Hand gestures are not used much during conversation. It is rude to talk with one's hands in one's pant pockets. Like most Europeans, Belgians do not talk with something in their mouths (gum, a toothpick, or food). Good posture is important, and people do not put their feet on tables or chairs. They avoid pointing with the index finger, scratching, yawning, or using a toothpick in public. Handkerchiefs are used discreetly.

Visiting

The importance of personal privacy extends to the home. Belgians enjoy inviting relatives and close friends to their homes, but other socializing is usually done in public places such as cafés, bistros, and restaurants.

It is rare for Belgians to visit one another without prior arrangement or at least calling ahead. Once a visit has been arranged, punctuality is important; arriving more than 30 minutes late is considered rude. A Belgian host or hostess appreciates a small gift or some flowers from an invited visitor. One should avoid giving chrysanthemums because they are associated with funerals. In rural communities, it may be appropriate to remove one's shoes, if dirty, before entering the home. Guests are usually offered refreshments (or appetizers if invited for a meal).

Eating

Most Belgians eat three meals a day, with the main meal served around 6:00 or 7:00 P.M. The family usually gathers for this meal, which consists of a main dish and dessert. A parent normally serves individual plates for each family member. Hosts also prepare individual plates for their guests. Meals are a social and cultural event in Belgium, and they are not to be finished quickly. The continental style of eating, with the knife in the right hand and the fork in the left, is most common. Belgians are thrifty and do not like waste; finishing one's food is expected. It is not impolite for guests to decline second helpings. In restaurants, one pays at the table and the tip is included in the bill. Still, one may also leave extra change if desired.

LIFESTYLE

Family

Even though the youth are becoming more independent, the family is still a strong and vital part of Belgian society. The average family has one or two children. Both parents often work outside the home. At home, they may share some household duties, but women are still generally responsible for most of them and for child care. Married children in Flanders seldom live with their parents, except in rural areas where families share farmland. Families often take excursions on holidays and Sundays. In the past, Wallonian extended families shared a large single house, but today they live separately. Still, they often remain in the same town or city as the rest of their family. In fact, throughout Belgium mobility tends to be low and people settle in or near the towns in which they were raised. This illustrates how important family and community roots are to Belgians. The elderly are generally well respected.

Dating and Marriage

Group dating usually begins by age 16, but it may vary according to regional traditions. The youth use public transportation and bikes at first, but when they reach driving age (18), they prefer private cars for dating. Young people go to movies, dances, and cafés. Long engagements are common. Living together before or instead of marrying is common. Only civil marriages are accepted by the government. Many families also have a religious ceremony.

Diet

Belgians eat a rich variety of foods, including pork, game birds, fish, cheeses, fruits, vegetables, breads, and soups. Wine,

beer, or mineral water is often served with meals. Belgium is famous for mussels, chocolates, three hundred varieties of beer, waffles, and french fries—which Belgians claim to have invented. French fries are served with mayonnaise rather than ketchup. Breakfast consists of a hot drink along with rolls or bread with jam or jelly. A snack at 4:00 P.M. is not unusual. Belgians take great pride in the quality of their food and the variety of cuisine—from domestically developed dishes to those adapted from other cultures. Restaurants offer a wide variety of international dishes.

Recreation

Participation in sporting activities is nearly universal; cycling and football (soccer) are most prominent. Belgium's national soccer team competed in the 1994 World Cup. The beach is a popular attraction, as are the beautiful forests in the south. Hunting, fishing, and pigeon racing have large followings in some rural areas. In pigeon racing, male pigeons are released far away from the females and owners bet on which will be the quickest to fly back to its mate. Families enjoy picnics, the theater, and movies. Festivals, local and national, such as *Carnaval*, are popular. Most families take a one-month vacation each year.

All Belgians are intensely proud of their rich cultural heritage, especially in art and architecture. Numerous theaters, festivals, and museums receive high patronage. Both modern and ancient art are prominent in art galleries. Belgium is known for such art masters as Brueghel, Van Eyck, and Rubens.

Holidays

Fairs, festivals, parades, and religious holidays are an integral part of the Belgian way of life. Legal holidays include New Year's Day, Easter Monday, Labor Day (1 May), Ascension Day, Whitmonday, Independence Day (21 July), Assumption (15 August), All Saints' Day (1 November), Veterans' Day (11 November), and Christmas. *Carnaval* is celebrated in February or March, depending on the city. This festival is characterized by parades, parties, colorful costumes, and traditional ceremonies. It has both medieval and ancient roots; the Catholic Church claims it to be the final celebration before the somber period of Lent, but pre-Christian tradition also claims it as a celebration to drive away the evil spirits of winter. Local spring and fall cultural and folklore festivals, such as the annual Cat Festival in Ieper, take place throughout the country.

Commerce

Because it is still customary to shop daily for fresh food, many open-air markets do business in the larger cities. Butcher shops are plentiful and well maintained. Supermarkets are available, although Belgium still has many small specialty shops. Businesses are open from 9:00 A.M. to 6:00 P.M., with a one- or two-hour break for lunch. Once a week (usually Friday), they remain open until 9:00 P.M. The average workweek is 35.8 hours.

SOCIETY

Government

Belgium is a constitutional monarchy under King Albert II, who holds executive power with the prime minister. All of the day-to-day affairs are handled by the prime minister and his cabinet. All governments have been coalitions, meaning no single political party has ever had a majority in Parliament. Parliament has two chambers: a 184-seat Senate and the more powerful 212-seat Chamber of Representatives. The cabinet contains an equal number of French- and Dutch-speaking ministers. Elections for Parliament are held at least every five years. The most recent elections were held in 1995, when Prime Minister Jean-Luc Dehaene's coalition was returned to office for a second term. All citizens older than 17 years of age are required to vote. The major political parties are split along linguistic lines: the Flemish Christian Democratic Party (DVP) is the strongest party in Flanders, and the Francophone Socialist Party (PS) dominates in Walloon. They work together with two other parties in a center-left coalition.

Constitutional reforms in 1981, 1988, and 1993 led to the organization of Belgium as a federal state. This move greatly reduced tensions related to linguistic divisions, as newly created government bodies have given greater decision-making authority to regions and communities (i.e., linguistic areas) in matters such as education, investment, welfare, and public works. The German-speaking minority is also protected.

Economy

Belgium's economy is one of the strongest in the world. Recovering from a recession in 1993, it grew 3 percent in 1995. Prospects within the expanded EU are strong; however, Belgium has the highest debt ratio among industrialized nations and must reduce its budget deficit to join Europe's single-currency plan. Unemployment is high (more than 14 percent in 1995). Real gross domestic product per capita is $18,630. The poorest 40 percent of the population earns more than 20 percent of the nation's income. Together, these figures indicate economic prosperity is available to most Belgians.

While less than 3 percent of the labor force is involved in agriculture, Belgium is a major world exporter of wool, beer, and meats and a key producer of automobiles for major foreign companies. Belgian steel, the principal export, is world famous. However, due to steel- and textile-market fluctuations in the 1980s, other industries such as engineering, chemicals, food processing, and biotechnology have grown. Exports now include items from each of these industries. Diamonds, crystal, and glass are well-established industries. Belgium is strong in foreign trade, partly because the third largest seaport in the world is located at Antwerp and because of its central location among EU countries. Most Belgian trade (74 percent) is conducted with EU members. The currency is the Belgian *franc* (BF).

Transportation and Communication

Belgium claims the most complete transportation system in the world, with the fourth most train tracks per mile and the fifth most roads per mile (all freeways are lit at night).

Coupled with a high population density, this system makes Belgium visible at night to orbiting space craft. Trains are the fastest and most practical form of public transportation between cities. Buses and streetcars are widely available, but most people also own cars. Bicycles are still popular for personal transportation. The efficiency of Belgium's postal system is recognized worldwide. Television and radio stations are government owned, although the number of private stations is increasing. Cable television is available in all parts of the country.

Education

Public education is free and compulsory between ages six and eighteen. Classes are often very demanding. Many Flemish families send their children to schools operated by the Catholic Church and subsidized by the state. A large portion of the federal budget is allotted to education, and 20 percent of the population is enrolled in school at any given time. All students learn at least one foreign language. Beginning at age 14, students have opportunities to choose between different career and educational paths; comprehensive examinations determine one's entrance to higher education. Those who do not go on to a university receive training in their chosen careers at vocational and technical schools. Schools for the arts are also popular. The adult literacy rate is 99 percent.

Health

Socialized medicine provides for the health care of all citizens. Doctors and clinics are private but are paid out of public funds. Health concerns are similar to those in the United States, as is the quality of care. Life expectancy ranges from 74 to 81 years, and the infant mortality rate is 7 per 1,000. Although the water is generally safe, Belgians drink bottled water rather than tap water.

FOR THE TRAVELER

U.S. and Canadian citizens do not need a visa for visits of less than three months, but a passport is required. English is widely understood. Art museums are excellent and recommended, as are the Ardennes forests, the castles throughout Belgium, the beaches in the north, and old cultural cities such as Antwerp, Bruges, Brussels, and Gent. If flying out of Brussels, hand carry all film, as it will otherwise be damaged by X rays.

The Belgium Tourist Information Office, located at Town Hall Grand Palace, Grote Market 1000, Brussels, Belgium, offers free help in arranging lodging and provides cultural information and maps. Information is also available from the Belgian Tourist Office, 780 Third Avenue, Suite 1501, New York, NY 10017; phone (212) 758–8130. Belgium's embassy is located at 3330 Garfield Street NW, Washington, DC 20008; phone (202) 333–6900. Consulates, which can provide the same services as the embassy, are located in Atlanta, Chicago, Los Angeles, and New York.

CULTURGRAM ™ '97

Belize

Boundary representations not necessarily authoritative.

THE AMERICAS

BACKGROUND

Land and Climate

Covering 8,866 square miles (22,963 square kilometers), Belize is about the size of Massachusetts. Located in Central America, it is bordered by Mexico, Guatemala, and the Caribbean Sea. The landscape is diverse for such a small area. The northern half of Belize is flat with marshes and lagoons, while coastal areas are covered by mangrove swamps. The land rises to the south and west, reaching an elevation of about 3,000 feet (915 meters) in the Maya Mountains. More than 60 percent of the country is forested. Belize has the world's second largest barrier reef with hundreds of small islands called *cayes* (pronounced KEYS). Beautiful rivers, greenery, the reef, and the *cayes* add to the nation's diversity.

Belize has two seasons: wet and dry. Humidity is high year-round. The south receives the most rain. Temperatures average between 80°F and 85°F (26–29°C), although they are cooler in the mountains. In Belmopan, the capital, days are hot and nights are cool. Belize is subject to hurricanes between June and October.

History

The Maya thrived in the area between the third and ninth centuries A.D. as part of a civilization that covered Guatemala, Honduras, Mexico, and El Salvador. Numerous city-states existed throughout Mayan lands, and these were often at odds with each other. Mayan ruins are still evident all over Belize. Little is known of the period after the decline of the Mayan people until the arrival of the first Europeans in the 16th century. The Spanish came in search of gold and found none. British pirates arrived during the 17th century and took advantage of the islands and reef to lure ships onto the rocks for looting. British woodcutters soon followed and brought slaves to help in logging the huge forests. The pirates also turned to woodcutting. The logwood and later mahogany trade became very lucrative for these British, who were known as the Baymen.

The Spanish tried to claim the region, but at the decisive Battle of St. George's Caye in 1798, the Baymen and their slaves fought back Spanish invaders. With the Spanish Empire all around them, the Baymen asked Britain for protection. Spain and Britain signed a treaty to allow Belize to become a crown colony in 1862. England had promised to build a road between Belize City and Guatemala City as part of that treaty. The fact that it never happened led to a long-term dispute between the two neighbors. Guatemala claimed the area as its own territory because of the treaty's failure.

Belize was called British Honduras until 1973. The British granted internal self-rule in 1964. In 1981, with support from the United Nations and a strong independence movement, Belize became a sovereign country within the Commonwealth of Nations. British troops remained to protect the borders, but after a 1991 agreement in which Guatemala relinquished its claim to Belize, Britain decided (in 1993) to withdraw its troops.

THE PEOPLE

Population

The population of Belize is about 214,000 and is growing at 2.4 percent. Belize's Human Development Index (0.883) ranks it 29th out of 174 countries and reflects the availability of choices needed to enjoy a decent quality of life. About one-fourth of all people live in Belize City. Each of the country's six districts has a main town where the bulk of that district's population lives. Many Belizeans live and work abroad.

Belize has a diverse blend of peoples. Creoles account for about 30 percent of the total population, and *mestizos* (mixed Spanish and Indian) 44 percent. *Mestizos* are descendants of 19th century immigrants from Mexico, as well as immigrants from other Latin American countries. Creoles, who dominate in Belize City, are persons with some degree of African ancestry. Many are descendants of early European (mostly English or Scottish) settlers and African slaves. Creoles were once the largest group but are now the group with the largest percentage of emigrants. Refugees from neighboring countries (mainly El Salvador and Guatemala) have significantly added to the *mestizo* share of the population.

Most rural villages are comprised of *mestizos*, Mayas (Kek'chi, Mopan, and Yucatan), or Garinagu (Caribbean and African mix). Mayas make up 11 percent of the population; the Garinagu, who live in the south, comprise 7 percent. East Indians (3.5 percent) have been in Belize for generations and are joined by other minorities, including Mennonites (3 percent), Arabs, Chinese, and North Americans.

Language

English is the country's official language and, with the exception of people in remote areas, everyone speaks it. Most people also speak Creole, and everyday speech is often a combination of Creole and English. Creole is a melodic English-based language with roots in the days of slavery. Although it is traditionally an oral language, current efforts are underway to establish grammar and spelling standards for a written form. Spanish is spoken by *mestizos* throughout the country (especially in the Cayo, Corozal, and Orange Walk districts), but not necessarily by all *mestizos*. Still, it has overtaken English as the first language of many Belizeans. While English must be used in school, Creole or Spanish may be used in the first few years to clarify certain things to children who do not speak English. Mayan groups speak their native languages. The Garinagu speak Garífuna and usually also English.

Religion

Freedom of religion is valued and respected in Belize. Most major Western Christian denominations are represented, but the Roman Catholic (60 percent) and Anglican (12 percent) Churches dominate. Most *mestizos* and Mayas are Catholic. Creoles generally belong to Protestant churches, but many are also Catholic. A number of other Christian faiths are practiced. Schools are generally run by churches, so most people are affiliated with a religion. The only distinct indigeneous religious practices are found among the Maya and Garinagu.

General Attitudes

Belizean society is nonconfrontational. Belizeans are fun loving, happy, and generally "laid-back." The pace of life is not regulated by a clock so much as by events or people. Punctuality may be admired but is not generally practiced. Men commonly practice *machismo*, the habit of demonstrating or claiming manliness through macho acts or sexually oriented language. Women usually ignore it and accept it as part of life.

For a small nation of so many ethnic groups and cultures, Belize is relatively free of racial tension. Equality and coexistence are important concepts. Prejudices exist but not on the level of hatred. A neighborhood in Belize City might consist of every possible ethnic group and have few racial problems. One reason is that the people don't mix; they coexist. But another more powerful reason is that most ethnic groups subscribe in some degree to Creole cultural practices, and Belizean Creoles have adopted aspects of the cultures around them. Most people can speak Belizean Creole, which further enhances harmony.

Although Belize is located in Central America, its culture is also closely linked to the Caribbean, which gives Belizeans great pride.

Personal Appearance

Belizeans are concerned about how they look, and U.S. fashions are the most popular in Belize City and other cities. The way a person is dressed is considered a mark of taste and status. Many office, bank, hotel, and school employees wear uniforms. Many men, especially professionals, wear *guayaberas*, untucked cotton shirts that are sometimes embroidered.

The Maya often wear traditional clothing. This might include long, brightly colored, heavy skirts with embroidered, white blouses for women, and work clothes and straw hats for men. Garinagu women also tend to retain traditional dress, which might include a simple, colorful blouse, a matching knee-length skirt, and a head scarf. The Mennonites, a group originally from Germany, maintain conservative, simple clothing and do not follow modern fashions.

CUSTOMS AND COURTESIES

Greetings

Belizeans are informal and friendly in greeting (hailing) one another. It is rude not to hail even a slight acquaintance or not to return a hail. When entering a place of business, one also greets the clerk or receptionist. When strangers pass on the street, a simple nod of the head or a wave is acceptable; acquantances might add "Hey, how?" or "Y'aright?"

When greetings precede conversation, a handshake is common. Friends might shake by clasping the palms and locking thumbs, or by locking all fingers, or just pressing fists together. Men often pat each other on the back when they shake hands. *Mestizos* greet by saying ¡Buenos días! (Good morning), ¡Buenas tardes! (Good afternoon), ¡Buenas noches! (Good evening), or just ¡Buenas! any time of day. In Creole, one might use *Wa di gwan?* (What's happening?) or a number of other phrases.

In formal settings, people address others with proper titles, but they use first names in informal situations. Children usually address their elders by adding "Miss" or "Mister" before the name, and they often answer questions by saying, "Yes, ma'am," or "No, sir."

Gestures

Belizeans, especially Creoles and *mestizos*, are very animated. Nonverbal communication plays a vital role in all situations. Hand and facial gestures are varied and often complicated. Belizeans might indicate direction with the head or lips. Staring or pointing at someone is rude. Sucking air through the teeth can mean "Give me a break." People might hiss to get one's attention, but this is offensive to many (especially women). To hail a taxi or bus, people move the hand up and down before the vehicle passes.

Visiting

Belizeans are very hospitable. Unannounced visitors are welcomed and made to feel at home, sometimes even if they are strangers. Arranged visits most often occur on weekends. Before television was introduced in 1980, visiting was an integral part of everyday life. It has since diminished in cities but is still important in villages. When one visits a home, it is polite to hail the occupants from the gate or street until they come out. A lengthy conversation might take place over the fence before one is invited into the yard or home. Offering a guest refreshments, usually at least a drink, is considered good manners. In areas without refrigeration, people might offer fresh coconut. Though not expected, it is also polite for the guest to bring the host something.

Eating

Families generally spend mealtime together, although in some Mayan and *mestizo* families, women eat after or separate from the men. Conversation is usually limited and mainly carried out between adults. An urban breakfast may include fruit, bread, cheese, beans, eggs, or cereal. Rural breakfasts usually consist of beans. For most, the main meal of the day is dinner, eaten at midday. Schools let out and businesses close so people can eat at home. In cities, people also often go to restaurants. The evening meal, called supper or *tea*, is lighter than dinner. For some groups (such as the Kek'chi Maya), the main meal is in the evening.

Meals in rural areas are usually less varied than in cities; rice, beans, tortillas, fresh fruit, and chicken are often the only available foods. In addition, urban people might eat burgers, *tamales*, fish, and a variety of other dishes.

LIFESTYLE

Family

Families tend to be large and often include the extended family. It is common for grandparents to raise grandchildren after their own children have left Belize for economic or other reasons. Leaving children behind has actually created quite a problem in Belize, as minors have become a majority of the population in Belize City. Adult children usually remain at home until they get married or have a child. Single-parent families are abundant among the Creole population, and women have become the leading family figure in that group. In a Creole village, it is common for households to have a female head and several generations together without any adult men.

In most other homes, the father takes the leading role. Younger mothers are more inclined to work outside the home than older women, but women are generally expected to take care of the home and family.

Apartment living is not popular. Most families own or rent homes. In rural areas, this may be a simple thatched hut. In coastal towns and villages, houses are built of wood or cement and rest on stilts because of the threat of hurricane flooding. As the elevation increases, the interior designs of houses remain similar, but stilts become less common. Because of the small population, the government can allot land to Belizeans who apply for it, making land and home ownership easier.

Dating and Marriage

Urban dating (courting) tends to follow the same basic pattern as in North America. Schools may prohibit their students from going to popular dating destinations, such as discos, so private parties and school dances are the primary way for young people to meet. Village dating revolves around church activities or dances. Among the Maya and some *mestizos*, boys are often only allowed to meet with a girl in her home.

Many Belizean young women become single mothers early and never marry. Likewise, many young men father a number of children by several women and never formally marry. Or they may enter into common-law marriage relationships. For those who do marry formally, a church ceremony is usually followed by a colorful reception that includes food, music, and dancing.

Diet

The most common staple is white rice and kidney beans. That dish may be accompanied by stewed chicken, beef, or fish. A staple among the Mayas is corn, which is usually present in some form (such as tortillas) at every meal. Fish and seafood are common on the coast. Other popular foods include *tamales*, *panades* (fried corn shells with beans or fish), meat pies, *escabeche* (onion soup), *chirmole* (soup), and *garnaches* (fried tortillas with beans, cheese, and sauce). Fruits (bananas, oranges, mangoes, papayas, limes, and so forth) are abundant and part of the daily diet. Vegetables are more limited and often imported.

Recreation

The most popular sports are football (soccer) and basketball. Organized leagues receive great local support, including fledgling semiprofessional leagues. Women often have softball teams. Volleyball, track-and-field, and boxing are enjoyed in many areas. Cycling is popular; the largest athletic event is the annual cross-country race held Easter weekend. It is a source of pride and a national tradition that attracts an international group of cyclists. Urban people like to go to the *cayes* for recreation.

Belizeans enjoy going to concerts and school fairs or watching the latest movies at home on cable and video. They appreciate reggae, calypso, *soca*, and various types of American music. A local favorite is *punta-rock*, which has its roots in the Garífuna culture.

Holidays

The largest and most celebrated national holidays occur in September. A street parade/party takes place the Saturday before St. George's Caye Day (10 September). Independence Day is 21 September. Various "September Celebrations" are held between these two holidays. Baron Bliss Day (9 March) honors a Portuguese noble who left his wealth to the country and its people. Garífuna Settlement Day (19 November) marks the arrival of the Garinagu to Belize. They originally came from Saint Vincent and had settled in Honduras before migrating to Belize.

Christmas is a time for family, religion, and community; it is a quiet holiday for most. Easter weekend is popular for vacations; religious ceremonies are limited. Belize also celebrates Labor Day (1 May) and a number of other holidays.

Commerce

Weekday business hours are 8:00 A.M. to 5:00 P.M. Stores generally open again in the evening for two hours. Most businesses close for lunch. Banks close at 1:00 P.M. On Friday, they open again from 3:00 to 6:00 P.M. Larger grocery stores are open all day Saturday and on Sunday morning. Small shops have varying hours and are usually part of someone's home.

SOCIETY

Government

Belize is a two-party democracy with a bicameral legislature. The two parties are the People's United Party (PUP) and the United Democratic Party (UDP). Britain's Queen Elizabeth II is officially the head of state and is represented in Belize by a governor general (currently Sir Colville Young). The head of government is the prime minister, who is the leader of Parliament's dominant party. General elections are held at least every five years, but they can be called sooner if politically necessary. The last elections were in 1993 and Manuel Esquivel of the UDP was elected prime minister. His term lasts until 1998. The voting age is 18.

Economy

Belize's economy has been expanding since independence, although its current growth rate has dropped to about 2 percent. Large amounts of foreign aid have greatly contributed to the economy's success. About half of the labor force is employed in agricultural production. The country's main exports are citrus fruits, sugar, molasses, bananas, wood and wood products, and clothing. Sugar has traditionally been the primary cash crop, but citrus fruits are now nearly as strong. Tourism is the fastest-growing source of income, with many people capitalizing on the natural beauty of the country. Environmental tourism and adventure tours are very popular. Unemployment tends to average more than 10 percent, and even higher for the youth. Real gross domestic product per capita is estimated between $3,000 and $5,600. However, poverty affects 65 percent of all rural people. These figures reflect economic progress in the country, even though it has not yet benefited the majority of the population. The currency is the Belizean dollar (Bz$).

Transportation and Communication

The Northern, Western, and Hummingbird highways are paved and link most cities. Getting to remote areas is more difficult, as roads are rough. The national network of private bus systems is inexpensive and widely used. In cities and towns, most people get around by walking or riding bikes. The number of private cars is growing. Several small, private domestic airlines provide commuter and tourist travel.

In major towns, most people have telephones; villages usually have at least one phone. Radio and television broadcasts together reach nearly all Belizeans, who remain informed not only on local matters but on regional and international news as well.

Education

The vast majority of primary and secondary schools are church operated, even though they receive large subsidies from the government. Students pay fees, buy their own books and supplies, and usually must wear uniforms. Because some families cannot afford these costs, a few government schools exist to provide their children an education, but there are usually not enough spaces to accommodate all. Children are required to attend school until standard six (equivalent to the eighth grade in the United States), but secondary schooling is not required. Many students are not able to complete their primary education due to cost, family obligation, or a number of other factors. The official literacy rate is more than 95 percent, but the actual figure is closer to 50 or 60 percent.

Space in secondary schools is limited and acceptance depends on one's passing the Belize National Selection Exam. Those who complete a secondary education can attend junior college, teacher's college, or the University College of Belize. The government is focusing reform efforts on standardizing curriculum in all schools and providing more vocational education in each district.

Health

Health care is accessible to all citizens, although many preventable diseases still afflict the country. Each district has a small hospital and there is a large hospital in Belize City. A health worker is assigned to each village but might not always be present. Clinics and private doctors serve those who can afford to pay. Rainwater tanks and municipal water systems are used widely, although some concern for water safety exists. The infant mortality rate is 35 per 1,000. Life expectancy averages between 66 and 70 years.

FOR THE TRAVELER

U.S. citizens need a valid passport to enter Belize, but a visa is not necessary for stays of up to 30 days. Belize has a great deal to offer tourists, from snorkeling, fishing, and relaxing in the spectacular *cayes* to beautiful scenery, Mayan ruins, and wildlife further inland. Avoid wearing expensive jewelry in public or going out alone after dark. For more information, contact the Belize Tourist Board, 421 Seventh Avenue, Suite 1110, New York, NY 10001; phone (800) 624–0686. You may also wish to contact the Embassy of Belize, 2535 Massachusetts Avenue NW, Washington, DC 20008; phone (202) 332–9636.

CULTURGRAM ™ '97

Republic of
Bolivia

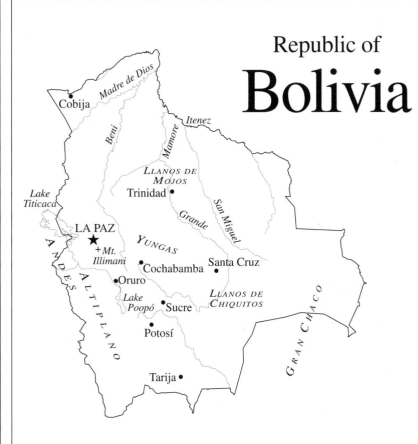

Boundary representations not necessarily authoritative.

THE AMERICAS

BACKGROUND

Land and Climate

Located in the heart of South America, Bolivia is a land-locked country. With 424,165 square miles (1,098,581 square kilometers), it is almost three times the size of Montana. There are three distinct geographical areas: the high, cold, and dry mountain-rimmed Altiplano to the west; the medium-elevation *yungas* (valleys) in the middle; and the *llanos*—wet, hot, forested lowlands in the east and northeast. Grasslands are common on these plains, which makes the area good for cattle ranching. Forests cover about half of Bolivia. The country shares the vast, resource-rich subtropical Gran Chaco plain with Paraguay and Argentina. The famous Lake Titicaca, the highest navigable body of water in the world (12,500 feet or 3,749 meters), lies on the north end of the Altiplano. It is shared equally by Bolivia and Peru.

Surrounding the Altiplano are the mineral-rich Andes Mountains, which climb to over 21,000 feet (6,400 meters) and are permanently covered with snow above 16,000 feet (4,800 meters). These mountains are known for their beauty, especially Mount Illimani near La Paz. The eastern foothills are home to a diverse variety of plants and animals; scientists have found more than seven hundred bird species there. Although Bolivia experiences four seasons, they are not all perceptible in some areas because elevation plays a more important role in climate than seasons do. Summer (December–March) is the rainy season. Winter is from June to September. In La Paz, the average annual temperature is 65°F (18°C).

History

Aymara and other groups were conquered in the 1400s by Incan armies, bringing the area into the Inca Empire. The Incas introduced the Quechua language and a new social system. The Spanish began their conquest in 1532, and by 1538 all of present-day Bolivia was under Spanish control. Known as Upper Peru during Spanish rule, Bolivia was one of the first colonies to rebel. Political uprisings occurred frequently in the 1700s, but they were always crushed. It was not until the independence movement of 1809 that Upper Peru began to see success. After a 16-year War of Independence, the area gained independence on 6 August 1825 and was named after its liberator, Simón Bolívar.

Bolivia's first president was overthrown in 1828, and the country experienced decades of factional strife, revolutions, and military dictatorships. Much of its original territory was lost between 1879 and 1935 in wars with Chile, Brazil, and Paraguay. The War of the Pacific (1879–84) was most significant because Bolivia lost its access to the sea. This event basically doomed the economy, and Bolivians regularly appealed to Chile for the return of the territory. In 1992, Peru granted Bolivia access to the sea via the Ilo port in southern Peru. With this access, Bolivia expects to increase international trade and improve its economy.

The government attempted to improve conditions and stabilize the country during the 1950s, but a military coup ended the reforms in 1964. A series of coups brought various dictatorships to power, each of them oppressive to the majority-indigenous populations. Terrible economic conditions in the 1980s, characterized by spiraling inflation that peaked at 11,700 percent, made it clear that military governments could not effectively lead the country.

A representative democracy was finally established in August 1985 with the election of President Víctor Paz Estenssoro. He reduced inflation to less than 20 percent and stabilized the economy. His term ended peacefully in 1989, when Jaime Paz Zamora was elected.

National elections in 1993 marked another peaceful transfer of civilian power, when Gonzalo Sánchez de Lozada was elected president. Significantly, his vice president, Victor Hugo Cárdenas, is Aymara. He is the first indigenous person to rise to such a high office in Latin America. He, along with a variety of native groups, seeks social change that will allow native peoples to participate fully in the economy, the government, and other social institutions without discrimination. Sánchez also plans to increase privatization and implement educational reforms.

THE PEOPLE

Population
Bolivia's population of 7.9 million is growing at 2.3 percent annually. About half of all people live in urban areas. Nearly 70 percent of the total population is composed of native Americans, including Quechua (30 percent), Aymara (25 percent), Guaraní, Mojeño, Chimane, and smaller groups. About 25 percent of the people are *criollo* (or *mestizo*), who are of mixed indigenous and European heritage. Another 5 percent are of European descent.

Bolivia's Human Development Index (0.588) ranks it 113th out of 174 countries. Limited access to adequate health care and economic prosperity affects the quality of life, particularly in rural areas. Adjusted for women, the index (0.519) ranks Bolivia 80th out of 130 countries, indicating that women have fewer economic opportunities than do men.

Language
Castellaño (Spanish), Quechua, and Aymara are all official languages. Spanish is used in government, schooling, and business and is the native tongue of about 40 percent of the population. Indigenous groups speak their own languages, but many also speak Spanish.

Religion
Approximately 95 percent of the people are Roman Catholic, although there are various other religions, including some indigenous systems and an active Protestant minority. Bolivians of the Altiplano also mix Aymaran and Quechuan traditions with their Catholic beliefs. For instance, *Pachamama*, or goddess Mother Earth, is very popular. People toast to her or bless things in her name. A *ch'alla* is the blessing of any material possession or event by offering symbolic articles and alcohol to *Pachamama* and *Achachila*, god of the mountains.

General Attitudes
Time is viewed differently in Bolivia than in North America. People enjoy getting as much pleasure out of an experience as possible, with less regard to how much time they spend. Scheduled events begin late, as all understand arriving on time is not expected. The Aymara view the past as something they can see in front of them but the future as unseen and therefore behind them.

Kindness, gentleness, and concern for another's welfare are the keys to friendship in Bolivia. The people like to remind others that they are also "Americans" because they live in South America. They call U.S. Americans *norteamericanos*.

Tensions exist in society between the ruling class—those of European or mixed heritage—and indigenous groups. The latter have often been barred from participating in society because of their race. Those who have wanted to assimilate into society have had to speak Spanish and change their way of dress. Many also adopt Spanish names. The indigenous movement would like to extend all the benefits of a democratic society to all of the peoples in the country without forcing them to abandon their traditions. The ruling class believes other groups should assimilate into society by leaving tradition behind and adopting a more Westernized culture.

Personal Appearance
Bolivians wear different clothing depending on where they live and their social class. Generally, urban residents wear Western-style clothing. Many women wear a *pollera* (a full, colorful skirt). Rural women wear a *pollera* with a shawl (*manta*). They may also wear hats (bowler derbies) that differ from area to area; one can tell where people come from by looking at their hat. Women often wear their hair in braids.

Some indigenous people make their own clothing out of wool. Common colors include red, black, and off-white. Native men might wear shin-length pants, a shirt, and a thick leather belt. They often wear a *poncho* and a hat. Native women wear a long, dark-colored dress tied at the waste with a colorful belt. They may also wear a small shoulder cape and oval hat. Women carry babies on their backs in an *aguayo*, a woven square cloth.

CUSTOMS AND COURTESIES

Greetings
Spanish-speaking Bolivians greet friends and acquaintances with a cheerful *¡Buenos días!* (Good morning), *¡Buenas tardes!* (Good afternoon), or *¡Buenas noches!* (Good evening). *Hola* (Hi) or *¿Cómo estás?* (How are you?) are also common. One adds the title *Señor* (Mr.), *Señora* (Mrs.), or *Señorita* (Miss) for first-time introductions or when greeting strangers (such as a store owner). *Señorita* is used for any woman, unless she is older or the speaker knows she is married. Bolivians show respect for others by addressing them as *Don* (for men) or *Doña* (for women) before their first name. Rural people (*campesinos*) even use these titles with close friends. Strangers do not address each other by first name.

Greetings are accompanied by a handshake. However, if a person's hand is wet or dirty, he or she may offer an arm or elbow. Bolivians maintain little personal space and stand close during conversation. Close friends and relatives frequently use the *abrazo*. It consists of a hug, a handshake, two or three pats on the shoulder, and another handshake. Women friends often embrace and kiss each other on the cheek. They commonly walk arm in arm. Teenage girls may also hold hands.

Common Spanish farewells are *Hasta luego* (Until soon) or *Hasta mañana* (Until tomorrow). Friends use the casual *Chau* or *Chau, chau*. *Adiós* implies good-bye for a long time; it might be used in seeing someone off on a trip. In southern areas, *Adiós* is also used as a quick greeting when people pass on the street.

Gestures

Bolivians often use hands, eyes, and facial expressions to communicate. To beckon children, one waves the fingers with the palm down. Patting someone on the shoulder is a sign of friendship. A raised hand, palm outward and fingers extended, twisting quickly from side to side, is a way of saying "there isn't any" or "no"—a gesture often used by taxi and bus drivers when their vehicles are full. Waving the index finger indicates a strong "no." One covers the mouth when yawning or coughing. Eye contact in conversation is essential. Avoiding another's eyes shows suspicion, lack of trust, or shyness.

Visiting

Bolivians enjoy visiting one another. It is customary and friendly to drop by unannounced, but arranged visits are also common. Visitors generally give flowers or small gifts to the host upon arrival. Hosts might also present visitors with gifts. They are not opened in the presence of the giver. Hosts try to make their guests as comfortable as possible. A dinner guest is expected to try all types of food offered. Compliments given during the meal instead of after will bring a second helping. Guests respectfully address hosts by first name, preceded by *Don* or *Doña,* to show familiarity with them.

Upon arrival, visitors are invited inside and offered a drink or light refreshments; it is impolite to refuse them. It is also impolite to start a conversation on the doorstep. Visitors staying a few days are welcomed with a hug and kiss on the cheek. Hosts provide special meals as a welcoming gesture and, if possible, all family members are present to greet the guest. Guests are not asked how long they will stay, as this is interpreted as a desire to have them leave soon.

Eating

Upon entering a room where people are eating, Bolivians often say *Buen provecho* (similar to *Bon appétit*). It is polite to say *Gracias* (Thank you) to all at the table when one is finished eating, and to wish them *Buen provecho* when they leave. Generally, one is not excused from the table until all are finished eating. It is proper to remain at the table to enjoy the company of the others. Everyone (including guests) is expected to eat everything on the plate. One should eat meat only with utensils, not hands. Eating on the streets is in poor taste. In restaurants, the host usually insists on paying for the meal. A tip generally is included in the bill (10 percent), but leaving a little extra (up to 5 percent) is polite.

LIFESTYLE

Family

The family is central to Bolivian society. Middle- and upper-class families have one or two children. Poorer families are traditionally much larger, but children often die in infancy. Although many rural couples live together in common-law arrangements, formal marriages are more common in cities. Children almost always live with their parents until they are married and sometimes even after marriage.

Most women work in the home. Without modern conveniences, their work is difficult and requires more time. This can prevent women from pursuing work in the labor force. But they often run small businesses (sewing, cutting hair, selling soda and gum, etc.) from their homes. Upper- and middle-class families often have maids. While the father makes most family decisions, the mother exerts much influence on household affairs. Although children are taught the importance of education, illiteracy is still high among the poor. Children are generally well disciplined and share in family responsibilities. The elderly live with their children's families.

Dating and Marriage

Chaperoned dating begins at about age 15. Dating is preceded by flirting. In many towns on Sunday evening, boys and girls enjoy *dar vueltas* (doing turns), where they walk in groups around the central plaza to make eye contact and flirt. The process of getting acquainted, dating seriously, and being engaged can take up to three years. Men marry between the ages of 20 and 25, while women marry between 19 to 23. People usually do not marry until they have acquired some sort of financial security or property. For a marriage to be legal, a civil ceremony must be performed. However, most couples also have a religious ceremony; a dance and reception generally follow the wedding. Because weddings are expensive, many rural people cannot afford them and choose common-law marriages instead. Bolivians wear their wedding rings on the right hand.

Diet

Potatoes, rice, soups, milk products, and fruits are common staples in the Bolivian diet. Bolivia has hundreds of potato varieties prepared in different ways. *Chuños* are a freeze-dried potato used in soups or side dishes when rehydrated. Most foods are fried and seasoned with spicy salsa. Chicken is the most common meat. Southern Bolivians eat a lot of beef and enjoy barbecues. Breakfast usually consists of tea or coffee, bread, and sometimes cheese. Lunch, the main meal, consists of soup and a main dish. In cities, people enjoy *salteñas* (meat or chicken pies with potatoes, olives, and raisins) as a mid-morning snack.

Recreation

Fútbol (soccer) is enjoyed through the country. Bolivia's national soccer team competed in the 1994 World Cup. Other popular sports vary with the region. Leisure activities include watching television (in urban areas), visiting and relaxing with friends, and attending festivals. In the Chaco region, people get together to drink several rounds of *yerba mate*, an herbal tea. Dancing and singing are popular at various events.

Music is an integral part of the Bolivian culture. Played and promoted throughout the world, it can be divided into three types: fast, happy rhythms from the east and northeast; slow, romantic, and melancholic rhythms from the Andes Mountains; and happy, romantic rhythms from the central valleys. A common instrument is the *charango*, a twelve-string, convex, guitar-like instrument made from armadillo shells. A *zampona* is many different flutes joined together to play a variety of notes.

Holidays

Holidays include New Year's Day, *Carnaval* (the Saturday before Ash Wednesday), *Día del Mar* (Sea Day,

23 March), Holy Week before Easter (March or April), Father's Day (19 March), Labor Day (1 May), Mother's Day (27 May), Independence Day (6 August), All Saints' Day (1 November, a day for the family to clean and decorate ancestral graves and enjoy a picnic), and Christmas. On Christmas Eve, some children place their old shoes in a window for *Papa Noel* (Santa Claus) to take them in exchange for new gifts. Children also receive gifts on 6 January (Three Kings' Day).

Dancing, costumes, and pouring water on people are common during *Carnaval*; a favorite treat at this festival is *confite* (candy stuffed with nuts or fruit). Each of the nine provinces also celebrates regional holidays rich in folklore. In fact, Bolivia has been called "The Capital of Folklore." These local events are noted for their wonderful music and colorful costumes. Almost every *pueblo* (village) has its fascinating and unique fiestas in honor of its patron saint or the Virgin Mary.

Commerce

Business is generally conducted Monday through Friday from 9:00 A.M. to noon and 3:00 to 7:00 P.M. The midday break or *descanso* allows people to have lunch and relax.

SOCIETY

Government

A president, vice president, and cabinet form the executive branch. The Supreme Court sits at Sucre, the legal capital. *El Congreso Nacional* (the national congress), based in La Paz, consists of a 27-seat Chamber of Senators and 130-seat Chamber of Deputies. The Nationalist Revolutionary Movement currently holds the most legislative power, but opposition parties have significant representation. Elections are held every four years. Voting is mandatory beginning at age 18 for married individuals and 21 for singles.

Economy

Although Bolivia has been one of the poorest and least developed Latin American countries, economic figures have improved since reforms, and current economic growth is encouraging. Unemployment remains at less than 10 percent, and privatization and other reforms are stimulating new ventures. Real gross domestic product per capita is $2,410. In 1995, inflation was close to 13 percent. The currency is the *boliviano* ($B).

With natural resources such as tin, natural gas, crude oil, zinc, silver, gold, lead, and tungsten, mining is Bolivia's major industry. Others include coffee and food production, textiles, and timber. Half of the labor force is engaged in agriculture, with coca (used in making cocaine) being the largest (illicit) cash crop. The government finds it difficult to stop coca trafficking because of the money involved and because the coca leaf has been a traditional crop for centuries. It has many legitimate uses in society, including medicinal and dietary, and is a basic part of the culture.

Transportation and Communication

Throughout its modern history, Bolivia has been handicapped by its landlocked location and lack of internal transportation and communication. Only a few major highways are paved. Airlines connect major cities and allow one to avoid travel over rugged terrain. But buses, taxis, and trains are the most common forms of transportation. Buses are often crowded. More expensive minivans are faster and less crowded. Taxis often stop to pick up other passengers going the same way. Several radio and television stations are in operation.

Education

Schooling is free and compulsory for ages six to fourteen. Yet, while illiteracy is declining, problems still exist. Less than half of all children complete their primary education, and only about one-third go on to secondary school. In the past, indigenous children could not receive instruction in their own language because Spanish was the language used in all schools. However, educational reforms now permit bilingual education in Spanish and local Indian dialects. The adult literacy rate is about 81 percent; it is higher in urban areas and for men. Since 1985, six universities have been built, bringing the total to fifteen. One must pass two entrance exams to be admitted to a university.

Health

Because of disease and widespread poverty, the infant mortality rate in Bolivia is 71 per 1,000. The average life expectancy ranges from 61 to 66 years. Sanitation facilities are poor, and tap water must be boiled. Local nurses and doctors have been training *responsables populares de salud* (community health-care workers) in basic skills. These trainees help serve the needs of the rural population.

Still, traditional medicine is used in many rural areas to cure illness. Only about half of the population has adequate access to medical care. Many illnesses affect the populace, including *chagas*, a parasitic disease that causes early death by heart attacks and intestinal problems in about one-fifth of the population.

FOR THE TRAVELER

U.S. visitors must have a passport, but a visa is only required for stays longer than 30 days. Bolivia is in the yellow fever endemic zone; vaccinations are recommended. Visitors entering from other infected areas must have proof of vaccination. Malaria is also a problem. La Paz is beautiful, but its extremely high altitude (11,910 feet or 3,360 meters) means there is less oxygen than most people are used to, and travelers may be weak and short of breath. Plenty of rest is recommended. The Bolivian remedy for altitude sickness is to drink a lot of water and coca tea. It is also a good idea to avoid a big evening meal, since digestion is also affected; make lunch the main meal. For travel information, contact the consulate office of the Embassy of Bolivia; phone (202) 232–4828. The Embassy of Bolivia is located at 3014 Massachusetts Avenue NW, Washington, DC 20008–3603; phone (202) 483–4410.

CULTURGRAM '97

Federative Republic of
Brazil

Boundary representations not necessarily authoritative.

BACKGROUND

Land and Climate

Brazil is the fifth largest country in the world and the sixth most populous. At 3,286,470 square miles (8,511,965 square kilometers), it is larger than the continental United States and makes up half of South America. Forests cover 65 percent of its territory and include the world's largest tropical rain forest in the Amazon River Basin. The Amazon is the world's largest river. Recent concerns over the destruction of this region for development have prompted a global effort to save the rain forests. Less than 5 percent of Brazil lies above three thousand feet.

The country is south of the equator and has a mostly tropical climate. Humidity is high in coastal and forest regions, but the highlands (such as those around São Paulo) have a more moderate climate. The south is more temperate than the north. The warmest month is January; the coolest is July. Freezing temperatures are possible in the southernmost areas.

History

Brazil does not have a written history prior to the arrival of Europeans, but various groups inhabited the area when Pedro Álvarez Cabral arrived in 1500 and claimed the region for Portugal. Brazil was colonized by Portugal. The French and Dutch both attempted to establish colonies but were eventually driven out. After Spain conquered Portugal, it controlled Brazil from 1580 to 1640. Colonization took several decades and expansion did not really begin until after 1650.

When Napoleon captured Lisbon, Portugal, in 1808, the royal family fled to Brazil and established Rio de Janeiro as the seat of the Portuguese Empire. Brazil ceased to be a colony and became part of the Portugal kingdom. The royal family returned to Portugal in 1821, leaving Dom Pedro I to govern Brazil. He declared Brazil's independence in 1822 after people in Portugal demanded that Brazil be returned to colonial status. He was followed by his son, Dom Pedro II, who was deposed in 1889 by a military coup.

Since that time, the military has seized control five times, although with relatively little violence. The dictator Getúlio Vargas ruled from 1930 to 1945, followed by elected presidents. A 1964 coup gave the military control, although the country eventually returned to civilian rule. In 1985, Tancredo Neves was appointed president by an electoral college, but he died before assuming office. His vice president, José Sarney, took office. A new constitution was ratified in 1988.

Elections in 1989 brought conservative Fernando Collor de Mello to office as the first directly elected president in 29 years; he took office in March 1990. Collor began an austerity campaign to revive the economy. Unfortunately for Brazil, the "shock" therapy crippled the economy, and many measures only covered Collor's corrupt activities. Upon discovering this in 1992, legislative leaders called for Collor's impeachment. Collor resigned in December 1992 before full impeachment proceedings could be carried out. The entire process was a historic test of democracy, since it marked the first time a leader was removed from office by legal, constitutional means.

Itamar Franco, Collor's vice president, assumed the presidency until elections in October 1994. During Franco's presidency, his finance minister, Fernando Cardoso, introduced an anti-inflation plan that was so successful, the economy began to boom in 1994. Cardoso, who had been in exile from 1964 to 1985, became extremely popular and upset the front-running presidential candidate, Luiz (Lula) da Silva. Since taking office in 1995, Cardoso has continued to implement economic reforms stabilizing the economy. He plans to address social problems, such as poverty, human-rights abuses, and clashes between wealthy landowners and landless peasants.

THE PEOPLE

Population

The population of Brazil is approximately 160.7 million and is growing annually at a rate of 1.2 percent. Ninety percent of the people live on 10 percent of the land—mostly in the 200-mile-wide (320 kilometers) east coast region. In fact, the two largest cities of the southeast, São Paulo and Rio de Janeiro, together hold more than 18 million people. Nearly 50 percent of the people are younger than age 20. Brazilians of European (mostly Portuguese) descent make up 55 percent of the population, while 32 percent are of mixed heritage and 11 percent have Black African ancestry.

There are only about 150,000 indigenous people in Brazil, many of whom inhabit the Amazon region (including some who have never been contacted by modern society). Many of the mixed peoples have some indigenous blood through intermarriage. Groups of German, Italian, and Japanese immigrants settled in the southern half of the country and still maintain ethnic communities. In fact, Brazil is home to the largest cohesive community of Japanese outside of Japan. The black population descended from African slaves brought to Brazil before the 1880s; they live mostly in northeastern states such as Bahia. All groups have had an influence on Brazilian culture through religion, food, festivals, music, and dances.

The country's Human Development Index (0.804) ranks it 63d out of 174 countries. Adjusted for women, the index ranks Brazil 53d out of 130 countries. Although conditions are improving, not all Brazilians have the access to health care, education, and economic prosperity they need to make choices in their lives.

Language

Portuguese is Brazil's official language. It differs somewhat in pronunciation from the Portuguese spoken in Portugal, but it is otherwise essentially the same. English and French are popular second languages. German descendants living in southern cities may also speak German. Although Portuguese speakers generally understand Spanish, some Brazilians are offended when deliberately spoken to in Spanish. Indigenous peoples speak a variety of more than one hundred Amerindian languages.

Religion

Brazil is traditionally a strong Roman Catholic country, at one time claiming membership of nearly 95 percent of the large population. However, membership has been dropping and is currently less than 70 percent. Membership in other Christian churches and Protestant groups is growing rapidly. Under Portuguese rule, the Catholic Church had great influence over politics. Since the founding of the republic in 1889, however, there has been a separation of church and state, and religious freedom is guaranteed. Although Brazilians consider themselves quite religious, most attend church only on special occasions. Some in the northeast and in large cities practice Afro-Brazilian religions (such as *Candomblé*) that combine tribal beliefs with Catholicism.

General Attitudes

Brazilians are friendly, warm, and free spirited. They are also outgoing and enjoy being around others. Brazilians are often opinionated and will argue for their conviction with a vigor that may seem like anger, but is not. Brazilians tend to view time more as a sequence of events rather than hours and minutes (except in São Paulo). Therefore, people in most regions appear to have an extremely casual attitude about time. Brazilians are polite in crowds and shoving is considered discourteous. Men tend to stare at and make comments about women passing by. This is not considered rude and is generally ignored by the women. In contrast to just a few years ago, most Brazilians are optimistic about their country's future as a stable democracy with a strong, growing economy.

Personal Appearance

In the cities, Brazilians prefer to wear European fashions, specifically Italian and French. The people are very fashion conscious, especially women, and wear the latest styles—sometimes even a season before the Europeans because of the opposite seasons south of the equator. Shoes are well kept and polished. Manicures and pedicures are popular. In rural regions, more traditional clothing is common, especially among the native peoples.

CUSTOMS AND COURTESIES

Greetings

Brazilians greet each other with a handshake; good friends often embrace. Women often kiss each other on alternating cheeks, although they may only touch cheeks and "kiss the air." Common terms are *Tudo bem?* (Is everything fine?) or *Como vai?* (How are you?). Young friends greet each other with a simple *Oi* (Hi). When one joins or leaves a small group, it is polite to shake hands with all who are present. A common term for parting is *Tcháu* (Good-bye); also common is *Até logo* (See you soon).

Gestures

The U.S. American "OK" sign, with the thumb and index finger forming a circle, is an offensive gesture. The "thumbs-up" sign shows approval. To beckon, all fingers of the hand wave with the palm facing down. To get someone's attention from a distance, people say "pssssst." Whistling at people is considered rude. Using a toothpick in public is rude if not done with discretion—by covering the hand holding the toothpick with the other hand.

Visiting

Brazilians enjoy visiting with one another. The tropical climate allows for much time outdoors, including chatting outside late into the evening. When invited to a home, guests generally arrive several minutes late, except perhaps in São

Paulo. If invited to dinner, one might take candy, wine, or a small gift to the hosts. One is generally expected to stay at least two hours. Guests may be invited to share in a meal, if in progress. Hosts normally offer their guests coffee or some other refreshment toward the end of the visit. While Brazilians enjoy conversation, they avoid controversial subjects (such as politics and religion) at social gatherings. Asking personal questions about one's age, salary, etc., is considered rude.

Eating

Brazilians eat in the continental style, with the knife held in the right hand and the fork remaining in the left. People wash their hands before eating and refrain from touching food while eating. One wipes the mouth each time before drinking. After-meal conversation often takes place over a cup of strong *cafezinho* (black coffee). In restaurants, diners call the waiter by holding up the index finger or by softly saying *Garçon*. The check is requested with the phrase *A conta, por favor*. While the bill usually includes the tip, one may leave extra change. If the bill does not include the tip, 10 to 15 percent is customary.

LIFESTYLE

Family

Families are traditionally large and may include the extended family. The elderly who cannot care for themselves live with their children because it is improper to send them to a nursing home. The family is strong and is led by the father. However, the mother does have an influence in decisions, especially those affecting the home. Children usually only leave the home when they marry and rarely before. Unmarried men may leave early for employment reasons, but they usually live at home until they are 30. Family members rely on each other for assistance and enjoy being together. Among the urban youth, however, some of these values are becoming less important. While middle-income families live in modest homes or apartments, the poor often lack the basic necessities of life, including food, sanitation, and shelter. Women and youth often work to help support families.

Dating and Marriage

Group dating starts at about age 14. Couples gradually emerge from the group. Serious dating and engagements may last as long as two or three years. Traditional families expect the young man to ask the girl's father for permission to be her boyfriend. Weddings may include two ceremonies: a legal civil ceremony and an optional religious ceremony. Wedding parties are lavish and elegant, with much food, drink, and music.

Diet

Breakfast usually consists of *café com leite* (coffee with milk), fruit, and bread with marmalade. The wealthy may also enjoy cheese. Lunch is the main meal and often includes beans, rice, meat, salad, potatoes, bread, and fruit. Dinner often includes a bowl of soup with bread, followed by coffee or milk with a piece of cake. Favorite foods vary by region. In Bahia and other states, foods may be spiced with *dendê* (palm) oil. In Rio de Janeiro, the favorite is *feijoada* (black beans with beef, pork, sausage, and sometimes even a pig's ears, feet, and tail). Areas in the south enjoy *churrasco*, a barbecue with a variety of meats. *Bife à cavalo com fritas* (meat with egg and french fries) is popular in many areas. Common drinks include lemonade, soft drinks, coffee, and *mate*, an herbal tea enjoyed in the southern states.

Recreation

The national sport is *futebol* (soccer); Brazil's soccer teams are among the finest in the world. In fact, the people have such a passion for soccer, they have been known to close businesses and schools during the World Cup or important national competitions. Brazil's team won the 1994 World Cup championship. The legendary soccer player Pelé is from Brazil. Basketball and volleyball are also popular. Because the nation has many fine beaches, both Brazilians and tourists enjoy boating, fishing, and swimming. Brazilians are avid fans of auto racing. People in major cities often join athletic clubs for recreation. Families often take vacations the week before Easter or during school breaks. Traditional dances and festivals are popular and vary by region.

Holidays

Carnaval, a five-day festival preceding Ash Wednesday, is the most famous holiday in Brazil. It is marked by street parades, *samba* and *bloco* dancing, parties, drinking, costumes, conga drums, and music. Some people spend months preparing costumes and saving for *Carnaval*. During this week, crime (and car-accident) rates are unusually high.

Tiradentes Day (21 April) celebrates the death of Joaquim José da Silva Xavier, a dentist and nationalist who was known as Tiradentes and died in the struggle for independence. The *Festas Junina* (June festivals) coincide with the feasts of St. John and St. Peter and are celebrated with local fair-type activities. During the Christmas celebration, people eat the big meal (turkey or ham) and exchange gifts on Christmas Eve. Gifts from *Papai Noel* (Father Noel) are found on Christmas, but all other gifts are given the day before. Other holidays include Easter, Labor Day (1 May), Independence Day (7 September), Memorial Day (2 November), and Republic Day (15 November).

New Year's Eve is a time for large parties. In some areas *Candomblé* believers dress in white and blue to honor the sea goddess *Iemanjá* and to get energy for the new year. Flowers and candles are placed on beaches as part of the celebration.

Commerce

Padarias (neighborhood stores that sell milk, bread, sandwiches, sweets, soft drinks, and sometimes alcohol) open as early as 5:00 A.M. Most other stores are open weekdays from 8:00 A.M. to 6:00 P.M. and until noon on Saturday, while some larger stores remain open until 9:00 P.M. on Fridays. Supermarkets are open every day of the week. Some business offices and stores close from noon to 2:00 P.M. for the afternoon meal. The 24-hour clock is used to schedule events so 3:00 P.M. is referred to as 15.00.

SOCIETY

Government

Brazil is a federative republic consisting of 26 states and one federal district (Brasília, the capital). Each state is technically autonomous, with a legislative body and elected governor, but all rights not delegated to the state are reserved by the federal government. The president is head of state and government. The National Congress has an 81-seat Federal Senate and a 513-seat Chamber of Deputies. In 1993, citizens rejected a referendum to switch to a parliamentary system, with a prime minister as head of government. Voting is universal and compulsory for ages 18 to 70. Voluntary voting is allowed for 16- and 17-year-olds and for those older than 70. The president and legislature face elections again in 1998. Brazil's major political parties include Cardoso's Brazilian Social Democratic Party (PSDB), Brazilian Democratic Movement Party (PMDB), Liberal Front Party (PFL), and Worker's Party (PT). Several other parties also hold seats in Congress.

Economy

Brazil has the largest economy in South America, and the ninth largest in the world. Real gross domestic product per capita is $5,240, which has more than tripled in the last generation. However, income distribution is highly unequal; the poorest 40 percent of households earn about 7 percent of the nation's income. Poverty is a serious problem in both rural and urban areas, affecting more than one-third of the total population.

Prior to 1992, inept government policies and corruption threatened to destroy the economy. When Franco became president, he named Cardoso as his finance minister. Cardoso introduced a new currency, the *real* (R$), as part of an anti-inflation program that cut monthly inflation from 50 percent to about 2 percent. This allowed foreign reserves to increase, unemployment to decrease, and gross national product to expand by about 5 percent in 1994. Assuming further reforms continue, Brazil's economy has great potential for the future.

Agriculture employs about 30 percent of the population. The nation is the world's largest producer of coffee, oranges, and bananas. It is second in soybean and cocoa production, third in corn and beef, fourth in pork, and eighth in rice. Much of Brazil's sugarcane is used to produce ethyl alcohol, a fuel used in more than 1.5 million Brazilian cars. Brazil's industrial sector exports automobiles and parts, textiles, minerals, iron ore, steel, and metals; other industries include cement and chemicals. Natural resources include gold, nickel, tin, oil, timber, and several minerals. Most electric power is generated by hydroelectric dams. Brazil is largely self-sufficient in food and consumer goods.

Transportation and Communication

While domestic air travel is well developed between hundreds of local airports, flights can be expensive. Travel by intercity bus is more common, although buses tend to be crowded. São Paulo and Rio de Janeiro have rapid transit systems. City buses do not stop automatically but are hailed by the wave of a hand. Readily available in large cities, taxis with red license plates have fixed meter rates. Brazil has a highly developed media, with one of the world's largest television networks. The most popular television programs include *telenovelas* (soap operas). A media-oriented society, Brazil also enjoys a large film and music industry. Televisions are found in even the poorest urban and rural areas. Urban telephone service is good. Pay phones are operated by tokens, not coins.

Education

A national adult literacy program has raised the literacy rate from 66 to 82 percent. Education consists of eight years of compulsory elementary education (to age 14) and three years of secondary education. About 40 percent of those who enter school proceed to the secondary level. Entrance into one of Brazil's top universities is difficult and is preceded by a special college-preparation course and entrance exams. About half of secondary school graduates go on to trade schools. Brazil has many fine libraries and research centers. There are hundreds of higher education institutions.

Health

Excellent medical care is available in big cities to those who can afford it. However, other areas are rarely equipped with adequate facilities. Water often is not potable. Sanitation in some areas is insufficient. Yellow fever and malaria are found in some rural areas. The infant mortality rate is 57 per 1,000. A grassroots effort is providing mobile health-care workers to rural areas to fight infant mortality through education and basic care. Life expectancy averages 64 to 69 years.

FOR THE TRAVELER

U.S. citizens need a passport and visa to travel to Brazil. Visas must be obtained in advance. Although not required, yellow fever, typhoid, and cholera immunizations are recommended. Travelers coming from yellow fever endemic zones are required to show proof of vaccination. Do not eat uncooked or unpeeled fruits and vegetables. To avoid dengue fever, take measures to prevent daytime mosquito bites (especially when visiting urban areas). A tourist visa may prevent travel to certain rural areas where disease is a problem. For current health advisories, call the U.S. Centers for Disease Control International Travelers' Hotline at (404) 332–4559.

Brazil offers visitors spectacular scenery, food, and festivals. One can visit modern cities as well as simple rural villages. An increase in crime against tourists prompted Brazil, in 1992, to deploy special tourist police units in areas where tourists tend to congregate; this has improved conditions, but visitors are urged not to wear expensive jewelry in public or be alone after dark. They should also be vigilant with luggage in airports. For information regarding travel and accomodations, contact the Brazilian American Cultural Center, 16 West 46th Street, Second Floor, New York, NY 10036; phone (212) 730–0515. You may also wish to contact the consular section of the Brazilian Embassy, 3009 Whitehaven Street NW, Washington, DC 20008; phone (202) 745–2828. The Embassy of Brazil, is located at 3006 Massachusetts Avenue NW, Washington, DC 20008.

Republic of
Bulgaria

Boundary representations not necessarily authoritative.

BACKGROUND

Land and Climate

Slightly larger than Tennessee, Bulgaria covers 42,823 square miles (110,910 square kilometers). Much of the terrain is mountainous; the Rila Mountains in the south are the highest on the Balkan peninsula. The northern and central regions are dominated by plains. To the east lies the Black Sea. The northern border is the Danube River, which separates Bulgaria from Romania. The climate is similar to that of the U.S. corn belt, with cold, damp winters and hot, dry summers. Northern regions tend to be colder than southern areas.

History

Thracians are the oldest known inhabitants of the area now called Bulgaria. They founded the Odrisaw Kingdom in the fifth century B.C. Slavic tribes began migrating to the area several hundred years later. In the seventh century A.D., Bulgars (a central Asian people) migrated to the area and mixed with the Slavs and Thracians. A Bulgarian state was recognized by the Byzantine Empire in 681. Two Bulgarian kingdoms existed before Bulgaria was conquered by the Ottoman Turks in 1396. The period that followed is known in Bulgaria as the "Turkish yoke." The struggle for political and religious independence gave rise to a cultural renaissance at the end of the 18th century. The Ottomans ruled until 1878, when Bulgaria became independent as a result of the Russian-Turkish War. It was briefly divided into the Kingdom of Bulgaria (to the north) and Eastern Romelia (to the south). Eastern Romelia remained part of the Ottoman Empire until it was reunited with Bulgaria in 1886. Until 1944, this was the period of the Third Bulgarian Kingdom.

Allied with Germany in World Wars I and II, Bulgaria was twice defeated. Communists seized control in 1944 and consolidated power when Soviet troops marched into the country later that year. The monarchy was abolished by referendum in 1946. The prominent Bulgarian Communist leader, Georgi Dimitrov, who had been a nationalist hero against the Nazis in World War II, died in 1949. The 1947 constitution was named after him.

From 1954 to 1989, Todor Zhivkov held power. His authority remained unquestioned until a 1989 palace coup removed him as reforms swept through Eastern Europe. In a transitional year, the Communists renamed their party the Socialists prior to free elections in 1990. They were victorious but had trouble forming a stable government. Their new leader, Petar Mladenov, soon resigned under pressure. A coalition government was formed under the leadership of Dimitar Popov (prime minister) and Zhelyu Zhelev (president). A new constitution was approved in 1991 and subsequent elections established a multiparty parliament. Zhelev, a popular former dissident, was reelected president in 1992. His government worked to privatize industry, liquidate collective farms, and return property confiscated in 1948 to its owners or heirs. In the 1994 general elections, Socialist Party leader Zhan Videnov became prime minister. The next presidential elections must be held by early 1997.

PEOPLE

Population

Bulgaria's population of 8.8 million is shrinking slightly. The majority of people (85.3 percent) are ethnic Bulgarians.

EUROPE

Of the rest of the population, 8.5 percent are Turks, 2.6 percent are Romas (Gypsies), and 2.5 percent are Macedonians. Armenians, Russians, and other smaller groups also inhabit Bulgaria. Sofia, the capital, has more than one million residents and is the largest city. The majority of people (68 percent) live in urban areas. Bulgaria's Human Development Index (0.796) ranks it 65th out of 174 countries. This indicates that the basic needs of the population are met, but compared to other industrialized nations, opportunities and choices are limited.

Language

The official language is Bulgarian, and nearly all inhabitants speak it. About half of the Turkish population speaks Turkish as its native tongue, but most also speak Bulgarian. Bulgarian is a Slavic language that uses an alphabet first developed in the ninth century by Cyril and Methodius. The Cyrillic alphabet preceded, and is similar to, the Russian alphabet. Russian was previously a required subject in school, so many people can speak it. English, German, and French are the most popular languages to study.

Religion

The Bulgarian Orthodox Church claims a membership of more than 85 percent of all Bulgarians. Muslims make up about 13 percent of the population. Orthodox monasteries are held in high regard for their religious and artistic significance. Many monasteries and churches contain frescoes and icons of significant historical value.

While religious worship was discouraged during the Communist era, it is unrestricted today. Rural people and the older generation are more devout in attending services, but the urban youth are showing an interest in religion. Once banned, religious holidays are now openly celebrated throughout the country. Numerous Christian and non-Christian organizations from other countries have sent missionaries to Bulgaria. Because a few groups have questionable practices, Bulgarians are developing animosity toward outside groups, and Parliament is considering a law to limit their activities.

General Attitudes

Bulgarians generally respect those who are open, strong, capable, gregarious, good humored, loyal to family and friends, and forthright. Families and group concerns are very important and play a role in individual decisions.

Bulgarians take considerable pride in their heritage and culture, which have been preserved despite centuries of foreign domination. They are particularly sensitive about Ottoman rule. Democracy has always been important to Bulgarians. In fact, the 1879 constitution was one of the most progressive in Europe at the time. People are interested in politics, both domestic and international, and try to be well-informed. Political discussions are popular. Art and science are appreciated.

Bulgarians face many challenges during the transition to democracy. They have faced economic hardship, difficult constitutional questions, and ethnic tensions, but they are generally optimistic about the future. The youth are particularly interested in Western pop culture. They admire the United States as a wealthy and fortunate country, and they also look to Western Europe as a model for their own development. At the same time, adults are wary of "foreign" influences in Bulgaria, and oppose "non-Bulgarian" ideas or items. An entrepreneurial spirit is emerging, but businesspeople are not admired on a personal level. In the past, wealthy people could only be so through corruption, a condition that still afflicts society today. So honest, private businesspeople have to work hard to gain respect and be regarded in a positive light. Bulgarians are also strengthening a work ethic that was weakened during the Communist years of guaranteed employment. Careers and professional skills are becoming more important.

Personal Appearance

European and American fashions are popular, but clothing is expensive. Many women knit sweaters for themselves and their families, and most people include sweaters in their wardrobe. Women are more concerned with their appearance than men, always making an effort to be well dressed and well-groomed in public. They may wear something more casual at home to keep nicer clothing in good condition. Professional women usually wear a skirt, a blouse or sweater, and high heels to work. Clothing is neatly pressed; wrinkled items are rarely seen in public. Sneakers are worn only with jogging suits. Young women wear blue jeans and either a sweater or a shirt with buttons. Flannel is a popular fabric. Older rural women often wear a house dress, sweater, and scarf with conservative shoes.

Professional men wear suits and ties to work, although older men prefer trousers and sweaters. Young men wear jeans, denim or sports jackets, flannel shirts, and sneakers or loafers. Young children are considered the best-dressed people in the country, wearing imported clothing and newly hand-knit items. Hats, boots, scarves, gloves, and winter jackets or fur coats are worn during the cold winters.

CUSTOMS AND COURTESIES

Greetings

When meeting, Bulgarians usually shake hands. The handshake might be accompanied in formal situations by *Kak ste?* (How are you?) or *Zdraveite* (Hello). Friends, relatives, and colleagues use the informal terms for these greetings: *Kak si?* and *Zdrasti* or *Zdrave*. Close female friends might kiss on the cheek. People do not shake hands when saying *Dobro utro* (Good morning), *Dober den* (Good day), *Dober vetcher* (Good evening), or *Leka nosht* (Good night). They use first names in informal settings but otherwise address others by title and family name. *Gospodin* (Mr.), *Gospozha* (Mrs.), or *Gospozhitsa* (Miss) are common titles, but professional titles are also used. When one joins a small gathering, it is polite to greet each person individually, beginning with the elderly.

Dovishdane (Till I see you again) is a common parting phrase. Friends might also say *Vsichko hubavo* (All the best) or *Ciao* (Good-bye). Urban people do not usually greet strangers passing on the street, but this is considered polite in rural areas.

Gestures

"Yes" is indicated by shaking the head from side to side, and "no" is expressed with one or two nods. One might shake the index finger back and forth to emphasize the "no" and even add a "tsk" sound to express displeasure. In conversation, people generally do not use hand gestures, but they often touch each other. Female friends might walk arm in arm down the street. Pointing with the index finger is rude. It is impolite for men to cross an ankle over the knee or for anyone to put feet on furniture. As a matter of cleanliness, it is rude to touch the lower leg, ankle, or foot when eating. One should ask permission of other passengers before lowering a bus or train window.

Visiting

Visiting (*na gosti*) is an important part of Bulgarian life. Friends and neighbors commonly drop by for a short visit without prior arrangement, but more typically, an invitation is extended. Hosting friends for afternoon coffee and cake is popular, as is inviting them over for dinner. If friends receive a plate of baked goods, they later return the plate full of a similar gift. People often socialize at a café. Outdoor cafés provide opportunities to spend warm summer evenings visiting.

Women guests usually enter the home before men. Many Bulgarians remove their shoes upon entering, unless the hosts object. Slippers might be offered, or guests wear their stockings. Hosts usually offer refreshments and a drink; alcohol is rarely served without food. Invited guests often bring flowers (odd numbers only; even numbers are for funerals) for the hostess, a bottle of alcohol for the host, or candy for the children. When visiting a newborn baby, people bring only odd numbers of gifts (even numbers bring bad luck), and they do not visit without invitation until the baby is 40 days old.

Evening visits usually start after 8:00 P.M. and may last until after midnight (until 3:00 A.M. for special occasions). Bulgarians enjoy showing hospitality to guests and having long conversations, so leaving early is rude. Eating and dancing are typical parts of an evening visit in urban areas. Rural families might get together to enjoy a meal made of produce from the family garden.

Eating

In addition to three meals a day, Bulgarians might have a mid-morning snack and afternoon coffee. Breakfast is usually light, consisting of coffee and a cheese-filled pastry or some other bread product (sweet roll, toast, etc.). Traditionally, the main meal is eaten at midday. It consists of soup and/or salad, a main course, and dessert. Alcohol is usually served with this meal. When family schedules conflict with the traditional mealtime, people eat a lighter lunch—at a fast-food establishment, kiosk, or café, if not at home—and eat their main family meal after 7:00 P.M. If dinner is not the main meal, it is light and consists of some of the same foods as lunch, but not soup or dessert. Salads are eaten from a common platter with individual forks.

The continental style of eating is most common, with the fork in the left hand and the knife in the right. It is polite for guests to accept second helpings. An empty plate and glass will usually be refilled. A small amount of food left on the plate (usually after second helpings) indicates one is full. Conversation is expected, and everyone waits for all to finish before leaving the table. Napkins are placed on the table, not in the lap. Meals for special occasions can include several courses and last many hours. Toasting (*Nazdravey*) is done at the beginning and throughout a meal; people maintain eye contact when clinking glasses during a toast.

Although Bulgarians generally eat at home, they are eating out more often because so many new restaurants are opening. Bills are paid at the table. A traditional eating establishment that is common in rural areas is called a *mehana*; it features traditional food, folk music, and dancing.

LIFESTYLE
Family

The family unit is strong and supportive of its members. The elderly are often cared for by their adult children. Unmarried adults live with their parents until they marry. Young couples often live with one set of parents until they are able to get housing for themselves. Most urban families live in apartments, which are in short supply. Rural families usually have their own homes. Many village homes are owned by urban families, who use them for summer retreats, for retired parents, and for keeping family gardens. Bulgarians still feel tied to their agricultural heritage.

Most families do not have more than two children. Some women may receive three years of maternity leave, two of which are paid. Because urban women usually work outside the home, grandmothers play an important role in child care. Men traditionally do not help with household duties, but the younger generation is assuming greater responsibilities.

Dating and Marriage

The youth associate in groups at first. One-on-one dating usually does not occur until people are in their twenties. Favorite activities involve getting together at a café to drink and talk, going to a movie, dancing at a disco, or relaxing in the park. Rural youth enjoy socializing in the town square. Most Bulgarians expect to marry and have children. The average age for women to marry is between 18 and 25. Rural men marry in their twenties and urban men in their thirties.

Weddings involve big celebrations. A legal civil ceremony is often followed by a church wedding. A big reception is held in the evening. Folk music, dancing, and eating are common at the reception. Many traditions are kept by families, including pinning money on the bride's dress to represent future prosperity, the groom serenading the bride at her home, and pulling on opposite ends of a loaf of bread (whoever gets the largest piece will be the boss of the family). Newlyweds only now are beginning to go on honeymoons.

Diet

Bulgarians eat pork, fish, or lamb with most main dishes. Dairy products such as yogurt and cheese are common ingredients in many dishes. Popular main meals include *moussaka* (a casserole with pork or lamb, potatoes, tomatoes, and yogurt) and *nadenitsa* (stuffed pork sausage). *Kufteta* is a fried meat patty mixed with bread crumbs. *Sarmi* is a pepper or cabbage stuffed with pork and rice. Grilled meat (*skara*), such as *shishcheta* (a lamb shish kebab), is popular, especially in restaurants. *Shopska* is a salad made with Bulgarian cheese (called *cerene*), cucumbers, and tomatoes. A favorite cold soup is *tarator*, which includes cucumbers, yogurt, garlic, dill, walnuts, and oil. Cheese *banitsa* (a layered pastry) is eaten as a snack or for breakfast, while pumpkin *banitsa* is a popular dessert. Various cakes and *baklava* (a thin, leafy pastry with a syrup-and-nut filling) are also enjoyed for dessert. Coffee is usually either espresso or Turkish style. Meals are usually accompanied by a soft drink, alcohol, or coffee.

Recreation

Skiing is extremely popular in Bulgaria. People also generally enjoy being out in nature, hiking, walking, or touring in the countryside. Soccer and basketball are popular sports. Bulgaria's national soccer team finished fourth in the 1994

World Cup. August is the favorite time to go to the beach on the Black Sea. Summer vacations also typically include a trip to the mountains. Many professional organizations, schools, and local governments own lodges in the mountains where their members can stay for minimal cost.

Folk dancing and music are very much alive in Bulgaria. Festivals held throughout the year highlight various aspects of traditional Bulgarian culture. Urban dwellers enjoy the performing arts (ballet, opera, and classical music), and even small towns have a local theater. Movie attendance is high, and U.S. American movies are quite popular. The youth enjoy rock, pop, disco, and folk music. The urban youth have access to recreation centers.

Holidays

Public holidays include New Year's Day, National Day of Freedom and Independence (3 March), Labor Day (1–2 May), the Day of Bulgarian Culture and Science (24 May), and Christmas Day (25 December). On 24 May, Saints Cyril and Methodius are honored for developing the Cyrillic alphabet, but the country's accomplishments in science and culture are also celebrated. Easter is popular but not a state holiday. Name days are celebrated with a family meal.

The most celebrated season stretches from Christmas Eve to New Year's Day. On Christmas Eve, products of the soil (no meat) are eaten to represent a successful past harvest and wish for a good future harvest. On New Year's Day, people eat a large meal and exchange presents. They often decorate a tree. Children go door-to-door wishing good fortune to friends and relatives, carrying with them a small decorated stick (*survachka*), with which they touch people they visit in exchange for candy and money.

At the beginning of March, Bulgarians celebrate spring with *Martenitza*. People exchange red-and-white yarn designs to symbolize luck and happiness. They wear the yarn designs on the clothing until they see a sparrow. They then either put the *martenitza* on a tree branch to bring on spring or hide it under a rock to represent the wish that the evil spirits in nature (and man) will go to sleep.

Commerce

Offices are open from 9:00 A.M. to 6:00 P.M. in most cases, but private shops often have additional hours. Some businesses close for the midday meal. Many close by noon on Saturday, and most are closed on Sunday. A strong capitalist spirit exists, and entrepreneurs are turning their garages or vacant buildings into shops or other small enterprises. Bulgarians shop daily for bread and other fresh foods. They purchase dairy, meat, and shelf products from small stores and fresh produce at open-air markets. Selection is best on a designated weekly market day.

SOCIETY

Government

Bulgaria is a multiparty democracy. The president is head of state and the prime minister is head of government. Members of the 240-seat National Assembly (*Narodno Sobranyie*) are elected directly by the people. Zhan Videnov's Socialist Party has control of the National Assembly. All citizens are eligible and required to vote at age 18.

Economy

Bulgaria's painful transition to a market economy has been slow. Divisions over privatization measures and economic reforms led to a recent currency crisis and have threatened the country's economic stability. High inflation (50–80 percent) and high unemployment (10–12 percent) are expected to continue. Private-sector growth is needed to improve conditions. Unfortunately, crucial foreign investment is lacking, public debt is high, and regional conflicts have hindered trade on the Danube River. Finding new markets for Bulgarian goods is essential to progress. Real gross domestic product per capita is estimated to be $4,250. This figure indicates Bulgarians can meet most basic needs but lack access to economic prosperity.

Bulgaria exports agricultural products (grains, tobacco, wine, dairy foods) and some machinery. It imports consumer goods, food, and heavy machinery. Tourism is an important source of foreign capital. The currency is the *lev* (Lv).

Transportation and Communication

Most people use the reliable public transportation system, which consists of buses, trams, trolleys, and trains. Most families own one car. Taxis are plentiful in urban areas.

Two national political newspapers and several private papers are increasing their circulation. Television broadcasts are changing rapidly, as American and European programming is becoming more popular. Telephone service is expensive and not fully developed.

Education

Education, compulsory to age 15, was once free at all levels. Extreme financial pressures have led even primary schools to charge some fees. Science and technical training are stressed in school, but the lack of modern equipment hampers advanced training. Entrance to secondary schools is determined by competitive exam, and urban students can often choose from five types of school, each offering a different focus (such as math and science or foreign languages). A number of universities and three-year training institutions offer higher education. The adult literacy rate is 93 percent.

Health

A national health-care system provides free medical care to all citizens, but facilities often are not well equipped. Private doctors offer better care to those who can pay for it. The infant mortality rate is 12 per 1,000; life expectancy averages 70 to 77 years.

FOR THE TRAVELER

U.S. visitors need a valid passport to enter Bulgaria, but no visa is required for stays of up to 30 days. Interesting sites include Plovdiv's old town and Roman ruins, Black Sea resorts, ski resorts near Blagoevgrad, Sofia's museums, and the Rila Monastery. For travel information, contact Balkan Holidays, 41 East 42d Street, Suite 508, New York, NY 10017. You may also wish to contact the Embassy of Bulgaria, 1621 22d Street NW, Washington, DC 20008; phone (202) 387–7969.

Printed on recycled paper

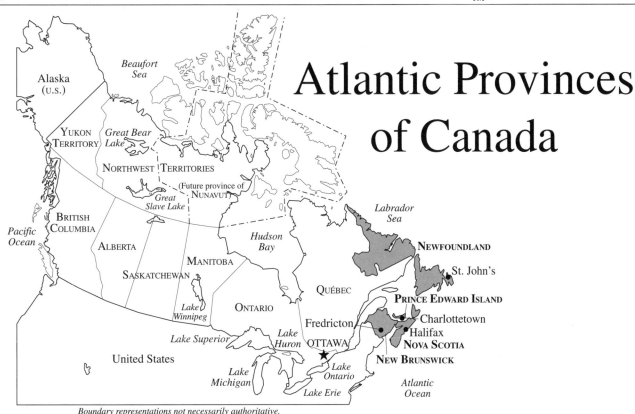

Atlantic Provinces of Canada

THE AMERICAS

Boundary representations not necessarily authoritative.

BACKGROUND

Land and Climate

Canada is the second largest country in the world, after Russia. It covers 3,851,788 square miles (9,976,140 square kilometers). However, much of the north is sparsely inhabited because of the arctic climate and permanently frozen ground. Therefore, most of the people live within 100 miles (160 kilometers) of the U.S. border. The combined Atlantic provinces are a bit smaller than Texas and cover only 5 percent of Canada's total land area. This area is generally subject to a humid continental climate, although the coast of Newfoundland experiences a subarctic effect from the Labrador current. Winters are cold; summers are warm and humid. Fog is common in the spring. During the warmest month (July), temperatures average between 60°F and 65°F (15–18°C). Although the four provinces are referred to as Atlantic Canada, three of them—New Brunswick, Prince Edward Island, and Nova Scotia—are also called the Maritime Provinces. Newfoundland includes the mainland area of Labrador. The Appalachian Mountains cover much of the lower Atlantic Provinces, but the region also offers plateaus, valleys, and rocky coasts.

History

In 1604, the French began to settle in an area they called Acadia. However, in 1713 the English began to gain control over the region. Because the Acadians were not trusted by the English, many were forced to leave the region in the 1750s for other parts of North America. Acadians were among the first people to settle in Louisiana, and the term *Cajun* is derived from the word *Acadian*. Not too many years after their expulsion, many Acadians returned to the Maritimes and settled throughout the region. At about the same time, English "Loyalists," who left the 13 colonies after the American Revolution, also began settling in the region.

In 1867, the British North America Act created the Dominion of Canada out of Nova Scotia, New Brunswick, and a colony called Canada (present-day Québec and Ontario). Prince Edward Island did not join until 1873, and Newfoundland remained a separate colony until 1949.

With the Statute of Westminster in 1931, Great Britain relinquished its formal authority over Canadian affairs, retaining only the right to have the last word on constitutional matters. In 1982, Britain agreed to give up that right, and Canada's constitution was altered to reflect its full formal sovereignty. A Charter of Rights and Freedoms was also ratified in 1982. The nation still acknowledges Britain's Queen Elizabeth II as the official head of state, but Canada operates independent of the British government. The queen is represented in Canada by Governor General Romeo LeBlanc.

In 1984, Pierre Trudeau retired after 15 years as prime minister. His Liberal Party had governed Canada for 42 of the previous 50 years. Trudeau was succeeded by Brian

Mulroney, head of the Progressive Conservative Party. Mulroney was reelected in 1988 but resigned in 1993 ahead of new parliamentary elections. The Liberal Party returned to power as a result of the 1993 elections, and Jean Chrétien became prime minister.

Canada is an active member of the United Nations (UN). It frequently contributes troops to UN peacekeeping missions and relief operations. Canadians proudly point to the efforts of a former prime minister, Lester B. Pearson, who won the Nobel Peace Prize for advocating in the 1950s the use of peacekeeping forces in international conflicts.

THE PEOPLE
Population

Canada's population is 28.4 million. The combined population of the four provinces of Atlantic Canada comprises about 9 percent of that total, or about 2.56 million. However, because these provinces are small, population density is much higher than the national average. The ethnic origins of the people are basically French and English, with some German, Dutch, Scottish, and Irish. But there are also native peoples (Abnaki, Micmac, etc.) and African-Canadian descendants of black slaves who fled the United States. The French are concentrated in New Brunswick, while more than 95 percent of the people of Newfoundland are of British descent.

Canada's Human Development Index (0.950) ranks it first out of 174 countries. Canada's strong egalitarian society affords its people excellent access to health care, education, and economic prosperity needed to make choices in their lives. Adjusted for women, the index (0.891) ranks Canada ninth out of 130 countries.

Language

English and French are both official languages in Canada. French is a key language in New Brunswick and is spoken as a first language by about 34 percent of that province's citizens. Most others in Atlantic Canada speak English as their first language, even those of non-British descent. Canadian spelling of English words follows U.S. standards in some cases (e.g., *organize* rather than *organise*) but British standards in others (*centre* not *center*), and Canadians call the last letter of the alphabet *zed,* not *zee.*

Religion

Religious beliefs in Canada follow traditional lines. The French are generally Roman Catholic while those of British descent are mostly Protestant. Many other Christian faiths and non-Christian organizations are represented in Atlantic Canada as well. Overall, Canada's population is 47 percent Roman Catholic, 41 percent Protestant, and 12 percent other groups. The largest Protestant groups are the United Church and the Anglican Church. Although there is an official separation of church and state in Canada, religion is publicly recognized and some private religious schools are subsidized by the state.

General Attitudes

Most Canadians are friendly and open to one another. The people are proud of their cultural heritage, which includes French, British, and other European influences. Atlantic Canadians are considered conservative and traditional, in part due to their rural heritage. They are very patriotic, as their area was one of the first to be part of Canada. Despite close ties and many similarities between their nation and the United States, Canadians emphasize they are not U.S.-type people just living in Canada. As *North* Americans, they share the title "Americans" with people in the United States. Canadians often see U.S. Americans as more aggressive and materialistic than themselves. They also feel they are more tolerant and community oriented than U.S. Americans and less condescending to foreigners. The preservation of Canadian culture, especially against influence from the United States, is important.

Atlantic Canadians see themselves as hardworking, unpretentious people who value nature, community involvement, and education. They feel their unique sense of humor and rural values set them apart from other Canadians in many ways. Due to economic difficulties in the region, they approach Atlantic Canada's future with cautious optimism and a will to preserve their way of life.

Personal Appearance

Although their dress habits are very similar to those in the United States, the people are somewhat more conservative in their attire. It is polite to remove sunglasses when speaking to someone and to remove hats in buildings.

CUSTOMS AND COURTESIES
Greetings

Because the people of the Atlantic Provinces have various cultural backgrounds, greetings vary from place to place. A handshake is the most common greeting. Nodding the head often replaces handshaking in informal situations. Some French speakers might greet friends with a light kiss to the cheek. French-speaking people are often more outgoing and open than those of British descent. French speakers might use *Bonjour* (Good day) or *Tu vas bien?* (How are you doing?) to greet others. Common for English speakers are "Hi," "Good morning," or "How are you?" Smiles are always appreciated.

When one passes a stranger on the street, a smile and a nod are appropriate. Rural people also often greet the person verbally, but this is less common in large cities. People use first names when addressing others in informal situations or when the more senior person requests it. Titles are used with new acquaintances and on formal occasions.

Gestures

Most gestures, positive and negative, are the same in Canada as in the United States. However, some gestures common in the United States might be offensive to a specific cultural groups or in a particular area. A visitor should use gestures conservatively. Pointing at someone with the index finger is rude; using the entire hand to motion to someone is more polite. Eye contact is important when talking to another person. French speakers use hand gestures somewhat more often than do others during conversation.

Visiting

Atlantic Canadians enjoy visiting with one another. Close friends might drop by unannounced, but most visits are otherwise arranged in advance, especially in urban areas. It is impolite to drop by during regular mealtimes. Guests are nearly always offered refreshments, usually including at least a drink and often a small snack. It would be rude of the hosts not to offer something. Refreshments are considered an unspoken invitation to stay a while. Invited dinner guests often receive appetizers and a drink before the meal. It is appropriate for them to take a gift, such as wine or chocolate and sometimes flowers, to the hosts. This is especially true if the guests are not related to the hosts. Etiquette is important to most people but will depend on the situation and the hosts. For example, removing street shoes upon entering is appropriate in some homes but is not important in others, unless one's shoes are muddy or wet.

Eating

The standard three meals a day are often complemented by afternoon tea (especially among those of English heritage) or snacks at work. It is important for the family to eat supper (dinner) together when possible. In some rural areas, the main family meal is at midday. When one eats as a guest, especially in a formal situation, it is often impolite to rest the hands in the lap during the meal. Taking second helpings is a way to compliment the hosts on the food. It is considered polite to offer another table guest a dish before serving oneself.

Adults dress well when dining at fine restaurants. Although younger people dress more casually, they are still well dressed when dining formally. There are, of course, a number of casual and fast-food restaurants where nicer clothing is not necessary. Tipping is generally the same as in the United States: 10 to 20 percent.

LIFESTYLE

Family

While the family unit is the center of society, both parents commonly work outside the home. Traditional norms have changed somewhat over the last decade, as in other industrialized countries. However, rural values continue to be important to most people. The average family size is comparable to that in the United States, but the divorce rate is lower in Canada. Family homes are generally wood-frame structures with various exteriors. Outside of large cities, where many live in rented apartments, the majority of homes (62 percent) are single-family dwellings owned by the occupant. In Newfoundland, this figure rises to more than 75 percent.

Dating and Marriage

Dating and marriage customs are similar to those in the United States. Dating usually begins around age 13. The youth enjoy going to movies, eating out, going to the beach, and attending sporting events such as hockey games. People generally marry in their twenties. Wedding traditions depend on a couple's religious affiliation. In some areas, a three-day celebration is popular.

Diet

Since Atlantic Canada is so closely associated with the ocean, fish and seafood are important to the diet. Lobster is a favorite and inexpensive food. Dulse, an edible seaweed, is popular in some areas. Despite a short growing season, fresh fruits are common, including apples and a variety of berries. Fruit pies are popular in season. Dairy products are consumed in fairly large quantities. *Donair*, popular throughout the region, is pita bread stuffed with meat and sauce. Commonly eaten meats include chicken, beef, and pork. A main meal might consist of meat or fish, a vegetable, potatoes, dessert, and a drink. Prince Edward Island is famous for growing 70 different types of potatoes.

Recreation

Both spectator and participant sports are popular. Favorites include swimming, hockey, speed and figure skating, football, baseball, soccer, rugby, curling, skiing, tennis, golf, track-and-field, and gymnastics. Since the Atlantic Ocean surrounds many of these provinces, lobster cookouts and beach parties are common social events. In their leisure time, people enjoy gardening, hiking, fishing, and other outdoor activities. Spending weekends at summer cottages is very popular. People also like to visit, shop, watch television, and read.

Art galleries and museums are numerous. Many old churches are popular centers of attraction, as they symbolize the heritage of the people. Atlantic Canadians are a people of the sea, so the ocean greatly influences songs, art, poetry, and prose. It also influences folk festivals and other leisure activities. Dance and music festivals with a Scottish flavor are common in Nova Scotia (New Scotland), and other areas hold Irish and Acadian events. Prince Edward Island, birthplace of Lucy Maud Montgomery (author of *Anne of Green Gables*), is a popular recreation spot for those interested in seeing places associated with her books.

Holidays

Official Canadian holidays include New Year's Day, Easter, Victoria Day (third Monday in May), Canada Day (1 July), Labour Day (first Monday in September), Thanksgiving Day (second Monday in October), Remembrance Day (11 November), Christmas, and Boxing Day (26 December). Boxing Day is a day to visit friends and relatives. It comes from an old British tradition of presenting small boxed gifts to tradesmen (postal carriers, delivery persons, and, in the past, servants). In addition to public holidays, local festivals are held throughout the region each year to commemorate everything from the shrimp harvest to military battles to cultural heritage.

Commerce

Many people in the Atlantic Provinces work in agriculture or fishing; both occupations require long hours of hard work. The service sector employs the most people. Business hours are similar to those in the United States. Offices are generally open weekdays between 8:00 or 9:00 A.M. and 5:00 P.M. Most stores close on Sunday, except for convenience stores or shops in tourist areas. Canadians usually begin full-time work between the ages of 16 and 25.

SOCIETY

Government

Officially, Canada is a confederation with parliamentary democracy. Basically, that means Canada's system is patterned partly after Great Britain's but also has a federal system like that of the United States. The federal government holds considerable power in areas of national concern, such as health insurance, trade, the military, and development. Still, individual provinces have great control over their regions. Relations between the provincial and federal governments have not always been smooth. For example, residents of the Atlantic region have felt in the past that the federal government has not done enough to stimulate economic development in their area; many young people leave the area to find jobs.

The provinces each have one-chamber legislatures, and the leader of the dominant political party is the province's premier. Parliamentary elections may be called at any time but must be held at least every five years. Currently, the three strongest parties in Canada are the Liberal Party, Bloc Québecois, and the Reform Party. Together, these parties hold the most seats in the 295-seat House of Commons. While members of the House of Commons are elected and form the working government, the Senate's members are appointed by the governor general (on the prime minister's advice) to serve until they are 75 years old. The Senate does not introduce legislation.

Economy

Canada has one of the strongest economies in the world. It ranks second in the world in gold and uranium production, third in silver, and fourth in copper. It is a world leader in the supply of wood pulp and other timber-related products. It has also been a leading exporter of wheat for many years. Other resources include nickel, zinc, lead, potash, oil, and natural gas. Barley, oats, and other agricultural products are also important exports.

In the Atlantic Provinces, people are generally employed in manufacturing, construction, fishing, mining, and the pulp and paper industries. Tourism is also important. Some Atlantic Provinces have developed offshore petroleum resources. In addition, Newfoundland is heavily involved in hydroelectric development, which provides energy to the area. The local economy was dealt a serious blow when cod fishing, a traditional occupation, was banned due to dwindling resources. This and other factors have driven regional unemployment higher than in the rest of Canada.

In Canada, inflation and unemployment rates vary according to region. Unemployment in 1995 was about 10 percent. Inflation is around 2 percent. The currency is the Canadian dollar (Can$). Real gross domestic product per capita is $20,520, indicating economic prosperity is available to the majority of the population.

Canada has a free-trade agreement with the United States. In 1993, it also signed the North American Free Trade Agreement (NAFTA) with Mexico and the United States. That agreement provides for the freer movement of capital and goods, more cross-national investment, and a large market for many goods from each country.

Transportation and Communication

In the Atlantic Provinces, the use of ferries between islands is common. On secondary roads, cars must often be driven with caution because of farm equipment traveling on the road. Major cities have bus systems. As in the United States, personal cars are important modes of transportation. Communication systems are well developed: 98 percent of the people have telephones; 95 percent have televisions. Numerous cable-television systems provide service to all segments of the population. Radio broadcasts and newspapers reach millions of Canadians each week.

Education

Each province is responsible for its own educational system. In all provinces, education is compulsory for eight years beginning at age six or seven. Primary and secondary education is free. Newfoundland has a public-denominational system; every school uses similar curricula, but the schools themselves are operated by different religious groups. All provinces have their own public universities. College attendance has risen from 16 percent (of college-age people) in 1960 to nearly 40 percent today. About 10 percent of the total population holds university degrees. The adult literacy rate is 99 percent.

Health

In general, Canadians enjoy very good health. Their infant mortality rate is 7 per 1,000, and life expectancy ranges between 75 and 82 years. Hospitals and quality of care are excellent. Canada has a universal, compulsory national health insurance that covers doctors' fees and most hospital costs for all Canadians. It is funded by taxes and premiums collected by the federal and provincial governments.

FOR THE TRAVELER

Visas are not required of U.S. citizens staying up to 180 days; only proof of citizenship and a photo ID are necessary. U.S. travelers entering Canada from a country other than the United States must have a valid passport. Drivers should be aware that the use of seat belts is required, radar detectors are illegal (they will be confiscated in Manitoba), and speed limits are calculated in metrics. In fact, all weights and measures are based on the metric system. For more specific information on the areas you plan to visit, contact the Canadian Consulate General, 1251 Avenue of the Americas, New York, NY 10020–1175; phone (212) 596–1600. You may also wish to call Canada's Atlantic Coast at (800) 565–2627 for travel guides and other free information. Canada's embassy is located at 501 Pennsylvania Avenue NW, Washington, DC 20001; phone (202) 682–1740.

Ontario and the Western Provinces of Canada

Boundary representations not necessarily authoritative.

BACKGROUND

Land and Climate

Canada is the second largest country in the world after Russia, covering 3,851,788 square miles (9,976,140 square kilometers). However, much of the north (incuding parts of the Yukon and Northwest Territories) is uninhabited due to the arctic climate and permanently frozen ground. Most of the population lives within 100 miles (160 kilometers) of the U.S. border. Ontario's climate is generally mild. Summers are warm and humid, while winters can be very cold, due to the Great Lakes. The southern prairies of Manitoba, Saskatchewan, and Alberta are flat and vast; they have a very dry climate, with cold winters and short, hot summers. The northern portions of these provices are characterized by forests and eventually tundra. British Columbia enjoys a wet, mild climate. Beautiful scenery can be found in every region: from lakes and the Niagara Falls in Ontario, to national parks and the towering Rocky Mountains in Alberta, to British Columbia's mountains and coastline.

History

Although Britain's John Cabot first landed in Canada in 1497, the French were mostly responsible for its early colonization. France established settlements in the 1600s at Québec and Montréal. The area was called New France. Britain fought often with France for control of the territory throughout the 1600s. Britain captured Québec in 1759 and Montréal in 1760. In 1763, the Treaty of Paris gave Britain control over all of New France, which was renamed Québec.

The 1774 "Québec Act" protected the distinct characteristics of French-Canadian culture in Québec, as well as in parts of Ontario and Manitoba.

Québec was divided in 1791 but united in 1840 as Canada. In 1867, Canada was divided into Québec and Ontario. In that same year, the British North America Act created a federal union, called the Dominion of Canada, from the provinces of Québec, Ontario, Nova Scotia, and New Brunswick. This new federal government was based on the parliamentary system. In 1869, the Dominion of Canada purchased "Rupert's Land" from Hudson's Bay Company (the British trading company); this land included present-day Manitoba, Saskatchewan, Alberta, and the northern provinces. British Columbia joined as a full province in 1871.

The prairie provinces are known for the 1920s cooperative movement that significantly influenced the way communities organized financial, agricultural, insurance, and food distribution industries—a system that remains largely intact today. Saskatchewan was the birthplace of Canadian agrarian socialism, and it and Manitoba have long histories of electing democratic-socialist governments provincially.

Although Canada still retains formal ties with Britain and Queen Elizabeth II is the official head of state, Britain has no control over Canadian affairs. These were deeded to Canada first through the 1931 Statute of Westminster and then through constitutional changes in 1982. A Charter of Rights and Freedoms was also established in 1982, guaranteeing many traditional personal freedoms. Ontario has generally supported more liberal political parties on the federal level—one reason why Pierre Trudeau was prime minister for 15 years. The prairie provinces and British Columbia have traditionally been more conservative in federal elections, giving strong support to governments such as the one led by Brian Mulroney's Progressive Conservative Party from 1988 to 1993. Elections in that year brought the Liberal Party to power. Its leader, Jean Chrétien, serves as prime minister.

In the west, self-government for aboriginal peoples and native land claims are two dominant political issues. For instance, in 1991, the government announced plans to create the province of Nunavut, effectively giving the native Inuit greater autonomy on 772,000 square miles (1,999,500 square kilometers) in the northeast. The measure was approved by Northwest Territory voters in 1992, and Nunavut will officially have provincial status in April 1999. Nunavut has long been considered the "true north" in Canada: a place where difficult challenges and a tough climate helped build Canadian character. Nunavut will cover about two-thirds of present-day Northwest Territories; after 1999, the remaining one-third will retain its name and provincial status.

THE PEOPLE

Population

The total population of Canada is 28.4 million. Approximately 37 percent (10.5 million) of the people reside in Ontario, making it Canada's most heavily populated province. Twenty-eight percent (nearly eight million) live in the combined region of the prairie provinces, British Columbia, Yukon, and Northwest Territories. Canada is made up of a mosaic of nationalities that have, for the most part, remained distinct. Ontario is not only populated by those of British and French descent but also by sizable German, Italian, Ukrainian, Chinese, and Japanese communities. Toronto, with four million residents, has evolved in the past 20 years to become Canada's most culturally diverse city. Large immigrant populations from Asia, the Caribbean, and Europe have added considerable diversity to the metropolis.

Immigration from Asia has increased over the last few years. In fact, Vancouver's population of 1.5 million is 15 percent Chinese (mostly from Hong Kong). Most European nations are represented. Native peoples live mainly in the northern territories. British Columbia was settled primarily by British, Chinese, and Japanese groups, while the prairies attracted many European nationalities in the 1800s.

Canada's Human Development Index (0.950) ranks it first out of 174 countries. Canada's strongly egalitarian society affords its people excellent access to health care, education, and economic prosperity needed to make choices in their lives. Adjusted for women, the index (0.891) ranks Canada ninth out of 130 countries.

Language

Both English and French are official languages in Canada. French is spoken by about 5 percent of the people in Ontario and Manitoba, but English dominates in these and all western provinces. In fact, in western provinces, less than 3 percent of the people are fluent in French, and many speak a language other than English or French as their mother tongue. Among native groups, more than 50 languages are spoken.

Canadian spelling of English words follows U.S. standards in some cases (e.g., *organize* rather than *organise*) but British standards in others (*centre,* not *center*), and Canadians call the last letter of the alphabet *zed,* not *zee*. In addition, Canadians have some unique phrases and idioms. For instance, *Eh!* is used much like "Ya know" or "Isn't it?" is used in the United States.

Religion

Most Canadians are Christians, but the beliefs and doctrines of the different Christian churches are diverse, and society is highly secularized. The United Church is the most prevalent in western provinces, followed by the Catholic, Anglican, Lutheran, and Presbyterian faiths. In Ontario, 29 percent of the people belong to the United Church, 25 percent are Roman Catholic, and 21 percent are Anglican. A number of other Christian churches are present, as well as various non-Christian denominations.

General Attitudes

The people of Ontario are fairly reserved and formal, while those in the prairie provinces and British Columbia are more open and friendly. As Ontario contains large urban areas, life is faster paced—similar to New York City—whereas the pace of life in the west is more relaxed. The people take great pride in their individual provinces and heritage, as well as in being Canadian. Despite close ties and many similarities between their nation and the United States, Canadians emphasize they are not U.S.-type people just living in Canada. As *North Americans,* they share the title "Americans" with people in the United States. Canadians often see U.S. Americans as more aggressive and materialistic than themselves. They also feel they are more tolerant and community oriented than U.S. Americans, as well as more polite. For example, Canadians respond to *Thank you* with *You're Welcome,* rather than with silence or some other phrase. Preserving Canadian culture against influence from the United States is important.

Canadians are known to be self-deprecating and have a sardonic sense of humor. They admire people who are well educated, skilled, modest, and polite. In relation to the rest of the world, Canadians see themselves as associated with "fairness" and humanitarianism. They consider themselves to be honest brokers in negotiations. Indeed, Canada frequently contributes troops to United Nations peacekeeping missions and relief operations. Canadians proudly point to the efforts of a former prime minister, Lester B. Pearson, who won the Nobel Peace Prize for advocating in the 1950s the use of peacekeeping forces in international conflicts.

Personal Appearance

Although dress habits are similar to those in the United States, the people are generally more conservative and somewhat more formal in their dress. Tattered or very casual clothing may only be acceptable in some parts of Ontario. Men who wear hats remove them in buildings.

CUSTOMS AND COURTESIES

Greetings

A firm handshake and sincere *Hello, how are you?* are the most common greetings when one meets new people. Otherwise, a wave of the hand or nod of the head are acceptable gestures when saying *Hello*. The majority of people in

Ontario, the prairie provinces, British Columbia, Yukon, and Northwest Territories speak English. Still, in cities near Québec with large French communities, French greetings are common. In Vancouver, British Columbia, the ethnic Chinese minority commonly uses Chinese greetings.

Gestures

Most gestures, positive and negative, are the same in Canada as in the United States, but they do vary between ethnic groups. People often use hand gestures in conversation, but not to the extreme. Eye contact is important during conversation and smiles are always welcome. However, Canadian reserve dictates that a generous amount of personal space be protected when conversing with others. Also, casual conversations with clerks, waitresses, and so forth are kept to a minimum.

Visiting

Although Canadians enjoy getting together often, unannounced visits are not common; it is considered polite to visit only when invited. In most areas, guests customarily remove their shoes when entering a home to avoid tracking in dirt. Guests follow the cue of the host or hostess. That is, if the host is fairly relaxed, guests will be the same. Refreshments are usually offered, but refusing them is not necessarily impolite. Guests arriving in the morning might be offered coffee or tea and fruit or light pastries. The same is true for afternoon visits, except for a heavier selection of sweets. Evening visitors typically receive a drink (often wine) and light foods. Guests invited for a casual dinner commonly offer to help with preparations and/or bring part of the meal. It is polite to compliment the hostess on the meal. Reaching for things on the table is impolite. Houseguests staying for more than one day usually write a letter of thanks and either send or leave a thank-you gift. Promptness in showing gratitude is important.

Eating

Canadian eating habits tend to be a bit more formal than U.S. habits. People normally eat with the fork in the left hand and the knife remaining in the right. Canadians eat breakfast soon after they wake up each morning, lunch some time between noon and 2:00 P.M., and dinner around 6:00 P.M. Mealtimes are later on weekends and holidays. Families eat their main meal together on most nights of the week, although busy schedules can sometimes prevent this. The main meal usually consists of an entrée and a salad. Dessert is sometimes included. Children are taught not to place elbows on the table, to sit still while eating, and to say *please* and *thank you*. Food is usually placed on the table in serving dishes so family members can choose their own portions. Guests are often seated at the right of the host and are served first. They may decline second helpings without offending the cook. When one finishes a meal, one places the utensils together on the plate.

When dining out, Canadians tend to dress well (except at fast-food restaurants). Tipping about 15 percent is expected.

LIFESTYLE

Family

While the family unit is the center of society, it is common for both parents to work outside the home. Licensed day-care and home-care facilities are widely available to assist working parents. Traditional norms have changed somewhat during the last decade; however, the father in a family usually takes the lead, while the mother exercises influence on all decisions. The mother also retains primary responsibility for household chores. The average family size is comparable to that in the United States. Families are close, although economic conditions (the need for employment) are taking relatives away from each other. This decreases daily contact between extended family members but encourages efforts such as family reunions to renew and preserve family ties. The number of single-parent homes is on the rise, creating a strain on social services. Outside large cities, most people (62 percent) own their home. Houses are of wood-frame construction as in the United States.

Dating and Marriage

Dating usually begins between the ages of 14 and 16. Favorite activities include dancing and going to the movies. While most couples have a formal wedding, more than 10 percent (and growing) prefer to live together in common-law arrangements. Another trend is that fewer young people expect to marry at all, and if they do, they expect to marry at a later age (e.g., at 30 or so). Weddings are celebrated with family and friends, but elaborate events are somewhat less common than in the United States. A typical honeymoon for Canadian newlyweds involves taking a few days off to be together; about half will travel somewhere.

Diet

Because Canada has a multicultural heritage, a variety of foods and dietary habits are represented, especially in Toronto and Ottawa, Ontario's two largest cities. Throughout the prairies, one can find wild rice, smoked fish, beef, ethnic dishes, Pacific salmon, and a variety of foods similar to those in the United States. A particular region's diet is a reflection of location and the largest ethnic group of the area. For example, grains are more common inland because they are grown there, seafood is most popular on the coast, and various immigrant groups eat foods common to the countries from which they came.

Recreation

Ice hockey is the most popular sport, but Canadians are certainly not limited in their interests or opportunities. They engage in such activities as boating, fishing, swimming, baseball, football, basketball, skiing, hunting, horseback riding, lacrosse, soccer, rugby, and curling. In curling, two four-person teams slide a large "stone" (with a gooseneck handle) over ice toward a target. Movies, local festivals and fairs, parks, and museums also offer recreational opportunities. From the Calgary Stampede in Alberta to the Vancouver Sea Festival to the Toronto Film Festival, there are many celebrations in which to participate.

Holidays

Official holidays include New Year's Day, Family Day (third Monday in February), Easter, Victoria Day (third Monday in May), Canada Day (1 July), Labour Day (first Monday in September), Thanksgiving Day (second Monday in October), Remembrance Day (11 November), Christmas, and Boxing Day (26 December). Boxing Day is a day to visit friends and relatives. It comes from an old British tradition of giving small boxed gifts to service employees or the poor.

In addition to official holidays, local festivals are held throughout the region to commemorate various events. Each province also has its own official holidays.

Commerce

A normal business day is from 8:00 A.M. to 5:00 P.M., Monday through Friday. Canadians usually begin full-time work between the ages of 16 and 25. Business habits are similar to those in the United States. Stores are open at least until 6:00 P.M., and many remain open until 9:00 P.M. on at least some weeknights. Some businesses also operate on Saturday and Sunday.

SOCIETY

Government

Officially, Canada is a confederation with parliamentary democracy. That means Canada's system is patterned partly after Great Britain's but also has a federal system like that of the United States. The federal government holds considerable power in areas of national concern, such as health insurance, trade, the military, and development. Still, provincial governments have administrative and legislative authority over issues of education, property laws, and medical facilities. The provinces each have one-chamber legislatures, and the leader of the dominant political party is the province's premier.

The federal Parliament includes a body of up to 104 appointed Senators and an elected body of 295 members of the House of Commons. The prime minister is the leader of the dominant political party in the House. Queen Elizabeth II is represented by a governor general, currently Romeo LeBlanc. Parliamentary elections may be called at any time but must be held at least every five years. The voting age is 18. Currently, the three strongest parties in Canada are the Liberal Party, Bloc Québecois, and the Reform Party.

Economy

Canada has one of the strongest economies in the world. Real gross domestic product per capita is $20,520, indicating that economic prosperity is available to the majority of the population. Canada ranks second in the world in gold and uranium production, third in silver, and fourth in copper. It is a world leader in the supply of wood pulp and other timber-related products, the most important of which is newsprint. Many U.S. newspapers are printed on Canadian paper.

Canada has a free-trade agreement with the United States. In 1993, it also signed the North American Free Trade Agreement (NAFTA) with Mexico and the United States. That agreement provides for freer movement of capital and goods, more cross-national investment, and a large market for many goods from each country.

As the industrial heart of the nation, Ontario leads Canada's economy. As the financial and political center of Canada, it plays a role much like both New York and California in the United States. Copper, nickel, and other minerals are mined in Ontario's Sudbury Basin. The western provinces produce vital raw materials, agricultural goods, and other products for export and manufacturing. The prairies are the breadbasket of the nation and also have important potash, oil, and natural gas reserves. Major products of British Columbia include timber, coal, oil, and minerals. British Columbia also serves as Canada's gateway to Pacific Rim markets. The north is rich in minerals and other natural resources. Economies in many provinces have expanded in recent years to include manufacturing, chemicals, and food processing. The currency is the Canadian dollar (Can$). Canadians refer to it as the *loonie*, after the image of the waterbird (the loon) minted on the gold-colored coin.

Transportation and Communication

There are more cars per capita in the west than elsewhere in Canada because public transportation systems cannot serve the wide expanses of the prairies and north. Domestic air transportation provides an important link to isolated regions in the north. The national railway ships freight from the west to the east and vice versa. Communications systems are highly developed, including satellite systems, fiber optics, cable television, and excellent broadcast networks. Television is often dominated by U.S. American–made programs, but the federal government actively supports the development of Canadian films and television shows.

Education

Each province is responsible for its own educational system. In all provinces, education is compulsory and free for at least eight years, beginning at age six or seven. Each province also administers its own colleges and universities. While colleges are subsidized by the federal and provincial governments, students must pay tuition. Many students choose to complete a two-year technical training program and enter the workforce; about 40 percent enter a university. While only about 10 percent have college degrees, an additional 20 percent have completed at least partial post-secondary training. The literacy rate is 99 percent.

Health

Canadians enjoy very good health in general. Their infant mortality rate is 7 per 1,000. Life expectancy ranges between 75 and 82 years. Hospitals and quality of care are excellent. Facilities and personnel are less available in rural and isolated regions. Canada has a universal, compulsory national health insurance that covers doctors' fees and most hospital costs for all Canadians. It is funded by taxes and premiums collected by the federal and provincial governments.

FOR THE TRAVELER

Visas are not required of U.S. citizens staying up to 180 days; only proof of citizenship and a photo ID are necessary. U.S. travelers entering Canada from a country other than the United States must have a valid passport. Drivers should be aware that the use of seat belts is required, radar detectors are illegal (they will be confiscated in Manitoba), and speed limits are calculated in metrics. In fact, all weights and measures are based on the metric system. For more specific information on the areas you plan to visit, contact the Canadian Consulate General, 1251 Avenue of the Americas, New York, NY 10020; phone (212) 596–1600. Canada's embassy is located at 501 Pennsylvania Avenue NW, Washington, DC 20001.

Québec Province of Canada

THE AMERICAS

Boundary representations not necessarily authoritative.

BACKGROUND

Land and Climate

Covering 3,851,788 square miles (9,976,140 square kilometers), Canada is the second largest country in the world after Russia. Much of the north is uninhabited due to the arctic climate and permanently frozen ground. Québec is the largest province and is one-sixth the size of the United States. The Canadian Shield—a vast, U-shaped, rocky expanse surrounding the Hudson Bay—covers most of the province and includes 470,000 square miles (1,217,300 square kilometers) of rocky, coniferous forest. The bulk of the population lives in the St. Lawrence Valley to the south. Winters are very cold and snowy; summers are humid and warm.

History

In 1534, Jacques Cartier landed in Gaspé and announced French sovereignty over the territory. The following year, he traveled up the St. Lawrence River to the present site of Québec and Montréal, but real colonization did not begin until the 1600s. Québec City was founded in 1608. More towns were eventually established and the number of French settlers gradually increased. By 1663, the area was under the firm control of Paris and was called New France. But the British also had settlements, and the two European powers fought for control of the land. In 1713, a war ended with France ceding most of its Atlantic coast holdings.

War also ensued from 1744 to 1748. But major fighting and conquest did not take place until the 1750s. In 1756,

France and England declared what became the Seven Years' War (French and Indian War). In 1759, the British conquered Québec City and, in the following year, Montréal. Peace was declared in 1763 with the signing of the Treaty of Paris, through which Britain gained control of all of New France. The area was then renamed Québec. At the time of the British takeover, the 70,000 French-speaking people in Québec outnumbered English speakers. The French culture remained firmly established during British rule and has continued to dominate the region. In 1791, Québec was divided into Upper and Lower Canada, but the two were joined again in 1840 as the province of Canada.

In 1867, Canada was divided into Québec and Ontario, as the British North America Act created the Dominion of Canada. The new federal union included Québec, Ontario, Nova Scotia, and New Brunswick. Much of western Canada (then known as Rupert's Land) was added a few years later, and British Columbia joined the Dominion in 1871. Canada eventually gained self-governing status within the Commonwealth. Throughout its history as part of Canada, Québec's inhabitants have debated the issue of their status within the federation. Various independence and "special status" drives were launched in the 20th century. The movement gained momentum after the 1960s and seemed to peak by the 1980s under the political leadership of the *Parti Québécois* (PQ).

Although a public vote on the question of independence was defeated in 1980, Québec opposed a new Canadian constitution in 1982. It then became necessary to seek compromise, which was embodied in the 1987 Meech Lake Agreement. The agreement would have recognized Québec as a distinct society within Canada and accorded its people certain rights that other provinces would not have. A crisis developed in 1990 when several provinces balked at signing the agreement and Québec threatened to secede. An emergency meeting between Prime Minister Brian Mulroney and opposing provincial premiers failed to pass the agreement and it was defeated.

Demands again in 1991 for secession led the federal government to seek an acceptable compromise between Québec and other provinces. By early 1992, many Canadians had determined secession would harm the economy. So an increasing number came to favor recognizing Québec's distinct status. However, a referendum on the issue failed to pass in October 1992. Still, Québec decided not to leave the union, opting to take advantage of other proposed constitutional changes and remain part of Canada's strong economy. Faced with increasing opposition, Mulroney resigned in 1993. Subsequent elections brought Jean Chrétien to power as Canada's new prime minister. He heads the Liberal Party.

Due to separatist demands, a referendum vote on Québec's independence came before the province in October 1995. In a surprisingly narrow vote, separation was rejected by a margin of 52,000 votes. In January 1996, separatist leader Lucien Bouchard, who was instrumental in leading the independence campaign to near victory, replaced retiring PQ leader Jacques Partizeau as premier of Québec. Bouchard remains committed to leading the drive to sovereignty but will focus first on overcoming high levels of unemployment and public debt.

THE PEOPLE
Population
Québec's 7.2 million people account for 25 percent of Canada's total population (28.4 million). The Human Development Index (0.950) ranks Canada first out of 174 countries. Canada's strong egalitarian society affords its people excellent access to health care, education, and economic prosperity. Adjusted for women, the index (0.891) ranks Canada ninth out of 130 countries.

Quebec's population density is slightly higher than the national average. However, its urbanization rate (79 percent) is comparable to that of British Columbia and Ontario. About 83 percent of the people are of French origin, while 10 percent have a British heritage. This latter group is generally called "Anglophones" (as opposed to the French-origin "Francophones"). Anglophones tend to emigrate from Québec more than Francophones, as young English speakers seek jobs in other parts of Canada.

Native peoples in Québec include the Montagnais, Mohawks, Atikamekw, Crees, Malacites, and Inuits. The Inuits are an Eskimo people who live in the north. Various other ethnic groups (principally from Europe or French-speaking Caribbean islands) are represented in the larger cities.

Language
Both French and English are official languages in Canada. However, French is the first language of most people in Québec and is used almost exclusively in some of Québec's regions. According to provincial law, all public signs must be

in French. Bilingual (French and English) signs are allowed inside buildings, but all street signs and external signs must be in French. Various groups have challenged this law and revisions are eventually expected that will allow bilingual signs on storefronts, and perhaps in other cases.

Fewer than one million people in Québec claim English as their first or primary language. Of these, about 60 percent also speak French. Many people, especially in large urban areas, mix French and English during conversation.

The Inuit speak Inuktitut, a complex and ancient language. Recent immigrants speak their native tongues at home but must learn French or English for public interaction.

Religion
Religious beliefs in Canada follow traditional lines. The French are generally Roman Catholic; those of British descent are mostly Protestant. Of course, other Christian and non-Christian groups are active in Québec, but the majority of people are Catholic. In fact, before Québec was controlled by Great Britain, it was largely ruled by the Catholic Church and French civil law. Although church and state are officially separate in Canada, religion is publicly recognized and private religious schools are often subsidized by the state. Religious organizations have played a greater role in Canadian politics than is typical in the United States.

General Attitudes
Both Francophone and Anglophone *Québécois* (Québec Canadians) are friendly and hospitable. Etiquette and politeness are important. People value a good education and comfortable lifestyle. French and English speakers have generally integrated well, but Anglophones sometimes express frustration over being a minority within a minority. In general, however, both Francophones and Anglophones view their bilingual society as a benefit rather than a drawback.

The French *Québécois* are particularly proud of their language and French heritage, insisting they are different from the rest of Canada and should protect their unique cultural institutions. A strong sense of nationalism motivates them to preserve French culture but does not necessarily require them to be independent. The majority still sees Québec as a vital part of Canada, despite voter support for separatist leaders. Occasional threats of secession have caused tensions not only within Québec but also throughout other provinces.

Personal Appearance
European and North American fashions are popular, with clothing trends very similar to those in the United States. Jeans, T-shirts, and tennis shoes are popular casual items. For formal events, Canadians tend to dress up a bit more than U.S. Americans.

CUSTOMS AND COURTESIES
Greetings
Due to past cultural and linguistic ties to France, Switzerland, and Normandy, Québec has experienced the most European influence of any Canadian region. Therefore, traditional European greetings are used in Québec, which include a firm handshake in most cases. *Bonjour* (Good day) is the common French greeting, although friends and young people often prefer *Salut* (Hey). Women who are close friends may embrace, and both men and women often exchange kisses on

both cheeks as a greeting. Of course, not all of Québec is French, and greetings in predominantly English areas are similar to those in other parts of Canada. Throughout Québec, first names and informal language forms are used by friends, relatives, or people of equal age/status. Conversation is direct and polite. The French term for "Good-bye" is *Au revoir*.

Gestures

Many gestures are the same in Québec as throughout the rest of Canada, but there are some differences. For instance, even if one excuses oneself, it is offensive to burp in public. The U.S. "thumbs-down" sign (meaning "no" or that something is bad) is an offensive gesture in Québec. Also, *Québécois* tend to use their hands during conversation more than other Canadians to express themselves or emphasize a point.

Visiting

Québécois enjoy visiting with one another in a relaxed, informal atmosphere. A quick call in advance is all that is needed before dropping by a friend's or relative's home. In other cases, visits are arranged in advance—usually upon the hosts' invitation. Visitors nearly always remove their shoes at the door, as well as any hats or coats. They are offered food or drink, even during short visits.

Etiquette is important in Québec and is adhered to on formal occasions. Guests invited to a home often bring the hosts a small gift of flowers, candy, or wine. Houseguests who stay overnight leave a thank-you letter and either leave or promptly send a thank-you gift to their host family.

Eating

In French-speaking areas, one keeps both hands above the table during a meal. Women rest their wrists on the table, men their forearms. Elbows may only be placed on the table after the meal is finished. Supper time is generally at 6:00 P.M. This time is so important to families that a telephone call between 6:00 and 7:30 P.M. is considered impolite. Québec City and Montréal are well-known for their fine French cuisine. Tipping rates are the same as in the United States—about 10 to 15 percent. Eating on the streets is improper unless one is sitting down at an outdoor café or standing outside a food stand. During a meal, it is polite to wipe one's mouth before drinking from a glass.

LIFESTYLE

Family

While the family is the center of society, the extended unit is loosely knit. In the nuclear unit, both parents often work outside the home. Although traditional norms have changed somewhat over the last decade, the father is usually head of the family, but the mother exercises influence on all decisions. The average family has one or two children. To encourage growth, the government gives parents approximately US$500 at the birth of a child and adds a small monthly stipend. This amount increases over time and with the addition of each child. In urban areas, nearly half of the people live in rented apartments; outside large cities, home ownership is 62 percent.

Dating and Marriage

Dating and marriage customs are similar to those in the United States. Dating usually begins before age 16. Favorite activities include dancing and going to the movies. Many couples enjoy sporting activities together. Going out to eat is one of the most common dates in Québec. In the summer, picnics and outdoor dance festivals are popular. In Québec, it is now common for couples to live together for years before officially getting married. After two years, even without an official ceremony, the government recognizes the union as a common-law marriage.

Diet

Québec regional cuisine displays a definite French influence and includes such foods as pea soup, French pastries and breads, crêpes, special cheeses, lamb, and veal. *Tourtière*, a regional pie dish of the Saguenay–Lac-St. Jean area, is served in various forms throughout Canada. Potatoes and red meats are common with evening suppers. A favorite fast-food is *poutine*, fries covered with spicy gravy and cheese curds. Maple syrup is produced in Québec and is a favorite in desserts. Food connoisseurs consider Québec's cuisine to be among the best in North America.

Recreation

Both spectator and participant sports are popular. The biggest sport is hockey. Young people learn to play at a fairly early age on the province's numerous ice rinks. National Hockey League teams enjoy a wide following. Other favored sports include swimming, biking, baseball, curling, rugby, skiing, tennis, golf, and lacrosse (Canada's official national sport). Québec offers a variety of outdoor recreational opportunities, such as fishing, hunting, and hiking. In Montréal and other cities, people also enjoy the fine arts. Montréal's annual film and jazz festivals are popular attractions.

Holidays

Two holidays unique to Québec include the *Carnaval de Québec,* a two-week period in February filled with activities (although normal working hours prevail), and St. Jean-Baptiste Day (24 June), which is celebrated as Québec's national holiday (quite distinct from Canada Day). Other holidays celebrated throughout Canada include New Year's Day, Easter, Victoria Day (for the English) or *Dollard Des Ormeaux* (for the French) held the third Monday in May, Canada Day (1 July), Labour Day (first Monday in September), Thanksgiving Day (second Monday in October), All Saints' Day (1 November), Remembrance Day (11 November), Christmas, and Boxing Day (26 December). Boxing Day comes from the British tradition of presenting small boxed gifts to service workers, tradesmen, and in the past, servants. It is now primarily a day for visiting family and friends or shopping. Almost every town has a winter carnival with parades and sports. Since Québec is "maple syrup country," people often have parties centered on syrup making during two or three weeks of spring. These are called sugaring-off parties. Dancing at these celebrations is similar to square dancing.

Commerce

A normal business day is from 8:00 A.M. to 5:00 P.M., Monday through Friday. Stores are open until at least 6:00 P.M., and many remain open until 9:00 P.M. on a few nights. Some businesses also operate on Saturday and Sunday.

SOCIETY

Government

Officially, Canada is a confederation with parliamentary democracy. That means Canada's system is patterned partly after Great Britain's but also includes a federal system like that of the United States. The federal government holds considerable power in areas of national concern, such as health insurance, trade, the military, and development. Provincial governments have authority over education, property laws, and medical facilities. Québec's one-chamber legislature has 125 seats. The leader of its dominant party serves as premier. In Québec, the governing party is *Parti Québécois* (*Bloc Québécois*). The Liberal Party is the main opposition.

Canada's federal Parliament includes a body of up to 104 appointed senators and an elected body of 295 members of the House of Commons. The prime minister is the leader of the dominant political party in the House. Britain's Queen Elizabeth II is represented by a governor general, currently Romeo LeBlanc. Parliamentary elections may be called at any time but must be held at least every five years. The voting age is 18. Currently, Canada's three strongest parties are the Liberal Party, Bloc Québécois, and the Reform Party.

Economy

Canada has one of the strongest economies in the world. Real gross domestic product per capita is $20,520, indicating that economic prosperity is available to the majority of the population. On the provincial level, Québec has the highest rate of unemployment (11 percent in 1995) and the largest budget deficit in Canada. Economic growth has been slightly lower than in other provinces.

Mining is a major primary industry in Québec. Overall, Canada ranks second in the world in gold and uranium production, third in silver, and fourth in copper. Forestry is also important in the province. Canada is a world leader in producing wood pulp and other timber-related products; many U.S. newspapers are printed on Canadian paper. Manufacturing industries are also important. Tourism has become an increasing source of revenue in the past several years. One-third of all U.S. international travel is to Canada. The St. Lawrence Seaway makes Montréal Canada's most important port city. The James Bay project and other hydroelectric power plants provide nearly 90 percent of all electricity in the province.

Canada signed a free-trade agreement with United States in 1988. This agreement led to the North American Free Trade Agreement (NAFTA), signed in 1993 with Mexico and the United States. NAFTA provides for freer movement of capital and goods, more cross-national investment, and a large market for many goods in each country. The Canadian dollar (Can$) is usually somewhat weaker than the U.S. dollar and can be affected by variations in the U.S. dollar's value.

Transportation and Communication

Transportation systems are excellent, especially in Montréal and Québec City, where bus systems are well developed. Montréal has one of the best subways in the world. Personal cars are used for transport in other areas. The national railroad network carries passengers as well as freight, and the airways present an increasingly popular way to travel. Communications systems are highly developed, as most people have telephones and televisions. Radio networks and newspapers service the entire populace. All systems are highly

modern, and Canada has several satellites in orbit to aid communication.

Education

Québec, as with all provinces, is responsible for its own educational system. School is free and compulsory for children ages six to sixteen. Local Catholic and Protestant school boards are supported by the government to direct school curricula. The education system allows the children of English-speaking parents to be educated in English, usually at Protestant schools. These English students have the opportunity to become bilingual through French courses offered in their schools. Immigrants who were educated in English schools in Québec can also send their children to an English school. However, new immigrants have to enroll their children in French schools.

While students may get permission to leave school at sixteen, high school continues another two years, and the government actively encourages students to finish. After graduation, students may enter a two-year technical training program (similar to a trade school or community college in the United States), or they may attend a two-year college preparatory program (similar to filling general education requirements in the United States). Those who opt for technical training then enter the labor force, while the others attend a three-year university. Although the provincial government subsidizes university education, students pay tuition costs. College attendance has risen from 16 percent (of college-age students) in 1960 to nearly 40 percent today. About 10 percent of the total population holds university degrees. The adult literacy rate is 99 percent.

Health

Canadians enjoy very good health in general. Their infant mortality rate is 7 per 1,000, and life expectancy ranges from 75 to 82 years. Hospitals and an advanced level of care are available to all citizens. Canada has a universal, compulsory national health insurance that covers doctors' fees and most hospital costs. It is funded by fairly high taxes and premiums collected by the federal and provincial governments. While patients must sometimes wait months for elective surgery and certain expensive procedures, all citizens have access to basic health care at public clinics.

FOR THE TRAVELER

U.S. citizens do not need visas for stays of up to 180 days, but they must present proof of citizenship and photo identification. U.S. citizens entering from another country need a valid passport. Travelers to Québec should make an attempt to speak French. Radar detectors are illegal in Québec; devices will be confiscated and drivers fined. Handguns are also not permitted in Canada and may be confiscated. For detailed travel information, contact the Canadian Consulate General, 1251 Avenue of the Americas, New York, NY 10020–1175; phone (212) 596–1600. You may also contact Tourism Québec, PO Box 979, Montreal, Canada H3C 2W3; phone (800) 363–7777; or the Embassy of Canada, 501 Pennsylvania Avenue NW, Washington, DC 20001; phone (202) 682–1740.

Republic of
Chile

Arica
Iquique
Antofagasta
Copiapó
La Serena
Valparaíso ★SANTIAGO
Juan Fernández Islands
Talca Rancagua
Concepción
Temuco
Osorno
Puerto Montt
Coihaique
Strait of Magellan
Punta Arenas

Boundary representations not necessarily authoritative.

BACKGROUND

Land and Climate

While Chile is slightly larger than Texas, it stretches along 4,022 miles (6,435 kilometers) of South America's western coast. Its average width is less than 100 miles (160 kilometers), but total square miles are 289,112 (748,800 square kilometers). Chile's territory includes *Isla de Pascua* (Easter Island) and *Isla Sala y Gómez.*

Because of its north-to-south distance, Chile has many different climates and landscapes. The climate ranges from subtropical in the north to moderate in the central region and subarctic in the south. One can find deserts, swamps, forests, the Andes Mountains, beautiful lakes, rich agricultural regions, volcanoes, and a wide variety of plants and animals. Chile has been called the "Switzerland of South America" for its natural beauty. The country is subject to earthquakes. Being in the Southern Hemisphere, Chile's seasons are opposite those in North America; summer is between December and March.

History

Ferdinand Magellan became the first European to sight Chilean shores in 1520, after successfully navigating around the southern tip of the American continent. Diego de Almagro claimed Chile as part of the Spanish Empire for Pizarro in 1536, and Pedro de Valdivia commenced the Spanish conquest in 1541 against very strong Indian resistance. Chileans now revere many early Indian warriors, such as Caupolican, as national heroes.

Chile began to fight for independence from Spain in 1810. Although initial revolts were suppressed, Chilean patriots eventually joined with the armies of José de San Martín in Argentina. In 1817, San Martín's forces invaded Chile by crossing the Andes mountains. The Spanish were quickly defeated and one of the revolution's heroes, Bernardo O'Higgins, became the new country's leader. Unable to establish a stable government, O'Higgins left the country in 1823 and Chilean politics remained unstable for several years. After 1830, however, stability and periodic reform allowed Chile to make progress. From 1879 to 1884, Chile fought the War of the Pacific against Peru and Bolivia. Victorious, Chile annexed the provinces of Arica and Antofagasta in the north.

A civil war in the latter 1880s was followed by less stable governments and military interventions until elections in 1932. During most of the 20th century, Chile concentrated on promoting economic growth and addressing social problems. By 1970, many people had become convinced that socialism could solve some of those problems without hindering growth. That feeling allowed Salvador Allende to become the first freely elected Marxist president in South America. But

Allende's policies were too radical and the country faced economic disaster by the end of 1972. Because of the chaos, General Augusto Pinochet Ugarte led a military coup in 1973 that ended Allende's socialist government.

Backed by the military, Pinochet ruled by decree. He determined that authoritarianism was better than liberal democracy. In 1980, a new constitution gave him the right to rule until 1988. In 1988, Pinochet subjected himself to a plebiscite to determine if he should continue in power or allow free elections. Upon losing the plebiscite, he called for elections in December 1989. Pinochet's choice for president was defeated by the centrist-left candidate, Patricio Aylwin Azocar. Aylwin took office in 1990 as the first elected president since 1970. Pinochet continues to wield significant power as head of the armed forces, a post from which he cannot legally be removed. Despite his reputation for years of human-rights abuses and a dictatorial style, Pinochet is credited for building a successful and productive economy. Aylwin built upon that strong base with innovative programs, allowing Chile to be among the most prosperous of Latin American countries. Aylwin is especially credited with implementing successful antipoverty programs and maintaining a delicate balance between opposing political forces.

Aylwin did not run for reelection in 1993 but supported Eduardo Frei Ruiz-Tagle, who took office in March 1994. The son of a former president, Frei is very popular in Chile. He has emphasized even more social spending for Aylwin's antipoverty measures. Frei seeks closer economic ties with the United States and Canada and constitutional reforms to reduce the military's political power.

THE PEOPLE

Population

The population of Chile is about 14.2 million and is growing annually at 1.5 percent, one of the lowest rates among all South American countries. Only about 15 percent of the population lives in rural areas. More than four million people live in the Santiago region. About 95 percent of the people have either a European heritage or are *mestizo* (mixed European-Native American descent). Only 3 percent are pure Native American (Indian) and 2 percent have other ethnic origins.

Chile's Human Development Index (0.880) ranks it 33d out of 174 countries. Adjusted for women, the index (0.759) ranks Chile 43d out of 130 countries. Chileans enjoy fairly good access to health care, education, and the economic resources necessary for a decent standard of living; however, women's wages are substantially lower.

Language

Spanish, called *Castellano*, is the official language. However, as in all South American countries, some terms common to Chile will not have the same meaning elsewhere. English is taught in the schools and understood by many in the larger cities. Small minorities also speak German (southern Chile), Italian, and Mapuche, an Indian language.

Religion

Most Chileans profess a Christian faith. It is estimated that more than 80 percent of the population belongs to the Roman Catholic Church. Most other people belong to various Protestant groups or other Christian churches. There is a small Jewish minority, and many Indians follow traditional beliefs. Church and state are separated, and religious freedom is guaranteed.

General Attitudes

The Chilean people are friendly, both among themselves and with strangers. The people are known for their sharp and witty sense of humor. This and their cultural and educational refinements have earned them the distinction of being called the "British of South America." They take pride in their literacy, their nation, and their heritage. Confidence and optimism are commonly expressed by people when asked how they view Chile and its future. There is a strong middle class in Chile, and education enables many poorer people to excel and build a better life. Chileans respect the elderly. They are a law-abiding, pragmatic people who believe in progress.

Personal Appearance

Fashions follow European styles and are quite sophisticated in urban areas. Individuals take considerable pride in their appearance. Even in rural areas, where people are not as wealthy, it is important to be neatly and cleanly dressed. People take as much care as possible with their clothing and accessories. Many Chileans consider sloppy or tattered clothing to be in poor taste.

CUSTOMS AND COURTESIES

Greetings

Greetings in Chile are very important because they stress an individual is welcome and recognized. The *abrazo* is the most common greeting among friends and relatives. It consists of a handshake and hug, sometimes supplemented with a kiss to the right cheek for women or family members. A handshake is appropriate when meeting someone for the first time. Eye contact is considered essential when greeting someone. Traditional verbal greetings include *¿Qui'ubo?* (What's up?), *¿Cómo está?* (How are you?), and *¡Gusto de verte!* (Nice to see you). Men stand to greet a woman entering the room. Chileans show significant outward affection to friends and relatives. The *abrazo* is repeated with each individual when one leaves a small social gathering of friends or family.

Chileans customarily use titles when addressing people. The title used depends on the situation. *Señor* (Mr.), *Señora* (Mrs.), and *Señorita* (Miss) are common for strangers and acquaintances, as are professional titles (*Doctor, Director, Profesor*). When speaking with elderly men and women and other respected individuals, one uses *Don* and *Doña* with their first name to show special respect and familiarity.

Gestures

Eye contact and correct posture are important during conversation, while excessive hand gestures are avoided. Yawns are suppressed or politely concealed with the hand. One does not beckon other people with hand gestures, except for a waiter in a restaurant. Items, including money, are handed, not tossed, to other people. Respect and courtesy are important to Chileans.

Visiting

Unlike in some other areas of South America, guests wait outside the door of a home until invited inside. Dinner guests often bring flowers, wine, or bread for the host family. Guests invited to lunch might offer to bring a dessert, such as cookies or ice cream. It is appropriate to greet the head of the family first. Chileans appreciate guests who show genuine interest in their family, especially their children. Light, casual conversation usually precedes any business discussion; political topics are avoided unless initiated by the host. Guests are usually offered something to eat.

Eating

Chileans converse freely at the table. The hostess is often complimented on the meal. Chileans use the continental style of eating, with the fork in the left hand and the knife remaining in the right. Both hands are kept above the table at all times. Asking for second helpings is impolite. Even if second helpings are offered, the guest is expected to decline. Only if the host insists should the guest take more food. It is impolite to leave directly after eating; guests should stay for conversation.

In a restaurant, a waiter can be summoned with a raised finger. It is usually considered bad manners to eat food, except for ice cream, while walking in public. As fast-food increases in popularity, however, this habit is changing.

LIFESTYLE

Family

The family unit in Chile encompasses the extended family. While men have tended to dominate private and public life in the past, recent years have seen a change in the attitudes about women in the home and professional world. Nearly 30 percent of the labor force is female. Many women hold key political and business positions in Chile. And while the father takes the lead in the family, the mother has considerable influence on decisions. The relationship between the husband and wife is characterized by reciprocity, with the man performing courtesies for the woman and vice versa.

It is customary for a child to bear two family names; the last name is the mother's family name and the second-to-last name is the father's family name. People use either their full name or go by their father's family name, which is the official surname. Therefore, a person named José Felipe Correa Peres could use his full name or be addressed as Señor Correa.

Dating and Marriage

Young people begin dating by the time they are 16. Group dating is emphasized early on. Men begin to marry at about age 22 and women marry between 18 and 23. Couples often date from one to three years before getting engaged. Getting an education before marriage is often important. Traditional

Christian wedding ceremonies are common. Divorce is not recognized by the Catholic church, but legal means of canceling or nullifying a marriage are available.

Diet

Many national dishes are prepared with fish, seafood, chicken, beef, beans, eggs, and corn. The main meal is eaten at midday, between 12:30 and 2:30 P.M. A lighter meal is eaten between 8:00 and 10:00 P.M. During the afternoon, teatime is customary. At teatime, a beverage, small sandwiches, and cookies or cakes are served.

There are large supermarkets in major cities. Traveling markets *(ferias)* provide fresh fruits, vegetables, meat, fish, and flowers to smaller cities and towns. What is eaten depends on the region, but some favorites include *empanadas de horno* (meat turnovers with beef, hard-boiled eggs, onions, olives, and raisins), *pastel de choclo* (a baked meal of beef, chicken, onions, corn, eggs, and spices), *cazuela de ave* (chicken soup), and seafood casseroles and stews. On rainy days, children enjoy eating *sopaipillas,* which are made from a deep-fried pumpkin dough sprinkled with sugar. *Manjar,* made by boiling an unopened can of sweetened condensed milk for hours, is a favorite bread spread or baking ingredient.

Recreation

Popular activities include sports, theater, music, and movies. *Fútbol (*soccer*)* is the most popular sport. Chileans also enjoy swimming and going to parks. During the summer, vacations to the coast or the countryside are common. In a nation with a very long coastline, Chileans enjoy fishing as well. Weekend or holiday barbecues are frequent social gatherings. In areas where cattle have been important, rodeo is very popular. Rodeo in Chile is very different from U.S. rodeo. Cowboys *(huasos)* wear handwoven capes and straw hats. The main event consists of a pair of *huasos* skillfully guiding their horses to trap a steer against a padded arena wall. Points are earned for the portion of the steer that is pinned.

Holidays

Chile's important holidays include New Year's Day, Easter, Labor Day (1 May), Naval Battle of Iquique (21 May), Independence Day (18 September), Armed Forces Day (19 September), Columbus Day (12 October), All Saints' Day (1 November), and Christmas. The independence holiday is celebrated at parks where people eat *empanadas,* drink *chicha* (a sweet drink made with fermented grapes), and dance the *cueca* (the national dance) to guitar music. Christmas is celebrated much the same way as it is in North America, but it takes place in summer rather than winter, making some activities different from those in the Northern Hemisphere.

Commerce

In Santiago, Chile's capital, and other large cities, people usually work from 9:00 A.M. to 6:00 P.M., five or six days a week. Depending on the location, however, siesta hours (midday meal break) are still observed, and shops and offices may close for a couple of hours. Chile has an active and modern business climate; its exports and investments link it to world markets.

SOCIETY

Government

The Republic of Chile is a multiparty democracy. President Frei is chief of state and head of government. His term expires in the year 2000. The National Congress has two houses: the Senate (46 members) and the Chamber of Deputies (120 members). Several political parties are officially represented in the government. However, a governing coalition of four main parties currently dominates the legislature. The parties, collectively called the Concertation of Parties for Democracy, include the Christian Democratic Party, Socialist Party, Party for Democracy, and Radical Party. The main opposition is provided by a coalition (Union for the Progress of Chile) of three parties: National Renewal, Independent Democratic Union, and Center Center Union. The legislature sits at Valparaíso in a recently constructed Congress building. The voting age is 18. All eligible citizens are required by law to vote.

Economy

Chile's economy is prosperous and growing. Growth has averaged 6.5 percent annually since 1991. Chilean foreign debt has decreased steadily, and the country enjoys considerable foreign investment. Unemployment and inflation are both at manageable levels. Real gross domestic product per capita is $8,410, which has more than doubled in the last generation. These figures indicate Chileans generally have greater access to economic prosperity than they did 30 years ago and the average person can earn an income sufficient to meet basic needs.

President Aylwin instituted a program aimed at helping the poor by extending special small business loans and other credits to them, investing more in the poorest schools, building permanent homes for low-income families, and sponsoring work-study programs for the youth. The income of the poorest Chileans has subsequently risen by 20 percent and more than one million people have been lifted above the poverty line. While much more progress is still needed, the program's success has encouraged greater productivity and prosperity in Chile.

Chile is one of the world's largest producers of copper, which accounts for about 50 percent of all exports. Fresh fruit has become one of Chile's main exports, with more than 40 countries importing Chile's grapes, apples, nectarines, peaches, and other fruits. Agriculture, fish products, wood products, metals, light manufacturing, and the mining of minerals are all important to the diverse economy. The currency is the Chilean *peso* (Ch$).

Transportation and Communication

Public transportation in Chile is fairly efficient, although many roads remain unpaved. Santiago has a subway, and elsewhere the bus systems provide inexpensive travel in and between cities. Several airports also serve domestic and international travelers. A satellite communications system, cable television, and other technological advances have helped Chile increase telephone access, establish global communication links, and improve radio and television service to the country.

Education

Chile has one of the best-educated populations in Latin America, with an adult literacy rate of nearly 95 percent. Schooling is free and compulsory between ages five and seventeen. In addition to public schools, there are many private, commercial, and industrial educational institutions. The people value education, viewing it as the way to a better life. There are eight universities in Santiago alone; others are located throughout the country. The Nobel Prize for literature was awarded in 1945 to a Chilean, Gabriela Mistral, for her verse and prose, and in 1971 to another Chilean, Pablo Neruda, for poetry.

Health

Currently, health care is nationalized. However, the system is being decentralized somewhat and private insurance institutions are taking over some portions of care payment (more than 10 percent). Citizens have a choice as to whether they use the private or public health-care system. Chileans have enjoyed increasingly good health over the past few years, with infant mortality rates dropping from more than 60 per 1,000 in the 1970s to 14 per 1,000 today. Life expectancy has also increased to between 72 and 78 years. Water is potable in most areas.

FOR THE TRAVELER

A U.S. citizen does not need a visa for a visit of fewer than 90 days. A valid passport is necessary. No vaccinations are required. Chile has a wide variety of attractions in every part of the country because of its natural beauty. A visitor can enjoy beaches, skiing, hiking, and other opportunities. The tourist industry is well developed. Santiago is subject to severe smog, particularly in the winter; those with respiratory problems should take precautions. For more information, contact the Chile National Tourism Board, 9700 South Dixie Highway, 11th Floor, Miami, FL 33156; phone (800) 825–2332. You may also wish to contact the Embassy of Chile, 1732 Massachusetts Avenue NW, Washington, DC 20036; phone (202) 785–1746.

CULTURGRAM ™ '97

Republic of
Colombia

Boundary representations not necessarily authoritative.

BACKGROUND

Land and Climate

With 439,733 square miles (1,138,910 square kilometers), Colombia is the fourth largest country in Latin America and is about the size of California and Texas combined. It is located at the juncture between Central and South America. Colombia has snowcapped mountains as well as tropical jungles. Divided by three branches of the Andes Mountains, Colombia has low coastal plains on the Caribbean Sea and the Pacific Ocean; cool mountain plateaus, valleys, and active volcanoes in the center; and an eastern region with plains in the north and jungle in the south.

There are no distinct seasons in Colombia, but differing elevations experience a variety of temperatures. Medellín, at 5,000 feet (1,500 meters) above sea level, averages 70°F (21°C), while Bogotá, the capital, averages 55°F (13°C) at 8,000 feet (2,400 meters) above sea level. The coast is hot and humid. With such diversity in temperature, altitude, and rainfall, Colombia produces an incredible variety and abundance of vegetation and animal life. When Middle Eastern coffee seeds were brought to Colombia by Spanish missionaries, they found a perfect climate in Colombia. Coffee has flourished ever since, becoming the country's most important export crop.

Earthquakes are fairly common in Colombia, but most are so minor they are not even felt by people. However, serious tremors have taken their toll in recent years. Following strong quakes in 1983 and 1992, a 1995 quake left dozens dead and hundreds homeless.

History

The history of Colombia before the arrival of Europeans is uncertain, but many peoples thrived in the area and were present when the Spanish began to settle the region in the 1500s. The area was soon part of New Granada, which encompassed present-day Venezuela, Ecuador, and Panama in addition to Colombia. Resentment against Spanish rule grew in the late 1700s until 1810, when nationalists claimed independence. However, independence was not really achieved until after several years of struggle, when Simón Bolívar assembled an army to defeat Spanish troops at the Battle of Boyacá in 1819. He established a new Greater Colombia (*Gran Colombia*) republic, from which Venezuela and Ecuador withdrew in 1830.

Known first as the State of New Granada, Colombia's name was changed several times before it became the Republic of Colombia. Panama declared itself independent in 1903 to make way for U.S. construction of the Panama Canal. Civil war between conservatives and liberals from 1948 to 1957 led to a constitutional amendment requiring the presidency to alternate between the Liberal and Conservative political parties until 1974. Elections have been held regularly since that time.

The M–19 guerrilla movement and the Medellín and Cali drug cartels caused unrest and violence in the 1980s. M–19 renounced terrorism and joined the democratic process in the 1990 presidential elections. Drug traffickers, often called *narcoterrorists*, killed several presidential candidates and committed violent acts to dissuade Colombians from voting. Despite the violence, elections were held and César Gaviria Trujillo was elected president.

Gaviria took a solid stand against violence and drug trafficking. However, to encourage peace in the country, he offered terrorist groups the right to participate in the 1991 constitutional convention if they would disarm and renounce violence. While most groups accepted the offer and began participating in the political process, two rejected it. Gaviria also offered drug traffickers leniency and certain rights if they would quit dealing in narcotics and confess their crimes. Many traffickers began accepting the offer in late 1990, and drug-related violence diminished for a time.

In December 1990, a national assembly was formed to rewrite the 1886 constitution. For the first time, nearly all segments of the population—including former terrorists, Indians, and nontraditional political parties—were represented in the process. The convention was given the right to make whatever changes it chose. The new constitution took effect in July 1991, and it enjoys wide support throughout the country. It encourages political pluralism, the rule of law, and special rights for the long-ignored Indians. Colombia's black population also eventually (1994) received special rights, such as reserved seats in Congress and a recognition of basic civil rights. Elitism is discouraged through a provision that prohibits two people in the same family from being members of Congress at the same time.

Drug-related violence increased in 1992 and 1993 as opposing factions battled for control over segments of the drug industry. In addition, some guerrilla groups continued their campaign against the government by sabotaging oil fields and other economic sites. Violence subsided somewhat by the end of 1993, partly due to the death of noted drug baron Pablo Escobar. National presidential elections held in 1994 were peaceful and democratic. Ernesto Samper Pizano of the Liberal Party was elected president to serve a four-year term. Samper has continued economic reforms begun in 1991. However, in contrast to past leaders, he plans to attack widespread poverty (affecting nearly 40 percent of the population) through increased social spending.

In July 1995, Samper was accused of receiving money for his 1994 election campaign from the Cali drug cartel. Calls for his impeachment led to one of the country's worst political crises in years. After months of speculation, Samper was absolved of wrongdoing in June 1996.

THE PEOPLE

Population

Colombia's population of 36.2 million is growing at 1.7 percent annually. The majority of Colombians live in the western half of the country; much of the southeast is covered by jungle. A mixed Spanish-Indian ethnic group *(mestizo)* composes 58 percent of the population. Whites account for 20 percent. Others include black-caucasian mix (14 percent),

black (4), Indian-black mix (3), and Indian (1). Blacks are descendants of slaves imported during the Spanish colonial era. Many mixed with other peoples, especially when slavery was abolished in 1851. Blacks generally live along the Pacific and Caribbean coasts, comprising the majority of some large cities; Quibdó has a population of 300,000, comprised mostly of black or mixed black peoples. The largest cities are Bogotá (4.35 million), Medellín (2.1), and Cali (1.4). Approximately 70 percent of the population lives in urban areas, and more than 40 percent is younger than age 20.

Language

The official language is Spanish. Most indigenous ethnic groups have their own languages; among 80 groups, there are 40 different languages. Dialects spoken by some blacks reflect their African roots. English is spoken by some in large cities and is a required course in school.

Religion

While Colombians are guaranteed freedom of religion, the Roman Catholic Church is the state religion, to which nearly 95 percent of the people belong. Through the courts, the church has jurisdiction over marriages and divorce. While religion remains an important influence on culture, society is nevertheless becoming more secularized. Many members of indigenous or black ethnic groups retain beliefs from non-Christian, traditional worship systems.

General Attitudes

Colombians value courtesy and smiles. The individual is important in society. For this reason, timetables and punctuality are not stressed. It is not impolite to be late for an appointment, especially in rural areas. Colombians are proud of their history of democracy and independence. They do not appreciate outside interference and are confident they can meet challenges on their own. This is evident in successful attempts to end the violence that gripped many of their cities in the late 1980s and early 1990s. Colombians are hardworking and peace loving, and are experiencing a new appreciation for cultural and political pluralism. The historical class structure and closed political system are slowly dying, but society faces many challenges to creating a truly egalitarian society.

Personal Appearance

An individual's appearance is important. Clothing is conservative, clean, and well kept. The proper clothing for each occasion is essential. Men wear suits, white shirts, and ties in urban areas. Women wear comfortable dresses, and urban youth dress casually. Dress in rural areas is less fashionable, but the people wear neat, clean clothing. Indians often wear traditional clothing, which can include wraparound dresses, bowler hats, and *ponchos*.

CUSTOMS AND COURTESIES

Greetings

The most common greeting is a handshake, although it is not too vigorous. Men often shake hands with everyone when entering a home, greeting a group, or leaving. Women kiss each other on the cheek if they are acquainted but offer a verbal greeting otherwise. Young people will also kiss each other on the cheek if they are good friends. It is customary to address people by a title (*Señor*, *Señora*, or *Doctor*, among others) when being introduced. First names are not used between strangers. The *abrazo* (hug) is common between close friends or relatives. Common terms include *¡Buenos días!* (Good day), *¿Cómo está?* (How are you?), and *¡Adiós!* (Goodbye).

Gestures

Yawning in the presence of strangers or in a group is impolite because it is a sign of hunger. People beckon others with the palm down, waving the fingers or the whole hand. People use toothpicks discreetly. Smiling is an important gesture of goodwill.

Visiting

Visiting is an important part of Colombian culture. Friends and relatives may visit unannounced, especially in rural areas where telephones are not widely available, but it is otherwise polite to call ahead or make arrangements in advance. Colombians are gracious hosts. They usually offer guests refreshments and make them feel comfortable. In return, guests treat hosts with courtesy and respect.

When invited for dinner, guests usually arrive at least a few minutes, and often 30 or more minutes, late. They may bring a small gift to the hosts, but this is not expected. On more formal visits, guests wait to sit until the hosts have directed them to a seat. Customs vary with ethnic group and region. Hosts often accompany departing guests out the door and even down the street. Politeness and proper etiquette are emphasized in Colombia. It is improper to put one's feet on furniture when visiting.

Eating

Good manners and courtesy when eating are important to Colombians. Pleasant conversation is welcome at the table, as it stimulates a feeling of goodwill. Overeating is impolite; a host may offer more helpings, but these should be politely refused. For many, it is important to keep hands above the table during the meal. In a group, it is impolite to take anything to eat without first offering it to others. Eating on the streets is not proper. In restaurants, a 10 percent service charge is usually included in the bill; if not, patrons leave a tip at the table.

LIFESTYLE

Family

The family is important in Colombian society, and family members share their good fortunes with one another. Traditional values still maintain a strong influence on family relations. The father feels the obligation to provide for his family. The mother is responsible for most of the affairs of the home. An increasing number of women work outside the home; more than 20 percent of the labor force is female. It is the custom for a child to bear two family names: the last name is the mother's family name and the second-to-last name is the father's family name. People either use their full name or go by their father's family name, which is the official surname. Therefore, a person named José Muñoz Gómez would be called *Señor Muñoz*.

Upper-class families enjoy many modern conveniences and can hire household help. However, most Colombians lead simpler lives. About one-third live in absolute poverty.

Dating and Marriage

Depending on family custom, dating begins around age 14 or 15. In large cities, the age is somewhat lower. Couples date and decide on marriage much as U.S. American couples do. Marriage ceremonies generally follow Catholic traditions.

Diet

Breakfast often consists of juice, coffee or hot chocolate, fruit, eggs, and bread. Some eat a smaller "continental" breakfast. Lunch, usually between noon and 2:00 P.M., is the main meal of the day. When possible, the family gathers at this time (many schools and businesses close) for the meal. However, in urban areas there is a trend to have the main meal in the evening. Soup, rice, meat, potatoes, salad, and beans are the staple foods. *Arroz con pollo* (chicken with rice) is a popular national dish. *Arepa* is a cornmeal pancake. *Sancocho* is a meat-and-vegetable stew. Supper is usually at 7:00 or 8:00 P.M. Coffee, the chief agricultural product in Colombia, is the favorite drink of many.

Recreation

Fútbol (soccer) is the most popular sport in Colombia. Most people, especially men, carefully follow World Cup action. Colombia's national team competed in the 1994 World Cup. Other favorite activities include cycle racing, swimming, track-and-field, volleyball, basketball, and baseball. Attending bullfights is also popular. Wealthy individuals belong to sport clubs offering golf and tennis. Aside from playing or watching sports, people enjoy dancing, especially at folk festivals, and music.

Holidays

Holidays in Colombia include New Year's Day, Epiphany (6 January), St. Joseph's Day (19 March), Easter, Labor Day (1 May), Feast of St. Peter and St. Paul (29 June), Independence Day (20 July), Battle of Boyacá (7 August), Assumption Day (15 August), *Día de la Raza* (12 October), All Saints' Day (1 November), Independence of Cartagena (11 November), and Christmas.

Commerce

The Colombian workweek is basically Monday through Friday, from 8:00 A.M. to 6:00 P.M., with lunch between noon and 2:00 P.M. Shops, however, are open from 9:00 A.M. to 6:30 P.M., Monday through Saturday, with some closing Saturday afternoon. Banks close at 3:00 P.M.

SOCIETY

Government

The Republic of Colombia has a bicameral Congress, with a 102-seat Senate and 161-seat Chamber of Representatives. Senators are elected in a national vote, while representatives are elected regionally. The president is head of state and head of government. He and a cabinet form the executive branch. The judicial branch is independent. All citizens may vote at age 18. The main political parties include the Liberal Party (of which Samper is a member) and the Conservative Party (which now forms the main opposition in Congress). A few smaller parties are also represented in the legislature. Colombia has 23 states called *departamentos*.

Economy

Colombia has a fairly strong, vibrant economy. It benefits from high rates of foreign investment and solid growth, which are possible because of its free-market policies. Colombians are proud of the fact that they are current on all foreign debt payments and have never defaulted. The country has a reputation for managing the economy according to sound principles. However, the government is challenged by high inflation, decaying infrastructure, illegal drug trade, and violence.

Colombia's Human Development Index (0.836) ranks it 57th out of 174 countries. Adjusted for women, the index (0.720) ranks Colombia 50th out of 130 countries. Real gross domestic product per capita is $5,480, which has more than doubled in the last generation. Despite these fairly impressive figures, the incidence of rural poverty and an unequal distribution of income indicate that economic opportunities are more accessible to the ruling class in urban areas. Blacks and indigenous groups are especially marginalized, but new laws recognizing their rights and providing for greater political integration are expected to lead to better economic conditions for these lower socioeconomic groups.

Agriculture plays a key role in Colombia's economy. Coffee is the most important export, accounting for 30 percent of all export earnings; freshly cut flowers and bananas also provide export earnings for the nation. Other agricultural products are sugar, cotton, rice, and corn.

The mining of Colombia's many natural resources as well as manufacturing are also key elements in the economy. More than 90 percent of the world's emeralds are mined in Colombia. Crude oil, natural gas, iron ore, nickel, gold, copper, textiles, chemicals, and other products all contribute to the economy. The production and export of illicit drugs (such as cocaine) also generates revenue for the economy—revenue that must be replaced through legitimate activities before the drug industry's significance decreases. With half of the country covered by forests and woodlands, the timber industry is becoming important. The currency is the Colombian *peso* (Col$).

Transportation and Communication

Domestic bus service is the most common link between cities, but air-passenger travel is on the rise. Although a minority of the people own cars, travel on highways has increased and with it so has road construction and repair. Still, only about 10 percent of the roads are paved. Colombia has coasts on two oceans, and its port cities provide shipping access to North American, European, and Asian markets. Communications systems have improved with various projects. There are more than 1.8 million telephones in the nation, and a fiber-optic system is scheduled to link the country with the United States. The country has a free press that has been active in resisting violence from terrorists.

Education

Primary education is free and compulsory, although many schools are private. Boys and girls often attend separate schools. Rural schools have increased in number in recent years, helping the literacy rate rise to about 87 percent. Unfortunately the literacy rate is only 40 percent for the indigenous and black populations. Overall, just fewer than 60 percent of all students actually complete their primary education and move on to the secondary level. Secondary and vocational schools are found in major cities, and several universities are now in operation; Bogotá has eight, the largest being the National University. Scholarly achievement has been important throughout Colombia's history.

Health

Hospital and personal health care are available in the cities but are lacking in rural areas. Private clinics and public or charity hospitals are available. As many tropical diseases have been eradicated, life expectancy has risen to between 70 and 75 years. However, malaria and yellow fever are still dangerous in rural and tropical regions, and tap water often is not safe for drinking. The infant mortality rate is 27 per 1,000. Infant mortality is significantly higher and life expectancy lower among blacks and Indians.

FOR THE TRAVELER

A tourist visa (from a consulate) or tourist card (obtained at the airport) is required of U.S. citizens staying more than 30 days. A valid passport and proof of onward passage are also required. Minors (younger than 18) traveling alone or with only one of their parents or guardians must carry a notarized authorization (authenticated by the embassy or consulate) from the absent parent(s) or guardian(s). Tourists leaving the country by air are charged an airport tax that must be paid in U.S. dollars or *pesos*. There are some restrictions on what one can bring into the country. Violence continues to affect a large portion of the country. The U.S. Department of State has issued travel warnings for U.S. citizens traveling to Colombia. For updates, call (202) 647–5225. One should take precautions against pickpockets operating in some cities. Also, officials recommend that only taxis with green and off-white paint be used, as those vehicles are registered and considered trustworthy. For additional information, contact the consular section of the Embassy of Colombia, 1825 Connecticut Avenue NW, Suite 218, Washington, DC 20009; phone (202) 332–7476.

Republic of
Costa Rica

Boundary representations not necessarily authoritative.

BACKGROUND

Land and Climate

Costa Rica covers 19,730 square miles (51,100 square kilometers) and is just smaller than West Virginia. About 60 percent of Costa Rica is covered by different types of forests. More than 11 percent of the total territory is reserved as national parks. This small nation has a diverse landscape of tropical rain forest, mountain cloud forest, volcanoes, green countryside, and beautiful rivers. Although the country lies entirely in the tropical climate zone, elevation changes allow for cooler temperatures in the central highlands. The coastal lowlands are hot and humid. Most people live at elevations where the climate is generally mild the entire year. Rainfall varies between the dry season (December–April) and the wet season (May–November). The land is subject to earthquakes, hurricanes, and volcanic eruptions.

History

A variety of native peoples lived in present-day Costa Rica before Columbus arrived in 1502. In the north, the indigenous cultures were influenced by Mayan civilization. Southern groups were more related to the indigenous peoples of South America. Today's museums offer a glimpse of pre-Columbian life. Spain eventually colonized the Costa Rican area along with most of Central America. Because minerals were scarce, the area was ignored by the Spanish crown and remained isolated. In 1821, Costa Rica joined other Central American nations in declaring independence from Spain during a nonviolent revolution. In 1824, it became a state of the Federal Republic of Central America. After the republic collapsed in 1838, Costa Rica became a sovereign nation.

Costa Rica has a long tradition of changes in government via democratic means. This tradition has been interrupted by military coups only three times in 150 years. Consequently, Costa Rica has one of the most stable democratic governments in Central America. Civil war erupted for six weeks in 1948 after a dispute over elections. José Figueres Ferrer led an interim government until 1949 when the election dispute was settled. Figueres (who was elected president in 1953 and again in 1970) abolished the army in 1948, and a new constitution was introduced in 1949. Costa Rica has enjoyed peace and democracy ever since.

The nation practices a philosophy of nonintervention in the affairs of foreign governments. Former president Oscar Arias Sánchez (who left office in 1990) was an avid supporter of the Central American Peace Plan. Arias won the Nobel Peace Prize for his efforts to bring peace to the region. The award is a great source of pride for all Costa Ricans, as they feel it emphasizes their distinct heritage.

The election of José Maria Figueres Olsen as president in 1994 marked the 11th peaceful transfer of power since 1948. Figueres is the son of the former three-term president.

THE PEOPLE

Population

The population of Costa Rica is 3.4 million and is growing at 2.2 percent a year. The population is relatively young, with more than 45 percent younger than age 20. Most people live in the central valley highlands. The majority of people (87 percent) have a European heritage. About 7 percent are of mixed heritage (European and Indian), although many of these are immigrants from other Latin American countries. Two percent of the population is black and lives mostly on the Atlantic Coast. These people are descendants of laborers brought from the Caribbean to build a railroad. They later worked on banana plantations and developed a distinct culture in the region around Puerto Limón. One percent of Costa Ricans are Native Americans, some of whom still live in the Talamanca mountain region. Another 1 percent are ethnic Chinese.

The country's Human Development Index (0.883) ranks it 28th out of 174 nations. Adjusted for women, the index (0.763) ranks Costa Rica 42d out of 130 countries, indicating that women have fewer economic choices than men.

Language

Spanish is the official language of Costa Rica. English is widely understood. Patua (Creole English) is spoken by the black population. Bribri, an indigenous language spoken by the Bribri people, is the most common native language. Ten other native groups speak Spanish or a native tongue.

Costa Ricans are known as *ticos* within their own country and throughout Central America. The nickname comes from their habit of ending words or phrases with the suffix *tico* (instead of the more common Spanish diminutive *tito*). So instead of saying *chico* (small) or *chiquitito* (very small), Costa Ricans say *chiquitico*. Individually, men are called *ticos* and women *ticas*, but the mixed company reference is *ticos*.

Religion

The Roman Catholic Church claims membership of about 95 percent of the population. Until the mid-1980s, the Catholic Church was the nation's official church, but it lost that status when the government decreed a democratic nation should support no particular religion. Although the Catholic Church continues to be very influential in the country, the constitution guarantees religious freedom to the people. As is the trend elsewhere, secularization in Costa Rica is leading some people away from organized religion. At the same time, a growing number of religious people are joining other Christian chur-ches—and religion still plays an important role in society.

General Attitudes

Costa Rica is a land of courtesy, domestic enterprise, hospitality, and gentleness. Militarism is despised by nearly all. Children are taught in school that armies are created to oppress rather than protect people. Aggressiveness, brusqueness, and violence are also shunned. *Ticos* say they are lovers of peace and conciliation. They avoid confrontation when possible. People value privacy and quiet behavior but vigorously defend personal honor. A strong work ethic is prevalent among most segments of society, and rural people especially accept hard labor as a necessary part of life.

Individuality is an important characteristic, expressed in Costa Rica's relations with other nations and, to a lesser extent, on a personal level. This is partly due to Costa Rican isolation during the colonial period; because they had little contact with colonial rulers, *ticos* developed greater independence. Still, group conformity in values, interests, and thought is important in society. Individuals are recognized as such and all people are given respect, regardless of their social class. There is little resentment between the classes, due to this traditional respect and a belief that some things are determined by God. A feeling that Deity controls some aspects of life, such as one's health or success at a given venture, is evident in daily speech. People often attribute their achievements to and place hope in God. This tradition is changing with greater education and people's desire for material progress.

Personal Appearance

Western dress is common throughout the country. Women generally pay more attention to their appearance than men and always try to be fashionably dressed. Still, all *ticos* consider it necessary to be well groomed in public. Clothing is neat, clean, and generally modest. People bathe every day and place great emphasis on personal cleanliness.

CUSTOMS AND COURTESIES

Greetings

Women friends or relatives greet each other with a light kiss on the cheek. If women are not yet acquainted, they often pat each other on the arm. Men shake hands. It is an insult not to shake every man's hand in a small group. Common terms for greeting include *¡Buenos días!* (Good day), *¡Buenas tardes!* (Good afternoon), and *¡Buenas noches!* (Good evening). Ticos often respond to the greeting *¿Cómo está?* (How are you?) with the expression *Pura vida* (Pure life). Also used as a way to say "Okay," *Pura vida* has endless uses in the country. *¡Hola!* (Hi) is a casual greeting popular among the youth; older people consider it disrespectful if used to greet them. In rural areas, people greet each other when passing on the street, regardless of whether or not they are acquainted. One might simply say *¡Adiós!* or *¡Buenas!* or be more formal and say *¡Adiós, Señora!* or *¡Buenos días!* This tradition is less common in urban areas. Rural people often bow their heads slightly and touch their hats in greeting. Greetings between strangers or acquaintances are brief, but people who know each other usually take a few minutes to talk about family, work, or health. Polite and respectful greetings are a social norm.

One addresses others by professional title either with or without a surname, depending on the situation. *Señor* (Mr.) and *Señora* (Mrs.) are also used, especially for people with whom one is not well acquainted. *Ticos* address friends, children, coworkers, and subordinates by first name. They use the title *Don* or *Doña* with the first name of an older man or woman, respectively, to show special respect for and familiarity with the person. For example, a child might call the mother of his best friend *Doña Maria*.

Gestures

Hand gestures are common and important to everyday conversation. In fact, Costa Ricans often use their hands to express an idea, either with or without verbal communication. To indicate "no," one vigorously waves the index finger (palm out, finger up). To express shock or when faced with a serious situation, *ticos* will shake the hand vigorously enough to snap (slap) the fingers together three or four times. There are many different hand greetings in addition to the handshake or wave. For instance, young people slap hands together in a greeting similar to a "high five." Eye contact is very important, especially when one is discussing a serious issue or talking to a superior. It is traditionally understood that the lack of eye contact means one cannot be trusted. Chewing gum while speaking is impolite.

Visiting

Urban Costa Ricans generally prefer that visits be arranged in advance. Only close friends or relatives drop by unannounced, and then mostly in the afternoon after household chores have been done. Otherwise, uninvited visitors may not be asked into the home. In rural areas, people visit unannounced more often and are rarely turned away. Hosts usually offer visitors something to drink (like coffee) and refreshments (pastries, bread, or crackers). Costa Ricans enjoy socializing but do not visit as often as people in other Latin American or Caribbean countries. Invited guests are generally expected to arrive a few minutes late (later in rural areas). Punctuality is not customary, but being very late is also not appreciated. Dinner guests usually bring a small gift to their hosts, such as flowers, wine, a plant, or something to share or mark the occasion. Close friends often bring more personal gifts. Gifts are also exchanged on special occasions.

Host usually serve dinner guests refreshments and drinks while they socialize for an hour or so before the meal is served. After dinner, coffee and dessert accompany more conversation. Guests generally leave shortly thereafter.

If a Costa Rican invites someone to dinner or to spend a few days at his home, the potential guest must determine whether the invitation is sincere or whether the host is just trying to be polite. Polite invitations are often extended as a gesture of goodwill rather than as an expectation that guests will come.

Eating

At the table, Costa Ricans enjoy active conversation on a variety of subjects. Mealtime is to be enjoyed and is extended by conversation. Costa Ricans eat rice and beans in various combinations for nearly every meal. Typical at breakfast is *gallo pinto* (mixture of rice and black beans). *Casado* (rice, beans, salad or eggs, meat, and plantains) is a common lunchtime meal. Bread is eaten with most meals, although tortillas are also common. Table manners vary from family to family, but as a general rule, one should keep both hands above the table rather than in the lap. In restaurants, the bill customarily includes a tip of 10 percent. Further tipping is not expected.

Most people eat three meals a day, with mid-morning and afternoon coffee breaks or snacks. Breakfast and dinner are the most important meals, as lunch is becoming more rushed and is more often eaten away from home. Business professionals make lunch dates, but dinner is otherwise the meal for entertaining guests.

LIFESTYLE

Family

Costa Ricans value family tradition and heritage. The immediate family has an average of three to five children. Rural families are usually larger. Rural extended families often either share a dwelling or live as neighbors. Women retain their maiden names when they marry. Children carry the surnames of both parents. The second-to-last name in a full name is the family surname. While the husband makes most final decisions in the home, he shares many responsibilities with his wife. Most women do not work outside the home, but a growing number are entering the labor force. Nearly 30 percent of the workforce is female. Many families, even many of the poor, own their own homes, which are either wood-frame or cement-block structures (or a combination, with block halfway up the wall and wood to the roof).

Dating and Marriage

Girls are generally more restricted in dating than boys. They can seldom have visitors past 10:00 P.M., unless courtship is close to marriage. When a young couple is dating, the boy is often allowed a certain schedule for sitting with the girl on the porch or taking short neighborhood walks. This may be for two hours during a few evenings each week. Early dating is usually done in groups, excepting in rural areas where there are fewer people. Movies, dances, picnics, the December bullfights, and a yearly civic carnival are favorite dating activities. A boy usually asks a girl's parents for permission to date her, but this custom is slowly disappearing, especially in urban areas.

Marriage is still a valued institution; Costa Rica has one of the highest marriage rates in Latin America. Families visit each other to show formal agreement on their children's marriage. Women generally marry in their early 20s, men somewhat later. Unmarried adults usually live with their parents, especially in rural areas. Typically, only university students live on their own if not married.

Diet

Many varieties of food are enjoyed in Costa Rica. Popular in some areas is *olla de carne*, a beef stew with potatoes, onions, and many vegetables. *Tamales* (meat, vegetables, and flour wrapped in plantain leaves and boiled) are served for Easter and Christmas. Bread, tortillas, and fruits, along with rice and beans, are staple items eaten with main meals. Also common are *lengua en salsa* (tongue in sauce), *mondongo* (intestine soup), *empanadas* (turnovers), *arroz con pollo* (rice with chicken), and *gallos* (tortillas with meat and vegetable fillings). *Ticos* of all ages enjoy coffee. Adults may take two or three coffee breaks each day.

Recreation

Fútbol (soccer) is the most popular sport, both for spectators and participants. Basketball, baseball, volleyball, surfing, auto racing, swimming, cycling, running, and tennis are also popular. Fishing is good in many parts of the country. The wealthy enjoy golf and polo. Beaches are crowded between January and April. Local carnivals, festivals, and bullfights are popular attractions at various times throughout the year.

Costa Ricans enjoy music that is popular in the Caribbean and Brazil, as well as music common throughout Central and North America. Dancing is a favorite activity among *ticos* of all ages. Cultural arts are popular, and people enjoy stories and poetry. Media broadcasts from the United States are popular and have a significant impact on urban trends.

Holidays

Costa Rican holidays include New Year's Day; Feast of St. Joseph (19 March); Anniversary of the Battle of Rivas against Walker (11 April), in which the national hero, Juan Santamaría, the drummer boy, lost his life; *Semana Santa*

(Holy Week) and Easter; Labor Day (1 May); Annexation of Guanacaste to Costa Rica (25 July); Feast of St. Peter and St. Paul (29 June); Feast of Our Lady of the Angels (2 August); Central American Independence Day (15 September); *Día de la Raza,* recognizing the indigenous roots of Latin America (12 October); Feast of Immaculate Conception (8 December); and Christmas. Christmas is celebrated with family, but New Year's is a time for friends, parties, drinking, and dancing. However, many people interrupt festivities before midnight on New Year's Eve to go home and eat a small, quiet meal with the family before returning to their party after midnight.

Commerce

Most businesses are open weekdays from 8:00 A.M. to noon and 2:00 to 6:00 P.M., although some shops do not close for the midday break. Many shops are open on Saturday, but most are closed on Sunday. Government offices close weekdays at 4:00 P.M. Few business meetings are strictly formal, and socializing is an important part of a business relationship.

SOCIETY

Government

Costa Rica is a democratic republic. The country has an elected president and two vice presidents in the executive branch. There is a unicameral National Assembly, whose 57 legislators are elected to four-year terms. The judicial branch is separate. Costa Rica has seven provinces. All citizens age 18 and older are required to vote in national elections. Election day is always a national holiday; people travel to their town of birth to vote and enjoy grand celebrations. Most Costa Ricans are affiliated with one of two major parties: the National Liberation Party (PLN), of which President Figueres is a member, and the Social Christian Unity Party (PUSC). The next national elections are in 1998.

Economy

Despite a relative lack of minerals and other traditional natural resources, Costa Rica has a fairly prosperous economy. Real gross domestic product per capita is $5,480, a figure that has more than doubled in the last generation. Since 1992, the economy has been growing at more than 4 percent annually. These figures reflect Costa Rica's stability; successful tourism, timber, and agricultural industries; and generally egalitarian society. Most people earn enough to meet basic needs and take advantage of a variety of economic opportunities. Unemployment is low, although inflation rose to more than 22 percent in 1995. Poverty still affects more than one-fourth of the population. Costa Rica has been a major recipient of foreign aid, and foreign investment in the country is increasing.

Agricultural products comprise the bulk (70 percent) of Costa Rica's exports; 27 percent of the people are employed in agriculture. Exports include coffee, bananas, beef, sugar, cocoa, and fertilizer. Ornamental flowers are becoming an increasingly important export. Cattle raising is concentrated in the Guanacaste province but is expanding to other areas. Other industries include food processing, textiles, and construction

materials. Costa Rica has excellent potential for hydroelectric power, and nearly all of its electricity comes from hydroelectric power plants. Tourism facilities are well developed, so the industry is prosperous and important to the economy. Currently, ecotourism is especially popular. The monetary unit is the Costa Rican *colón* (C) or plural *colones.*

Transportation and Communication

While personal automobiles are becoming more affordable, the most common form of transportation within and between cities is the bus. Fares are inexpensive and the system is efficient. Almost every town and tourist destination can be reached by paved roads. Taxis are commonly available; legal taxis are red. There are 26 airports with paved runways. The domestic telephone system was expanded between 1989 and 1994; telephones are located throughout the country, although remote areas still lack service. Rural homes usually do not have phones, but each town has at least one public phone. Satellite systems are used for international communication. Radio stations transmit throughout the country. There are also a number of television stations in Costa Rica. Several national newspapers have wide circulation. The postal system is very efficient.

Education

Costa Rica has one of the finest urban public education systems in the Americas. Primary education is compulsory and free for six years, beginning at age seven. Where facilities exist, children also attend kindergarten at age five and a preparatory year at age six. Enrollment in secondary schools is not mandatory, but more than 40 percent of all pupils advance to that level. Secondary schooling is also free. The adult literacy rate is 94 percent. Four public universities, and a number of private universities, serve the population. Evening schools educate the older generation as well as young people who cannot attend secondary school during the day. Gaining a high school diploma is considered very important. Costa Rica is home to four international education centers.

Health

Medical care is considered very good and a national healthcare system serves all citizens. Life expectancy has risen in recent years to between 76 and 80 years, and the infant mortality rate has fallen to 10 per 1,000. Infant malnutrition and inadequate prenatal care remain problems in rural areas. Malaria is common along the Nicaraguan border and at lower elevations, and dengue fever (spread by mosquitoes) has been reported on both coasts since 1993. Dysentery and typhoid are found in areas outside the capital.

FOR THE TRAVELER

U.S. travelers need a passport to visit Costa Rica, but a visa is not required for stays of fewer than 90 days. Those who stay longer must have an AIDS test performed in Costa Rica and apply for permission to stay. For lodging and travel information, contact the Costa Rican Tourist Bureau, ICP PO, Box 777–1000, San José, Costa Rica; phone (800) 343–6332. You may also contact the Embassy of Costa Rica, 2114 S Street, NW, Washington, DC 20004.

July 96

CULTURGRAM '97

ZAGREB
Drava
PANNONIAN VALLEY
Danube
Osijek
Sava
Slavonski Brod
Rijeka
KRAJINA REGION
Knin
Zadar
Split
Ploče
Dubrovnik

Republic of
Croatia

Germany
Czech Republic
Poland
Slovakia
Ukraine
Austria
Hungary
Slovenia
Croatia
Romania
Italy
Bosnia-Herzegovina
Serbia and Montenegro
Bulgaria
Former Yugoslav Republic of Macedonia
Adriatic Sea
Albania
Greece
Turkey
Mediterranean Sea

Boundary representations not necessarily authoritative.

BACKGROUND

Land and Climate

Croatia is situated along the eastern coast of the Adriatic Sea. Its hinterland stretches close to the slopes of the Julian Alps in Slovenia and into the Pannonian Valley to the banks of the Drava and Danube Rivers. Covering 21,829 square miles (56,538 square kilometers), Croatia is about the size of West Virginia. Along the Adriatic are hundreds of islands that hug the highly indented coastline. The coast enjoys a Mediterranean climate with hot, sunny summers and pleasant winters. Many famous cities, including the medieval port of Dubrovnik, lie along the long coast. In mountainous regions, winters are cold and snowy, while summers are cool. In the Pannonian area, winters are cold and dry; summers are hot. The capital, Zagreb, lies on the Sava River.

History

Slavic peoples began settling the Balkan Peninsula in the seventh century A.D. Croatians were first united into a single state by King Tomislav in 925. Following Catholicism's Great Schism in 1054, Croats accepted Roman Catholicism and became associated with the West. In 1102, the Croatian and Hungarian monarchies came together in a personal union. In the 1500s, Croatia and Hungary became part of the Austro-Hungarian (Hapsburg) Empire, where they remained until the 20th century.

After two destabilizing Balkan wars in 1912 and 1913, the entire region was embroiled in World War I—sparked by the assassination (in 1914) of Austria's crown prince in Sarajevo (Bosnia). Upon Austria's and Germany's defeat, the Austro-Hungarian empire collapsed. Several new states were created from it in 1918, with Slavs uniting together in the Kingdom of Serbs, Croats, and Slovenes. Relations between ethnic groups were hostile and not conducive to a peaceful union. By 1929, Serbia had increased its domination of the country and declared it the Kingdom of Yugoslavia (meaning, "kingdom of southern Slavs"). Croats suffered repression under Serbian rule. So when Germany and Italy invaded in 1941, Croat fascists declared an independent Croat state under their leadership (called *Ustashe*) and allied with the Nazis. While Croats welcomed independence, they did not fully realize that the *Ustashe* regime was a puppet of the Nazis. At the hands of Croat fascists, many thousands of civilian Jews, Serbs, and Gypsies died in concentration camps or in massacres. The actual record of events from that era is hotly disputed even today, but the memory of Croat brutality (perceived and real) was one catalyst to Serbian attrocities committed in the 1990s.

During World War II, a great many Croats joined other Slavs in the antifascist movement that waged a civil war for control of Yugoslavia. Communist forces (antifascist partisans) emerged victorious over the *Chetniks* (royalists) as Germany was falling to Allied advances. Croatia subsequently became part of the Socialist Republic of Yugoslavia created under partisan leader Josip Broz Tito. The Yugoslav federation was quickly consolidated and Tito became its president in 1953. To keep opposing groups together, Tito's Communist Party carefully controlled nationalist sentiments among all ethnic groups and promoted the federalism concept. Attempts to revive Croat nationalism and culture were suppressed. When Tito died in 1980, his authority was transferred to a collective state presidency, which had a rotating chairman. That body was not able to rule effectively for long before simmering ethnic tensions erupted. By the end of the 1980s, the federation was on the verge of collapse.

With the fall of communism elsewhere in Europe, Croatia held elections in 1990. The newly elected leadership under President Franjo Tudjman declared independence in 1991. Croatia was recognized by the international community in January 1992, but it faced heavy military intervention from the Yugoslav army and Serbian government, which strongly opposed independence. Entire cities were nearly destroyed in fierce fighting between these forces, as well as between local Serbs and Croats.

The United Nations helped broker a cease-fire in 1992. Many people had been killed; thousands had been forced to leave their homes, creating a serious refugee problem; and historically rooted ethnic hatred boiled over on Croatian soil. Local Serbs had gained control of Krajina, or roughly one-third of Croatia's territory. They declared a Republic of Serb Krajina, but this was never recognized outside of Serbia. Rebel Serbs, supported by Serbia's government, launched rocket attacks on civilians in Zagreb and threatened other violence if their independence were not recognized.

After negotiators and the United Nations failed to solve the crisis peacefully, Croatia forcefully recaptured Krajina in August 1995. Thousands of Serbs fled to neighboring Serb-held regions; by 1996, nearly 200,000 Serbs had left Krajina. Eastern Slavonia (near the border with Serbia), also held by rebel Serbs opposed to Croatian independence, was returned to Croatian control without violence. Croatia agreed to a two-year transition period to avert another mass Serbian exodus. On the heels of his victory in securing Croatia's borders, President Tudjman called for early parliamentary elections near the end of 1995. His Croatian Democratic Union (HDZ) Party won 60 percent of the seats. Tudjman faces reelection in 1997. The new prime minister, Zlatko Matesa, is focusing on economic development.

Croatian support for Croats and Muslims fighting Serbs in Bosnia added to tension and violence in the region during the 1990s. Under pressure from Western allies, Croatia eventually supported the Dayton Peace Agreement in 1996 and pledged to support a resolution of the Bosnian civil war.

THE PEOPLE

Population

Croatia has between 4 and 4.5 million residents. The actual number is difficult to determine because of the refugee situation: Croat refugees left in 1992, Bosnian Croats came throughout the war, and Croatian Serbs left in 1995 and 1996. Croats form about 78 percent of the population. Serbs accounted for 12 percent before 1995 but may account for less than 5 percent today. About 2 percent of the people claim to be Yugoslavs, although such an ethnic group does not really exist. It was promoted under Communist rule to suppress nationalism and provide an optional ethnic distinction for children of mixed marriages. Muslims of Slavic origin comprise 1 percent of the population, and another 1 percent is Hungarian. Slovenes and other small groups make up the rest of the population. More than 300,000 Croatians live abroad; most are in Bosnia, but some work in other European countries as guest workers. These Croatians have representation in the *Sabor*, Croatia's Parliament.

Language

Croatian is the country's official language. It is a Slavic language that adopted a Latin alphabet in the 14th century. Because the Cyrillic alphabet is used in some neighboring countries, it can be used by Serbs and other ethnic groups to write their own languages or Croatian. Although the Cyrillic alphabet does not appear on signs or in public documents, recent laws guarantee the right to teach and use it. Serbian, Hungarian, Czech, Slovakian, Italian, Albanian, and Slovenian are all spoken by their respective groups in Croatia. Students may study English, French, German, and Italian in school beginning at age ten.

Religion

Religion traditionally has been important to Croats. With the demise of communism and Yugoslav socialism, religion is once again playing an important role in Croatian society. It was a primary dividing feature between Croats and other Slavs because most Croats are Roman Catholic; some are Protestant or Jewish. Serbs are mostly Orthodox Christian. There are also many Muslims. Freedom of worship is guaranteed. The Catholic Church plays an active role in political and social affairs.

General Attitudes

The people of Croatia are sociable, optimistic, proud of their heritage, and hospitable to strangers. They value their families, education, and good careers. For centuries, Croats did not have their own independent state, and for decades, Croatia was part of Yugoslavia. Croats now have an internationally recognized sovereign country. They are extremely proud of their nation and are anxious for other countries to accept them and learn of Croatian history and culture. Their historical ties to western Europe also bring Croatians much pride, and they have worked to again integrate with European organizations. Most Croatians hope for the establishment of democratic principles and rights for all citizens. It is a difficult goal, since mutual tolerance and respect must precede any lasting peace.

Personal Appearance

It is important for clothing to be neat and clean. Adults do not wear shorts in public, except for recreation or on the coast. Women wear skirts and dresses more often than pants. In the workplace, women customarily wear dresses. Urban men wear suits and ties for special occasions and in some business or professional circles. The European tradition of wearing a tie (*kravata*) comes from the 18th century Croatian soldier's uniform. For informal situations, men prefer more practical daily clothing, such as jeans, knit shirts or sweatshirts, and casual shoes or sneakers. Natural fiber fabrics (cotton and wool) are generally preferred over synthetics. Rural women often wear scarves on their heads.

CUSTOMS AND COURTESIES

Greetings

A handshake is the most common greeting in Croatia, along with a phrase such as *Dobro jutro* (Good morning), *Dobar dan* (Good day), or *Dobra večer* (Good evening). The most common phrases used among friends and neighbors for saying hello are *Zdravo* (Health) and *Bok* (literally "God," it means "Hi"). Good-bye can be either *Zbogom* (With God) or *Do vidjenja* (Until we meet again). When friends and relatives greet, they may embrace and appear to kiss cheeks. Croats kiss twice—once to each cheek—while Serbs generally add a third kiss. Actually, most people brush cheeks and "kiss the air." In formal situations, a man waits for a woman to extend her hand. In formal greetings, the family name is preceded by *gospodine* (Mr.), *gospodjo* (Mrs.), *gospodjice* (Miss), or a professional title. The younger person greets first. Close friends and relatives use first names. Kinship is important and terms used when addressing family depend on that relationship. For example, the word for "aunt" can be either *teto* (mother's sister) or *ujna* (father's sister or mother's brother's wife).

Gestures

Hand movement is common during conversation and includes gestures popular throughout Europe. One indicates "money" by rubbing the thumb and index finger of the right hand. People beckon with the index finger or by waving all fingers inward with the palm up. Yawning in public is impolite. On public transportation, it is polite to offer one's seat to pregnant women or the elderly. While public approval is displayed by applause, whistling or shouting "ouuuu" shows disapproval.

Visiting

Croats enjoy visiting one another to socialize. Most visits are arranged in advance, but unexpected guests are also welcomed. When invited to a home, guests bring a gift to the hosts. It is usually a bottle of wine, sweets, or an odd number of flowers. Gifts are unwrapped in the presence of the giver, whom the hosts thank. Flowers are given to the hostess, other types of gifts to the host. Flowers, if wrapped, are unwrapped before the hosts open the door. The hostess puts them in a vase and places them in the room where the guests are seated. The host offers something to drink or a snack, and the hostess makes coffee (usually Turkish) and offers biscuits or cookies. It is impolite not to accept refreshments. At small gatherings, newly arrived guests greet each person separately. Evening visits usually end before 11:00 P.M., except on special occasions. Hosts who live in an apartment accompany departing guests out the door; those who live in a house accompany them a little way down the street.

Eating

Breakfast is light and usually accompanied by black coffee. Lunch is the main meal of the day and consists of soup, meat, salad, bread or potatoes, and a dessert. In urban areas, dinner usually consists of cold cuts, bread, cheeses, and eggs. Rural people might have this or a cooked meal. People eat in the continental style, with the fork in the left hand and the knife remaining in the right. They keep hands above the table. Conversation at the table is often lively. Regional cuisine varies, with northern food being somewhat heavier and spicier than southern food. In coastal areas, people might break at mid-morning for *marenda*, a light meal of fish, cheese, and bread. A light midday snack is common in other areas, too.

In restaurants, one pays the bill at the table. A 5 to 10 percent tip is customary; it is given to the waiter with the bill and not left on the table. Among friends or colleagues, one person often pays for the entire meal. Over time, these people will take turns paying the bill.

LIFESTYLE

Family

Rural families traditionally include grandparents, parents, and two or more children. The father or grandfather has a dominant role in the family. Urban families usually have two children. Both husband and wife work and share in decision making. Grandparents may also be included, but less often than in rural areas. Children of working mothers may go to day-care centers or be cared for by family members (usually grandparents). Parents often feel obligated, especially in rural areas, to support grown or married children by giving them money or housing. In turn, children are expected to care for their elderly parents. Adult children often live with their parents until they marry or are able to be on their own.

Dating and Marriage

The youth begin dating around age 15, beginning with small groups. They like to gather downtown in cities or at the town square in rural areas. Small cafés and disco clubs are popular dating destinations. Rural people marry in their early twenties and urban dwellers in their late twenties to early thirties. To be legally married, one must have a civil ceremony. Having a church wedding before the civil one has become popular since 1991. After the ceremony, the wedding party is usually held at a restaurant or home. Weddings in rural areas are a particular cause for celebration, and the festivities may last for days.

Diet

The Croatian diet is influenced by its varied climate, landscape, and neighboring countries. Seafood and vegetables are most popular in coastal areas. Dishes made from chicken, beef, fish, pork, and lamb are common throughout Croatia. An inland specialty is *štrukli* (boiled or casseroled salt cottage cheese strudel). Meals in the countryside are large and made with seasonal ingredients. The main meal of the day usually consists of some sort of meat or fish, potatoes, and rice or corn. Urban families have less time to cook than their rural counterparts and, therefore, eat foods more convenient to prepare. Wine is the most popular drink with a meal. Also popular are beer, mineral water, and fruit drinks.

Recreation

People are sociable and enjoy getting together for historical, religious, cultural and sporting events, or on family occasions.

Folk festivals and cultural arts are well developed and enjoyed. The most popular sport is soccer, followed by basketball, handball, water polo, and sailing. Other favorite sports include tennis, chess, volleyball, archery, hockey, boxing, skiing, swimming, bowling, rowing, fishing, and hunting.

People enjoy going on walks and having picnics. Families usually have summer vacations of one to four weeks. Urban people enjoy outings in the countryside, vacationing on the Adriatic Coast, and traveling abroad. In many northern villages, people enjoy painting on glass. Television is watched in the evening and on weekends. Movie theaters and museums are popular.

Holidays

Official public holidays include the New Year (1–2 January), May Day (1 May), Day of Croatian Statehood (30 May), Day of the Antifascist Struggle (22 June), Ascension (15 August), All Saints' Day (1 November), and Christmas (25–26 December). Orthodox Christians celebrate Christmas on 7 January and receive a paid holiday for it. Muslims may take paid leave to celebrate *Ramasan Bairam* (the feast at the end of the month of fasting) and *Kurban Bairam* (Feast of the Sacrifice). Jews may also have paid leave for *Yom Kippur* and *Rosh Hashanah*.

Commerce

Weekday business and work hours begin at 8:00 A.M. and end at 4:00 P.M. Stores are open until 8:00 P.M. On Saturday, stores close at 1:00 P.M., except in tourist areas, where they stay open later. Socializing, especially after meetings, is important among business associates.

SOCIETY

Government

The Republic of Croatia has 21 counties. President Franjo Tudjman, first elected in 1990, was reelected in 1992 to a five-year term. He is head of state. He appoints the prime minister as head of government. Parliament (*Sabor*) consists of a 130-seat Chamber of Deputies and a 68-seat Chamber of Counties. The constitution enacted in December 1990 is called the "Christmas Constitution." Croatia's voting age is 18. Dominant political parties include the governing HDZ and the Croatian Social Liberal Party (HSLS). A number of smaller parties also have legislative representation.

Economy

Central planning and state domination were ineffective in developing Croatia's economy when it was part of Yugoslavia, even though it was among the most prosperous of the federation's republics. In 1991, the Croatian government began to institute market-oriented reforms by encouraging privatization and entrepreneurship. Progress was interrupted by the war and refugee situation, but by 1995 inflation had been reduced to less than 15 percent and unemployment to 16 percent. The estimated gross national product per capita is $2,640. In 1996, the government announced plans to attract more foreign investment and build a stronger economy. Economic growth may exceed 5 percent in 1996.

Croatia has a developed industrial sector and exports ships, equipment, chemicals, textiles, and furniture. Many factories and workers, idled by the region's conflicts, have the potential to be highly productive. Tourism is a vital source of revenue and jobs, but it has declined sharply because travelers have avoided the area. This has crippled the economies of some cities. Remittances from expatriate workers living in other European countries continue to be a key source of income for the country. The currency is the Croatian *kuna* (HK).

Transportation and Communication

Although many own private cars, people often use public streetcars and buses for urban transportation because they are inexpensive and convenient. In small cities and rural areas, bicycles are popular for getting around. Air and waterway links connect Croatian cities together and with other countries. The communications system functions well but lags behind western European standards. The government is updating and improving it. The number of private newspapers is increasing, but the government still has considerable influence over the media.

Education

Eight years of basic education are required, beginning at age seven. There are a number of secondary schools and four universities. Secondary schooling lasts four years but is not mandatory. Education is free to citizens at all levels. Those who gain entrance to a university may attend at no cost. Those who can or will pay tuition are allowed to enroll above the normal entrance quotas. Ethnic minorities may run their own schools. The literacy rate is about 97 percent.

Health

Health care is provided by the government, paid for by income taxes. Care is available to all and is of good quality. Facilities are most modern in large cities. People can pay to see private doctors. The infant mortality rate is 8 per 1,000. Life expectancy averages 70 to 77 years.

FOR THE TRAVELER

U.S. citizens need a valid passport and visa to visit Croatia. The tourist industry is well developed. Despite the fighting in 1995, most areas are safe to visit. To obtain any current travel warnings, call (202) 647–5225. Questions regarding travel opportunities may be answered by your travel professional, the Croatian Embassy Information Office, or the Ministry of Tourism, Ulica Grada, Vukovara 78 Zagreb, Croatia. You may also contact Pan Adriatic, 34–08 Broadway, Second Floor, Astoria, NY 11106; phone (718) 777–0555. Croatia's embassy is located at 2343 Massachusetts Avenue NW, Washington, DC 20008; phone (202) 588–5899 ext. 28.

Printed on recycled paper

CULTURGRAM '97

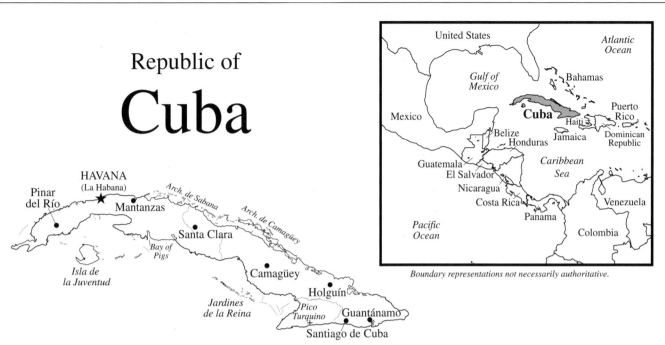

Republic of
Cuba

Boundary representations not necessarily authoritative.

BACKGROUND

Land and Climate

Cuba is an archipelago of two main islands, Cuba and *Isla de la Juventud* (Isle of Youth), and about 1,600 keys and islets. The total area of 42,803 square miles (110,860 square kilometers) is nearly as large as Pennsylvania. Cuba lies about 90 miles (145 kilometers) south of the United States. The island of Cuba has about 2,335 miles (3,735 kilometers) of coastline, with some 280 beaches; the most famous is Varadero in Matanzas province.

Low hills and fertile valleys cover more than half of the country. Mountain ranges divide the country into three regions: west, center, and east. The highest peak, Pico Turquino, rises to 8,320 feet (1,974 meters) in the east. Tropical forests in the east contrast with central prairies and western hills and valleys, where the royal palm is the dominant tree.

Cuba's subtropical climate is warm and humid. The average annual temperature is 75°F (24°C). Cuba experiences a dry season from November to April and a hotter, wet season from May to October. About two-thirds of all precipitation falls in this latter season, when hurricanes are also frequent.

History

Prior to the arrival of Columbus in 1492, Cuba was inhabited mainly by the indigenous Taino people. In 1511, a Spanish colony was firmly established and the Taino, forced into slavery, were wiped out. Havana, founded in the early 1500s, became the capital and a gathering point for Spanish treasure fleets from the New World. In 1762, Havana fell into British hands for a short period until it was returned to Spain in exchange for Florida the following year. Beginning in the 18th century, African slaves were brought to Cuba to work on plantations. In the 19th century, sugar production became the basis of the economy. Despite numerous rebellions, and unlike much of Latin America, Cuba remained in Spanish hands. The various uprisings culminated in the Ten Years' War (1868–78), which ended in failure after the loss of 200,000 lives.

José Martí, Cuba's national hero, led another revolt in 1895 but died early in the struggle. International protests over Spain's treatment of Cuba led to U.S. involvement and the Spanish-American War of 1898. Cuba gained independence, but it was not official until the end of the U.S. occupation in 1902. Other occupations (1906–9 and 1912) were based on the Platt Amendment to Cuba's constitution, which allowed U.S. intervention to maintain stability. In 1934, the United States canceled the amendment, receiving a 99-year lease on Guantánamo Bay—territory still held by the U.S. military.

U.S. investment was crucial to the Cuban economy through the 1950s, and sugar remained the chief export. In 1952, Fulgencio Batista's military coup established a dictatorship that increased corruption and turmoil. Popular opposition was organized into a rebel movement under the leadership of young Fidel Castro. After a two-year guerrilla war, Castro overthrew Batista, who left the country in 1959.

After the revolution, extensive economic and social change took place. Agrarian reform, nationalization of industry and banking, the creation of rural cooperatives, and other reforms were part of Castro's socialist-oriented path of development. These measures clashed with U.S. interests, and Washington, D.C., responded by breaking off relations and imposing a trade embargo that is still in effect.

Cuba, however, enjoyed the support of the Communist world through the 1970s and 1980s. Economic growth was steady, and important advancements were made in education, public health, and social security. The dissolution of the socialist bloc in the early 1990s seriously harmed Cuba's economy and standard of living. The government responded by liberalizing some economic policies and welcoming more international investment. Hopes for better relations with the United States were dashed in 1996 when Cuban jets shot down two U.S. civilian planes near Cuba's territory. Washington soon passed a law designed to punish international firms that do business in Cuba.

PEOPLE

Population

Cuba's population of 10.9 million grows annually at 0.6 percent. More than 70 percent of the people live in urban areas; Havana has 2.1 million residents. Cubans of Spanish descent make up about 66 percent of the population, while 12 percent have Black African ancestry. Another 21.9 percent are of mixed heritage. The remaining 0.1 percent are of Asian origin. The Cuban culture is highly integrated, with each ethnic group influencing society in a variety of ways. More than half of all Cubans are younger than age 30. The Cuban-American community in Florida has some one million members. Cuba's Human Development Index (0.769) ranks it 72d out of 174 nations. People are skilled and educated; given the proper opportunities, they can successfully achieve personal goals.

Language

Spanish is the official language spoken by all Cubans. The slight accent and pronunciation differences between Cuba's three main regions do not inhibit communication. Many words, expressions, and idioms are unique to Cuban society and not used in other Spanish-speaking countries. Some examples are *pelotear* (to pass the buck), *plan jaba* (a special shopping plan for working women), *amarillo* (traffic official), and *rebambaramba* (a free-for-all).

English is popular and a required course in secondary schools. Language teachers may teach private lessons.

Religion

Historically, Cuba has been among the least religious of all Latin American countries. Today, despite constitutionally guaranteed freedom of worship, society is highly secularized. Most people show no preference for organized religion. At the same time, recent years have seen growth in some congregations and a revival of religious devotion. This is due partly to a 1991 change in a policy that had excluded persons with religious beliefs from the Communist Party. The economic crisis has also led some people to seek comfort in churches.

Catholicism is the most prevalent faith, although many people combine it with ideas of African origin to form beliefs known as *Santería*. A number of Protestant churches also function in Cuba, including Baptist, Methodist, and Presbyterian. Spiritualism, emphasizing communication with the dead, and *brujería* (witchcraft) are practiced by small groups.

To operate in Cuba, Churches must register with the government and satisfy rules of association. Religion is not discussed in school, but it can be taught in any of Cuba's 1,800 churches and chapels.

General Attitudes

Cubans are friendly, warm, communicative, enthusiastic, and hospitable. It is uncommon to meet a Cuban who is not outgoing and fond of festivals, music, and dancing. Cubans' sense of humor allows them to joke about almost anything, even hardships. This does not mean Cubans are shallow—indeed they are hardworking—but they face difficulties with a positive attitude. In hard times, they look to friends and family for support. Cubans are patriotic and value their national dignity and their many social achievements. They honor the memories of those who died fighting invaders, counter-revolutionaries, and foreign powers. Cubans are often impassioned in their opinions and will argue their convictions with energy. Men especially like to debate the economy, international politics, and baseball.

Cubans have a casual view of time. Punctuality is not stressed and schedules are not strict. The joy of an event is more important than how long it should last.

Personal Appearance

Most people prefer lightweight, casual clothing. Cleanliness is important, even in the current period of austerity. Women of all ages wear slacks, jeans, short skirts, blouses, and canvas shoes or sandals. Dresses are seen at more formal events. Men wear long pants, jeans, and shirts or T-shirts in everyday situations. More formally, they may wear a *guayabera*, a traditional square-cut shirt. Shorts are popular in urban areas and at the beach, especially among the youth. Primary and secondary school students wear uniforms, as do students in medical colleges.

CUSTOMS AND COURTESIES

Greetings

Men greet with a handshake and *¿Qué tal?* (How are you?). They often shake hands with everyone when entering a home or greeting a group. Most women kiss each other once on the cheek and offer a verbal greeting. Kissing on the cheek is also common between friends of the opposite sex, especially among younger people. Greetings between strangers are brief; friends spend a short time talking about their families or health. Common verbal greetings include *¡Buenos días!* (Good morning), *¡Buenas tardes!* (Good afternoon), *¡Buenas noches!* (Good evening), and *¡Adiós!* (Good-bye). *¡Adiós!* is also a typical greeting when passing someone on the street. When parting, people may say *¡Hasta luego!* (So long).

People usually address others by first name, or they may use a professional title without a surname. Strangers frequently use *Compañero/Compañera* (Comrade), *Señor* (Mr.), and *Señora* (Mrs.). Nicknames are common among friends, acquaintances, and coworkers.

Gestures

Cubans use hand gestures while talking to reinforce ideas and emotions, which makes conversation rather lively. It is not considered rude to interrupt a friend or acquaintance during conversation. Maintaining eye contact while talking is important, especially in a formal situation. The lack of eye contact may be considered a sign of insincerity or spite. People stand close when talking, often touching or tapping each other when making a point.

One beckons with the palm down and fingers together waving inward. Beckoning people with the palm up is considered hostile. Yawning in the presence of others may be interpreted as boredom, so it is polite to cover one's mouth.

Visiting

Cubans are extremely social, and visiting in the home is common. Friends also socialize on the street, while waiting in lines, and at gatherings in neighborhoods and work centers.

Daytime visits are often unannounced but welcome. They may be long or short without too much concern for schedules. Weekends and holidays are the most popular times to visit. Hosts usually offer guests something to drink, such as black coffee, wine, or a soft drink. Declining such offers is not impolite. If visitors arrive at mealtime, hosts politely offer to share the meal, but guests respectfully decline and leave. When rural people visit urban friends, they may take a gift of food; urbanites visiting in rural areas may offer money to help pay expenses related to their stay.

While Cubans enjoy inviting friends over for an evening meal or party, the practice has become less common due to shortages and evening energy blackouts. Such socializing is casual, and guests often bring small gifts of rum, wine, or food to be consumed during the evening.

Eating

The daily meals are *desayuno* (breakfast), *almuerzo* (lunch), and *comida* (dinner). A light breakfast usually includes a cup of black coffee. Most workers and students eat lunch at work or school. The family gets together for dinner, the most important meal.

Table manners vary from home to home. Generally, however, diners keep hands above the table and pleasant conversation accompanies meals. Hosts expect to offer guests second helpings, but guests have the option of declining.

With the exception of expensive home restaurants, all restaurants are state owned. Prices are reasonable, but waits for a table can be long. Most customers leave a tip for the server.

LIFESTYLE

Family

Cubans maintain strong family ties. The nuclear family is standard, but many households include grandparents as well. Extended family members often build homes near one another to remain close. Families rely on each other for assistance when needed. When adult children marry, they usually live with a parent until they can obtain housing, which is in short supply. The average family owns a small house or apartment with all major utilities available.

Women account for 37 percent of the labor force and 55 percent of the country's specialists. They hold 28 percent of leading government and administrative posts. However, traditional values maintain a strong influence on family relations, and consequently, women are also responsible for most household chores and caring for children. This situation is changing among younger couples.

As in most Latin American countries, a person bears two family names: the last name is the mother's family name and the second-to-last name is the father's family name and the person's surname.

Dating and Marriage

Young people have many opportunities to socialize. Couples usually meet at school, youth parties, dances, music festivals, beach outings, movies, and through conversations on park benches. A common, though declining, custom is for a boy to ask a girl's parents for permission to become her formal boyfriend, in which case he is allowed to visit her at home on specific evenings each week. Most adults expect to marry, and most weddings occur for people in their twenties. A civil ceremony is held in an urban wedding palace, followed by a small family party. An increasing number of couples are also having church ceremonies. Common-law marriages are not common. Honeymoons last about a week.

Diet

At present, with a drastic reduction of imports and industrial production, the Cuban diet is based on foods grown locally. *Arroz y frijoles* (rice and beans) is the traditional staple meal. Indeed, rice is served at most meals, along with a favorite food such as potatoes, *boniatos* (sweet potatoes), *yuca* (cassava), *plátanos* (plantains), and tomatoes. Eggs are eaten boiled, fried, or as an omelet (called a *tortilla*). Corn is the basis of many foods, the most popular being *harina de maíz* (cornmeal).

Roast pork, currently a luxury, is the most appreciated meat and is eaten on special occasions. Seafood is eaten in coastal areas. *Tilapia*, a freshwater fish found in Cuba's numerous reservoirs, is also popular. Favorite tropical fruits—mangoes, avocados, guavas, oranges, lemons, pineapples, and papayas— are eaten in season. Sweets (often homemade) are usually eaten as desserts or snacks; ice cream is a favorite but is in short supply. Coffee is generally served sweet and strong after meals.

Recreation

Sports are highly developed in Cuba, which ranked fifth in the 1992 Olympic Games in terms of medals won. The most popular sport is baseball. Boys begin playing in leagues as early as age seven. Adult and college competition is well organized.

Boxing, basketball, swimming, volleyball, and cycling are widely enjoyed. Girls enjoy sports in school, but women usually do not play sports. The game of dominoes is a national pastime, played by males of all ages (especially the retired) in front of homes and practically everywhere else. Cubans dance at discos, go to music festivals or movies, watch videos or television, and converse with each other. They especially cherish music and dancing. The *rumba*, *mambo*, and *cha-cha-cha* originated in Cuba.

Holidays

Liberation Day (1 January) commemorates the revolution of 1958–59; it is preceded by New Year's Eve (31 December) festivities. Other holidays are Labor Day (1 May), the Anniversary of the Attack on the Moncada Garrison in Santiago de Cuba in 1953 (26 July), and the Beginning of the War of Independence from Spain (10 October). Mother's Day (second Sunday in May) is popular.

Religious holidays are not officially recognized, but many are celebrated with feasts and religious services. Christians attend services during Holy Week and on Easter. Often, a particular holiday honors a deity from Catholicism and *Santería* as one-in-the-same. For instance, St. Lazarus's Day (17 December) honors both that Catholic saint and the African god *Babalú Ayé*. A chapel near Havana dedicated to St. Lazarus/*Babalú Ayé* draws tens of thousands of annual pilgrims. St. Barbara's Day (4 December) represents both a

Catholic martyr and the African goddess *Chango*. And *Virgen de la Caridad del Cobre* (8 September) honors the patron saint of Cuba and the African goddess *Ochún*.

Commerce

Most establishments are open from 8:00 or 9:00 A.M. until 5:00 or 6:00 P.M. Banks close at 5:00 P.M. and many stores close on Sunday. In the current crisis, basic foods are rationed and sold in state-owned *bodegas* (neighborhood grocery stores). The state recently has opened stores where customers can purchase hard-to-find items with foreign currency. There are also markets for craftsmen's goods and free markets where farmers sell agricultural products at unregulated prices. Bargaining is common in these private markets.

SOCIETY

Government

Cuba is a socialist state and its constitution regards the Communist party as the leading force of society. The country has 14 provinces and one special municipality (Isle of Youth). Legislative authority is vested in the National Assembly of People's Power, with 589 deputies elected to serve five-year terms. The National Assembly elects from its membership the Council of State as the sitting legislature. Its president is both chief of state and head of government. This post is held by Fidel Castro Ruz. Last reelected in 1993, Castro has governed since 1959. The next elections are in 1998. The voting age is 16. Special commissions nominate approved candidates to run for seats in the Assembly.

Executive authority is vested in the Council of Ministers, appointed by the National Assembly upon the proposal of the head of state. Municipal and provincial assemblies deal with local affairs.

Economy

Cuba's centrally planned economy depended on trade with the Soviet bloc. When trade links were lost in the early 1990s, declining living standards were partly responsible for a large wave of Cuban rafters attempting to reach Florida in 1994.

Cuba's government responded to the crisis by opening free markets for crafts and produce, granting 2.6 million hectares of state land to farming cooperatives, increasing soybean production to boost protein consumption, promoting self-employment, reorganizing some state enterprises, and establishing joint ventures with foreign firms in tourism, mining, communications, and construction. By 1995, conditions had improved somewhat, but further progress may be difficult if relations with the United States do not improve. The estimated real gross domestic product per capita is $3,412.

Agriculture employs about 20 percent of the labor force. The main crops are sugarcane, tobacco, citrus fruit, coffee, rice, grains, and vegetables. Sugar is the most important export, but others include nickel, tobacco, cement, and fruit. Tourism is the second largest source of revenue, and biotechnology and pharmaceuticals are gaining importance. The labor force is mostly skilled: three-fourths of all workers have a secondary or higher education. The official currency is the *peso* (Cu$), but the U.S. dollar is also legal tender (although the United States prohibits sending dollars to Cuba). Mexico and Canada are Cuba's most important trading partners.

Transportation and Communication

In cities, people travel by bicycle or on crowded buses. More than one million bicycles have been sold since 1990. Taxis are scarce. In the countryside, horse-drawn carts are widely used. Trains and buses travel between cities; an extensive highway system connects all parts of the country. Motorcycles are more common than cars, and fuel is rationed.

The telephone system is old; few homes outside Havana have phones. Media operations, including a well-developed film industry, are owned and controlled by the state. Most homes have televisions. There are more than fifty radio stations and two television stations. Several weekly newspapers are published, but a paper shortage restricts circulation. Postal and telegraph services cover the entire country.

Education

Education is a priority in Cuban society, and the state provides free primary, secondary, technical, and higher education to all citizens. Education is mandatory between ages five and twelve (kindergarten through the primary level). More than 90 percent of all children continue with secondary education. Secondary graduates may take college entrance exams or go to a technical training institute. Cuba has an average of one teacher for every 45 inhabitants. The literacy rate is 98.5 percent, the highest in Latin America. Preschool education is available in urban areas. Special schools educate the mentally or physically challenged, and there are schools for students gifted in sports and the arts. Cuba has 46 centers of higher education. Despite a shortage of basic supplies like textbooks and paper, no child is without schooling.

Health

Cuba's health-care system is a government priority; Cuba has some 267 hospitals. More than 420 clinics provide various services, including maternal and infant care. Family doctors are assigned to serve each community, large and small, and there is one doctor for every 260 Cubans. Despite a shortage of medicines and other supplies, Cuba's average life expectancy is 77 years, and the infant mortality rate is 8 per 1,000—both the best in Latin America. More than 20 medical schools and other institutions train health-care workers. When a 1993 outbreak of optic neuropathy affected thousands, the government invited international experts to support Cuban physicians in controlling the disease.

FOR THE TRAVELER

Cuba has an active tourism industry. The United States and Cuba have no formal diplomatic ties. U.S. citizens are prohibited from visiting Cuba without U.S. government permission. A visa from the Cuban government is also required. For information, contact the U.S. Department of Treasury, Office of Foreign Assets Control, Licensing Division, 1500 Pennsylvania Avenue NW, Second Floor Annex, Washington, DC 20220; phone (202) 622–2480. Visa information is available through the Cuban Interests Section of the Swiss Embassy, 2630–2639 16th Street NW, Washington, DC 20009.

---

*A *Culturgram* is a product of native commentary and original, expert analysis. Statistics are estimates and information is presented as a matter of opinion. While the editors strive for accuracy and detail, this document should not be considered strictly factual. It is a general introduction to culture, an initial step in building bridges of understanding between peoples. It may not apply to all peoples of the nation. You should therefore consult other sources for more information.*

Czech Republic

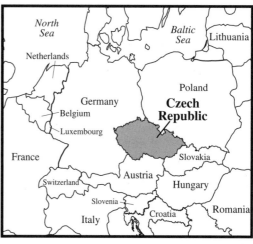

Boundary representations not necessarily authoritative.

BACKGROUND

Land and Climate

Covering 30,387 square miles (78,703 square kilometers), the Czech Republic is just smaller than South Carolina. It is roughly divided between Bohemia in the west and Moravia in the east. Bohemia's rivers flow north to the *Labe* (Elbe) River, while Moravia's rivers flow south to the Danube. The *Vltava* (Moldau) River flows through Prague. Bohemia is slightly more industrialized, while Moravia is known for its agriculture. Rolling hills typify both regions. Agricultural products include wheat, rye, hops, corn, potatoes, and some vineyard grapes. Mountains run along the western and northern borders, as well as in the south. The Bohemian Forest is located on the southwest border.

A continental climate prevails. Summers are warm and sunny; fall and spring tend to run long, with high temperatures ranging between 40°F and 55°F (4–13°C). Winters can be cold and snowy, with temperatures often below freezing.

History

In the fifth century, Slavic tribes began settling the area, and by the middle of the ninth century they lived in a loose confederation known as the Great Moravian Empire. Its brief history ended in 907 with the invasion by the nomadic Magyars (ancestors of today's Hungarians). The Slovak region became subject to Hungarian rule, while Czechs developed the Bohemian Empire, centered in Prague. In the 14th century, under the leadership of Charles IV, Prague became a cultural and political capital that rivaled Paris. In the 15th century, Bohemia was a center of the Protestant Reformation led by Jan Hus, who became a martyr and national hero when he was burned at the stake in 1415 as a heretic. Civil war in Bohemia and events elsewhere in Europe led the Czechs (as well as Hungary and Slovakia) to become part of the Hapsburg (Austro-Hungarian) Empire in 1526.

When the Hapsburg Empire collapsed upon defeat in World War I (1918), Czech and Slovak lands were united to form a new Czecho-Slovak state (the hyphen was dropped in 1920). Tomas Masaryk became the first president. Democracy flourished and affluence began to spread, but the country was not able to withstand German aggression. Hitler first annexed the Sudetenland, a region of German-speaking people, in 1938. By 1939, all Czech lands had fallen into German possession. The Czechoslovak people then suffered through World War II, in which more than 350,000 citizens (250,000 Jews) lost their lives. After the war, three million Germans were forced out of the country.

Liberated in 1945 by Allied forces, Czechoslovakia held elections in 1946 under Soviet auspices. Left-wing parties performed well, and by 1948 the Communists had seized control of the government. The Soviet-style state promoted rapid industrialization in the 1950s. Social and economic policies liberalized in the 1960s in response to a deteriorating quality of life. This led to discussions about easing political restrictions. In 1968, reform-minded Alexander Dubček, a Slovak, assumed leadership and put into motion a series of reforms known as "socialism with a human face." But the Soviet Union-led Warsaw Pact crushed the movement. The Communist Party was purged of liberals and reforms were abolished.

In the 1970s, many dissident groups organized against the regime. Members of these groups joined with workers,

EUROPE

university students, and others in peaceful demonstrations in 1989 in what was called the "Velvet Revolution." A crackdown on a student protest in November 1989 prompted a general strike that led General Secretary Miloš Jakeš to resign. Dubček returned to prominence and was elected leader of Parliament. Václav Havel, dissident playwright and leader of Civic Forum, became president in 1990.

Full multiparty elections under a new constitution were held in 1992. Havel remained president of the federal union, while Václav Klaus became prime minister of the Czech national government. Vladimír Mečiar became prime minister of the Slovak national government. Differences between Slovak and Czech leaders regarding such issues as resource distribution, infrastructure investment, and the course of economic reform led the two governments to agree to split into two sovereign states. Havel resigned, refusing to oversee the dissolution of the country, but he was reelected president of the Czech Republic after the country peacefully split on 1 January 1993. Ties between the countries remain strong.

With widespread support, Klaus launched an impressive program of economic reform that made the Czech Republic the envy of Europe. However, in June 1996 elections Klaus's ruling coalition lost its majority. Klaus formed a three-party minority government a month later.

THE PEOPLE
Population
The Czech Republic has 10.4 million people. About 81 percent are ethnic Bohemian and 13 percent are Moravian. Ethnic Slovaks (3 percent) also live in the republic. The rest (2.5 percent) of the population is comprised of several groups: Poles and Silesians in northern Bohemia; Germans in the west (Sudetenland); and Romanians, Bulgarians, Ukrainians, Russians, and Greeks in the south and east. The Romany ethnic group (Gypsies) is nomadic and difficult to count but officially forms 0.7 percent of the total population. The Romany are subject to intense discrimination throughout Europe and have not integrated into mainstream society.

The Human Development Index (0.872) ranks the Czech Republic 38th out of 174 nations. Most Czechs have good access to health care, education, and economic prosperity needed to make choices in their lives. Adjusted for women, the index (0.858) ranks the Czech Republic 15th out of 130 countries, indicating women earn a comparable share of the nation's income.

Language
Czech is a Slavic language; it is similar to Slovak but also related to others (such as Polish, Croatian, and Russian). Czech uses a Latin alphabet with several distinct accent marks and letters. The marks ˇ, ´, and ° appear over consonants or vowels to soften or lengthen the sound. Minority groups speak their own tongues. Czechs also often speak German, Russian, or English, depending on their generation.

Religion
Although 80 percent of Czechs consider themselves Christians, many were influenced by 40 years of official (Communist) atheism. Therefore, their link to religion may involve more of the country's historical heritage than belief. In addition, Czechs tend to think of worship as a private matter. While they believe in a Universal Being, they may not necessarily be devoted to a religious institution. Still, more than 40 percent belong to the Catholic Church and many are Protestant. The Czech Brethren (a Lutheran/Calvinist group) claims 2 percent of the population as members. Many younger people are joining churches, some of which have been imported or established since 1990.

General Attitudes
Czechs value education, cleverness, social standing, modesty, and humor. Czech humor is dry and ironic rather than slapstick, and jokes and rustic parables are commonly used in conversation. Irony also colors Czech realism, making it seem more like pessimism. While Czechs are individualistic to the degree that they may be stubborn in stating opinions or wishes, society's emphasis is on conformity and cooperation. For instance, community leaders (those who organize others) are held in high esteem. Young people are encouraged to belong to organizations such as the Boy Scouts or sports teams. Professionals (doctors, engineers, etc.) are admired, but so are skilled manual workers.

Moravians and Slovaks are known to be more lighthearted and jovial than Bohemians. Moravians tend to preserve traditional culture through costumes and folk music more than Bohemians. Still, all Czechs pride themselves on their support of the cultural arts. The country has a rich tradition of musical composers, including Dvořák and Smetana. Theater performances, concerts, and exhibits are held throughout the year. In the summer, small towns often sponsor informal, outdoor "forest theaters."

Personal Appearance
European fashions are commonly worn, and the youth wear the latest styles. Jeans and T-shirts are popular. Work attire for men is generally more casual than in some western European nations (e.g., sports jackets instead of suits, or blue overalls or jogging suits instead of shirts and ties). Older women generally do not wear slacks like the younger generation, and they wear hats more often. Adults wear shorts in parks or for recreation but not on city streets. Czechs dress up to attend cultural events; not being properly dressed is frowned upon. People in Moravia still wear traditional national costumes on festival days or for weddings and other special events.

CUSTOMS AND COURTESIES
Greetings
When strangers meet or when a young person greets an older person, they shake hands firmly and say their last names, followed by a verbal greeting, such as *Těší mne* (Pleased to meet you) or *Dobrý den* (Good day). A man usually waits for a woman to extend her hand before shaking. To show respect, one addresses both men and women by their professional titles (engineer, doctor, professor) and last names. It is common to preface the title with *Pán* (sir) or *Paní* (madam) when greeting the person: *Dobrý den, Paní Doktorká Čekanová*. One also uses *Pán* and *Paní* for persons without professional titles. People do not use first names until they are well acquainted, but relatives generally hug upon meeting and address each other by first names, as do young people of the same age.

To say good-bye, one uses the formal *Na schledanou* or the informal *Čau* (Ciao). *Ahoj* is an informal "Hi" and "Bye."

One responds to *Děkuji* (Thank you) with *Prosím* (Please), meaning "You're welcome."

Gestures

People maintain eye contact while conversing. Czechs may often look at or even stare at other people in public, but usually with no ill intentions. People often gesture with their hands to emphasize conversation. They beckon and point with their index finger. When one counts on the fingers, the thumb (not index finger) is number one. Speaking loudly is impolite.

Visiting

Czechs consider the home to be private. They do not often visit one another unannounced; even spontaneous visitors (only relatives and very close friends) call ahead when possible. Others are not invited to a Czech's home for more than a drink or coffee. Most guests invited to dinner are taken to a restaurant; it is an honor to be invited to a home for a meal. Friends often socialize in pubs, coffeehouses, and wine bars.

Czechs remove their shoes when entering a home and leave them in the entryway. Visiting etiquette is fairly formal, but the atmosphere is warm. Guests are offered something to drink or, prior to a meal, hors d'oeuvres. Women guests may offer to help prepare the meal in the kitchen or to clear dishes, but the offer will be politely declined. Invited guests usually bring an odd number of flowers to the hostess. Any type of flower is acceptable, except chrysanthemums (used mostly in funeral arrangements). Small gifts for the children are appreciated. Guests might also bring wine or chocolates for the hosts. Flowers are given to students at graduation.

Eating

Czechs eat three meals a day and often a mid-morning snack. For most families, lunch is the main meal. Dinner and breakfast are light. Women prepare meals, and men might help with cleanup. Few Czech men cook. Plates usually are prepared in the kitchen and carried to the table. The head of the household is served first, unless guests are present. People eat in the continental style, with the fork in the left hand and the knife remaining in the right. Hands, but not elbows, are kept above the table. Depending on the family, there is little dinner conversation unless the head of the household speaks first or special guests are present. The hostess generally offers seconds to guests, but it is not impolite to decline them after commenting on how good the food is.

Most Czechs do not eat out often. In restaurants, mineral water and bread and butter can be ordered, but they do not come with the meal. In pubs, there may be two waiters, one for the drinks and the other for the food. The headwaiter adds up the bill at the table. Drinking and toasting are common for formal and informal events. An empty glass is always refilled. When drinking socially, people do not pour for themselves.

LIFESTYLE

Family

Czech families traditionally are close and tight-knit. Urban families usually are small, rarely with more than two children. Rural families tend to be larger. Both parents generally work outside the home, but women are also responsible for the household and children. Urban housing is in short supply, so many families live in large apartment complexes on the outskirts of the city. Mothers receive several months of paid maternity leave, a subsidy for each birth, and child-care services when they return to work. Grandparents often help with child care, especially when a young couple is just starting out. Parents feel responsible for their adult children until they are financially independent. At the same time, adult children expect to take care of aging parents. Parents and children tend to share more expensive things like cars or *chaty* (cottages) for many years. Pets, especially dogs, are cherished members of many families.

Dating and Marriage

Young people tend to date in groups; they enjoy going to movies or the theater, hiking or camping, attending music festivals, or dancing at discos. Most men are married by the age of 30; women marry a few years earlier. Young couples tend to live with their parents after marriage because of a housing shortage, but they strive to become independent as soon as possible. Most urban weddings are held at city hall, with only the immediate family and closest friends present. A family luncheon or dinner is held afterward at a nearby hotel. Suit jackets and short dresses have been the standard wedding attire, but more formal gowns and tuxedos are being worn today. A church wedding, now legally binding, is becoming increasingly common. Honeymoons are also gaining in popularity. Rural weddings tend to incorporate more people, such as village members. Traditional costumes might be worn and celebrations can last all day.

Diet

Traditional Czech food is heavy and arduous to prepare. In the last decade, a healthier diet (fewer heavy sauces, leaner meat, more vegetables) that is easier to prepare has become more popular. Lunch usually begins with a hearty soup, followed by a main dish of meat and potato or bread dumplings. A common dish is *vepřo-knedlo-zelí* (pork roast, dumplings, and sauerkraut). Ham on bread and sausages in buns are popular snack foods that can be purchased from sidewalk vendors.

A wide variety of breads and bakery items are available. Breakfast usually consists of rolls, coffee cake, butter, jam, and coffee. Many desserts are made from fruit. Beer, soda, and juice are common drinks.

Recreation

Czechs are known for their love of nature, and hardly a weekend goes by without forests, fields, mountains, and lakes being filled with Czechs (especially urban residents). A surprising number of families own cottages. Urban families often tend garden plots of flowers, fruit trees, and vegetables that are either near their cottage or in communal garden areas on city outskirts. Camping, hiking, swimming in lakes, gathering mushrooms and berries, and snow skiing are all favorite outdoor activities.

Popular sports are soccer, tennis, and ice hockey. Leisure pursuits include watching television, going to movies or concerts, dancing, taking walks, or getting together with friends. Gardening and home-improvement projects are also widely enjoyed. In the evening, men often gather in pubs to drink beer and talk, while women visit close friends at home. In smaller towns, people socialize while doing errands.

Czechs enjoy touring in a car or taking bus tours. Forty years of travel restrictions led to a pent-up desire for travel outside of the republic. However, because the currency is not yet convertible, there is an annual limit on how much one can exchange for other currencies. This limits vacations to short weekend trips or requires vacationers to go where the bill can be paid (usually in advance) with the Czech *koruna*.

Holidays

Public holidays include New Year's Day, Easter Monday, End of World War II (8 May), Cyril and Methodius's Day (5 July), Jan Hus Day (6 July), Founding of the First Republic in 1918 (28 October), and Christmas (24–26 December). Cyril and Methodius are honored for introducing Christianity and creating the Cyrillic alphabet (used before the current Latin alphabet). Christmas Eve is the most important part of Christmas, and people eat carp for dinner in honor of their Catholic heritage. They also eat *vánočka*, a fruit bread, in the days leading to Christmas and during Lent. Small marzipan candies or paper cards in the shape of pigs are given in the new year for good luck.

All Saints' Day (1 November), Velvet Revolution Day (17 November), and St. Nicholas Day (6 December) are celebrated but are not days off from work. Each village or town also celebrates a day for its patron saint with fairs, dancing, feasting, and Mass.

Commerce

The workday usually begins between 7:00 and 8:00 A.M. and ends between 3:00 and 4:00 P.M. Businesses and offices often close for lunch. Women might shop for fresh foods during this time. Government offices usually are open until 6:00 P.M., but people often leave for home by 4:00 P.M. Since 1989, more stores in town centers have been staying open later in the evening. Czechs shop weekly for groceries and other items, but they rely on small shops and market stalls for daily purchases of bread, fruit, and vegetables.

SOCIETY

Government

The Czech Republic is a parliamentary democracy divided into eight regions. The president is head of state. The prime minister is head of government and leads Parliament's majority party or coalition. Parliament (or National Council) is composed of a Senate (81 seats) and a Chamber of Deputies (200 seats). The voting age is 18. The Civic Democratic Party, Christian Democratic Party, and Civic Democratic Alliance form Václav Klaus's minority government coalition. It is opposed by the Social Democrats.

Economy

With Klaus's measured approach, the Czech Republic has enjoyed success in its transition from a planned to a free-market economy. When the country applied for membership in the European Union in January 1996, it already met most of the basic criteria for monetary union. Strong fiscal policies have enabled the government to balance its budget the last four years. Inflation remains high (about 9 percent).

Real gross domestic product per capita is $7,690. Low salaries have made it hard for people to earn a living, but most at least have jobs. Unemployment is 3 percent (0 percent in Prague). Private enterprises have absorbed many who were laid off by sagging industries. Exports of manufactured goods are booming due to low labor costs and high quality. Agriculture is important to the domestic economy, and the country is nearly self-sufficient in food. Tourism is especially important; 70 million people visited the country in 1993 alone.

Czechs form a cohesive, well-educated, and hardworking labor force that has attracted substantial foreign investment. At the same time, the country's privatization program concentrates on selling stock to Czechs rather than outside interests or large firms. This means everyone has a stake in economic performance. The currency is the Czech *koruna* (Kc).

Transportation and Communication

Public transportation is extensive and reliable in most urban areas and between towns and cities. The fleet of trams, buses, and trains is aging, and the industry is being pressed to privatize and modernize. This will increase prices and decrease service along unprofitable routes. More people are buying cars, and the Czech-manufactured *Škoda* is popular.

Daily newspapers are widely read, as is an abundance of other printed media. Many homes have cable television and access to international programming in addition to local broadcasts. People without phones in the home have access to public phones. Post offices sell transit tickets, accept utility payments, and provide many other services; postal delivery is efficient.

Education

The literacy rate is 99 percent. Young children go to nursery school or kindergarten, but compulsory education begins at age six. Public education is free. Primary education used to last for eight years, followed by four years of secondary school. In 1994, the structure changed so grade school lasts five years. At age 11, children begin eight years of secondary school in one of three basic tracks: academic (leading to university studies), technical (for learning an occupation such as electrician, mason, etc.), or teaching. Two-year, postsecondary job training programs are increasingly popular.

Higher education was free, but new university students must now pay tuition. There are several institutions of higher learning, the oldest of which is Charles University, founded in 1348.

Health

Health care is universal and the government covers most costs. People pay a minimal insurance premium and pay for some prescriptions. Employers assist in covering these costs. Pollution is the most serious threat to health. The infant mortality rate is 9 per 1,000; life expectancy ranges from 69 to 77 years.

FOR THE TRAVELER

U.S. travelers do not need a visa for stays of up to 30 days, but a passport is required. Czech architecture, which remained relatively unscathed during World War I and II, rivals that of any in Europe. For information about travel to the Czech Republic, contact your travel agency or the Czech Embassy, 3900 Spring of Freedom Street NW, Washington, DC 20008; phone (202) 274–9100.

A *Culturgram* is a product of native commentary and original, expert analysis. Statistics are estimates and information is presented as a matter of opinion. While the editors strive for accuracy and detail, this document should not be considered strictly factual. It is a general introduction to culture, an initial step in building bridges of understanding between peoples. It may not apply to all peoples of the nation. You should therefore consult other sources for more information.

CULTURGRAM '97

Kingdom of
Denmark

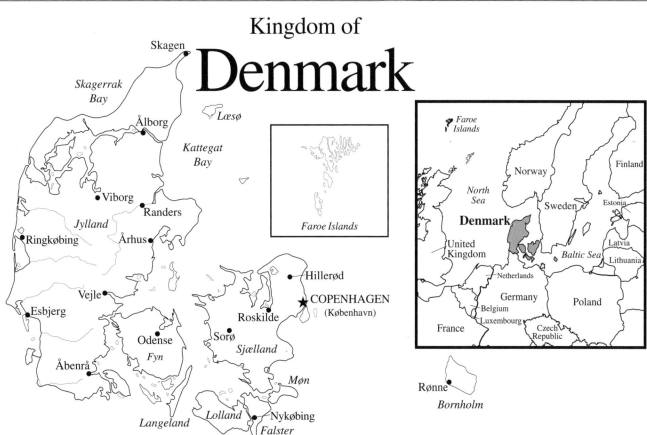

Boundary representations not necessarily authoritative.

BACKGROUND

Land and Climate

Located between the North and Baltic Seas, Denmark is a flat country with low to gently rolling plains. It consists of more than four hundred islands, of which only ninety are inhabited. Its total area is about twice the size of Massachusetts and covers 16,629 square miles (43,070 square kilometers). The largest landmasses include *Jylland* (Jutland), connected to the European continent, and the islands of *Sjælland* (Zealand), *Fyn* (Funen), *Lolland*, *Falster*, and *Bornholm*. Fertile agricultural land dominates the country's landscape of moors, lakes, and woodlands. Moderated by the warming influence of the Gulf Stream, Denmark's temperate maritime climate is usually cool, humid, and overcast. Winters are windy, but mild compared to other Scandinavian countries. In January, high temperatures average about 34°F (2°C). Summers are cool, with July daily temperature highs averaging 72°F (22°C).

History

The Kingdom of Denmark (*Kongeriget Danmark*) has been a monarchy as long as it has existed. During the rule of the Vikings (c. 750–1035), Denmark was a great power, but it is not known exactly when and by whom it was controlled in the first decades of that time period. The first known king was Gorm the Old, who ruled in the early 900s. His son, Harald Bluetooth, united the country under Christianity and ruled in the latter half of the 900s. Gorm's grandson, Canute the Great,

commanded a vast empire that included England until 1035. Queen Margrethe I united Denmark, Norway, and Sweden in the Union of Kalmar in 1397. Sweden left the union in 1523 and Norway in 1814. King Frederik VII signed a liberal constitution in 1849, making the country a constitutional monarchy rather than an autocracy. Some territory was lost to Prussia (Germany) in 1864, but the country remained stable.

Denmark was neutral during World War I, but Nazi Germany occupied it during World War II. Denmark joined the North Atlantic Treaty Organization (NATO) in 1949 and the European Community (now European Union, or EU) in 1973. During the 1970s and 1980s, Denmark concentrated on maintaining its social welfare system, broadening opportunities, and increasing the standard of living. During the mid-1980s, Denmark became interested in environmental protection and has since passed some of the world's toughest environmental legislation.

In 1992, Denmark rejected the Maastricht treaty that would have led to a common currency and stronger political ties within the EU. In 1993, voters accepted a modified version of the treaty granting Denmark exemption from the European single currency, European citizenship, a unified European military, and the elimination of borders. Although they see the benefits of the EU's internal market, Danes are somewhat skeptical and fearful of integration. Half of all Danes support European integration, but even some supporters fear that small countries such as Denmark will be overpowered by larger EU nations. They worry that expansion of the EU's powers would weaken Denmark's national identity, independence, and legislation, including its tough environmental standards.

THE PEOPLE
Population
Denmark's population of 5.2 million is growing annually at 0.2 percent. Fears that the population will someday decline seem to be influencing the Danes, as a slight increase in births has occurred over the past few years. The majority of the population lives in urban areas. In Denmark, most people (99 percent) are Danish. Greenland and the Faroe Islands are part of the Danish Kingdom but are autonomous nations. These areas have small populations: 58,000 and 49,000, respectively. The Faroese belong to the old Nordic, and mostly Danish, ethnic background. The Greenlanders are Eskimos or are of mixed Eskimo and European origin. Because these groups are autonomous, with their own languages and cultural heritages, they are only mentioned here as part of Denmark's kingdom; their cultures are not discussed.

Denmark's Human Development Index (0.920) ranks it 16th out of 174 countries. Adjusted for women, the index ranks Denmark 4th out of 130 countries. Excellent access to health care, education, and economic prosperity affords men and women many opportunities and choices in their lives.

Language
Danish is the official language. Because Danish is a Scandinavian language, Swedes and Norwegians can understand its written form. But spoken Danish is more difficult for other Scandinavians to understand because of differences in pronunciation and intonation. Vocabulary also differs. Members of a very small German-speaking minority live along the border with Germany, but they also speak Danish. English is widely understood and spoken; in fact, it is part of the school curriculum after the fifth grade. German is also a popular language to study in school.

Religion
The Evangelical Lutheran Church is Denmark's national church. Its members, who comprise 91 percent of the population, are automatically enrolled and support it through taxation. Membership is expected and not considered a choice by Danes unless they belong to another religion.

The Lutheran Church and its value system permeate daily life in Denmark, although with little visibility. Danes do not generally attend church outside of Christmas and Easter, when attendance is very high. Although fewer than 5 percent attend Sunday meetings, most Danes still participate in religious ceremonies such as baptism and confirmation. Tolerance is extended to most other religious groups, such as Islam, whose numbers are increasing due to emigration.

The Lutheran influence on Danish values, public school curricula, and everyday life has been partially credited to N. F. S. Grundtvig, a Danish 19th-century bishop and poet who revitalized the Danish church and founded the movement *Grundtvigianism* or "the happy Lutheranism."

General Attitudes
Denmark's high standard of living reflects a progressive and egalitarian attitude. Danes have a strong tendency to create equality by supporting weaker members of society. Because of their respect for every citizen's right to a good life, they are willing to share responsibility for their nation's social welfare through heavy taxes. This attitude has also encouraged their contributions to the development of Third World countries. Danes see the government as the benevolent supporter of all of its members and know they can count on access to a high level of social services.

Danes are known for their tolerance of other people and diverse points of view. They admire individuals with a friendly attitude, a sense of humor, intelligence, sociability, personal stamina, integrity, and an open mind. They also appreciate those who do not take themselves too seriously. Their European neighbors perceive them as socially progressive, self-confident, relaxed and friendly, and liberal. Danes are considered to be less formal and introverted than those in other Scandinavian countries. Danes are also well educated and respected for their accomplishments in science, art, literature, and architecture.

Most matters of common wisdom directly relate to the Lutheran viewpoint. A love for understatement, rather than exaggeration, prevails. In Jylland, for example, rich people are known to remove the labels off their expensive cars and to dress down rather than up.

Personal Appearance
Clothing varies according to the season. However, the windy and rainy climate makes waterproof clothing (and sturdy shoes or boots) essential year-round. As the saying goes, "There is no such thing as bad weather. You just have to dress right." From late fall to early spring, wool coats and knitted sweaters are important to the Danish wardrobe. With the arrival of warmer temperatures and brighter days, Danes enjoy wearing lighter fabrics and jackets, particularly in pastel colors.

In general, Danes wear relaxed, casual clothes and avoid flashy dress. Even at the most elegant restaurants, men are not required to wear a jacket and tie, though most do. Danes follow general European fashion trends. Businessmen wear suits. Professional women are expected to dress fashionably; both skirts and jackets or dressy pants are acceptable. Dressing up for special occasions is expected.

CUSTOMS AND COURTESIES
Greetings
Although usually informal, Danes shake hands when introduced to strangers, at the end of business meetings, and on formal occasions. However, this gesture is not considered necessary when greeting friends. Young people and close acquaintances usually greet each other with a nod or a wave and say *Dav* or *Davs* (pronounced DOWSE), which is like saying "Hello." The youth also say *Hej* (pronounced HEY) or even "Hi" when greeting or parting. The term for "Good day" is *Goddag*. Using a person's first name is the most common way of addressing others. Only in rare formal situations do people use last names. Even managers and university professors are usually addressed by first name.

Gestures
Danes appreciate courtesy in all interactions. Eye contact is important during conversation. Danes generally do not use many hand gestures. The few gestures used include "thumbs

up" to signal "well done" or a circle formed with the thumb and index finger to indicate appreciation. Yawning or coughing without covering the mouth is impolite. Keeping hands in one's pockets during conversation is also considered rude. Displaying affection in public is accepted to a certain point. It is considered polite to give one's seat to pregnant women or the elderly. Most women allow men to open doors for them. Busy stores often have an automatic queue or number system for customers standing in line.

Visiting

Proper etiquette is important when visiting. Except when calling on close friends, Danes always plan visits in advance; they never arrive unannounced. Most invitations are for dinner or for a cup of coffee, which includes some kind of cake or biscuit. Because of the weather and the dark winters, Danes take great pride in keeping a nice and cozy home. They enjoy having visitors in their homes and do their best to make guests feel welcome; however, one should not follow a host into other rooms unless invited. Guests should arrive on time and follow the host's suggestions of where to sit. It is considerate to bring a gift to the hostess, such as flowers, wine, or chocolates, or something for children, nothing expensive. Leaving directly after a meal is impolite, and conversing about one's personal life is avoided.

Although most Danes socialize in the home, young people enjoy socializing at cafes, which in urban areas are gaining popularity among people of all ages. Socializing is also common at local community clubs known as *foreninger*. These clubs are based on a wide range of interests such as hobbies, sports, political and professional organizations, etc.

Eating

For many busy families, dinner is the only occasion during the day to meet and discuss family matters. Most families make an effort to have dinner together every evening. Danes eat in the continental style, with the fork in the left hand and the knife remaining in the right. At family meals, the father and mother sit at opposite ends of the table. Everyone is seated and served before anyone begins to eat. A parent will often say *Vær så god* (Please, eat well) to begin the meal, especially if guests are present. When passing and receiving food, one might say *Vær så god* and *Tak* (Thank you).

Hosts customarily offer their guests second helpings, as it is their duty to see that the guests are satisfied. One does not leave the table until the hostess rises. Then, upon leaving, the guest thanks the hostess for the meal by saying *Tak for mad!* (Thanks for the meal!). In restaurants, a service charge is included in the bill, but some people also leave a small tip.

LIFESTYLE

Family

Danish families are generally small, close-knit, and stable. More than one-third of children are born out of wedlock, often to couples living together. With women making up 47 percent of the workforce, both father and mother usually work outside the home. Government-funded day-care centers are crucial to working mothers. Women in the workforce get a six-month paid maternity leave; men get an optional two weeks. As the mother also shares the burden of earning an income, the father is increasingly expected to share household duties. Parents usually are liberal and allow their children a large measure of freedom in making decisions for themselves. As an ethnically homogeneous people, 65 percent of Danes have surnames that end in -*sen* (Hansen, Christensen, Andersen, etc.).

Dating and Marriage

Dating begins by age 15. Youth enjoy dancing, sporting activities, and going to movies. Today, young Danes seldom get engaged. Most live together before deciding to marry. Although a large number of couples have children outside of marriage, they generally decide to marry after a while. Weddings are held in either a church or a town hall. Rice throwing and dancing the bridal waltz are important wedding traditions. About one in four marriages ends in divorce.

Diet

Breakfast consists of coffee or tea, pastries or rolls, cheese, eggs or cereal, and milk. For lunch, Danes enjoy traditional open-faced sandwiches known as *smørrebrød*. Pumpernickel bread, known as *rugbrød* or "rye bread" is the traditional bread used for sandwiches. *Smørrebrød* is often served with slices of salami, *frikadeller* (Danish meatballs), hard-boiled eggs, or liver paste and topped with cucumber slices, dill, or parsley. Staple foods include pork roast (a favorite), fish, beans, brussels sprouts, potatoes, various fresh vegetables, and breads such as wheat and "rye."

For dinner, Danes enjoy dishes such as *frikadeller* or *hakkebøf* (Danish hamburger) served with gravy, white potatoes, pickled red beets, and a salad. Salads are becoming a more popular part of dinner. *Bøf* (hamburger steak with a brown sauce and fried onions) and *frokostbord* (a cold buffet of many different foods) are also favorites. Popular desserts include fruit, apple cobbler, ice cream, and sweet waffles or pancakes served with ice cream. For Christmas, Danes enjoy goose or pork roast, which is broiled until its skin is crisp. At Easter, lamb roast is served. Favorite drinks include coffee, tea, milk, beer, soft drinks, and mineral water.

Recreation

Soccer is by far the most popular spectator sport in Denmark. Danes also enjoy handball, badminton, swimming, sailing, rowing, and jogging. Among women, gymnastics, handball, horseback riding, and badminton are popular. Watching television, going to the movies, and reading are popular leisure activities.

Danes pride themselves on their attention to culture. Music, theater, ballet, and other cultural activities are popular. Copenhagen is home to a large number of jazz artists. Well-known Danish writers include Hans Christian Andersen, author of "The Ugly Duckling," and Isak Dinesen (Karen Blixen), author of the novel *Out of Africa*. Danes like to travel. During vacation, families enjoy traveling throughout Europe by car and camping along the way.

Holidays

Danes enjoy great holiday traditions. For example, on New Year's Eve people attend parties, listen to the queen's and the prime minister's annual speeches, wait for Copenhagen's City Hall bells to mark midnight, and then light fireworks to welcome the new year.

Other traditions follow throughout the year. On 5 January, the eve of Twelfth Night, Danes light the Christmas tree for the last time. In February or March, Danes participate in Mardi Gras–type activities during *Fastelavn*. At Easter, people take a long Easter holiday (Thursday–Monday) to eat, drink a special potent Easter beer, and have family gatherings. Queen Margrethe's Birthday (16 April) is a school holiday, and Constitution Day (5 June) is a half holiday. Although they celebrate Christmas over three days, Danes enjoy Christmas Eve night the most. With the Christmas tree lit, they sing songs while dancing in a circle around the tree. They later exchange gifts and eat a special meal.

Commerce

The Danish workweek, one of the shortest in the EU, averages 32 hours. Businesses are usually open from 8:00 A.M. to 4:00 or 5:00 P.M., Monday through Friday. Shops open at 9:00 or 10:00 A.M. and close around 5:30 P.M., except on Thursday or Friday when they stay open until 7:00 P.M. and Saturday when they close at 2:00 P.M. On the first and last Saturday of the month, shops are open until 4:00 P.M. Wages and working conditions are determined jointly by employer and employee organizations for two-year periods. Each worker receives five weeks' paid vacation each year.

SOCIETY

Government

Denmark is a constitutional monarchy. The 1849 constitution (revised in 1953) gave the monarchy and Parliament joint legislative authority. The monarch must sign all legislation passed by Parliament, but executive power rests with the prime minister. Queen Margrethe II presides over the Council of State and performs numerous other duties as well. She came to the throne in 1972 as the first female monarch to rule since Margrethe I. Between 1513 and 1972, all kings were named either Christian or Frederik. The crown prince's name is Frederik.

Parliament is called the *Folketing*. Elections are held at least every four years and those older than age 18 may vote. Both Greenland and the Faroe Islands have representatives in Parliament. Prime Minister Poul Nyrup Rasmussen was reelected in 1994. The main parties are the Social Democratic Party, Conservative Party, and Liberal Party.

Economy

Denmark has a shortage of natural resources, but it has been able to rely on its high-quality agricultural produce for revenue. About 60 percent of the land is arable, employing 6 percent of the population in agricultural pursuits and producing 15 percent of the nation's exports. Meat, beer, dairy products, and fresh and processed fish are also shipped around the world. Economic diversification has allowed manufacturing to become the most important exporting sector. Small and medium-sized companies are most prominent, producing furniture, medical goods, and machinery. Lego building blocks originated in Denmark and are known worldwide.

The economy grew 4 percent in 1994. Inflation is 2 percent and unemployment is at 12 percent. Real gross domestic product per capita is $19,080. With one of the highest standards of living in the world, Denmark also has one of the highest tax rates. For example, taxes and duties on a new car cause its price to triple. The currency is the Danish *krone* (DKr).

Transportation and Communication

Although personal automobiles are important, bicycles are also a primary source of transportation for many Danes. Bicycles have been a popular means of commuting to work and an integral part of city life for decades. Some cities even have special bicycle paths along the busiest streets and traffic lights especially designed for bikers. Rail traffic, bus lines, and ferry services also continue to meet the transportation needs of the country. Copenhagen has a rapid-transit system for daily commuters. The Great Belt waterway, the bridge-tunnel system connecting the islands of Fyn and Sjælland, is expected to open for trains in 1997 and for motorists in 1998. When completed, it will be the site of the world's largest suspension bridge. A bridge between Copenhagen and Malmöe, Sweden, is expected to open in the year 2000.

All communications systems are modern and efficient. Denmark has two national television stations: one state-owned television channel and the other partially funded by commercials. Most Danes access television stations in other countries through cable networks or their own satellite dishes. The majority of households receive at least one daily newspaper.

Education

Primary education is free and compulsory for nine years at the *Folkeskole* (People's School). Among other required courses, students must study a foreign language. About two-thirds then choose practical training schools for job training, and the rest choose a secondary school to prepare for a college education. Entrance to universities is determined by a highly competitive examination, but the education is free. Denmark was a pioneer in the community college (*Folkeshøjskole*) concept. Today, *Folkeshøjskoler* instruct resident students in such subjects as literature, history, sports, photography, religion, etc. The focus is on personal development without exams. The adult literacy rate is 99 percent. Denmark ranks among the highest in the world in per capita expenditures on education.

Health

Health care is provided through a comprehensive socialized medicine system. Each citizen may choose a family doctor to coordinate services, nearly all of which are provided free of charge (paid for by taxes). Danes boast a life expectancy of between 73 and 79 years. The infant mortality rate is 7 per 1,000. Medicine is available at a low cost. A few can get medicine free of charge.

FOR THE TRAVELER

While passports are required, U.S. citizens do not need visas when staying less than three months in Scandinavia. Denmark offers a variety of interesting sights, from Legoland (a theme park with giant Lego statues and structures) to castles and clean beaches. For more information, contact the Danish Tourist Board, 655 Third Avenue, New York, NY 10017; phone (212) 949–2333; or the Royal Danish Embassy, 3200 Whitehaven Street NW, Washington, DC 20008.

Dominican Republic

Boundary representations not necessarily authoritative.

BACKGROUND

Land and Climate

The Dominican Republic occupies the eastern two-thirds of the island of Hispaniola, which it shares with Haiti. Covering 18,815 square miles (48,730 square kilometers), it is about twice the size of New Hampshire. The central mountain range, Cordillera Central, boasts the highest point in the Caribbean, Pico Duarte, at just higher than 10,000 feet (3,048 meters). The Cibao Valley lies in the heart of the country and is the major agricultural area.

This nation has a variety of landscapes, from deserts in the southwest to alpine forests in the central mountains. Sugarcane fields spread over coastal plains in the north and east, and coconut plantations cover most of the tropical peninsula of Samaná. Pebble beaches under rocky cliffs afford spectacular views on the southern coast. Elsewhere, white sand beaches and warm waters attract tourists to resort areas.

Weather generally is tropical, warm, and humid, especially in summer months and along southern and eastern coasts. A dry, desert-like climate, due to deforestation and little rainfall, prevails in the western and southwestern regions. Rainy seasons may vary in different parts of the country, but they generally are in the late spring and early fall.

History

In pre-Columbian times, Arawaks and Tainos occupied the island. The arrival of Christopher Columbus in 1492 brought Christianity, colonization, slavery, and disease, decimating the native population within decades. With the vanishing indigenous workforce came the increased importation of West Africans to provide cheap labor for mines, sugar plantations, and cattle farms.

The first permanent European settlement in the New World was established in 1496 as Santo Domingo, the city from which Spain set out to conquer the Americas. Here stands the first New World university and Catholic Church building. Santo Domingo's Colonial Zone is one of the great treasures of Spanish America today, with many original buildings intact and restored.

In 1697, the western portion (now Haiti) of Hispaniola was given to France. In 1795, the entire island was ceded. Rebellious slaves seized Santo Domingo in 1801 and established Haiti as the first independent country in Latin America. The resulting Haitian domination of the Dominicans (1822–44) left a legacy of mistrust and strained relations that still endures. The Dominicans declared independence in 1844. Spain returned intermittently between local attempts at government. After an occupation by U.S. Marines (1918–24), a constitutional government was established.

The Trujillo era followed, bringing the country under a military dictatorship. Rafael Leonidas Trujillo gained the presidency in 1930 and ruled for three decades until he was assassinated in 1961. His merciless persecution of Haitians in the late 1930s further added to the list of grievances between the two countries. His death brought a division of the army, civilian unrest, and political revolt. U.S. Marines and an inter-American peacekeeping force stepped in (1965). With stability restored, elections were held and in 1966 the constitutional government was reestablished. Continuing under this system, today's Dominican Republic is the largest and most populous democracy in the Caribbean region.

An ally of Trujillo, Joaquín Balaguer, was appointed president in 1960. For the next three decades, power rested in either his hands or those of rival Juan Bosch (of the Dominican Liberation Party). As head of the Social Christian Reformist Party, Balaguer narrowly won the 1994 elections and began his seventh term in office. Constitutional reforms called for elections two years later but did not allow Balaguer to run for an eighth term. In June 1996, centrist Leonel Fernández of the Dominican Liberation Party was elected president.

THE PEOPLE

Population

The population is about 7.8 million. More than one million of these people live full- or part-time in New York City and are called *Dominican Yorks*. Nearly 40 percent of the population is younger than age 16. The rural population is steadily decreasing through migration to cities. Mixed-race people account for 73 percent of the total population, while 16 percent is Caucasian and 11 percent black. The mixed-race group is a combination of Spaniards and other Europeans, descendants of West African slaves, and descendants of natives. A Haitian minority is included in the black population.

The Human Development Index (0.705) ranks the Dominican Republic 96th out of 174 countries. Adjusted for women, the index (0.590) ranks the Republic 69th out of 130 countries. Although the people's basic needs are met, most (particularly women) do not have access to economic prosperity.

Language

The official language is Spanish, but Caribbean phrases, accents, and regional expressions give it a distinct personality. For example, when eating, people request *un chin* instead of the Spanish *un poquito* (a little bit) of something. Many people drop the *s* at the end of words, turning *dos* (two) into *do'*. Cibao Valley residents, or *Cibaeños* may pronounce the *r, l,* and *i* differently. The formal Spanish form of address for "you" (*usted*) is used, but urban people prefer the more familiar *tú*. Some Creole is spoken near the Haitian border and in the *bateys* (sugarcane villages) where many Haitian workers live.

Religion

Dominicans are 95 percent Catholic by record, but a much smaller number regularly attends church or follows a strict doctrine. Rural residents might combine Catholic traditions with local practices and beliefs. Although Dominicans are fairly secular, Catholic traditions are evident in daily life. Some children are taught to "ask blessings" of their parents and other relatives upon seeing them. They might say *Bendición, tía* (Bless me, aunt), and the response is *Dios te bendiga* (May God bless you).

Evangelical Christian, Seventh-Day Adventist, Latter-day Saint (Mormon), and other denominations also exist throughout the country. A Jewish colony in Sosúa dates from World War II immigration policies that welcomed refugees.

General Attitudes

Dominicans are warm, friendly, outgoing, and gregarious. They are curious about others and forthright in asking personal questions. Children are rarely shy. *Machismo* permeates society, especially among rural and low-income groups, with males enjoying privileges not accorded to females. A proud and aggressive attitude is admired in sports, games, or business, and many people have a sharp entrepreneurial sense. That does not mean, however, that business etiquette is aggressive.

The common expression *Si Dios quiere* (If God wishes) may make Dominicans appear fatalistic or indifferent to goals. However, it more fully expresses the attitude that personal power is intertwined with one's place in the family, community, and grand design of Deity. Friends and relationships are more important than schedules, so being late for appointments and spending time socializing instead of working are socially acceptable.

Confianza (trust) is highly valued and not quickly or easily gained by outsiders. Borrowing is common, and although an item may be forgotten and never returned, everyone is generous and helpful. Class divisions, most evident in larger cities, are economic, social, and political, favoring historically prominent families. Light skin and smooth hair are preferred over strong African features, but most social relationships are not openly affected by race.

Personal Appearance

Dominicans are clean and well-groomed. They take pride in their personal appearance and place importance on dressing well. Dominicans draw on New York fashions, wearing the latest in dresses, jeans, or athletic shoes. Clothes tend to be dressy, always clean and well pressed, with bright colors, shiny fabrics, and for some people, a lot of jewelry. Jeans and short skirts are acceptable for women in urban areas, but dresses or skirts and blouses are more common in the countryside. A special event, such as a town meeting, always requires dressing up. Men wear long pants and stylish shirts, except at the beach or if doing manual labor. Professional men wear business suits or the traditional *chacabana*, a white shirt worn over dark trousers. Children are also dressed up, especially for church or visiting.

CUSTOMS AND COURTESIES

Greetings

Men shake hands firmly when they greet. One offers a wrist or elbow if one's hand is dirty. Friends may also embrace. Most women kiss each other on both cheeks. A man with the *confianza* of a woman will also kiss her. A handshake and *¿Cómo está usted?* (How are you?) is a common formal greeting. The *usted* is dropped for more casual situations. It is polite to ask about a person's family. *¡Hola!* is an informal "Hi," as is *¡Saludos!* Adults, particularly in the *campo* (countryside), often address each other as *compadre* (for men) or *comadre* (for women). One might not greet a stranger on the street, but one would never enter a room without greeting everyone present. Nor would a person leave without saying good-bye to everyone.

Formal introductions are rare, but professional titles are used to address respected persons. Older and more prominent people may be addressed as *Don* (for men) or *Doña* (for women), with or without their first names.

Gestures

Dominicans are animated in conversation and have many gestures. They point with puckered lips instead of a finger. Wrinkling the nose indicates one does not understand, rubbing fingers and the thumb together refers to money, and an upright wagging forefinger means "no." To express disapproval, one points (with lips) at the object and rolls the eyes. "Come here" is indicated with the palm down and fingers together waving inward. One also says "psssst" to get another's attention. To hail a taxi or bus, one wags a finger or fingers (depending on the number of passengers needing a ride) in the direction one is going. Numbers are often expressed with one's fingers instead of with words. Patrons may clap to request a check in a restaurant.

Sitting with legs apart is unladylike, and most women ride "sidesaddle" on the backs of motorcycles. Personal space is limited; touching is normal and crowding is common.

Visiting

Visiting is an important form of social recreation, especially in rural areas and poor *barrios* (neighborhoods). Visits in the home are common, but much socializing also takes place in public (while shopping, washing, and so forth). Women often get together in the kitchen. A visit may be long or short and may occur at any time, usually without prior notice. Urbanites with telephones may call ahead, but whether expected or not, company is always genuinely welcomed. In rural areas doors are kept open; people consider it strange to close them and not accept visitors. To Dominicans, privacy is unimportant; they perceive the desire for solitude as sadness and equate being alone with being lonely. Sitting in *mesadoras* (rocking chairs) talking or just sharing time is common. Nearly all homes have *mesadoras*. Hosts offer visitors something to drink (coffee or juice) and invite them to eat if mealtime is near. Refusing such offers is not impolite.

If guests interrupt (or passersby happen upon) someone eating, the person will immediately and sincerely invite them to share what is left by saying *A buen tiempo* (You've come at a good time). Guests may decline by saying *Buen provecho* (Enjoy), or they may sit down and eat.

Eating

The main meal, *comida,* is served at midday and often lasts two hours. Families prefer eating at home. Urban workers unable to return home may eat at inexpensive cafés or buy from vendors. *Desayuno* (breakfast) is usually light: sweetened coffee and bread, and a bit more in urban areas. *Cena* (the evening meal) is also light, often not more than a snack or leftovers from *comida*. Guests are served first, and sometimes separately and more elaborately. Table conversation is often lively. Dining out is only popular among those who can afford it. Service is included in the bill.

LIFESTYLE

Family

Family ties are important. Extended families are common, especially in rural areas and poor *barrios*. Many households are led by women—widows, women who are divorced, women whose husbands work elsewhere, or older women with adult children and grandchildren. Women, men, and often boys all work outside the home. The boys shine shoes or sell snacks on the streets. Large families are normal, and many rural villages are composed of interrelated families. Within the extended family, informal adoption is common, with other family members taking in and raising children whose parents need help. Likewise, siblings raised by one

mother may have different fathers, but all children are cared for equally. Cousins are often as close as siblings. Some men have more than one wife and family. Smaller, nuclear families are more common among the educated urban population.

Most families live in small houses, either rented or self-built. They may be constructed of cement, wood, or palm bark. They are brightly painted, have cement or dirt floors, and are covered with zinc roofs. Electricity and running water are luxuries. Affluent urban houses are larger and often have walled and landscaped grounds. Urban apartments are becoming popular, as are newly constructed condominiums.

Dating and Marriage

Attending movies, discos, dances, baseball games, and sitting on park benches are social activities for couples. Dating is relatively open and increasingly free of parental control. Girls are more closely supervised than boys and they often go out in groups. Rural couples might have a sibling tagging along as chaperone. Marriages are often common-law (*por la ventana*), but many couples also marry in a church or civil ceremony. Elaborate urban weddings are major social events.

Diet

If Dominicans do not eat rice and beans at midday, they feel they have not eaten. Rice is served at most meals in large quantities, along with such favorites as *habichuelas* (beans) and *yuca* (cassava). *Yuca* usually is boiled or prepared as fritters; it is also baked into rounds of crisp cracker bread called *casabe*. *Plátanos* (plantains) and bananas are plentiful. Mangoes, papayas, pineapples, guavas, avocados, and other tropical fruits (passion fruit, coconuts, and star fruit) are grown locally and eaten in season. People may eat small quantities of chicken, beef, pork, or goat with a meal. *Bacalau* (dried fish, usually cod) is eaten in some areas; fresh fish is only eaten along the coast. Food usually is not spicy.

The national dish is *sancocho*, a rich stew made with vegetables and meats and served on special occasions. *Habichuelas con dulce* (a sweetened drink made from beans) is popular at Easter. Dominican coffee is usually served sweet and strong. National beers and rums are highly regarded and widely consumed, as are bottled soft drinks and sweetened fruit juices.

Recreation

Dominicans love music and dancing. The country is alive with *merengue*, a fast-paced, rhythmic music. *Salsa* and other Latino styles are popular, as are North American pop and jazz. Discos are found in rural communities.

The game of dominoes is a national pastime. Outdoor tables in front of homes, bars, and rural *colmados* (neighborhood markets) are surrounded by men who play for hours, especially on Sundays. Outdoor players are almost exclusively men, but everyone may play at home. Even young children become adept. Cockfighting is another national pastime. Cockfight gambling stakes can be high. The lottery has high participation.

Baseball is the most popular sport. Competition is keen, and many Dominicans have become famous major league players in the United States and Canada. Strolling in parks, visiting friends, and watching television are popular activities. Various cultural activities (theater, concerts, etc.) are available in large urban areas.

Holidays

National holidays include New Year's Day (1 January), *Día de los Reyes* (Day of Kings, 6 January), *Nuestra Señora de la Alta Gracia* (Our Lady of High Gratitude, 21 January), Duarte's Day (26 January), Independence Day (27 February), Easter, Labor Day (1 May), Corpus Christi, Restoration of Independence (16 August), *Nuestra Señora de las Mercedes* (Our Lady of Mercies, 24 September), Columbus Day (12 October), and Christmas. Urban families go to beach or mountains during *Semana Santa* (Holy Week before Easter). *Carnaval* is celebrated for several weeks in the early spring with costume parades, complete with masked participants hitting spectators with pig bladders, and other festivities. Gifts are not exchanged at Christmas, but they may be given to children on 6 January. The government may call special holidays to celebrate an event or project completion.

Commerce

Business hours vary, but most establishments open around 8:00 or 9:00 A.M., close between 12:00 and 2:00 P.M., and open again until 5:00 or 6:00 P.M. Banks close by 3:00 P.M. Telephone offices do not close at midday and remain open until 10:00 P.M. Most shops are closed on Sunday. Small *colmados* have their own hours. Street vendors are most busy at midday. Bargaining is common in open-air markets, in some owner-operated stores, and on the streets. Prices in supermarkets and elsewhere are fixed.

Family ties and social relationships are important in obtaining employment or doing business. Business arrangements are seldom made between strangers.

SOCIETY

Government

The president and vice president are elected by the people. A bicameral Congress of 30 senators and 120 deputies is also directly elected, as are local officials. National and local elections are held simultaneously every four years. The voting age is 18. There are 29 provinces. A nine-member Supreme Court is appointed by the Senate.

Economy

The economy is based on agriculture. Coffee, sugar, pineapple, cocoa, tobacco, and rice are key crops, both for export and domestic use. Fluctuating world prices impact earnings and contribute to a volatile domestic market. Inflation is usually high. *Dominican Yorks* often send earnings back to families in the Republic; the money constitutes an important source of revenue. Tourism is another vital source of income. The currency is the Dominican *peso* (RD$).

Industrial activity includes sugar refining, cement, and pharmaceuticals. Assembly plants for various products are located in duty-free zones. The environment has suffered from the exploitation of mineral and natural resources, but efforts at conservation are being made.

Real gross domestic product per capita is $3,280, which has more than doubled in the last generation. Yet poverty affects more than 40 percent of people, and a wide gap exists between rich and poor.

Transportation and Communication

Main roads are paved and heavily traveled. Rural roads often are not paved and may not be passable during rainy seasons. Public transportation varies between a ride on the back of a motorcycle, a local or long-distance trip in a *guagua* (economical van or bus), or a ride on a larger bus. Pickup trucks or small vans travel to and from rural villages carrying passengers, animals, and cargo together. Urban Dominicans travel locally by *carros públicos* (public cars), taxis that follow certain routes. Private cars are expensive but by no means rare. More people have motorcycles.

Telephone service is available throughout the country; middle- and upper-class families have phones at home. Daily newspapers are widely read. Postal service is slow and unreliable. Most businesses use private messenger services. Private radio and television stations broadcast regionally and nationally.

Education

Free public education is provided through the high school level. Attendance is mandatory to sixth grade, but many children, especially in the *campos,* cannot attend or do not complete school for various reasons (work, lack of transport, or lack of money to buy required uniforms). Whereas three-fourths of Dominicans begin school, only one-third finish.

Scarce funding results in limited resources and understaffed facilities. Parents and teachers must provide basic supplies like pencils and paper. Textbooks and other materials are scarce. Many urban families send their children to private schools called *colegios*. University education is available, and trade schools provide technical training. The adult literacy rate is estimated at about 75 percent.

Health

Public hospitals and clinics provide free care, but private doctors are preferred when affordable. Public institutions tend to be poorly equipped and understaffed. Village health-care workers have enough training to administer basic services, but rural areas often have no doctors and people must travel elsewhere for care. Many people still consult *curanderos* (native healers). Lack of early treatment and preventive care are genuine concerns. Vaccination campaigns are helping fight disease, but such things as intestinal parasites and malaria pose serious challenges. The infant mortality rate is 50 per 1,000; life expectancy is 67 to 71 years.

FOR THE TRAVELER

U.S. citizens require proof of citizenship (a passport is the best form) and a tourist card (available through the airlines) to visit the Dominican Republic. The departure tax is $10. Food and water are generally safe in tourist areas, but it is best to drink bottled water. Cook vegetables and peel fruits. Information on travel opportunities can be obtained through the Dominican Tourist Information Center, 1501 Broadway, Suite 410, New York, NY 10036; phone (212) 575–4966. For more information, contact the Embassy of the Dominican Republic, 1715 22d Street NW, Washington, DC 20008; phone (202) 332–6280.

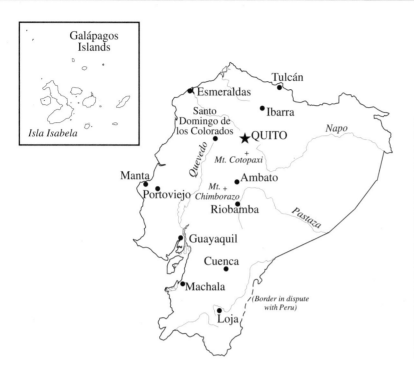

Galápagos Islands
Isla Isabela

Tulcán
Esmeraldas
Santo Domingo de los Colorados
Ibarra
★ QUITO
Napo
Quevedo
+ *Mt. Cotopaxi*
Manta
Ambato
Mt. Chimborazo +
Portoviejo
Riobamba
Pastaza
Guayaquil
Cuenca
Machala
/*(Border in dispute with Peru)*
Loja

Republic of
Ecuador

Cuba
Mexico
Atlantic Ocean
Caribbean Sea
Nicaragua
Guatemala
Panama
Guyana
Costa Rica
Venezuela
Suriname
Colombia
French Guiana
Ecuador
Galápagos Islands
Brazil
Pacific Ocean
Peru
Bolivia
Chile

Boundary representations not necessarily authoritative.

THE AMERICAS

BACKGROUND

Land and Climate

Ecuador was named after the equator and is located on it. The country is just smaller than Nevada, covering 109,483 square miles (283,560 square kilometers). Ecuador has four major geographical regions: *La Costa* (coastal lowlands), which contains rich agricultural land; *La Sierra* (Andean highlands), with snow-capped mountains; *El Oriente* (eastern lowlands), beginning at the eastern foothills of the Andes and containing mostly tropical rain forest; and the *Archipiélago de Colón* (or Galápagos Islands), a group of islands in the Pacific about 600 miles (960 kilometers) off the coast. Charles Darwin did the majority of his evolution studies on these islands. Ecuador is subject to earthquakes and volcanic eruptions, although they are rare. In the central highlands, the Avenue of the Volcanoes consists of some 30 volcanoes in two mountain ranges. Most are extinct. The two highest peaks are Chimborazo at 20,561 feet (6,267 meters) and Cotopaxi at 19,347 feet (5,897 meters).

The climate varies with elevation more than with season, but the rainy season is generally from November to May. The driest months are June to September. The coastal lowlands are hot and humid, while the highlands include everything from subtropical valleys to frigid mountains. Quito's temperature averages 71°F (22°C) year-round. The rain forest, which is part of the upper Amazonian basin, has a tropical climate, while the Galápagos Islands are rather cool.

History

Various groups of indigenous peoples, whose ancestors first inhabited Ecuador, were conquered in the latter 1400s by Incas from the south. The Inca Empire ruled the area until, during an internal power struggle, the Spanish conquered it in 1534. The Spanish era was characterized by Spaniards taking ownership of large tracts of land and large numbers of local people. In the early 1800s, Antonio José de Sucre, a compatriot of Simón Bolívar, led a successful military campaign against the Spaniards. Ecuador, along with Colombia and Venezuela, gained its independence in 1822 and became part of *Gran Colombia* (Greater Colombia), a federation led by Bolívar that was dissolved a few years later. Ecuador declared itself a republic in 1830.

In 1941, Peru and Ecuador battled over ownership of an area in the southern Amazon region then controlled by Ecuador. The dispute was mediated by Argentina, Brazil, Chile, and the United States. A treaty signed in 1942, the Rio de Janeiro Protocol, gave Peru most of the territory. This took Ecuador's access to vital mineral wealth and the Amazon River system, so Ecuador later rejected the treaty. Ecuador continued to claim the territory, and the two neighbors exchanged hostilities from time to time. Although international maps show the territory as part of Peru, maps sold in Ecuador reflect pre-1941 boundaries. In January 1995, Ecuador attacked a remote area of the border in the Cordillera del Condor region that had not yet been marked. Fighting lasted for several days before a cease-fire was called and international observers from the 1941 mediating nations were sent to help negotiate a settlement. While Peru insists the 1942 protocol be recognized and Ecuador withdraw, Ecuador claims the treaty was unfair and demands restoration of the land (even beyond the border area).

Between 1830 and 1948, Ecuador had 62 presidents, dictators, and military juntas. In 1948, Galo Plaza Lasso became the first freely elected president to serve a full term. His presidency was followed by two other peaceful administrations, but military rule followed again in 1963. The military alternated with civilian governments until 1979 when a new constitution allowed for a freely elected president.

The 1992 elections marked Ecuador's fourth consecutive peaceful transition of power and commitment to democratic rule. However, Sixto Durán Bellén's economic and constitutional reform policies proved unpopular. Political scandals, the cost of the border dispute, and other problems contributed to the 1996 election of Abdala Bucarem, a populist lawyer representing the center-left Roldosista Party. Bucarem's challenge will now be to lead a government in which his party holds only 19 of 82 legislative seats.

THE PEOPLE

Population

Ecuador's population is nearly 10.9 million and is growing at 2 percent annually. The majority (55 percent) is *mestizo* (Spanish-Indian mix). About 25 percent is native Indian (descendants of various ancient peoples). Another 10 percent is of Spanish descent, and 10 percent is black. Quito, the capital, is one of the oldest continuously inhabited cities in the Western Hemisphere and has 1.3 million people. The largest city is Guayaquil, with 1.8 million inhabitants. About 56 percent of all Ecuadorians live in urban areas.

Indigenous groups, long marginalized by the effects of colonization, have begun to organize themselves to regain lost rights, press for environmental protection of their lands, and achieve recognition for their language and culture. Ecuador's Human Development Index (0.784) ranks it 68th out of 174 countries. Access to health care, education, and the resources needed for a decent standard of living has improved, but opportunities to progress are still limited. Adjusted for women, the index (0.641) ranks Ecuador 60th out of 130 countries.

Language

Spanish is Ecuador's official language, although the Indian language Quechua is spoken by the Sierran (highland) Indians, including the Quichua, Saraguro, Otavalan, Cañari, and Chimborazo groups. Quechua is recognized by the constitution as an important part of Ecuadorian culture, but it is not an official language. Many Quechua words have been adopted into the colloquial language to replace Spanish words or describe something for which there is no Spanish term. Indeed, many Ecuadorian interjections come from Quechua and not Spanish. Indian groups (Shuar, Auca, Cofan, Cecoya, Cayapa, and Colorado) in other regions of the country speak their own languages. Many Indians are bilingual in a native tongue and Spanish. English is understood by many people in business, but is not widely spoken outside of tourist areas. Spanish tends to be spoken faster on the coast than in the Sierra highlands. Some consonants are pronounced differently between the two regions.

Religion

As a country settled by the Spanish, Ecuador is predominantly Catholic. In fact, more than 80 percent of the people belong to the Catholic Church, and many official holidays center on the Catholic faith. However, the constitution guarantees religious freedom. Many other Christian churches are growing in popularity, and people are generally tolerant of other beliefs.

General Attitudes

General attitudes vary throughout Ecuador, as there is a great diversity of cultures in the country. However, most Ecuadorians are proud of their country and history. Overlaying Ecuador's ethnic diversity are regional differences that tend to influence politics and internal relations. The *Serranos* (people from mountainous areas, including Quito) are considered more formal, conservative, and reserved than their countrymen in coastal regions, the *Costeños*. *Costeños* are considered cosmopolitan, open, and liberal; they are generally the businesspeople of Ecuador. *Serranos* are associated with government and banks. The two groups, political rivals, distrust each other in many respects but are united in others. One common trait for all Ecuadorians is that once a family opens its doors to a guest, the door is always open.

Indigenous peoples maintain strong cultural identities. In the past, many factors hindered their assimilation into mainstream society, including cultural differences and how the majority viewed them. Today, some changes have brought about greater contact and cooperation between Indians and other Ecuadorians. Still, indigenous peoples that remain in their home regions retain their traditional culture. Some who move to urban areas adopt parts of the *mestizo* culture, but others remain culturally distinct.

Personal Appearance

Clothing habits differ between rural and urban areas. In urban areas, many wear standard Western-style clothing. While younger women wear pants, older women tend to prefer skirts. Every rural region has its own traditional clothing, colors, and fabrics. Generally, people from coastal areas wear bright, clear colors (white, yellow, and red), while those from the highlands prefer blues, browns, and blacks. Rural women usually wear skirts and often wear hats—made of straw in coastal areas and wool or leather in the highlands. New clothing is often purchased for special celebrations. These items might be purchased at a store but are more often made by local tailors.

CUSTOMS AND COURTESIES

Greetings

People usually shake hands when meeting for the first time. A handshake is then used in subsequent greetings, along with the exchange of good wishes. Close friends appear to kiss each other on the cheek. Actually, they "kiss the air" while brushing or touching cheeks. Men often embrace if well acquainted. It is customary to address people by a title (*Señor, Señora, Doctor, Doctora*, etc.) when being introduced. Strangers generally do not address each by first names. Among friends, the title *Don* or *Doña*, followed by the first name, is a common greeting because it indicates both respect and friendship.

Common greetings include *¡Buenos días!* (Good day) or *¿Cómo está?* (How are you?). It is courteous to greet people in small stores or restaurants, or when passing on rural roads.

Friends commonly greet each other with *¡Hola!* (Hello). After a long absence, one might greet another with *¿Cómo has pasado? A los tiempos que nos vemos.* (How have you been? It has been a long time.).

Gestures

Yawning in public, whistling or yelling a name to get someone's attention, or pointing with the index finger are considered impolite in Ecuador, as they show a lack of respect for others. Ecuadorians might point by puckering or pursing the lips. One can also indicate "up the road" by lifting the chin, and "down the road" by lowering the chin. Hands are often used to emphasize or replace verbal communication. Drawing a circle or two in the air with the index finger means "I'll be back." To indicate, "Sorry, the bus is full," or "Sorry, we're out of tomatoes," or anything along that line, a person sticks out the hand, as if to shake hands, and twists it almost as if waving. During conversation, a person might touch another person of the same sex to show friendly concern.

Visiting

When Ecuadorians (both families and friends) visit, it is usually for a meal and conversation. However, unannounced visits are common and welcomed. Even if unexpected guests arrive during mealtime, they will be offered a full meal. It would be impolite to refuse. When guests leave the home, they are often given a small gift (*regalito*) of something the family has on hand (fruit, candy, etc.). Guests are typically offered something to drink, and it is generally impolite to refuse the offer. When inviting a guest to visit, the host will state the starting time, but specifying an ending time is considered bad taste. Instead, an ending time is generally understood depending on the nature of the visit. Guests are not expected to arrive on time and can be anywhere from ten minutes to an hour late, depending on the event. Guests invited specifically to dinner do not leave right after the meal, but stay for conversation.

Evening socials (for birthdays, reunions, parties) might extend past midnight. They usually involve eating, dancing, and drinking. Furniture is placed near the wall so everyone, including children, can dance in the middle of the main room. The hosts serve refreshments on serving trays; guests do not serve themselves from a central location. A meal is then usually served late in the evening, after which many guests will leave and others will stay for more socializing.

At small gatherings, arriving guests greet each person individually. The host introduces the guests to people with whom they are not yet acquainted. Guests who fail to say hello to those they know are not placing enough worth on their relationship. When leaving, a person should also say good-bye to each individual. Among the youth, more formal customs are being replaced by informal ones. For instance, young people often use group greetings rather than personal ones.

Eating

Food and eating habits play an important part in Ecuadorian culture. Every holiday is associated with a special kind of food and every town has a specialty dish. Mealtime is considered a good time for conversation—catching up, conducting business, or socializing. When inviting a guest to a restaurant, the host is expected to pay for the meal. Youth, however, will often split a bill.

LIFESTYLE
Family

Families are important in society and are generally close-knit. The elderly are respected and treated well. Several generations may live under the same roof. Many families dwell in small homes or rented apartments. While most families follow traditional roles, urban families are changing as more women work outside the home and more men share household duties. Other traditions are changing as well. Children used to live with their parents until they got married. Now they often leave to get an education or to work. A young woman would traditionally go directly from her parent's home to her husband's, but more are living independently for a time before marriage. Families are also getting smaller. Urban families average two children, while rural families average three or four.

Dating and Marriage

Dating usually begins in groups, when the youth get together for dances or other activities. In couple dating, a girl must ask for her parents' approval when invited out. Girls often do not begin dating until after their *quinceañera* (coming out party) at age 15. A Catholic ceremony officially presents the girl to society. If the family can afford it, a party with food, drinks, and dancing will follow. Women usually marry by age 23 (younger in some rural areas) and men around age 25. Families often emphasize that young people should complete their education before marrying. Many urban couples do not live together before their church wedding, even if they have already been married by law. Common-law marriage (referred to as *estilo manabita*) is common in rural, coastal areas. It is accepted as a legal marriage, even though no ceremony has been performed. For most of these unions, the ceremony is only lacking because of the expense of a wedding.

Diet

Of the three daily meals, the midday meal is most important. *Serranos* favor corn and potatoes, while *Costeños* favor rice, beans, and bananas, of which there are several varieties. Fresh fruits are abundant and fish is a staple item, along with chicken and meat. Soup is almost always served at both the midday and evening meals. Hot bread is a popular afternoon snack. Some favorite dishes include *arroz con pollo* (fried chicken with rice), *locro* (a soup made with potatoes, cheese, meat, and avocados), *llapingachos* (cheese and potato cakes), *seviche* (raw or cooked seafood marinated in lime and served with onions, tomatoes, and various spices), *fritada* (fried pork), *empanadas* (pastries filled with meat or cheese), *arroz con menestra* (rice with spicy beans, barbecued beef, and refried plantains), *caldo de bola* (plantain-based soup with meat and vegetables), and *cuy* (roast guinea pig).

Recreation

Fútbol (soccer) is the favorite sport in Ecuador, followed by volleyball and track. Others include tennis, basketball, and boxing. Ecuadorian volleyball (*Ecuavolley*) is played with a heavy ball by three players on each side. Most sports are played by men and boys, although a few girls may also participate. Various museums, cultural sites, and outdoor activities offer other forms of recreation to many people. Quito offers an active cultural life for the wealthy.

Holidays

Ecuadorians celebrate the new year by burning effigies of the Old Year in the streets on New Year's Eve. *Carnaval* (in February or March), Easter, Labor Day (1 May), and the Battle of Pichincha (24 May), which marks Ecuador's liberation, are all national holidays. But the most important national holiday is Independence of Quito Day (10 August), the day in 1809 when efforts were first made to become independent from Spain. When a new president is elected, he takes the oath of office on 10 August. The independence of Guayaquil is celebrated 9 October. All Souls' Day (2 November) is observed by visits to cemeteries; many people place bread-dough dolls on gravestones to honor the dead. The founding of Quito (6 December) is celebrated with large festivals, bullfights, and sporting events. Of course, Christmas is an important holiday. Several local festivals and fairs are held throughout the year in various regions. Each city and province celebrates the anniversary of its own founding.

Commerce

Stores are generally open weekdays between 8:00 A.M. and 12:30 P.M., when they close for lunch. They open again between 2:30 and 6:00 P.M. Urban stores remain closed after 12:30 P.M. on Saturday and do not open on Sunday. Some rural stores may be open on Sunday to accommodate farmers who cannot shop on other days. Banks close at 1:30 P.M. each weekday. Most local businesses are family owned and operated.

Urban families often shop at large supermarkets and department stores, but they also enjoy frequenting open-air markets. Rural Ecuadorians usually shop at open-air markets and small local businesses. The open-air markets operate a few days a week, but not every day. The particular days depend on the region. These markets offer a variety of goods from food to clothing to household items and crafts. They are often the only source of certain locally grown fruits and vegetables.

SOCIETY

Government

The Republic of Ecuador has a president and vice president in the executive branch. The unicameral legislature has 12 nationally elected members and 70 provincial representatives. Elections are held every four years for national offices and two years for provincial representatives. All those 18 and older have the right to vote, but those who are literate are required by law to vote. A number of political parties are active, but the largest include the Roldista Party, Christian Democrats, Democratic Left Party, and Democratic Popular Movement. The next national election is scheduled for 2000.

Economy

The economy enjoyed steady growth in 1994 despite relative poverty and various setbacks. Opportunities for greater foreign investment and trade have been hindered by the uncertain political climate, as well as by energy shortages and high unemployment. Real gross domestic product per capita is $4,350, which has more than doubled in the last generation. A growing number of people have the opportunity to earn a decent income, although more than half of the population still lives at subsistence levels.

Much of the population (28 percent) is employed in agriculture, producing bananas, coffee, sugarcane, fruits, corn, potatoes, rice, and other foods. Petroleum accounts for 47 percent of the nation's exports, followed by coffee, bananas, cocoa, shrimp, and fish. Industry employs 18–20 percent of the labor force, while services and other activities employ the rest. Important industries include food processing, textiles, chemicals, fishing, and timber. The currency is the *sucre* (S/), named for the national hero Antonio José de Sucre.

Transportation and Communication

In cities, transportation is provided by buses, taxis, and *colectivos* (small minibuses that are more comfortable and faster than buses). In rural areas, *busetas* replace the *colectivos*. Roads connecting cities have been improved and about half are fully paved. About 650 miles (1,048 kilometers) of railroad provide some train transportation within the country. Communication systems function fairly well, with telephone services as well as radio, television, and newspaper organizations. Seaports provide shipping to other nations. Air travel to and within Ecuador is increasing.

Education

Education is mandatory for six years, beginning at age six. Children attend school daily either from 7:00 A.M. to 12:30 P.M. or from 1:00 to 6:00 P.M., eating lunch at home. They usually wear uniforms. The government controls both public and private educational institutions. The school system is comprised of nursery schools, kindergartens, rural and urban elementary schools, secondary and vocational schools, night schools, and special-education schools. The adult literacy rate is 88 percent. There are 21 universities; the largest is in Quito and has 45,000 students.

Health

The government provides medical care to all citizens at low (sometimes no) cost to the patient. Yet rural clinics are not always well equipped. Those who can afford it might go to a private clinic or doctor. The country still battles such diseases as typhoid, cholera, polio, malaria, and yellow fever. Dengue fever is carried by mosquitoes in some coastal areas. Medical care has improved over the years and the infant mortality rate dropped from 60 per 1,000 in 1988 to 38 per 1,000 in 1995. Life expectancy has risen to between 68 and 73 years.

FOR THE TRAVELER

With a valid passport, U.S. visitors must show proof of onward transportation (e.g., a return ticket) and adequate finances. With such proof, visitors may obtain a migratory control card that permits stays of up to 90 days. If departing by plane, one must pay a tax upon leaving. While no vaccinations are required for entry, you may want to take precautions against typhoid, cholera, polio, tetanus, hepatitis, malaria, and yellow fever. Consult your physician. Altitude sickness is common in Quito, which has an elevation of 9,300 feet (2,800 meters). For more information, contact the Embassy of Ecuador, 2535 15th Street NW, Washington, DC 20009.

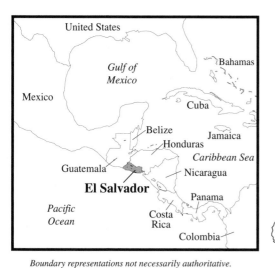

Boundary representations not necessarily authoritative.

Republic of
El Salvador

BACKGROUND

Land and Climate

With 8,124 square miles (21,040 square kilometers), El Salvador is just smaller than Massachusetts. A narrow band of coastal lowlands is divided from the mostly mountainous east and north by a central plateau. El Salvador is called the "land of the volcanoes" for its more than two hundred extinct volcanoes that have enriched the country's soil. Lush cloud forests are found in the mountain tops. Some peaks rise to between 6,000 and 8,000 feet (1,800–2,400 meters). Although deforestation has taken a heavy toll on the country's natural forests, the government and private citizens are now working to protect endangered species of animals and plants. Small earthquakes are frequent in most areas; one region or another suffers a significant quake every 30 years or so. The climate is tropical in the lowlands, with a yearly average temperature around 85°F (29°C); semitropical on the plateau, with lower temperatures and less humidity; and temperate in the mountains. Temperatures rarely fluctuate more than ten degrees year-round. El Salvador has only two seasons: the rainy *invierno* (winter) from May to October and a dry *verano* (summer). Most of the rain falls in short evening storms. San Salvador, the capital, lies on a plateau at the foot of the San Salvador volcano.

History

Various native civilizations (including Maya, Lenca, and Nahuat) inhabited the area long before the Spanish conquest. Ruins of their cultures remain at Tazumal, Joya de Cerén, and Quelepa. The Pipil of Aztec origin were those encountered by the Spaniards. The natives called the region Cuscatlán. In 1524, Pedro de Alvarado conquered the area in the name of Spain, which then ruled for almost three hundred years. The native population was nearly wiped out under harsh colonial rule. For most of its early history, El Salvador was a minor province of Guatemala. Attempts by Father José Matías Delgado to gain independence from Spain in 1811 and 1814 were unsuccessful but earned Delgado a hero's recognition.

A wider regional attempt to gain independence was successful in 1821, but this was followed by two years of instability as Mexico's Emperor Agustín de Iturbide tried to annex Central America. When his empire collapsed, El Salvador and its neighbors formed the United Provinces of Central America. Political strains between liberals and conservatives led to the Union's collapse in 1838. El Salvador claimed sovereignty in 1841 but was intermittently dominated by Guatemala through the end of the century.

The 1871 constitution marked the true birth of the nation. It was during the relatively stable period of 1871 through 1931 that most present-day educational, artistic, and government institutions and large businesses were formed. It is also the time when a new wave of upwardly mobile European and Palestinian immigrants arrived; their descendants comprise the bulk of today's affluent urban class. Much of the prosperity was built on the success of the coffee industry. Coffee had become so successful, however, that the government seized Pipil lands on which most of it was grown; small farmers were marginalized. When coffee prices collapsed during the depression, farmers rebelled in 1932. Many Pipil joined Augustín Farabundo Martí, a Communist, in destroying property and killing scores of people. They were quickly defeated by government forces, who carried out a massacre of at least ten thousand natives. Native culture nearly died with the massacre as the indigenous people feared to be considered anything but Spanish.

For more than 50 years, El Salvador was plagued with internal strife and military dictatorships. Governments were hard on those who voiced dissent. A rebel movement born in the 1960s began to mature in the late 1970s. The dictators faced a deteriorating situation and splintered. In 1979, a rival faction of the military overthrew the government. In 1980, rebels came together to form the Farabundo Martí National Liberation Front (FMLN), named for the executed leader of the 1932 rebellion. The FMLN launched a civil war to force a change in leadership. In the midst of war, a new constitution was adopted (1983) and the Christian Democratic Party's candidate, José Napoleón Duarte, was elected president in 1984. His government was accused of serious human-rights violations, corruption, and other abuses of power.

Elections were held in 1989 and Alfredo Cristiani, the National Republican Alliance (ARENA) candidate, became president. Violence marred the elections, and the war intensified. Peace talks that had begun earlier broke off and rebel forces mounted large offensives around the capital. Cristiani reopened discussions with FMLN leaders in 1990, and both sides accepted the United Nations (UN) as a mediator. Fighting continued into 1991 and peace talks faltered several time. However, both sides finally made key concessions, thereby facilitating a 1992 UN-sponsored peace agreement between the leftist FMLN and the right-wing government. As many as 75,000 people died during the years of violence.

The subsequent cease-fire held, and formal peace was declared in December 1992 amid huge celebrations. As part of the peace agreement, the FMLN became a legal political party. A police force separate from the military was established. During the war, right-wing death squads associated with the military and police often killed citizens who opposed the government; hence, a new security force was necessary. Peaceful elections were held on schedule in March 1994. Armando Calderón Sol, ARENA's leader, was elected president.

PEOPLE

Population

El Salvador's population of 5.9 million is growing at 2 percent annually. About half of all people live in rural areas. Major cities include the greater San Salvador area (1.5 million residents), Santa Ana (250,000), and San Miguel (200,000). The majority of people (95 percent) are *mestizos* (mixed Spanish and Native Americans), while about 4 percent are Native American and approximately 1 percent are of European and Palestinian descent.

El Salvador's Human Development Index (0.579) ranks it 115th out of 174 nations. Adjusted for women, the index (0.533) ranks El Salvador 76th out of 130 nations. The country ranks well behind many of its neighbors in development, mostly due to the effects of war on health-care, educational, and economic systems. A minority of people have opportunities for personal advancement and economic prosperity.

Language

Spanish is the official language of El Salvador. Although the Native American language is Nahua, only a few thousand people continue to speak it. The educated speak English in addition to Spanish.

Religion

El Salvador is a Christian nation with about 70 percent of the people belonging to the Roman Catholic Church. Another 25 percent belong to a variety of other Christian faiths, including several Protestant movements. The state itself is secular; the only reference to religion in the constitution is a provision preventing clergy from holding public office.

General Attitudes

Salvadorans are proud of their country and its accomplishments. Having endured 12 years of war, they now look forward to a future of peace and democracy. Past feelings of hatred and revenge gradually are being replaced with hope, optimism, and cooperation. It has been difficult for some people, given the suffering, to reach out to former enemies, but Salvadorans have done a remarkable job so far. Parents hope for a bright future for their children, even if they must continue to struggle with the devastation the war brought to the country.

On a personal level, some may be discouraged by the slow pace of reconstruction and reconciliation, but most are patient and willing to help rebuild the nation. Salvadorans have a strong work ethic. One's honest work is considered to give one equal social standing with others. All family members contribute to the family's well-being. Salvadorans value personal relationships, friendships, and security. Devotion to the group is more important than individualism. Time is considered flexible: people are more important than schedules, and social events usually begin later than planned.

Personal Appearance

Because of the warm climate, summer clothing is suitable all year. Business representatives often wear suits. Women wear dresses more often than slacks. During *verano* months, light jackets are sometimes necessary at night. Although the poor do not have extensive wardrobes, they keep their appearance neat and clean. Daily showers are considered a must. People without running water will go to considerable lengths to keep themselves, or at least their children, bathed as frequently as possible.

CUSTOMS AND COURTESIES

Greetings

A brief, strong handshake is the customary formal greeting for both men and women; people sometimes also use a slight nod of the head. Children appreciate adults shaking their hands. In cities, friends and relatives of the opposite sex kiss lightly on one cheek. Friends or relatives who have not seen each other for a while exchange hugs. Placing an arm around the shoulders of another person shows friendship. Friends often stand very close when conversing.

The most common daily greetings include *¡Buenos días!* (Good morning), *¡Buenas tardes!* (Good afternoon), and *¡Buenas noches!* (Good evening). *Adiós* or *Hasta luego* are formal parting terms, while less formal good-byes are *Chao* or *Nos vemos*.

When addressing people older than themselves, Salvadorans show friendly respect by using the title *Don* (for men) and *Doña* (for women) with the first name (e.g., *Doña Mélida*).

Among peers, professional and courtesy titles are used with the family name (e.g., *Señor Moreno*) or with full names (*Doctora Isabel Pérez López*). Only close friends or relatives address each other by first name.

Gestures

In some circles, using excessive hand gestures is considered in poor taste. But for many Salvadorans, hand gesturing is so important that people jest they could not talk at all if their hands were tied. Although pointing directly at people with the index finger is impolite, pointing at objects or animals is acceptable. One points at an angle to the street to hail a taxi or bus. To indicate "no," one can wag the vertical index finger from side to side. Touching the tip of the thumb and index finger while facing the palm in means "money," but facing out it means "OK." A person can beckon to a friend with a hand wave, but strangers are summoned verbally.

Visiting

Friends and relatives visit one another frequently as a way to maintain strong relationships. Most people drop by without prior arrangement, although urban residents with phones try to call ahead when possible. Hosts usually serve guests refreshments or coffee. Visiting in the evening or on weekends is most popular. Visitors from out of town, or who have not visited for a while, commonly bring small gifts—fruit, pastries, and so on.

Guests are expected to show dignity, courtesy, warmth, and friendship. It is appropriate to stand when a woman enters the room and when meeting other people. Polite hosts wait for their guests to decide when to leave. They walk their guests to the door and wait there while the guests walk or drive away.

Eating

Families usually eat at least the main meal together, whether it is at midday or in the evening. In cities, food is usually served on dishes from which diners choose their portions. In rural homes, plates are more often served prepared.

Guests compliment their hosts on the meal as a way of assuring the hosts they feel welcome. Hosts usually offer second helpings and feel complimented when they are accepted. However, one is careful in a poorer home not to eat too much since the family may be low on food. Hosts will continue to offer food until the guest says *No, gracias; estoy satisfecho* (No, thanks; I am satiated). In many households, it is rude to say *Estoy lleno* (I am full). In rural areas, the wife will eat alone after the guests have been properly fed and attended to. Men often stand when a woman leaves the table. People leaving the table say *Buen provecho* (roughly, May you benefit from the meal).

LIFESTYLE

Family

The nuclear family is the basis of Salvadoran society. The father is typically head of the family, which has an average of five members. Single-parent families are also common, and a large number of babies are born to unwed mothers. Men sometimes consider it a sign of virility to father children by more than one woman.

Most young adults remain at home until they marry. Excepting urban professionals, unmarried adults with children also usually live with their parents. Elderly parents often move in with their married children.

Women care for the children and household, but a significant number are also employed in the labor force. They may till the ground, clean homes, sew, tend a small grocery store in the home, work as skilled labor, or direct a business or institution. The majority of families belong to the peasant class (*campesinos* who work on the land but do not own it) and the blue-collar working class. The gap between rich and poor is wide and expanding.

Dating and Marriage

Dating for both genders begins after the 15th birthday, when many girls celebrate a *Quince años* (Fifteen years) party—the traditional entrance for girls into the social world. Urban youth often begin dating earlier. Traditionally, it is improper for couples to date openly unless engaged, but mostly only rural couples maintain this tradition today. Asking a girl's parents for her hand in marriage is more or less a polite formality and often an occasion for a festive dinner. In most cases, wedding ceremonies follow Catholic traditions, even among the secularized population. *Campesinos* often enter into common-law relationships because they cannot afford the expense of formal weddings.

Diet

Salvadoran food is much less spicy than that of many other Latin American countries. Most people eat red beans (*frijoles*) cooked in many ways, thick corn tortillas, rice, eggs, and fruit. One of the most common dishes is *pupusas* (meat, beans, and cheese wrapped in tortillas). People who can afford to eat meat regularly consume beef, chicken, or fish for lunch and/ or dinner. Poorer rural families eat tortillas, whatever they can grow, and an occasional pig or chicken, a number of which are usually kept around the house as domestic livestock.

Recreation

The national sport in El Salvador is soccer (*fútbol*). Basketball (*baloncesto*) is also very popular. Most towns have a gym and athletic field. In their leisure time, people like to visit, enjoy movies or music, or just relax. Many Salvadorans enjoy dancing at parties, discos (in larger cities), or dancing halls (smaller towns). During holidays and on weekends, people often go to the beaches for the sunshine, fishing, and oysters.

Holidays

The Salvadoran love for beauty and gaiety finds expression in the many colorful festivals held throughout the country during the year. National holidays include New Year's Day; Easter Week (*Semana Santa*); Labor Day (1 May); Mother's Day (10 May); Father's Day (17 June); August religious festivities (1–5 August); Independence Day, which commemorates the day Father José Matías Delgado declared the country independent (15 September); Columbus Day (12 October); and Christmas.

Commerce

Most businesses are open from 8:00 A.M. to noon and from 2:00 to 6:00 P.M., Monday through Friday. They close at noon on Saturday, except retail shops at large malls, which remain open through Sunday. Government offices open at 7:30 A.M. and close at 3:30 P.M. on weekdays. While fixed prices prevail in the stores, bargaining is common in open markets.

People in small towns and in rural areas purchase produce and meat at open markets but other groceries (bread, milk, soap, rice, etc.) at small, family-owned stores. This traditional retailing structure is quickly being replaced in urban areas by *supermercado* (supermarket) shopping.

SOCIETY

Government

El Salvador is a democratic republic. The executive branch is led by President Armando Calderón Sol and Vice President Enrique Borgo Bustamante, both elected in 1994. They serve a five-year term and are ineligible for immediate reelection. The unicameral National Assembly has 84 members, all of whom are elected. The voting age is 18. In addition to ARENA, major political parties include five factions of the FMLN, the Christian Democratic Party, and the National Conciliation Party. The country is divided into 14 departments and 262 municipalities. Although still weak, municipal power and autonomy, strengthened in the 1983 constitution, has been steadily increasing since 1990.

Economy

Mostly due to the effects of war, El Salvador has one of the weakest economies in Latin America. Prospects for the future are bright, however, as evidenced by the success of important reforms initiated in 1992, including privatization and deregulation. Annual economic growth since 1993 has averaged more than 5 percent. Real gross domestic product per capita is $2,250. High inflation has been lowered to 10 percent and unemployment is 7 percent. Problems remain in such areas as underemployment, land reform, income inequality, and pollution. However, Salvadorans are working to solve what problems they can. At the same time, they rely heavily on remittances from family members who emigrated to the United States. Aid also comes from the U.S. government. Although training programs have been established to teach new skills, there remains a shortage of skilled labor in El Salvador.

Coffee is the most important export, accounting for nearly half of all export earnings. It is grown on the steep mountainsides. The higher the altitude, the higher the coffee bean quality. Children often help their parents pick coffee during school vacations. El Salvador also exports sugar, cotton, shrimp, and clothing. Important domestic industries include food processing, cement, textiles, and petroleum processing. The currency is the Salvadoran *colón* (¢).

Transportation and Communication

Because relatively few people own cars, most travel by bus. Rural people also travel on foot. Taxis are available in larger cities. Roads in and around cities are mostly paved or gravel. However, rural roads are rarely paved and can be impassable during the rainy season. Many roads fell into disrepair during the war and are not yet repaired.

An effort is being made to improve communications, which are not well developed. Phones are concentrated in larger towns. Distant relatives and friends in rural areas often communicate through telegrams. The free press is growing, and there are two major daily newspapers in addition to a few smaller ones. Of the eleven television stations in El Salvador, nine are privately owned. There are also many private radio stations.

Education

El Salvador's adult literacy rate is 70 percent, but only about 35 percent of all rural adults are literate. The government is engaged in a vigorous campaign to increase that rate, building rural schools and encouraging enrollment. El Salvador, as a by-product of war and consequent poor quality of public schools, has hundreds of private schools and dozens of private universities. In all, there are 45 universities (public and private) in the country.

Elementary school (ages 7–12) is compulsory. It is followed by an optional three years of *Educación Básica* (Basic Education), after which the student may choose between three years of technical school or three years of *Bachillerato*, the college track. The school year begins in mid-January and runs through October. Most children wear uniforms. Although public schooling is free, including at the university level, most people stop attending school at various ages to begin working and contributing to the family income.

Health

Medical care in El Salvador is free at all state health facilities, but many were damaged during the war. Rural areas often lack clinics, while urban clinics and hospitals are in poor condition. A large, higher-quality private health-care system is available in cities to those who can afford it. The government is trying to improve health conditions through free immunizations, hygiene and sanitation education, water and sewage system development, and more modern hospital administration. The infant mortality rate is 39 per 1,000. Life expectancy ranges from 65 to 70 years. Malaria, measles, intestinal disorders, and other diseases continue to afflict people, especially in rural areas.

FOR THE TRAVELER

U.S. citizens need a valid passport and tourist card to enter El Salvador. A tourist card can be obtained from the airlines. Visitors planning to stay more than 30 days need a visa. One must have at least $300 on arrival. No vaccinations are required unless one is coming from a yellow fever endemic zone, but cholera and other diseases may be active in certain areas. Call the Centers for Disease Control International Traveler's Hotline for updates: (404) 332–4559. Avoid uncooked or unwashed foods. Crime is a serious problem. Do not travel between towns after dark. Some Salvadorans are offended when people from the United States introduce themselves as *Americans* because Salvadorans also consider themselves Americans—Central Americans. It is best to identify oneself as a U.S. citizen (*estadounidense*).

To apply for a visa, contact the Consulate General of El Salvador, 1010 16th Street NW, Third Floor, Washington, DC 20036. The Embassy of El Salvador is located at 2308 California Street NW, Washington, DC 20008; phone (202) 265–9672.

CULTURGRAM ™ '97

England

(United Kingdom)

Boundary representations not necessarily authoritative.

BACKGROUND

Land and Climate

England is located in the British Isles, which include Great Britain, Ireland, the Isle of Man, and the Channel Islands (in the English Channel). England, Scotland, and Wales are located on the island of Great Britain. Politically, Great Britain and Northern Ireland make up the country known as the United Kingdom (UK), which is about the size of Oregon. England itself covers 50,363 square miles (130,357 square kilometers) and is about the size of New York state.

Low mountains and rugged hills in the north contrast with flat countryside in the east and level and rolling plains in the southeast and southwest, the direction from which the prevailing wind blows. Nearly 30 percent of the land is cultivated. Almost half is meadows or pasture. The climate is temperate, but skies are overcast more often than not. The north is wetter and slightly cooler than the south. Winter temperatures rarely drop below 25°F (–4°C) and summer averages seldom rise above 75°F (24°C). Humidity levels, ranging from medium to high, can make it seem colder or warmer than temperatures indicate.

History

Julius Caesar's expeditionary forces reached Britain in 55 B.C., but the Romans did not invade until A.D. 43 in the reign of Tiberius. They incorporated the area into the Roman Empire and stayed until 426, when Rome was in decline and raiding Angles and Saxons (two Germanic tribes) drove them out of Britain. Vikings began raiding the islands in the late eighth century. In 865, Danish-led forces invaded and ushered in two centuries of Viking domination. Other groups also invaded, including the Norsemen. The last invasion was in 1066, when William the Conqueror (or William of Normandy) won the Battle of Hastings. This Norman conquest ushered in a new chapter in English history of great political and social change. The signing of the Magna Carta in 1215 was one such change; it established important principles of human rights and limits on the monarchy.

A long period of dynastic struggle ended in the 15th century with the War of the Roses. Henry Tudor emerged with the crown. His son, King Henry VIII, created the Church of England with the Crown as its head. Henry VIII's daughter, Elizabeth I, reigned in an age when the empire began to span the globe, leading to the saying that "the sun never sets on the British Empire." Through acts of union, Wales (1535) and Scotland (1707) joined England, and the empire was known as the United Kingdom of Great Britain. An act of union in 1801 brought Ireland to the empire, which was then called the United Kingdom of Great Britain and Ireland. When most of Ireland became independent in 1921, the name changed to the United Kingdom of Great Britain and Northern Ireland.

Britain established itself as a great naval power by defeating the mighty Spanish Armada in 1588. It became the world's most powerful economy during the Industrial Revolution. With these strengths and by acquiring colonies around the globe, Britain was firmly established as an international force and one of the Great Powers of Europe. Although its U.S. American colonies were lost in 1776 (Canada was a colony until 1867 and then became an autonomous part of the Commonwealth), Britain acquired new lands in the Mediterranean, the Caribbean, Africa, and Asia.

After World War I, expansion halted and the empire began to shrink (some colonies had already claimed independence

E
U
R
O
P
E

well before the war). During World War II, under the leadership of Winston Churchill, the British withstood intense Nazi bombings, which nearly destroyed many areas. After the war, Britain granted most of its colonies (more than 50) independence. The majority remained voluntarily in the Commonwealth and some even retain Queen Elizabeth II as their nominal head of state. Britain was a founding member of the North Atlantic Treaty Organization (NATO) in 1949. It joined the European Union (EU) in 1973.

The country established itself as a modern welfare state in 1945; however, the Conservative governments of Margaret Thatcher and John Major have placed more emphasis on the private sector. Despite strong opposition to Tory (Conservative) policies, Major was reelected in 1992. The Conservatives narrowly hold a parliamentary majority. European integration, the economy, and peace efforts in Northern Ireland are crucial to elections, which must be held by May 1997.

THE PEOPLE

Population

England is the largest nation of the UK, which has an overall population of 58.3 million and is growing at only 0.3 percent annually. The English comprise about 81 percent (about 47 million) of that total. The nation is highly urbanized, with nearly 90 percent of the people living in cities. Although most people living in England are Caucasian, Britain's past colonial heritage has brought many cultures together. Therefore, various ethnic groups from India, Africa, and Asia also reside in England (comprising 2.8 percent of the population).

The Human Development Index (0.916) ranks the UK 18th out of 174 nations. Good access to health care, education, and economic prosperity affords people opportunities and choices in their lives. Adjusted for women, the index (0.862) ranks the UK 13th out of 130 countries.

Language

English is the official language of the UK. Different dialects are spoken throughout England, as are the foreign languages of minority groups. But nearly everyone speaks British English, also known as BBC or Oxford English.

Religion

During the reign of Henry VIII, England split from the Roman Catholic Church to form the Church of England (Anglican Church), which became the country's established religion. The Church of England exercised great influence over the country throughout history, but it no longer has political power. Still, the queen is head of the church. At least 27 million Anglicans reside in the UK. Throughout the country, there are also large Catholic (more than five million), Presbyterian (two million), Methodist (0.7 million), and Jewish (0.4 million) populations. Other Christian and non-Christian religious organizations are also active in England. Society is generally secular, despite the presence of an established church. That is, the English generally are not actively involved with religion. The Anglican Church, for example, as representative of its English heritage, is high on ceremony but is not as involved in evangelical activity. Only about one-tenth of all adults regularly attend Sunday church services; of that number, only about one-third attend the Church of England. The

English consider religion a very private matter. It is impolite to ask about one's religious beliefs.

General Attitudes

Having a long and rich history, the English enjoy tradition and custom more so than do U.S. Americans. They often find U.S. Americans to be too casual, especially with the English language. In fact, they do not consider the language spoken in the United States (American English) to be the same language spoken in Great Britain (British English). In general, the English are suspicious of extremes and may be embarrassed by displays of emotion or excessive enthusiasm. Rather, they value moderate behavior and emotional reserve. Britons are known for a wry sense of humor that allows them to be self-critical, but this does not give the same freedom to visitors. Britons appreciate visitors who have some knowledge of their history and system. A fairly dominant feature of society is the class system. It is not strictly related to wealth or education, nor is it discussed. But it is carefully observed and impacts daily life. Accents, educational backgrounds, clothing, tastes in furnishings, and leisure activities are all indicative of one's position in the class structure.

Personal Appearance

The English dress much the same as people do in the United States, except that fashion trends are more closely tied to Europe. Older women tend to wear dresses more often than women in the United States. Business attire is conservative.

CUSTOMS AND COURTESIES

Greetings

A handshake is the most common form of greeting among the English, whether for formal occasions, visits, or introductions. Handshakes generally are firm but not aggressive. When people are already acquainted, they often use verbal greetings instead. Among friends, women are often kissed (by men and women) lightly on both cheeks. When one passes a stranger on the street, it is appropriate to smile and say *Good morning*, *Hello*, *Good afternoon*, or *Good evening*, if one establishes eye contact with that person. Such an exchange occurs less frequently in large cities. Most people call friends and young people by first name but use titles (*Mr.*, *Mrs.*, *Doctor*, etc.) in formal situations or to show respect.

Gestures

The English are in general a reserved people. They do not approve of loud or demonstrative behavior (except in very informal gatherings). People respect each other's personal space and feel uncomfortable when someone stands too close to them during conversation. Touching is generally avoided. Manners are important, although standards are not as high among the youth, who comprise nearly one-fifth of the population.

Visiting

It is a common courtesy to telephone ahead before visiting someone. In fact, just showing up is considered impolite, even among friends. Hosts do not always serve refreshments to visitors. While not customarily required, it is not uncommon for guests to bring gifts. In informal situations, a friend might ask to bring something to the meal (such as a bottle of wine), or a guest might bring chocolates, flowers, or wine as a gift to the hosts. In formal settings, gifts are less likely, but guests will likely send a thank-you note afterward. The English admire good manners and expect visitors to practice them. Traditionally, men hold doors open for women and stand when a woman enters the room. The English enjoy discussing a wide variety of topics during *tea*. This is a 4:00 P.M. snack of tea, *buns* (cupcakes), or *biscuits* (cookies). The food is often substantial enough to act as a meal. When one uses someone's phone, it is courteous to offer to pay, as even local calls are billed separately. However, hosts rarely accept the offer.

Eating

The English eat in the continental style, with the fork in the left hand and the knife in the right. Proper manners are a must at the table; loud behavior is avoided. The English generally eat three meals a day. What each meal (except breakfast) is called depends on family background and local tradition. The majority call the noon meal *lunch* and the evening meal *dinner*. Some, however, call the noon meal *dinner* and the evening meal *tea*. Others call the evening meal *supper*, while still others use *supper* to refer to a snack before bedtime. At a restaurant, diners summon a waiter by raising the hand. The waiter brings the bill on a plate, on which a 10 to 15 percent tip should be left.

LIFESTYLE

Family

English families are small and tightly knit. The traditional standard has been two children in a family. This pattern is changing, however. Fewer people are marrying and those that do, marry later. Women are having fewer children and having them later. More women work outside the home, and there are more single-parent families.

Most families enjoy a comfortable standard of living. The middle class represents Britain's majority. The English ideal is to have a house and garden. Two out of three families have their own homes. Apartment (*flat*) living is not popular and is only common in large cities. There is a trend away from urbanization. People are moving to the countryside to develop an attachment to the land and to avoid big-city problems.

Dating and Marriage

Dating activities in England are similar to those in the United States, but dating patterns are different. While U.S. teenagers enjoy casual dating, British youth generally have only one boyfriend or girlfriend at a time and do not date other people during that time. A person may legally marry at age 16, but most marry in their mid- to late twenties. Marriage customs are much the same as in the United States.

Diet

A full traditional breakfast consists of bacon, sausages, grilled or fried tomatoes, mushrooms, eggs, and bread fried in fat or oil. Fewer people now eat this heavy meal on a regular basis, preferring to stick with various combinations of cereal, toast, juice or fruit, and tea or coffee. The British eat a wide variety of European and ethnic foods. Many traditional foods such as beef and potatoes have given way to poultry and pasta dishes. Fast-food has also become more prevalent, and hamburger restaurants now rival the traditional fish-and-chip (french fries) shops in popularity. Numerous Chinese and Indian restaurants and pizza houses provide *take-away*

service, and many *pubs* (public houses) serve anything from snacks to full meals. Traditional English dishes include roast beef and Yorkshire pudding (a baked batter usually served in muffin form) and steak and kidney pie.

Recreation

A variety of activities are enjoyed in England, which developed many of the world's favorite sports. *Football* (soccer) was first codified in England. It and rugby are the most popular sports. There are two types of rugby, Union and League, the latter of which is played in the north. One of the most popular spectator sports is horse racing (over jumps in the winter and on a flat track in the summer). The English enjoy cricket in the summer. Modern lawn tennis was first played in England, and modern boxing rules came from the country. Other favorite forms of recreation include badminton, sailing, swimming, *snooker* (a billiards game), darts, and squash.

The English like to walk and golf, and many participate in *angling* (fishing). Gardening represents a favorite way to relax and is a huge industry (gardening books can become bestsellers). Gardens of flowers, shrubs, and other decorative plants are most common, but some people also plant vegetables. *Pubs* offer a place to meet, socialize, and relax with friends and neighbors. Relaxing in the home, however, is more popular. The English watch more television than any other people except U.S. Americans. They claim it is because of the quality of their programming. Videos are also popular, but many people equally enjoy the cinema. The English also support the performing and cultural arts.

Holidays

The English have the fewest public holidays in Europe. They include New Year's Day, Good Friday and Easter Monday, May Day (1 May), spring and summer bank holidays, Christmas, and Boxing Day (26 December). For New Year's Day and May Day, workers receive a day off on the holiday's closest Monday. Virtually everything closes for Christmas, including shops and restaurants. More and more offices now close between Christmas and New Year's because it is a slow business period. Boxing Day is named for the tradition of giving small, boxed gifts to servants and tradesmen. It is now a day for visiting friends and family.

Holidays that are celebrated but not treated as days off from work include the Queen's Birthday (second Saturday in June), Remembrance Day (closest Sunday to 11 November), and Guy Fawkes Day (5 November). Guy Fawkes Day, or Bonfire Night, commemorates the capture of Guy Fawkes, who plotted to destroy the houses of Parliament in 1605. In some areas, huge bonfires are lit and firework displays are put on for the public. Most people receive four or five weeks of personal vacation from work. July and August are popular months for taking trips, and many people also vacation in the winter.

Commerce

Businesses generally are open from 9:00 A.M. to 5:00 P.M., Monday through Friday. An increasing number of shops are lengthening business hours and staying open on weekends. Government offices and some rural shops close for lunch between 1:00 and 2:00 P.M. and stay open until 5:30 P.M. Most stores and businesses are closed on Sunday.

SOCIETY

Government

Britain has no written constitution. The constitutional arrangements are the result of acts of Parliament, common law, and precedent. The importance of a parliament was established following the 1649 civil war and execution of King Charles I. Upon the death of Oliver Cromwell, who had led the violent revolution, the monarchy was reestablished but parliamentary sovereignty remained prominent. The monarch, Queen Elizabeth II, is head of state, but elected officials govern through Parliament.

The House of Commons is the main legislative body. It has 651 members, 524 of which are from England. The party with the most members of Parliament (MPs) forms the government, and that party's leader becomes the prime minister (officially appointed by the queen). The prime minister and cabinet govern as the executive body. The voting age is 18, and elections are held at least every five years. In practice, they are held more often, as the prime minister can call them at any time.

Parliament's upper chamber is the House of Lords, which has 1,200 members. About two-thirds are hereditary members and the other third are appointed members for life, including those who sit on Britain's highest court of appeals. Anglican archbishops and bishops also sit in the House of Lords. The chamber's chief legislative role is to veto legislation, which in practice simply delays it. Since the House of Lords is not an elected body, it rarely chooses to completely block legislation.

Economy

England has always been a global economic power, even though its per capita income is lower than in many other European countries. Real gross domestic product per capita is $17,160. Most people enjoy a good standard of living, although there is a fairly large gap between the upper and lower classes. Unemployment remains about 8 percent.

Britain does the bulk of its trading within the EU. Natural resources include oil, coal, natural gas, tin, iron ore, and salt. Important exports include crude oil (from the North Sea), manufactured goods, and consumer items. The service sector is more important than manufacturing, and London is one of the world's most important financial centers. Britain's farmers supply the country with about 60 percent of its needs. However, the beef industry collapsed in 1996 due to health concerns over "mad cow" disease and an EU ban on British beef exports. The currency is the pound sterling (£).

Transportation and Communication

Travel by road is the favored method of transportation for both people and freight. The British drive on the left side of the road, and a car's steering wheel is on the right side of the car. Taxis are common in the cities. Public transportation is well developed in most urban areas, with a subway in London called the *Tube* or the *Underground* and subways in such cities as Manchester and Newcastle. Buses and trains service major cities, but public transport in rural areas is not as extensive. Domestic and international air travel is well developed. London's Heathrow Airport is the busiest in the world.

The Channel Tunnel (or "Chunnel") connects England and France by rail under the English Channel. Prior to 1994, people could only cross the channel by ferry or air. The tunnel offers a three-hour ride between London and Paris (about 35 minutes in the actual tunnel) for passengers, freight, and private cars. High-speed trains operate on the French side and will be in place on the English side by 2002.

Telecommunications are well advanced, with fiber optic cable links and satellite systems. Most British homes have telephones and televisions. Several daily newspapers are available throughout the nation.

Education

England's education system has produced a 99 percent literacy rate. A large portion of tax revenues is spent on education needs. Schooling is free and compulsory between ages five and sixteen. Many students begin earlier with nursery school and some stay beyond age 16 to prepare for entrance to college. A grade is called a *form*. Public schools are called *state schools* and private ones are called *public schools*. At age 16, students take an exam to earn the General Certificate of Secondary Education. At 18, they may take the General Certificate of Education, which is used as an entrance exam by England's universities and colleges. In addition to more than 40 universities and various professional schools, England has an Open University, which offers correspondence and broadcast courses to anyone interested. England's quality of higher education is evident in many important scientific and technological contributions made by the British, as well as British achievement in the arts and other areas.

Health

Britain's National Health Service (NHS) provides, on the basis of taxation, free medical treatment and many other social services. Only prescriptions and some dental services must be paid for by the individual. Quality of care and facilities is high, but the country struggles under the increasing cost of financing NHS. Private care is also available, and many people now have private insurance programs to avoid long waits for surgical treatment covered by the NHS. Life expectancy averages 77 years; the infant mortality rate is 7 per 1,000.

FOR THE TRAVELER

While a valid passport is necessary, no visa is required of U.S. citizens staying in the UK less than six months. There is much to see and do in England. For suggestions and lodging information, contact the British Tourist Authority, 551 Fifth Avenue, Seventh Floor, New York, NY 10176; phone (800) 462–2748. You may also contact the Embassy of the United Kingdom, 3100 Massachusetts Avenue NW, Washington, DC 20008; phone (202) 462–1340; or the British Information Service, 845 Third Avenue, New York, NY 10022; phone (212) 752–5747.

CULTURGRAM™ '97

Republic of
Estonia

Boundary representations not necessarily authoritative.

EUROPE

BACKGROUND

Land and Climate

Estonia is a small European country, similar in size to Switzerland or the combined states of New Hampshire and Vermont. It is one of the three countries known as the Baltic States (Estonia, Latvia, and Lithuania). While Russia lies to the east and Latvia to the south, Estonia is otherwise bordered by the waters of the Baltic Sea and the Gulf of Finland. More than 1,500 islands in the Baltic Sea make up nearly 10 percent of Estonia's total 17,400 square miles (45,100 square kilometers). The two largest islands are Saaremaa and Hiiumaa, each of which is populated.

Estonia is mostly flat, with hills in the south. The highest hill is *Suur Munamägi* (Great Egghill) at 1,043 feet (318 meters). Historically an agrarian country, Estonia is also endowed with oil shale deposits and phosphorite, particularly in the northeast. The country's major rivers include the *Emajõgi* (Mother River), *Pärnu*, *Narva*, and *Pirita*. Lake Peipus dominates the eastern border. A number of smaller lakes and rivers, many rich in fish, dot Estonia's landscape. Forests, wetlands, and meadows harbor wildlife, berries, and mushrooms.

The climate is usually wet, with many cloudy days. Winters are cold and snowy with temperatures often below freezing. Summers are cool; temperatures average around 65°F (18°C). Estonia is warmed by the Gulf Stream, which also brings rain at the end of summer.

History

The Estonian people belong to the ancient Finno-Ugric tribe that has inhabited the region for thousands of years. Before the 13th century, Estonians generally lived in free association, without an aristocracy of any kind. This changed with the invasion and domination of German and Danish crusaders in the 1200s. Baltic Germans remained the ruling class into the 20th century. Estonia came under Swedish control in 1561 but became linked to Russia beginning in 1710.

Estonia took advantage of the chaotic conditions of Russia's Bolshevik Revolution in 1917 to declare its independence. The Red Army invaded but was defeated in the Battle of Võnnu. Estonia maintained its independence for 22 years. However, under the secret Molotov-Ribbentrop pact between Germany's Adolf Hitler and Russia's Josef Stalin, Estonia was invaded in 1940 by the Soviet Union (USSR). Until it was defeated in World War II, Germany occupied the territory from 1941 to 1944. The Soviets then reestablished their power and incorporated Estonia into the USSR.

With the relaxed political climate under Soviet leader Mikhail Gorbachev, Estonia's quest for independence became visible outside the USSR. At large demonstrations and nighttime festivals, people sang outlawed nationalistic songs to show their determination. As the Soviet Union weakened and finally collapsed in 1991, Russian president Boris Yeltsin accepted Estonia's declaration of restored independence. Estonia has since moved steadily toward reestablishing its sovereign and democratic government.

THE PEOPLE

Population

Estonia's population of about 1.6 million is growing at 0.5 percent per year. The majority is ethnic Estonian (61 percent), although Russians comprise 33 percent of the population. Other groups include Ukrainians (3 percent), Belarusians (2 percent), and Finns (1 percent). Most non-Estonians migrated to the area during the Soviet era. They are eligible for citizenship if they meet language, residency, and other requirements. Many ethnic Russians, heartened by Estonia's current economic and social development, are choosing to seek formal citizenship. Citizenship is vital for property ownership, social benefits, and other privileges of living in Estonia.

During World War II, thousands of Estonians fled their homeland and settled all over the world. The largest expatriate communities are located in Toronto, Canada, and New York City. Groups are found throughout the United States, in Australia, and in Sweden. These communities retain their roots through festivals, church worship, and newspapers.

Tallinn, the capital, is the largest city with about 500,000 inhabitants. Tartu (116,000) and Narva (83,000) are the next largest cities. Three-fourths of all people live in urban areas. Estonia's Human Development Index (0.862) ranks it 43d out of 174 countries. Adjusted for women, the index (0.839) ranks Estonia 21st out of 130 countries. Although in a period of economic transition, Estonia affords women access to economic opportunities and choices related to their future.

Language

Estonian uses a Latin alphabet and is similar to Finnish. In fact, many Estonians also speak Finnish. English is popular, particularly with the youth, and is taught in school.

During the Soviet era, Russian was imposed on the Estonian population. Although most Estonians can speak Russian, they prefer to speak Estonian. After the country's independence in 1991, Estonian became the official language. Passing an Estonian language test is now a specific requirement for citizenship, even though many ethnic Russians cannot yet speak Estonian. Ethnic Russians are proud of their language and feel it is unfair to have to learn Estonian in order to retain their homes and employment. The language requirement for citizenship remains a contentious issue between the Russian and Estonian populations.

Religion

Estonia was one of the last nations in Europe to convert to Christianity. Before the 13th century, Estonians followed a religion closely tied to nature that included the worship of a god called Taara. The adoption of Christianity came through foreign invasions and missionary work. Following the Reformation, the Lutheran Church became dominant in Estonia.

Because religious worship was suppressed during the Soviet era, the country today is quite secular. Indeed, less than one-fourth of the population is religious. Most of these people still attend the Lutheran Church, although other Christian denominations are also active. Religious freedom is guaranteed. Although the government is not tied to a particular religion, prayers are sometimes offered at official functions.

General Attitudes

Estonians view themselves as an industrious and efficient people who maintained these values even during the Soviet era. They are patriotic and proud of their ancient heritage. Although they are not part of Scandinavia, Estonians tend to identify with the Scandinavian value system and way of life. Estonians cherish freedom and their traditional culture. Despite occupation by other nations, particularly since 1940, Estonians are proud that they have retained their traditions and language. They look forward to closer ties with the West.

Estonians place a high value on family, education, and work. They value a good personal reputation for themselves and others. People desire future opportunities to travel and to obtain a higher standard of living.

Personal Appearance

Estonians tend to have fair-colored hair and blue eyes, so they appear to be Scandinavian or Nordic. They like to dress well in public. People always dress more formally when going out to eat, going to theater, or visiting friends. Women generally wear dresses more than slacks, although the youth are adopting a more varied approach. Young people prefer European fashions. People dress warm during the winter, preferring coats to jackets. Clothing styles in rural areas are more relaxed than in cities. Each county has its own traditional costume that is worn for special occasions, such as festivals, holidays, or weddings.

CUSTOMS AND COURTESIES

Greetings

Estonians usually greet with a simple *Tere* (Hello) and a handshake. The younger person initiates the greeting, and men greet women first. In a group, the elderly are first to be greeted. People often begin a conversation with *Kuidas käsi käib?* (How are you?) or *Kuidas läheb?* (How is it going?). Other greetings include *Tere hommikust* (Good morning), *Tere päivast* (Good day), and *Tere Õhtust* (Good evening).

When one is approached, it is polite to stand and acknowledge the other person's presence, maintaining eye contact during the greeting. It is a courtesy to use the formal pronoun *Teie* (you) when meeting someone for the first time, with older people, and with those in authority. The informal *Sina* (you) is used with friends and relatives.

Gestures

It is polite to offer a greeting when passing someone on the street. Chewing gum in public is impolite, especially when talking to someone. Estonians use the "thumbs-up" gesture to indicate things are going well. Pointing with the index finger is impolite, as is talking with one's hands in the pockets. Hand gestures are kept to a minimum during conversation.

Visiting

An important aspect of social life is visiting or receiving friends. Punctuality is expected. When visiting friends or visiting someone for the first time, people commonly bring flowers to the hosts. Hosts usually offer tea or coffee to their guests. People enjoy inviting friends over for dinner. Estonians appreciate conversation during the meal.

Hosts often give departing guests a bouquet of flowers as a token of friendship. Guests staying in the home generally give a gift to thank the hosts for their hospitality.

Eating

Dark rye bread, eggs, cheese, pastries, sandwiches, and porridge are common breakfast foods, accompanied by milk or coffee. The main meal is at midday. It consists of three courses: soup, a main dish of meat or fish and potatoes, and dessert. Common soups include bouillon, cabbage, or pea. Dessert is often cake, ice cream, fruit, or fruit preserves. Dinner is a lighter meal and is eaten after 6:00 P.M. It might include potatoes, stew, pasta, or soup.

Hands are generally kept above the table during a meal. One waits for all to finish before leaving the table. Requesting second helpings pleases the cook.

LIFESTYLE

Family

Families tend to be small, commonly with one to three children. Ties with extended family members are important. Grandparents often care for their grandchildren while both parents work. In many cases, newlywed couples live with their parents until they are financially established. Parents try to assist their adult children financially, if possible. Adult children take direct responsibility (financial and physical) for their aging parents. Nursing homes are used only for those who have no close relations.

Urban families tend to live in apartments or small, single-family homes with a fence and garden. Those living in apartments usually have a plot of land in the countryside for growing fruits and vegetables. Most rural families live on farms and enjoy larger homes.

Dating and Marriage

Common dating activities include attending cultural events, going to the theater, dancing, participating in sporting events, and eating and drinking. Estonians usually marry after they have finished their education, which is usually in their early twenties. Some couples live together before or instead of marrying. Weddings are generally secular, but church weddings are becoming more popular. Parents from both sides help organize the celebration, to which plenty of friends and relatives are invited. Estonians often have their first child early in their marriage.

Diet

Dark rye bread and fish (salmon, cod, herring, sole, pike, perch, and whitefish) are commonly eaten. Potatoes, cabbage, carrots, and beans are the prevalent vegetables. The most common fruits are apples, cherries, pears, and a number of wild berries (raspberries, strawberries, cranberries, cloudberries, and blueberries). Pork, beef, lamb, veal, and chicken are common meats. Dairy products such as milk, butter, yogurt, sour cream, and cottage cheese are staples of the diet. Most people drink tea and coffee each day. Vodka is also enjoyed. *Pirukas* (a pastry with meat and vegetables) is popular. A favorite Russian dish is *rosolje*, pink potato salad made with beets and herring. Sauerkraut soup is served with sour cream. At Christmas, people eat *verivorst* (blood sausage), jellied meats, *sült* (head cheese), roast pork or goose, sauerkraut, potatoes, rye bread, and homemade ale.

Recreation

Music is highly appreciated and attending concerts of all types is a frequent form of recreation. Nearly all age groups and professions have their own choirs. These choirs, and the more famous *Hortus Musicus* professional group, often play and sing folk music. Estonia is one of the few countries in the world that has a national epic poem, *Kalevipoeg* or "Son of Kalev," which tells the mythical story of Estonia's early development. Every city has a theater or community playhouse and their performances are enjoyed by many. This has been true throughout history. Estonians have always been quick to perform popular Western plays along with works from their own playwrights.

A national song festival has been held roughly every four years since 1869. A combined choir with as many as 30 thousand voices sings a variety of traditional folk songs. Usually held the first weekend in July, the festival begins with a parade through Tallinn. Dance festivals and colorful costumes add to this celebration of history and culture. The festival's international and local audience has been as large as 500,000 people.

Estonians love sports. The country has produced a number of Olympic champions and has a strong national basketball team. Other recreational activities include volleyball, sailing, ice boating, ice skating, cross-country skiing, swimming, and cycling. In their leisure time, Estonians like to relax in saunas (often on a weekly basis) and work in their gardens. Even in urban areas, the people feel tied to the land and their agricultural heritage. A favorite summer pastime is picking wild berries and mushrooms in the forest.

Holidays

New Year's Day (1 January) is followed by a number of holidays throughout the year. For *Vastlapäev* (15 February), people go sledding and eat special foods; a long sledding ride indicates good luck with the fall harvest. Independence Day (24 February) celebrates freedom in 1918. Even though 20 August marks Estonia's reestablishment of freedom in 1991, the 24 February holiday remains the primary focus of independence celebrations. Easter is celebrated Friday through Sunday and includes the tradition of painting eggs and eating special foods. On Fool's Day (1 April), people play tricks on each other. Two days in June commemorate historical events: 14 June honors those who were deported to Siberia by Stalin in 1949, and 23 June marks the Day of Victory at Võnnu.

Jaanipäev (Midsummer's Day) is 24 June. This marks the beginning of the summer's "white nights," during which the sun sets for only a few hours. People light huge bonfires or place fires on small rafts. Parties, dances, and concerts are held. People also traditionally search for a fern blossom on this night because it will bring happiness to them (but ferns do not have blossoms). Girls pick seven types of flowers to put under their pillows in hopes of dreaming about their future husband.

The Day of the Souls (2 November) remembers the dead. *Kadri* Day (25 October) and *Mardi* Day (10 November) are days for girls and boys, respectively, to paint their faces, dress up in old clothes, and go to their neighbors' houses. They knock, sing special national songs, and sometimes dance, asking to be let in out of the cold. They are given candy and fruit. Estonians celebrate Christmas over three days (24–26 December) and eat a special meal on Christmas Eve.

Commerce

Businesses are usually open between 8:00 or 9:00 A.M. and 5:00 P.M. Offices often close for lunch, but shops and restaurants do not. Goods are sold in stores, open-air markets, and kiosks. Food stores are usually open until 9:00 P.M. on weekdays and are open on weekends. Other stores may be open on Saturday but close by noon and are closed on Sunday.

SOCIETY

Government

The Republic of Estonia has 15 counties. It is governed by a combined parliamentary and presidential system. The first democratic elections since the 1991 independence were in 1992. National elections in 1995 brought former communists (from the Republican Coalition Party and Rural People's Union) to power in place of the reformist government elected in 1992. President Lennart Meri is chief of state. A prime minister is head of government. The 101 members of Parliament (*Riigikogu*) are elected by region. Several parties have legislative representation and most support Estonia's economic and democratic progress. The voting age is 18.

Economy

A free-market economy is rapidly being reestablished. Widespread support to reintegrate into Western Europe has enabled the government to implement ambitious programs of privatization and economic reform. Privatization of small state enterprises is nearly complete. Consumption per capita is high, and the economy is growing by 5 percent annually. Production is up, unemployment is dropping, and inflation rates are among the lowest in the region. Real gross domestic product per capita is $6,690. Estonia has the necessary infrastructure for the average person to take advantage of increasing economic opportunities and higher standards of living.

The country's economic strengths include a skilled, industrious workforce and highly efficient agricultural sector. The main industries include textiles, agriculture, tourism, and chemicals. Lumber, meat products, and textiles are exported. The country is generally self-sufficient in food production.

The Estonian currency is the *kroon* (EEK). In 1995, Estonia signed an economic agreement with Europe that entitles it to participate in European Union (EU) conferences and to work toward eventual EU membership. Foreign trade has shifted quickly from the East to the West. Estonia has strong trade links with Finland, Germany, Sweden, and several other countries, although Russia is still an important market for Estonian goods. Estonian businesses are meeting the challenges of operating in a capitalist, democratic environment.

Transportation and Communication

In cities, both public transportation (buses, streetcars) and private cars are used. Many families own a car. Tallinn has both trams, which run on tracks, and trolleys, which run without tracks. Electric trains are used in suburban areas. People older than 75 years of age do not have to pay for public transportation. Trains and buses are used for transport between cities. Train service is also available to neighboring countries. Ferries travel between Estonia and Finland, Sweden, and Germany.

Not every family has a telephone, but the system is expanding. Several commercial radio and television stations now broadcast in Estonia, replacing only one of each during the Soviet era. Broadcasts from other European countries are also received via satellite or by airwaves from Finland.

Education

Estonia's adult literacy rate is 99 percent. Tallinn is home to several universities and technical colleges. Tartu University, located in Tartu, was built in 1632 by Swedish King Gustav Adolphus and is one of Europe's oldest academic institutions. Its library holds more than three million scientific dissertations.

Day-care centers and kindergartens provide preschool education before age six, when primary schooling begins. Students are required to attend school until age 14, at which time a student can choose to attend a technical school to learn such trades as carpentry or mechanics. Most students, however, go on to four years of high school. Many then continue on to a university or technical school.

Estonia's education system is currently under reform, which involves the time-consuming process of rewriting textbooks and curricula to more accurately reflect Estonia's history, culture, and values.

Health

Public and private health-care facilities exist in Estonia, and more than 93 percent of the population has access to health care. Most hospitals are run by the government and care is free. People must pay for care provided by private doctors and visits to the dentist. The health-care system is under reform. Improvements are being considered, including a new insurance system. One challenge is the modernization of hospitals, clinics, and other facilities that have outdated equipment. Estonian physicians are also making contacts with Western counterparts to improve their expertise and understanding of new technology. The infant mortality rate is 19 per 1,000; life expectancy averages between 65 and 75 years. The leading causes of death in Estonia are cardiovascular disease, cancer, and accidents (mainly traffic).

FOR THE TRAVELER

U.S. travelers planning to stay fewer than 90 days do not need visas to enter Estonia, but a valid passport is required. May and June are the months for many popular festivals; however, travelers should take an umbrella, as unexpected rain showers can develop quickly. Tallinn's Old Town is one of Europe's best-preserved medieval villages, complete with cobblestone streets, Gothic buildings, and defense towers. Other interesting sites include the ruins of St. Birgita's convent (where outdoor concerts are often held) and Rocca-al-Mare, an open-air museum that features early farmhouses and traditional folk dancing. Credit cards and traveler's checks are widely accepted. For further information, contact the Consulate General of Estonia, 630 Fifth Avenue, Suite 2415, New York, NY 10111; phone (212) 247–1450, or the Embassy of Estonia, 1030 15th Street NW, Suite 1000, Washington, DC 20005; phone (202) 789–0320.

Republic of
Finland

Boundary representations not necessarily authoritative.

BACKGROUND

Land and Climate

Finland is a Scandinavian or Nordic country that borders Russia. Just smaller than the state of Montana, it covers 130,127 square miles (337,030 square kilometers). Forests, lakes, and rivers dominate the Finnish landscape, covering more than 70 percent of the land. Only 8 percent is arable. Known as the "Land of 10,000 Lakes," Finland actually has more than 187,800 lakes. The terrain is low and flat in the south but gives way to rolling plains farther north and low hills in the far north. A few minor mountains are found in the far north of Lapland and in Saariselkä.

Finland is located at about the same latitude as Alaska, Siberia, and southern Greenland, but the climate is not as harsh because of the warming North Atlantic current, the Baltic Sea, and Finland's lakes. Still, winters are long and cold, averaging temperatures below freezing. Summers are short and cool, averaging from 63°F to 68°F (17–20°C). North of the Arctic Circle, the sun remains above the horizon day and night in the summer and below the horizon day and night in the winter. The aurora borealis lights up the northern night in winter. South of the Arctic Circle, where most of the population lives, the summer day lasts 19 hours and the nights are only partly dark. By contrast, midwinter daylight lasts only six hours. Finland has implemented tough environmental standards and initiatives to protect its environment.

History

Finnish people have lived in the area known as Finland since about 3000 B.C. Germanic peoples and other tribes also inhabited the area thousands of years ago, including the Tavasts, Lapps (Sami—pronounced SAY-me), and Karelians. Over time, the Finno-Ugric tribe became dominant. In 1155, a crusade from Sweden to Finland brought Catholicism and Swedish rule to the region. Finland was part of the Swedish kingdom for the next several hundred years, although Protestantism replaced Catholicism during the Reformation. Upon losing a war to Russia in 1809, Sweden ceded Finland to Russia.

Under Sweden, Finland did not exist as a unified entity but was only a group of provinces. The Russian czar, Alexander I, promised to grant Finland extensive autonomy and he did so. Finland thus became a grand duchy of the Russian Empire, with Alexander as the grand duke. Finnish historians consider the years under Alexander one of the best periods in Finnish history. A Finnish national movement led to the switch from Swedish to Finnish as the official language (in 1863), and the Finns had a semiautonomous legislature to administer local affairs. This autonomy was eventually resented in Russia, and in 1899, attempts were made to integrate Finland more fully into Russia. These "Russification" policies were resisted in Finland and would have eventually led to armed rebellion. Before that could happen, however, the Bolshevik Revolution gripped Russia. On 6 December 1917, Finland declared its independence, which was recognized by the Bolsheviks.

After a brief civil war, the Finns adopted a republican constitution in 1919. During World War II, Finland twice fought the Soviet Union: in the 1939–40 Winter War and then in the Continuation War until 1944. As a result, Finland was forced to cede one-tenth of its territory (roughly Karelia) to the Soviets. Finland avoided Soviet occupation, however, and preserved its independence.

In 1948, the Finns signed a friendship treaty with the Soviet Union that bound Finland to repel any attack on the Soviet Union that involved Finnish territory. The treaty still allowed trade and good relations with the West, but it created a situation where the Soviet Union could influence Finnish foreign policy. In 1989, Soviet President Mikhail Gorbachev officially recognized Finland's neutrality for the first time. In 1992, Russian President Boris Yeltsin signed a treaty with Finland's president to void the 1948 agreement. The new treaty recognizes Russia's and Finland's equality, sovereignty, and positive economic relations. Also in 1992, Finland decided to integrate more fully with Europe by applying for membership in the European Union (EU). Finland did not formally apply until after an October 1994 referendum gave public approval. The EU accepted the application and welcomed Finland as a full member on 1 January 1995.

Elections in 1991 brought Finland its first nonsocialist government in several years, sending the once-ruling Social Democrats into the Parliament's opposition. The new center-right coalition government took office during the global recession and suffered a loss of popularity when the economy weakened. Despite rebounding in 1994, the economy and other issues helped return the Social Democratic Party to dominance in 1995. Paavo Lipponen serves as prime minister.

THE PEOPLE

Population

The population of Finland is slightly more than five million, growing at a rate of only 0.3 percent annually. The majority of the people are Finns, although there is a significant Swedish-speaking minority. Finland also has very small minorities of native Sami and Russians. The overall population density is only six persons per square mile, but most people live in the southern Finland. More than 60 percent of Finns live in towns or cities, with nearly 40 percent residing in rural areas. Urbanization is a relatively new trend, so most people still have roots in the countryside and their home villages.

The country's Human Development Index (0.934) ranks it fifth out of 174 countries. Adjusted for women, the index (0.918) ranks Finland second out of 130 countries. Excellent access to health care, education, and the resources needed for a decent standard of living affords men and women many choices and opportunities in their lives.

Language

More than 93 percent of the population speaks Finnish, a Finno-Ugric language belonging to a different language family than other Scandinavian languages. It is most closely related to Estonian. Swedish is also officially recognized and is spoken by about 6 percent of the people. While only the Sami minority speaks Sami, Finland recognizes it as a language (but not an official one). English is a popular second language, especially among the youth and the educated. Those who speak Finnish as a native language must study Swedish for three years in school. Likewise, Swedish speakers learn Finnish. Finnish has very few consonants but many vowels. With 15 different cases, it is often difficult for foreigners to learn.

Religion

Although about 86 percent of the population belongs to the Evangelical Lutheran Church of Finland, the government has an official policy of religious neutrality. In fact, since 1923, freedom of religion has been guaranteed. The Evangelical Lutheran Church still performs important functions as a state church, however, including population registration and cemetery maintenance, and it is supported by state taxes. The Finnish Orthodox Church, which is also supported by the state, claims the next largest following in Finland (1 percent). Several other Christian groups and other religions are also active. As in many European nations, growing secularization has caused a decline in church attendance and membership. Approximately 12 percent of Finns are not affiliated with any religion.

General Attitudes

Finns maintain high ideals of loyalty and reliability, taking promises and agreements seriously. The people are generally reserved, and they appreciate etiquette and punctuality. They are, of course, proud of their Finnish heritage, as their language, culture, and national identity survived centuries of domination by other powers. Finns are especially proud of their small nation's status in the world. Finland has been a leading nation in peace conferences and initiatives. Finns are proud to have one of the cleanest environments in the world, and they stress values that maintain this. Enjoying nature (through activities such as berry picking in the forests) is an important part of their lives. Finland is also a leader in women's rights. Indeed, there is little talk of "feminism" because women expect to be involved in careers, politics, social issues, and motherhood all as a matter of course. In addition, an increasing number of men expect to share household responsibilities with their wives.

Personal Appearance

Finnish fashion standards are very high and internationally recognized. Finnish designs follow European lines. Formal wear is popular on festive occasions. Hats are worn during the winter. Men remove their hats when entering a building or elevator, or when speaking to another person. Colorful native Finnish costumes can be seen during festival times, at weddings, or at some graduation balls. They vary from region to region but usually involve a layered dress (including apron) and bonnet or cap for women and trousers, shirt, and waist-length jacket or vest for men. Young women wear ribbons like a headband instead of a cap. Men also usually wear a peaked cap, felt hat, or woolen cap. These costumes have their origins in the 18th and 19th centuries. Stripes are popular for the dresses and jackets, but there are literally hundreds of variations.

CUSTOMS AND COURTESIES

Greetings

It is customary to shake hands with men and women when greeting. People may sometimes use both hands, but they usually avoid further physical contact. When introduced, people mention their full names or a title and last name. Traditionally, Finns did not use first names until invited to do so, but using first names on first meeting is now quite common, especially among the youth. Men may raise hats (if worn) to greet people at a distance; otherwise, a nod is acceptable. A general greeting is *Hyvää päivää.* (Good morning/afternoon), or even just *Päivää.* Another expression for "Good morning" is *Hyvää huomenta.*

Gestures

It is considered bad manners to talk with one's hands in one's pockets. During conversation, maintaining eye contact is important but folding one's arms can be a sign of arrogance and pride. While it is proper to cross the legs with one knee over the other, it is inappropriate to sit with one ankle over the other knee. When yawns cannot be suppressed, one covers the mouth.

Visiting

Finns expect visitors to be punctual. Visitors usually take cut flowers as a gift, or they may send them afterwards to thank the hosts. Visits are nearly always an occasion for coffee and cakes or cookies. Guests wait until the host has taken a first sip before they drink. Most visits are more informal and involve relaxing and socializing. On special occasions, guests may be invited to sit in a sauna with the hosts. Spending time in the sauna is a national pastime.

Eating

When invited to dinner, visitors sit where the host asks them to and they do not begin eating until the hostess or host begins. Table conversation is generally light, but topics such as religion or politics are not avoided. Guests do not ask personal questions of their hosts. Finns eat in the continental style, with the fork in the left hand and the knife remaining in the right. Dress is conservative in restaurants but may vary between casual and formal, depending on the restaurant. The check is presented on request and is paid at the table. While some people leave small change on the table, a 15 percent tip is usually included in the bill and is therefore not otherwise expected. However, porters, doormen, and coat checkers receive tips.

LIFESTYLE

Family

The average Finnish family has one or two children. Population growth is so low that the Finnish government is trying to increase the birthrate because the number of working people is declining compared to the number of people receiving retirement benefits. Women are offered paid maternity leave of up to 11 months, and their husbands can share a portion of that leave. In addition, women receive a small monthly allowance for each child until the child is 17. Day-care facilities are provided by the government free of charge. Both parents usually work outside the home. In fact, half of all Finnish wage earners are women. Women hold more than one-third of Parliament's two hundred seats, and many women hold important government and business positions.

Most families own their own homes. Traditionally, houses were made of Finland's plentiful wood. Over time, however, brick has become more common; it lasts longer, requires less care, and is less flammable than wood. Taxes are high and housing is expensive, but Finns enjoy a high standard of living. Most families have access to summer cottages for vacations.

Dating and Marriage

Dating begins at about age 15, first in groups, then in couples. Movies and dances are popular activities. Many young couples choose to live together before or instead of marrying. The youth are moving away from many traditions and accepting more secular views of personal relationships. When two people marry, they both have the right to keep their original surname or to take that of their spouse. Their children may also bear either surname.

Diet

Finnish cuisine has been influenced by many cultures, from French to Russian, but it includes a wide variety of Finnish specialties using fish and seafood, wild game, and vegetables. Reindeer steak is a traditional specialty, as is salmon. Wild berries (blueberries, cloudberries, strawberries, and raspberries) are popular in desserts and liqueurs. Potatoes, cheeses, and a Finnish buffet (such as the *smörgåsbord*) are also very popular. Rye bread is common and open-faced sandwiches are eaten for snacks and at breakfast. Milk and coffee are the most common beverages for everyday drinking. Traditional Christmas foods include salmon, ham, herring, and various casseroles. Ginger cookies and other sweets are also common at Christmastime.

Recreation

Recreation and general fitness are important to Finns, whose favorite hobbies include fishing, hunting, camping, and other sporting activities. Ice fishing is popular on winter weekends. Favorite sports include skiing, track-and-field, basketball, Finnish baseball (*Pesäpallo*), ice hockey, cycling, and boating activities. Golf is gaining popularity; some even play on the ice in the winter. The sauna is a traditional way to relax for people of all ages. During retreats to summer cottages, people like to run from their hot saunas for a swim in the cold, clear lakes nearby. *Sauna* is a Finnish word that has been adopted by English and other languages. Because Finns traditionally relate to the forest, many of their favorite recreational activities revolve around the forest, from picking wild berries and mushrooms to hiking and taking vacations. Lakes likewise play an integral role in recreation.

Holidays

The most important holidays include New Year's Day (1 January), Easter (two days), *Vappu* or May Day (1 May), Whitsunday (Pentecost), Midsummer (summer solstice), Independence Day (6 December), and Christmas (24–26 December). The Finland Festivals (16 of them) are held between

June and September around the country and include art, music, dance, opera, theater, and other festivities.

At Easter, families decorate Easter eggs and grow grass on plates in the home. On Palm Sunday (a week before Easter), children dress up as Easter witches and recite charms door to door. They receive sweets or money for their verses. During *Vappu*, people enjoy street carnivals and other celebrations in honor of both springtime and laborers. Finns celebrate Midsummer with huge bonfires by the lake; people usually leave cities and towns to go to the countryside for this day. The blue and white Finnish flag is also prominent on this day. Christmas is a time of peace, family, and gifts. A main meal is eaten Christmas Eve after a visit to family graves. Later, Father Christmas (who looks like Santa Claus) arrives with gifts for the children. Rural families enjoy time in the sauna on Christmas Eve as well. Christmas Day and 26 December are days for visiting and relaxing.

Commerce

Stores are usually open from 9:00 A.M. to 6:00 P.M., Monday through Friday, and Saturdays from 9:00 A.M. to 2:00 P.M. Some shops and department stores are open until 8:00 P.M. on weekdays and 5:00 P.M. on Saturdays. Shops in Helsinki's subway stay open even later. Banks close at 4:15 P.M. on weekdays and do not open on weekends. The Finnish worker enjoys a workweek averaging 37.5 hours.

SOCIETY
Government

The Republic of Finland has 12 provinces. The republic's constitution provides for an elected president who serves as head of state for a six-year term. Martti Ahtisaari was elected president in 1994. Members of Parliament (*Eduskunta*) and the prime minister serve four-year terms. All men are expected to serve at least 18 months in the military. The voting age is 18. In addition to the Social Democrats, the Center Party and National Coalition Party are the largest political parties. Several smaller groups have representation in Parliament.

Economy

The Finnish economy is based on the free market and relies heavily on imports for many raw materials and important goods. Finland's most important exports are timber and timber-related products. Also important are shipbuilding, chemicals, and textiles. Natural resources include timber, silver, iron ore, and copper. High-technology industries are growing in importance. Economic growth for 1995 was about 5 percent. Unemployment remains high (about 16 percent). Finland is self-sufficient in grains, dairy products, and some meats. Other foods are imported. The currency is the *markka* or *Finmark* (FMk).

Finns enjoy a high standard of living. Real gross domestic product per capita is $16,270. Most people have access to economic prosperity in spite of a high cost of living.

Transportation and Communication

Although fuel is expensive, most Finnish families own at least one car. Overall, the roads in Finland are in good condition. The railway system is an excellent form of transportation. Buses, a good domestic air service, taxis, and ferries (for transport on lakes and across rivers) also serve the public. Helsinki has a subway. Finland's modern communication network includes numerous television and radio stations, an efficient phone system, and more than 250 newspapers.

Education

Education is a major priority for the Finnish government. Beginning at age seven, children are required to attend a free comprehensive school for at least nine years, after which they may attend a vocational school or complete three years of senior secondary school. Finland has a high rate of enrollment in secondary schools. Many students go on to further studies at one of Finland's several university-level institutions. The University of Helsinki was founded in 1640. Although university students do not pay tuition, they do pay small annual fees (for health insurance and student services). The adult literacy rate is 99 percent. Finns are well-read, and public libraries have high attendance.

Health

Finland takes great pride in its health programs. Health care is socialized, reliable, and modern. It is funded by national and local taxes. Citizens receive free basic health care from municipal health centers, but they can also pay to visit a private doctor if they choose. Public and private hospitals provide specialized care. Finland has one of the lowest infant mortality rates in the world at 5 per 1,000. This is due, in part, to an extensive network of maternity clinics. Life expectancy ranges from 73 to 80 years. Finland has one of the world's highest doctor-patient and nurse-patient ratios.

FOR THE TRAVELER

While passports are required, U.S. citizens do not need visas for visits of up to three months' total time in Scandinavia—Denmark, Iceland, Finland, Norway, and Sweden. No vaccinations are required, and the water is safe to drink. Numerous travel packages and different types of vacations are available in Finland, from skiing on the ice pack to camping by lakes. For information on travel possibilities, contact the Scandinavian Tourist Board, 655 Third Avenue, Suite 1810, New York, NY 10017; phone (212) 949–2333. You may also contact the Embassy of Finland, 3301 Massachusetts Avenue NW, Washington, DC 20008.

Boundary representations not necessarily authoritative.

France
(French Republic)

BACKGROUND

Land and Climate

Slightly smaller than Texas, France covers 211,208 square miles (547,030 square kilometers). The terrain is varied, from plains to mountains and forests to farmland. The north coast lies along the English Channel and the west coast along the Atlantic Ocean. The southeast coast is on the Mediterranean Sea. Mountains stretch along the borders with Spain, Italy, and Switzerland. France boasts Europe's highest peak, Mount Blanc (15,771 feet or 4,807 meters). The Rhine (*Rhin*) River forms part of the border with Germany; the northern border with Belgium is a flat plain with rolling hills. The southern climate is Mediterranean, with warm, moist winters and hot, dry summers. The north is temperate and prone to rain. The west is also rainy and is influenced by the Atlantic, which moderates winter temperatures. The central east and upland areas have a continental climate, with fluctuating temperatures; in the mountains, thunderstorms are prevalent in summer. French sovereignty extends to the island of Corsica as well as ten overseas *départements* and territories.

History

By 51 B.C., the Romans had conquered the area's Celtic inhabitants, the Gauls, who then adopted the Roman's customs, language, and laws. Clovis I, king of the Franks, defeated the last Roman governor in A.D. 486. In the late eighth century, France was just one part of the vast empire ruled by Charlemagne. In 987, France emerged as one of the empire's successor kingdoms. The following centuries brought intermittent conflict, particularly with the English, including the Hundred Years' War from 1337 to 1453. In 1429, after 80 years of war, Joan of Arc led the French in victory over the English.

Later burned by the English (1431), she remains a French heroine today.

By the late 1600s, France dominated Europe. Under Louis XIV (the Sun King), the movement toward centralized government reached its peak. His palace at Versailles was the envy of the continent. But by 1789, royal extravagance and defeats in foreign wars resulted in the French Revolution. The monarchy of Louis XVI was toppled and the country entered the "reign of terror." Despite the conflict, the French Revolution marks a milestone in world history: the general movement toward democratic government. After a decade of instability, Napoleon Bonaparte took power, declaring himself emperor in 1804. Napoleon conquered most of Europe before embarking on a disastrous campaign in Russia in 1812. In 1814, Austrian and Prussian forces seized Paris and Napoleon was exiled. He returned in 1815 for the Hundred Days' War, which ended in his defeat to the English at Waterloo.

The monarchy was restored but was followed by the Second Republic (1848–52) and then the Second Empire (1852–70) under Napoleon III. Defeat at the hands of Germany led to the Third Republic in 1871. France was a major battleground during both world wars. It was occupied by the Germans between 1940 and 1944 and is famous for the D-Day invasion that turned the tide of World War II in favor of the Allies. In 1946, the Fourth Republic was declared, and after a referendum in 1958, a new constitution for a Fifth Republic was approved. Charles de Gaulle became president. France was a founding member of the European Community and is a central force in European Union (EU) politics today.

In 1968, students and workers protested over poor working conditions and a rigid educational system, resulting in

EUROPE

lasting social change. The 1968 events were still fresh in the public mind when students in the early 1990s took to the streets, protesting conditions in public schools and proposed changes in wage laws. The social unrest and economic difficulties led three successive prime ministers to resign before a conservative was given the job in 1993. Maintaining support in the 1995 elections, the conservatives enjoy a majority in both houses of Parliament.

THE PEOPLE

Population

France's population of 58.1 million is growing annually at 0.5 percent. Three-fourths of the population lives in urban areas. Greater Paris claims eight million inhabitants and Marseilles one million. Ethnically, the French have a Celtic heritage that has mixed with various other European groups (Latin, Nordic, Teutonic, Slavic, and others) over the centuries. Immigrants and descendants of immigrants from France's old colonial possessions also inhabit France. These include North Africans (Algerians, Tunisians, and Moroccans), West Africans, Caribbean peoples, and Asians from the former Indochina region. Although they have integrated into French society, the various ethnic groups generally do not mix with one another. North Africans remain the most separate because of their Islamic religion.

The French enjoy a high standard of living. France's Human Development Index (0.930) ranks it eighth out of 174 countries, indicating most people benefit from economic prosperity and the country's strong social welfare programs. Adjusted for women, the index (0.898) ranks France seventh out of 130 countries.

Language

French is an important international language. It is an official language of the United Nations and is second only to English in use between nations for communication, business, and diplomacy. The French government has stressed the language so much that almost everyone in France speaks French, despite the different nationalities represented. Even regional dialects have lost their importance in recent years.

Despite the prominence of French, France has recognized its citizens' need to learn other languages. In 1992, it announced that traditional language learning in school would start earlier (age nine) and that all students will be required to learn a second foreign language beginning at age thirteen. In addition, past emphasis on grammar and theory will be replaced by a focus on communication skills. English is the most common foreign language. Even before 1992, children were learning English outside of school. Despite this move toward other languages, the French government resists the inclusion of foreign words and phrases in the French language.

Religion

The majority of the French (nearly 90 percent) are Roman Catholic and practice their faith by celebrating the various religious holidays and attending mass once or twice a year. While regular attendance at mass is increasingly rare, many people visit places of special devotion, such as shrines, to worship. A small percentage of the people belong to other Christian churches (2 percent), the Jewish faith (1 percent), and Islam (1 percent). About 6 percent claim no religion.

General Attitudes

The French believe success is judged by educational level, family reputation, and financial status. They are extremely proud of their culture, heritage, and way of life. They are among the most patriotic people in the world, which is illustrated by their attempts to limit the influence of other cultures in France. This patriotism includes a general expectation that visitors have some knowledge of French and show appreciation for French culture. While French attitudes have traditionally been dominated by Paris, there seems to be a growing decentralization in administration as well as attitudes. The French are reserved and private, and people tend to be more hospitable outside Paris. Politeness is valued in human interaction, and *s'il vous plaît* (Please) is a valued phrase.

Political and social trends have caused the French to reexamine their national identity. Society seems divided over issues related to the central government's structure, education, immigration, economics, and even language. This introspection has led some to predict that French society will experience fundamental change during the next generation.

Personal Appearance

In general, the French take great care to dress well and fashionably, whether they are wearing formal or casual attire, and they feel more at ease with visitors who show the same degree of attention to appearance. Paris is the home of many of the world's leading fashion designers. Professional attire, depending on the business and location, tends to be formal. Parisians dress more formally than people in other cities. In the southern sunbelt, dress is more casual but not less stylish.

CUSTOMS AND COURTESIES

Greetings

Shaking hands upon greeting and parting is customary in France. An aggressive handshake is considered impolite. The French handshake is a light grip and a single, quick shake. Generally, a woman does not offer her hand to a man but waits for him to initiate the greeting. If their hands are dirty or wet, some Frenchmen will offer their elbow or arm to shake. It is normal for women to be kissed on both cheeks by male and female friends. Actually, they touch cheeks and kiss the air. The standard phrases for greeting include *Bonjour* (Good day) and *Comment allez-vous?* or the more informal *Ça va?* (both meaning "How are you?"). Greetings are usually combined with the person's name or a title and always precede any conversation or request. Good-bye is *Au revoir* (Until we meet again) or the less formal *A bientôt!* (See you soon!). A favorite among young people is *Salut!* for both greeting and parting. Friends and close colleagues use first names; otherwise titles are important and customary. Besides professional titles, *Monsieur* (Mr.), *Madame* (Mrs.), or *Mademoiselle* (Miss) are commonly used.

Gestures

The American "OK" sign (rounded index finger touching the tip of the thumb) means "zero" to the French. The French gesture for "OK" is the "thumbs up" sign. Slapping the open palm over a closed fist is vulgar and should be avoided. Sitting with legs spread apart is impolite; one should sit straight with knees together or with legs crossed at the knee. Feet are not placed on tables or chairs. The French are careful about their personal habits, being discreet when sneezing, blowing the nose, etc. They do not use personal items, such as combs and toothpicks, in public. It is improper to speak with hands in the pockets or to chew gum in public.

Visiting

The French are formal in their visiting customs, and people do not often visit unannounced. Guests usually arrive on time because punctuality is a sign of courtesy. However, for some social events it is also polite to arrive a few minutes late, allowing the hosts extra time for final preparations. Guests do not enter a home until invited inside. They generally sit where the host directs. It is a polite gesture to bring candy, wine, or flowers to the hostess, except red roses (which express love) and chrysanthemums (used in cemeteries). When ending a visit, a guest waits for a polite silence before rising. At the door, small talk, expressions of thanks, and repeated good-byes continue; it is impolite to be in a hurry to leave. Dinner guests often send a thank-you note the next day. At mealtime, pleasant conversation is appreciated as much as fine food. However, because the French are private people, it is best to avoid personal questions and sensitive topics such as politics and money. The hosts should be complimented on the meal; good cooking is a matter of pride in French homes.

Eating

Etiquette is important. Both hands remain above the table at all times. A man may rest his wrists, and a woman her forearms, on the table edge. One does not place the elbows on the table. Speaking with food in the mouth is impolite. It is improper to help oneself twice to cheese. The French eat in the continental style, with the fork in the left hand and the knife remaining in the right. Lettuce is folded into small pieces with the fork but never cut. Fruit is peeled with a knife and eaten with a fork. Bread is broken with the fingers and used to wipe the plate. One places the knife and fork parallel across the plate when finished. Formal lunches and dinners may last more than two hours, with as many as eight to twelve courses. Social meals begin with an appetizer in the living room, then hors d'oeuvres, followed by a course of fish or pasta or something cooked in a crust or sauce, the main course with vegetables, salad, cheese, fruit, and then a dessert. Coffee finishes the evening. A typical family meal has two to four courses. When eating out, the person who invites or makes the suggestion is the one who pays.

Wine is consumed with most meals, except breakfast; dozens of varieties are available. The French are knowledgeable about wine quality. Unless certain of its high quality, foreign guests should not give wine as a gift.

LIFESTYLE

Family

While the nuclear family is still the most important unit of society, many people are now moving away from their extended families to work or study. Still, many children remain at home until they finish their education, and families enjoy getting together when possible. Most families enjoy a comfortable standard of living, although class distinctions are still fairly visible. In cities, most people live in apartments. The average family has one to two children. Pets outnumber children in France and receive special attention.

Dating and Marriage

The average youth starts dating around age 15. Favorite activities are going to dances and movies. The French cinema is well developed, and American films are also popular. Because French teenagers do not normally have jobs, their finances for social activities are limited. Social class, wealth, and level of education are important in the choice of a mate. Civil ceremonies are required by law. Religious ceremonies are optional but common. Many couples choose to live together before or instead of marrying. Many also choose not to have children.

Diet

The French consider cooking an art, and French cuisine is famous and popular around the world. French cookbooks date back to the Middle Ages, and French standards were the early gauge of fine cooking. Regional traditions are strong. There are several types of cooking, ranging from hearty, inexpensive fare to sophisticated dishes with costly ingredients and rich, complex sauces. *Nouvelle cuisine*, which emerged in the 1960s, was a reaction to the heaviness of this style of cooking. While still made of expensive ingredients, it is much lighter, portions are smaller, and the presentation is more artistic.

Most French eat a light continental breakfast (croissants or bread and coffee). Lunch was once the main meal of the day, but urban society has changed and many people now have a light lunch and eat their main meal in the evening. In Paris, lunch (*déjeuner*) is usually eaten around noon or 1:00 P.M. and dinner frequently is not before 9:00 P.M. In other parts of the country, particularly rural areas, people eat earlier.

The French resist fast-food. Filled croissants and sandwiches in their traditional form can be purchased in vending machines, shops, and cafés. Cafés also offer toasted ham and cheese (*croque-monsieur*) and a plate of salad-type vegetables for a light meal. *Pâtisseries* sell cakes and some places sell crêpes. The resistance to foreign fast-food has not been entirely successful, as many hamburger restaurants operate across the country.

Recreation

The French are enthusiastic spectators, but fewer participate in team sports than might be expected. Soccer and rugby are popular spectator sports. Participation is highest in individual sports: fishing, cycling, tennis, hiking, skiing, and sailing. Others enjoy hunting, horse riding, and golf. People of all ages enjoy *pétanque*, a form of bowling that originated in southern France. Leisure activities include watching television, visiting museums, or attending plays and concerts. The annual *Tour de France* cycling race is a popular national event. Most people take five weeks of vacation each year, four weeks in the summer and one week at Christmas. Camping is popular in the summer. During August, when many people travel, some shops and factories close. Summer music festivals occur throughout France. Recent years have seen increased support for concerts, theater, and the opera.

Holidays

The French celebrate several holidays each year. For New Year's (*Etrennes*), they often present flowers to older family members, and some exchange gifts. People celebrate New Year's Eve with parties and fireworks. In February, Mardi

Gras (Shrove Tuesday) is celebrated with parades and parties. Easter Sunday and Monday are legal holidays. Labor Day (1 May) is marked by parades and celebrates the coming of spring. French Armistice Day (*Le Huit Mai*) is 8 May and Bastille Day (*La Fete Nationale*) is 14 July. Bastille Day commemorates the storming of Bastille prison in Paris during the French Revolution. At Christmas (*Noël*), the tree is decorated on Christmas Eve, followed by a big meal and midnight Mass. Shoes are left by the fireplace for Santa Claus to fill. Other holidays include Ascension, Pentecost, Assumption (15 August), All Saints' Day (1 November), and World War I Armistice Day (11 November).

Commerce

Businesses and non-food shops open from 9:00 or 9:30 A.M. to 6:00 or 6:30 P.M., Monday through Saturday. Some large stores stay open until 9:00 P.M. one or two evenings a week. Small shops, especially in rural towns, may close for lunch and on Mondays. Many food shops open as early as 7:00 A.M. and on Sunday mornings. Banks close at 4:30 P.M. Many businesses close on holidays. The average workweek is 39 hours.

SOCIETY

Government

The French Republic has 22 regions subdivided into 96 departments, not including overseas possessions. France's president serves as both head of state and executive head of government for a seven-year term. The president also appoints a prime minister from the majority party in the National Assembly and has the right to dissolve the assembly to call for new elections. The president has no veto power but can rule by emergency decree in a crisis. Conservative Jacques Chirac (Rally for the Republic Party) became president in 1995, replacing retired President Françios Mitterrand (Socialist). Alain Juppe serves as prime minister. The voting age is 18. The National Assembly's 577 members are elected for five-year terms. The Senate's 321 members serve nine-year terms and are elected every three years by about 130,000 local councilors.

Economy

France has one of the world's most highly developed economies enabling its people to enjoy the benefits of economic prosperity. Real gross domestic product per capita is $18,510, which has tripled in a generation.

As one of Europe's leading agricultural producers, France is self-sufficient in most foods. The agricultural sector employs about 7 percent of the workforce and is a world leader in wine, milk, butter, cheese, barley, and wheat production. Major industries include steel, motor vehicles, aircraft, textiles, chemicals, and food processing. Exports include machinery and transport equipment, steel products, and agricultural goods. The service sector employs two-thirds of the labor force. More than half of France's power is generated by nuclear power plants.

France is a signatory of the Maastricht treaty, which calls for greater European economic integration. Although France has benefited from success within the EU, efforts to integrate have slowed down. High unemployment (12 percent) and wide public deficits remain the nation's greatest socioeconomic problems. Efforts to overhaul the welfare system were met with crippling strikes at the end of 1995. The currency is the French *franc* (F).

Transportation and Communication

The public transportation system is well developed. Buses serve most cities, and train service extends to even the smallest towns. Trains are best for long-distance travel. The TGV (*train à grande vitesse*) is one of the world's fastest passenger trains with a top speed of 300 MPH (480 KPH). Most people own private cars, which are generally French brands, such as Renault or Peugeot. Taxis in urban areas are expensive. Paris has a subway. The French domestic air system is efficient, and car ferries link France with Corsica and Great Britain. In 1994, a new rail link to England opened. A trip from Paris to London, crossing under the English Channel, takes three hours. The actual time in the tunnel is 35 minutes.

The communications system is modern. Pay phones generally use phone cards (*telecarte*) purchased at a post office. They are based on time used and can be used more than once—until the time paid for runs out. The post office is the center for various forms of communication and transactions.

Education

Schooling is free and compulsory from ages six to sixteen. The literacy rate is 99 percent. Nearly 20 percent of all children attend Catholic schools that are partly subsidized by the state. Secondary education, lasting seven years (11–18), is offered by *lycées* and *collèges*. *Lycée* students gain the equivalent of a U.S. junior college education with an additional emphasis on philosophy. After secondary education, students take an exam to determine if they may go on to higher education.

Education is practically free at France's 60 universities, including the Sorbonne in Paris. However, the best students take further preparatory classes in order to attend the *Grandes Ecoles*, where they study for careers in government, the military, education, and industry (engineering, marketing, and management).

Health

Medical care is generally good and is available to all citizens through a socialized system. Prices and fees are fixed by the government. Many French also carry private insurance to pay fees not covered by the government. In addition to public hospitals, private clinics are available. The French enjoy good health, with an infant mortality rate of 7 per 1,000 and life expectancy rates ranging from 75 to 82 years.

FOR THE TRAVELER

U.S. citizens can travel in France for up to three months without a visa, but a valid passport is required. Visas for longer stays can be obtained through an embassy or consulate. Try to learn some French before going, as the people not only appreciate the attempt but may expect visitors to use French when possible. For more information, contact the French Tourist Office, 444 Madison Avenue, 16th Floor, New York, NY 10022; or the Embassy of France, 4101 Reservoir Road NW, Washington, DC 20007–2185; phone (202) 944–6200.

Boundary representations not necessarily authoritative.

Republic of
Georgia

BACKGROUND

Land and Climate

Georgia covers 26,912 square miles (69,700 square kilometers) and is slightly larger than South Carolina. Most of the country is mountainous, including the highest peaks, Shkhara (17,656 feet) and Mkinvartsveri (16,677 feet) of the Great Caucasus Range. The Lesser Caucasus Range is in the south, and the Surami (*Likhi*) Range divides the country between east and west. Several rivers supply hydroelectric power, and natural and thermal springs are abundant.

Georgia's climate ranges from subtropical in coastal areas to a continental climate further inland. The capital, Tbilisi, is located in a valley and along the slopes of high hills; its winter is windy and chilly with Fahrenheit lows in the 30s and highs in the 40s (0°–10°C). Snow falls mostly in mountainous regions. Spring begins late and summer is hot and dry, with temperatures reaching above 90°F (32°C). Rain is most heavy in coastal regions.

History

Georgia is Greek for "the land of farmers." The native name is *Sakartvelo*, or "the land of the Kartvels," as Georgians call themselves. Historically this name applied only to central Georgia. Western Georgia was known between the sixth century B.C. and third century A.D. as Colchis; the east was part of Iberia. The Egrisi (Lazica) Kingdom flourished in the third and fourth centuries. Situated on strategic territory, Georgia was invaded or otherwise influenced by Arabs, Persians, and Turks prior to the tenth century.

Georgia's "Golden Age" occurred in the 11th and 12th centuries. King David the Builder (ruled 1089–1125) created a strong, ethnically mixed, and internationally active state. Under the rule of Queen Tamar (1184–1213), Georgia's territory and population (12 million) were at their largest. A 13th-century Mongol invasion ushered in a gradual decline.

Exhausted by repeated wars and famines, Georgia sought protection from the Orthodox Christian Russian Empire. A protectorate treaty was signed in 1783, but it did not protect the region from a devastating Persian invasion in 1795. In 1801, the last Georgian king, Giorgi XII, asked Russia for autonomous incorporation into the Russian Empire. Russia obliged but, by 1864, had fully annexed the entire region.

Despite intense Russification, the 19th century was marked by a Georgian cultural revival led by nobleman Ilia Chavchavadze. He was assassinated in 1907 by opponents of Georgian nationalism. The 1917 Russian revolution reopened the door to Georgian independence, which was declared in May 1918. The door closed quickly in 1921 when the Red Army invaded and began the period of Sovietization.

Although Joseph Stalin was an ethnic Georgian (real last name: Jugashvili), Georgia suffered his repression like all Soviet republics. While resistance to Moscow's rule was not overtly apparent for many years, with the exception of a 1956 protest that was put down by tanks, Georgians never accepted Soviet ideology. In April 1989, several political protesters were killed by Soviet troops, and Georgians pressed for independence. It was declared in April 1991 following elections that removed Communists from power.

The Soviet Union soon disintegrated, but peace did not come to Georgia. The policies of Georgia's President Zviad Gamsakhurdia led some ethnic minorities to seek their own independence. After a series of insurgencies, the economy collapsed and 350,000 people became refugees. The problem was most severe in Abkhazia (a northwest autonomous republic created in 1921), where ethnic Georgians were driven from the region by Abkhazians who wanted independence. A bitter struggle finally ended in an agreement to let the refugees return home, but implementation of the 1994 accord was hindered by continuing disagreements. Russia, which had been

EUROPE

aiding Abkhaz rebels, cut off supplies and sealed its border with the region in January 1996. Abkhazia's economy collapsed with the subsequent blockade, and rebel leaders participated in formative negotiations for peace later in the year.

South Ossetia (an autonomous political unit on the Russian border) also seeks autonomy, desiring to unite with North Ossetia in Russia. That situation remains unresolved.

After Gamsakhurdia was forced to flee in 1992 (he died in 1994), leadership was assumed by former Soviet Foreign Minister Eduard Shevardnadze. Georgia joined the United Nations and instituted democratic, market-oriented reforms. It also joined the Commonwealth of Independent States (CIS) to help ensure its territorial integrity.

An assassination attempt wounded Shevardnadze in 1995, but it did not keep him from becoming president through the nation's first fully democratic elections in November 1995.

PEOPLE

Population

Georgia's population of 5.6 million is growing at less than 0.9 percent. About 55 percent of the people live in urban areas. Ethnic Georgians comprise 70 percent of the population. Minorities include Armenians (8 percent), Russians (6.3 and declining), Azeris (5.7), Ossetians (3), Abkhazians (1.8), and several smaller groups (Kurds, Ukrainians, Germans, Greeks, and others). Exact tallies are impossible due to the refugee crisis. Georgia's Human Development Index (0.709) ranks it 92d out of 174 nations. This indicates that existing social institutions have potential to allow for personal advancement, but they are not yet functioning at the desired level.

Georgians are divided into a dozen distinctive regional groups. Their differences are not unlike those between people in different U.S. states. For instance, eastern Kartlians and Kakhetians consider themselves more composed and even-tempered than Mingrelians, Gurians, Imeretians, and others. Mingrelians speak a unique ancient dialect.

Tbilisi, founded in A.D. 459, is home to 1.25 million people. The second largest city is Kutaisi, followed by Sukhumi (partially destroyed during the Abkhaz rebellion) and Batumi. Large Georgian communities are found in France, Russia, Turkey, and Iran. Those in Iran are Muslim descendants of Georgians taken to Persia in the 17th century.

Language

The official and common daily language is Georgian. Most urban Georgians can speak Russian. Minorities speak their native language in addition to either Russian or Georgian.

Georgia's alphabet was created in the second century B.C. by King Parnavaz and is one of the world's 14 original alphabets. It has 33 letters and uses the original, but slightly modernized, script. Georgia's oldest known literary work, "The Martyrdom of Saint Shushanik," dates to the fifth century.

Abkhazian also ranks as an official language but is only used and understood in Abkhazia. English is the most popular foreign language, followed by German, French, and Turkish.

Religion

Georgia adopted Christianity by A.D. 337. St. Nino is revered for doing much of the "enlightening," and is one of the most worshiped saints in Georgia. Despite lengthy periods of non-Christian domination, Georgia remains a Christian nation. The Georgian Church is autonomous but affiliated with the Greek Orthodox Church; its patriarch, Ilia II, is respected for preaching interreligious tolerance and nonviolence.

Even during seven decades of Soviet rule, people considered religion crucial to cultural survival. Most people (65 percent) belong to the Georgian Church, but some are Russian Orthodox (10 percent) and Armenian Orthodox (8).

The Ajara Autonomous Republic near the Black Sea in southwest Georgia is the only region to have a Muslim Georgian population, as the region spent considerable time under Turkish rule. Overall, 11 percent of Georgians are Muslim. Roman Catholics, Baptists, and Jews also live in Georgia. There are several working synagogues.

General Attitudes

Georgians are committed to their land of ancient history and tradition; even in the most difficult times, emigration has been minimal. Centuries of multicultural interaction have made Georgians tolerant of other religions and cultures. For instance, Jews have lived in the land for at least 2,500 years without notable discrimination.

Despite a geographical link to Asia Minor, Georgians identify with Western culture and see their future as tied to Europe. Georgians are proud of their country and are pragmatic and positive about the future. They view themselves as a peaceful, beautiful, nonchalant, and romantic people with a difficult destiny—difficult because of their history of having to fight for a national identity and independence. Georgians value friendship and passing time in pleasant company. To outsiders they sometimes seem boastful and verbose, as Georgians like to create an impression of abundance. Pessimism has increased in recent years because of growing hardships, but Georgians try to remain cheerful and not too self-critical.

In Georgia, abstract norms and rules are generally less important as social regulators than are the mores and values formed between relatives, colleagues, and peer groups.

Personal Appearance

The standard dress is European. Traditional costumes are seen only at folk dance performances and during national holidays. Georgians pay attention to how they dress, choosing quality clothing even if it is not affordable. Sloppy or careless dress is considered improper, even in casual situations. Jeans are popular among all segments of society. Adults and teenage girls do not wear shorts in public. Dress, hairstyles, and public behavior remain conservative. Eastern Georgians tend to have darker hair and eyes than western Georgians.

CUSTOMS AND COURTESIES

Greetings

When greeting, Georgians shake hands and say *Gamarjoba* (literally, "Let you win"), which means "Hello." Responses differ; the term is repeated for official greetings, or *Gagimarjos* serves as a responding "Hello" in informal cases. *Rogora khar?* (How are you?) is an informal way to begin a conversation. *Rogor brdzandebit?* is more formal. *Kargad ikavit* means "Bye, take care." *Mshvidobit* (Peace be with you) is used for a more substantial parting. In cities, it is uncommon for people to greet strangers on the street; in rural areas, however, people commonly greet, smile at, and sometimes speak to strangers passing by.

Shaking hands is common even at casual meetings. Embracing in a friendly manner or kissing on the cheek is also common, especially among young people and women. Small children might receive hugs and kisses. Adults are addressed by professional title and last name, or by first name following *Batono* (Sir) or *Kalbatono* (Madam). Using *Batono/Kalbatono* with just the last name is heavily formal, so first and last names are used in correspondence or in the media.

Gestures

Conversations can be animated and Georgians often use their hands to express themselves. Eye contact is appreciated. People sometimes express appreciation for something by raising a "thumbs up." Pointing with the index finger is improper but practiced. Chewing gum in public, especially when talking, is impolite but also practiced. Legs may be crossed at the knee, but feet never touch the furniture. Public displays of affection between young couples are inappropriate. People usually stand when an elderly person enters a room.

Visiting

Georgians are sociable and hospitable, known for friendly and generous treatment of even unexpected guests. A Georgian saying is "Any guest is God's messenger." Oral and phone invitations to the home are traditionally popular. The hardships of the 1990s have changed cultural habits; once-frequent visits to friends and relatives have declined. This is due not only to social unrest but also the economic situation; hosts feel they cannot provide as adequately for guests as in the past. Still, hosts expect to offer at least a cup of coffee or cookies to guests. They offer full dinners to invited guests when possible. Guests bring gifts only on special occasions, but flowers are a polite and welcome gesture; something for the children is always appreciated.

In Tbilisi, people have long enjoyed strolling down Rustaveli Avenue in the evenings to meet friends, eat at sidewalk cafés, or attend theater or opera performances. During the civil unrest, they retreated to the safety of their homes. With life slowly stabilizing, these old pleasures are returning.

Eating

Family meals are shared together. Breakfast is light if eaten early and more substantial when eaten around 9:00 A.M. Lunch is called a "second breakfast" if eaten before noon and "dinner" if eaten after noon. The evening meal is called "dinner" if eaten before 5:00 P.M. and "supper" if eaten after that hour. Most people eat after 6:00 P.M. Georgians eat in the continental style, with the fork in the left hand and knife in the right. They eat some fish and meat dishes with the hands. Georgians prefer to eat with a neighbor or someone else than to eat alone.

Georgian is known for a traditional table ritual. Before a meal, a toastmaster (*Tamada*) proposes toasts, to anything from national values to each person at the table, and drinks the entire glass after each toast. Women only drink symbolically, but men do as the *Tamada*. It is improper to serve alcohol without first proposing a toast. Traditionally, people drank Georgian wine from *Kantsi* (embroidered deer, bull, or goat horns) passed around the table. Today, *Kantsi* are displayed in homes or sometimes used by the *Tamada* but not passed around.

When guests are present, the hostess prepares and serves the meal, although she eventually joins the group if other women are present. Hosts traditionally provided more than could be eaten, but hard times have changed that. Guests might not ask for seconds and can decline offers of such without insulting the hosts. They are, however, expected to eat everything on their plates and compliment the hosts on the food.

LIFESTYLE

Family

Family attachment is highly valued in society. In most families, at least three generations have lived together for a considerable portion of their lives. The father is responsible for economic support, major financial transactions, and protecting the family's old and young. The mother is most influential in the decision-making process. Parents usually have two children. Most women care for the household and children, as well as hold jobs outside the home. Grandparents often provide day care in these cases.

Traditionally a newlywed couple lives with the groom's parents until they can afford an apartment or home. This is changing now and families try to accommodate couples who cannot rely on traditional arrangements. Also, more young adults are working to help support the household.

Urban families typically rent apartments, which until recently were government owned. The law now allows families to buy apartments, but many are waiting for society to stabilize before making the investment. A typical apartment has one or two bedrooms, a living room, a small kitchen, and a bathroom. Rural homes are more spacious, but constructing such houses is difficult due to the price of scarce building materials.

Dating and Marriage

When dating, couples might go to movies or concerts, visit each other's homes, listen to music, walk in city parks, or meet at cafés. Social unrest and economic hardship have made it unsafe and expensive to do some things, but greater stability is allowing for more recreational choices.

A person generally is free to choose a spouse, and families do not often interfere. A traditional wedding is rather flamboyant, with large feasts, folk dancing, and singing. Today's weddings are not as extravagant, with urban ceremonies being fairly quiet family events. Virginity on a girl's wedding day is a traditional value. Fidelity is extremely important in marriage, although men traditionally have enjoyed some liberties that more wives now refuse to accept.

Diet

Georgians grow a variety of fresh fruits and vegetables, as well as wine grapes and tea. Variety and abundance in midautumn are celebrated by the rural harvest holiday *Rtveli*. Salads, vegetables, eggs, bread and butter, cheese, ham or sausage, and coffee or tea are eaten for breakfast. The "second breakfast" or "dinner" typically consists of soup and/or meat, potatoes, beans, vegetables, fruit, bread, and wine. Supper comprises the same basic foods as dinner; good wine is indispensable.

Dishes in the west tend to be lighter than in the east. Spices are popular everywhere. The most common meats include beef, pork, chicken, and lamb. Abundant vegetables include tomatoes, cucumbers, beans, eggplant, and cabbage. Popular fruits are apples, pears, and peaches. Among the favorite national dishes are *Satsivi* (fried chicken or turkey soaked in walnut sauce with spices), *Khatshapuri* (twisted, salted cookies, sometimes with a fried egg in the center), and *Gozinaki* (a honey-and-walnut confection).

Recreation

In their leisure time, people might watch television or videos, read, or go to theaters, movies, exhibitions, or concerts. Georgia boasts high-quality theater performances. Favorite sports include soccer, basketball, skiing, and tennis. People also follow figure skating and hockey competitions. Georgians enjoy weekend outings. Urban residents with summer cottages spend as much time as possible there enjoying nature, gardening, or tending to greenhouses. Rural people generally are occupied by farming and have less time to relax.

Holidays

The main official holidays include New Year's Day (1 January), Christmas (7 January), Easter Sunday, and Independence Day (26 May). New Year's is celebrated mostly in families, but parties are also arranged. Special meals and champagne are common for New Year's Eve celebrations. People usually do not exchange gifts for Christmas, as this is primarily a religious holiday. Colored eggs and special cakes are prepared for Easter. Other prominent religious holidays include Epiphany (19 January), Our Lady's Day (28 August), and St. George's Day (23 November).

Commerce

Businesses are mostly open from 10:00 A.M. to 7:00 P.M., with a break around midday. Prior to national holidays, offices close early but stores are open longer. State stores, private businesses, and kiosks have fixed prices. Bargaining occurs at farmers' markets or with spontaneous street traders.

Georgia's private industry is in its infancy, as are the standards of commerce. The most recent trend is the "trade fair," where prices are lower than in stores and bargaining for the wide variety of goods and foods is acceptable. Such fairs are held regularly in a growing number of cities.

SOCIETY

Government

Georgia is a republic with a Western-style government and legal system. It is headed by a strong executive president, elected for a four-year term. A new constitution was ratified in October 1995. Parliament has 250 seats. The largest party is Shevardnadze's Citizens Union Party, but various other parties also have representation. Georgia's Law of Citizenship allows every permanent resident to become a citizen regardless of ethnic origin. It also sets generous guidelines for new settlers. In cooperation with President Shevardnadze, Parliament is strengthening democratic institutions and working to curb crime and corruption. The voting age is 18.

Economy

Georgia traditionally has had a strong agricultural and industrialized economy, with exports of wine, tea, brandy, fruit, vegetables, manganese, marble, and arsenic. But in the post-Soviet economic crisis the system of supply and distribution collapsed. Many enterprises closed and Georgia began importing basic necessities. Still, the country has the potential for food self-sufficiency. And as the economy stabilizes, tourism, agriculture, and mineral sectors can expand. Even amid crisis, private enterprises are emerging in light industry, construction, transportation, food, and finance.

Georgia's inflation moderated in 1995, allowing for the introduction of a national currency named *lari.* Real gross domestic product per capita is estimated to be $3,670. Economic prosperity cannot be realized in the near future but certainly later as conditions improve.

Transportation and Communication

Georgia has a well-developed transportation system, with taxis, buses, trolleys, and streetcars serving urban areas. Tbilisi has a subway. The expense and scarcity of fuel have hampered transportation, but private enterprises and government efforts are filling gaps as the economy improves. Buses running between towns are crowded. Most roads are paved but are not in the best condition. Bicycles are not common, partly due to steep terrain in many areas. Airports operate in all major cities and Tbilisi Airport receives daily international flights. Two large ports at Poti and Batumi are vital to shipping throughout the Transcaucasian region.

Most urban families and businesses have phones, and many in rural areas do as well. Media broadcasts reach most homes with independent television and radio programs. People read newspapers regularly. The postal system, a remnant of the Soviet network, still depends on Moscow. It can take months for a letter from abroad to reach an addressee; those who can afford it use fax machines or electronic mail to communicate internationally.

Education

Children begin school at age six and graduate at seventeen, whereupon they receive a certificate of completion that entitles them to begin work or seek higher education. Major ethnic minorities have their own schools, some of which use their native language for instruction along with Georgian. Private and specialized schools are becoming more popular.

There are 21 state-run institutions of higher education and more than 100 private or cooperative ones. Obtaining a good education is a high priority, and literacy is 99 percent.

Health

The public health-care system lacks the efficiency and quality of expensive private services. Georgian physicians are highly skilled, but the nation lacks ambulances and fuel, heated and supplied hospitals, and so forth. Rural inhabitants suffer particular difficulties in obtaining care. At present, regular humanitarian aid from abroad is vital. The infant mortality rate is 23 per 1,000; life expectancy is 73 years.

FOR THE TRAVELER

U.S. citizens need a visa and passport to enter Georgia. Driving in the countryside is advisable only if one is accompanied by local people. To ask directions, begin the inquiry with "Excuse me" (*Ukatsravad* or *Bodishi*). For travel information, contact the Embassy of Georgia, 1511 K Street NW, Suite 424, Washington, DC 20005; phone (202) 393–6060.

Germany

(Federal Republic of Germany)

Boundary representations not necessarily authoritative.

BACKGROUND

Land and Climate

Covering 137,803 square miles (356,910 square kilometers), Germany is just smaller than Montana. There are four main geographic zones: the broad lowlands in the north; the central uplands, including various small mountain ranges; the wide valley and gorge of the Rhine River in the southwest; and the forested mountains and plateaus of the south. About 40 percent of Germany is forested. The Rhine, Danube, and Elbe Rivers flow through Germany. The climate is generally temperate and mild, with warm summers and wet winters.

History

Before becoming a nation-state (1871), Germany was divided into a patchwork of small separate principalities and was once part of the Holy Roman Empire. Through three wars (1864–70), Prussian leader Otto von Bismarck united Germany into a powerful, industrialized nation. In World War I (1914–18), Germany allied with Austria and Turkey. The United States joined (in 1917) Britain, France, Russia, Italy, and Japan to defeat the German Empire. Germany was made to pay huge reparations, admit guilt for the war, and cede about one-tenth of its territory. A democratic government, known as the Weimar Republic, was established in 1918.

The country's humiliation was made worse by the economic depression of the 1930s and a lack of support for Weimar leaders. Germany's distress gave rise to Austrian-born Adolf Hitler and his National Socialist (Nazi) Party. In 1933, President von Hindenburg named Hitler chancellor after the Nazis emerged as the dominant party in elections. In 1934, the day after von Hindenburg died, the posts of president and chancellor were combined, and Hitler declared himself *Führer* (leader) of the Third Reich. He soon embroiled Germany and the world in World War II. Before being defeated by the Allied forces in 1945, the Nazis occupied much of the continent, killing many, including six million Jews.

Germany was split into occupation zones to facilitate disarmament and organize a democracy. When the Soviet Union did not comply with the agreement, the zones occupied by the Western Allies became the Federal Republic of Germany (FRG), a democratic nation. The Soviets in turn created out of the eastern zone the German Democratic Republic (GDR), which followed the Soviet model of development. When thousands of people fled the east, the GDR built the Berlin Wall (1961) to shut off access to West Berlin. The wall remained a symbol of the Cold War until late 1989 when it was opened to traffic on both sides. The wall was eventually torn down and the two nations became the reunified Federal Republic of Germany on 3 October 1990. Berlin regained its status as the country's capital, but the actual transition from Bonn to Berlin will not be complete until the year 2000.

(Western) Germany was a founding member of the European Community, now known as the European Union (EU). It joined the North Atlantic Treaty Organization (NATO) in 1955, but German troops were restricted by constitution to German soil. In 1993, policy changes allowed troops to participate in United Nations relief operations in Somalia. Midway through his fourth term in office, Chancellor Helmut Kohl faces several challenges: record-high unemployment, the continued cost of German reunification, low economic growth, European integration, and immigration.

E U R O P E

THE PEOPLE
Population

Germany's population is slightly more than 81 million and is growing at 0.6 percent annually. About 86 percent of all Germans live in urban areas. The population is primarily ethnic German. Noncitizen minorities from Turkey, the former Yugoslavia, Italy, Greece, and other nations live in Germany as guest workers (*Gastarbeiter*). They comprise up to 20 percent of some western metropolitan populations. In western states, numerous political refugees from the Middle East, India, Africa, and Asia receive room and board until their applications for asylum are processed. A small Slavic (Serbian) minority resides in the east, and a Danish population lives in the north. Many ethnic Germans from eastern European nations have emigrated to Germany to find work. The much-publicized violence against immigrant groups reflects the feelings of only a small minority of Germans. Most Germans do not support such activity but do support stemming the flow of "economic" refugees. New laws restrict the definition of a valid asylum seeker and limit other forms of immigration.

Language

German is the official language. However, the German taught in school and used in the media often is not the German spoken daily. Various dialects are used in most areas. In fact, a German from Bonn or Hannover may have trouble understanding a person from München (where Bavarian is spoken) or Halle (Saxon). While the dialects are mostly verbal, they are part of folk literature and music and are also written. English, widely understood, is a required school subject. Many Germans in eastern states know Russian.

Religion

Germany is essentially a Christian, but secular, society. About 35 percent of the population belongs to the Roman Catholic Church, 36 percent is Protestant (mostly Lutheran), and 2 percent is Muslim. A number of other Christian denominations are active throughout the country. About 25 percent of the people have no official religious affiliation. Historically, entire towns and regions belonged to one faith, according to the local ruler's choice. These lines are still visible today, as Catholics reside mostly in the south and west and Protestants in the north and east.

General Attitudes

Germans are industrious, thrifty, and orderly. They appreciate punctuality, privacy, and skill. They have a strong sense of regional pride, a fact that the federal system of government recognizes and accommodates. World War II broke down class distinctions because most people lost their possessions and had to start over again. Germany emerged as a land of freedom and opportunity. Germans appreciate intelligent conversation but are often wary of unfamiliar or different ideas. Many are also prone to pessimism. Most Germans have a strong classical education because of the nation's rich heritage in music, history, and art, and they expect others to appreciate that background. Former East Germans share this approach to culture and are proud of how they have nurtured their cultural heritage through the performing arts and museums. After four decades of life under communism, however, it is not surprising that those in the east have somewhat different attitudes toward daily life and work.

Tensions exist between people in the west and east over matters relating to reunification. Easterners feel they are treated as second-class citizens, receiving lower salaries, getting blamed for tax hikes, and being ridiculed by their western counterparts. Westerners resent the economic burden of rebuilding the east; they believe easterners are less capable and unrefined. Such tensions will continue to exist at least until living standards in the east more nearly equal those in the west. Despite the emotional divisions, reconstruction and revitalization are building a united Germany.

Personal Appearance

Germans follow European fashion trends and take care to be well dressed in public. Sloppy or overly casual attire is inappropriate. Shorts and sandals are common leisure wear in summer. Women wear cosmetics sparingly. In southern Germany (mostly southern Bavaria), traditional clothing such as *Lederhosen* (leather pants, either short or knee-length), *Dirndlkleider* (dresses with gathered waists and full skirts, worn with an apron), Bavarian suits, and alpine hats may be part of one's modern daily wardrobe. Traditional costumes of other regions are worn during festivals and celebrations.

CUSTOMS AND COURTESIES
Greetings

A handshake is the most common form of greeting. If one's hand is dirty, one may offer an elbow or forearm to be shaken. A man waits for a woman to extend her hand before shaking it; in mixed company he shakes a woman's hand before a man's. In groups, several people do not shake hands at once; crossing someone else's handshake is inappropriate. Germans generally do not greet strangers on the street, although sincere smiles are appreciated. The most common verbal greeting is *Guten Tag!* (Good day). Some may use a simple *Hallo* (Hello). Many people in southern Germany use *Grüß Gott!* By tradition, only family members and close friends address each other by first name. Others use titles and surnames. However, this is changing among the youth. When addressing a stranger, acquaintance, or colleague, one combines *Herr* (Mr.), *Frau* (Mrs. or Miss), *Fräulein* (Miss for girls), or other titles with the person's professional title and last name. The titles can also be used without the name. For example, a male professor with a doctorate degree is addressed as *Herr Professor Doktor*; a female head of a department in business or government could be addressed as *Frau Direktorin*.

Gestures

Chewing gum in public is inappropriate, as is cleaning one's fingernails. Talking with one's hands in the pockets is disrespectful. People cross the legs with one knee over the other and do not place feet on furniture. Pointing the index finger to one's own head is an insult to another person. To wish luck, instead of crossing fingers, Germans "squeeze the thumb." That is, they fold the thumb in and close the fingers on it.

Visiting

Germans appreciate punctuality, but hosts are not insulted if guests arrive a few minutes late. Dinner guests often bring an odd number of flowers, avoiding roses (symbols of love) or carnations (for mourning). They unwrap flowers before giving them to the hostess. Guests usually stand when the host enters the room and remain standing until offered a seat again. It is also courteous to stand when a woman enters the room. Not everyone adheres to these rules of etiquette, but it is polite to do so. Hosts almost always serve refreshments to guests, even during short visits. Spontaneous visits, even between neighbors, are not very common. Arrangements are generally made in advance. Germans enjoy gathering for conversation and social events. While dinner parties may last well into the night, daytime visits are usually short, except afternoon *Kaffee-trinken*, where tea or coffee and cakes or cookies are served.

Eating

Germans eat in the continental style, with the fork in the left hand and the knife remaining in the right. They keep hands above the table, with wrists resting on the edge. Potatoes and fish are not cut with a knife because this indicates they are not fully cooked. Leaving food on the plate is considered wasteful. Most Germans prefer beer, wine, or mineral water with meals; they rarely drink tap water. Soft drinks and fruit juices are also popular. Germans prefer their drinks without ice, as they do not consider cold drinks to be healthy. Germany does not have drinking fountains because of the tradition of bottled water. In restaurants, the bill usually includes a service charge and is paid at the table. Customers often round up the total to the next *Mark* or even five *Marks*, giving the waiter the difference as an extra tip (*Trinkgeld*). This is more common in western states. If the restaurant owner serves the meal, leaving a tip is inappropriate.

LIFESTYLE

Family

Traditionally, the father is the head of the family. Both parents often work, more so in the east than in the west. Large families are not common, even in rural areas. The average family has only one or two children. While order, responsibility, and achievement are still traditional family values, a greater variety of lifestyles exists today, especially among those in the west. Most young adults prefer to live away from home once they become wage earners or go on to a university. Most families live in apartments. Single-family homes are by no means rare, just very expensive. About 40 percent of all western homes (whether houses or apartments) are owned by the occupants. The rate is lower in the east. In urban areas, people often own or rent small garden plots in or near the city.

Dating and Marriage

Dating is different in Germany than in the United States. The German language does not even have a word for *dating*. Young men and women socialize on a casual basis. If one wants to go out with another, either sex can suggest a *Verabredung* (appointment). They each pay for their own food and entertainment (unless one offers to pay for a special occasion). Young people usually marry in their twenties, but they often wait until they have some financial security. It is common for young people to live together before or instead of marrying. Legal marriages are performed at city hall; religious ceremonies are optional.

Diet

While regional dishes vary among Germans, potatoes, noodles, dumplings, sauces, vegetables, cakes, and pastries are common. Pork is a popular meat, along with beef and, to a lesser extent, chicken. Pork is prepared according to regional tradition; it may be boiled with cabbage in Frankfurt, roasted with dumplings in München, or prepared as ham in Westphalia. Lamb is widely available in the north. Fish is popular in North Sea areas such as Hamburg but also in Bavaria, where trout is plentiful. Every region has its own type of *Wurst* (sausage).

Breakfast consists of rolls, marmalade, and coffee or another hot drink. The main meal, traditionally served at midday, includes soup, a main dish, and dessert. For the lighter evening meal (*Abendbrot*), open-faced sandwiches (cheese, meats, and spreads) are common, unless people eat in a restaurant, where full meals are served. Two-income families rarely have a big midday meal; they eat the main meal in the evening and may or may not have *Abendbrot*. Germans buy groceries often and prefer fresh foods for cooking. Ethnic dishes (especially Italian and Greek) and fast-foods are popular. Germans are known for their beer making and drinking. They also enjoy domestic and other wines. However, the youth consume less alcohol overall than the older generation.

Recreation

Germans enjoy hiking, skiing, swimming, cycling, touring in cars, and playing tennis, among other things. Garden plots with small gazebos offer relaxation on summer evenings. People also enjoy watching television or visiting with friends. Soccer (*Fußball*) is the most popular sport and millions belong to soccer clubs. Germany's team traditionally participates in World Cup competitions. Organized sports participation is changing because of reunification. A uniform club system is being organized. Germans in the west have long relished travel, something those in the east are also beginning to enjoy. Carnival (*Fasching*) is important in some regions, where dances, parades, and other celebrations take place before the Catholic Lent. Of the performing arts, music and theater are most popular. Generous government subsidies have allowed even the smallest cities to have professional orchestras and opera companies. Summer arts and music festivals are held throughout the country.

Holidays

New Year's celebrations begin on *Sylvester* (31 December) with midnight fireworks and parties, followed by a public holiday on 1 January. Easter is celebrated with Sunday worship services and Monday family gatherings. Labor union parades mark Labor Day (1 May). Various religious holidays (Catholic and Protestant) are celebrated, such as Pentecost, Ascension, and All Saints' Day (1 November). The Day of German Unity is celebrated on 3 October. At Christmas, people exchange gifts on Christmas Eve (*Heiliger Abend*); the family relaxes on Christmas day. Germans enjoy visiting on 26 December, also a legal holiday.

Commerce

Before reunification, shops in the east were open late to accommodate workers, while stores in the west closed by 6:30 P.M. to comply with labor laws. However, Germany recently passed legislation permitting stores to remain open until 8:30 P.M. on weekdays. On Saturday, shops may close at 4:00 P.M. rather than 2:00 P.M., and bakeries can open for three hours on Sundays. Business hours range from 8:00 A.M. to

5:00 P.M. on weekdays. Banks close for lunch and then at 4:00 P.M., but they remain open a bit later on Thursdays. Many Germans shop daily for fresh produce (often at open-air markets) and bread (at bakeries).

SOCIETY

Government

Germany's president, currently Roman Herzog, is elected as head of state by members of the federal and state legislatures for up to two five-year terms; his duties are mostly ceremonial. Chancellor Kohl is head of government. He governs in a center-right coalition, led by his Christian Democratic Union (CDU) Party. Germany's legislature has two houses, the Federal Council (*Bundesrat*) and the lower Federal Assembly (*Bundestag*). The country has 16 states (*Länder*), each of which has its own legislature and autonomy over schools and other matters. State governments elect the 69 members of the *Bundesrat*, while the 662 members of the *Bundestag* are elected by popular vote. The voting age is 18. CDU's allied parties include Bavaria's Christian Social Union (CSU) and the Free Democratic Party (FDP). In opposition, the Social Democratic Party (SPD) is joined by the Greens, the Party of Democratic Socialism (PDS), and smaller parties.

Economy

Germany is one of the top five economic powers in the world. Germany's Human Development Index (0.921) ranks it 15th out of 174 countries. Real gross domestic product per capita is $21,120, although the figure for the east is less than half of that. Eastern prices are typically as high as those in the west, but salaries, rents, and overall living conditions remain lower. Germany's prosperity generally reaches all levels of society through the social network but to varying degrees, according to region and socioeconomic status.

The shift to a market economy in the east took more than one million jobs. Money from economically powerful western states is being used to revive the eastern economy, and some areas are beginning to do well. Western companies are buying many eastern factories and shops; the government is rebuilding roads, railways, and public transportation facilities; and workers are being retrained. More private investment is required in the east to revitalize industry and relieve the west of heavy tax burdens. Germany exports cars, steel, aluminum, televisions, and other manufactured goods. Germany's construction and service industries are strong components of the domestic economy. The German currency, the *Deutsche Mark* (DM), is one of the strongest in the world.

The economy rebounded slightly in 1994 from reunification costs and the global recession of the early 1990s, but it remained almost stagnant in 1995. Unemployment remains a serious problem for the country at 10 percent (9 percent in the west and about 15 percent in the east). Workers also face cuts in social benefits due to recent government austerity measures.

Transportation and Communication

Most families own cars; the car is more important to Germans than to many other Europeans. They especially favor cars for touring or traveling long distances. Public transportation and bike riding is more efficient for daily travel in major cities because of heavy traffic and limited parking. Subways, buses, streetcars, and trains form the main transportation network. Trains travel to nearly every town and city. Drivers and cyclists carefully obey traffic rules. One must attend expensive and rigorous driver-training schools to qualify for a driver's license. While there is no speed limit on sections of the *Autobahn* (freeway), there are strict limits on all other roads. The communications system is fully developed. Telephone and postal services are centralized and efficient.

Education

Education is a source of pride, especially in the areas of technology and craftsmanship. The states administer public education. Preschool begins around age four. Full-time schooling is mandatory between the ages of six and fifteen, and part- or full-time schooling continues on a chosen track until age eighteen. Students may enter a job-training program, train for specific professional careers, or study to enter a university. Nearly every occupation, from mechanic to waiter to accountant, has a school or program designed specifically for it. For example, waiters and waitresses might attend school for up to four years before certifying as servers. Because of this training, their salaries are much higher than their U.S. American counterparts.

German literacy is 99 percent. Education is free at all levels, but entrance to universities is difficult and can only be gained through success on the *Abitur* exam, taken at the end of *Gymnasium*, or college preparation school. Adults can continue their education through evening classes.

Health

Medical care is provided free or at minimal cost to all citizens. Private doctors also practice, but most people have access to care in hospitals and clinics. The government controls fees and some co-payments are required. In addition to government health insurance, private insurance is available. When workers become ill, they receive up to six weeks of full pay while they recover. People in eastern states suffer more often from pollution-related illnesses. Germany's infant mortality rate is 6 per 1,000. Life expectancy ranges from 73 to 79 years.

FOR THE TRAVELER

U.S. visitors do not need a visa to travel for up to three months in Germany, but a valid passport is required and should be carried at all times for identification. Tap water is safe, but people drink bottled water. When traveling on any public transit system, riders retain their tickets until the ride is over, as conductors may check them anytime. On subways and buses, travelers validate their own tickets in machines on board. Germany offers beautiful scenery, historical sites, and many recreational activities. Travel in the east offers a unique look at German culture. For travel information, contact the German National Tourist Office, 122 East 42d Street, 52d Floor, New York, NY 10168. You may also contact the Embassy of the Federal Republic of Germany, 4645 Reservoir Road NW, Washington, DC 20007; phone (202) 298–4000.

A *Culturgram* is a product of native commentary and original, expert analysis. Statistics are estimates and information is presented as a matter of opinion. While the editors strive for accuracy and detail, this document should not be considered strictly factual. It is a general introduction to culture, an initial step in building bridges of understanding between peoples. It may not apply to all peoples of the nation. You should therefore consult other sources for more information.

Greece

(Hellenic Republic)

Boundary representations not necessarily authoritative.

BACKGROUND

Land and Climate

Covering 50,942 square miles (131,940 square kilometers) in southern Europe, Greece is just smaller than Alabama. Although it lies farther east than most of western Europe, Greece is generally considered part of the West because of its heritage and its membership in the North Atlantic Treaty Organization (NATO) and the European Union (EU). It is situated south of Albania, Bulgaria, and the former Yugoslav Republic of Macedonia. The latter nation has been independent from the defunct Yugoslav federation since 1991, but its name is an issue of serious contention for Greece and other regional powers. Greece's northern province is called Macedonia, and Athens considers the neighboring country's use of the name a territorial threat.

Sparsely populated mountain areas cover much of Greece. Earthquakes are possible in these regions. The fertile valleys, plains, and coastal areas are more densely populated. Nearly 25 percent of the entire territory is arable. An archipelago of more than 2,000 islands is part of the country, but only 166 islands are suitable for habitation. A warm, temperate Mediterranean climate prevails in the south, while the north is wet and cool. In general, winters are mild but wet; summers are hot and dry.

History

Although the history of ancient Greece stretches back to 3000 B.C., Athens had its beginnings in 1300 B.C. and city-states began forming around 1000 B.C. From this point, Greek culture began to thrive. The first Olympics were held in 776 B.C., and literature, philosophy, and art began to flourish. By 400 B.C., the glory of ancient Greek civilization reached its peak. During that period, Athens was the center of a vast overseas empire. Many of the West's first studies of government, law, and the concepts of justice and liberty began in Greece. Its rich heritage of architecture, sculpture, science, drama, poetry, and government established a foundation for Western civilization.

Philip of Macedonia conquered Greece in 338 B.C., but he was assassinated. His son, Alexander the Great, led the Greeks to an empire that covered much of what is now the Middle East. After Alexander's death in 323 B.C., the empire declined, and by 146 B.C. it had become part of the Roman Empire.

Centuries later, along with Constantinople (now Istanbul, Turkey), Greece was the center of the Byzantine Empire, which fell in A.D. 1453. In 1460, Greece became a Turkish province. After four centuries of Turkish rule (the Ottoman Empire), the Greeks began a war of independence, supported by Britain, France, and Russia. In 1832, Prince Otto of Bavaria was made king of Greece. In World War II, Greece was occupied by German and Italian forces and lost one-eighth of its population to fighting and starvation. After liberation in 1944, a civil war between the government and Communist guerrillas cost another 120,000 lives. The government, with aid from the United States, was victorious in 1949.

EUROPE

In 1965, a political crisis developed between Prime Minister George Papandreou and King Constantine II, which resulted in Papandreou's dismissal. A group of army colonels staged a coup in 1967, and the royal family fled. From 1967 to 1974, the colonels ruled as a repressive dictatorship. Their eventual fall allowed for general elections, through which a republic was established when voters rejected a return to a monarchy. In 1981, Andreas Papandreou's Socialist Party won a majority in Parliament and he became prime minister. He was reelected in 1985 but lost the majority in 1989 in the face of various financial and political scandals.

Elections had to be held three times before Konstantinos Mitsotakis and his New Democracy Party received enough votes to form a government in 1990. Mitsotakis worked to privatize state enterprises, cut government spending, and prepare Greece for greater economic integration within the EU. Austerity measures that were necessary to accomplish those goals led to voter discontent. Hence, in the 1993 elections, the Socialist Party regained parliamentary leadership and Andreas Papandreou was returned to office as prime minister. He immediately began to reverse various privatization efforts and other economic policies. After experiencing months of poor health, Papandreou resigned as prime minister in January 1996; he was replaced by Costas Simitis. Simitis became party leader of the Panhellinic Socialist Movement (PASOK) after Papandreou's death in June 1996. Simitis seeks to revive the country's ailing economy and move it closer toward meeting the EU's Maastricht treaty convergence criteria.

THE PEOPLE

Population

The population is about 10.6 million and is growing annually at 0.7 percent. Nearly 98 percent are ethnic Greeks, but there is a small Turkish minority. Much smaller minorities include Albanians, Pomachs, and Slavs. Almost two-thirds (64 percent) live in urban areas. Athens, the capital, is the largest city, with a population of more than 3.5 million.

Greece's Human Development Index (0.907) ranks it 22d out of 174 countries. Most people enjoy good access to education, health care, and economic prosperity. Adjusted for women, the index (0.825) ranks Greece 27th out of 130 countries. Compared to women in other European countries, Greek women earn a lower share of their nation's income.

Language

Greek is the official language of Greece. It has a long tradition, remaining relatively the same since the days of Homer (9th–8th century B.C.). About 1 percent of the population speaks Turkish. English and French are widely understood, and English is a popular subject in schools.

Religion

About 98 percent of the people belong to the Eastern (Greek) Orthodox Church, which is the official religion in Greece and quite powerful. Although freedom of religion is guaranteed, the state supports the Eastern Orthodox Church through taxes, and other religions are not allowed to proselyte. The Orthodox Church is a Christian church directed by an archbishop (independent of the Roman Catholic Church) and the Holy Synod. Eastern Orthodox principles are taught in the schools. Religion is an inseparable part of the Greek way of life; however, Greeks generally are not religious. Older people, particularly women, attend church more frequently than young people.

About 1 percent of the people (mostly of Turkish origin) are Muslim; there are also members of other Christian churches and some of the Jewish faith in Greece. Jewish communities are located in Thessaloníki and Athens.

General Attitudes

Greek society traditionally is dominated by males, although in the last generation women, particularly those in urban areas, have gained greater prominence and rights. Men consider it a matter of personal honor to fulfill obligations to their families and others. They may attribute their failures to external circumstances rather than to personal inadequacies. Also, a man may praise the food served in his home as especially good or be the hero of his own tales. Such self-praise is not considered bragging. While Greece's older generations value family, religion, tradition, and education, the younger generation tends to view status and friends as also very important. Greeks are very proud of their cultural heritage, which they view as being central to Western civilization. Greeks see themselves as individualistic, brave, and hardworking.

Personal Appearance

Greeks generally wear clothing influenced by European fashions. Fashionable clothing is popular among the youth and has become essential for working professionals. Rural and older people generally prefer to dress more conservatively. Greek women wear dresses more often than do North American women. Traditional costumes are worn at folk festivals and on special occasions.

CUSTOMS AND COURTESIES

Greetings

Greeks are often expressive in their greetings. Friends and relatives hug and kiss when they greet each other. Otherwise, people shake hands. Young men often slap each other's back or arm at shoulder level instead of shaking hands. There are many different verbal greetings; their usage depends on the situation. One term for "Good morning" is *Kaliméra sas.* "Good evening" is *Kalispéra sas.*

Close friends and family members call each other by first name, but most people address acquaintances and strangers by their title ("Doctor," "Professor," "Mrs.," etc.) and surname. In urban areas, people do not greet strangers while passing on the street. When getting on an elevator, one usually nods at the others present and might give a short, general greeting. Villagers briefly greet passing strangers in rural areas.

Gestures

Gestures are frequently used among people of a similar social status; using some gestures with superiors or elders may be improper. To indicate "no," one tilts the head either backward or side to side. To indicate "yes," one nods the head slightly forward. Pointing a finger at someone is impolite; it often indicates anger, a threat, or authority. A Greek may smile not only when happy but sometimes when angry or upset. A person may release a puff of breath through pursed lips to ward off the jealousy of the "evil eye" after he or she has given or received a compliment. People use the hands a great deal in conversation, both to accompany and replace verbal expressions.

Visiting

Ancient Greeks believed a stranger might be a god in disguise and were therefore kind to all strangers. This tradition of hospitality continues to the present. In small towns, friends and relatives commonly drop by unannounced. However, in urban areas it is polite to inform friends and family before visiting them. Greeks enjoy inviting friends to their homes for dinner or for special occasions—such as name days or New Year's Day. Christmas and Easter present opportunities for family gatherings.

Invited guests usually take a gift to the hosts, including flowers, a bottle of wine, or cookies. All guests, invited or unannounced, are offered refreshments. A cup of coffee is most common, but other drinks, a homemade fruit preserve, or cookies are also popular. If Greek hosts insist several times about anything (that a guest stay longer or eat more, for example), they usually mean it, and guests try to accommodate them so as not to hurt their feelings.

Eating

Traditionally, lunch was the main meal of the day and was served in the early afternoon (between noon and 2:00 P.M.). However, due to changing work schedules, this is no longer practical for many families. Dinner is often eaten as late as 8:00 or 9:00 P.M. Leaving the table before everyone has finished eating is impolite. Greeks are careful to finish everything on the plate so as not to insult the cook. Taking second helpings is the best way to show appreciation for the meal and to compliment the hostess.

At restaurants, a group will often order a number of different dishes that everyone shares. It is not unusual for guests to go into the restaurant kitchen and choose their dinner by looking into the different pots of food. People leave tips not only for the server but also for the busboy.

LIFESTYLE

Family

The family unit is strong in Greece. It is vital that no member bring shame or dishonor to the family. If the parents of a family die, the oldest child usually helps younger siblings finish their education and get out on their own. The elderly are respected, addressed by courteous titles, served first, and have much authority. Greeks care for their elderly parents at home when possible. If the parents must live in a home for the elderly, their children take care of all arrangements and make frequent visits. Parents traditionally treat their children with firm discipline; however, this practice is changing. Still, parents (even the poorest) usually spend a large portion of their income on clothing, feeding, and educating their children. In fact, parents believe it is their duty to provide for a good education. And they will always help their children,

married or not, if they can. Some newlywed couples live with their parents or in-laws until they can afford a home of their own.

Dating and Marriage

Traditionally, the man asks the woman's parents for permission to marry her. If the parents approve, the two date and become better acquainted during a formal engagement. Such formalities are now quite rare, except among rural people. Young people socialize as they do throughout Europe, and it is common for a couple to live together before or instead of marrying. On Sunday afternoon in rural areas, the youth often gather in the village square to socialize. The average age for women to marry is 25; men usually marry at age 30.

Diet

While tastes vary between urban and rural dwellers, certain foods are common to all Greeks. These include lamb, seafood, olives, and cheese. People also eat potatoes, rice, beans, breads, chicken, fruits, and vegetables. Olive oil is used in cooking. Garlic, onions, and spices are also popular. Salads are often eaten with the main meal. *Souvlaki* is a shish kebab with cubes of meat (pork or lamb), mushrooms, and vegetables. Eggplant, zucchini, stuffed tomatoes, and pasta are all favorites. Bean soup is popular in the winter. For Easter, Greeks enjoy roast lamb and *kokoretsi* (lamb liver, lungs, and spleen wrapped in intestines and roasted on a spit).

Recreation

Coffeehouses were once the focal point of leisure activity for men. Now rare in urban areas, they still provide a place for rural men to play cards and discuss politics. Rural women stay at home with other women to do crafts and enjoy conversation. Movies (both Greek and foreign) and the theater are also popular. People enjoy festivals throughout the year that highlight ancient Greek theater and literature. With an Olympic tradition, the Greeks love sports, especially soccer, basketball, swimming, and sailing. Greece's national soccer team competed in the 1994 World Cup. On weekends, urban dwellers like to go to the beach or go skiing or fishing. Folk dancing is also common.

Holidays

Almost every city and village has a patron saint who is honored with a yearly festival. Easter is by far the most important holiday, celebrated with special feasts, processions, and gatherings. Greeks celebrate 1 January as St. Basil's Day and as a traditional day to give gifts, although many people now prefer to exchange gifts on Christmas (25 December). For many holidays, a traditional greeting is *Chronia polla* (Many years). At midnight on New Year's Eve, a special cake (*vasilopitta*) with a coin in it is cut into various pieces. Whoever gets the coin is supposed to have good luck during the new year. Other holidays include Independence Day (25 March), St. Constantine and Helen Celebration (21 May), Assumption (15 August), and Ochi Day (28 October). Ochi Day commemorates the day that Joannis Metaxas, then prime minister, said *Ochi* (No) to Hitler and Greece entered into World War II on the side of the Allies. It is considered a heroic decision because of the size of the German and Italian Armies.

Commerce

Work and business hours vary, depending on the season and type of business. Banks and government offices generally are open between 8:00 A.M. and 3:00 P.M. Shops may open and close when they want. During the hot summer months, many close between 2:00 and 5:00 P.M. In the past, most Greeks worked from 8:00 A.M. to 1:30 P.M. and from 5:00 to 8:00 P.M., Monday through Friday; however, this practice has nearly disappeared. Continuous shifts (9:00 A.M.–5:00 P.M.) are common in corporations and large department stores.

SOCIETY

Government

Greece is a presidential parliamentary republic, with a president, currently Kostis Stephanopoulos, as head of state. The president has a few statesman and executive duties, but the prime minister is head of government. The unicameral Chamber of Deputies (*Vouli ton Ellinon*) has three hundred members. Informally, the body is called simply *Vouli*. Elections are held at least every four years, the next being scheduled for 1997. All citizens are eligible and required to vote at age 18. The two main political parties include PASOK and the conservative opposition, New Democracy. Smaller parties have legislative representation and can sometimes have a significant impact on political events.

Economy

Greece traditionally is an agrarian nation; more than 25 percent of the labor force works in agriculture. Greece produces wine, wheat, wool, cotton, olives, raisins, and tobacco. The industrial sector has made important advances in recent years, and it accounts for 50 percent of export earnings. In addition to manufactured goods, exports include food, fuels, and raw materials.

Real gross domestic product per capita is estimated at $8,310, the lowest among EU countries. Still, this figure has doubled in the last generation. Most people are able to earn enough to meet their needs, and a growing number have access to economic prosperity. Inflation has dropped to 8 percent. However, the country faces decaying infrastructure and large budget deficits. Greece's currency is the *drachma* (Dr).

Transportation and Communication

Principal highways connect Athens with Thessaloníki and Pátrai. Roads may be poor in mountain areas, making travel to remote villages difficult. Buses and trains are the most common forms of public transportation. There are 37 commercial airports. In Athens, people commute by car and bus. Young people often drive motorbikes. Athens has one short subway line that cannot accommodate many travelers, so the government began building the Athens metro subway in 1992. It is scheduled for completion by 1996. Because traffic congestion is so bad in Athens, cars with license plates ending in an even number are allowed to drive in the center of town only on even days of the month (with odd numbers driving on odd-numbered days). There are more than one hundred daily newspapers in Greece and at least thirty are published in Athens. The government owns and administers the telephone, radio, and television systems.

Education

Education is free and mandatory. Although some start kindergarten earlier (age five), all children begin elementary school at age six. Students are required to complete six years of elementary school and three years of *gymnasia*. *Lyceums* are alternately available in three- or four-year courses that generally prepare a student for higher education. Universities, technical colleges, and schools of higher education are free to those who achieve enrollment through entrance exams. The literacy rate is 94 percent.

Health

All workers are required to have health insurance from either state-supported health-care systems, such as the Institute of Social Insurance (IKA), or through other agents. While the IKA provides all citizens with health benefits, it is not as efficient as people would like. Hospitals generally are understaffed and overcrowded. Doctors who work in public hospitals are not allowed to have private patients. A few private clinics do exist, but their services are not covered by state insurance. Many people feel they would obtain better care through a private system. Still, Greeks enjoy good health, with a life expectancy of 75 to 81 years. The infant mortality rate is 8 per 1,000.

FOR THE TRAVELER

While no visa is necessary for U.S. citizens to enter Greece, a valid passport is required. Visas are required for stays lasting longer than three months. Water outside of Athens and major resorts may not be safe for drinking. Greece offers beach resorts, historical sites, and both modern and ancient cultural events. For information on travel opportunities, contact the Greek National Tourist Organization, 645 Fifth Avenue, New York, NY 10022; phone (212) 421–5777. The organization has other offices in Los Angeles and Chicago. You may also wish to contact the Embassy of Greece, 2211 Massachusetts Avenue NW, Washington, DC 20008; phone (202) 939–5818.

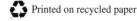 Printed on recycled paper

July 96

Grenada

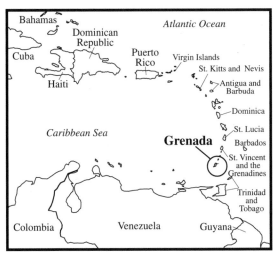

Boundary representations not necessarily authoritative.

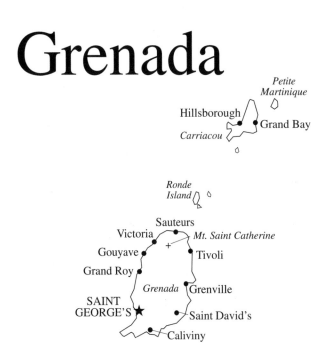

BACKGROUND

Land and Climate

Grenada, Carriacou, and Petite Martinique occupy 131 square miles (340 square kilometers) of territory in the Caribbean. Grenada is some 100 miles (160 kilometers) north of Venezuela and about 20 miles (32 kilometers) from its sister islands. Marked by a central range of hills and mountains—the highest of which is Mount Saint Catherine (2,700 feet or 800 meters)—the island is lush, tropical, and humid. Coastal areas are prized for fine beaches and a warm surf. The rainy season runs from June to December, with November being the wettest month.

Carriacou and Petite Martinique are drier, more barren, and marked by cactus. Such small islands do not attract much rainfall, presenting a water supply problem for residents. Hurricane season is August to October. Average annual temperatures of 85°F (29°C) in the day and 74°F (23°C) in the evening vary only slightly, becoming hotter in July and August and cooler in January and February. The heat is moderated by a near constant breeze.

History

Grenada was originally inhabited by Arawak Indians, who were supplanted by the war-like Caribs. Christopher Columbus sighted the island (but did not land) in 1498, naming it Concepción. The origin of the name *Grenada* remains obscure. In 1650, the French government of Martinique purchased Grenada from a French company that had taken it from the Caribs. British forces captured the island in 1762. The Treaty of Paris (1763) formalized the acquisition and, except for a brief French occupation (1779–83), Grenada remained a British colony.

The French and then the British imported African slaves to work on plantations until slaves were emancipated in 1833. From 1855 to 1958, Grenada served as headquarters for the Government of the British Windward Islands. From 1958 to 1962, Grenada was a member of the West Indian Federation.

In 1967, it became a self-governing state in association with the United Kingdom. Eric Gairy, trade unionist turned politician, led Grenada to independence (7 February 1974). As prime minister, he governed with a strong hand until March 1979, when the left-wing New Jewel Movement under Maurice Bishop staged a coup d'état. Bishop formed the People's Revolutionary Government (PRG) and served as prime minister. He enjoyed popular support and is still regarded by many as a national hero. Most were drawn to Bishop's personality, if not his policies.

The PRG soon developed close ties with Cuba and the Soviet bloc, alienating neighboring states. Particularly alarming was the size of Grenada's People's Revolutionary Army (PRA). In October 1983, General Hudson Austin of the PRA and Bernard Coard, PRG Finance Minister, led an internal coup that resulted in the violent execution of Bishop and several key government officials. On 25 October 1983, U.S. Marines and a coalition of Caribbean peacekeeping forces invaded to safeguard foreigners and restore law and order. Democratic elections were held in 1984 and the peacekeepers left in 1985.

Subsequent elections in 1990 did not result in a clear mandate; Governor General Sir Paul Scoon appointed Nicholas Braithwaite of the National Democratic Congress to be prime minister. In June 1995, the New National Party received the most votes and Keith Mitchells became prime minister.

PEOPLE

Population

Grenada's population of 94,000 is growing at 0.4 percent annually. The birthrate is higher than that, but emigration keeps net growth static. Most people (94 percent) live on Grenada, 5 percent live on Carriacou, and a few hundred reside on Petite Martinique. Saint George's, the capital and largest city, is home to 7,500 people. Most people reside in small villages. Grenada's Human Development Index (0.786) ranks it 67th out of 174 countries. Although most Grenadians are able to meet their basic needs, access to adequate health care and economic prosperity is limited.

Most Grenadians (84 percent) are descendants of African slaves. Other groups include mulattoes (mix of black and European, 12 percent), East Indians (3 percent), and whites of European origin (1 percent). East Indians descend from laborers who came to work on plantations after the slaves were freed. Many also mixed with Africans to produce a group known locally as the *duglas*.

Language

English, the official language, is used in education, government, business, and the media. Grenadian English differs from U.S. English in idioms and some spelling. For instance, *now for now* means "urgent," and *one time* means "at the same time." One says *Happy* (not *Merry*) Christmas or *Happy returns* (on holidays or special events). A car accident is a *bounce*.

Informally, Grenadians speak a French-English-African patois, sometimes referred to as creole or "broken English." Grenada's patois is noticeably different from that on Carriacou and Petite Martinique. The dialect has no past or future tense. Inflection and body gestures are primary tense indicators. Rastafarians (see Religion below) have affected Grenadian patois to a small degree, introducing such terms as *Irie* (Everything is cool) and the affirmative *Yes I*. Children are urged to use standard English in public, and Grenadians generally do not like outsiders to speak patois to them. But even spoken English contains patios elements, such as in the phrase "Don't *mamaguy* me" (Don't flatter me).

Religion

Roughly 60 percent of the population is Roman Catholic, while 35 percent belongs to various Protestant churches (mostly Anglican). The remaining 5 percent belongs to other Christian churches or practices Islam or Rastafarianism.

Christians generally worship on Sunday morning, with prayer meetings at various times during the week. Politicians freely invoke the powers of heaven, and school children pray at the beginning and end of the school day.

Rastafarianism is not practiced by many, but its stylistic influence (fashion, vocabulary, etc.) is widespread. Practicing "Rastas" generally believe that Haile Selassie I (emperor of Ethiopia from 1930 to 1974) was "the living God," that marijuana is a sacred herb, that one's hair should be grown long in dreadlocks, and that all Afro-West Indians must eventually move to Ethiopia, the promised land.

General Attitudes

Grenadians are warm, friendly people who enjoy doing and returning favors. Their generous sense of humor helps them deal with difficult circumstances in a casual way.

Disputes sometimes explode into angry shouting, but hard feelings seldom remain for long. Time schedules are not as important as people, and events usually start later than planned; it is customary to wait for everyone to arrive. Grenadians enjoy a strong sense of community. People often come together to finish a work project and share a meal or have a party. This cooperative effort is called a *maroon*.

How individuals feel about the 1983 U.S. military occupation is summed up by how they describe the event: American Rescue Mission (positive), American Intervention (neutral), or American Invasion (negative).

Personal Appearance

Grenadians, especially women, take great pride in their public attire. They make it a point to appear neat and well dressed, especially for church and certain social functions. Sloppy or very casual clothing is frowned upon, as are tourists who are skimpily clad away from the beach. Men wear trousers and either a button-down shirt or *shirt-jac* (square-cut, untucked shirt). Women typically wear a skirt and blouse or a dress. In rural areas, or around one's home, dress is more casual. Men may be barechested and people often go barefoot.

Youth fashions include blue jeans, T-shirts, and basketball shoes. Schoolchildren wear uniforms. Boys often untuck their shirts or unfasten their belts in the "ragamuffin" style, much to the chagrin of older Grenadians. Rastafarian colors (red, yellow, and green) are ubiquitous in Grenada, seen on everything from belts to shoes to caps. These colors are also on the Grenadian flag, but their use in fashion is tied to Rastafarianism and not patriotism.

CUSTOMS AND COURTESIES

Greetings

Grenadians greet one another with a handshake. Friends sometimes nod upwards or tap the faces of clenched fists instead. In a formal setting or among strangers, *Good morning*, *Good afternoon*, or *Good night* are typical greetings, followed by *Mr.*, *Miss*, *Mistress* (for married women), or *Madam* (for married women of higher social status) and the person's last name, if known. If the speakers know each other, they might combine the title with a first name. Grenadians express a verbal greeting before conducting business, beginning a conversation, or asking a question.

Rural acquaintances and friends casually greet each other with such patois phrases as *W'happen dey?* (What's happening?) or *Hows tings?* (How are things?) Typical responses include *Ah dey* (I'm all right) or *Just cool* (Everything is fine). Throughout Grenada, friends address each other by a *call name* (nickname).

It is considered rude to *pass a friend straight* in the street without at least nodding or saying hello. Grenadians often call out a friend's or relative's name as they pass his or her house and may stop briefly to chat if time permits. When parting, friends often say *Later!* or *We go see* (See you later). Formally, people might say *Until we meet again*.

Gestures

Waving the hand at waist level, palm down, means "no." Extending the thumb up from a closed fist means "good." To beckon, people wave the fingers with the palm facing down.

Hissing can mean different things. Men and women hiss to get a friend's attention, but when a man hisses at a passing woman, she ignores it as suggestive.

Visiting

Grenadians are considered among the friendliest people in the Caribbean; stopping to chat or socialize on the street or at a person's home is a favorite pastime. Such impromptu visits usually take place in the afternoon or early evening. Sitting on the porch, chatting at the roadside, or going to sporting events with friends is particularly popular after about 4:30 P.M. Visitors verbally announce their presence and wait to be invited in. Since most rural yards have watchdogs, this helps one avoid being mistaken for an intruder.

Grenadians nearly always offer guests refreshments and it is impolite to refuse these entirely. At a *fete* (party or gathering), if one cannot eat, it is polite to take something home for later. Funerals are social events. Men wear black suits and women wear hats with black or white dresses. People linger long at the graveside to talk. Men may go to a local rum shop to continue their conversations. In fact, rural men often socialize at rum shops—small bars where they can drink and play dominos, cards, or draughts (like checkers).

Women socialize less in the evening, except in family situations, and more through church and neighborhood organizations. They may also visit friends during the day.

Family visiting reaches a peak during Christmas. Relatives and close friends expect a visit during this season, and people typically visit from house to house for days. With each visit, they are offered food and something to drink (beer, rum, whiskey, black wine, or sorrel—a red, clove-spiced drink made from the flower of a sorrel bush).

Eating

Grenadians usually eat breakfast early in the morning, a main meal around noon, and supper at dusk. Families try to eat the main meal together. Supper is light, often consisting of bread and cheese. Most people eat from a bowl with a spoon. Wealthier families may add a fork and a knife. People drink coffee with breakfast and tea in the afternoon, but with lunch or supper they prefer soft drinks, fruit juice, or water. When eating at restaurants, Grenadians normally do not tip the server.

LIFESTYLE

Family

The extended family is central to Grenadian society, and one household often holds parents, children, grandparents, and cousins. Children might live at home well into adulthood. Family members look after one another and share resources and labor. Since most children are born out of wedlock and men typically do not consider it their role to raise them, they are often nurtured by the mother, aunts, grandparents, and cousins. Women run the household and men generally provide income. However, women are increasingly working outside the home as well. Wealthier and urban households more often include a nuclear family with both a father and mother.

Homes are constructed of wood and/or cinder block. They usually have one to three rooms, electricity, and water (except on Carriacou and Petite Martinique, which lack public water systems). Wealthy urban families often have other modern conveniences. Some rural homes have detached kitchens for cooking on coal pots. All Grenadians take pride in the appearance and cleanliness of their homes and yards. They often paint their houses bright colors and give them names (Hideaway, De Fort, Fair Winds, etc.). Domestic livestock (sheep, goats, chickens) share the rural yard with the dog. Each school day, children take sheep and goats to a grassy area for grazing and pick them up after school.

Dating and Marriage

Young people like to meet and date at dance halls or frequent street dances (*blockos*). Dancing (often called *wind and grind*) can be quite physical and older Grenadians think it is lewd. Dating is otherwise inconspicuous, and public displays of affection are generally frowned upon. Couples often live together before or instead of marrying, but when weddings do occur they are gala events. After a church ceremony, the entire village can enjoy plenty of food, music, and dancing.

Diet

Staple foods include plantains, corn, rice, breadfruit, and peas. Produce includes onions, green peppers, *callaloo* (green, leafy plant similar to spinach), tomatoes, and carrots. Chicken, fish, mutton, goat, pork, and beef are the most popular meats. Grenadians also like *manicou* (a type of opossum) and iguana. The variety of available seafood includes reef fish (barracuda and parrot fish), shark, snapper, sea turtle, tuna, lobster, and conch (*lambi*), as well as canned sardines and salmon. Many staple items are imported, including powdered milk, canned vegetables and meats, salt pork and salt fish, rice, cheese, coffee, and tea.

Locally favorite fruits include bananas, mangos, grapefruit, coconuts, and *paw paw* (papaya). Guavas are eaten fresh, stewed, as a jelly, or as *guava cheese* (a confection). A typical daily meal includes rice and peas (chickpeas or pigeon peas), a vegetable, and stewed meat. Soups, *souses* (boiled meat in a seasoned broth), fish broths, barbecues, and roasted foods are popular. Grenadians generously use hot pepper sauce, curries, and spices when cooking. The national dish is called the *oil down*, a stew of *callaloo*, breadfruit, meat or salt fish, and coconut oil. People also like *roti* (curried meat and vegetables wrapped in a flat bread) and *dahl* (curried chickpeas).

Recreation

Grenadians have a passion for cricket and closely follow the status of West Indian teams. Each town has cricket and *football* (soccer) teams, and boys begin playing at age ten. Basketball is becoming popular in urban areas. Girls play *netball* and watch other sports; both boys and girls participate in *athletics* (track-and-field). Men and boys like to fish, dive, or sail. Annual regattas draw fierce competition from around the region. Carriacou's Windward village is widely known for its hand-built sailing vessels. Most people like to watch television, and urban residents can go to movie theaters.

Music is extremely popular, and people of all ages love calypso, *soca*, reggae, ragamuffin, *dub*, and steel drum (or *pan*) music. U.S. American and British pop music, particularly slower, romantic *lovers' rock*, is also favored. Many Grenadians are competent on the guitar, violin, ukulele (often called *tenor banjo*), or drums.

Holidays

Grenadians celebrate Christmas, Good Friday, Easter (Saturday–Monday), Whitmonday, and Corpus Christi. Secular holidays include New Year's Day, Independence Day (7 February), Labor Day (1 May), Thanksgiving (25 October), Emancipation Day (first Monday in August), and Carnival. Thanksgiving, related to the 1983 U.S. intervention, is marked by official ceremonies but is generally ignored in the countryside.

Grenada's national Carnival is held in August in St. George's. Celebrations run from Sunday through Tuesday evening, with street dancing, concerts, and colorful parades. Carriacou celebrates Carnival three days before the Catholic Lent. Each parish (Saint George's, John's, Mark's, Andrew's, Patrick's, and David's) has a festival to honor the saint for which it was named. Villages and towns also hold local festivals, including Fisherman's Birthday (Saint Peter's Day) in Gouyave and Windward, Grenville's August Rainbow Festival, and Carriacou's August Regatta and December Parang festival (a competitive folk-music event).

Commerce

Businesses are typically open weekdays from 8:00 A.M. to 4:30 P.M., and 8:00 A.M. to noon on Saturday, though longer hours are common in urban areas. Shops close on Sunday. Banks open from 8:00 A.M. to 2:00 P.M. weekdays, except on Friday when they stay open until 5:00 P.M. Each large village or town has a Saturday open-air market for fresh fruits and vegetables. These markets are also a center for socializing. Street vendors are common and licensed.

Rural people buy staples from *cum-rum* shops (small family-owned shops that carry various goods), fresh produce from the open-air market, and meat and fish from roadside butchers and vendors. Supermarkets are found in larger urban areas.

SOCIETY

Government

Grenada is a parliamentary democracy and a member of the Commonwealth. A governor general, currently Reginald Palmer, represents the British queen, who is head of state. The prime minister is head of government and is usually the leader of the dominant party in the House of Representatives. Grenada's Parliament includes an elected 15-member House of Representatives and an appointed 13-member Senate. The voting age is 18.

Economy

Grenada's developing economy centers on agricultural exports and tourism. Known as the Isle of Spice, Grenada is the world's second largest nutmeg producer and is well-known for cocoa, cinnamon, cloves, pepper, and ginger. Other exports include bananas, coconuts, and mangoes. Agriculture accounts for 40 percent of employment, most of it on small, private plots. Tourism is important in and around St. George's. Remittances from Grenadians working abroad provide the country with needed income.

Real gross domestic product per capita is $3,822. This figure reflects the fact that one-fourth of the rural population lives in poverty and the economy lacks diversification. Most families work hard to meet basic needs. Unemployment is about 25 percent. The currency is the East Caribbean dollar (EC$).

Transportation and Communication

Air service and regular, inexpensive boat service link the islands. Paved roads connect major towns and villages. While there is a public bus system, most people rely on private minibuses for local transportation. Minibuses wait in market areas until full and then depart for their destination, dropping and adding passengers along the way. Private taxis are available, and groups can charter a *board bus* (truck-turned-bus with a canvas top and wood sides) for special events. People commonly walk short distances, especially in more remote areas. The youth like to ride bicycles.

Grenada has a number of radio stations, and television provides a mixture of local news and overseas (usually U.S.) programming. Several weekly newspapers are published, but radio remains the primary source for news. Residential phone service is available, and most communities have public phones.

Education

Education is compulsory for ages five to sixteen. Churches own most schools, but the government sets the curriculum. Students may choose a school based on their religion, but the choice is most often based on a school's reputation, location, or other factors. About 88 percent of Grenadians finish primary school; students must then pass the Common Entrance exam to enter the secondary level. Of the roughly half that do advance, the vast majority graduate. Postsecondary education can be obtained at the University of the West Indies, which has a branch in St. George's; various technical centers; or a teacher-training college. Grenada's literacy rate is 98 percent.

Health

Free health care is available to all Grenadians. Parishes and some towns have a clinic staffed with health assistants who perform preventive care and see minor cases. Government doctors make regular visits to the clinics. General Hospital in St. George's is somewhat crowded and under equipped. Two other hospitals (in St. Andrew's and Carriacou) provide basic services. High costs prohibit most Grenadians from visiting private doctors, whose level of care is generally better. Average life expectancy is 68 to 73 years. The infant mortality rate is 12 per 1,000.

FOR THE TRAVELER

Although not required, a passport is recommended for U.S. citizens traveling to Grenada. Water is safe to drink on the main island but is untreated elsewhere. Avoid being out alone at night because of petty crime. Tourism centers on St. George's, where one can visit Grand Anse beach, Fort Frederick, the National Museum, and the picturesque Carenage. More than 200 old sugar mills and 31 forts (many with cannons in place) can be seen. Carriacou offers a quiet, remote experience. For more information, contact the Grenadian Embassy, 1701 New Hampshire Avenue NW, Washington, DC 20009; phone (202) 265–2561; or call the Grenada Board of Tourism at (800) 927–9554.

Republic of
Guatemala

Boundary representations not necessarily authoritative.

THE AMERICAS

BACKGROUND

Land and Climate

Covering 42,043 square miles (108,890 square kilometers), Guatemala is just smaller than Tennessee. About two-thirds of Guatemala is mountainous and volcanic. Some volcanoes are active and tremors are frequent; the last major earthquake was in 1976. Rich forests covering 40 percent of Guatemala, particularly in the northwest Petén region, are subject to rapid deforestation due to cutting. Most people live on the slopes of the highlands or in the fertile, well-watered lowlands along the Pacific Coast. In the coastal lowlands, hot, humid weather prevails. In the highlands, days are warm and nights are usually cool. The people call Guatemala "The Land of the Eternal Spring" because 75°F (24°C) is the average annual temperature in the capital, which is on a plateau 4,800 feet (1,400 meters) above sea level. November to May is the dry season. Rain is abundant from May to October. The Caribbean Coast is wet year-round.

History

The Mayan Empire flourished in what is now Guatemala for more than one thousand years until it began to decline in the 1100s. As one of the chief centers of the Mayan culture, Guatemala abounds in archaeological ruins, notably the majestic ceremonial city of Tikal in the Petén region. From 1524 to 1821, the Spanish ruled Central America. After winning its independence in 1821, Guatemala was briefly annexed by Mexico and then became a member of the Central American Federation until the federation dissolved in 1838.

Military dictatorships controlled Guatemala until a 1944 revolution. From 1945 to 1982, leaders tried to cure some of Guatemala's social ills, but democracy was still absent. Violence was common, and rebels began a civil war in 1954 after an elected president (Jacobo Arbenz Guzmán) was overthrown by a U.S.-backed military coup. Coups and civil war made political stability seem impossible until 1984, when a constituent assembly was elected to write a new constitution.

In 1986, Guatemala returned to civilian rule under Marco Vinicio Cerezo Arévalo. Cerezo withstood two military coups, but the military has strong ties to the country's principal landowners and therefore wields much power. In fact, it has more control over some regions than civilian authorities. Because the military is primarily responsible for human-rights abuses, such control presents enormous problems for political and economic progress.

Elections in 1990 brought the first transfer of power from one elected official to another. President Jorge Serrano Elías began peace talks with the rebels in 1991. The end of decades of civil war seemed possible early in 1993. Unfortunately, talks were interrupted by a May 1993 political crisis when Serrano dissolved Congress and the Supreme Court and suspended the constitution. Backed by the army, he announced emergency rule, which touched off civilian street protests. As pressure mounted, the military withdrew its support, forcing Serrano to flee to Panama. Military leaders recalled Congress, which chose its ombudsman for human rights, Ramiro de León Carpio, to finish Serrano's term in office.

Talks with rebels opened again in 1994 and continued into 1995. Alvaro Arzu Irigoyen, a conservative businessman, narrowly won the November 1995 presidential elections. After beginning a new round of negotiations with Arzu, rebels announced an open-ended cease-fire in March 1996. Several important accords have been reached since 1994 as a result of continued negotiations. Both sides hoped to sign a full peace agreement by the end of 1996.

THE PEOPLE
Population

Guatemala's population of almost 11 million is growing at 2.5 percent annually. While 56 percent is *ladino* (*mestizo*), 44 percent is composed of some 28 indigenous groups descended from the Maya. Some of the largest are Quiché, Cakchiquel, Kekchí, Ixil, and Mam (Pocomam). They live throughout the country, but significant numbers reside in western highlands. Collectively, they refer to themselves as Maya or Indigenous. *Ladinos* descend from the Spanish and Maya, but they relate more to their Spanish heritage. The Human Development Index (0.591) ranks Guatemala 112th out of 174 countries. Adjusted for women, the index (0.481) ranks it 87th out of 130 countries, one of the lowest in Latin America.

Language

Spanish is Guatemala's official language, but each indigenous group speaks its own language. Male indigenous Guatemalans generally are bilingual, speaking their own language and Spanish. Indigenous women have fewer opportunities to attend school and have less contact with Spanish-speaking *mestizos* than men do; therefore, they often do not learn Spanish. English is understood in tourist centers.

Religion

Roman Catholicism has traditionally dominated Guatemala, although many indigenous members combine it with their Mayan beliefs. Some indigenous groups have not accepted Catholicism. Guatemala guarantees freedom of religion. While Catholicism influences most celebrations and habits, regardless of people's religious preference, devotion to the Catholic Church is declining. In the last 20 years, many have converted to Protestant and other Christian churches. Protestants are usually referred to as *evangélicos* (evangelicals). About 45 percent of the people are now *evangélicos*. Increased religious devotion is credited with decreasing alcoholism and other social problems. However, tension between Catholics and *evangélicos* is rising.

General Attitudes

Guatemalans are generous, warm, polite, and humble. They value honesty, family unity, personal honor, work, and education. Optimism is less common than the acceptance of misfortune. People often believe they are not able to change their condition, either for lack of empowerment or because some things are God's will. Personal criticism is taken seriously and should be avoided. Punctuality is admired but not strictly observed because people are considered more important than schedules.

Family status and wealth are important to *ladinos*. The Maya desire to be treated as equals. Tension exists between *ladinos* and the Indigenous. *Ladinos* consider the Maya to be inferior and uncivilized. They avoid contact with the Indigenous who do not adopt *ladino* ways. Those Maya who wear Western clothing and assimilate into *ladino* culture are treated somewhat better. The Maya have been subjected to discrimination and human-rights abuses for centuries. There is hope

their condition may improve, especially considering that a Quiché Maya, Rigoberta Menchú, won the 1992 Nobel Peace Prize for her fight to have the plight of the indigenous population heard.

Personal Appearance

In cities, people generally wear Western-style clothing. However, most rural Maya, particularly women, have retained traditional dress. Each group's clothing has unique qualities, but basic features include a *faja* (woven belt worn by both sexes), wraparound skirts (*corte*) for women, and knee- or calf-length trousers for men. Women often wear ribbons in their hair. Men generally wear hats, usually made from straw or blocked felt. Skirts, pants, and blouses are often colorful. A woman treasures her *huipil* (blouse); its design identifies her status and hometown. Jackets and shawls are also worn.

CUSTOMS AND COURTESIES
Greetings

When meeting for the first time, people greet with a handshake and *¡Mucho gusto!* (Pleased to meet you). Among general acquaintances, the most common greetings are *¡Buenos días¡* (Good day), *¡Buenas tardes!* (Good afternoon), and *¡Buenas noches!* (Good evening). Among friends, a casual *¡Buenas!* or *¡Hola!* (Hi) might be used. After an initial greeting, one might ask *¿Cómo está?* (How are you?). Shaking hands heartily is common in most areas. Among friends, men usually shake hands and sometimes embrace, and *ladino* women kiss each other on the cheek. A younger woman will kiss a male friend, but older women only kiss relatives. Some older women greet by grasping the person just below each elbow.

In small groups, it is important to greet each individual. In larger groups, it is acceptable to offer a group greeting or simply to greet as many persons as possible. Guests greet hosts individually, regardless of the size of the group. When addressing others, using a title (*Señor, Señora, Señorita, Doctor*, etc.) shows respect. People show special respect for older individuals by using *Don* and *Doña* with the first name. Common parting phrases include *Que le vaya bien* (May you go well), *Nos vemos* (See you later), and *Mas tarde* (Later).

Gestures

Guatemalans beckon by waving the hand downward and in. One hails a taxi or bus by sticking the hand out horizontally, palm facing down. A "tssst tssst" sound gets someone's attention in public. Pointing with the finger or the hand can be misinterpreted because many finger and hand gestures are vulgar. To point, people often purse (pucker) their lips in the direction of whatever they are indicating. To emphasize something, express surprise, or indicate "hurry," one shakes the hand quickly so that the index and middle fingers slap together and make a snapping sound. "No" can be indicated by wagging the index finger from side to side.

Urban couples tend to be more affectionate in public than rural ones. Rural people hold hands but rarely kiss or show other affection. Personal space during conversation is relatively close, although touching is not common.

Visiting

Visiting friends and relatives is important to building strong relationships. One's frequent visits reflects the value of a relationship. People who live close, especially in rural areas, drop by unannounced (or send a child to announce the adults are coming later); nearly any time of day is acceptable. Frequent visitors may establish a pattern of visiting at certain times so they can be expected. Socializing also takes place outside the home; friends and relatives may meet at the market, community meetings, church, or the water well. Still, it is proper to visit the home to show that a person's hospitality is valued. Visits are often prearranged for formal events, longer stays, or if people do not live close. When extended, invitations may be for dinner, a special event, or celebration.

Frequent visitors usually do not bring gifts to the hosts, but anyone staying more than one day will give flowers, chocolates, or something for the home. The longer the stay, the nicer the gift. Gifts are also given for birthdays and weddings. Hosts often send dinner guests home with food or something from the garden. People usually serve their guests coffee, tea, water, or another drink and sweet bread or other snack. Refusing is impolite. When leaving a home, guests graciously thank the hosts and often invite them to visit.

Eating

Most people eat three meals a day; poorer families might eat only one meal and then snack on tortillas the rest of the day. A rural breakfast may consist of tortillas and leftover beans. The main meal is eaten at midday; anyone in the family not working eats this meal. Dinner, usually eaten after 7:00 P.M., is lighter than lunch. The entire family gathers for the main meal on weekends; these meals are important for socializing. In some cases, women serve the meal and eat later. Many people have coffee and sweet breads around 4:00 P.M., and men working in the fields might have a snack at midmorning. School children are served hot cereal at 10:00 A.M.

Guatemalans often use tortillas as a scoop for some foods. They may also eat some foods with the hands but otherwise use utensils at most meals. They keep hands above the table, not in the lap. Upon finishing the meal, each person (even the cook) often thanks all others at the table with *Muchas gracias,* to which all reply *Buen provecho* (Good appetite).

Guests finish everything on their plates and wait for the host to offer more food. Asking for more might embarrass a host who is out of food, but eating more compliments the cook. When offered additional food, one first politely declines but then always accepts and eats it completely.

LIFESTYLE

Family

The extended family forms the basis of society and exerts significant influence on an individual's life and decisions. The father is the head of the family, but the wife controls the household; she is considered the heart of the family. Rural extended families often share a single home or live next to each other in a family compound. This includes parents, married sons and their families, unmarried children, and often grandparents. Urban families generally live in nuclear family settings, although grandparents are often present. Unmarried adults live with their parents unless they must go elsewhere for work. Family members are expected to share responsibilities and be devoted to the unit. Adult children are responsible for the care of their elderly parents.

Ladino women often work as secretaries, teachers, nurses, and in other professions. One-fourth of the labor force is female. Mayan women also work but less often in professional capacities. They may sell produce at markets, embroider or weave products for sale, or work in community groups. Within the home, women are responsible for the food, household, children, education, and religion. Men work professionally or do field work and other physically demanding labor.

Ladino families generally live in urban areas or towns in small, single-family homes. Although they often must live in apartments, people prefer the privacy of homes. Housing for indigenous groups follows their various traditions, such as a modest adobe or bamboo dwelling with a thatched or tin roof. Poverty is a serious problem for many in Guatemala, and land ownership is not available to most. In poorer families, children must work as soon as they are able to help support the family. Many rural families have no running water or electricity, although the cities are well equipped with these.

Dating and Marriage

Urban youth begin socializing in groups around age 15. They enjoy going to movies, eating out, or just being together at home or elsewhere. Rural youth take walks, meet after school, visit at church or community events, or meet in town (at the market or water well). A girl's honor is important; a proper couple is "chaperoned" by younger siblings or cousins.

Among *ladinos*, social status is important in choosing a spouse. Traditionally the boy's parents asked for the girl's hand in marriage; now the boy asks the girl's father. Women often marry by age 20 (earlier in rural areas) and men by 24. Common-law marriages are accepted and often necessary, especially if the groom cannot afford his responsibility to pay for the wedding, new clothes for the bride, and any celebrations.

Diet

Corn tortillas or, in many regions, *tamalitos* (cornmeal dough wrapped in corn leaves and steamed) are eaten with every meal. Other foods include black beans, rice, tamales, greens, and fried *plátanos* (bananas) with honey, cream, or black beans. Meats (beef, pork, and chicken) are usually stewed, and sauces are important. Often a particular dish is unique to a certain village since key ingredients (such as spices) are found only in that village. Papaya and breadfruit are among the many fruits eaten in Guatemala. The poorest rural families eat only tortillas (or *tamalitos*), whatever food they can grow, and foods gathered in the forest.

Recreation

The most popular sports are soccer, basketball, and volleyball. People most often enjoy family outings to a beach or lake or other recreational activities on holidays and during festivals. Guatemala is noted for the *marimba*, a musical instrument made of wood and played with sticks padded with rubber. The *marimba* can be heard at many of the yearly festivals. *Cofradías* (religious fraternities dedicated to a particular saint) offer a variety of recreational and leisure activities. Urban people enjoy watching television, but visiting is the most common leisure activity for all Guatemalans.

Holidays

A popular Guatemalan saying claims there are more celebrations than days in the year. This describes the events that occur in villages and towns all year long. Each town has an annual *feria* (fair) to honor the local patron saint. This is often the most important holiday in rural areas.

Major celebrations are divided into two periods: Christmas and Easter. The Christmas season begin 7 December, when people clean house and burn their garbage to ceremonially cleanse their homes of evil in preparation to receive Christ. On Christmas Day, people set off firecrackers and eat special foods. Firecrackers accompany most celebrations, especially New Year's. Easter is celebrated with Holy Week, during which numerous large processions fill the streets. In these, figures representing Christ are carried on special platforms by men wearing purple robes (black robes on Good Friday). On Saturday, effigies of Judas Iscariot are burned.

National holidays include Labor Day (1 May), Army Day (30 June), Independence Day (15 September), *Día de la Raza* (Day of the Race or Columbus Day, 12 October), Revolution Day (20 October), and All Saints' Day (1 November).

Commerce

Business hours vary from town to town, but they generally range from 8:00 A.M. to 6:00 P.M. in the cities, with a one- or two-hour break around noon. Work hours also vary because so many are involved in agriculture. Urban residents purchase food and other basics from small shops and large supermarkets. Fresh produce is available at open-air markets. In rural areas, farmers produce some of their food and buy basics and other produce at open-air markets or small shops. Villages might have a market just twice a week, with one day offering only basic goods. All neighborhood stores operated out of homes stock about the same items, so one buys from family and friends first. Farmers sometimes have another job to earn a wage. Other family members may sell handicrafts or livestock to make money. Landless people might work on farms for a wage.

SOCIETY

Government

Guatemala's president is head of state and head of government. The Congress of the Republic has 116 seats. The voting age is 18. The two largest political parties are Arzu's Party of National Advancement (PAN) and the Guatemalan Republican Front (FRG).

Economy

Guatemala is a relatively poor country. Real gross domestic product per capita is $3,330, but wealth is concentrated among the upper class; three-fourths of rural residents live in poverty. Even in urban areas, where economic conditions are better, poverty affects two-thirds of the people. Progress is hindered by thirty years of civil war, the existence of large commercial farms that produce for export but keep rural farmers landless and poor, and the lack of a diverse manufacturing sector. About 60 percent of the people are employed in agriculture. Coffee accounts for 25 percent of all export earnings. Other leading products include cotton, cacao, corn, beans, sugarcane, bananas, broccoli, and livestock. Nickel, oil, fish, rubber, and chicle (used in chewing gum) are important natural resources. Tourism and manufacturing are also vital to the economy. The currency is the *quetzal* (Q).

Transportation and Communication

Buses are relatively inexpensive and provide the main form of long-distance travel. Paved roads connect the capital to major cities and neighboring countries, but most other roads are unimproved. For short distances, most people will walk, ride a bicycle or motorcycle, or take the bus. The wealthy have private cars. Commuter airlines fly domestically. The communications system is fairly modern and efficient. Telephones are widely used in cities but not in rural areas. Urban newspapers are available, but rural people rely on radio for news and entertainment. Television is popular where there is electricity.

Education

Although there are several thousand primary schools, more than half of primary-age children do not attend. The adult literacy rate is 54 percent. It is higher for males than females and for urban dwellers. However, girls now tend to stay in school longer than boys. Children often leave school because of family needs or inadequacies in the system. In rural areas, many primary school students do not speak Spanish, the language of instruction. Facilities are often crowded, books in short supply, and teachers underpaid. The school day runs for about five hours. Primary school lasts five years. After primary and middle school, three years of secondary schooling (vocational training) are possible. Those desiring to go on to one of Guatemala's five universities must have college preparation, which usually is available only to the wealthy.

Health

Guatemala faces serious health problems, including malnutrition, a lack of potable water in many areas, and disease. Medical resources are concentrated in urban areas, although a national system is structured to provide health posts to outlying areas. Care generally is free or costs a small fee, but medicines must be purchased. Public funding is often inadequate and rural posts are not properly supplied. The infant mortality rate is 52 per 1,000; life expectancy is between 62 and 68 years.

FOR THE TRAVELER

U.S. visitors need a passport and visa or tourist card to enter Guatemala. A yellow fever vaccination is required if one travels to other countries after Guatemala. Other vaccinations may be advisable. Cholera is active: eat only well-cooked meat served hot, and drink only boiled or bottled water. Wash and peel fresh produce. Because of potential violence against U.S. citizens due to crime, terrorism, and unfounded rumors of U.S. Americans abducting children, call the State Department at (202) 647–5225 for travel warnings. On arrival, register with the U.S. embassy for more details. Avoid travel outside of tourist areas and do not travel between cities after sunset. Violent highway robberies are common. Theft is a problem anytime. For information on Guatemala's historic sites, contact the Guatemala Tourist Commission, 299 Alhambra Circle, Suite 510, Coral Gables, FL 33134; or the Embassy of Guatemala, 2220 R Street NW, Washington, DC 20008.

CULTURGRAM '97

Cooperative Republic of
Guyana

BACKGROUND

Land and Climate

Covering 83,000 square miles (214,970 square kilometers), Guyana lies just north of the equator and has a tropical climate. Trade winds moderate coastal humidity. Rain falls primarily between April and August and from November to January. Guyana is interlaced with rivers. In fact, its name is an Amerindian term for "Land of Many Waters." The major rivers (Essequibo, Demerara, Berbice, and Corentyne) flow north to the Atlantic. The coastal plain, which supports agriculture, lies slighty below sea level but is protected by drainage canals, dams, and walls. White sand hills are south of the coastal plain. Although unfit for agriculture, these hills support rain forests rich in hardwood trees and are home to a varied and abundant animal population. The interior is characterized by plateaus, flat-topped mountains, and savannas.

History

Little is known about the area's early inhabitants, but historians speculate they gradually migrated from center of South America as early as A.D. 1000. These Amerindians were divided into at least nine tribes, the largest of which were the Warrau, Wapisiana, Machushi, Patamona, Arawak, and Carib. The Amerindians were nearly decimated by Spanish conquistadors.

The Dutch established the first European trading post in 1580 but were soon joined by the English, French, and Spanish. In 1621, the Netherlands established the Dutch West India Company and gave it control of their colony, known as Essequibo. Dutch colonies were later established on the Berbice River (1627) and Demerara River (1741), despite Spanish claims to the entire region. The colonies changed hands between the British, French, and Dutch with confusing frequency until the British purchased and united them and, in 1831, renamed the area British Guiana.

African slaves were brought to the area in the mid-1700s to meet labor needs. By 1807, when the slave trade was abolished, about 100,000 Africans lived on plantations. After full emancipation in 1838, many freed slaves formed their own villages. Plantation owners then hired Portuguese and Chinese laborers, but these workers did not stay. Finally, planters brought indentured workers from India. By 1917, when Indian immigration ended, 341,000 Indians had settled permanently in British Guiana.

After World War II, the British gradually prepared for the colony's independence. Political parties formed to participate in elections; 1953 was the first year of universal suffrage. The most dynamic new party was the People's Progressive Party (PPP), established by Cheddi Jagan. The son of Indian immigrants, Jagan embraced Marxism while studying dentistry in the United States. The PPP splintered in the late 1950s after the British tried to halt its rise to power. The new party, the People's National Congress (PNC), was led by leftist Linden Burnham. His support came from Afro-Guianese, while Jagan's came from the Indo-Guianese community.

After Britain granted internal self-rule (1961), an anticommunist party formed to challenge the PPP, which had gained a majority in 1961 elections. The party became the United Force (UF) and joined with the PNC and other groups to oppose the government. Violence and turbulence characterized the next few years, and the three parties met to negotiate a solution. When they could not agree, Britain stepped in to revise electoral law to include proportional representation.

In 1964 elections, the PPP gained 45 percent of the vote, but it was not enough to form a government. Therefore, the PNC and UF formed a coalition under Burnham's leadership. Independence was granted in 1966, and British Guiana became Guyana. The PNC consolidated power in 1968 elections, and Burnham used that power to commit Guyana to socialism. In 1970, he renamed the country the Cooperative Republic of Guyana, and by 1974, it was essentially a one-party state.

For the next decade, the country was wracked by political and economic turmoil. Burnham's sudden death in 1985 brought some relief to the nation because his successor, Vice President Desmond Hoyte, introduced political and economic reforms. Nevertheless, the standard of living remained low and Hoyte was urged to hold free and fair elections. Despite some violence and charges of fraud, elections in 1992 were declared fair by international observers. The PPP returned to power, and Jagan continued to reform the political, social, and economic systems that had been corrupted by Burnham.

PEOPLE

Population

The population of Guyana is estimated to be 725,000. It is not growing, as emigration generally keeps up with birth rates. More than 30 percent of Guyanese live in three urban areas: Georgetown, Linden, and New Amsterdam. The villages and fertile acres of the coastal lowlands are home to another 65 percent of the population. The remaining 5 percent, mostly Amerindians, are scattered throughout the interior.

Guyana is ethnically diverse. The Indo-Guyanese are the largest group with nearly 50 percent of the population. They are followed by the Afro-Guyanese (36 percent), "mixed" (7 percent), and Amerindians (6 percent). Small groups of ethnic Chinese, English, and Portuguese make up 1 percent. The "mixed" people are, for the most part, descendants of Afro- and Indo-Guyanese but may also descend from other groups.

Warrau and Arawak Catholics fled to British Guiana from Venezuela in the 19th century to escape religious persecution. Their settlement in Santa Rosa produced Guyana's first Amerindian member of Parliament. Settlements like Santa Rosa are protected reservations. Today's Amerindians are seeking title to the lands they occupy, as they feel increasingly threatened by local and international companies looking for mineral and timber wealth. At the same time, many Amerindians are taking jobs with these companies in hopes of overcoming poverty on the reservations.

Guyana's Human Development Index (0.622) ranks it 105th out of 174 nations. Adjusted for women, the index (0.584) reflects a gap in their share of income. Due to the years of turmoil, most Guyanese still lack access to resources that would allow for personal advancement.

Language

English is the official language and is use by the media, for education and commerce, and in government. However, the spoken English that many people use on a daily basis is a dialect known as *Creolese*. This oral (unwritten) dialect is unlike the French-based Creole of the Caribbean in that it is based on English. *Creolese* adds flavor to the country's cultural life and is especially popular for songs and colloquialisms such as *Awe a go a Georgetown fore day morning* (We're going to Georgetown before sunrise). Older Amerindians speak their native languages in addition to English.

Religion

Christianity came to Guyana with the colonists. Other religions came with later immigrants. The Guyanese are a religious people. Even such socialists as Burnham professed some religious beliefs. Under the British, the Anglican Church had official status, but today all major religious groups have equal recognition under the law.

More than half of the Guyanese (57 percent) are Christians. The major congregations (Roman Catholic, Anglican, Protestant) are joined by various other Christian churches. Hinduism is practiced by 33 percent of the population; its adherents are almost exclusively Indo-Guyanese. About 9 percent of the people are Muslims. Islam also came to Guyana with the East Indians, but in Guyana, there is no friction between Hindus and Muslims. Traces of African folk practices and traditional Amerindian religious beliefs are still found, but their impact on society is negligible.

General Attitudes

The Guyanese are warm, outgoing, friendly, and fun loving. They are also resilient, as evidenced by how they survived terrible hardships associated with plantation life in colonial times. Personal goals center on providing a better life and an education for their children. Hence, individuals work to purchase and develop a plot of land, acquire a milk cow and a good fishing net, and perhaps open a small shop, all the while working odd jobs if necessary. However, as the standard of living declined sharply after independence, the allure of a seemingly better life abroad has caused thousands to emigrate. For most families today, the thing most desired is a visa to the United States or Canada.

Personal Appearance

The Guyanese generally follow North American and European fashion trends. Burnham had at one time decreed all men would wear trousers and *shirtjacs* (open-necked shirts with side pockets worn over the trousers). Although the *shirtjac* is still widely worn, suits are now also common. Informal dress includes slacks or shorts and T-shirts for both men and women. Special occasions call for women to wear dresses and considerable jewelry, often crafted from Guyanese gold. Schoolchildren wear uniforms, but after school they prefer T-shirts with slacks, jeans, or shorts.

CUSTOMS AND COURTESIES

Greetings

Relatives and friends may greet each other with a hug and, between women, a brief kiss on each cheek. A handshake is the norm between business and professional associates. Young people say *Hi* or *Hi, man, how you doin'?* They may add backslapping or a "high five." They might also ask *Wha' it saying?* to which the response is either a "thumbs up" signal (for good) or an open palm turned down (for bad).

Amerindian greetings vary according to the language. The Wapisiani use *Kaimen Pugar* (roughly, "Peace be with you").

The Machushi say *Morogeh koman honah* (I'm glad to see you) and respond *Enah* ("yes," meaning "hello").

The youth address most adults who are not members of their families as *auntie* or *uncle*. If the adults are gray haired, they are *grannie* or *grandpa*. Teachers and school personnel are addressed not by name but as *Miss* or *Sir*. Adults do not address each other by their given names until they become close friends. Using the titles *Mr., Miss, Professor, Doctor,* etc., with the family name is appropriate.

Gestures

The Guyanese talk with their hands, especially when angry or excited. They point their fingers into one another's faces to stress a point and shake the forefinger to alert one to their displeasure. Most Guyanese do not wear shoes inside their homes; on entering someone's house, guests leave their shoes at the door as well.

Visiting

Unannounced visiting is an accepted practice. If the weather is nice, the host and caller may visit outside; otherwise the visitor is invited in. Once the guest is seated, a cold drink and something to snack on is offered and conversation begins. Such visits usually occur in the late afternoon or on weekends. Oral or written invitations are extended for informal parties and family dinners. Gifts are not expected, but guests may bring the hostess something from the garden or another small token.

An invitation to one's home for a special event is an invitation to a feast. On arrival, one is offered a cold drink; dinner is served after most guests have arrived (which may be long after the appointed hour). The food usually is presented buffet style. Guests seat themselves. If the event is a wedding or birthday, guests bring gifts that are opened after the party.

Eating

Guyanese usually eat breakfast at home. Those working outside the home either carry their midday meal or eat it in a small restaurant or at a *snackette* stand. Schoolchildren go home to eat, bring their lunch, or buy it from vendors who operate stalls outside the schools. Dinner, shared by the family at a common table, is usually the main meal of the day. In addition to regular meals, Guyanese enjoy snacks. *Snackettes* sell finger food and drinks; vendors offer highly seasoned barbequed meat; and ice cream is popular anytime. The better restaurants in Georgetown serve both local favorites and quasi-continental dishes.

LIFESTYLE

Family

Urban couples customarily have three to five children; rural families may have five or more. Both urban spouses usually work outside the home; the husband is head of the household and primary breadwinner, and the wife is the homemaker. Men generally do not help with household chores. It is not uncommon for grandmothers to care for young children while mothers are at work. Although rural people generally marry within their respective ethnic groups, mixed marriages are common in cities.

Indian indentured laborers came and worked as families. Today, Indo-Guyanese parents carefully monitor unmarried daughters. Should a young woman become pregnant before marriage, the entire family is disgraced. Slavery, on the other hand, did not encourage marriage and reserved child care for older women. The impact on the Afro-Guyanese, especially among lower-income families, is clear: when an unmarried girl bears a baby, she commonly brings it to her mother to raise. Grandmothers may rear the children of more than one daughter and, as a rule, both the mother and grandmother work to provide for the family. These single-parent and multi-generational families are increasingly common.

Dating and Marriage

Young people socialize in groups until they finish their formal schooling. When couples date, they go to the cinema, public celebrations, church functions, and other activities they enjoyed in groups. Weddings are important events and are celebrated according to traditional religious rites. A Christian marriage takes place in a church, followed by a reception that includes food, drink, and dancing, as well as speeches honoring the couple and their parents. After a Hindu wedding, guests are served a traditional supper of seven vegetarian curries on a water lily pad. They return the next day for a Western-style reception. Muslim festivities can last three days.

Diet

Guyanese cuisine is as diverse as the population, with each ethnic group contributing favorite cultural foods. Rice, eaten at both lunch and dinner, is grown locally. Beef, pork, mutton, chicken, and both freshwater and saltwater fish are abundant. Many Guyanese, especially Hindus, are vegetarians.

Breakfast might include coffee and toast with perhaps a piece of fruit. Heartier eaters may add eggs, salt fish, and boiled *ground provisions* (plantains, cassava, yams). Meat pies, cheese rolls, *roti* (unleavened bread wrapped around chicken or beef and potatoes), and rice with bits of vegetables or meat are popular lunch items. Spicy curry is a favorite dinner. Another, *cook-up rice*, is made with coconut milk, rice, meat or fish, and—as the name implies—almost anything the cook has on hand. *Metemgee* is like *cook-up rice*, but with a *ground provision* instead of rice.

Adults drink soda, fruit juices, or beer with lunch and dinner. Coffee and milk are for breakfast; tea can be served at breakfast or between meals. Locally produced beer, sodas, and homemade fruit drinks are party-time favorites, but men drink substantial amounts of rum when they socialize.

Christmas calls for special treats: garlic pork, *pepper pot*, *black cake*, and ginger beer. No Christmas breakfast is complete without garlic pork. *Pepper pot*, served throughout the season, is a meat stew flavored with *casareep*, a cassava extract. Dried local fruits, soaked in rum and caramelized sugar, give *black cake* its unique color and distinct sweet taste.

Recreation

Cricket is an obsession, while *football* (soccer) comes in a distant second. Both men and women play field hockey, tennis, and golf. Large crowds usually attend regular car races near the Timehri International Airport. Boxing is popular among Afro-Guyanese men. Dominoes is a favorite table game during the lunch hour at schools and in offices.

The Guyanese like action movies made in India or the United States. Bars, discos, and karaoke clubs are places to relax with friends and enjoy the latest Caribbean music. Church and school fairs draw crowds on weekends. While they are designed to raise money for the sponsoring organization, the fairs offer an inexpensive and pleasant way for families to spend an afternoon.

Holidays

The Christmas season is popular in Guyana, celebrated by all with gift giving and feasting. Boxing Day (26 December) is a day to relax after Christmas. New Year's Day is also quiet, as revelers recuperate from the parties of Old Year's Night.

Republic Day (23 February) marks the date Guyana became The Cooperative Republic of Guyana. The holiday is known as *Mashramani*, an Amerindian word for the celebration at the end of a cooperative project. Fireworks and a presidential address are traditional on Independence Day (26 May). On CARICOM Day (first Monday in July), the Guyanese celebrate their relationship with Caribbean nations. Freedom Day (first Monday in August) marks emancipation.

Easter (Friday–Monday) is very popular and features kite flying along the seawall as a rite of spring. *Devali*, the fall Hindu Festival of Lights, features a light parade. *Phagwah* welcomes spring, and the Indo-Guyanese greet each other with a sprinkling of water, powder, and *abeer* (a red liquid). Official Muslim holidays are *Id ul Fitr*, the feast at the end of *Ramadan*, and *Id ul Azha*, the feast of sacrifice. For the latter, people distribute food and clothing to the poor. Muslims also commemorate *Yaum an Nibi* (Muhammad's birthday), but it is not a public holiday.

Commerce

Businesses and urban markets are open from 8:00 A.M. until 4:30 P.M.; markets close at noon on Wednesday and Saturday. Except for food vendors open between 10:00 A.M. and 2:00 P.M., urban markets are closed on Sunday. Village markets are open one or two days a week. Family-run stores sell mostly packaged goods. Gasoline stations are adding convenience stores. Unlicensed street vendors flourish despite efforts to curb their activities. As part of the black market before 1992, they were essential to the local economy. Today, they mainly undermine established retailers.

SOCIETY

Government

Guyana is a democracy divided into ten regions. Cheddi Jagan is Guyana's president and chief of state. Sam Hinds, the prime minister, is head of government. All but ten of the 65-seat National Assembly members are directly elected; the ten are indirectly elected through regional Democratic Councils. The voting age is 18, and the next elections are in 1997.

Economy

Guyana's economy is showing signs of growth after years of decline. Sugar continues to be the chief export, but rice is also benefiting from high world prices. Gold and diamond mining have potential, but the nation's substantial bauxite reserves are less profitable to extract. Economic growth is hampered by poor roads, insufficient energy, lack of skilled labor, and a large debt load.

In addition to expanding fish processing, Guyana is experimenting with shrimp farming. Although the country is rich in timber, an inadequate infrastructure and environmental concerns have so far spared Guyana's forests. Real gross domestic product per capita is $1,862; most people can provide for their basic needs but not much else.

Transportation and Communication

Pedestrians, bikes, scooters, and cars compete with minibuses and *lorries* for space on Guyana's roads. Minibuses have designated routes and fares but no schedules. Drivers wait at a *car park* until their bus is full (and crowded) before they set out. Outside the coastal plain, the only roads lead to the airport and to Linden. Access to the rest of the country is by air or water. Guyana Airways serves the interior, but seats are limited. Speedboats provide passenger and cargo service along the rivers. In many locations, the family boat is essential to get to market, school, church, or the nearest village.

Dependable phone service is available in most areas along the coast. Efforts are underway to expand service in Georgetown and elsewhere. Communication with remote areas is possible via radiophone. A free press circulates several daily and weekly newspapers. Two radio stations broadcast throughout the country, and Georgetown has a choice of television channels.

Education

Education is free and compulsory, but the cost of uniforms and books keeps some children from attending school or advancing to secondary school. Children attend nursery school at age three, primary school by age six, and secondary school (first *form* or year) by age ten. After the fourth *form*, a student may enter the job market, seek additional training, or prepare for university. Education standards declined sharply after 1976, when the government took over private schools. Teachers are poorly paid and schools are not well supplied. Parents who can afford to do so send their children to after-school "lessons" for tutoring, and private schools are beginning to reopen.

Students pay tuition to attend the University of Guyana. Higher education is also offered through a teachers' college, several technical institutions, and three schools of nursing.

Health

Guyanans receive free medical and dental care at public clinics and hospitals, but these are not always well equipped or supplied. A national health insurance plan reimburses income lost to illness, maternity leave, or disability. Most clinics operate with a *medex* (an individual trained in primary health care), a nurse, or an untrained village matron. Community health workers provide basic care to interior villages. Six private (expensive) hospitals operate in Georgetown. The infant mortality rate is 48 per 1,000. The life expectancy rate is between 62 and 68 years.

FOR THE TRAVELER

U.S. citizens must have a passport to enter Guyana, but visas are not required for stays of up to 30 days. No immunizations are required, but those visiting the interior will need malaria prophylactis. For information, contact the Chancery of Guyana, 2490 Tracy Place NW, Washington, DC 20008.

A *Culturgram* is a product of native commentary and original, expert analysis. Statistics are estimates and information is presented as a matter of opinion. While the editors strive for accuracy and detail, this document should not be considered strictly factual. It is a general introduction to culture, an initial step in building bridges of understanding between peoples. It may not apply to all peoples of the nation. You should therefore consult other sources for more information.

Republic of
Honduras

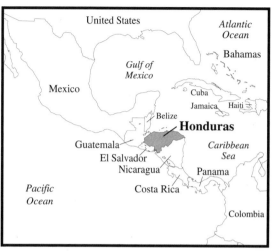

Boundary representations not necessarily authoritative.

BACKGROUND

Land and Climate

Covering 43,278 square miles (112,090 square kilometers), Honduras is just larger than Tennessee. Located east of El Salvador and Guatemala in Central America, Honduras shares its southern border with Nicaragua and has Pacific and Atlantic Ocean coasts. La Mosquitia, an area of wetlands, mountains, and tropical forests, covers the lower eastern coast. The largest pine forest in Latin America, the Olancho Forest Reserve, is about the size of Connecticut. The climate varies according to elevation: subtropical in the lowlands and temperate at higher levels. The capital, Tegucigalpa, enjoys a relatively mild climate year-round. The rainy season extends from May to November, although rains sometimes may not begin to fall until as late as October. March through May are the hottest months.

While Honduras is mountainous, it is the only Central American country without volcanoes, which is a factor in its low food production. Soil in volcanic regions is usually rich and good for agriculture. Due to the poor soil, many people have practiced migratory agriculture, moving every few years to clear new land and plant crops. This and timber operations have caused Honduras to lose 30 percent of its forest over the past 25 years. Wildlife has also been affected. Many efforts are now underway to reverse this trend and preserve the forests for wildlife, indigenous peoples, and the environment. Precious woods, gold, silver, copper, lead, zinc, and other such minerals are found in Honduras.

History

The great Mayan Empire flourished in present-day Honduras until about A.D. 800, when the Mayan population began to decline. Smaller empires controlled various regions until the arrival of Spanish *conquistadores*. Columbus landed in 1502 and called the area *Honduras* (depths) because of the deep waters off the north coast. The Indians battled against Spanish occupation until 1539, when the last of their chiefs (Lempira) was killed and the Spanish established a provincial capital at Comayagua. Honduras was incorporated into Spain's Captaincy General (colony) of Guatemala. Immigration increased when silver was discovered in the 1570s.

The Misquito Indians of the Mosquitia region requested and received a British invasion, but troops were only able to occupy that area of the country. The British withdrew in 1859. In September 1821, Honduras and four other provinces declared independence from Spain and briefly joined the Mexican Empire. Complete independence for Honduras came in 1838, when a republic was established. By the end of the 1800s, the government had become unstable and the country came under Nicaraguan influence. Instability continued until Tiburcio Carías Andino took power in 1932. His military rule ended in 1949, but military leaders continued to exercise control until 1981, when elections restored civilian rule. The elections of 1989 marked the third free election in a decade, as well as the first peaceful transfer of power to an opposition political party in half a century. Rafael Leonardo Callejas took office in 1990, but the military continued to exercise a great deal of power and influence in the country. Callejas was not allowed by the constitution to run for a second consecutive term, so two new candidates vied for the presidency in 1993. Carlos Roberto Reina Idiaquez was elected and took office in 1994. Reina promised to reduce the military's budget and has already reformed military recruitment methods. He continues to attack corruption and promote human rights.

THE PEOPLE

Population

Nearly 5.5 million people live in Honduras, a population that is growing annually at 2.6 percent. Ninety percent of the population is *mestizo* (a mixture of indigenous Indian and Spanish), while only 7 percent is native Indian. Two percent is black and 1 percent is white (of European descent). The Indians live mostly in isolated regions such as La Mosquitia. The principal Indian ethnic groups include Misquito, Payas, and Xicaques. The blacks are primarily Garinagu. There is also a group known as the Sambos—a mixture of black and Indian inhabitants.

Honduras's Human Development Index (0.578) ranks it 116th out of 174 countries. Adjusted for women, the index (0.524) ranks Honduras 77th out of 130 countries. Most people do not have access to opportunities for personal development and economic prosperity.

Language

Spanish is the official and dominant language. However, some Garinagu speak Garífuna, and Indians speak a number of different indigenous languages. About ten thousand people, mostly on the Bay Islands, speak Creole English. English is a required course in secondary schools, but few people are fluent. Major hotels have bilingual employees.

Religion

About 88 percent of the population is Roman Catholic, but various other Christian groups are active and freedom of religion is guaranteed by law. Protestantism is growing rapidly with a variety of churches present in even the smallest towns. Most Protestants (or *evangélicos*) attend church regularly. Some follow specific rules affecting their lifestyle (no coffee, dancing, etc.). The Catholic Church maintains a strong influence on the culture through festivals, family celebrations, and politics. Many public holidays center on religious themes. Each town and city has a patron saint for whom it holds an annual festival.

General Attitudes

In Honduras, as in much of Latin America, social philosophies such as fatalism, *machismo*, and *hora latina* are evident. Fatalism exists partly due to the difficulties of life in poverty; people are aware of limited social mobility and try to accept their position in life as something they cannot control. This attitude may seem counterproductive, but it can actually relieve frustration and allow people to enjoy what is good in life rather than focus on what is unpleasant. During conversation, people often add the phrase *Si Dios quiere* (God willing), particularly when making commitments. *Machismo* is indicative of a male-dominated society in which women are expected to remain submissive. Women only comprise about 18 percent of the formal labor force, and most rural women do not work outside the home. *Hora latina* refers to

the concept of time and schedules. Since individual needs are more important than schedules, being late for appointments or social events is a way of life. For example, a person would not hesitate to stop and talk to a friend on the way to an appointment, even if it means being late. This occurs even in urban settings, where punctuality is a bit more important, because personal contacts and relationships are often necessary to conduct business and work with the government.

Hondurans value their Christian beliefs, as well as their ties to the land and to agriculture. Environmental issues are also important to Hondurans.

Personal Appearance

Hondurans normally wear Western-style clothing. Shorts are rarely worn in public except in the coastal areas where it is hot and humid. Urban men often wear a *guayabera* (a decorative shirt of light fabric that hangs to just below the waist) instead of a more formal shirt and tie. Urban women are especially stylish with respect to clothing, hair, and makeup. In rural areas, where the majority are poor, many people wear secondhand clothing imported from the United States. Men wear rubber boots when working in the fields while women wear flip-flops. T-shirts with English slogans are popular throughout Honduras, even though the wearer probably does not speak English. Dressing up for special occasions is important to Hondurans. People are careful to keep dress clothes separate from clothes worn at work and at home. The wealthy wear the latest Western fashions.

CUSTOMS AND COURTESIES

Greetings

A handshake is an appropriate greeting for men and urban women. Middle- and upper-class women kiss male and female friends on the cheek. Rural women greet one another by placing one hand on the upper arm of the other woman. The *abrazo* is a warm embrace shared by close friends and relatives. When meeting someone for the first time, a person addresses the other by official title or *Señor, Señora,* or *Señorita* (Mr., Mrs., or Miss). The titles *Don* (for men) and *Doña* (for women) are also used before first names to show respect. *Usted* (the formal version of "you" in Spanish) is appropriate among acquaintances or those meeting for the first time. One customarily gives a general greeting when entering a room. In small groups, people greet and say good-bye to each person individually. People commonly say *Que le vaya bien* (May it go well with you) when parting. While passing someone in the street, one says *Adiós.* Literally meaning "Good-bye," *Adiós* in this case is meant as a general greeting. One always says *Buen provecho* (Enjoy your meal) at the table before a meal. A person approaching or passing a table in a restaurant also says *Buen provecho* to the people at the table.

Gestures

Hand and body language are important to communication. Waving the index finger is often used to say "no." Clasping both hands indicates strong approval. Touching the finger below the eye warns caution. And a hand placed under an elbow usually means someone is thought to be stingy. People often point with their lips or their chin. To express enthusiasm, they place their middle finger and thumb together and shake their hand, producing a snapping noise. One beckons by waving the hand with the palm facing down. Beckoning with the index finger is rude.

Visiting

Visiting is a common pastime on Saturday afternoons and Sundays, and people often visit unannounced. People in rural areas also visit on days when they are not in the fields. Hondurans are courteous and generous to guests in their homes. Hosts almost always offer their guests refreshments, such as juice, soda, coffee, or sweets; refusing is impolite. Unexpected visitors arriving at mealtime are often extended an invitation to eat with the family. Even people of humble circumstance will share whatever they have to make a guest feel welcome. If a guest does not feel like eating, the host may wrap up a little food to send home with the visitor. When leaving a home, guests are especially respectful to the head of the household.

Social events may have an indicated starting time, but hosts and guests understand this is very flexible; being several minutes or an hour late is not uncommon.

Eating

Hondurans eat breakfast between 6:00 and 8:30 A.M., the main meal around noon, and a lighter evening meal sometime between 6:00 and 8:00 P.M. Meals are eaten in a leisurely manner. Diners keep both hands (but not elbows) above the table. People customarily use the fork in the right hand and knife in the left, although rural people might also use pieces of corn tortillas instead of utensils. Families do not necessarily eat together, due to lack of plates or table space or simply as a matter of convenience. At finer restaurants, a 10 to 15 percent tip is appropriate; tips are not necessarily expected at less formal restaurants.

LIFESTYLE

Family

Family ties are strong in Honduras. Members of the extended family, including grandparents and other relatives, often occupy the same household. While the father is respected as the head of the household, the mother often has the greatest responsibility and influence in everyday family life. Hondurans carry both their paternal and maternal surnames. The father's surname is the individual's family name, but the mother's surname appears at the end of the person's name. Both surnames follow one or two given names. When a woman marries, her name does not change.

Unfortunately, a large number of families live in poverty. Most Honduran homes do not enjoy modern conveniences. Small adobe houses with dirt floors are common in rural areas. Cities have both modern, luxurious housing as well as poor slums. People in remote areas lack electricity and other modern conveniences.

Dating and Marriage

Girls have their formal initiation (*La Fiesta Rosa*) into social life at age 15, when elaborate parties are held to recognize their coming of age. Dating usually begins as a group activity or with the girl being accompanied by one or more other girls. Later on, couples date without accompaniment. Activities are simple and usually just involve socializing. Couple often get together and establish themselves at dances.

In rural areas, most poor people start their families without marrying, often as young as age 14. Common-law marriages are generally accepted, so many people never officially marry. Single mothers are common in all social classes, and many siblings in these families have only the one parent in common. Young single mothers often return to live with their parents until they are older or find another spouse.

Diet

Beans, corn, tortillas, and rice are the staple foods. Bananas, pineapples, mangoes, citrus fruits, coconuts, melons, avocados, potatoes, and yams are the most common fruits and vegetables. Special dishes include *tapado* (a stew of beef, vegetables, and coconut milk), *mondongo* (tripe and beef knuckles), *nacatamales* (pork tamales), and *torrejas* (similar to French toast and served at Christmas). *Topogios* or *charamuscas* (frozen fruit juice in plastic bags) are popular during the summer months. People also enjoy soda. Coffee and coffee with milk are traditional and usually are served with the main meal of the day. Some restaurants in major cities serve pizza, hamburgers, and other North American dishes.

Recreation

Fútbol (soccer) is the national sport. Young boys play the game almost anytime, anywhere, and professional competition is available as well. Although in recent years more girls have become involved in *fútbol*, they are still more likely to play basketball. Boys and men in rural areas enjoy playing card and dice games. In villages on the north coast, men like to play dominoes after they return home from a day's work of fishing. Wealthy Hondurans enjoy cycle races, baseball, golf, tennis, and swimming.

Holidays

Public holidays include New Year's; Day of the Americas (14 April); Labor Day (1 May); Independence Day (15 September); Birth of Morazán, the national hero (3 October); Columbus Day (12 October); Armed Forces Day (21 October); and Christmas. Independence Day is the most popular national holiday. School children practice for months in preparation for parades and programs. Constructing nativity scenes is a popular Christmas tradition. Since money is scarce, the scenes are made from scratch each year with natural resources and clay figures.

During Easter's Holy Week (*Semana Santa*), businesses close from Wednesday through the end of the week. Many people go to the beaches while others may swim in the rivers. The Day of the Child (10 September) is not an official holiday but is still popular. Children receive sweets and gifts at school, and adults congratulate the children when passing them on the street. Private home celebrations may also take place among the wealthy. In addition to these holidays, Honduras has community celebrations honoring patron saints and regional fiestas such as *Carnaval* in La Ceiba.

Commerce

Government office hours are from 8:00 A.M. to 4:00 P.M. or 7:30 A.M. to 3:30 P.M., Monday through Friday. Private businesses operate from 8:00 A.M. to noon and 1:00 to 5:00 P.M., although some do not close at noon for the *siesta* (midday break). Banks usually close by 3:00 P.M., while post offices may remain open as late as 9:00 P.M., depending on the city.

On Saturdays, most businesses close between noon and 2:00 P.M. In marketplaces and shops where prices are not posted, bartering is common; otherwise prices are fixed.

SOCIETY

Government

The Republic of Honduras is divided into 18 departments (provinces). Its president is chief of state and head of government. He governs with a cabinet and serves one four-year term. The judicial branch of government is independent. The unicameral National Congress (*Congreso Nacional*) has 134 seats. National elections are next scheduled for November 1997. All citizens are required to vote beginning at age 18. Two parties dominate in Congress, although smaller parties have representation. President Reina is a member of the governing Liberal Party (PLH). The opposition National Party (PNH) has two factions (Monarca and Oswaldista), each devoted to an individual leader.

Economy

The economy in Honduras is based largely on agriculture, which employs more than 60 percent of the population. Honduras is one of the poorest countries in the Western Hemisphere, and income and productivity rates are low. The most profitable exports are bananas and coffee, followed by seafood, timber, cotton, sugar, and metals. Global price fluctuations for these raw materials can be major and can cripple the economy from one year to the next. Manufactured items are slowly becoming more important. Unemployment is more than 15 percent. Underemployment, a condition where people do not have full-time or steady work, is more than 30 percent. Economic reforms implemented in the early 1990s and scaled back by President Reina are beginning to improve some conditions. However, infrastructure (services, roads, markets) is weak and the large bureaucracy is inefficient. The Honduran currency is the *lempira* (L), but it is sometimes referred to as a *peso*.

Real gross domestic product per capita is estimated at $2,000, which has doubled in the last generation. About half of all people live in poverty. Most do not earn an income sufficient for their needs. Economic prosperity is only enjoyed by the wealthiest Hondurans.

Transportation and Communication

Highways connect Tegucigalpa with some other principal cities. The people rely on buses for public transport because few own cars. Rural areas are isolated from cities due to poor transportation and communication. In areas without buses, pickup truck owners may provide travel on specific routes. Tegucigalpa, San Pedro Sula, La Ceiba, the Bay Islands, Puerto Lempira, and some villages in La Mosquitia are accessible by airplane. Private telephones are found only in major cities. Most large towns have one public telephone and a telegraph service. Many people communicate by placing messages on the radio. Mail service is slow but fairly reliable.

Education

Schooling is required for six years beginning at age seven. However, while nearly all children begin their schooling, many drop out before the end—especially among the rural poor. Fewer than half of all children actually complete the full six years, and fewer than one-third advance to the secondary level. Children are often needed at home to help with farming or household chores, and having them gone all day at school can be too great a sacrifice for many families. The literacy rate is 71 percent. The National University of Honduras and some trade schools provide higher education, but only 9 percent of the population advances to those levels of study. Honduras has some of Central America's best agricultural and forestry schools.

Health

Various health challenges face Honduras, which is in the yellow fever endemic zone. Malaria is prevalent below 3,000 feet (about 900 meters), and rabies, typhoid, hepatitis, parasites, and dysentery, as well as intestinal disease, present problems for the population. A serious cholera epidemic struck the country in 1991. The infant mortality rate is 43 per 1,000, and life expectancy ranges from 66 to 71 years. Vaccinations are provided free of charge, and nearly all people have access to them. But, while most Honduran children (83 percent) are immunized, up to half suffer from malnutrition.

Rural areas have health centers, but many villagers must walk hours to reach one. Facilities are often not equipped with medicine. Urban medical care is more adequate but still lacking by modern standards. Basic health care is subsidized throughout the country, but patients must pay small fees for each visit. Poorer citizens cannot often afford prescription medicine.

FOR THE TRAVELER

A valid passport is necessary for travel to Honduras, but U.S. citizens staying for a short time do not need a visa to enter the country. Yellow fever and typhoid vaccinations are recommended, as is a gamma globulin shot. If you plan to travel to areas with malaria, take prophylactics. Water is not safe for drinking. Overland travel between Nicaragua and Honduras is very hazardous due to highway robbery. Off-road travelers along that border risk injury by land mines. Petty theft is common in many areas; do not wear expensive jewelry or carry large amounts of cash.

Honduras offers many vacation opportunities. The Bay Islands off the north coast are popular for their excellent scuba diving and snorkeling. Honduras is also home to the famous Mayan ruins called Copán, located near the Guatemalan border. For more information, contact the Honduras Travel Information Center, 80 Wall Street, Suite 915, New York, NY 10005; phone (212) 269–3612; or the consular section of the Embassy of Honduras, 1612 K Street NW, Suite 310, Washington, DC 20006; phone (202) 223–0185. Other consulate offices, which offer the same services as an embassy, are located in several major U.S. cities. The Embassy of Honduras is located at 3007 Tilden Street, POD 4M NW, Washington, DC 20008.

CULTURGRAM™ '97

Republic of

Hungary

Boundary representations not necessarily authoritative.

EUROPE

BACKGROUND

Land and Climate

Hungary is a landlocked nation in central Europe. Covering 35,919 square miles (93,030 square kilometers), it is slightly smaller than Indiana. Most of the east is flat, but the northwest has rolling hills and low mountains. Almost 55 percent of the land is suitable for cultivation, allowing Hungary to be nearly self-sufficient in food. The capital, Budapest, is actually the union of two cities (Buda and Pest) lying on opposite sides of the Danube River. They united in 1872 as Budapest, once called the "Paris of the East." The climate is continental, with cold winters and warm, pleasant summers. The average temperature in winter is 32°F (0°C) and in summer is 70°F to 75°F (21–24°C).

History

Present-day Hungary became part of the Roman Empire in 14 B.C. as the province of Pannonia, but the east remained in the hands of Germanic and other tribes. In the fifth century, Magyars began migrating from the east. By the end of the ninth century, the Magyars had conquered the resident Moravians and begun permanent settlement. They were led by Árpád. Christianity was introduced by his grandson Géza, in the late tenth century. Géza's son, Stephen, became Hungary's first king in A.D. 1000, and Stephen converted the people to Christianity. The dynasty lasted until the 14th century, after which time nonnative powers controlled the area. During the Renaissance of the 15th century, the country reached a high level of culture and political power but was conquered by the Ottoman Turks. Later, Hungary was united under the crown of the Austrian Hapsburgs during their rise to world prominence (16th–18th centuries). Hungarians rose in rebellion in 1848 but were defeated after two years of fighting.

In 1867, the Dual Monarchy, a sharing of power between Austrians and Hungarians in Central Europe, was established. The Austro-Hungarian Empire was later shattered by heightened national awareness and desire for self-rule among Slavic minorities. This division contributed to the beginning of World War I in 1914. In treaty settlements following the war, Hungary became an independent republic but lost two-thirds of its former territory and three-fifths of its people to new neighbor states. Hungary fought as a German ally through most of World War II, but Germany invaded in 1944 after Hungary talked of declaring neutrality. Soviet troops liberated the country in 1945, and free elections again established a republic. The Communist Party, under heavy influence from the Soviet Union, seized power within two years and by 1949 had declared Hungary a socialist state called the People's Republic of Hungary.

Communist reformer Imre Nagy tried to change the system that emerged. He even withdrew Hungary from the Warsaw Pact and declared the country neutral in 1956. In response, the Soviet Union attacked Hungary, repressed the movement, executed Nagy, and buried him in disgrace. Until 1988, when he was forced to resign under pressure for reform, János Kádár was the leader of the Communist government. By October 1989, Hungary had changed its name to the Republic of Hungary and abolished the Communist monopoly on power. Nagy was reburied as a national hero.

In 1990, free elections were held and József Antall became the new prime minister. Antall died in 1993 and was replaced briefly by Peter Boross. Their party, the Hungarian Democratic Forum, which had swept the Communists from power in 1990, was defeated in May 1994 elections. The Socialist Party (MSZP), which gained the parliamentary majority in that vote, was the Communist Party before 1989. Gyula Horn became prime minister. The MSZP received its majority largely because of people's disillusionment with the course of economic reform. Horn promised to continue market reforms but also meet people's basic needs. His government faces a serious budget deficit, inflation, and the task of privatizing inefficient state industries.

In addition to economic concerns, regional issues also challenge Hungary's leaders, particularly the status of ethnic Hungarians living in Slovakia and Romania. Treaties promoting their rights were signed in 1995. Hungarians have especially close ties to their past cultural center of Transylvania (in Romania since 1920), where Hungarian kings lived in exile during Turkish rule.

THE PEOPLE

Population

Hungary's population of 10.3 million is currently not growing. Magyars (Hungarians) form the largest ethnic group and 90 percent of the population. The Romany (Gypsies) comprise 4 percent of the people and are usually the poorest of the poor. Germans (2.6 percent), Serbs (2), Slovaks (0.8), and Romanians (0.7) comprise significant minorities. Two million people reside in Budapest. Hungarians comprise 10.8 percent of Slovakia's population and 7 percent of Romania's.

The country's Human Development Index (0.856) ranks it 50th out of 174 countries. Most peoples' basic needs are met, which allows them a certain degree of choice in their lives. Adjusted for women, the index (0.836) ranks Hungary 23d out of 130 countries. This figure indicates women have good access to employment opportunities.

Language

The official language is Magyar, or Hungarian, as it is referred to in other countries. Ninety-eight percent of the population speaks it. Magyar is part of the Finno-Ugrian group of the Uralic language family, which includes Estonian and Finnish. It is a "vowel harmony" language. The sounds of vowels are marked by various accents and change to better agree with other vowels in a word. Accents (or a lack of accents) may completely change the meaning of a word. Most minority groups speak their own languages in addition to Hungarian. German and English are popular courses in school.

Religion

Roughly two-thirds of the population is Roman Catholic. Various other Christian groups make up the other third, including Calvinists (20 percent) and Lutherans (5 percent). During Communist rule, religious groups were carefully regulated through a government agency. In 1990, religious freedom was granted to all. While religion does not affect daily life much, many people consider themselves devout Christians.

General Attitudes

As a nation that experienced a form of democracy before most other European nations, the new democratic Hungary is proud of its heritage. Even during the Communist regime, Hungary was considered one of the most prosperous and open countries in Eastern Europe. It was one of the first to announce sweeping reforms and was able to accomplish them without violence or serious upheaval. The people earnestly wish to become part of an integrating Europe. Hungarians also view their past achievements and their artists and composers with pride. Franz Liszt and Béla Bartók are just two names that are well-known throughout the world. Hungarian folk music and food are also renowned.

Accompanying pride, however, is a historical tendency for pessimism. Individual Hungarians will express doubt about their own future or condition, even if their neighbors are worse off. Hungarian humor incorporates pessimism, which then becomes a whimsical, light-hearted cynicism. Some say pessimism is only natural for Hungarians, who as traditional farmers found it bad luck to predict good harvests. Individually, Hungarians value independence, a strong and stable family, education (including good performance in school and an advanced degree), security (be it a job, home, or social benefits), property (a home, garden, and car), access to or ownership of summer cottages, and travel outside of Hungary. People admire professionals but do not generally admire the wealthy, who are often associated with corruption.

Personal Appearance

Clothing styles in urban areas generally follow those in Western Europe, with blue jeans being the most popular among the youth. Businessmen wear conservative suits. Women pay particular attention to style and their appearance.

Traditional costumes are seen only in rural areas and during special celebrations. They may include intricately embroidered blouses and skirts for women, who also wear colorful hats or scarves. Each region has its specialty. The men often wear vests over loose-fitting shirts. Pants may be pleated, baggy, and less than full-length—or tight, black, and tucked inside boots. Men wear a variety of hats.

CUSTOMS AND COURTESIES

Greetings

Adults greet each other with a firm handshake. A man usually waits for a woman to extend her hand first. If one's hand is dirty, one may offer a wrist or elbow. Except between men, many Hungarians also *puszi*, or hug and kiss each other lightly on each cheek. Polite verbal greetings include *Jó napot kívánok* (Good day), *Jó reggelt kívánok* (Good morning), and *Jó estét kívánok* (Good evening). *Kívánok* is often left off in more casual circumstances or is replaced by a person's name. Children greet older women with *Kezét csókolom* (I kiss your hand). Men might also use this with older women to show special respect.

Popular informal greetings include *Halò, Szervusz,* or *Szia*, which all mean "Hello." The latter two terms come from the Latin *servus*, which once meant "I am here to serve you." One might follow a greeting with *Hogy vagy?* (How are you?) or another question. When addressing someone, it is polite to use the person's professional title with his or her surname. People introduce themselves by surname, usually followed by the given name. Greetings on a first-name basis are limited to close friends and relatives. However, adults address the youth, and the youth address each other, by first name. Urban Hungarians do not usually greet strangers on the street, but rural people will. When parting, Hungarians say *Viszontlátásra* (See you again) or simply *Halò*, *Viszlát*, or *Szia*.

Visiting

While close friends, relatives, and sometimes neighbors make short unannounced visits, urban or extended visits are arranged in advance when possible. Relatives visit often. Guests remove shoes upon entering a home; hosts may have a pair of guest slippers for them to wear. First-time guests do not stay long, leaving just after coffee is finished. When guests arrive, hosts often help them remove their coats. An informal atmosphere prevails. Hosts accompany departing guests outside.

Hungarians enjoy socializing in the home but also frequently meet at restaurants, coffeehouses and tearooms. Guests in the home are usually offered such refreshments as coffee, tea, fruit juice, brandy, or one of many popular regional wines. When one is invited to dinner, it is polite to bring a small gift of flowers, boxed chocolates, or wine. Flowers are presented in odd numbers; they remain in cellophane wrapping until the hostess puts them in a vase. The hosts will usually display the flowers in a room where the guests will be after dinner, or sometimes on the table.

Eating

Breakfast may be a light meal with only rolls and a drink, or it may be heartier and include eggs, salami, cheese, yogurt, and even hot peppers. Lunch is often the main meal in rural areas, including soup, often salad, a main dish of meat and potatoes, and dessert with coffee. In urban areas, lunch is light and dinner is the main meal. Rural people eat a light dinner of cold cuts, fruit, bread or rolls, and a drink.

Before eating or when entering a room where someone is eating, Hungarians say *Jò èt vagyat*, which means something similar to *Bon appétit* (Enjoy the meal). They keep hands above the table but do not rest the elbows on it. Napkins are kept on the table throughout the meal. Leaving food on the plate is impolite. Although tap water is safe to drink, many people prefer mineral water or some other beverage. As throughout Europe, the continental style of eating is used, with the fork in the left hand and the knife remaining in the right. Tips are customary in restaurants at the same levels as the rest of Europe (10–15 percent).

LIFESTYLE

Family

The average Hungarian family has three people. Urban families tend to be smaller than rural ones. The cost of living is high in cities and housing is often limited. The father maintains a dominant role in the family. Both parents usually work. In fact, nearly 80 percent of all women work. Men share some household responsibilities but traditionally take the "outside" chores (yard work, gardening, etc.). Adult children often live with their parents until married. Aging parents are generally cared for by their children, who may live in the same house or nearby. Urban families live in either small apartments or small single-family homes, while rural families have single-family homes.

Dating and Marriage

Young people like to go to movies, concerts, and theaters. They enjoy dancing, watching television, and just talking together on park benches. Many ski and hike together. Most Hungarians expect to marry and raise a family (in that order). Urban newlyweds tend to be older than rural couples. Most people wait until after they have finished schooling or are working before they marry. Traditional weddings were elaborate three-day affairs but are rare today. Still, the ceremony at city hall is often followed by a lavish dinner. With housing in short supply, young couples often must live with parents for their first few years of marriage.

Diet

Hungary's location in central Europe makes it a prime gathering point for many ethnic culinary specialties. One of the most famous Hungarian specialties is *goulash*, a stew of meat, potatoes, onions, and paprika. Paprika is a familiar spice in many dishes. Pork is the most common meat in the Hungarian diet, but chicken is also popular. Side dishes include noodles, potatoes, and dumplings. A cabbage-and-vinegar salad is popular with main meals. Except for certain seasonal varieties, vegetables and fruits are in ample supply year-round. Bread and pastries are available in a wide variety. Fish soup (*halászlé*), stuffed paprika, stuffed chicken, and various kinds of strudel and pancakes are all part of the diet. Hungary is also proud of its many wines.

Recreation

Hungary's most popular sport is soccer. Other important sports include swimming, tennis, fencing, and sailing. Hunting and fishing are popular activities as well. In their leisure time, many Hungarians like to take walks, visit parks or local museums, attend concerts, watch television, or work outside in the garden. They meet in town for afternoon tea or an ice cream treat or relax at the local thermal bath. For vacations, many like to go to resort spas. Longer vacations are often spent at Lake Balaton. Many also travel to neighboring countries.

Hungary was once known as a nation of horsemen, especially for the time when the Hussars (15th-century light cavalry) were famous for their horsemanship. Today, horses are used mostly in the tourist industry, but some Hungarians enjoy riding them for recreation.

Hungarians consider their performing arts companies, art galleries, and other cultural institutions to be national treasures, and they attend when possible. Hungarian folk music and dancing are still very popular. The youth also enjoy modern music.

Holidays

Public holidays include New Year's Day, War of Freedom Day (15 March, a day marking the 1848 rebellion and war), Easter (Sunday and Monday), Labor Day (1 May), Pentecost, St. Stephen's Day (20 August), National Holiday (23 October, in honor of the 1956 uprising), and Christmas (25–26 December). In addition, local festivals commemorate various folk or religious events throughout the year. At Easter, it is customary in some places for boys to "sprinkle" girls with water or cologne as a sign that the girl is a flower that should not fade. Also popular at this time are elaborately painted Easter eggs. St. Stephen's Day celebrates the harvest and honors the first king of Hungary.

Commerce

Businesses open around 8:00 A.M. and remain open until 6:00 P.M. Some close for an hour at lunch. Many, but not all, businesses are open on Saturday until 2:00 P.M. All close on Sunday. Produce stands often operate on sidewalks, and open-air markets are found in most towns. Produce, fresh bread, and other items are available at these markets. People shop often for fresh produce and dairy products, which are easily obtained at neighborhood stores. Supermarkets are located in large cities.

Formalities are important in business dealings. People tend to use formal names, discuss business politely, and treat people with respect. Refreshments are usually served. Important business discussions may be followed by an invitation to dinner, regardless of the progress made in the meeting.

SOCIETY

Government

Hungary is composed of 19 counties. An elected president (Arpad Goncz) is chief of state, and a prime minister (Gyula Horn) is head of government. Parliament has one 386-seat house, called the *Országgyulés* (National Assembly). The voting age is 18. In addition to the MSZP and Democratic Forum, the Alliance of Free Democrats and other parties hold seats in Parliament.

Economy

Having started its initial economic reforms prior to 1989, Hungary has been a leader in the transition toward a free-market economy. Nevertheless, the transition remains difficult for many of Hungary's citizens who have endured higher prices, higher taxes, and a lower standard of living. Unemployment is about 12 percent and inflation remains around 20 percent. The country still faces a large budget deficit despite cuts in 1995 that caused personal wages to drop by 10 percent. Further budget reforms may require unpopular cuts in social benefits (some of the most generous in the region).

Overall, Hungary is performing better than some other former Communist countries and has the potential for a bright future. The economy grew 3 percent in 1994, ending a four-year period of decline. Strong foreign investment, stable government institutions, a booming small business sector, and a hardworking labor force are key strengths. The government is selling all state-owned small businesses and pledges to accelerate privatization of larger industries. A stock market was established in 1990. Real gross domestic product per capita is $6,580. Most people can meet basic needs, and many are able to afford the flood of consumer items now available on the market.

Industries account for 40 percent of the gross national product. Important natural resources include bauxite, coal, and natural gas. Hungary welcomes foreign investment and trade in order to build its economy and increase its hard currency reserves. The currency is the *forint* (Ft).

Transportation and Communication

Public transportation in Hungary is well developed. Budapest has a subway. Taxis are also available. More and more people own private cars, but public transport is still the principal mode of travel. Bicycles are used for short distances. An extensive train network serves most of the country. Some transportation (mostly for tourists) is provided on the Danube River.

The communications system is modern, although many homes lack telephones. Most families have a television and radio. There are several local broadcast channels and cable television is available but expensive. *Kossuth Radio Budapest* is popular. Four daily national newspapers and several regional papers service the country. Magazines and other publications abound. The free press is active and striving to be competitive with foreign media companies that are investing in Hungary.

Education

Schooling is free and compulsory for all children ages six to fourteen. Most then go on to secondary schools for technical training or preparation for higher education. Teachers are well trained and students receive a solid education. Beginning in elementary school, foreign language classes are offered. Those who successfully complete secondary school may go on to any of the five academic, four medical, and nine technical universities in Hungary, provided they pass tough entrance exams. Several other institutions of higher learning are also available. University education was free before 1994, but students must now pay tuition. The adult literacy rate is 99 percent.

Health

Hungary's health-care system is well organized and modern. Standards in hospitals and clinics are high. Hungary's infant mortality rate is 12 per 1,000. All citizens receive free care in public institutions and most medicine is paid for. Patients must pay to see private doctors. Health-care professionals are well trained but not necessarily well paid. Major health hazards include pollution, a traditionally high-fat diet, high alcohol intake, and widespread smoking. These factors combine to give Hungary a life expectancy rate of 68 to 76 years, one of the lowest in Europe.

FOR THE TRAVELER

U.S. visitors need a valid passport to enter Hungary, but a visa is only necessary for business travelers or for persons staying longer than 90 days. Hungary has a fairly well-developed tourist industry, offering horseback tours, Danube River cruises, train excursions, or stays at traditional country inns. English is understood in tourist areas. Travelers can enjoy interesting architecture in many cities and towns, high-quality and inexpensive performing arts, sailing on Lake Balaton, mountain resorts, fine pastries, and much more. For details on travel opportunities, contact the Hungarian Tourist Board, 150 East 58th Street, 33d Floor, New York, NY 10155; phone (212) 355–0240. You may also wish to contact the Embassy of Hungary, 3910 Shoemaker Street NW, Washington, DC 20008; phone (202) 362–6730.

A *Culturgram* is a product of native commentary and original, expert analysis. Statistics are estimates and information is presented as a matter of opinion. While the editors strive for accuracy and detail, this document should not be considered strictly factual. It is a general introduction to culture, an initial step in building bridges of understanding between peoples. It may not apply to all peoples of the nation. You should therefore consult other sources for more information.

Republic of
Iceland

Isafjördhur

Siglufjördhur

Húsavík

Saudhárkrókur

Akureyri

Blönduós

Seydhisfjördhur

Egilsstadhir

Olafsvík

Hofsjökull

Langjökull

Vatnajökull

Borgarnes

Hafnarhreppur

REYKJAVÍK ★

Hafnarfjördhur

Myrdalsjökull

Vík

Greenland

Greenland Sea

Denmark Strait

Norwegian Sea

Iceland

Norway

Sweden

United Kingdom

Denmark

Netherlands

Atlantic Ocean

Ireland

Germany

France

Italy

Spain

Boundary representations not necessarily authoritative.

BACKGROUND

Land and Climate

Slightly smaller in area than Kentucky, Iceland (39,768 square miles or 103,000 square kilometers) is the second largest island in Europe and is surrounded by many smaller islands. The land is rugged with varied scenery. About 80 percent uninhabited, this "land of fire and ice" is one of the most active volcanic countries in the world. It is, in fact, a volcanic island and averages one eruption every five years. Earthquakes are also frequent, but they are rarely strong enough to cause damage. Iceland has more hot springs than any other country in the world; in fact, the English word *geyser* comes from Icelandic. The uninhabited interior is a popular place for horse riding and camping. Accessible except during winter, it has many beautiful features, including glaciers, mountains, lakes, volcanoes, and even deserts.

Despite the country's northerly location, the climate is much milder than one would expect. The warm Gulf Stream nearly encircles the island. The average annual temperature in Reykjavík is 41°F (5°C). It does, however, often become bitterly cold in both summer and winter when the polar winds blow. There are two or three months of continuous daylight in the summer, while during the winter (mid-November–January) there may only be four or five hours of daylight (10:00 A.M.–3:00 P.M.).

History

The first permanent settlers in Iceland were Norwegian and Celtic peoples. Iceland claims the Norwegian Ingólfur Arnarson as the first settler in 874; he founded Reykjavík, the current capital. In 930, Icelanders created the *Althing*, their national assembly, but they had no central government or monarchy. The *Althing* established laws and also served as a court. Christianity was adopted by the *Althing* in the year 1000, the same year that Leifur Eiríksson is said to have discovered America, landing at Newfoundland.

In 1262, Iceland became subject to the Norwegian crown, partly to end civil war between various local chieftains. Despite the new ruler, Iceland remained fairly autonomous. In 1380, both Iceland and Norway united with the Danish crown. Denmark introduced Lutheranism to Iceland in the 1530s but met with stiff opposition to the Reformation. The last Catholic bishop, Jón Arason, was beheaded in 1550 and the Lutheran Church was established. Even though today's Iceland is Lutheran, Arason is a national hero because he resisted the Danes.

By the 1600s, Denmark had established a trade monopoly with Iceland, and Iceland became little more than a Danish colony. Accordingly, the 17th and 18th centuries are now considered a dark period in Iceland's history, a time when it lost its self-government and free trade. This period had a profound

EUROPE

influence on later political developments and is one reason why Icelanders are very nationalistic. It is also why Iceland is usually among the first nations to recognize new countries. Iceland was first to recognize the independence of Latvia, Lithuania, and Estonia in 1991.

The 18th century brought famine and economic troubles, but an independence movement did not really begin until the 1800s, when the people experienced a revival of national literature and history. When Denmark's monarchy became subject to a constitutional democracy, Iceland was given an opportunity to regain home rule. A constitution was granted in 1874, but Iceland remained responsible to Denmark.

It was not until 1918 that Iceland became an independent sovereign state under a common Danish king. During World War II, the United States and Great Britain helped defend Iceland, and Iceland's ties with Denmark were essentially broken. The Republic of Iceland was formally declared in June 1944 and a new constitution was adopted. Iceland developed a progressive economy and stable political system. Cooperation between political parties has always been high because nearly all governments have been coalitions, with no one party dominating the *Althing*. David Oddsson of the Conservative Party, first elected prime minister in 1991, was returned to office through elections in 1995.

THE PEOPLE

Population

In terms of population, Iceland is a small country with about 265,000 people. The population is growing at 0.9 percent a year. Very few people emigrate to other countries. About half of the population lives in the capital, and the central part of the country is uninhabited. Icelanders are descendents of the Norwegian and Celtic peoples who settled in the ninth and tenth centuries. They are considered a homogeneous people. The country's Human Development Index (0.933) ranks it sixth out of 174 countries. Excellent access to health care, education, and economic prosperity affords Icelanders a high standard of living and freedom for individual choices.

Language

The official language is Icelandic. Icelanders are taught Danish and English in primary and secondary school, and nearly everyone can speak both of these languages. During the Viking era (8th–10th centuries), all Nordic peoples shared a common language. After that, separate tongues evolved in the areas of present-day Norway, Sweden, and Denmark. Iceland retained the old language, which remained essentially unchanged through the centuries. (In fact, modern Icelandic is more similar to ancient Norwegian than modern Norwegian is.) As a result, Icelanders can read medieval Icelandic *sagas* (stories) from the "Age of Sagas" (1200–1400) with little difficulty. Because of this heritage, Icelanders enjoy tracing their ancestral roots. The *sagas* cover centuries of Scandinavian

and British history. Through them, the lives and exploits of the Vikings and peoples that came after them are known to the world today.

Religion

The bulk of the population (more than 90 percent) belongs to the state church, the Evangelical Lutheran Church. Despite the existence of a state-sponsored church, religious freedom is fully guaranteed, and other Christian churches (Roman Catholic and Protestant) have members in Iceland. Two percent of the population has no religious affiliation. Attendance at the state church is generally sparse; people usually go to church only twice a year. But while religion is not a public matter, Icelanders are privately very religious. There is a strong belief in spiritual and supernatural things, and people are quite devout.

General Attitudes

Icelanders are proud of their society, which is very egalitarian and highly literate. People's abilities are more important than their station in life. In general, the people are known to be individualistic and independent. There is little crime and very little pollution in the country. Most areas are heated almost entirely by geothermal energy produced naturally by hot springs. A source of pride for Icelanders, geothermal springs provide the country with renewable, clean energy.

Literature and language are extremely important in Iceland. Whereas many languages will adopt or adapt foreign words (often English) into their language to describe a new item or habit, Icelanders want to keep their language as pure as possible. In fact, an official committee exists for the sole purpose of creating new Icelandic words, for terms such as *telephone* or *computer*, when necessary.

Personal Appearance

Icelanders dress well, especially when attending theaters and fine restaurants. Because the climate is generally cool, warm clothing is necessary during much of the year. Iceland is known for its woolens, especially sweaters. Dressing neatly in public is important, and most people spend a lot of money on clothing. European fashions are most common.

CUSTOMS AND COURTESIES

Greetings

A handshake is the normal way to greet someone, along with saying *Saell* (to a man) or *Sael* (to a woman). The phrase roughly means "Blessed." A more casual greeting, especially among children, is *Halló* (Hello). All Icelanders are properly and officially called by their first name, even though they also have a last name. A first name is used after a person's title as well. A woman does not change her name with marriage. A woman's last name is formed by the possessive form of her father's first name, followed by *dóttir*, meaning daughter. A man's last name is the possessive of his father's first name, followed by *son*. Names in a phone book are alphabetized by the first given name, but it is necessary to know the last name as well.

Gestures

Body language traditionally has not been important to communication in Iceland. Consequently, few hand expressions are used during conversation. People don't normally eat on the street, with the exception of foods like ice cream and hot dogs. Smoking is prohibited in public buildings.

Visiting

Icelanders are usually casual about visiting; they commonly drop in on people unannounced or telephone just before visiting. Truly formal invitations are rare. Hosts may offer a cup of coffee. Because society is home centered, people entertain in the home more often than they go out. Due to the cold weather, Icelanders spend a lot of time indoors and devote plenty of time, effort, and money to making their homes pleasant. Indeed, beautification of the home is a lifetime pursuit, and creating a nice atmosphere brings much prestige. Icelandic homes are usually larger and better furnished than the average Scandinavian or European homes and, therefore, are natural places for entertaining guests.

Guests invited to dinner usually bring a gift (flowers or candy) to the hosts. At the end of a meal, or even refreshments, guests customarily shake hands with their hosts and thank them. It is not enough simply to make a comment or say thank you at the table; guests actually approach the hosts, offer the hand, and express their appreciation for the hospitality.

Eating

Breakfast is usually a light meal and includes cereal or toast with tea or coffee. Icelanders typically eat lunch around noon and dinner between 7:00 and 8:00 P.M. The continental style of eating is followed, with the fork in the left hand and the knife remaining in the right.

At restaurants, service charges and tax are included in the bill. Before the mid-1970s, going out to eat was not popular and being a waiter or waitress was a demeaning job. Offering a tip was an insult and emphasized the waiter's position as a servant. Consequently, there is no tradition of tipping in Iceland. Since the 1970s, restaurants have increased dramatically in number and waiting tables is fully respectable. Icelanders still do not tip, but the practice would no longer be considered an insult. The increase in restaurants has also led to a wider variety of foods available in the country. Most European and Scandinavian dishes can be found in Reykjavík.

LIFESTYLE

Family

Family ties are strong and families tend to be larger than other Scandinavian families. Even though people are individualistic, family members rely heavily on each other. Because the country is small, personal ties are important and family relations play a key role. This is evidenced by the tradition of asking "Who are your people?" when meeting someone for the first time. This inquiry is an attempt to place a person in a family or professional level. The initial response is to name one's parents. If they are not known, the parents' professions might be named or the grandparents' names given. Today's youth do not practice this, but their parents' generation still does.

More than 80 percent of Icelandic families own their own homes. Family patterns are changing as more women are becoming part of the workforce. Though relatively young, the feminist movement is gaining power. For example, in 1983 an all-woman political party won several seats in Parliament. They hold fewer seats today, but women's issues are more readily addressed than before.

Dating and Marriage

Dating begins around age 15 or 16. Parties and dances are among the most popular activities. The government recognizes common-law marriage, so many couples choose to live together without formal marriage. Some choose to marry at a later date.

Diet

The basics of the Icelandic diet include fish, lamb, and dairy products. Fresh fish is plentiful and includes such varieties as cod, haddock, halibut, plaice (a type of flounder), herring, salmon, and trout. Popular dishes are *hangikjöt* (smoked mutton) and *skyr* (similar to yogurt). Potatoes (usually boiled) are served with most meals. *Hangikjöt* is the traditional meal on Christmas day. For many years, greenhouses have made it possible for Iceland to service its need for tomatoes, peppers, cucumbers, and other produce. Water is safe to drink and clean throughout the country.

Recreation

Traveling and camping are favorite pastimes in Iceland. Hiking, trout and salmon fishing, swimming in pools heated by natural hot springs, soccer, skiing, and golf are other common forms of recreation. Many enjoy riding the small horses unique to Iceland. Chess is popular. Iceland is known as a bird-watcher's paradise. Merchants Holiday provides a three-day weekend that is popular for camping. Cities practically empty as everyone heads to the countryside, especially the interior, to camp. There are many large, established campgrounds where people gather. Some also camp in more private areas.

Holidays

Public holidays include New Year's Day, Easter (Thursday–Monday), First Day of Summer (usually third Thursday in April), Labor Day (1 May), Ascension Day, Whitsunday and Whitmonday, National Day (17 June), Merchants Holiday (first Monday in August), and Christmas (24–26 December). Christmas Eve is the most sacred and important day of Christmas. It is the evening for exchanging gifts and celebrating the birth of Christ. The 25th is a day for the big family meal and visiting, while the 26th is spent relaxing or enjoying some form of recreation.

New Year's Eve is extremely popular. Icelanders celebrate with many parties, fireworks, and bonfires. These light up the dark winter night and create excitement throughout the country.

Commerce

Business hours are generally from 9:00 A.M. to 6:00 P.M., Monday through Friday. Some businesses close for one hour at midday and many stay open until 7:00 P.M. on Fridays. Workers often stay much later into the evening, working overtime to earn more money. Saturday's hours depend on the business and season. Stores usually close an hour earlier in the summer. Kiosks or small vending-type shops remain open until 11:30 P.M. All workers receive a mandatory five-week vacation each year, which they definitely take advantage of. In fact, one reason for all of the overtime is so people can afford to take a nice vacation. July is the most popular month for vacationing because it is warm. Many people also vacation abroad; southern Europe is a favorite destination.

SOCIETY

Government

The Republic of Iceland is divided into 23 counties and 14 independent towns. A president is head of state. In June 1980, Icelanders selected Vigdís Finnbogadóttir as president. She was the world's first freely elected female head of state. The popular president choose not to run for reelection in June 1996, when Olafur Ragnur Grimsson, a veteran left-wing politician, defeated three rivals with 41 percent of the vote. Although the position of president has been largely ceremonial, with the prime minister running the government, that may change with the election of a career politician. Iceland's legislative body, the *Althing,* has 63 seats, which are shared by five parties, of which the Independence and Progressive Parties are the largest. The voting age is 20. The next election for prime minister is scheduled for April 1999.

Economy

Fish, the country's most abundant natural resource, is the most important export industry. Even manufacturing efforts tend to focus on the fishing industry; Iceland produces and exports machinery used in fish processing. Thirteen percent of the population is employed in fishing or fish processing, which accounts for about 75 percent of all export earnings. Only 1 percent of the land is suitable for cultivation; agriculture (including raising livestock) employs 6 percent of the population. There are many pastures and meadows used for livestock grazing. Sheep are the most important animals and wool is a primary product.

Industrially, Iceland has great potential for geothermal and hydroelectric power and is developing ways to exploit these renewable resources. Aluminum and aluminum smelting have become profitable industries. Other industries include publishing, cement, and diatomite. Some factories are able to use geothermal energy for power. Iceland is one of the most affluent countries in the world, known for low unemployment rates and strong economic performance. Real gross domestic product per capita is $17,660, which has tripled in the last generation. These figures indicate that the majority of Icelanders earn a good income and have access to economic prosperity. The currency is the *króna* (IKr) or plural *krónur.*

Transportation and Communication

Most Icelandic families have at least one car. In and around Reykjavík, the capital, there is also an excellent bus system. Iceland has no railroad. Some roads outside the capital are not paved, but most are passable year-round. One cannot travel inland or in certain remote areas in the winter. The communications system is modern and efficient.

Education

School attendance is compulsory for ages six to sixteen. Every child must know how to swim to graduate from elementary school. Education has always been important; about 99 percent of the population is literate. Iceland has the highest percentage of children enrolled in school in the world. Students learn Danish and English in school. A large percentage of youth continue their education through specialized training schools or college preparation schools, which lead to a university education. The University of Iceland is the only full university and many go abroad for advanced degrees. A small university in Akureyri offers some programs.

Health

Icelanders have one of the world's highest life expectancy rates in the world, living between 77 and 81 years. The infant mortality rate is extremely low at 4 per 1,000. All citizens have compulsory health coverage through a national system. Dental care is partially paid for by the government, although school children receive free care. There are no major health problems in the country.

FOR THE TRAVELER

While passports are required, U.S. citizens do not need visas for visits of up to three months in Scandinavia—Denmark, Iceland, Finland, Norway, and Sweden. No vaccinations are required. Iceland offers some unique vacation ideas. For information about travel opportunities, contact the Scandinavian Tourist Board, 655 Third Avenue, Suite 1810, New York, NY 10017; phone (212) 949–2333. You may also wish to contact the Icelandic Embassy, 1156 15th Street, NW, Suite 1200, Washington, DC 20005; phone (202) 265–6653.

Republic of
Ireland

Boundary representations not necessarily authoritative.

BACKGROUND

Land and Climate

Covering 27,135 square miles (70,280 square kilometers), the Republic of Ireland is somewhat larger than the state of West Virginia. The Republic of Ireland covers five-sixths of the island of Ireland, which is off the northwest coast of Europe. It shares the island with Northern Ireland, which is part of the United Kingdom (UK). Rugged coastal hills and low mountains surround the island's fertile, central plains and numerous lakes and bogs. Some say Ireland is like a badly baked pie—crusty around the edges and soggy in the middle. No part of the country is more than 70 miles (112 kilometers) from the coast. The Shannon is the longest river. Snow falls only on a few days in winter and quickly melts because of the moderating effect of the North Atlantic Current; winters are therefore wet and mild. The coldest temperatures average 30°F to 40°F (-1–4°C). Summers are cool; the warmest month of July has an average temperature below 65°F (18°C). Ireland's dampness, fog, and rain make the country's lush and green.

History

Although the Irish can trace the history of their island back several thousand years, the period of the Celts offers the most famous historical record and marks the beginning of Ireland's modern history. The Celts conquered the island in the fourth century B.C. Legend has it that St. Patrick came to Ireland in A.D. 432, bringing Christianity and converting the people. Norse Vikings invaded in 795 and established seaports in Ireland. The Norse eventually were defeated in 1014, but then the English began invading in the 12th century. In 1171, King Henry II of England forced Irish nobles to recognize his supreme rule. Over time, though, the English invaders adopted local culture and allowed the Irish some autonomy. In 1603, England established rule over all of Ireland after defeating the last major Gaelic leaders. Irish Anglicans, supported by England, excluded Catholics from controlling land and politics. In 1801, the United Kingdom of Great Britain and Ireland was established with the Act of Union, but it was not popular with Irish Catholics.

The country was devastated in the 1840s by the great potato famine; at least one million people died in five years and another two million emigrated to other countries, particularly the United States. Political conflict intensified after the famine, bringing rebellions and agitation for independence. The movement climaxed in 1921 with the signing of the Anglo-Irish Treaty. This treaty established the Irish Free State as a British dominion and allowed six northern counties (with a Protestant majority) to remain in the UK as Northern Ireland.

Under a new constitution in 1937, The Irish Free State changed its name to Ireland (*Éire*). The country began to decrease its association with the British Commonwealth. In 1949, Ireland formally withdrew from the Commonwealth and declared itself completely independent. The six northern counties remained part of the UK.

The Republic of Ireland has often sought the return of Northern Ireland to Irish sovereignty, but talks over the years regarding unification have not been fruitful. The issue was clouded with significant violence in Northern Ireland between militant forces favoring unification (namely, the Irish Republican Army or IRA) and those opposed (namely, loyalist Protestant paramilitary groups). In the 1990s, talks opened and

EUROPE

repeatedly failed. When the IRA finally called a cease-fire in 1994, the gesture was soon returned by loyalist militias. Encouraged by this, Great Britain, Ireland, and some Northern Ireland leaders pressed forward with a peace plan.

By 1995, all-party talks on the issue of power sharing between Northern Ireland political/religious groups were met with optimism on all sides. However, after British insistence that all-party talks depend on the disarmament of IRA guerillas, talks stalled, and in February 1996 the IRA broke its 17-month cease-fire. Efforts to revive the talks continued, despite sporadic violence. Sinn Fein, the IRA's political wing, was excluded from all-party talks held in June due to the IRA's broken cease-fire. Unionists (groups favoring Northern Ireland's association with Great Britain) oppose any contact with Sinn Fein, but Nationalists (Irish groups traditionally in favor of reunification) insist Sinn Fein's complete exclusion would doom the peace process.

Sovereignty, IRA disarmament, and the participation of Sinn Fein remain sensitive issues in the peace process. The prime ministers of both Great Britain and Ireland, as well as moderate leaders in Northern Ireland, continue to seek fair and reasonable solutions to the conflict.

THE PEOPLE

Population

Ireland's population of about 3.5 million is growing annually at 0.3 percent. Emigration tends to increase or decrease population growth more than the natural birthrate does. Many young people emigrate to the United States or the UK to secure employment, but others simply move to Dublin from rural areas. Nearly one in four people lives in the metropolitan Dublin area. Ethnically, the people of Ireland are Celtic. There is also a strong Norman influence and a small English (Anglo-Irish) minority.

Ireland's Human Development Index (0.915) ranks it 19th out of 174 nations. People enjoy good access to economic prosperity, education, and health care needed to make choices in their lives. Adjusted for women, the index (0.813) ranks Ireland 30th out of 130 countries. Compared to other Europeans, Irish women earn a lower share of their nation's income.

Language

Although Irish (called Gaelic) is the first officially recognized language, it is only spoken on a daily basis in the small Gaeltacht areas of the western seaboard. English, recognized as Ireland's second language, is spoken by everyone. Government documents and road signs are in both languages, and Gaelic is taught in schools. The government is trying to increase fluency in the primary language.

Religion

About 93 percent of the population is Roman Catholic. Three percent belongs to the Anglican Church. The remaining 4 percent holds various other beliefs—both Christian and non-Christian—or has no religious affiliation. The Catholic Church has played an important role in Ireland's cultural and political history. The Catholic faith has shaped the values of the people and laws of the land. For instance, the constitutional ban on abortion (and previously divorce) remains in effect largely due to efforts of the Catholic Church. Despite Catholicism's dominance, freedom of religion is guaranteed.

General Attitudes

The Irish are easygoing, lighthearted, good-humored, polite, and cheerful. They are quick-witted and have the ability to laugh at themselves. A general attitude that things will work out in the end affects their daily lives. The pace of life is somewhat influenced by the old maxim "God gave us time and he gave us plenty." Traditions are important and material goods do not have the same priority as in the United States. Still, some groups are calling for social and political liberalization, including greater tolerance for nontraditional lifestyles.

Traditional Irish values include having a good education and a secure job, owning a home, and possessing talent or humor. Individualism is admired but aggressiveness, arrogance, and fanaticism are not. The Irish avoid personal confrontation; they rarely say "no" to a person's face but communicate it in a different way. Most Irish resent outside criticism of their society or politics, preferring to be the only ones openly critical of themselves.

Some people wonder what the differences are between the people of the Republic of Ireland and those in Northern Ireland. Because both nations share a common cultural heritage, many things are similar. The differences that do exist have their roots in centuries-old conflicts over exploitation, political affiliation, and religion.

Personal Appearance

European fashions are most common, although traditional Irish styles influence those styles. For example, earth tones and warm colors are more popular. Sweaters and other woolen items are common because of the cooler climate. Fine-quality tweeds and linens are produced in Ireland. Casual dress is acceptable in most situations, but attire worn in public is generally conservative. Light rainwear is necessary for anyone living or traveling in Ireland.

CUSTOMS AND COURTESIES

Greetings

The Irish shake hands and greet one another with English phrases such as *Hello* and *How are you?* Depending on the situation, they may say *Good morning*, *Good evening*, *Hello*, and so on. The most typical Irish-language greeting is *Dia Dhuit* (Hello). Good-bye is expressed with *Slan* (Bye) or the more formal *Slan agus Beannacht* (Good-bye).

When addressing friends, relatives, and acquaintances, the Irish generally use first names. However, titles (*Mr., Mrs., Ms., Miss, Dr.*) and last names are used formally or with persons of higher status. Rural Irish greet each other when passing on the street, even if not acquainted, but urban residents reserve such greetings for neighbors and people they know.

Gestures

The Irish do not use hand gestures excessively during conversation, but they do not keep hands entirely still—some gesticulation is common.

The Irish value politeness and generally do not push (even if in a hurry), eat on the street (or on the run), comb hair in public, or otherwise offend those around them. If one breaches social norms, apologies are usually in order.

Visiting

The Irish are warm and hospitable, but it is not especially common for people to invite others to their home for dinner.

Rural people might sometimes drop in on friends unannounced, as was common practice in the past, but this is not the norm elsewhere. People like to have conversation in *pubs* (public houses) and on special occasions. Some say conversation is the national pastime. Many *pubs* feature folk music as entertainment. Visiting in the home takes place during holidays, especially between Christmas and New Year's Day. Parties are also popular during holidays. Because visiting is not frequent outside of holidays, it is not customary to take a gift when invited to someone's home.

Eating

The Irish eat three meals a day, with the main meal either at midday (if a family's schedule allows) or supper. When possible, families sit down together for their meals. Supper is often served later in the evening. The Irish eat in the continental style, with the fork in the left hand and the knife remaining in the right. Most people appreciate and adhere to good table manners, including not placing elbows on the table, not putting the knife in the mouth, not taking second helpings before asking permission, and so on.

Traditional Irish dishes are hearty, simple, and delicious. In addition to Irish cuisine, European dishes are popular. Many types of restaurants, including U.S. fast-food, are found in Ireland. "Farmhouse" restaurants feature traditional recipes. Tea kitchens serve hot drinks and homemade cakes and pastries in the afternoon. In restaurants, a service charge is often included in the bill. If not, a 10 to 15 percent tip is customary.

LIFESTYLE

Family

Family cohesiveness in Ireland is very important. Extended families often live near one another. When work or study takes members to distant parts of Ireland or to other countries, they make great efforts to return home for family celebrations—especially Christmas.

The average family has two or three children. Irish women stay at home to care for the children and household more often than do women in some other countries. Still, many younger women are becoming career oriented, and some 32 percent of the workforce is comprised of women. Competitive salaries and support services for women lag behind those for men. But Ireland's president presses her agenda for greater women's equality.

Although many young families rent an apartment (*flat*) or house, most eventually own a home. In fact, home ownership is high in Ireland. Houses usually are constructed of brick or concrete. Traditional thatched cottages can still be seen in some western areas, but these are no longer built today. Many families also have resort homes or chalets for summer vacations.

Dating and Marriage

While couples commonly married in their late twenties or later during the 1960s and 1970s, some are now marrying in their early twenties. This may be due to the fact that young people begin dating at an earlier age. Teenagers enjoy going to movies and dancing. The tradition of taking a special date to the graduation ball (similar to the *prom* in the United States) has developed in the last decade. The graduation ball calls for formal suits and dresses, a large meal, and a dance at a local hotel. Going to *pubs* is a popular social activity for people of all ages. *Pubs*, which serve more than alcohol, are open to those under drinking age and are prized for their food and atmosphere.

Most weddings are performed in a church and are automatically accepted as legal, but some are also performed in a registry office. Until 1995, Ireland's constitution prohibited divorce. The Irish traditionally had supported the ban due to influence of the Catholic Church. Efforts to lift the ban arose in the 1980s but did not succeed, and controversial debate between liberals and conservatives continued in the 1990s. Government efforts led to a national referendum in November 1995 in which voters chose to legalize divorce by a margin of 1 percent. The current law permits Irish couples to divorce after four years of separation.

Diet

As an agricultural country, Ireland produces many fresh vegetables. Fresh dairy products, breads, and seafood are also widely available. Potatoes are a staple food. Apples, oranges, and pears have long been integral to the Irish diet but are now being joined by a wider variety of fruits that have become available since Ireland joined the European Union (EU). Smoked salmon is considered an Irish specialty, as are Irish stew and Irish lamb. Tea is the most common drink. Breakfasts usually are large, including such foods as bacon and eggs. The main meats eaten for dinner include chicken, pork, beef, and mutton.

Recreation

The Irish are sports oriented, and most weekends include some sporting activities for the family or individual. Popular sports include the two national pastimes: Gaelic football and hurling (the women's version of hurling is called *camogie*). Hurling is played on a soccer-type field with wooden sticks and a small leather ball. Gaelic football is played with a round ball and seems like a cross between soccer and basketball. Players can touch the ball with their hands, but they cannot pick it up from the ground. The ball is punched, not thrown, and it can be kicked. Teams score for getting the ball into a soccer-type net but can also make points for putting it over the top of the goal. Soccer, rugby, sailing, cycling, golf, and horse racing are also favorite activities. Ireland's national soccer team competed in the 1994 World Cup. Fishing (*angling*) is also a common recreational activity, featuring mainly trout and salmon fishing.

Ireland's music industry is flourishing and has a strong international reputation. Contemporary rock often mixes elements of traditional folk music to create a unique style popular throughout the world. When strictly traditional music is played, one or more of the following instruments is usually involved: fiddle, guitar, banjo, tin whistle, button accordian, concertina, and harp.

Holidays

The main public holidays in Ireland are New Year's Day, St. Patrick's Day (17 March), Easter (Friday–Monday), Labour Day (1 May), the bank holidays (the first Monday in both June and August, and the last Monday in October), Christmas, and St. Stephen's Day (26 December). St. Patrick's Day features street parades in every city, but the largest is in Dublin. In honor of St. Patrick, Ireland's patron saint, the Irish wear a shamrock and have banquets. Some U.S. Americans, however, celebrate the day more fervently than the Irish. Christmas is the main family and social celebration. Everyone comes home from wherever they are to share a traditional meal of turkey and ham. It is a popular time for the wealthy to take a "sun" holiday in a warmer climate.

Commerce

Generally, business and banking hours are from 9:00 A.M. to 5:00 P.M., with an hour break for lunch in all but the major cities. Shopping centers remain open until 9:00 P.M. on Thursday and Friday evenings. Most people buy basic goods from shopping centers, which have replaced the more traditional corner shops and open markets.

SOCIETY

Government

The Irish Republic is headed by a popularly elected president who serves a seven-year term. The current president, Mary Robinson, was elected in 1991 as the first woman to hold the position. The president has only a few executive powers but can exercise considerable influence on national politics. A prime minister serves as head of government. The cabinet is drawn from members of Parliament. The current prime minister, John Bruton, took office in December 1994 after the resignation of Albert Reynolds. Bruton leads a coalition government composed of his Fine Gael Party, the Labor Party, and the Democratic Left Party.

The bicameral legislature is structured to provide both vocational and proportional representation. All members of the 166-seat House of Representatives (*Dail*) are directly elected. Of the Senate's 60 members, 49 are elected and the rest are appointed. All citizens may vote at age 18. Elections are held at least every five years. The next elections must be held by November 1997. Ireland has 26 counties. Many people in Ireland refer to Northern Ireland as the *six counties*.

Economy

Ireland has a small, open economy that relies heavily on trade, especially with nations of the EU. In fact, nearly 73 percent of Ireland's gross domestic product is exported. Real gross domestic product per capita is $12,830. That figure has more than tripled in the last generation. A serious unemployment problem affects 13 percent of the labor force. Still, the government has been able to drastically reduce inflation, encourage more exports, and attract foreign investment. As a result, consumer spending has increased and the economy is growing at 7 percent, the highest in Europe. EU assistance to counties bordering Northern Ireland has also boosted local economies.

While agriculture was once the main sector of the economy, only 15 percent of the population is now employed in it, and it is less able to generate export earnings. Instead, a diversified economy now relies more heavily on industry, including textiles, chemicals, and machinery. In agriculture, animal husbandry and dairy farming are important. Key crops include potatoes, sugar beets, turnips, barley, and wheat. Ireland is generally self-sufficient in foodstuffs, although fruits and some other items must be imported. The currency is the *punt* (£Ir).

Transportation and Communication

Buses (single- and double-decker) are the most common form of public transportation. They are efficient within and between cities. Taxis are expensive and not regulated by the government. Irish rail systems provide links to major cities. Nearly all roads are paved and in good condition. Most families have at least one car. Vehicles travel on the left side of the road. Although the communications system is small, it is modern and efficient. There are several radio and television stations in Ireland. A variety of daily newspapers are published throughout the country.

Education

The Irish constitution recognizes that parents have the freedom to provide for the education of their children, either in their own homes, in private schools, or in schools established by the state. Schooling is compulsory between ages four and fifteen, and about two-thirds of all children are still in school full-time at age sixteen. The government provides free education in primary and secondary schools and gives substantial aid to institutions of post-secondary education. University education is free.

Primary schools are managed by local boards composed of parent representatives, teaching staff, and relevant religious authorities. To be accepted as a pupil in secondary school, a child must be at least 12 years old and have completed primary education. Following secondary school, one may attend vocational or technical colleges, or a university if one passes proper examinations. Ireland's literacy rate is about 99 percent.

Health

Ireland's population is generally healthy. Well-equipped public medical clinics are located throughout Ireland. Care in public hospitals is provided at government cost. Many people choose to go to private doctors and facilities to avoid the waiting lists and other inconveniences of the public system. Long-term medical services are free to persons with infectious diseases and to children suffering from certain conditions. The infant mortality rate is 7 per 1,000. Life expectancy averages between 73 and 79 years.

FOR THE TRAVELER

U.S. citizens do not need a visa for trips of up to three months, but a valid passport is required. Citizens of some nations must obtain a visa upon arrival, while others must apply in advance. In Ireland, accommodations for tourists vary from bed-and-breakfast establishments to castle hotels. Travel packages are offered by the Irish Tourist Board (*Bord Fáilte*). For more detailed information, contact the Irish Tourist Board, 345 Park Avenue, 17th Floor, New York, NY 10154–0004; phone (800) 223–6470. You may also wish to contact the Embassy of Ireland, 2234 Massachusetts Avenue NW, Washington, DC 20008; phone (202) 462–3939. Consulates, which offer the same services as the embassy, are located in Boston, Chicago, New York, and San Francisco.

CULTURGRAM™ '97

Northern Ireland

(United Kingdom)

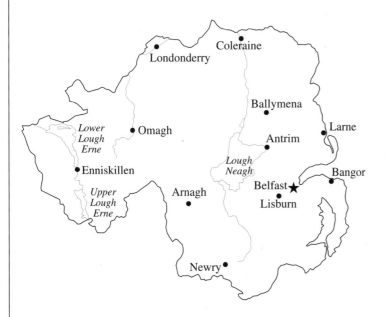

Boundary representations not necessarily authoritative.

BACKGROUND

Land and Climate

Northern Ireland is the smallest of the four nations that make up the United Kingdom (UK). Covering 5,482 square miles (14,199 square kilometers), it is about the same size as Connecticut. Summers are mild (average 55°F or 13°C) and wet; winters are cold (average 32°F or 0°C) and windy. The climate makes for a lush, green countryside.

Northern Ireland consists of the six northern counties on the island it shares with the Republic of Ireland. The six counties, together with three in the Republic of Ireland, make up what is called *Ulster*. Northern Ireland is often just referred to as *Ulster*. A large lake (*Lough Neagh*) dominates the terrain near Belfast. Rolling hills, a few low mountains, a rugged coastline, and forests are all part of the Northern Ireland landscape.

History

Celtic tribes invaded the island during the fourth century B.C. In the fifth century A.D., legend holds that St. Patrick converted the island to Christianity. The English began invading in the 12th century. In 1603, Irish revolts caused England's King James I to force Irish Roman Catholics in Northern Ireland to give up their land to English and Scottish Protestants. In 1801, the United Kingdom of Great Britain and Ireland was formed by the British Parliament.

In southern Ireland, the Easter Rebellion against British rule took place in 1916. This led to the Irish Free State, established in 1921 under British dominion. However, the south was largely Catholic. Meanwhile, the mainly Protestant northern counties of *Ulster* chose to remain in the UK as Northern Ireland. In 1949, the Irish Free State (not including Northern Ireland) became the Republic of Ireland and formally withdrew from the Commonwealth. The six northern counties remained part of the UK.

Seeking to unite all of Ireland, the Irish Republican Army (IRA), which is made up primarily of Catholics, began a campaign of assassinations and bombings against the Northern Ireland Protestants and British soldiers stationed in the country since 1969. The soldiers had been sent to maintain order after rioting broke out in Londonderry over issues of religious discrimination. Protestant extremists retaliated in similarly violent ways, making it impossible for frequently started negotiations on Northern Ireland's status to succeed. The British government instituted direct rule in 1972, precipitating further violence.

In 1975, Protestant and Catholic voters elected a 78-member convention with the responsibility of drafting a constitution and organizing a government for home rule acceptable to both sides. Unable to come to an agreement, the convention disbanded ten months later. Although widely publicized, the subsequent struggles of the past two decades have been initiated by extremists on both sides and are not generally supported by either Catholics or Protestants.

In 1985, after talks with the UK, the Republic of Ireland was awarded a consultative role in the affairs of Northern Ireland. In 1991, talks opened again on the issue of home rule, relations with the Irish Republic, and power sharing between Catholics and Protestants. Many hoped that compromises would be reached between Nationalists (those who seek union with Ireland) and Unionists (those who support the current union with the UK). The talks collapsed after only a few months. They resumed again in 1992 but ended after four months with little hope for future talks. Inflexibility on the part of leaders from both sides, as well as continued violence, made it difficult for talks to proceed. They did take place, however, in secret for several months in 1993.

Near the end of the year, a framework for peace was jointly announced by Ireland and Britain. Gerry Adams, leader of Sinn Fein, the IRA's political wing, expressed support for the plan. In 1994, the IRA announced a voluntary cease-fire, a gesture soon returned by Protestant paramilitary groups. By 1995, all-party talks on the issue of power sharing between Northern Ireland's political/religious groups were met with optimism on both sides of the border. For the first time, most people believed peace was at hand.

Negotiations continued but stalled in September 1995 after Ireland and Sinn Fein refused to link all-party talks to Britain's insistence that IRA guerrillas disarm. Frustrated by London's demands for disarmament, the IRA ended its 17-month cease-fire in February 1996 with a bombing in east London. Efforts to revive the peace talks continued despite sporadic violence. Delegates chosen in Northern Ireland's May elections met together for all-party talks in June without Sinn Fein, which was excluded from the talks because of the IRA's broken cease-fire. Sovereignty, disarmament, and Sinn Fein's participation in the talks remain sensitive issues unlikely to be resolved soon.

THE PEOPLE

Population

The population of Northern Ireland is about 1.7 million and is growing at only 0.2 percent per year. Northern Ireland is basically homogeneous; nearly all inhabitants are Irish, while some have Scottish roots. Belfast is the capital and largest city with about 360,000 people. The Human Development Index (0.919) ranks the UK 18th out of 174 nations. Good access to health care, education, and economic prosperity affords people opportunities and choices in their own lives. Adjusted for women, the index (0.862) ranks the UK 13th out of 130 countries.

Language

English is the official language. Although regional accents and expressions may vary, the Irish speak basically the same form of English that is spoken throughout the UK. Also known as British English or Oxford English, it often varies from U.S.

American English in spelling, pronunciation, idiomatic phrases, etc. In recent years, Gaelic, the ancient language of Ireland, has become popular.

Religion

In contrast to the Republic of Ireland (*Éire*), which has a Catholic majority, Northern Ireland (*Ulster*) has a Protestant majority. There are 950,000 Protestants, compared to some 650,000 Catholics. The largest Protestant churches include the Presbyterian Church, the Church of Ireland, and the Methodist Church. The division between Catholics and Protestants has been a major source of conflict throughout Irish history and not just during the 20th century.

General Attitudes

The Irish believe in hard work, but on the whole the pace of life is more relaxed than in the United States. Religion and politics have long been sources of conflict in this politically troubled nation and generally are avoided as topics of conversation. The Irish are friendly, sincere, and keenly sensitive to the beauties of nature. They appreciate honorable people and those who keep their word. Those loyal to the British Crown are proud of the queen of England. Although Northern Ireland is part of the UK, the people are not English, but Irish. The majority support Northern Ireland's position as part of the UK, and many therefore think of themselves as British in addition to Irish. Being British is not the same as being English.

Despite the political turmoil, the ordinary person in Northern Ireland longs for peace. Daily interaction between both communities is common on a grassroots level. Catholics and Protestants may attend different schools and churches, but most adults work together and shop at the same stores. Government initiatives strive to create a more tolerant and pluralistic society.

The Irish consider their land as one of ancient tales and rich history. They believe this endows their nation with a certain "magic" that is hard to express but easy to feel. Folklore plays an important role in creating that magic.

Personal Appearance

The Irish wear popular European fashions but add their own styles as well. They often wear sweaters in the summer because of the cool climate. Wool clothing is popular. Jeans and sweatshirts are common casual wear. Many tend to dress more conservatively than in the United States. Businesspeople generally dress formally; dark suits with ties are common for men. The youth follow clothing fads in the entertainment industry.

CUSTOMS AND COURTESIES

Greetings

Handshakes are common during initial meetings. Firm and brief, yet friendly, handshakes are characteristic of the *Ulster* people. Greetings between people who know each other include *Hello, Hi*, and *How are you?* In formal situations or when meeting strangers on the street, one may say *Good morning, Good afternoon*, or *Good night*, depending on the time of day. Men who know each other well may greet each other with a hearty slap on the back. People wave at others who are too distant for a verbal greeting. Strangers may offer a brief greeting or wave on uncrowded streets. Rural people often wave to strangers in passing vehicles and expect similar greetings in return. People generally call each other by first name, a practice that is becoming increasingly common even in the business world. Only close friends (particularly those at school) use nicknames.

Gestures

The Irish do not use hand gestures excessively during conversation, but they do not keep hands entirely still; some gesticulation is common.

The Irish value politeness and generally do not push (even if in a hurry), eat on the street (or on the run), comb hair in public, or otherwise offend those around them. People traveling on buses usually offer their seats to the elderly. Men generally open doors for women. It is polite for drivers to give way to pedestrians and other cars entering from side roads. If one breaches a social norm, an apology is usually in order.

Visiting

Among good friends, people often drop by unannounced and are always warmly welcomed. If the host is in the middle of something, guests will probably be told to make themselves at home—or be asked to join in. Dinner guests are expected to arrive on time. They usually bring a gift, such as wine or chocolates. It is customary for the hosts to open the gifts immediately in the presence of the guests. People often socialize for a while before dinner is served. Women usually are seated first. When finished eating, one places the utensils together vertically on the plate. Formal rules of etiquette depend largely on the event and the preferences of the hosts; however, many people follow less formal practices.

Hosts nearly always serve refreshments during informal visits, but they do not insist their guests eat. Socializing not only takes place in the home but also in *pubs*.

Eating

The Irish eat in the continental style, with the fork in the left hand and the knife remaining in the right. They keep the hands above the table. In restaurants, the waiter brings the bill to the table. The bill usually includes a 15 percent value-added tax and a 15 percent service charge. If it does not include the tip, patrons leave money on the table. Families gather on Sunday to enjoy a large, formal meal and to spend time together. The evening meal eaten around 6:00 P.M. is called *tea*.

LIFESTYLE

Family

Although the father dominates in the home, the mother exercises considerable influence in family affairs. Women traditionally have played conservative roles by staying at home, but this is changing as many now work outside the home. Men generally do not participate in household chores, and some continue to maintain a separate social life with their male friends after marriage. Still, there is a very low divorce rate in Northern Ireland. Commitment to family ties is important. Visiting one's parents is a popular weekend activity. The elderly often live alone and are proud to be independent as long as possible. However, as fewer adult children can take aging parents into their homes, the number of nursing homes or *shared accommodations* are increasing. Most families, including many newly married couples, own their own homes. Houses typically are two-story buildings made of brick or concrete.

Dating and Marriage

Teenagers generally start dating between ages 14 and 16. Most either associate with groups of friends or go out as couples. Dancing and going to movies are popular activities. Dating more than one person at a time usually is not accepted. Engagements generally are long and may last two or more years. Women marry at about age 23; men at about 25. Church weddings are still common. Receptions include an elaborate meal (for up to two hundred guests) often held in hotels, followed by speeches and dancing. Many couples live together before marrying. Civil marriages are becoming more common.

Diet

Mealtime traditionally has been important to the people in Northern Ireland. In the past, this called for large meals and a great deal of preparation. However, as women spend more time working, this is no longer possible and meals are becoming less formal. Fried foods are a traditional favorite, but this is also changing as health issues become more important. Fresh produce, especially vegetables, are readily available. Potatoes have remained an important staple in the Irish diet. With many types of potatoes available, most people eat potatoes in some form every day. Fresh seafood, fish, lamb, pork, and beef are eaten frequently. There are many different bread varieties to choose from, as well as scones and pastries. Irish stew, homemade tarts, and *pasties* (meat pies in the shape of burgers) are traditional dishes.

Recreation

Soccer, hurling, Gaelic football, lawn bowling, golf, fishing, cricket, bicycling, sailing, hiking, and rugby are all popular sports in Northern Ireland. Hurling is played on a soccer-type field with wooden sticks and a small leather ball. Gaelic football is played with a round ball and is like a cross between soccer and basketball. Players can touch the ball with their hands, but they cannot pick it up from the ground. The ball is punched, not thrown, and it can be kicked. Teams score by getting the ball into a soccer-type net but can also make points for putting it over the top of the goal.

Horse, dog, and car racing are also common. The Irish are avid movie fans. Amateur clubs and societies (such as bingo clubs) are enjoyed by some. The Northern Irish are proud of their cultural heritage. In contemporary literature, poetry is especially popular. *Ulster* poet Seamus Heaney recently won the Nobel Prize for literature.

Holidays

Official holidays include New Year's Day; St. Patrick's Day (17 March); Easter (Thursday–Monday); Labor Day (1 May); Battle of the Boyne (12 July), a part of Orange Day festivities that can last a full week and consist of parades, speeches, and other celebrations; Halloween (31 October); Christmas; and Boxing Day (26 December). Boxing Day comes from the British tradition of giving small boxed gifts to service workers. It is now a day for visiting friends and relaxing. Fairs that celebrate the harvest, historical figures, or folk traditions are also common throughout the area.

Commerce

Business hours extend from 9:00 A.M. to 5:00 P.M., Monday through Friday. Government offices are often closed for an hour at lunch time and remain open until 5:30 P.M. Banks are open from 9:30 A.M. to 4:30 P.M. Most shops are open from 9:00 A.M. to 5:30 P.M., Monday through Saturday. Businesses usually are closed on Sundays.

SOCIETY

Government

Northern Ireland comprises 26 districts within the United Kingdom of Great Britain and Northern Ireland. It is represented in the UK's 651-seat House of Commons (Parliament) by 17 elected members. The majority of those seats are held by leaders who support Northern Ireland's union with Great Britain. The UK's head of state is Queen Elizabeth II. A prime minister (John Major) is head of government. Northern Ireland had a regional assembly prior to 1972, and plans are being developed to restore local authority. The voting age is 18.

Economy

Farming, fishing, tobacco, shipbuilding, and aircraft manufacturing are the major economic enterprises. Farmers commonly raise cattle, hogs, and sheep and produce dairy products, poultry, and potatoes, among other things. Many farmers suffered in 1996 from the EU's ban on British beef, Northern Ireland's largest export.

Northern Ireland's standard of living is comparable to England's. Real gross domestic product per capita in the UK is $17,160, a figure that is generally lower than in other European nations. Still, most people earn an income sufficient to meet basic needs and provide some luxuries. The years of violence have depressed economic development and investment in Northern Ireland. The economy was boosted by increased investment and international aid during the 17-month cease-fire. However, continued progress toward peace is needed to create a stable environment that can attract more investment, international aid, and new industries and can eventually lower unemployment. Unemployment remains one of Northern Ireland's biggest economic challenges. The currency of the UK is the British pound sterling (£).

Transportation and Communication

Transportation is excellent, with buses being the most common and best means of travel within a city. On two-level omnibuses, nonsmokers use the lower level and smokers go to the upper level. On one-level buses, smokers must use the back of the bus. Taxis are also available. Private cars provide long-distance transportation. Traffic moves on the left side of the road. Communications systems are modern. Private and public television and radio broadcasts are available throughout the nation. All phone calls, including local ones, are billed by the length of the call. Therefore, a person borrowing someone's phone usually offers to pay for the call.

Education

Children attend either Catholic or Protestant schools. Primary school is required for children between ages four and eleven. At age 11, all students take a difficult, government-sponsored exam. If they do well, they go to grammar school, which prepares them for a university education. If they fail to score high marks, they go either to a secondary (or intermediate) school or a technical college to prepare for a profession or trade. They can still choose to go to grammar school if the family is able to pay tuition and fees. After this first exam, students must take two more government-sponsored exams to gain admission to a university. Programs of study are much stricter than those in the United States. A bachelor's degree can be obtained in three years, but the exams taken before one is admitted to a university are recognized as being equal to a first-year university exam. The government pays for public education at the university level. The adult literacy rate in the UK is 99 percent.

Health

As throughout the UK, the residents of Northern Ireland enjoy relatively good health. Hospital facilities are readily available. Northern Ireland is served by the National Health Service, which provides free or low-cost medical care to all citizens. The individual pays for prescriptions and some dental costs. The infant mortality rate is 7 per 1,000; the average life expectancy is between 74 and 80 years.

FOR THE TRAVELER

U.S. travelers do not need a visa to visit Northern Ireland, but a valid passport is required. Visitors should be careful to fully cooperate with police officers in the event violence erupts again. Northern Ireland's green and beautiful countryside is inviting to tourists, and tourist facilities are well developed. For information regarding travel opportunities in Northern Ireland, contact the Northern Ireland Tourist Board, 551 Fifth Avenue, Suite 701, New York, NY 10176; phone (800) 326–0036. You may also wish to contact the Northern Ireland Bureau of the Embassy of the United Kingdom, 3100 Massachusetts Avenue NW, Washington, DC 20008; phone (202) 789–6268.

CULTURGRAM '97

Italy
(Italian Republic)

Boundary representations not necessarily authoritative.

BACKGROUND

Land and Climate

Italy, including the islands of Sardinia and Sicily, covers 116,305 square miles (301,230 square kilometers) and is slightly larger than Arizona. It surrounds two independent nations, San Marino and Vatican City (Holy See). San Marino has been independent since the fourth century. As part of the Papal States, Vatican City was protected by France in the 19th century. It was occupied by Italy in 1870 but recognized as the sovereign State of Vatican City in 1922.

Italy is shaped like a boot. The "heel" and some coastal areas are fairly low in elevation, but the country is generally mountainous. The Italian Alps run along the northern border, and the Apennines form a spine down the peninsula. Sicily and Sardinia are also rocky or mountainous. The Po River basin to the north holds some of Italy's richest farmland and most of its heavy industry. Agricultural areas in the south are subject to droughts. The climate is temperate. Winters are cold and rainy in the north, cool around Rome, and mild in the south. Summers are moderately hot but can be very hot in the south (up to 104°F or 40°C).

History

Italy's early history is also the early history of Western civilization in that much of the West's culture comes from the Italian Peninsula. Although the area's history dates back several thousand years, one of the first civilizations to flourish was that of the Etruscans between the eighth and second centuries B.C. They influenced mostly central Italy and later the Roman Empire. Before the Romans became prominent, Greek civilization dominated the south. Rome later adopted much of the Greek culture and became a major power after 300 B.C. as it expanded throughout the Mediterranean region. By the fifth century A.D., the western Roman Empire had fallen to a number of invasions. The peninsula was then divided into several separate political regions. In addition to local rulers, French, Spanish, and Austrian leaders governed various parts of Italy. The Italian Peninsula was the center of many artistic, cultural, and architectural revolutions, including the great Renaissance of the 15th and 16th centuries.

Risorgimento, the Italian unification movement, began in the 1800s. National unification was declared in 1861 by the first Italian Parliament in Turin. A king (Victor Emmanuel II) was named and unification was completed in 1870 when Rome unified with the rest of the area.

Italy experienced a fascist dictatorship under Benito Mussolini from 1922 to 1943 and initially aided Germany's Hitler in World War II. In 1943, the fascists were overthrown and Italy supported the Allies. Italy established itself as a republic in the 1946 elections, officially abolishing the monarchy by national referendum. Political violence and terrorism marked the 1970s. Conflicts within the coalition governments led to frequent government collapses during the 1980s. Political changes in Eastern Europe led Italy's powerful Communist Party to change its name and structure to maintain voter loyalty.

Elections in April 1992 hurt the ruling coalition but failed to bring a strong government to power. The proportional system of voting, originally designed to prevent totalitarianism, was blamed for consistently bringing weak coalitions to power. On its 16th vote in May 1992, Parliament finally chose Oscar Luigi Scalfaro, a Christian Democrat, as president. Political stability still could not be achieved, as the country was soon rocked by dozens of political scandals. Numerous top officials resigned, including the prime minister, and charges of past corruption became even more widespread. By 1994, six thousand individuals were under investigation for corruption. In the midst of this serious crisis, voters were asked to determine whether the proportional system of voting for Parliament should be replaced by a majority system. In April 1993, more than 80 percent of voters supported the change.

In May 1993, a new prime minister (Carlo Azeglio Ciampi) committed the government to political reform. Ciampi resigned amidst charges of corruption in January 1994. President Scalfaro dissolved Parliament and called elections under the "new" electoral system.

On promises of running a clean government and stimulating the economy, Silvio Berlusconi's Forza Italia Party won the elections in March, but it soon became clear that electoral reforms had not sufficiently addressed Italy's political problems. Berlusconi finally become prime minister in May, only to have his government fall in December 1994.

Scalfaro named Treasury Minister Lamberto Dini, a member of no political party, prime minister in January 1995. Calls for elections soon surfaced, even from Dini's supporters, but many factions supported waiting until the entire political system could be constitutionally changed. Dini's caretaker government, Italy's 54th since World War II, pressed ahead with fiscal and other reforms until it fell in December 1995. Wanting a clean and workable government, voters in the April 1996 elections brought economist Romano Prodi of the Democratic Party of the Left (formerly the Italian Communist Party) to power as prime minister.

THE PEOPLE

Population

Italy's population is slightly more than 58.2 million and is growing at 0.2 percent annually. Most people are ethnic Italians, but there are small groups of ethnic Germans, French, and Slovenes, as well as Albanian-Italians, and Greek-Italians. Although traditionally a country of emigrants, Italy has experienced a large influx of immigrants in the last fifteen years. Italy's Human Development Index (0.912) ranks it 20th out of 174 countries. Adjusted for women, the index (0.861) ranks Italy 14th out of 130 countries. Italians enjoy access to health care, education, and economic prosperity needed to make choices in their lives.

Language

Italian is the official language, although dialects differ from city to city. The Florentine and Roman dialects had a major influence on modern Italian. Most youth also speak English, the most common second language, while older generations prefer to speak French. There are significant French-, German-, and Slovene-speaking minorities. An ethnic minority in southern Tyrol speaks Ladin.

Religion

Nearly all Italians are Roman Catholic, although many neglect religious devotion. Attendance at services is not high, and secularism is more appealing to many segments of society. At the same time, many Catholics are finding alternate ways to worship (through pilgrimages, informal gatherings, praying at shrines, and so forth). The Catholic Church does, however, wield significant social and even political influence in Italy. Vatican City, home of the Roman Catholic pope and headquarters for the Roman Catholic Church, is located within Rome.

General Attitudes

Due to improved economic and social conditions in southern regions and the influence of the media, differences between northern and southern Italians are diminishing. However, Italians still refer to one another by their city of origin (Milanese, Roman, Florentine, etc.) and some regional attitudes remain. Adopting practices of their German and Austrian neighbors, people in the industrialized north traditionally value punctuality, reliability, organization, and economic success. They often feel more pressure and view time as a resource not to be wasted. They take pride in having a low tolerance for high levels of criminality and public corruption. In contrast, Southerners are appreciated for their warm character and friendliness. They enjoy a leisurely life and take their time to accomplish business. Family values prevail in the south and are often more appreciated than economic success.

Regional economic differences have led to tensions within the country. Many in the more prosperous north feel they are too heavily taxed to subsidize special projects in the south. Those in the south often resent the higher incomes and better employment rates of the north. Political movements calling for more regional autonomy in a federal system have gained some momentum, particularly in the north. However, most Italians still oppose a political separation.

Italians consider social life and interaction very important; they try not to miss social events such as parties and celebrations. People desire a good reputation in their social circle and seek approval from their peers. Often the ability to influence others is associated with how well one can accommodate different interests or points of view. Humor, agreeability, reliability, and success in business and social life are regarded more favorably than individual assertiveness. Italians value their health, family, serenity, and financial security.

Personal Appearance

Italians take care of their appearance and tend to dress up, even for an evening stroll. They seldom wear worn, dirty, or sloppy clothing. Although attitudes vary among the youth, many people base their opinions of others on how they dress. Older women generally wear dresses, but the youth follow European fashion trends. Italy is a major center of the European fashion industry.

CUSTOMS AND COURTESIES

Greetings

Men and women greet each other by shaking hands. In groups, Italians avoid crossing other people's handshakes. If a person's hand is dirty, he or she may offer a forearm, a finger, or a simple apology instead. When a man and a woman are introduced to each other, the man waits for the woman to extend her hand first. Close friends often greet each other with a hug or with a kiss on both cheeks. Actually, they touch cheeks and "kiss the air." Except in southern Italy, the kiss on both cheeks between men is reserved for family members. Friends and family members say *Ciao* (Hi or Good-bye) as an informal greeting. Other terms include *Buongiorno* (Good morning) and *Buonasera* (Good afternoon or Good evening). Persons of the same gender often walk arm in arm in public.

Gestures

Italians are known for their use of hand gestures during conversation, especially in the south. In fact, they often communicate with their hands instead of words. A common gesture is rubbing the thumb rapidly against the fingers to indicate "money." A finger placed under the eye and pushed down slightly on the skin says someone is smart or clever. In some areas of the south, a person might indicate "no" might by nodding the head up. Gestures are so numerous that there is actually a dictionary of Italian gestures. Men remove their hats when entering buildings. Removing one's shoes in the presence of others is impolite. One covers the mouth when yawning or sneezing.

Visiting

As a people inclined to long friendships, Italians enjoy visiting one another, especially on holidays and Sundays. In urban areas, visits are usually planned due to busy schedules. In villages, people are used to unannounced visits by friends and neighbors. Hosts might offer their guests coffee, cake, ice cream, or drinks. Dinner guests often bring a bottle of good wine, a box of chocolates, or flowers (in odd numbers) as a gift for the hosts. Unless instructed otherwise, guests wait for the hosts to sit before they are seated and to begin eating before they eat. In the north, guests are expected to eat all that they are served. In the south, if guests are served more generous portions, they may leave some food on the plate. Guests wait for the host to offer second or third helpings.

If visiting before supper, guests generally are expected to stay for the meal. Not staying may be considered impolite, especially in the south. In the evening before supper or on holidays, Italians enjoy taking a walk in town.

Eating

Italians eat in the continental style, with the fork in the left hand and the knife remaining in the right. During the meal, they keep their hands above the table; keeping hands in the lap is improper. When finished eating, a person places the utensils parallel on the plate. One does not leave the table until everyone has finished eating.

Although Italian families traditionally eat lunch together, this custom is disappearing, especially in large cities. Most families at least try to get together for supper. When eating with guests, Italians usually do not hurry; a meal may last one to four hours. Regular family meals are much shorter. Dinner conversation often includes soccer, politics, family matters, business, and local events. Hosts appreciate compliments on the home and meal. Guests do not volunteer to help clean up. It is appropriate for guests to give some attention to children in the family. At restaurants, the bill often includes a service charge, but leaving a small tip for the waiter is also appropriate.

LIFESTYLE

Family

Italians enjoy strong ties and, when being together or helping each other is possible, they honor their family obligations. Parents are willing to help their children, even as adults, when necessary. Many will help their children buy a home or pay for an apartment—even if it means a sacrifice for the parents. With a faster pace of life and more family members working, fewer families can care for elderly members. Most families in the north live as nuclear units, and the average family has one or two children. Southern families are traditionally larger, and many generations often live in the same town or house. However, recent trends indicate that extended families throughout the country get together less often and fewer live near each other. Urban dwellers generally reside in apartments; houses are common in suburbs and rural areas.

Dating and Marriage

As in other Western countries, Italians date either in groups or as couples. Dancing and going to movies are frequent activities. Women usually marry by age 26, while the average age for men is 29. A man will rarely marry before he has finished his education and found employment. Therefore, engagements can last several years. Some couples live together before marrying. Marriage ceremonies most often follow Catholic traditions. Divorce is granted only after three or more years of legal separation.

Diet

An Italian breakfast is light, consisting of a cup of coffee or cappuccino (warm milk for children) and a *cornetto* (cream-filled croissant) or bread with jam or honey. Lunch, the main meal, is around 1:00 P.M. It usually includes three courses: pasta, fish or meat, and vegetables. In the north, pasta or rice is part of every main meal. Pasta is dominant in the south. A simple salad (lettuce and tomatoes) is served with the second course (meat dish). The standard salad dressing contains oil and vinegar but not spices. Italians eat a light dinner in the evening. Wine commonly accompanies meals and also is used widely in cooking. Meat and tomato sauces are popular with various types of pasta. Veal is a favorite meat. Italian pizza is not the same as U.S. American pizza and differs from region to region. Contrary to popular belief in North America, spaghetti and meatballs is not a typical Italian meal. While some pasta sauces have small amounts of meat in them, Italians usually eat the main meat dish after the pasta course. Italians enjoy literally hundreds of different cheeses, including mozzarella and parmesan.

Recreation

For recreation, Italians go to the beach, countryside, movies, dances, or sport events. Soccer is by far the most popular sport. Avid fans follow the World Cup competition. Italy's national soccer team, which competed in the 1994 World Cup, has won the World Cup three times. Bicycling, horse racing, skiing, tennis, boxing, fencing, swimming, and track-and-field are also popular.

Opera theaters are found in all main towns. Italians enjoy cultural events and are proud of their country's cultural and artistic heritage. Italy was a birthplace and center of the arts for centuries, shaping art movements throughout Europe and the world. During the day, Italians often go to bars to socialize. Bars, which are more like coffee shops, have a light, open atmosphere and serve both coffee and drinks.

Holidays

Italians celebrate both religious and national holidays, including New Year's Day; Epiphany (6 January); Easter (including Easter Monday); Liberation Day (25 April), which commemorates Italy's liberation in World War II; Labor Day (1 May); the Anniversary of the Republic (2 June); the Assumption of the Virgin Mary (15 August); All Saints' Day (1 November); Immaculate Conception (8 December); Christmas; and St. Stephen's Day (26 December). Nearly every city and town honors the local patron saint with an annual celebration, and various other festivals are also held throughout the year.

Commerce

The Italian work schedule is from 8:00 or 9:00 A.M. to 1:00 P.M. and from 3:00 to 6:00 or 7:00 P.M., Monday through Friday. Government offices close by 2:00 P.M. Many Italians work six days a week. Grocery stores close one afternoon of the week, and barber shops close on Mondays. Businesses are generally closed on Sunday.

SOCIETY

Government

The Italian Republic is divided into 20 regions. Some regions favor a more federal system of government that would give them increased autonomy from the central government in Rome. Italy's president is chief of state, while the prime minister is head of government. The prime minister is usually the head of a majority party or a majority coalition of parties but can also be appointed from other parties. In all cases, a proposed prime minister must be approved by a parliamentary vote of confidence. Prime ministers can be removed from office at any time if Parliament passes a vote of no confidence.

Italy's upper legislative chamber is the 326-seat Senate. Eleven Senators are appointed for life and the others are elected to seven-year terms. The 630 members of Italy's Chamber of Deputies also hold office for seven years unless Parliament is dissolved early for new elections. Citizens may vote in senatorial elections at age 25. The voting age for all other elections is 18.

Because numerous parties often hold seats in Parliament, it is difficult for one party to gain a majority. Coalitions are usually necessary, and these often fall apart during disputes, power struggles, or scandals. Parties usually are grouped as rightists, centrists, and leftists when forming coalitions, although some coalitions have been between opposing forces. Forza Italia and the National Alliance dominate on the right, with the Democratic Party of the Left (formerly the Communist Party) leading parties on the left. The small Popular Party and the Northern League are the largest parties in the center.

Economy

Italy's economy is based on agriculture in the south and industry in the north. Agriculture employs less than 10 percent of the labor force, but agricultural products are important and allow Italy to be nearly self-sufficient in food production. Italy is one of the world's largest wine producers and a major producer of cheese. Other important crops include wheat, potatoes, corn, rice, fruits, and olive oil. Italy is a major steel and iron producer; industry accounts for more than one-third of the gross national product. Tourism is also a vital source of revenue.

The economy is still recovering from the recession of the early 1990s. Growth rose to 2 percent in 1994 but has been low, compounded by high unemployment, budget deficits, and Italy's need to make policy changes to qualify for the European Union's monetary union. Real gross domestic product per capita is $18,090, which has more than tripled in the last generation. Most people earn a decent income and enjoy a standard of living consistent with Italy's standing as one of the world's seven major industrialized countries. The currency is the Italian *lira* (Lit).

Transportation and Communication

The principal means of public transportation are buses and trains, which are both punctual and inexpensive. Most households have at least one car. Subways operate in Milan and Rome; taxis are available in all cities. A domestic air system flies between major cities. Seas surrounding Italy are also used for transportation of goods and people. The communications system is modern and extensive but is not always well maintained. Mail delivery is also unreliable at times. Numerous radio and television stations broadcast on a regional basis, and Italians have access to many daily newspapers.

Education

School attendance is compulsory from ages six to fourteen. Classes are held Monday through Saturday. Education is a serious matter, and most young people spend a great deal of time doing homework. The adult literacy rate is 97 percent. The oldest university in Europe was founded in Bologna in the 12th century. Italy has more than 50 universities and institutes of higher learning.

Health

Health-care services are coordinated through government agencies. Individuals can choose their family physician; the government pays for most services. Private care is also available, but the patient must pay for it. Italians enjoy a life expectancy rate that ranges from 75 to 81 years. The infant mortality rate is 7 per 1,000.

FOR THE TRAVELER

A visa is not necessary for stays of up to three months, but a valid passport and proof of return passage are required. Italy has long been a favorite travel destination. Numerous museums, art galleries, historical sites, beautiful beaches, mountains, and lakes attract many tourists each year. Care should be taken in large cities against pickpockets. For travel information, contact the Italian Tourist Office, 630 Fifth Avenue, Suite 1565, New York, NY 10111; phone (212) 245–4961. You may also contact the Embassy of Italy, 1601 Fuller Street NW, Washington, DC 20009; phone (202) 328–5500.

Jamaica

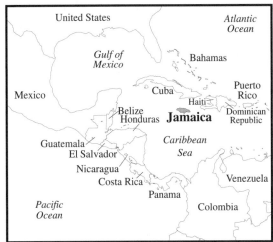

Boundary representations not necessarily authoritative.

BACKGROUND

Land and Climate

Jamaica is part of the Greater Antilles, a chain of islands that forms the northern boundary of the Caribbean Sea. Its nearest neighbor is Cuba (about 90 miles to the north). Only 51 miles across at its widest point, Jamaica covers 4,243 square miles (10,990 square kilometers) and is just smaller than Connecticut. Eighty percent of the island is mountainous. Less than 20 percent is suitable for continuous cultivation. Jamaica has a tropical maritime climate, but rainfall varies depending on the region. The rainy seasons occur in May and October. Hurricanes are possible from June to November. The tropical island climate prevents extreme temperature variations; temperatures are generally 80°F to 90°F (26–32°C) on the northern coast. Jamaica's capital, Kingston, is a large port city.

History

Jamaica's original inhabitants were the Arawak Indians, who called the island *Xaymaca*, meaning "land of wood and water." Columbus landed on the island in 1494. Because of the harsh life imposed on them by settlers, the Arawaks were virtually wiped out within a few decades of Spanish colonization. The Spanish occupied the island until 1655, when it was captured and colonized by the English. By the late 17th century, the English had established sugarcane plantations and were importing large numbers of slaves from Africa. Slavery was abolished in 1838. Some Spaniards stayed in Jamaica, having fled to the hills to fight the British. Over time, the Spanish mixed with the African peoples. Today this small group is called the Maroons, a people that has some political autonomy within Jamaica.

In the 1860s, Jamaica's status was upgraded to a British crown colony rather than just a colonial possession. During the 1930s, people began calling for self-determination. In 1938, serious social unrest was fomented by long-standing injustices and labor problems. Alexander Bustamante, aided by Norman Manley, championed the cause of the workers and sparked important social change. The two also formed today's key political parties. In 1944, a new constitution was written, ending rule by the British crown colony government and granting adult suffrage. Jamaica remained under nominal British rule, however, until it gained full independence in 1962.

A socialist government ruled in the 1970s before being replaced by a conservative government in the 1980s under Edward Seaga. In 1989, socialists again took control through national elections and promised to tackle the country's foreign debt. Seaga challenged the incumbent socialist prime minister, P. J. Patterson in 1993 elections, but Patterson won in a landslide. He heads the People's National Party.

THE PEOPLE

Population

The population of Jamaica is slightly more than 2.5 million and is growing at 1 percent annually. The majority of people are Black African (76 percent). Afro-Europeans (15 percent) and Afro-East Indians plus East Indians (3 percent) make up significant minorities. There are whites of European descent (3 percent), some Chinese, and other groups as well. More than 50 percent of the people live in urban areas. Kingston is the largest city and Montego Bay is the second largest. Because of heavy emigration, nearly as many Jamaicans live outside of Jamaica as on the island. Most of these expatriates live in England and the eastern United States. The Human Development Index (0.721) ranks Jamaica 88th out of 174 countries. Although economic conditions are improving, opportunities for personal advancement are somewhat limited. Adjusted for women, the index (0.710) ranks Jamaica 53d out of 130 countries.

Language

English is the official language of Jamaica. However, *Patois* (Creole), a combination of English and some African languages, is spoken in rural areas and is gaining popularity in urban areas. Most Jamaicans can speak or understand *Patois*, but it is not a written language. Jamaican speech, even in English, has a distinctive rhythmic/melodic quality.

Religion

Most Jamaicans are Christians, and all major denominations are represented on the island. The Anglican Church is the official national church. Anglicans and other Protestants represent about 55 percent of the population. Five percent of the people are Roman Catholic. Religion plays an important role in society through the spiritual values and social opportunities it provides. Church gatherings are particularly valuable to rural women. Small groups practice, to varying degrees of authenticity, ceremonies and rituals from India, China, and Africa. These practices have been Jamaicanized from their original Hindu and Islamic roots. Ecumenism (unity among all churches) comes naturally to Jamaicans.

Jamaica is home to a long-standing Jewish community, whose first members arrived with Columbus as ship hands to escape the Spanish Inquisition. Although Jews usually attend services as families, the vast majority of churchgoers in other religions are women and children. Religious education is commonly included in school curricula.

General Attitudes

Jamaicans like to be with people and are generally outgoing. They enjoy lively conversation and often hold strong views. People are warm and hospitable, but they may hold back with strangers until they get to know them. Jamaicans have a fairly flexible approach to life. A common good-natured answer to life's challenges is *No problem, man*, even if there is no solution at hand. Flexibility is also evident in the attitude toward time and schedules. A common phrase is *Soon come*, which can mean anything from five minutes to next week. Events and meetings do not necessarily begin on time, although people are more punctual in urban areas.

Rural Jamaicans particularly appreciate honesty and hard work. Urban Jamaicans are increasingly building a strong professional and cooperative atmosphere for business and work. Throughout the country, having wealth or connections with someone who is wealthy or powerful is important. Financial security, prestige, a home and property, and a motor vehicle are valued possessions. Jamaicans are generally aware of others' opinions of them. Men are often judged by sexual prowess, while women are often judged by physical appearance.

Personal Appearance

Jamaicans are conscious of clothing fashions and like to wear jewelry. Women are generally mindful of appropriate dress for themselves and their children, though many reserve the right to dress according to their own tastes. Women usually wear skirts or dresses; professional women are well dressed in colorful clothing. Their clothing is often made by local seamstresses rather than purchased in a store. Many institutions (banks, insurance companies) provide their employees, particularly women, with uniforms. Women often wear headdresses to match or complement their dresses. Men tend to dress more casually than women. They wear Western-style clothing for most occasions. Sunday is the day for women and children to wear their best clothes to church. Rural children often have shoes only for church or school. The youth wear colorful clothing, following trends set in the music industry. On weekends, for example, they commonly wear *dance hall* (a popular form of music) outfits. These include tight dresses for young women and baggy pants or long shorts for young men.

CUSTOMS AND COURTESIES

Greetings

In Jamaica, greetings range from a nod or bow, to a handshake or a slap on the back, to a kiss—all depending on the persons involved and the occasion. People who are being introduced usually shake hands and say *Good morning*, *Good afternoon*, or *Good evening*. Jamaicans are formal in their introductions: *Mr.*, *Mrs.*, *Miss*, or professional titles are used with the surname unless people are well acquainted. Children usually refer to adults other than family (parents, aunts, uncles, or grandparents) as *Sir*, *Mr.*, *Mrs.*, or *Miss*. Elderly people in rural areas occasionally curtsy when greeting. People passing on the road often call out greetings to friends and acquaintances and receive a warm response. It is considered rude not to greet someone properly before beginning a conversation or asking a question. Greetings among friends are casual. A common phrase is *Wha-apun?* (What's happening?) or *Alright, alright* (as if to bypass asking and responding to "How are you?"). Common phrases for saying good-bye include *Later*, *Tomorrow then*, and *Next time*.

When addressing others in formal situations, people use titles and surnames. But in casual situations, they commonly use nicknames. A Jamaican might have many nicknames (also called "pet" or "yard" names) given to him (usually men) by various friends or groups. The nickname usually has to do with a physical trait or station in life. Some examples include *Fatty* (for a fat person; it is a compliment because it indicates the person must be wealthy and does not have to work hard); *Whitey* (white person; also not an insult, but one would never call a Black Jamaican *Blacky*); or *Juicy* (man who sells juice on the street). In addition, people often shorten their names (*Nicky* for Nicholas) or slightly alter their given names to create a nickname by which they want to be called.

Gestures

Jamaicans can be very animated when speaking and tend to use many hand gestures to help make a point (especially if men are talking about cricket or politics). They like to emphasize greetings by holding on to an initial handshake, or by touching the person's arm or shoulder during the greeting or the conversation. People show respect for or approval of shared ideas by touching fists. To hail a taxi, one keeps the hand down (rather than holding it above the head) and waves. To get someone's attention, one might say, "pssssst," clap hands, or tap on a grill or gate of a home. Jamaicans, particularly women, make a sound by sucking air through their teeth to express "give me a break."

Social gestures generally follow traditional lines in Jamaica. Men offer seats on a bus to older women, women with young children, or pregnant women. Seated passengers often offer to hold packages or children for standing passengers. Men open doors for women in urban areas. Kissing, chewing gum, or combing one's hair are not common in public. Women rarely smoke in public.

Visiting

Informal visits are accepted at the house gate. People usually do not approach the door until greeted and invited past the gate. Visitors simply knock, ring a buzzer, or otherwise call attention to themselves, and the person at home greets them. Conversations held on the street are referred to as *meet-and-greet* activities. Visitors inside homes are usually offered a drink and sometimes a meal. Guests often take a small gift for the host or hostess. A gift, even in urban settings, might be fresh produce, flowers from the guest's garden, or a bottle of wine. Families and friends find time to get together often and always enjoy a good laugh. Because Jamaica traditionally has not had telephones and many rural homes still lack them, visits are commonly unannounced. There is no need to call ahead; surprise guests are nearly always welcome. Urban visitors will often keep the visit brief if they have not called ahead.

Eating

Rural families tend to eat dinner together each day after 4:00 P.M., while urban families might not have the opportunity to eat together except on weekends. Meals are casual and specific table manners are less important than enjoying the food. Many Jamaicans say grace before or after meals.

When guests are invited for a meal, the occasion is usually relaxed and sociable. Buffet meals are popular. Invitations are sometimes extended for breakfast or brunch, in addition to the usual lunch and dinner. Dress and table settings vary according to degree of formality. Eating outdoors is popular, especially in gardens and on patios. Jamaicans eat in the continental style, with the fork in the left hand and the knife remaining in the right. Good public table manners are considered an important social refinement. Restaurants range from informal diners that serve simple Jamaican dishes to sophisticated gourmet establishments.

Take-away (take-out) meals served in boxes are common. These may be purchased from caterers, restaurants, or street vendors. Different foods sold by street vendors are plentiful and relatively inexpensive. Pineapples, melons, and water coconuts are often sold from roadside stalls or carts as quick snacks or thirst quenchers. Because eating while walking is considered inappropriate, people often eat snacks on the spot. In restaurants, the bill usually includes a service charge, but if not, one leaves a 10 to 15 percent tip.

LIFESTYLE

Family

The family structure varies in Jamaica according to several factors, including one's social standing. For example, families in lower socioeconomic groups usually are larger than those in the middle or upper classes. In addition, women of the lower groups commonly have several children by different men, known as *baby fathers*. The men refer to these women as their *baby mothers* (as opposed to wives or girlfriends). Most who have more than one child out of wedlock believe men prove their virility by fathering a child and that women must give birth to prove their femininity. Women assume the primary responsibility for child care, but children often live with grandparents, other relatives, or godparents when the mother works outside the home. In these circles, therefore, the extended family plays a crucial role.

Most families live in houses or town houses. Apartments are not common. Homes typically are built of concrete or, in rural areas, wood.

Diet

Jamaican food is generally very spicy. Breakfast usually includes akee and salt fish, the national dish. Other favorites include rice and peas or beans, stews, and various types of fish. Fish may be eaten at least twice a week. Curries are popular. Curried goat is a common meal. Most meals are served with rice and peas (red beans) and may also include boiled green bananas or fried dumplings. A typical salad includes cabbage and carrots. Vegetables (yams, green peppers, etc.) and fruits (mangoes, bananas, papaya, pineapple, oranges, grapefruit, tomatoes) play an important role in the diet. Fruit is plentiful and one or more types is usually in season. *Jerk* is a favorite of Jamaicans and visitors alike. It is a spicy hot piece of barbecued pork or chicken, roasted in open pits or on makeshift grills. *Jerk* is often served with a bland, hard-dough bread. *Bammy* (cassava/manioc bread) is a standard food; it is still prepared in the style of the Arawak Indians. *Bammy* with fried fish is a frequent combination, as is *festival* (fried dough) with fish. Many enjoy Indian and Chinese dishes. Drinks made from boiled roots, herbal teas, fruit juices, and a variety of alcoholic beverages are common. Coffee and tea are popular; all hot drinks are customarily called *tea* (coffee, cocoa, green tea, etc.). Beer and white rum are especially popular. Women usually do not drink alcohol in public.

Recreation

Cricket and football (soccer) are the most popular sports in Jamaica. Dominoes is the favorite indoor game. Many also enjoy table tennis, field hockey, tennis, and *athletics* (track-and-field). Girls play *netball* in school. Music of all types, theater, and dancing are popular activities. Comedies written and performed in *Patois* are popular. Young Jamaicans enjoy reggae, Social Calypso (SOCA), and *dance hall* music. The latter incorporates elements of reggae, disco, and rap. SOCA is popular during *Carnival*, a grand springtime festival involving parades, costumes, and parties. A frequent pastime is listening outside of rum bars to prerecorded music from stereo systems.

People attend discos, community centers, and clubs. Other leisure activities include going to movies and enjoying spectator sports, such as boxing or team competitions. Various festivals, community events, and church activities provide entertainment and recreation. Jamaicans also take advantage of the many outdoor activities their island offers.

Holidays

Official Jamaican holidays include New Year's Day, Ash Wednesday, Easter (Friday–Monday), Labor Day (23 May, a day for community improvement projects), Independence Day (first Monday in August), National Heroes Day (third

Day (first Monday in August), National Heroes Day (third Monday in October), Christmas, and Boxing Day (26 December). Boxing Day is a day to visit family and friends. The Maroons celebrate 6 January as their independence day.

Commerce

Business hours generally extend from 9:00 A.M. to 5:00 P.M., Monday through Thursday, and until 4:00 P.M. on Friday. Banks close weekdays around 2:00 P.M. except on Friday, when they stay open for a few more hours. Grocery stores and other shops might open earlier and stay open later, depending on the town and type of shop. Street vendors sell goods and food from early in the morning until late at night. Open-air markets sell fresh produce. Prices in these markets are fixed. Rural people shop more often than urban residents, as few have access to refrigeration.

SOCIETY

Government

Jamaica's government is based on a Westminster (British) model parliamentary democracy. The People's National Party (PNP) and Jamaica Labour Party (JLP) are the only two parties represented in Parliament. Elections must be held at least every five years, but the prime minister can call them earlier. The voting age is 18. In Jamaica's bicameral Parliament, members of the House of Representatives are elected, but members of the Senate are appointed. The cabinet, led by the prime minister, holds executive power. Although Jamaica is independent from Great Britain, it is part of the Commonwealth of Nations and recognizes Queen Elizabeth II as head of state. She is represented in Jamaica by a governor general.

Economy

Bauxite and tourism are key elements of Jamaica's economy. Tight fiscal and monetary policies have lowered inflation to about 27 percent but have restricted economic growth. Still, gains in the bauxite and aluminum industries in recent years have allowed the economy to grow moderately by 1 to 2 percent. Sugar, bauxite, bananas, and coffee are important exports. Agriculture employs more than 20 percent of the population. Jamaica is part of the Caribbean Basin Initiative (CBI), a program designed to improve economic relations between the United States and nations of the Caribbean. Stronger ties with the United States have boosted Jamaica's tourist industry. The government is moving to reduce the foreign debt and stimulate further economic growth. Unemployment is 15 percent. The currency is the Jamaican dollar (J$).

Real gross national product per capita is $3,200, which has improved significantly in the last generation. A growing portion of the population earns a decent income and has access to improving economic conditions. However, rural poverty and slow economic growth inhibit greater prosperity.

Transportation and Communication

Buses serve all parts of the island. Cars and buses are the most common form of transportation. Most roads are paved. Following the British tradition, traffic moves on the left side of the road. Buses are often crowded; they are numbered but accurate schedules are not always available. *Route cabs* are taxis that follow certain local routes. Regular taxis are plentiful; fares are negotiated. Jamaica's communications system is modern and adequate, although rural people seldom have phones in their homes. Public phone booths, usually found near police stations or post offices, require phone cards (not coins) that are purchased at post offices and some stores. There are several radio and television stations and various daily newspapers.

Education

Children attend basic schools (ages three to six) and primary schools (six to twelve). Secondary schools (ages 12 to 17) include technical, comprehensive, vocational, and high schools. Secondary enrollment is limited and admission is determined by competitive examinations each year. A lack of money for fees, uniforms, lunch, or transportation makes attendance difficult for some rural poor. The government tries to help those who cannot afford these expenses. With rare exception, children must wear uniforms to school. Most children (93 percent) who enter school finish the primary level. About 60 percent of all eligible children are enrolled in secondary schools. Most Jamaican adults have completed at least five years of education.

The adult literacy rate is 84 percent. Boys value education less than girls do. Young women are increasingly influenced by Jamaicans living in other countries and by their desire for economic autonomy; they recognize the benefits of an education in providing for a better future. More girls than boys attend secondary school, and the number of women in postsecondary institutions is approaching that of men. Higher education is provided at six teacher-training colleges; a college of art, science, and technology; a college of agriculture; schools of music, art, dance, and drama; and the University of the West Indies.

Health

Most large towns or cities have a hospital. Medical clinics are community based and are available across Jamaica. The public health-care system covers basic care for all citizens at no or low cost. Fees might be required in some cases or for more complicated care. Private facilities are available. Kingston and resort areas have doctors available 24 hours a day. Facilities and care are generally of high quality. Piped water is safe to drink. The infant mortality rate is 16 per 1,000. Life expectancy has risen in recent years to between 72 and 77 years.

FOR THE TRAVELER

Visas are not required of U.S. tourists. However, proof of citizenship (such as a passport) and onward passage are necessary to travel to Jamaica. No immunizations are required. The tourist industry is well developed. For information on travel opportunities, contact the Jamaica Tourist Board, 801 Second Avenue, 20th Floor, New York, NY 10017; phone (212) 856–9727. You may also wish to contact the Embassy of Jamaica, 1520 New Hampshire Avenue, Washington, DC 20036; phone (202) 452–0660.

A *Culturgram* is a product of native commentary and original, expert analysis. Statistics are estimates and information is presented as a matter of opinion. While the editors strive for accuracy and detail, this document should not be considered strictly factual. It is a general introduction to culture, an initial step in building bridges of understanding between peoples. It may not apply to all peoples of the nation. You should therefore consult other sources for more information.

Principality of
Liechtenstein

Boundary representations not necessarily authoritative.

BACKGROUND

Land and Climate

Covering 61.8 square miles (163 square kilometers), Liechtenstein is the fourth smallest state in Europe, situated between Austria and Switzerland. The principality enjoys a beautiful Alpine landscape that is dominated by the valley of the Rhine River and the Rhaetikon Massif. The highest point is Grauspitz at 8,525 feet (2,599 meters). Small vineyards are found in the foothills. The climate is temperate and strongly influenced by the *Föhn*, a warm southerly wind. The *Föhn* was one of the three "national plagues" that once endangered the country. It sometimes kindled extensive fires, jeopardizing the then mostly wooden houses. Today, building materials are mainly brick and concrete, and each village maintains a well-equipped voluntary fire brigade. Like the *Föhn*, the other two sources of natural disaster have also been brought under control. High embankments contain the formerly wild Rhine River; the last big flooding (*Rheinnot*) of the river took place in 1927. The debris slides (*Rüfen*) coming down from the mountains have been enclosed and rendered harmless.

History

The area of Liechtenstein has been permanently inhabited since 3000 B.C. It was colonized by Celts and Rhaetians. In 15 B.C., the Romans conquered the territory. In the fifth century, the Alemanni settled it and, in the twelfth century, the German language established an exclusive foothold. Historically Liechtenstein is composed of two areas, the Lordship of Schellenberg and the County of Vaduz. The two domains had been owned by various dynasties of counts before Prince Johann Adam Andreas of Liechtenstein purchased them in 1699 and 1712, respectively. As territories under the direct suzerainty of the German Empire, they provided the prince with a seat in the Diet of the Princes.

In 1719, the two domains were united and elevated to the Imperial Principality of Liechtenstein. It is the only country that still carries the name of its dynasty. Napoleon made Liechtenstein and 15 other regions part of the Rhine Confederation in 1806, granting each independence in exchange for loyalty. At the Vienna Congress of 1815 (after Napoleon's defeat), Liechtenstein became part of the German Confederation. It remained a member until the Confederation was dissolved in 1866. Since then, Liechtenstein has remained fully sovereign. It has had no army since 1868 and is a neutral country. From 1852 to 1919, it formed a customs union with Austria-Hungary. Since 1924, Liechtenstein has benefited from a customs union with Switzerland and the use of the Swiss *franc* as its currency.

The constitution of 1921, which is still in force today, established "a constitutional hereditary monarchy upon a democratic and parliamentary basis." Prince Franz Josef II became the first prince to reside in Liechtenstein rather than in Vienna, Austria. He ruled from 1938 until his death in 1989. He was succeeded by his son, Prince Hans Adam II, who rules today. Liechtenstein joined the United Nations in 1990. It has always enjoyed political stability. A rare interruption was a vote of no confidence in 1993 for a newly appointed prime minister. Parliament was dissolved and new elections were held to seat the current government.

EUROPE

THE PEOPLE

Population

The population of Liechtenstein is slightly more than 30,000 and is growing at 1 percent annually. It expanded rapidly after World War II due to an increased demand for imported labor. Approximately 38 percent of the inhabitants today do not possess Liechtenstein citizenship. The large number of foreign nationals, who come mainly from German-speaking countries, has led the government to pursue a restrictive immigration policy. As a result, the nation's growth has stabilized, but the numbers of daily commuters from the Swiss and Austrian border regions have increased. Only 40 percent of the workforce is native to Liechtenstein.

Liechtenstein's Human Development Index is 0.931, meaning most people have access to a good income, a useful education, and adequate health care.

Language

The language spoken in Liechtenstein is German. High German is taught at school and used as a written language, but people speak an Alemannic dialect. This dialect is similar to Swiss German (*Schwiizertütsch*) and is difficult for people from other German-speaking countries to understand. Its nuances vary from village to village. The mountain commune of Triesenberg was founded in the 13th century by people from southwestern Switzerland. Their descendants still speak a Walser dialect. The primary foreign languages taught at school are French and English.

Religion

The constitution guarantees religious freedom. The people of Liechtenstein are mostly Roman Catholics (80 percent). The Catholic Church is the state church. The priests are employed by the communes. Almost 20 percent of the people belong to a variety of other Christian churches or to no church at all. Religion still has some impact on daily life, but society has become more secularized in recent years.

General Attitudes

Liechtensteiners are proud of their high standard of living and modern achievements, but they cherish tradition as well. They value hard work and a good sense of humor. Conservative, deliberate, and pragmatic, they are also sincere and warmhearted. Many view Liechtenstein as one of the most beautiful spots on earth and consider it good luck that the country is so small and unimportant. Despite the lack of an army, for instance, it has escaped war since the end of the 18th century. Moreover, people tend to know each other well. This creates a sense of personal responsibility but also encourages gossiping and envy. The small society depends on the commitment of its citizens to participate, and civic duties are taken seriously. Liechtensteiners like to talk politics and many are somehow involved in it.

The national identity of Liechtensteiners is closely linked to their respective communes and to the princely house. The prince plays an important role in public life and enjoys far-reaching constitutional rights. In contrast to other European monarchs, his tasks are not just representational. Liechtensteiners have always held the princely house in high esteem. It is only recently that attitudes toward the monarchy have become more critical. In addition to a current debate on constitutional reform, Liechtenstein faces the challenge of defining its place in international society. A more active foreign policy has recently opened Liechtenstein to the outside world. This has heightened awareness of being a distinct nation but also of the limits of independence. Political efforts to participate in European integration are likely to have a profound impact on the way Liechtensteiners view themselves.

Personal Appearance

People in Liechtenstein generally dress well and neatly. They prefer modern European fashions that tend to be more colorful than those in the United States. Overly casual or sloppy attire in public is frowned upon. *Trachten* (traditional costumes) are worn only on special occasions, especially by women. The typical woman's *Tracht* consists of a dress with gathered waist and full skirt, an apron, and a headdress. A man's traditional attire includes knee breeches, a straight loden jacket, and a flat, black hat.

CUSTOMS AND COURTESIES

Greetings

A handshake is usually the appropriate form of greeting. To waive or nod to somebody across the street is acceptable. People also commonly greet one another verbally when passing on the street or entering a store. The traditional terms to address strangers are either the Swiss German *Grüezi!* or the *Grüss Gott!* used in Austria and southern Germany. Both terms mean "Greetings." It is appropriate to add the other person's name, if known. Among friends, young and old greet each other with a short *Hoi!* Most people in Liechtenstein address each other with the familiar *du* form, and young people generally use first names. However, this is only common among locals and not toward foreigners. The prince is addressed as *Durchlaucht* (Your Serene Highness). Greetings in languages other than German are also acceptable; keeping silent might be considered impolite. English, French, and Italian are the foreign languages most likely to be understood.

Gestures

Liechtensteiners do not use the hands much during conversation, but they consider talking with hands in the pockets to be impolite. People remove gloves before shaking hands. Pointing the index finger to one's head is an insult. Any acts of personal hygiene, such as cleaning one's fingernails, are not appropriate in public. If one cannot suppress a yawn, one covers the open mouth with a hand. Both men and women may sit with legs crossed, with one knee over the other.

Toasting with alcoholic beverages is common. Whether in the home or at a restaurant, a toast usually precedes any drinking. It is extremely impolite to begin sipping or drinking from one's glass before the host proposes the first toast. The host will not do this until all persons have a full glass. Once the first toast is made, all guests are free to take a drink and propose additional toasts. In a group, pairs next to each other, not across from each other, lightly tap their glasses simultaneously while maintaining eye contact.

Visiting

For business meetings, punctuality is important. Dinner guests are expected to arrive no more than a quarter of an hour late. They often bring flowers, candy, or a bottle of wine. Flowers are unwrapped before being given to the hostess, but other small gifts are not. Red roses are reserved for romantic occasions. In formal situations, guests wait to sit down until they are invited to do so. Even during short visits, guests are usually offered refreshments such as coffee, beer, wine, or mineral water. It is appropriate to give notice of a visit in advance. Dropping by is only common between neighbors or close friends and relatives. While dinner invitations may last well into the night, daytime visits are usually short.

Eating

Lunch is typically eaten at noon and dinner around 6:00 or 7:00 P.M. When going out for dinner, people meet around 8:00 P.M. Liechtensteiners eat in the continental style, with the fork in the left hand and the knife remaining in the right. They may rest their wrists on the table edge. Soft food such as potatoes, dumplings, and fish are cut with the fork. Fish may also be cut with a special knife. Lettuce and spaghetti are not cut at all. It is considered polite to not leave any food on the plate. Second helpings are a compliment to the cook. When finished, one places the utensils side by side on the plate.

In restaurants, diners do not take home leftovers. Most people drink bottled mineral water, wine, or beer with meals. Soft drinks are served without ice. The bill is paid at the table. The waiter usually asks whether each person prefers to pay separately. Service charges are included, but customers usually round the total up to the next *franc* or more as a *Trinkgeld* (an extra tip).

LIFESTYLE

Family

The nuclear family is the most important social unit in Liechtenstein's society. Family bonds play an important role. The father generally is the head of the household. Both men and women train for careers, and an increasing number of married women work outside the home. The size of the average family has decreased to about two children. While singles and couples often live in apartments, families tend to prefer houses. The majority live in single-family homes, but more and more young families are becoming tenants because real estate is expensive. Many people prefer to settle in the village where they grew up. Adult, unmarried children usually move out of their parents' homes by the time they finish their professional training.

Dating and Marriage

Young people socialize on a casual basis in school and in numerous recreation clubs. There are close to three hundred clubs and *Vereine* (associations). Dating practices differ from those in the United States and there is no German word that precisely means "dating." Either sex can suggest an activity and it is assumed that they each pay for their own entertainment.

People usually marry in their late twenties. It is considered important to first complete one's education and enjoy some financial security and independence. Some couples live together before or instead of marrying. Legal marriages are performed at the national Registry Office. Having a church wedding is optional but common. It usually takes place the day after the civil marriage. Some old wedding customs are still practiced, such as decorating the door frames of the couple's home with garlands or organizing a mock kidnapping of the bride.

Diet

Zmorga (breakfast) usually consists of bread with jam and coffee. There are many different kinds of bread. *Zmittag* (the main meal) is served at midday and includes a soup or salad, a main dish, and dessert. *Znacht* (dinner) is typically light and often consists of open-faced sandwiches with cheese and meat. Full meals are served for dinner invitations and in restaurants. The national dish, *Riebel*, is made of cornmeal stirred in a frying pan with milk, water, and salt. It is often eaten with elderberry purée. Other traditional dishes are *Käsknöpfle*, a sort of pasta with sharp cheese, and *Rösti*, grated and fried potatoes.

Recreation

People in Liechtenstein love nature and outdoor activities such as hiking, cycling, and skiing. They enjoy a diversity of leisure-time clubs. Among the most popular team activities are soccer, gymnastics, music bands, and choirs. Many clubs organize public festivals and other social events. People also enjoy traveling abroad. A great cultural attraction is the prince's art collection, which includes world-famous paintings. A small part of this extensive private collection is exhibited in connection with the State Art Collection in Vaduz. A new, larger art museum has been planned but is not yet built.

Holidays

Liechtenstein recognizes many Catholic holidays as public holidays: Epiphany (6 January), Candlemas (2 February), Feast of St. Joseph (19 March), Easter (Good Friday–Easter Monday), Ascension, Whitmonday, Corpus Christi, Nativity of our Lady (8 September), All Saints' Day (1 November), Immaculate Conception (8 December), and Christmas (24–26 December). Christmas is the biggest celebration of the year. On Christmas Eve, the family gathers around the Christmas tree and exchanges gifts. Most people relax on Christmas Day and visit relatives and friends on 26 December. In addition to these religious holidays, New Year's Day (1 January) and Labor Day (1 May) are public holidays. The national holiday is celebrated on 15 August with festivities, speeches, and fireworks. Mother's Day is celebrated the second Sunday in May. Many old customs, partly pagan in origin, are still continued as folklore, such as *Funkasunntig* (Bonfire Sunday) or *Fasnacht* (Carnival).

Commerce

Business hours may vary. In general, they are from 8:00 A.M. to noon, when everything closes for lunch, and from 1:30 to 6:30 P.M., Monday through Friday. On Saturdays, stores close at 4:00 P.M., and some shops are closed Monday morning. There are no supermarkets in Liechtenstein, so people buy food and other consumer goods in a variety of small shops.

SOCIETY

Government

Liechtenstein is divided into 11 communes that uphold their traditional autonomy. They enjoy extensive rights, are organized as cooperatives with a strong sense of community, and have their individual coats of arms. The capital is Vaduz. It has about five thousand inhabitants. The communes form two regions that correspond to the two historical domains. They are called the *Oberland* (Upper Country) and the *Unterland* (Lower Country). The principality of Liechtenstein combines democracy and monarchy, as people and prince govern together. The *Fürst* (ruling prince) is head of state. He sanctions all laws and can issue pardons and emergency decrees.

Landtag (Parliament) has 25 members elected for four years. The traditional two parties (Fatherland Union and Progressive Citizens' Party) are both conservative people's parties. In 1993, a more liberal third party (Free Electoral List) joined Parliament for the first time. The government has traditionally been a two-party coalition, governed by a *Regierungschef* (prime minister). The courts are presided over by Liechtenstein judges as well as Swiss and Austrian judges; this is due to the country's size and the fact that its legal system is a combination of Austrian, Swiss, and Liechtenstein law. The right to vote was extended to women only in 1984. The people enjoy direct democratic rights, such as the rights of political initiative and referendum.

Liechtenstein is currently facing some crucial political questions. On the domestic level, a debate on constitutional reform aims to clearly define the authority of the prince, government, and Parliament. Internationally, negotiations are underway to modify the customs treaty with Switzerland. This became necessary after Swiss voters rejected, but Liechtenstein voters approved, the Agreement on the European Economic Area (EEA), a free-trade agreement between the European Free Trade Association, of which Switzerland and Liechtenstein are both members, and the European Union. While maintaining its open border with Switzerland, Liechtenstein formally joined the EEA in May 1995.

Economy

Despite a lack of natural resources, Liechtenstein has a strong, modern economy. It enjoys one of the highest standards of living in the world. There are no budget deficits, and inflation and unemployment rates are low.

After World War II, Liechtenstein experienced an economic boom as many companies invested heavily in the country. They took advantage of low taxes and other favorable conditions to build firms and factories, rapidly transforming the agrarian economy into an industrial state. Today, only about 2 percent of the gainfully employed still work in agriculture. Industry is highly technical, manufacturing capital- and research-intensive products. The largest branch is engaged in metal finishing, mainly machines and machine parts. Textiles, ceramics, and chemicals/pharmaceuticals all have long traditions in Liechtenstein. While industry produces mainly for export, a large number of small enterprises produce goods for domestic consumption. Industry and trade used to be the most important employers, but the service sector has recently caught up and today provides about 48 percent of all jobs.

Liechtenstein's high level of economic prosperity is due mainly to the economic and monetary union with Switzerland, the favorable tax situation, and political stability. The currency is the Swiss *franc* (CHF).

Transportation and Communication

Liechtenstein's road network is well developed. Private cars are the most important means of transport. Public transportation is provided by postal buses at low cost. Only one railway line crosses the country; it is operated by the Austrian Federal Railways. Good international connections are available through the nearby Swiss train stations and *Autobahn* (expressways). The closest international airport is in Zürich, Switzerland.

Communications facilities are good. The telephone and postal services are managed by Switzerland, but Liechtenstein issues its own postal stamps. They are renowned for their beautiful design and collected throughout the world. With regard to media, Liechtenstein is rather underdeveloped. There are two daily newspapers, which function as the mouthpieces of the two main political parties. The first radio station began broadcasting in August 1995. Television broadcasts come from other countries.

Education

School education is free and mandatory between the ages of seven and sixteen. Pupils may thereafter continue to study in preparation for entering a university or vocational training. The system of apprenticeships is quite popular and successful. Up to the level of the university entrance qualification, the *Matura*, Liechtenstein has a well-developed educational system. For further training, agreements with Switzerland and Austria ensure that Liechtensteiners have places in educational institutions abroad. There is no illiteracy, and adult education is actively promoted.

Health

Medical care is provided by a relatively high density of private doctors. There is one small public hospital in Liechtenstein. In addition, the country has concluded agreements with its Swiss and Austrian neighboring regions that ensure the availability of beds in hospitals there. The government provides for age and disability insurance, unemployment benefits, and social welfare. It requires people to purchase private health insurance. The infant mortality rate is very low at 5 per 1,000; life expectancy averages 78 years.

FOR THE TRAVELER

U.S. visitors do not need a visa for stays of up to three months, but a valid passport is required. No vaccinations are necessary. There are no customs formalities on the Liechtenstein-Swiss border, but normal practices apply on the Austrian border. Tourism is well developed. The country offers beautiful scenery, historical sites, and recreational activities. For further information, you may contact the Liechtenstein National Tourist Office, PO Box 139, 9490 Vaduz, Liechtenstein. In addition, Switzerland Tourism provides information about travel to Liechtenstein: 608 Fifth Avenue, Swiss Center, New York, NY 10020; phone (212) 757–5944. It also has offices in Chicago and El Segundo, California. The Embassy of Switzerland represents Liechtenstein's diplomatic interests in the United States: 2900 Cathedral Avenue NW, Washington, DC 20008; phone (202) 745–7900.

CULTURGRAM '97

Republic of
Lithuania

Boundary representations not necessarily authoritative.

BACKGROUND

Land and Climate

Lithuania is about the same size as Washington state (25,174 square miles or 65,200 square kilometers). It lies on the western fringe of the east European plain and has a short coastline on the Baltic Sea. It is a green country with more than 750 rivers and 2,800 lakes. The two longest rivers are the Nemunas and the Neris. Summers are short and winters are cold and foggy. The general climate is comparable to that of southeastern Canada. Forests cover about 30 percent of the country and are rich in wild animals, mushrooms, and berries. Forests and the Ciuronian Lagoon, a large freshwater lagoon on the Baltic are favorite destinations for recreation. Rain falls throughout the year but less so in the summer. A westerly breeze is common. The average temperature in January is 23°F (–5°C) and in July is 63°F (17°C).

While the country is technically divided into 44 regions and 11 municipalities, Lithuanians tend to identify with one of five main regions: Dzukia (around Vilnius), Aukstetia (northeastern lakes), Suvalkia (far south), Zemeitia (center/northwest) and Mazos Lietuvos (Lithuania Minor, in the southwest).

History

Although the Lithuanian people had existed for centuries, it was not until 1236 that Duke Mindaugas united the lands inhabited by them with those of the Yatwingians and Couronians to form the Grand Duchy of Lithuania. The new state grew in prominence, especially during the 14th century when it annexed neighboring lands and was ruled by strong monarchs. Vilnius became the capital in 1323. In 1386, reacting to a serious threat from Germanic invaders, the Grand Duke Jogaila married the Polish crown princess and became king. This alliance brought Lithuania into a dynastic union with Poland, which eventually allowed the two nations to defeat the German (Teutonic) invaders in 1410. Because of the union, the Lithuanians adopted Roman Catholicism in 1387 and began to adopt Western culture. Poland and Lithuania tightened their association in 1569 when they united under the Lublin Union.

After the Polish-Lithuanian state was partitioned by its neighbors (in 1772, 1793, and 1795), the Grand Duchy of Lithuania was left largely a part of the Russian Empire. Many attempts were made to regain independence, but all were unsuccessful. In World War I, it was occupied by the Germans. Then after the Russian Revolution in 1917, the Germans permitted Lithuania to elect its own officials. In February 1918, those officials declared Lithuania an independent state. But in December of that year, Communists in Lithuania established a government and the Bolsheviks invaded from Russia.

Later, in 1919, the Soviet army was driven from most of Lithuania, whose people were determined to regain sovereignty. At about the same time, Poland fought the Soviets, seeking to restore the territory it had claimed before 1795. Lithuania resisted Polish plans and signed a peace treaty with the Soviets that recognized Vilnius as belonging to Lithuania; the same treaty was later signed with Poland, which was to give up its claims to the city and region. Unfortunately, the Polish army ignored the treaty and seized Vilnius. Kaunas then became the capital of Lithuania.

In the interwar period (1920–40), Lithuania was independent and had a free-market economy, trading agricultural products with European and Scandinavian countries. After

E
U
R
O
P
E

the joint German-Soviet attack on Poland in 1939, Lithuania was forced to accept Soviet military bases on its territory. As compensation, the Soviets took Vilnius from Poland and returned it to Lithuanian sovereignty. Unfortunately, the Soviets soon dismissed the government and officially occupied the entire nation in 1940. When Germany's Hitler reneged on the 1939 Ribbentrop-Molotov agreement, in which Germany and Russia claimed respective territories, Germany invaded and occupied Lithuania from 1941 to 1944. Gestapo forces killed thousands of Jews and brought suffering to the entire country. The Soviets returned in 1944, only to incorporate the country into the Soviet Union (USSR).

Thousands of armed partisan fighters, known as "Forest Brothers," fought unsuccessfully for independence between 1940 and 1954. As a result of the resistance and Stalin's policies toward the Baltics, Lithuania suffered mass deportations and other difficulties. Relations were less confrontational after the 1950s, but Lithuanians never gave up their goal for independence. Their desires were realized in 1990 when the freely elected legislature of Lithuania re-declared independence (first declared in 1918). Since the Soviet government had been weakened by various international and domestic factors, it could not force Lithuania to cancel the declaration.

After the entire USSR collapsed in 1991, Russia recognized Lithuania's independence, which had already been recognized by many countries. The government, led by members of the political movement called *Sajudis*, embarked on an aggressive campaign to reform the economy and other social structures. Hampered by a poor global economy and soaring energy prices, among other variables, progress was slow and painful. In 1992, voters rejected the *Sajudis* leadership in favor of former Communists, who had formed a new political party. Although pledging to remain committed to democracy, the new government slowed privatization and other reform measures to soften the impact of political and social change. In late 1993, through more cooperative relations with Russia, Lithuania's leaders were able to effect a full withdrawal of Russian troops.

Still struggling with the effects of reform, the country faced a banking crisis at the end of 1995 that led to the dismissal of the prime minister. The country continues to seek ways to strengthen and stabilize fledgling democratic institutions and improve its economic performance.

THE PEOPLE

Population

The population of Lithuania is 3.9 million, with nearly 70 percent living in urban areas. Most people (80 percent) are ethnic Lithuanian, but the country is also home to Russians (8.6 percent), Poles (7.7), Belarussians (1.5), and Ukrainians (1.2), among a few other small groups. The term *Lithuania* was first used by Tacitus in the first century A.D. in reference to one of many peoples emerging from the Balts, who inhabited the Baltic region between the first and fourth centuries. Lithuanians began to form their distinct society in the early 100s. In Lithuania, all national minorities have full citizenship rights and are treated as equals. Except for Russians, minorities generally maintain their own customs and have not adopted Lithuanian culture. Most Russians have

integrated with mainstream society, combining their own customs with those of ethnic Lithuanians.

Lithuania's Human Development Index (0.769) ranks it 71st out of 174 countries. Access to education, health care, and economic opportunities is available, but differences between the standard of living of the rich and the poor are widening. Adjusted for women, the index (0.750) ranks Lithuania 44th out of 130 countries, indicating that women earn a significant share of the nation's income.

Language

Lithuanian, the country's official language, is known as one of the oldest Indo-European languages still in everyday use. It belongs to the Baltic language group, along with Latvian and some extinct tongues like Yatvangian and Old Prussian. Grammatically, Lithuanian is similar to Sanskrit and Homeric Greek. The formation of standard Lithuanian was not completed until the 19th century because Polish (and sometimes other languages) had been used as the state language after the 13th century. By the 17th century, Lithuanian survived only among rural peasants because urban dwellers spoke Polish. After 1795, when Lithuania and Poland ceased to exist, Russian was introduced and encouraged among Lithuanians. When Lithuanian was later revived, a number of dialects assimilated into four main dialects: Dzukian, Aukstecian, Suvalkian, and Zemeitian. Russian was reintroduced by the Soviets and today about 80 percent of Lithuanians can speak Russian. English and German are popular foreign languages.

Religion

Most Lithuanians belong to the Roman Catholic Church. Under Soviet occupation, churches were closed, clergymen repressed, and teachers forbidden to teach religion. People practiced their faiths mainly at home. In 1990, the Act of Restitution of the Catholic Church restored it to its prominence and allowed religious freedom. Many different Christian churches also operate in the country. Muslims and Jews have active congregations.

General Attitudes

Lithuanians are generally reserved, even somber, although they are sincere and full of emotion. They simply mask their feelings to maintain privacy. They appreciate skill and intelligence. They are often critical of their own personal faults and are openly critical and distrustful of public institutions. They commonly describe their nation as melancholy (due to its past history). Individually, people are also nostalgic for such things as old friends, youth, and fond memories. Lithuanians are patient and industrious. They value moderate thrift but view "excessive" thrift as stingy. They also value education, family, and loyalty to one's nationality.

Lithuanians are proud of their heritage but not of the Soviet period. For the future, they wish to be politically neutral and peaceful; however, they are willing to defend themselves to maintain Lithuania's independence. Many people are frustrated with the current period of transition and are uncertain of the future.

Personal Appearance

It is important to be cleanly dressed. Styles are mainly from Europe and increasingly from the United States. Lithuania's national dress is worn only on special occasions.

Because clothing is expensive and the market does not always meet demand, people often wear handmade clothing, especially rural dwellers or persons wishing to create their own style. As Lithuania's economy continues to integrate with the world's, the use of handmade clothing is expected to decline. Older rural women wear scarves on their heads. *Fedoras* (fur caps worn by men) and European-style hats are common in winter. Men remove their hats in a building. Wool and fur are commonly used for clothing when it is cold. Older women wear cosmetics sparingly.

CUSTOMS AND COURTESIES

Greetings

Shaking hands with men and, less often, women is customary when greeting. A handshake is nearly always used in professional contacts. Men sometimes kiss the extended hand of women in greeting, and good friends may kiss cheeks. When introducing a man, one uses *ponas* (Mr.) before the last name; for a woman, the term is *ponia* (Mrs.) or *ponele* (Miss). A person's professional title is also used before the last name when applicable. Doctors and teachers are respectfully addressed by title alone. Adults do not address each other by first name until invited to do so, but young people are called by their first names. Men raise their hats or nod to greet people at a distance. The most common terms for greeting are *Laba diena* (Good day), *Labas rytas* (Good morning), *Labas vakaras* (Good evening), *su Diev* (Go with God), and *Viso gero* (Good-bye). Friends use the more informal *Labas* (Hello), *Viso* (Bye), and *Iki* (Bye-bye). *Sveikas* (for a man), *Svieka* (for a woman), and *Svieki* (for a group)—all roughly meaning "How are you?"—are friendly ways to say hello. Urban Lithuanians do not greet strangers passing on the street.

Gestures

It is impolite to talk with one's hands in one's pockets. Lithuanians appreciate eye contact during conversation. People sometimes extend the thumb up to express approval, but verbal communication is preferred. Using the hands during or instead of conversation is not uncommon, only less formal. Chewing gum in public is not appropriate for adults.

Visiting

Visiting in the home is popular because outside social opportunities are somewhat limited and expensive. Spontaneous visits, even between friends and neighbors, are not very common. It is polite to call before any visit, but unannounced guests will be welcome. Hosts expect punctuality of invited guests. It is customary to bring an odd number of fresh flowers for even a brief visit. An even number is for funerals. Dinner guests may also bring wine. Guests should unwrap flowers before giving them to the hostess. White flowers are usually reserved for brides and carnations are for mourning or certain other occasions. In formal situations, guests wait to sit down until invited or until the host sits. For informal gatherings, guests may act more at home. Hosts always offer guests refreshments, which may include coffee (or tea) and cake or cookies. They offer an abundance of food to indicate their home's prosperity. Drinking vodka (usually only men) or other alcohol is typically part of most social visits. The length of an evening visit depends on the occasion. If the hour is late, a host may accompany departing guests outside.

Eating

Lithuanians eat in the continental style, with the fork in the left hand and the knife remaining in the right. They usually eat three meals each day. Breakfast is between 7:00 and 9:00 A.M., dinner 1:00 and 3:00 P.M., and supper 6:00 and 8:00 P.M. Rural inhabitants eat meals as much as two hours earlier. The midday meal is the main meal, and most businesses close for it. People either go home or eat at work-site canteens. Leaving food on the plate is impolite, as it suggests to the hostess that the meal was not good. In a restaurant, one must request the bill from the waiter and pay at the table. Toasting is common for dinner and supper, whether guests are present or not. Tipping is not customary but is becoming more common.

LIFESTYLE

Family

The average family has one or two children. The father is generally the head of the family, but both parents share in raising children and working outside the home. Women do household chores; men handle repairs. The elderly prefer to live alone, but many live with their adult children. In cities, most people live in apartments. Due to limited space, apartment furniture often serves multi-purposes. Single-family homes are more common in rural areas. As land confiscated by the Soviets is returned to people throughout the country, they are building more private homes. All families have gardens either near their rural home or on the outskirts of cities. Each family member helps tend the "kitchen garden," a source of fresh food, relaxation, and contact with the land.

Dating and Marriage

Young people enjoy dancing, going to clubs, and traveling together. They usually marry in their early twenties, but some wait until they are financially secure. Young couples often rely for a time on financial support, and even housing, from their parents. It is becoming more popular to live together before, or instead of, marrying. Legal marriages are performed at city hall; many couples now also have a church ceremony.

Rural weddings can be lavish, and it is becoming popular to practice older traditions. For example, after the wedding ceremony, the wedding party's way home is blocked by "ropes" of branches and flowers. The groom's friends and the matchmaker have to "buy" their way out with candy and whiskey. Sweets are also given to children along the way. The last rope is usually stretched across the gate of the couple's home. Parents meet the newlyweds at the door with bread, salt, and wine glasses filled with water. Many customs surround the two-day wedding celebration, including the mock punishment (and eventual rescue) of the matchmaker for convincing the bride to marry the groom.

Diet

Lithuanian cuisine has adopted many dishes from neighboring cultures, including *blynai* (pancakes), *barscai* (beet soup), and *balendelai* (stuffed cabbage leaves). Traditional specialties include smoked sausage, various cheeses, *cepelinai* (meat cooked inside a ball of potato dough, served with a special sauce), and *vedarai* (cooked potatoes and sausage stuffed into pig intestines). Soup is commonly served with dinner. Local fruits (apples, pears, plums, and strawberries) and vegetables (potatoes, carrots, cabbage, peas, and beets) are popular. People grow much of their own produce, and perserve some for winter consumption. They regularly eat rye bread and dairy products. Tea, milk, and coffee are the most common drinks.

Recreation

Basketball is the favorite sport in Lithuania, followed by soccer, boating (rowing), volleyball, cycling, tennis, cross-country skiing, and others. Camping is popular for family outings, as is picking mushrooms or berries in the forest, fishing (for men), and going to the beach. Watching television, knitting and sewing (for women), or visiting are common leisure activities. People also relax by visiting at their garden plots. Many enjoy caring for pets (mostly dogs), reading, and going to cultural events, especially those involving national dance and song.

Holidays

Official public holidays include New Year's Day, Independence Day (16 February), Mother's Day (first Sunday in May), Anniversary of the Coronation of Grand Duke Mindaugas of Lithuania (6 July), National Day of Hope and Mourning (1 November), and Christmas (25–26 December). Families traditionally have a 12-course meal on Christmas Day. The Day of Hope and Mourning, also known as All Souls' Day, is a day to remember the dead. For the pre-Lent Uzgavines, people dress in costumes and children go door-to-door asking for treats. Easter is celebrated with family. St. John's Day (24 June) marks the advent of summer. Various local festivals are held throughout the year.

Commerce

Business is generally kept separate from socializing. Offices are open weekdays 9:00 A.M. to 6:00 P.M., with an hour break at 1:00 P.M. Food shops are open 8:00 A.M. to 7:00 P.M., Monday through Saturday, with a break at 2:00 P.M. Some shops are open 10:00 A.M. to 10:00 P.M., with a break around 2:00 P.M. Banks are open weekdays 9:00 A.M. to 3:00 P.M. Kiosks and small shops have more flexible hours. Most Lithuanians shop at open-air markets, which operate at least twice a week in every town. These feature a wide array of foods, clothing, and household items.

SOCIETY

Government

Lithuania's 1992 constitution provides for a president as head of state. Algirdas Brazauskas was elected in 1993 to a five-year term. The prime minister, currently Mindaugas Stankevicius, is head of government. The 141-seat Parliament (*Seimas*) is the highest body of state power. The voting age is 18. The two largest political parties are the governing Democratic Labor Party of Lithuania and the opposition Conservative Party. A few other parties also hold *Seimas* seats.

Economy

Lithuania is an industrial state, producing precision machinery, processed foods, and light industrial products. The country has few natural resources, so it depends on imported raw materials. Main exports include machinery and parts, meat and dairy products, and consumer goods. Imports include oil and gas, chemicals, metals, and equipment. Production declined with independence, as traditional supply arrangements were interrupted, but ties are being established with Western Europe and neighboring countries to increase revenue, investment, and productivity.

The current government has slowed the pace of privatization and price liberalization to address reform's short-term results: high inflation, low wage growth, and poverty. Real gross domestic product per capita has dropped to $3,700. Although the basic needs of the population are met overall, the standard of living has fallen in the last few years due to difficulties associated with the transition to a market economy. The national currency is the *litas*.

Transportation and Communication

Public transportation is convenient and important because most families do not own private vehicles. Local buses and trolleys operate in cities, and a country-wide bus service radiates from the main towns. Lithuanian Aviation flies to and from various European destinations. Sea ferries connect Lithuania with Germany; trains provide service to Poland and Germany, as well as within the country. In addition to many private newspapers, there are three state-owned government newspapers, one each written in Lithuanian, Russian, and Polish. Several private television stations also broadcast in addition to the state-run station. The telephone system is not extensive but is fairly efficient.

Education

Children attend elementary school for nine years, assigned in the second form (grade) to one of three levels ("A" being for advanced students). Students may then pursue three years of secondary school, go to a vocational school, or begin working. The adult literacy rate is 98 percent. Education is provided free at all levels. General education schools offer an optional course in religion. Sunday schools are open for Jews, Karaites (a small group descended from the 14th-century Tatars), and other religious minorities. Ethnic minorities have the option of attending schools that teach in their language. Difficult entrance exams are required for the 16 institutions of higher education, including Vilnius University, the University of Vytautas Magnus, and Kaunas Technical University.

Health

Lithuania has a national health-care system, but some aspects are scheduled to be privatized; several private clinics already exist. The system provides for basic needs, although modern equipment and supplies are lacking. Home remedies and long recuperations are standard practices. The infant mortality rate is 17 per 1,000. Life expectancy averages 71 years.

FOR THE TRAVELER

U.S. travelers need a valid passport to enter Lithuania, but no visa is necessary for stays of fewer than 90 days. Vaccinations are not required, but a diphtheria booster is recommended. Tourist facilities are improving rapidly. For information, contact the Embassy of the Republic of Lithuania, 2622 16th Street NW, Washington, DC 20009.

CULTURGRAM ™ '97

Grand Duchy of
Luxembourg

BACKGROUND

Land and Climate

Luxembourg is a small, landlocked country bordered by France to the south, Belgium to the north, and Germany to the east. Covering 998 square miles (2,586 square kilometers), it is about the same size as Rhode Island. Nearly 25 percent of the land is suitable for cultivation. Luxembourg has gently rolling hills with shallow valleys and many forests, including those in the Ardennes uplands of the north. The south (the "Good Land") is dominated by farmland and woods. The landscape is dotted by castles and the ruins of castles and fortresses. The Moselle River forms the southeastern border. The climate is mild. Winter temperatures are generally above freezing and summer temperatures average 75°F (24°C). The sunniest summer months are May and June.

History

Luxembourg is one of Europe's oldest and smallest independent countries. But before it became independent, the area was ruled by many kingdoms, including that of the Romans and, much later, Charlemagne's. In 963, Count Siegfried of the Ardennes built a castle in present-day Luxembourg and founded the Luxembourg Dynasty. Charles of Luxembourg became the king of Bohemia in the 14th century and strove to make Prague (now in the Czech Republic) as beautiful as Paris. Indeed, Luxembourg gave more than one monarch to other countries during the medieval period.

Luxembourg was ruled by the Austrian Hapsburgs in the 17th and 18th centuries and then by the Netherlands. In 1815, it became a Grand Duchy in the Dutch Kingdom. The Luxembourgers revolted in 1830 after the Belgians also revolted against Dutch control. After the revolt, Luxembourg was divided between Belgium and the Netherlands. The Netherlands's portion is what eventually gained independence as today's Luxembourg. The 1867 Treaty of London declared Luxembourg an independent neutral state, although it remained closely tied to the Netherlands. Personal union between the monarchs of the Netherlands and Luxembourg ended in 1890 when both died without leaving heirs to their thrones. In Luxembourg, the crown passed to the House of Nassau, which holds it today.

Although neutral, Luxembourg was invaded by Germany in both world wars. After its liberation, Luxembourg ended its neutrality (1949) and joined the western European alliances, including the North Atlantic Treaty Organization. In 1964, the Grand Duchess Charlotte abdicated, allowing her son, Grand Duke Jean, to become ruler. Since that time, Luxembourg has enjoyed peace, economic growth, and beneficial relations with other European nations. Luxembourg is particularly well represented in the European Union (EU), of which it is the smallest member. Former Prime Minister Jacques Santer became the EU Commission president in 1995, and Luxembourg is a frequent site for EU conferences.

THE PEOPLE
Population

After remaining steady for several years, Luxembourg's population of 404,000 is currently growing at 0.6 percent annually. Nearly one-quarter of the population lives in the city of Luxembourg. The Luxembourgers, who are an ethnic mixture of French and German origins, account for about 75 percent of the population. The rest consists of guest and worker residents from Portugal, Italy, France, and other European countries. The immigrant population is growing faster than the number of native Luxembourgers. The country's Human Development Index (0.893) ranks Luxembourg 27th out of 174 countries. Access to economic prosperity, education, and health care affords people choices and opportunities in their lives. Adjusted for women, the index (0.790) ranks Luxembourg 35th out of 130 countries.

Language

Luxembourgish is the native tongue of Luxembourgers. It comes from a Franco-Moselle dialect, mixed with many German and French words. It was declared the national language in 1984, although it had always been used as the daily language of the people. Luxembourgish is used more as a spoken language than a written one. French and German also have official status. German is often used for newspapers, while French is the official language of the civil service, law, and Parliament. Children begin learning German in school at the age of six and French at seven. English is also taught in the schools and is widely understood.

Religion

The Roman Catholic Church claims membership of more than 90 percent of the population. While most adhere to Catholic traditions, society is basically secular. Most of the rest of Luxembourg's residents either belong to various Protestant and other Christian churches or are Jewish. A small number claim no affiliation. Most Christians do not attend church services on a regular basis, but many show their devotion through actions or attitudes (such as tolerance, charity, etc.).

General Attitudes

Although the people of Luxembourg are descendants of different nationalities and speak several different languages, they maintain a strong feeling of national pride. Their independence and separate identity in Europe are important. This character is reflected in the national motto: *Mir wëlle bleiwe wat mer sin!* (We want to remain what we are!). By both conquest and peaceful exchange, Luxembourg has been influenced by the neighboring countries of Belgium, Germany, and France. Many traditions of each of these countries are evident in the customs of the Luxembourgers. There are differences, however. For example, the pace of everyday life in Luxembourg is not as hurried as in other European countries. Luxembourgers value education, privacy, friendship, and humor. They do not appreciate loud behavior in polite company or in public.

Personal Appearance

Luxembourgers follow European fashion trends, chiefly those from France, Germany, and Italy. Men wear suits to work. Many men wear hats. Women wear dresses somewhat more often than pants. The youth follow the latest fashion trends. Luxembourgers stress cleanliness and neatness in appearance. People are always well dressed in public; tattered clothing is inappropriate. Very casual clothing is reserved for the home or recreational activities.

CUSTOMS AND COURTESIES
Greetings

A gentle handshake is most common and most appropriate when greeting acquaintances or meeting someone for the first time. Close female friends may hug three times. Other close friends who have not seen each other for a long time may kiss each other's cheeks three times. Polite inquiries about a friend's health or colleague's work might accompany a greeting. The most common verbal greetings in Luxembourgish include *Moien* (Morning), *Gudden Owend* (Good evening), and *Wéi geet et?* (How are you?). Also common is *Bonjour*, French for "Good day." Upon parting, one might say *Äddi*, a casual "Good-bye," or the more formal *Au revoir*. Young people like *Salut* or *Ciao* for a quick good-bye. Friends and acquaintances also use longer phrases, such as *Bis eng aner Kéier* or *Bis härno*, both of which roughly mean "See you later." *Äddi, bis mar* (Until tomorrow) is also appropriate. Like most Europeans, Luxembourgers are reserved when first meeting strangers. They are friendly, however, and remember those who befriend them. Friends and relatives address each other by given names or nicknames, while acquaintances use titles and surnames. High-ranking persons may be addressed by more than one title, such as *Här Minister* (Mr. Minister), with or without the surname.

Gestures

Although Luxembourgers might use hands to emphasize their speech during conversation, specific gestures are rarely used to complement or replace verbal communication. Proper behavior in public is expected; one refrains from yawning, shouting, or using offensive language. Handkerchiefs are used inconspicuously. Chewing gum while speaking is impolite.

Visiting

The people of Luxembourg enjoy visiting friends and relatives at home, but they rarely drop by unannounced. Most visits are prearranged, usually by invitation. Hosts take care to make their guests feel welcome. They nearly always offer refreshments, usually in the form of something to drink. Before a meal, a cocktail is common.

Good friends visiting a couple that has just moved into a new home bring bread, salt, and a bottle of wine to wish them well. Dinner guests normally bring flowers, chocolates, a small gift, or a bottle of wine to their hosts. Among younger people, the guests often bring dessert. Good friends and relatives might bring gifts on holidays or for special occasions (first communion, final exams at secondary school, obtaining a college degree, birthdays, and so forth).

When guests depart, they thank the hosts and are accompanied outside of the home. Guests are seldom invited to the home to discuss business. Such matters are taken care of in public places, such as restaurants, cafés, or offices.

Eating

Luxembourgers usually eat breakfast between 7:00 and 9:00 A.M., lunch at noon, and dinner around 7:00 P.M. Some people have coffee around 4:00 P.M. The main meal of the day was traditionally at midday, but this is not possible for people who work all day or are too far from home each day to eat at that time. For these families, lunch is light and dinner is the main meal. At the family meal, serving dishes are placed on the table for each person to choose his or her portion. When guests are present, each person's plate is usually prepared in advance. Hosts expect their guests to ask for second helpings. Some cooks will believe their food is not liked if guests do not eat seconds. People eat in the continental style, with the fork in the left hand and the knife remaining in the right. They keep both hands, but not the elbows, above the table at all times. It is not proper to have one's hands resting in the lap during a meal. Burping at the table is not appropriate.

In a restaurant, the waiter usually is paid at the table. The bill often includes a service fee. If so, an extra tip is not necessary but is appreciated. If service is not included, one normally leaves a tip of 10 to 15 percent.

LIFESTYLE

Family

The importance of the family is well established in Luxembourg. Parents still exert influence on the social and professional choices of their children. Parents are required by law to pay for their children's education, and adult children are required to meet certain financial obligations of their parents if in need. Over the past decade, traditional family ties have been weakened somewhat as more young people travel abroad for study or employment. Bonds are still maintained, however, through family gatherings and celebrations. Families usually are small, having on average fewer than two children. Many women work outside the home, comprising one-third of the labor force. If working parents have younger children, grandparents may be called upon to care for them during the day. Day-care facilities and other options are also available. More than 60 percent of all families own the homes or apartments in which they live.

Dating and Marriage

Dating usually begins at age 15, after compulsory education requirements have been met. Parental approval, although less important that in the past, is still a factor in a young person's dating choices. The youth enjoy going to movies and theaters, eating at cafés and restaurants, having parties or dinners, and dancing. Couples may postpone marriage until they are financially established or complete their educational goals. Some couples choose to live together before marriage, but this is not an official union, and most Luxembourgers expect to marry eventually.

Only civil marriages are recognized by law. To be married in a church, a couple must present a certificate showing that they have been legally married by a civil authority. A reception for acquaintances and friends may follow a civil wedding, while a dinner for close friends and relatives traditionally follows a church ceremony.

Diet

Food in Luxembourg is influenced by French and German traditions, but it has its own unique flavor. People appreciate fine foods and there are many national favorites. Popular dishes include *Judd mat Gaardebounen* (smoked collar of pork with broad beans), *Bouneschlupp* (bean soup), *Kachkéis* (a soft cheese known as *cancoillotte* in French), *Quetschentaart* (plum tart), *Fritten, Ham an Zalot* (french fries, ham, and salad), *Träipen* (black pudding commonly eaten on Christmas Eve), and freshwater fish (usually trout). Sausages, potatoes, and sauerkraut are common elements of the diet. Fresh fruits and vegetables are eaten in season. A variety of cheeses and other dairy products are important. Coffee, wine, juice, and beer are popular drinks. Luxembourg also exports some domestic wines and beer to other countries in Europe.

Recreation

Cycling and hiking are favorite activities in Luxembourg, mostly because of the beautiful scenery. Part of the famous *Tour de France* bicycle race passes through Luxembourg. People also enjoy soccer, jogging, and volleyball. There are facilities for golf, tennis, squash, and water sports. Hunting and fishing are popular seasonal activities. Numerous parks, theaters, movie theaters, and museums are available. Gardening and watching television are popular leisure activities. The cultural arts are important. Besides attending performances or museums, Luxembourgers like to paint, play musical instruments, or perform in village playhouses.

Holidays

In addition to some national holidays, several religious holidays are celebrated in Luxembourg. The national holidays include New Year's Day, Labor Day (1 May), the Grand Duke's Birthday—also called National Day (23 June), and Fair Day (early September). Fair Day occurs during fair season in the capital city. An ancient shepherds' market serves as the fairgrounds and many traditions focus on shepherding.

Religious holidays include Shrove Tuesday (February), Easter (including Monday), Ascension, Whitmonday, Assumption (15 August), All Saints' Day (1 November), All Souls' Day (2 November), and Christmas (24–26 December). Christmas and Easter are the most important holidays.

At Easter, young children take part in a tradition called *klibbere goen*. According to legend, all church bells go to Rome three days before Easter for confessional. So the boys use rattles to announce church services, since the bells cannot ring. When the bells return on the Saturday before Easter, the children collect money and colorful Easter eggs from each home in the neighborhood as their reward. Every family colors Easter eggs during this season, and on Easter Sunday, children receive the eggs and other gifts hidden in the garden.

Christmas celebrations begin weeks before the actual holiday. Some time before 6 December, small children place a shoe outside their bedroom before bedtime and expect to receive a piece of chocolate from St. Nicholas (*Kleeschen*) if they have been good. Otherwise they might receive a birch twig from his helper, *Housecker*. Then, on 6 December, *Kleeschen* visits good children and brings them gifts. Small parades are often held in various cities to celebrate the event. On Christmas Eve, families have a big meal and Catholics go to mass. Nearly all families have a tree in the home; many have a nativity scene. Christmas Day is a family day.

Carnival is celebrated in the spring in many cities. There are also wine fairs, art festivals, and festivities to mark historical events.

Commerce

Business hours are generally from 8:30 A.M. to 5:30 P.M., Monday through Friday. Some shopping and recreational facilities are open longer. Some small shops may close for an hour at lunchtime. Most people shop in large supermarkets for their groceries, but a fresh produce open-air market operates on Wednesday and Saturday. Luxembourg has a favorable business climate and there are few labor disputes. All workers receive 25 vacation days each year. Women receive from four to six months' maternity leave.

SOCIETY

Government

The Grand Duchy of Luxembourg is a constitutional monarchy, led by the Grand Duke Jean. However, the constitution vests sovereignty in the people. The 60 members of Luxembourg's unicameral legislature (Council of Deputies) are directly elected. A prime minister is head of government. A Council of State advises the legislature. Most governments are coalitions. The major political parties include the Christian Social People's Party, Socialist Workers Party, and Democratic Party. Several smaller parties also hold legislative seats. All citizens older than age 18 are required to vote in national elections. Parliamentary elections were last held in 1994. Jean-Claude Juncker is the current prime minister; highly popular, he heads the Christian Social People's Party.

Economy

Luxembourg enjoys a high standard of living. Real gross domestic product per capita is $21,520, the fourth highest in the world. More important is the economy's constant stability. Despite its lack of natural resources and its policy to no longer exploit its iron ore reserves, Luxembourg has been able to develop, diversify, and keep its economy strong. Inflation and unemployment remain low. The agriculture sector is modern and employs less than 5 percent of the labor force. About one-third of all workers in Luxembourg are foreign laborers from Portugal, Italy, France, Belgium, and Germany. The service sector of the economy has grown substantially as the manufacturing sector of the economy, which is based on the steel industry, has become less important. Today, services (especially financial) employ almost half of the workforce. Nevertheless, steel, chemicals, rubber, and other products are still important exports.

Luxembourg has benefited from European economic integration and cooperates closely with Belgium and the Netherlands in the BENELUX economic union. Luxembourg is also a member of the European Union. Inflation and unemployment generally have been low in Luxembourg. The government actively encourages foreign investment. Both the Belgian *franc* (BF) and the Luxembourg *franc* (LuxF) are accepted as currencies of equal value.

Transportation and Communication

Luxembourg is a hub of travel in Europe. Trains connect to most major European cities and are well maintained. Roads and railways are in excellent condition. Most families own cars. Taxis are plentiful in the cities. The urban bus system is efficient. The communications system is modern and efficient. The government administers telephone, telegraph, and postal systems. Television, radio, and newspapers are privately owned.

Education

Luxembourg's education system is well developed; literacy is 99 percent. Children attend primary school for six years and secondary school for seven years. Upon successfully passing exams at the end of the secondary level, students may go on to university studies. This might include a two-year banking course at Luxembourg's university, *Cours Universitaire*; training for primary-level teachers at the *Institut Supérieur d'Etudes et de Recherches Pédagogiques*; or the first year of college studies at the *Cours Universitaire*. That first year in humanities, law, economics, secondary education, science, or medicine is recognized by many foreign universities to which Luxembourgers must transfer to complete their studies. Various technical and vocational schools exist to train those who seek careers outside of these professions.

Health

Public health standards are high, facilities are modern and advanced, and the cost to patients is low because of a compulsory social insurance system. People may also carry private insurance to cover certain expenses. Clinics serve local needs, and hospitals are located in large towns. The infant mortality rate is 7 per 1,000. Life expectancy ranges from 73 to 81 years.

FOR THE TRAVELER

No visa is required of U.S. visitors staying up to three months, but a valid passport is necessary. No vaccinations are required. Interesting attractions include the old fortress of Luxembourg, the Battle of the Bulge museum at Diekirch, the Moselle Valley, and the newly restored exhibition "The Family of Man" by Edward Steichen in the castle of Clervaux. For more detailed information on travel opportunities in Luxembourg, contact the Luxembourg National Tourist Office, 17 Beekman Place, New York, NY 10022; phone (212) 935–8888. You may also wish to contact the Embassy of Luxembourg, 2200 Massachusetts Avenue NW, Washington, DC 20008; phone (202) 265–4171.

Mexico
(United Mexican States)

Boundary representations not necessarily authoritative.

THE AMERICAS

BACKGROUND

Land and Climate

Covering 761,602 square miles (1,972,550 square kilometers), Mexico is about three times the size of Texas or about one-fifth the size of the United States. It shares its northern border with the United States and its southern border with Guatemala and Belize. Mexico is rich in natural resources, including oil, natural gas, silver, iron ore, coal, copper, gold, lead, and zinc. Much of the north is dry and hot, while tropical jungles are found in the south. The high and cooler central plateau, where Mexico City is located, is bounded by two mountain ranges, the Sierra Madre Oriental on the east and the Sierra Madre Occidental on the west. In all, two-thirds of the country is covered by mountains, many of which contain extinct volcanos. Temperature and rainfall vary with elevation and region. In the mountains, alpine conditions prevail. In Mexico City, the climate is more temperate. Rain falls mainly between November and May on the plateau. In the south, humidity and temperatures are higher.

History

The history of Mexico boasts a long line of advanced Indian civilizations whose accomplishments rival those of the Egyptians and early Europeans. They had accurate calendars, understood astronomy, were skilled artisans, and built huge empires. The Olmecs are considered to have been among the first inhabitants of the area around 2000 B.C. The Mayan Empire built incredible cities throughout North and Central America but fell in the 12th century. The Aztecs were the last great empire and were conquered by the Spanish in 1519. The Spanish virtually destroyed the Aztec culture. They also brought Christianity to the land and ruled until the 19th century.

A drive for independence began in September 1810, led by Miguel Hidalgo, a Mexican priest. Independence was gained in 1821. Mexico was one of the first countries to revolt against Spain. A constitution was adopted in 1824 and a republic was established. However, Antonio López de Santa Ana took power in 1833 and ruled as a dictator. During his regime, Texas seceded (1836) and joined the United States. Mexico also fought a war (1846–48) with the United States and lost more territory (much of the current western United States). Santa Ana resigned in 1855 and Benito Juárez became president. In 1861, French troops invaded Mexico City and named Austrian Archduke Maximilian the emperor of Mexico. Forces under Juárez overthrew Maximilian in 1867. Another dictator, Porfirio Díaz, came to power in 1877 and was overthrown in 1910, when Mexico entered a period of internal political unrest and violence.

That period, ending in the 1920s, became known as Mexico's social revolution. The Institutional Revolutionary Party (PRI) emerged as the leader of the nation in 1929. Political unrest continued in the 1930s, but Mexico has been basically stable since 1940. However, the PRI ruled the country as a single party and restricted political dissent for many years. In 1988, when Carlos Salinas de Gortari was elected president, he promised to bring greater democracy to Mexico through political and economic reform. Many changes did take place, but none to challenge the PRI's position.

Two 1994 events, however, seemed to weaken the party's future. The first was the January Zapatista rebellion in the state of Chiapas (bordering Guatemala). Rebel Indians protesting poverty conditions and the centralization of power demanded the government's resignation and democratic change. While the actual rebellion was put down, rebels remained under arms, and Mexicans began questioning government policy toward minorities. The other incident was the assassination of a leading presidential candidate, Luis Donaldo Colosio, who was expected to replace outgoing President Salinas in the August 1994 vote. The PRI chose another candidate, Ernesto Zedillo Ponce de Leon, who took office in December 1994. His first several months in office were marked by an economic and currency crisis, which turned more voters against the PRI. As the country seeks to recover from this crisis, people are waiting to see if Zedillo's new six-year economic and social policy plan will improve living standards for the average Mexican.

THE PEOPLE

Population

Mexico has nearly 94 million people, a population that is growing at 1.8 percent annually. Mexico City, the capital, has a population of more than 19 million and is one of the largest cities in the world. About 60 percent of the population is *mestizo* (mixed Spanish and Indian). Thirty percent belongs to various Amerindian groups. Most of these are descendants of the Maya and Aztecs. About 9 percent is of European ancestry. Most Mexicans tend to identify with their Amerindian and Spanish heritage.

Mexico's Human Development Index (0.842) ranks it 53d out of 174 countries. Adjusted for women, the index (0.741) ranks Mexico 46th out of 130 countries. Most Mexicans have access to basic resources (education, health care, and a decent standard of living) that are necessary for them to make choices in their lives.

Language

Spanish is the official language. Written Spanish in Mexico is the same as written Spanish in Spain or South America. However, there are differences in the pronunciation of some words and in the use of idioms. As many as one hundred Amerindian languages are still spoken in parts of Mexico, including Tzotzil and Tzeltal (Mayan dialects), Maya, Nahuatl (Aztec), Otomi, Zapotec, and Mixtec. Most people who speak an Amerindian language also speak at least some Spanish. English is understood by many in large urban areas.

Religion

The majority of Mexicans (89 percent) are Roman Catholic. The Catholic Church is very much a part of the culture, attitudes, and history of all Mexicans, but it does not have much political influence. Other Christian churches are very active in Mexico. Some are growing quite rapidly. The constitution guarantees freedom of worship. Until recently, however, public displays of worship were banned and churches did not have the right to own property or exist as legal entities. The Mexican constitution, drafted after the revolution in an attempt to take power from the Catholic Church and give

it to the people, banned all churches from teaching religion in public schools.

In 1992, however, the law was changed so any church can become legal, own property and buildings (although existing buildings remain property of the government), open schools, and worship openly. Members of the clergy are allowed to vote, and foreign clergy are now allowed to be in Mexico. The law also gives religious groups access to radio and television. While the previous restrictions were often ignored, even by many government officials, the new law relieves a great deal of tension between the state and various religions— without forcing the government to endorse a specific church.

General Attitudes

The concept of time is less precise in Mexico than in the United States, although this is changing in urban areas. Generally, Mexicans feel individuals are more important than schedules. If a visitor or business associate drops in unexpectedly, most Mexicans will stop to talk, regardless of how long it takes and even if it makes them late for something else. Business contacts are often made during the two- or three-hour lunch break. Actually, these are social meetings, for the most part, and business is conducted in the last few minutes. Mexicans value friendship, honesty, and personal honor. The Mexican people are generally proud of their country, despite the challenges it continues to face. Mexicans call citizens of the United States *norteamericanos*, but they also like to remind U.S. citizens they are not the only North Americans.

Personal Appearance

Most Mexicans wear clothing that is also common in the United States, especially in urban areas. But rural residents might also wear traditional clothing—either daily or for festivals. This is most common among Amerindian groups. In some areas, a man wears a wool *poncho* (*sarape*) over his shirt and pants when it is cold. He also may wear a wide-brimmed straw hat. A woman may wear a long, full skirt. In cooler weather, a shawl (*rebozo*) covers her blouse. The designs and colors are often markers of a specific region. Regardless of the style of clothing, color and beauty are features appreciated by all.

CUSTOMS AND COURTESIES

Greetings

The usual greeting is a handshake or a nod of the head, although a full embrace between friends is common. Women often greet with a kiss on the cheek, and men may greet close female friends in the same way. Mexicans typically stand close to each other while talking, sometimes touching their friend's clothing. Mexicans generally are very friendly and polite in their greetings. Verbal greetings vary, but some common ones are *¡Buenos días!* (Good morning), *¡Buenas tardes!* (Good afternoon), *¡Buenas noches!* (Good evening or Good night), and *¿Cómo está?* (How are you?). A casual greeting is *¡Hola!* (Hello). Men are referred to as *Señor* (Mr.), women as *Señorita* (Miss). One only uses the title *Señora* (Mrs.) when one is sure a woman is married.

Gestures

A person can indicate "no" by shaking the hand from side to side with the index finger extended and palm outward. The "thumbs up" gesture expresses approval. One hands items, rather than tossing them, to another person. Tossing an item shows a lack of manners and is offensive. If someone sneezes, a person may say *¡Salud!* (Good health). Hand and arm gestures are often used in conversation.

Visiting

Mexicans are very hospitable. Unexpected visitors are usually welcomed and served refreshments. It is impolite to refuse refreshments. Unannounced visits are fairly common, but as more people get telephones, more are calling ahead first. Mexicans enjoy conversation and socializing with relatives or friends. If they invite people over for dinner, the meal might not be served until after 8:00 P.M., partly because many people work late and because they socialize for a while before eating. On special occasions such as birthdays or Mother's Day, gifts are important and serenading is still popular (usually in rural areas). First-time visitors usually receive a tour of the host's home.

Eating

When eating, Mexicans keep both hands above the table. Guests do not leave directly after the meal but stay for conversation. On weeknights, guests might leave a bit earlier than on weekends, when conversation could last until very late. Lunch is usually the main meal of the day. A light meal, called a *merienda*, may be eaten between lunch and dinner. Dinner might be light or heavy, depending on the family. Food purchased on the street usually is eaten at the stand. It is inappropriate for adults to eat while walking on the street. Bland foods such as bread or rice are eaten with spicy foods to relieve the burning sensation. Many also use a pinch of salt for relief. Hot, spicy food is called *picante*, while hot (temperature) food is called *caliente*. Some foods are eaten with utensils, others with the hand. *Tortillas* are often used as scoops for sauces.

LIFESTYLE

Family

Except in urban areas, where the trend is to have smaller families, Mexican families generally are large (more than three children). Family unity is very important. Indeed, family responsibilities often come before all other responsibilities. Divorce is relatively low, due in part to the dominance of the Catholic faith. The father is the leader of the family, but the mother runs the household. A household, especially in rural areas, may include members of the extended family.

Dating and Marriage

When dating, a boy often meets the girl at a prearranged place rather than picking her up at her home. However, parental approval of the boyfriend is important. In some rural areas, it is considered a mark of poor character for a girl to go out alone after dark, so a boy may call on her at home. It is common for Mexican males to make *piropos* (flattering personal comments) in passing to females, to which the females generally do not respond. Marriage customs follow Catholic traditions. Common-law marriage is also practiced and recognized.

Diet

Staple foods include corn, beans, rice, and chiles. They are combined with spices, vegetables, and meats or fish in the daily meals. Of course, different foods are eaten in different parts of the country, but some are common throughout the nation. For example, cornmeal or flour tortillas are eaten everywhere, either alone as bread or as part of a meal. Some common foods include *frijoles refritos* (refried beans), *torta* (hollow roll stuffed with meat or cheese), *quesadilla* (tortilla baked with cheese), *mole* (spicy sauce), *taco* (folded tortilla filled with meat, cheese, and onions), and many others. Two popular soups are *pozole* (vegetable soup with pork) and *birria* (goat soup). *Enchiladas* are tortillas with chicken inside, covered with a hot sauce. *Enfrijoladas* are chicken-filled tortillas covered with a bean sauce and cheese. Many names of Mexican food and Mexican restaurants are popular in the United States, but many Mexicans doubt the authenticity of U.S.-produced Mexican food.

Recreation

Fútbol (soccer) is the most popular sport in Mexico. Mexico's national soccer team competed in the 1994 World Cup. The sport that draws the next highest number of spectators is the bullfight. *Jai alai*, a fast-moving type of handball, is both a spectator and participation sport. Other participation sports include baseball, basketball, tennis, golf, and volleyball. Mexicans enjoy their own form of rodeo called *charreada*, which is often accompanied by a fair-like atmosphere. The people's love for music and dancing is evident in the many recreational activities that involve both. Daylong *fiestas* and weeklong festivals nearly always include a *mariachi* band or other type of musical group playing for dancing or just listening. Fireworks, feasts, and bullfights are also common festival activities. Watching television is a favorite leisure activity, especially in urban areas.

Holidays

As a predominantly Catholic nation, Mexico celebrates many Catholic holidays. Every village, town, and city has a patron saint, for which there is an annual celebration. Some of the main religious holidays include St. Anthony's Day (17 January), when children take their pets to church to be blessed by St. Anthony, the patron saint of animals; *Carnaval* Week, the week of parties and parades before Lent; Easter (Thursday–Sunday); Corpus Christi (May or June); Assumption (15 August); All Saints' Day (1 November); and All Souls' Day (2 November). The period from 31 October to 2 November is also called *Día de los Muertos* or Day of the Dead. Graves are swept, special altars are built to honor the newly dead, food or other items are placed on graves to accompany spirits on their journey to heaven, and families gather to celebrate life while they honor the dead. Festivities in some areas are quite lavish and include parades, markets, and concerts. Christmas celebrations begin as early as 16 December with nightly parties (*posadas*). The poinsettia flower originated in Mexico and is associated with the legend of a poor boy's gift to the Christ child. Many Mexicans attend a midnight mass on Christmas Eve.

National public holidays include New Year's Day, Birthday of Benito Juárez (21 March), Labor Day (1 May), *Cinco de Mayo* (5 May, which celebrates an 1867 victory over the French), Independence Day (16 September), Columbus Day (12 October), Revolution Day (20 November), and Day of the Virgin Guadalupe (12 December). This last holiday is not technically a public holiday because of its religious connections. But it is so popular that most offices and businesses honor it as a holiday. Guadalupe is the Catholic patron saint of Mexico.

Commerce

Businesses generally are open from 9:00 A.M. to 6:00 P.M., although many shops in smaller towns close between 2:00 and 4:00 P.M. for the midday meal. Street vendors and open-air markets are common and are often open to bargaining. Purchased items customarily are wrapped or placed in a bag before being carried in public. Government offices usually close by 2:30 P.M. In rural areas, weekly market days provide foods and other goods to the people.

SOCIETY

Government

Mexico's federal republic of 31 states operates under a central government that is led by a directly elected president. While states are technically autonomous, the central government controls things such as education, security, and national industries. A president may serve only one six-year term, and a legislator is not allowed to serve two consecutive terms. The legislature is composed of a 128-seat Senate and 500-seat Chamber of Deputies. The National Action Party (PAN) and Democratic Revolutionary Party (PRD) are just two of many opposition parties that hold legislative seats along with the PRI. Voting is compulsory (but not enforced) for all adults 18 and older.

Economy

Mexico is slowly recovering from its worst recession in more than 50 years. At the end of 1994, after a series of political shocks, high interest rates, and a sharp devaluation of the *peso* (40 percent), investor confidence weakened, foreign capital fled, and the economy plunged into a deep financial crisis. As the crisis continued through 1995, the economy shrank by 7 percent, inflation rose to 52 percent, and more than one million people lost their jobs. Restructuring and a U.S. loan package helped Mexico regain its footing, but people remain cautious about the future.

Boosted by growth in exports, the economy is expected to grow in 1996 and 1997. Export industries have enjoyed strong growth since 1993, when Mexico signed the North American Free Trade Agreement (NAFTA) with the United States and Canada. NAFTA lowered trade barriers between countries and led to a dramatic increase in the number of *maquiladoras* (border industries), where U.S. investment employs Mexican labor. The 1995 economic crisis highlighted the need for fiscal and other reforms. As foreign capital fled, it also alerted Mexicans to NAFTA's negative short-term impact.

Real gross domestic product per capita is $7,300, which has more than doubled in the last generation. Economic opportunities have improved, but poverty continues to affect several regions. Unemployment remains at more than 8 percent.

Mining and petroleum are the two most important industries, but they employ less than 2 percent of the labor force.

Tourism earns foreign exchange and provides employment for many people. In addition to oil, Mexico exports coffee, agricultural products, and engines. Agricultural pursuits employ about 26 percent of the labor force. Major crops include corn, cotton, wheat, coffee, sugarcane, sorghum, oilseed, and vegetables. The agricultural sector also produces rubber, cocoa, and chicle (used in making chewing gum). Unfortunately, Mexico is also a major supplier of marijuana. Efforts to stem the drug trade have been significant but very costly. The currency is the new Mexican *peso* (Mex$).

Transportation and Communication

Personal cars are common in urban areas, but most people use public transportation. Buses are plentiful and inexpensive. Mexico City has a fine subway system. There are numerous taxis, but many operate illegally. Mexico has an extensive system of roads, although many remain unpaved or semi-paved. There is a national railway system and a domestic airline. Buses also provide service between cities. Communications are well developed and modern, although many rural families do not have telephones in their homes. Numerous radio and television stations and several daily newspapers serve the public.

Education

Education is compulsory and free between ages six and fourteen. After six years of primary education, students enroll in either three years of secondary school, five years of college preparatory education, or a six-year teacher-training school. There are also numerous vocational schools to choose from. After secondary school, a student may enter one of the above tracks or may enroll in a professional school. A university education lasts from three to seven years. The National University of Mexico is prestigious, and only one-third of all applicants pass its entrance exams. Still, enrollment has increased rapidly in the last decade. The literacy rate is 88 percent.

Health

Medical facilities are good in large cities, but facilities are limited in rural areas. Sanitation is a problem in some regions. The infant mortality rate is 27 per 1,000, and life expectancy ranges from 70 to 77 years.

FOR THE TRAVELER

No visa is necessary for U.S. citizens staying up to three months, although proof of citizenship is required. Children traveling without their parents or with one parent must either have a passport or a notarized consent letter from the absent parent(s) to enter Mexico. No vaccinations are needed. For some locations, malarial suppressants may be advisable. Mexico's tourist industry is well developed and offers beaches, archaeological sites, grand colonial cities, and many other attractions. For information, contact the Mexican Government Tourist Office at the embassy address; phone (202) 728–1650. The Embassy of Mexico is located at 1911 Pennsylvania Avenue NW, Washington DC 20006; phone (202) 728–1600.

Printed on recycled paper

CULTURGRAM '97

Republic of Moldova

Boundary representations not necessarily authoritative.

BACKGROUND

Land and Climate

Moldova, the second smallest (after Armenia) former Soviet republic, covers 13,010 square miles (33,700 square kilometers) in southeastern Europe. The Prut River defines Moldova's border with Romania, and the Nistru (Dniester) River flows north to south in the east. Both rivers drain into the Black Sea. Moldova's hilly terrain, or rolling steppe, and rich black soil allow for 50 percent of the territory to support agriculture. There are few forests; ancient woodlands were plowed under for farming.

Moldova's climate is characterized by cold winters and warm summers. Average winter temperatures hover around freezing, while summers average between 70° and 80°F (21°–26°C). Humidity intensifies both cold and warm temperatures. The south is slightly warmer than the north. Rainfall is variable but can be heavy in the summer. Dry spells are not uncommon, and crop irrigation is necessary in some areas.

History

Known in centuries past as Basarabia, the main area now occupied by Moldova has had a long, troubled history of shifting borders and foreign domination. In 1359, it was incorporated into a principality called Moldavia. Basarabia became a tributary state to the Ottoman Empire in the 15th century. In 1792, Turkey ceded land on the Nistru River's east bank (now called Transniester) to Russia. Then, following the Russo-Turkish War (1806–12), Russia annexed Basarabia as well.

With the exception of small territorial shifts in 1859 and 1878, the region remained as is until Russia's Bolshevik Revolution in 1917. In March 1918, Basarabia's ethnic Romanian majority (between the Prut and Nistru Rivers) voted to unite with Romania, with which they shared cultural and historical (pre-Turkish) roots. The new Soviet government opposed such a union and established, in 1924, the Moldavian Autonomous Soviet Socialist Republic in Transniester.

In the course of World War II, the Soviets claimed and eventually fully annexed Basarabia to Moldavia, renaming the entire area the Moldavian Soviet Socialist Republic. By 1947, Moldavia was incorporated into the Soviet Empire but primarily served as an agricultural supplier to other Soviet republics. It remains a mostly agrarian nation.

Freedoms introduced by Soviet President Mikhail Gorbechev in the late 1980s allowed Moldavia to join other republics in a quest for independence. Elections in 1990 brought the Moldovan Popular Front to power, forcing out the Communists and leading to Moldavia's 1991 declaration of independence as the Republic of Moldova. The new country was immediately beset with ethnic divisions, economic chaos, and extremist political tendencies. The Popular Front, prior to independence, had severely alienated ethnic Russians in Transniester (and elsewhere) and ethnic Gagauzi in the south by introducing legislation to effectively marginalize minorities in the new state. The two minorities declared their independence. In Transniester (called Dnestr by ethnic Russians), where the elite Russian 14th Army under General Alexander Lebed had been and is still based, the situation erupted into open civil war in 1992. Russian troops participated and then helped establish a cease-fire. The Popular Front and political parties polarized and factionalized. The result was parliamentary gridlock. A 1993 vote disbanded Parliament.

In February 1994, a new, smaller parliament was elected. Several parties posted candidates, but those (such as Popular Front) strongly advocating unification with Romania or suppression of ethnic minorities were defeated in favor of more moderate groups (primarily the Agrarian and Socialist Parties). The new parliament quickly ratified a new constitution that guarantees minorities their rights and worked to implement further political, constitutional, and economic reforms. The government signed an agreement with Russia over the eventual (1997) withdrawal of its troops from Transniester. Moldova's moderate leaders extended greater autonomy to both separatist regions while maintaining Moldovan sovereignty. A "republic-within-Moldova" status was accepted in 1996 by Transniester leaders and Russia. However, Russian politics, General Lebed's new power in Russia, and pro-Russian, pro-Communist sentiment among Transniester's 750,000 residents may complicate troop withdrawal and lasting peace.

PEOPLE

Population

Moldova's population of 4.5 million is growing at 0.36 percent annually. Roughly 64 percent of the people are ethnic Moldovans (of Romanian descent). Ukrainians (13.5 percent) and Russians (13) are the largest minorities. They tend to live in cities and in Transniester. The Gagauzi (3.5 percent), a Turkic people originally from Bulgaria, are found in southern Moldova and inhabit no other country. Moldova is also home to some ethnic Bulgarians (2 percent) and smaller groups. The capital of Chisinau is home to more than 650,000 people. Tiraspol (186,000 residents), Balti (164,000), and Tighina (141,000) are the next largest cities.

Moldova's Human Development Index (0.757) ranks it 81st out of 174 nations. People are well educated, and with long-term political stability and further economic expansion, they will have increasing access to resources that allow for personal development.

Language

During the Soviet era, Russian was the official state language and Romanian, the language of ethnic Moldovans, had to be written in the Cyrillic alphabet. In 1990, Romanian was declared the sole official language and efforts were implemented to help schools, businesses, and government agencies shift to using Romanian and the Latin alphabet. The transition is necessarily slow and costly, and Russian is still heavily used in urban areas, especially among minorities.

By law, non-Romanian speakers have six years to learn Romanian as a condition of their continued employment. Flexibility exists if the six-year target proves impossible to reach. Ethnic minorities may continue to speak their own languages. Russians and Ukrainians speak Russian, while the Gagauzi speak Gagauz, a Turkic dialect. Bulgarians speak Bulgarian. These latter two minorities also generally speak Russian.

Religion

Most people in Moldova are Eastern Orthodox Christians. There is a small Jewish (1.5 percent) population, and a few other Christian churches have members. The practice of religion was repressed during the Soviet era, but people are now rebuilding their churches, attending services, and celebrating religious holidays. Religious devotion is rising, and religion is expected to play a greater role in the society's future.

General Attitudes

Moldovans value strong personal relationships with friends and relatives. Educated persons are respected above others, including the wealthy, as education generally is not associated with wealth. Material possessions are increasingly desired, which has given rise to greater corruption but has also encouraged private enterprise. Moldovans appreciate their agricultural heritage and tend to be politically and socially conservative. They are cautious toward people they do not know but warm and trusting with good friends. Moldovans tend to be pessimistic about their individual circumstances; even if they are inwardly optimistic about something, they more readily express any doubts before hopes.

As with many newly created countries, Moldova's hardships and social upheaval have confused attitudes toward society's goals. Those who initially favored unification with Romania were disappointed by the feeling in Romania that Moldovans had lost their "Romanian-ness" and were not culturally equal. Others have been disappointed by the economic hardships of the transition and have expressed fondness for the Soviet era. But most of these attitudes are as transitional as the political and economic situation; they will change and improve as the country does.

Personal Appearance

Moldovans wear the best clothing they have whenever in public. Women wear dresses or skirts and high heels. Young women prefer flashy outfits, jewelry, and considerable makeup. Urban youth favor jeans and T-shirts. Urban professional men wear suits with ties. Men otherwise wear sweatsuits and tennis shoes; jewelry indicates their social status. Older rural women (*batrana*) wear scarves on their heads, a practice that originally denoted one's marital status (unmarried girls did not wear scarves). Men often wear fur hats in colder weather.

CUSTOMS AND COURTESIES

Greetings

Urban Moldovans generally shake hands when they greet, although a man waits for a woman to extend her hand first. In mixed company, a man shakes a woman's hand before another man's. Good friends and relatives often hug as well. Rural Moldovan men, and increasingly urban ethnic Moldovan men, greet a woman by kissing her on the hand and saying *Sarut mina* (I kiss your hand). Other verbal greetings include *Buna Ziua* (Good day), *Ce mai facetz* (How do you do?), *Noroc* (Cheers, meaning "Hi"), and the Russian *Privet* (Hi) or *Zdravstrvuite* (Hello).

When addressing others, young people generally use first names. Adults use titles (*Domnul* for "Mr.," *Doamna* for "Mrs.," *Dominsoara* for "Miss") with the family name for all but close friends and relatives. Some adults introduce themselves by first name and patronymic (e.g., Ion Petru), often preceded by the family name (e.g., Chorbu Ion Petru). A patronymic is formed by the possessive of the father's first name. Use of this Russian custom is decreasing. Urban people do not greet people they do not know and rarely even smile (as a greeting) at strangers on the street. Rural people are more likely to greet strangers. A young woman is called a "girl," since the term "woman" is considered an insult that implies the person is old or married.

Gestures

Moldovans generally do not point with the index finger; they prefer using the open hand. They consider it impolite to put feet on furniture, cross legs in front of elders, or chew gum while speaking. Eating while walking in public is rude unless one is eating ice cream or *pirozhki* (a stuffed pastry). Society generally frowns on public displays of affection. Moldovan men usually remove their hats when entering a building or home. It is rude for men not to open doors for women or to neglect other such chivalrous acts.

Visiting

Most socializing takes place at home. Visitors remove their shoes at the door before entering. On special occasions, guests are treated to large meals. Otherwise, people sit in the kitchen or living room to chat for hours. Hosts generally provide guests with something to drink (coffee, tea, wine, cognac, etc.). Vodka is popular among ethnic Russians. Close friends and family feel comfortable visiting without prior arrangement, but a telephone call among those with phones is usually appreciated. If visitors plan to stay only a few minutes, they indicate this upon arrival so as not to make the hosts feel their quick departure indicates they did not like something.

Guests often take small gifts, such as flowers or wine. It is impolite not to take at least flowers to people on special occasions or holidays. Hosts, especially in rural areas, usually reciprocate with a small gift (cake "for the next morning" or wine). Foreign visitors, especially U.S. Americans, are considered honored guests and are treated to the family's best.

Eating

The urban breakfast is usually light, consisting of open sandwiches with sausage or cheese, coffee or tea, and fruit preserves. Rural people often eat more substantial meals of *kasha* (hot porridge), potatoes, bread, and sheep cheese. Indeed, breakfast can be the main meal, as the rest of the day is spent farming. Lunch and dinner are light. On weekends, however, lunch is the main meal. The urban lunch is generally the main meal, consisting of soup, salad, and an entrée. For dinner, people eat only an entrée, though it is not necessarily light. Children at elementary schools usually have an afternoon "tea" (juice and a sweet roll). Coffee and juice are common beverages among urban people, while rural people drink wine, tea, juice, milk, or stewed fruit. Ice is almost never served with drinks, as cold drinks are considered unhealthy.

Food is prepared by a woman; it is considered embarrassing for a man to admit he cooks. Serving dishes, from which each person takes his or her portion, are placed in the middle of the table. Urban Moldovans eat with the fork in the left hand and the knife in the right. They keep the hands and forearms above the table throughout the meal. Hosts offer guests additional helpings at least three or four times. Initially declined, they should then be accepted. One is expected to eat everything on the plate; the presence of leftovers is considered a sign that guests did not like the food.

Moldovans rarely eat at restaurants, which are too expensive, except during vacations and for business functions. Families go out for ice cream, coffee, or dessert. When one does eat out, the host expects to pay the bill; tips are not given.

LIFESTYLE

Family

Moldovans value their families. They often marry early in life because of their rural lifestyle, in part, and because young people desire to be treated as adults. Urban families usually have only one or two children, while rural families may have three or more. Children remain close to their parents throughout life. Young urban couples often have difficulty finding housing, so they usually move in with the bride's parents. Hence, many families have two or three generations living in a small one- or two-bedroom apartment. Rural extended families share a larger home, but they often lack modern conveniences (such as running water). Gender roles are clearly defined, especially in the countryside. Men lead the family, work the fields and raise livestock, or have a wage-earning job. Women are responsible for all household chores and child care, as well as farm work, if applicable. A successful career is less important for a woman than being a good cook and housekeeper, but more women are also becoming merchants, selling at outdoor markets goods they produce or buy in Romania and other countries.

Dating and Marriage

Young people date with the goal of getting married. They go to movies or for walks in the park, watch videos, and dance at large holiday or birthday parties. Couples marry at a Wedding Palace, the Soviet-era office where the only legal weddings could be held. Today, many get married in a church first and then go to the Wedding Palace for the civil ceremony. Fall is the most popular time for a wedding because it is the season of new wine. After the ceremony, the bride takes off her veil and puts on a scarf to indicate she is now a wife and a mature woman. The veil is given to the maid of honor, who is expected to marry next. Wedding guests usually stay through the morning and sometimes for an entire weekend. Divorce is common, but second marriages are not. Women with children find it especially hard to remarry.

Diet

Romanian, Russian, Ukrainian, and Bulgarian cuisine are all part of the Moldovan diet. The most common soup eaten at lunch is Ukrainian *borscht* (made of tomato juice and beets). Meat, bread, potatoes, and vegetables are staples for the main meal. Bread is served with most meals; wine is served with lunch and dinner. Traditional Moldovan dishes include *mamaliga* (cornmeal mush that resembles pudding) with *brinza* (sheep cheese), *mititei* (grilled meat sausages), fried onions with sour cream, and *placinte* (flaky stuffed pastry). Garlic, onions, and herbs are used in cooking many foods. Fruits (apples, grapes, plums, cherries, strawberries, watermelon) are eaten in season. Typical vegetables are eggplant, peppers, cabbage, potatoes, and tomatoes. As fresh produce is expensive for urban dwellers, many families have gardens on the outskirts of town. All meats are popular but expensive; chicken and pork are most affordable.

Recreation

In their leisure time, Moldovans visit, go to movies, or read. Soccer is the most popular sport, followed by chess. Some enjoy basketball. A small number of urban adults jog or exercise. Public exercise and swimming facilities are available but need repair. Moldovans love music and art. They particularly enjoy concerts. A number of ensembles perform folk music on a professional level. Folk music is especially popular at national festivals. Common instruments include the violin, flute, accordion, and cembalo.

Holidays

New Year's Day is a favorite day for decorating trees and for children to go to parties with *Mos Craciun* (Santa Claus) and *Alba-ca-Zapada* (his granddaughter, Snow White). Adults enjoy New Year's Eve parties with family and friends. Christmas (7 January) is only now being revived after a ban under the Soviets. People are rediscovering a rich tradition of caroling, folklore, trees, ornaments, and gifts. Some of the nonreligious aspects of Christmas had been transferred to New Year's by the Soviets, and that date remains the biggest holiday of the year. For non-Orthodox Christians, Christmas is 25 December and 7 January is St. John's Day. Easter (Saturday–Monday) is the most important religious holiday. An all-night ceremony ends with a dawn feast on Easter morning, followed later by visits and other celebrations.

National holidays include International Women's Day (8 March), Independence Day (27 August), and *Limba Noastra* (31 August, to celebrate the proclamation of Romanian as the official language). For *Hram*, each village and city celebrates its birth or the birth of its patron saint. People visit from house to house and eat; community activities include wrestling, concerts, and dancing.

Commerce

Offices typically open at 8:00 or 9:00 A.M., close for a lunch hour around 1:00 P.M., and reopen until 5:00 or 6:00 P.M. Grocery stores have a slightly longer lunch break and stay open until 8:00 P.M. Only grocery stores, restaurants, cafés, and farmers' markets are open on Sunday. Prices at most stores are set, as are open-market and street prices. Serious business cannot be conducted between strangers. Personal contacts are necessary, and major transactions are preceded by social interaction.

SOCIETY

Government

The Republic of Moldova has a president (Mircea Snegur) as head of state and a prime minister (Andrei Sangheli) as head of government. The 104-member Parliament is directly elected; the voting age is 18. Citizenship is granted to ethnic Moldovans and others who meet certain residency and ancestry requirements. The next national elections are in 1999.

Economy

Moldova's economy is based on its fertile land; agriculture employs more than one-third of the workforce. A significant number of people are also involved in food processing and related industries. Chief products include fruits and vegetables, wine, sugar beets, grains, sunflower seeds, tobacco, and dairy items. Most exports go to neighboring countries. Moldova also exports small appliances, textiles, leather goods, and tools. The government is encouraging tourism, which is still in its infant state. Fuel and energy are imported, as are some consumer items. The national currency is the *leu* (plural, *lei*).

To achieve create a capitalist economic system, the government is carefully privatizing firms, transferring ownership of state farms to peasant joint-stock associations, and reforming investment and other market-related laws. Most programs have the support of international lenders such as the World Bank. Thousands of state enterprises are being or will be sold to private investors. Real gross domestic product per capita is estimated at $3,670. While life is still difficult for many, high inflation is coming under control and more jobs are being created in the private sector. Still, it will take time before the benefits of an open market reach the average person, especially in rural areas.

Transportation and Communication

Urban dwellers benefit from an extensive and inexpensive public transport system of buses, trolleys, and minivans. Taxis are uncommon, expensive, and unregulated. Commuter buses and trains travel between cities. In rural villages, people may use horse-drawn carts (*karutsa*). Some Moldovans own cars, but most cannot afford them. Fuel and spare parts are expensive for those who drive.

Many people do not have phones, but post offices have public phones. An urban home is more likely to have a telephone than a rural one. Moldovans enjoy reading daily newspapers, and the free press is growing and changing rapidly. Television and radio facilities are state-owned.

Education

Moldova's basic education system consists of primary, secondary, and high schools. Children begin attending at age six or seven and finish high school eleven years later. An additional year of gymnasium is optional at the high school level. Students who do not go to or complete high school may attend vocational school to learn a trade. Even in high school, students may learn one of several trades by going to a professional education center one day a week. Successful students receive a professional license in the given trade upon graduation from high school. Students often gain hands-on experience in their chosen trade during summer vacations. Moldovans value higher education, and many compete for the limited number of available university spots. An increasing number are studying abroad. The adult literacy rate is 96 percent.

Health

Moldova's health-care system lacks modern facilities, skilled staff, and supplies. Preventive and maternal care are especially lacking. This contributes to a high infant mortality rate of 30 per 1,000 and a relatively low life expectancy rate of 65 to 71 years.

FOR THE TRAVELER

U.S. citizens need a visa and passport to enter Moldova. No vaccinations are required. Travelers should carry a first-aid kit, personal toiletries, tissues, and a full supply of film. Travel to Moldova is more of an educational experience than a vacation, but there is much to experience in the small country. For information, contact the Moldovan Chancery, 1511 K Street NW, Room 329, Washington, DC 20005; phone (202) 783–3012. You may also wish to contact Moldova's Permanent Mission to the United Nations, 573–577 Third Avenue, New York, NY 10016.

Montserrat

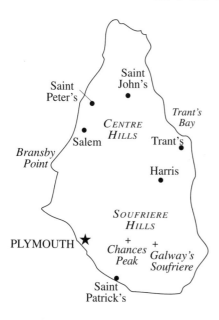

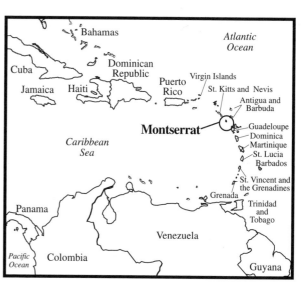

Boundary representations not necessarily authoritative.

THE AMERICAS

BACKGROUND

Land and Climate

Montserrat is located in the Caribbean Sea about 250 miles (400 kilometers) southeast of Puerto Rico. Part of the British West Indies, it is considered one of the Leeward Islands of the Lesser Antilles. Montserrat is known as the Emerald Isle and has a land area of only 39 square miles (101 square kilometers), or about half the size of Washington, D.C. The island is volcanic in origin and several fumaroles still emit sulfur fumes, steam, and boiling water. Chances Peak is the highest mountain at 3,000 feet (914 meters). Natural vegetation is confined mostly to the summits of the Soufriere Hills (in the south) and the Centre Hills. Sheltered bays are few and all beaches but one have black volcanic sand.

The climate is tropical, with temperatures ranging from 76°F to 86°F (24–30°C) year-round. Abundant rainfall keeps the island green, and the sea breeze is constant. The wettest months are September, October, and November, with the dry season lasting between March and June. The hurricane season usually occurs between June and November. In 1989, Hurricane Hugo devastated the island, but the international community helped rebuild it.

In July 1995, a long-dormant volcano on Chances Peak began rumbling and spewing ash. The southern half of the island, including Plymouth, the capital, was ordered evacuated for the third time in less than one year (April 1996).

Many residents have relocated in the north, while others have temporarily left the island. As mild eruptions continue, it is uncertain when normal activity on the island will resume.

History

The pre-Columbian name of Montserrat was *Alliouagana* (land of the prickly bush); it was named by the Carib Indians who overtook the Arawaks long before the coming of Europeans. Christopher Columbus named Montserrat in 1493 after a monastery near Seville, Spain. The Spanish, however, did not settle the island. In 1632, Thomas Warner from neighboring Saint Kitts came to settle Montserrat with English and Irish Catholics. These colonists were uncomfortable in Protestant St. Kitts, and soon Montserrat was established as an Irish-Catholic colony. Montserrat developed into a sugar and slave colony in the 17th century. With sugar and slavery firmly established, overbearing rich planters emerged. As the slave population grew, so did fear, repression, and rebellion, which culminated in the slave uprising on St. Patrick's Day in 1768. All of the leaders of the uprising were executed, and the rebellion failed.

In the 17th and 18th centuries, France and Britain fought for dominance over the sugar islands of the Caribbean. Montserrat changed hands several times, being occupied briefly by France in 1667 and 1782 before finally coming into permanent English possession after British Admiral Rodney's victory at Les Saints, near the French island of

Guadeloupe. The Treaty of Versailles in 1783 made Montserrat permanently British. It remains a dependent territory of the United Kingdom.

The sugar industry peaked in about 1791. In 1834, Britain's Parliament abolished slavery in the Caribbean and the slaves were freed. Many properties became burdened with debt and were sold. Former estates were cultivated by sharecroppers and black laborers. The cultivation of limes and cotton replaced the sugar industry when it collapsed. Montserrat lime juice was particularly in demand by the British Navy for combating scurvy, and the juice is said to have been the source of the nickname *Limey* used for the British.

After the decline of cotton and limes in the 20th century, many Montserratians emigrated. Some went to work on the Panama Canal, others went to Cuba, the Dominican Republic, the United States, and the United Kingdom in search of work. Those employed sent money home to relatives. When these remittances declined, the island turned to real estate and construction. Many U.S. American, Canadian, and British citizens now own plush winter homes and villas in Montserrat.

THE PEOPLE

Population

Montserrat has an estimated population of 12,700. The figure was as high as 14,000, but emigration and smaller families have led to the decline. The population grows by only 0.3 percent each year. Between 1959 and 1962, nearly one-third of the population emigrated to England; since then, another one-fifth has gone to North America. The greatest concentration of people live in the capital of Plymouth. The majority of Montserratians are of African descent, with an infusion of North American, European, and East Indian residents in recent years.

Language

The official language is English, but most people speak a West Indian dialect. The dialect is a form of English mixed with elements of Irish brogue and various African tongues. People commonly employ idiomatic expressions taken from this dialect. This is referred to as *speaking Montserratian*, or *speaking dialect*. Some people consider using the dialect as improper, but most enjoy the way it makes speech more colorful and even poetic.

Religion

Montserratians are religious, with Anglican, Methodist, and Roman Catholic being the main Christian denominations. Seventh-Day Adventists, Pentecostals, and other Christian churches are assuming an increasing importance.

Religion affects many aspects of daily life. Public schools have prayer and gospel singing every day before classes begin. Most public functions are opened and sometimes closed with prayer. Adults participate in many gospel choirs and concerts. People are genuine about their religious devotion. This is manifest by the dignity and respect with which Montserratians treat each other and strangers.

General Attitudes

Montserratians take great pride in their country and (recently) in their African roots. Friendliness, forthrightness, and honesty are viewed as proud assets of the island. Interactions are easy and amiable and most people display politeness, courtesy, and respect to all. The general attitude is one of tolerance and "live and let live." People take time to talk to each other, and the concept of time is not as literal as in industrialized countries. An event will sometimes go on much later than advertised. Similarly, being late is not a problem, as people are more important than schedules. Montserratians are observant of people and things; very little goes unnoticed when they watch a passersby, a group, a scene, or an activity.

Personal Appearance

Montserratians dress up in their finest clothes for church or any other important social function. Women wear dresses or dressy skirts and blouses to work, along with sandals. Men wear sport shirts or a shirt-jacket (square-cut, cotton shirt that is worn like a jacket), slacks, and shoes. Most men do not wear ties due to the climate. Jeans and tight-fitting clothing are also too hot for most people. Loose-fitting clothes made of lightweight fabric are most comfortable and popular. Older, rural women rarely wear pants, but younger and urban women do. All public schools require students to wear uniforms; each school has its own color for boys and girls. Teachers stress neatness and cleanliness.

CUSTOMS AND COURTESIES

Greetings

Montserratian greetings include the more polite *Good morning*, *Good day*, *Good evening*, and *Good night* (after dark), as well as the casual *You alright?*, which means "How are you?" The response is *Okay*. When parting, people might say *Good-bye* or *All the best*.

People often shake hands or touch when greeting. The youth sometimes touch clenched fists after a traditional handshake to show solidarity. When addressing friends and relatives, Montserratians use colorful nicknames that are usually acquired in childhood. Some nicknames may also be acquired in adulthood as a result of one's occupation or something else, but these do not stick to the person throughout life as the childhood name does. Acquaintances might also use one's nickname instead of one's given name, but formal situations call for the use of given names and titles. An older person or superior at work might be called *Mas* (for men) or *Miss* (for women), but most people use *Mr.*, *Mrs.*, or *Miss*.

Gestures

Montserratians are affectionate and loving. They commonly touch each other's hands, arms, or shoulders while talking. Hand gestures might be used to complement verbal expressions, especially between friends. People often use a quick "pssst" or hissing sound to get one's attention while walking by or when in a crowd.

Visiting

Montserratians are friendly with their neighbors and often stop by to see how they are doing or to *talk up* the latest island news. When neighbors visit, they might bring homemade gifts such as banana bread or guava juice. People often have house parties for birthdays, anniversaries, graduations, or other special occasions.

When Montserratians get together, the atmosphere is amiable, courteous, and relaxed. Invited guests are usually offered at least something to drink (soft drinks, juice, etc.).

The most popular form of socializing for men takes place at the local rum shop, a small neighborhood tavern. Friends and neighbors socialize, watch television, listen to music, or eat chicken or bread. Women more commonly socialize in the home or in connection with their children's activities.

Eating

Lunch and dinner are the main meals, as breakfast is usually light. Many Montserratians in Plymouth eat lunch at restaurants. They might have fried chicken and chips, a hamburger, or *peleau* (rice, beans, and chicken). Bread and cheese are eaten for a quick meal. Families usually eat dinner together at home. Barbecues are popular for community or family gatherings.

LIFESTYLE

Family

The extended family is the primary social unit in Montserrat. Grandparents often live with their children's families and help raise the grandchildren. Siblings usually have the same mother, but they may have different fathers. Women generally hold the family together. They care for the household and also usually work outside the home (in schools, stores, hotels, and restaurants). Men support their families and help raise children with a firm but loving hand. Discipline is stressed and children are well behaved.

Dating and Marriage

Dating begins in secondary school and centers on social or school functions. Young couples enjoy going to basketball games, cricket matches, or concerts. When churches have *fetes*, young people enjoy getting together for the games, music, food, and fun. The few nightclubs and discos are popular on weekends.

Couples marry in their twenties or thirties and begin to raise a family. Churches stress formal marriage, but common-law unions are not unusual. There are many single mothers, but they generally receive support from the fathers of their children.

Weddings are traditionally held in a church, and a reception follows the ceremony. At the reception, the bride and groom and their parents will give testimonials in tribute to each other's families while toasting with champagne. Musical entertainment follows, and guests enjoy plenty of food.

Diet

Local and imported chicken, rice, white potatoes, and breadfruit are the main staples of the diet. Meats and fish are popular, but chicken is by far the most consumed protein food. Bread is also important, and many small bakeries operate on the island.

Foods imported from Miami via Puerto Rico are expensive, and the island is trying to become more self-sufficient. The production of meats and vegetables to replace imports is actively encouraged. Locally grown produce includes potatoes, tomatoes, mangoes, papayas, and yams. Popular dishes include *goat water* (stewed mutton), *mountain chicken*

(actually frog), *saltfish* (usually dried cod), and dumplings. Meals often include soft drinks, homemade fruit juices, or beer. Coffee, tea, lemonade, and iced tea are also popular drinks for mealtime and at other times.

Recreation

Cultural activities such as school arts festivals, folklore and gospel choir concerts, and local plays and shows all have community support and participation. Calypso, *soca*, reggae, gospel, folk, steel pan, and *dub* (disc jockeys rapping street poems) are the favorite types of music. They are often part of social activities. On weekends, many people get together at dance clubs or *street blockoramas* (open-air parties) to enjoy music with friends. *Jumpups* (block parties that involve street dancing) are popular during the Christmas festival or on other special occasions.

The national sport of Montserrat and the West Indies is cricket. During a "test match," schools and businesses often close for a half day so people can go to Sturge Park (the main stadium) to watch Montserratian athletes compete. Basketball, *netball* (for girls), football (soccer), tennis, swimming, biking, boating, jogging, and hiking are increasingly popular.

Some Montserratians travel in July and August when school is out. The festival season in December is anticipated and planned in detail months in advance. This is generally the happiest and most popular time of year for people.

Holidays

Christmas and Easter are the most important holidays on Montserrat. Traditional Christmas practices (giving gifts, singing carols, and attending church) are combined with other celebrations. In Plymouth, many people celebrate Christmas Eve with a large block party. The Montserrat Festival, a Caribbean carnival, is held every December during the Christmas season. Cultural shows, calypso competitions, dancing, and parades are all part of the celebrations. Many Montserratians who live overseas return every year for the festival, which culminates in the Festival Day Parade on New Year's Day. Easter is also a time for family gatherings and church services.

St. Patrick's Day (17 March) is celebrated as a national holiday in memory of the 1768 slave uprising. The holiday serves to raise awareness of Montserrat's turbulent history and honor Irish influence on the island. Other important holidays include Emancipation Day (1 August, but celebrated on the first Monday in August), Whitmonday, Labor Day (1 May, but celebrated on the first Monday in May), and Queen Elizabeth II's Birthday (second Saturday in June).

Commerce

Normal business hours are from 8:00 A.M. to 4:00 P.M., with an hour taken for lunch. Businesses close at noon on Wednesdays and Saturdays. With the exception of convenience stores and gas stations, most businesses are closed on Sunday. An open-air market in Plymouth is open every day, but the variety and quantity of food is largest on Friday and Saturday. Fresh produce and meats are the market's main features.

SOCIETY

Government

Montserrat, as a territory of the United Kingdom, recognizes Queen Elizabeth II as head of state. According to the 1960 constitution, the island has a crown-appointed governor who maintains responsibility for defense, external affairs, internal security, administration of public services, and the judicial system. The governor, currently Frank Savage, has an Executive Council that includes a chief minister and five other members. Reuben T. Meade was elected chief minister in 1991 for a five-year term. The Legislative Council has eleven members, seven of whom are elected. It is presided over by a speaker (currently Howard Fergus), who is elected by the council from outside its membership. The next general elections for the Legislative Council were set for October 1996; the voting age is 18. Montserrat has three parishes (Saint Anthony, Saint George, and Saint Peter). The legal system is based on English common law, and the highest judicial authority is the East Caribbean Supreme Court.

Economy

Montserrat's economy is based on tourism, construction, real estate, agriculture, and some light industry (mostly assembly). Incentives, promotions, radio shows, and an agricultural fair are being used to encourage agricultural self-sufficiency. The island can support a variety of animals and crops. Cattle, chicken, local fruits and vegetables, and sea-island cotton are a few of the products being produced.

Tourism and construction of holiday villas and condominiums provide jobs and bring visitors and revenue to the island. As the island's leading industry, tourism accounts for about 30 percent of the gross domestic product. A deep-water port in Plymouth that accomodates cruise ships brings additional tourist business. Small factories assemble electronic components and manufacture plastic bags. A number of offshore banks are in business, but they are regulated by the government to ensure they remain reputable.

Montserratians generally enjoy a decent standard of living. The country has low unemployment, steady economic growth, and a gross domestic product per capita of about $5,800. Montserrat is a member of the Caribbean Community (CARICOM) and other regional bodies that are important to the economy. The stable East Caribbean dollar (EC$) is the currency.

Transportation and Communication

Villages are linked to each other and to Plymouth by paved roads on the western side of the island. Private cars and trucks account for a large portion of traffic. Public minivans travel between villages and Plymouth. Taxis are available in Plymouth. Children walk to schools located near their village or town, and a few older men ride donkeys for their transport.

There is no ferryboat service between islands in this part of the Caribbean, so many Montserratians travel off island by air. All regional business, government, and pleasure travel is by small plane. The government plans to realign the airport runway to accommodate small jets.

Telephone and telecommunication services are available islandwide. Radio Montserrat is government owned, and GEM Radio Caribbean broadcasts from Plymouth. Cable television was introduced during the rebuilding of Montserrat after Hurricane Hugo. All major channels are available and most homes have televisions. There are two newspapers.

Education

The education system reflects a strong British influence. Free primary and secondary education is provided for all school-aged children. There are a number of public and private preprimary schools; children can attend these beginning at age three. Pupils usually attend school for 13 years and most complete secondary school. School-leaving (graduation) exams are set by London and Cambridge syndicates, and the Caribbean Examinations Council is the examining board. The literacy rate is 97 percent.

When students graduate, some go on to Montserrat's Technical College, the University of the West Indies, or overseas colleges. Others begin to work; a small number of pupils drop out before graduation to begin working. An offshore medical school (American University of the Caribbean) is located in Montserrat, but it caters to students from abroad and does not supply doctors to Montserrat.

Health

Montserrat is a healthy island with an abundance of clean drinking water. Glendon Hospital in Plymouth provides surgical, medical, obstetric, and dental services. For special treatment or certain emergencies, patients are flown to Barbados or Jamaica. Twelve district health centers provide care and health education. Free care is provided to children and the elderly. Working adults have health insurance to cover their medical costs. A number of private doctors are in practice, and ear and eye specialists from other countries visit at times to provide care. The infant mortality rate is 12 per 1,000; life expectancy ranges from 74 to 78 years.

FOR THE TRAVELER

U.S. citizens require proof of identification (a passport is the best form, but a birth certificate and driver's license is acceptable) and a return ticket to enter Montserrat. Vaccinations are not required. A departure tax of $10 is charged at Blackburne Airport. Montserrat has a number of small hotels and other accommodations for the traveler. Visitors will enjoy a museum in a restored sugar mill, Galway's Plantation ruins, Trant's Estate (sight of an Amerindian village), and other ruins. Beaches, bays, fumaroles, and Galway's Soufriere (a volcano) are also interesting. For more information, contact the Montserrat Tourist Board, PO Box 7, Plymouth, Montserrat, British West Indies; phone (809) 491–2230; or the Montserrat Tourist Information Office, 1208 Washington Drive, Centerport, NY 11721; phone (516) 351–4922.

CULTURGRAM ™ '97

Kingdom of the
Netherlands

Boundary representations not necessarily authoritative.

BACKGROUND

Land and Climate

The Netherlands is about the size of Massachusetts and Connecticut combined. It covers 14,413 square miles (37,330 square kilometers). Areas in the west that have been reclaimed from the sea are called *polders*. In the past, windmills pumped water from the land and dikes held back the ocean. Today, modern machines do the pumping, but about 930 windmills (out of an original 10,000) still dot the landscape. Close to 300 continue to function, mostly for tourists, but some mill grains or perform other work. In the east, the land is above sea level and even has a few hills. Grasslands used for grazing are common in the north, while the south has a more varied landscape. The climate is temperate. Rain is common throughout the year. Excessive winter rain in 1995 caused substantial damage to many towns near rivers. The Rhine and other rivers flooded wide areas and prompted the largest peacetime evacuation in the country's history. Winters can be cold, but some are quite mild. Likewise, summers can be warm and sometimes cool.

History

Although its official name is the Kingdom of the Netherlands, Holland is the name by which most U.S. Americans know the country. However, its use is not appreciated by the Dutch who do not live in either North or South Holland provinces. In medieval times, the entire area was a group of autonomous duchies and counties. They were known as the Low Countries in the 1500s, along with Belgium and Luxembourg. During this time, the countries were ruled by a Spanish monarch. In 1568, Prince William of Orange rebelled against the Spanish crown and began an 80-year war for independence. In 1648, with the Peace of Westphalia, the Netherlands became independent. In the years following, it built a vast overseas empire, becoming for a time the world's leading maritime and commercial power. In 1795, French forces made the Netherlands a vassal state, and Napoleon completely annexed the territory in 1810. The Congress of Vienna ended French occupation, and the United Kingdom of the Netherlands was created in 1815. It originally included Belgium, which seceded in 1830.

The Netherlands remained neutral during World War I but was invaded by Germany in World War II. After World War II, the Netherlands played an important role in European economic development. Most overseas holdings were granted independence after World War II, including Indonesia and Suriname. In 1980, Queen Juliana abdicated in favor of her daughter, Queen Beatrix, who is head of state today. The heir to the throne is her son, Crown Prince Willem Alexander. If he ascends to the throne, he will be the first male monarch since 1890. The United States and the Netherlands have enjoyed unbroken diplomatic relations since 1782.

THE PEOPLE

Population

The Netherlands has a population of slightly more than 15.4 million, which is growing annually at 0.5 percent. More than 40 percent of the population lives in the two western provinces of *Noord* (North) Holland and *Zuid* (South) Holland. These two provinces, from which the Netherlands received

EUROPE

its nickname, "Holland," contain the three largest cities of the country: Amsterdam, Rotterdam, and The Hague. The population is 95 percent ethnic Dutch, although there are some Indonesians (50,000) and Surinamese (210,000). Turkish and Moroccan guest workers and their families or descendents number more than 250,000.

Also included in the Kingdom of the Netherlands are the Caribbean islands of Aruba (population 62,500) and the Netherlands Antilles (183,000). These islands have unique cultural aspects and, therefore, are not discussed in this *Culturgram*. The country's Human Development Index (0.923) ranks it fourth out of 174 countries. Excellent access to health care, education, and a decent standard of living affords the Dutch opportunity and choice in their lives. Adjusted for women, the index (0.851) ranks the Netherlands 20th out of 130 countries, reflecting a lower earned income among women compared to other European nations.

Language

The official language is Dutch, a Germanic language. Frisian is also spoken in the northeastern province of Friesland. English, German, and French are commonly understood and spoken and are taught in the secondary schools. Flemish, a form of Dutch, is spoken in a region of Belgium called Flanders.

Religion

About 36 percent of the people are Roman Catholic. Most Catholics live in the southern provinces of Brabant and Limburg. Another 27 percent are Protestant (mostly Dutch Reformed), 6 percent belong to other churches, and the rest are not officially affiliated with any religion. The royal family belongs to the Dutch Reformed Church. The Netherlands, like many European countries, is a secular society, in which the role of religion has diminished steadily for some time. There is a strong tradition of maintaining church and state separate.

General Attitudes

There is a noticeable difference in attitudes among those who live north of the Rhine Delta, a traditionally Protestant (Calvinist) region, and those who live in the traditionally Catholic south. By reputation, people in the south are more gregarious.

As a small, trade-dependent nation, the Netherlands has throughout history recognized the importance of being internationally minded. It has a strong tradition of involvement in international affairs, primarily European since World War II. It is active in the United Nations. Dutch attitudes about society helped them create one of the most extensive welfare systems in the world, which remains a high priority in the country despite the increasing difficulty of supporting it.

Dutch openness to the world has made the people no less proud of their own culture and heritage, whether it be in the arts, politics, technology, or a strong tradition of liberalism. Through hard work and engineering skill, the Dutch took much of their territory from the sea by pumping water from land that is below sea level and building dikes to keep the water back. Because of this feat and their pioneering spirit, the Dutch have a saying: "God made the earth, but the Dutch made Holland." However, these diligent efforts eventually led to sinking land, water pollution, and problems with the water table. So the government is buying thousands of acres of agricultural land in the reclaimed territory and returning it to

nature. Some dikes are being destroyed, and marshes and wetlands are gradually being allowed to return to their original state.

Personal Appearance

European fashions are popular. The Dutch enjoy stylish casual attire, as long as it is neat and clean. Traditional attire is rarely worn. The Dutch are famous for the wooden shoes or clogs *(klompen)* they produce. There are different *klompen* for different purposes, such as working in the fields, spending leisure time, and even getting married. Today, most *klompen* are exported. In the Netherlands, *klompen* are no longer worn in everyday situations, except on the farm, where field workers might still wear them.

CUSTOMS AND COURTESIES

Greetings

A warm and hearty handshake is an appropriate greeting for both men and women. It is also popular among friends to kiss on alternating cheeks three times when greeting. A common phrase is *Hoe gaat het* (How are you?). While people may wave if greeting from a distance, shouting is impolite. The use of given names is generally reserved for close friends and relatives, except among the youth. Otherwise, the Dutch address others by their titles and family names. When answering the telephone, both the caller and the receiver identify themselves before starting a conversation. It is rude not to do so.

Gestures

Eye contact and facial expressions are important. One covers the mouth when yawning. When someone sneezes, a person nearby will say *proost* or *gezondheid*, the equivalent of saying "Bless you." It is impolite to chew gum while speaking. Pointing the index finger to the forehead to imply someone is crazy is an insult. Wagging the index finger emphasizes a point.

Visiting

The Dutch are hospitable and enjoy having visitors. Unannounced visits are not common, except between very close friends or relatives. If a time to visit is stated, it is important to be punctual. If no time is stated for an evening visit to new acquaintances, it is usual to arrive after 8:30 P.M. and to leave between 11:00 P.M. and midnight. When visiting, one customarily shakes hands with everyone present, including children. Hosts nearly always offer refreshments and serve them to guests. Guests do not help themselves or go into the kitchen to get something. On a first visit to someone's home, a guest does not expect a meal (unless specifically invited to dinner). Rather, coffee or tea is served with sweet biscuits, and then drinks are served later in the evening. Dinner guests usually bring flowers or another small gift to their hosts. The Netherlands is known for its flowers, which are purchased regularly to adorn window boxes, other parts of the home, restaurants, and businesses. Greenhouse plants are also extremely popular.

Eating

The Dutch generally eat three meals a day. Dinner (around 6:00 P.M.) is the main meal for most people, but some rural families and older people retain the tradition of eating the main meal at midday. For them, the evening meal is light and often consists of bread, cold cuts, cheese, and salad.

It is impolite to begin eating before others at the table. A parent or host often indicates when to eat, usually by saying *Eet smakelijk* (pronounced ATE smahk-AY-lick), which literally means "Eat deliciously" but is used in the same way as *Bon appétit* (Enjoy the meal). It is proper to keep hands above the table (rather than in the lap) but not to rest elbows on the table. The Dutch use the continental style of eating, with the fork in the left hand and the knife remaining in the right. Forks are not used to eat dessert; small spoons are provided. One does not leave the table until all have finished eating.

LIFESTYLE

Family

The Dutch have strong families, which are moderate in size. Most have only one or two children, but southern (Catholic) families tend to be a bit larger. People generally live close to extended family, and mobility is not as high as in the United States. Many holidays emphasize family gatherings. As is the case throughout Europe, both parents often work outside the home. However, Dutch women are somewhat less likely to work outside the home than women in other European countries. Thirty-five percent of the labor force is female. However, more and more younger women are entering the job market, partly due to better access to education. Women hold one-fifth of all legislative seats. Young people often leave home at age 18 to continue their education or to work.

Dating and Marriage

Dating habits are similar to those throughout Europe. Teenagers begin with group activities. Dancing, watching movies, and going to cafés are popular. It is common for couples to live together before or instead of marrying.

Diet

Bread or toast with jelly, Dutch cheese or meats, and coffee or tea are the most common foods for a Dutch breakfast. The most popular breads include multi-grain and dark-grain varieties. Most people, especially children, eat something sweet on their bread for breakfast or lunch. Typical are chocolate sprinkles (*Hagelslag*) or chocolate spread. Children often eat hot cereal for breakfast. *Krentebollen* (raisin rolls) are also a favorite. Open-faced sandwiches are common for lunch, as is *kroket* (a deep-fried sausage). The main meal usually consists of potatoes and gravy with seasonal vegetables and meat or fish. Typical dishes include herring, smoked eel, pea soup, *poffertjes* (small puffed pancakes served on special occasions), and *hutspot* (mashed potatoes with carrots and onions).

Dutch pastries are world famous. Favorite snacks include fries (eaten with mayonnaise, not ketchup), *stroopwafels* (syrup waffles), and Dutch licorice (many varieties). Restaurants in larger towns offer a wide variety of cuisine, and Indonesian food has become an established part of the Dutch diet. Eating out is a special affair and is not as common as in the United States. Most families continue to eat most meals in the home.

Recreation

The most popular sport is soccer. The Netherlands's national soccer team competed in the 1994 World Cup. Tennis, field hockey, swimming, sailing, ice-skating, wind surfing, basketball, badminton, and many other sports are also enjoyed. Many Dutch participate in cycling; nearly every person old enough to ride a bicycle has one. Bike paths (*Fietspaden*) run throughout the country. A few Dutch ride in competition, but most ride for their health and for transportation. People ride to work, to go shopping, for fun, or just to get around town. A visitor could easily tour the entire country on a bicycle. People participate in sports through clubs. Games are organized locally, regionally, or nationally depending on the level of the players. Each sport has a national association that oversees its organization.

Some people enjoy *korfbal*, a sport played on a grass field (or indoors) that combines some principles of soccer and basketball. A ball must pass through a basket high above the players' heads for points to be scored. Men and women play together in teams of twelve or eight. Some people in Friesland play *Kaatsen*, a team sport similar to baseball; players hit a small, soft ball with the hand. Poles were traditionally used for jumping over ditches, and pole vaulting (for distance, not height) is popular in the north. It is called *Fiereljeppen*. In years when the ice is hard enough, a day-long ice-skating race takes place on a route that encompasses Friesland's 11 main towns and involves going across some parts of the sea. As many as 80,000 people participate.

The Dutch and tourists alike take advantage of sandy beaches on the North Sea, although it is windy and the water is often cold. Discos are popular gathering places for young people. Most people also enjoy drama, music, and art. There are more than six hundred museums in the Netherlands, and with good reason: some of the world's most famous artists are Dutch, including Rembrandt, Vermeer, and Van Gogh.

Holidays

Official public holidays include New Year's Day, Easter (Friday–Monday), the Queen's Birthday (30 April), Ascension, Liberation Day (5 May), Whitmonday, and two days for Christmas (25–26 December).

Christmas festivities actually begin well before Christmas day. The Dutch usually do not exchange gifts on Christmas day; it is a day for families and feasts. Some families exchange gifts on Christmas Eve, but gift giving is traditionally associated with St. Nicholas Day (6 December). St. Nicholas is the Santa Claus (*Sinterklaas*) for the Dutch. *Sinterklaas* is dressed like a Catholic bishop, rides a white horse, and leaves gifts in shoes. Children place hay or a carrot in their shoes for the horse, and it is replaced with candy or a small present. *Sinterklaas* also rides in parades and visits children wherever they may be. His servant throws small pieces of gingerbread candy (*pepernoten*) for children to gather and eat. Family members and friends who exchange gifts at this time (evening of 5 December) must disguise or hide the presents. They are all anonymous (said to have come from *Sinterklaas*) and are accompanied by an amusing poem about the receiver. Good-natured kidding and embarrassing others accompanies this festivity.

Each region is also known for local festivals throughout the year, often in celebration of the harvest. *Vlaggetjesdag* (Little Flag Day) is celebrated in coastal areas. Held in May, it marks the beginning of the herring season. Ships leave the harbor decorated with little flags. In the south, Carnival celebrations are popular. They begin on the Sunday before Lent and end at midnight Tuesday. Businesses may close or cut back hours, and many people enjoy festivities in Den Bosch, Breda, and Maastricht. The Dutch receive a month of paid vacation each year. Many people take a week at Christmas, a week at Easter, and two weeks in the summer.

Commerce

Business hours are usually between 8:30 or 9:00 A.M. and 5:00 or 5:30 P.M., Monday through Friday. Summer hours might begin and end earlier. Shops often close one morning each week, usually on Monday. Some also close at lunch, although not in large urban areas. Except in large cities, all shops close by 6:00 P.M. Amsterdam's so-called "night stores" are open later but charge higher prices. No businesses are open on Sunday and there is no Sunday newspaper.

SOCIETY

Government

The kingdom is a constitutional monarchy. The queen is head of state, but the prime minister is head of government. Willem (Wim) Kok was appointed prime minister after parliamentary elections in 1994. He had previously been vice prime minister under long-serving Ruud Lubbers. A Council of State, of which the queen is president, serves as an advisory body that must be consulted before legislation is passed. Amsterdam is the capital, but the government is headquartered at The Hague.

Legislation can be introduced by the crown or the lower house of Parliament. The prime minister and other ministers are responsible to the bicameral Parliament (States General). Members of Parliament's 75-seat upper house (First Chamber) are elected by the nations's 12 provincial councils. Members of the 150-seat lower house (Second Chamber) are elected directly by the people. The most recent elections were in 1994 for the lower house and in 1995 for the upper house. Several minor parties are represented in Parliament, but four are dominant: the Christian Democratic Appeal, Labor Party, Liberal Party, and Democrats '66. Voting is open to all citizens at age 18.

Economy

The Netherlands has a strong economy. Based on private enterprise, it is highly industrialized and efficient. Real gross domestic product (GDP) per capita is $17,780, which has tripled since 1960. The distribution of income is among the most equitable in Europe. Inflation is low. As the country prepares for European integration, high unemployment and a large budget deficit remain challenges.

Although agriculture and horticulture employ less than 6 percent of the labor force, the Netherlands produces food for export, as well as large numbers of cut flowers and bulbs for Europe and other parts of the world. The Netherlands accounts for more than half of the world's flower exports. Animal husbandry is a chief agricultural activity, producing meats, cheeses, and other dairy items. Leading industries include petroleum refining, machinery, chemicals, and construction. Trade accounts for half of the country's GDP. Banking and tourism are also key sectors of the economy. The currency is the *guilder* (g)—or plural *gulden*—formerly known as the *florin*.

Transportation and Communication

The public transportation system in the Netherlands is one of Europe's best. An efficient network of trains connects major and minor cities. Most people also own cars. In fact, with the high cost of public transportation, many people prefer to use their cars for daily travel. Buses and streetcars are common in urban areas, and Amsterdam and Rotterdam have subways. The country is divided into zones for public transportation. A universal ticket called a *Strippenkaart* is purchased at stations or from drivers or machines. When entering a bus, streetcar, or most trains, a passenger pushes the ticket into the slot of a machine that stamps it. The number of zones being traveled is thereby subtracted from the ticket. Rotterdam is one of Europe's most important ports, handling 30 percent of Europe's sea transit; it is the world's largest port.

The communications system is efficient and well maintained. Television and radio stations are privately owned and there are dozens of newspapers and periodicals. The national radio and television associations affiliated with each station have certain backgrounds, such as liberal, socialist, Protestant, Catholic, or neutral.

Education

Schooling is free and compulsory between the ages of five and sixteen. Children may be enrolled for an optional year at age four. Primary education ends at age twelve. Students may go to a Catholic, Protestant, or "nonreligious" school, but the basic curriculum is the same. Secondary school begins with three years of "basic education"; all students study the same 15 subjects that emphasize practical application of knowledge. After that, they can choose between different types of high schools, ranging from pre-vocational to pre-university. The number of years varies with the program. Vocational schools train students in such professions as accounting, nursing, or teaching. Graduates of vocational programs and general high schools often enter apprenticeships. Higher education is subsidized by the government. There are 13 universities, the oldest of which, Leiden, was founded by William of Orange in 1575. The adult literacy rate is 99 percent.

Health

Medical facilities are excellent and subsidized by the government. For persons earning less than a specified amount, the government coordinates insurance and health care. Those making over the specified amount are required to have private insurance. The government also provides unemployment and disability benefits. The average life expectancy for the Dutch is 78 years. The infant mortality rate is 6 per 1,000.

FOR THE TRAVELER

U.S. travelers do not need a visa for visits of up to three months, but a valid passport is required. Tourism is important in the Netherlands, and facilities are well developed. For brochures on travel opportunities in the country, contact the Netherlands Board of Tourism, 225 North Michigan Avenue, Suite 326 Chicago, IL 60601; phone (312) 819–0300. You may also wish to contact the Royal Netherlands Embassy, 4200 Linnean Avenue NW, Washington, DC 20008.

CULTURGRAM '97™

Republic of
Nicaragua

Boundary representations not necessarily authoritative.

THE AMERICAS

BACKGROUND

Land and Climate

Covering 49,998 square miles (129,494 square kilometers), Nicaragua is about the size of Iowa. Although it is the largest country in Central America, only about 9 percent of the land is suitable for cultivation. *Lago de Nicaragua* borders the Pacific Ocean and is the only freshwater lake in the world to have sharks and sawfish. Low central mountains and hills separate the populated west from the east. Forests cover about one-third of the country. Large pine forests are located in the northwest and mountain areas while tropical rain forests and coastal wetlands spread across the east. Natural resources include gold, silver, copper, lead, zinc, and timber. Nicaragua's climate is tropical, although the highlands are cooler. Humidity is generally high and temperatures average 80°F (27°C). Several volcanoes along the Pacific coast are active; eruptions and earthquakes are common. Occasional hurricanes and tidal waves can be very destructive.

History

Columbus was the first European to visit Nicaragua (1502), which was later explored by Spanish *conquistadores*. Spanish settlements date from the 1520s. Indigenous groups resisted the Spanish until they were finally conquered in 1552. Britain established settlements along the Mosquito Coast (the Caribbean coast) in the 17th century and claimed sovereignty over the coast in 1740. By and large, however, Nicaragua was ruled by Spain until 1821, when it declared independence. With independence it became a member of the United Provinces of Central America but chose to be an independent republic in 1838. Political power alternated between liberals and conservatives over the next few decades. The competition sometimes led to violence.

Internal chaos and U.S. economic interests led to the beginning of U.S. military intervention in 1909. During the 1920s and 1930s, guerrillas led by Augusto Cesar Sandino fought the U.S. occupation. Sandino was assassinated in 1934. In 1936, General Anastasio Somoza García seized the presidency. He ruled as dictator until his assassination in 1956. After his death, the Somoza family continued to rule the country, beginning with Somoza's son, Luis Somoza Debayle, who died in 1967. He was followed in that year by his brother, General Anastasio Somoza Debayle.

In 1962, the Sandinistas, a revolutionary group named after the martyr Sandino, was formed with the goal of overthrowing the Somozas. For the next 15 years, Sandinistas carried out various unsuccessful terrorist attacks on Somoza's National Guard, which was armed by the United States. In 1978, after the assassination of Pedro Joaquín Chamorro, a prominent anti-Somoza newspaper editor, riots broke out, Sandinistas stormed the national palace in Managua, and civil war followed. Somoza was forced to flee the country in July 1979, when the Sandinistas took control. Fifty thousand people were killed in the civil war.

The new Marxist-oriented government seized the Somoza fortune, redistributed their lands to the peasants, suspended the constitution, and began tightening controls. Concerned that Sandinistas were aiding Marxist rebels in El Salvador, the U.S. government suspended economic aid to Nicaragua in 1981, beginning a decade of strained relations between the two nations. Throughout the 1980s, U.S. funds supported the *Contras'* opposition to Sandinista rule. General elections brought Sandinista leader Daniel Ortega Saavedra to power in 1985. The United States responded by imposing a trade embargo that severely handicapped the country's economy.

In spite of 1987 peace negotiations, fighting continued on both sides. Eventually, the Sandinista government agreed to ensure free elections if the *Contras* would disarm. Free elections were held in February 1990 and Ortega was defeated by Violeta Barrios de Chamorro, the widow of the assassinated newspaper editor. The United States supported Chamorro's presidency, ended trade restrictions, and pledged aid to rebuild the economy. The *Contras* began to disband in 1990.

Strikes, hyperinflation, and the slow progress of land distribution led to severe economic difficulties for the new government. The currency became nearly worthless and had to be replaced in 1991. Sporadic violence erupted in many areas throughout the early 1990s. Some feared fighting would resume, but many supported efforts to negotiate peaceful solutions. In 1993, with support for Chamorro's government dwindling and Sandinistas still controlling the army, questions were raised as to Nicaragua's ability to maintain a lasting democracy. By 1995, the most serious threats had subsided and Nicaragua did not experience widespread fighting or unrest.

THE PEOPLE

Population

The population of Nicaragua is 4.2 million and is growing at 2.6 percent annually. The majority of the people (69 percent) are *mestizo*, a mixture of Indian and Spanish. Seventeen percent are of European descent. About 9 percent are black and 5 percent are native Indian. Most people live on the western plains. The population of Managua, the capital, is more than one million. The Caribbean side is sparsely populated—mostly by smaller ethnic groups. Nicaragua's population is young; about 45 percent is younger than age 15.

The country's Human Development Index (0.611) ranks Nicaragua 109th out of 174 countries. Although people are able to meet some basic needs, opportunities for economic prosperity and personal advancement are limited, especially in rural areas. Adjusted for women, the index (0.560) ranks Nicaragua 73d out of 130 countries.

Language

Spanish is the official and predominant language. Along the Caribbean coast, small groups speak English or other ethnic languages. Garífuna is common among the black population, while some Indian groups speak Miskito, Sumo, and Rama. Some Managua residents understand English.

Religion

Approximately 95 percent of the population is Roman Catholic. Protestant, Evangelical, and other Christian organizations are also present. Although relations between the Catholic Church and the government were strained during the Sandinista period, the Church has maintained its strong influence within the country. Catholic traditions, such as baptism, communion, and weddings, remain a significant part of family life. Some older women attend mass daily. Religious icons, particularly pictures of the Virgin Mary, decorate many homes. When parting or making future plans, people often add *Si Dios quiere* (God willing) as a qualifier to their commitment. Freedom of religion is guaranteed.

General Attitudes

Nicaraguans enjoy being with others and are sociable. They value honesty, friendliness, respect, and good humor. Individuals are more important than schedules, so punctuality at meetings may be admired but not strictly observed. Nicaraguans defend honor vigorously, sometimes even physically. Those in power are esteemed for their opinions and are generally afforded wealth. Therefore, power is highly valued and often sought. Personal criticism is taken seriously and usually avoided. Getting a job, having a large family, and owning a home or a plot of land are important long-term goals for Nicaraguans.

The Sandinista influence still pervades civilian life. Collectivism and helping each other are common values in all social classes. Years of strife have caused many to become wary and distrustful. Some now look to the government as a source of problems as well as possible solutions.

Personal Appearance

Physical appearance is important to Nicaraguans. Even if they cannot afford expensive clothing, they will make special efforts to be neat and well-groomed.

People throughout the country wear lightweight clothing. In rural areas, men wear cotton shirts and pants. Jeans are also common. Rural women usually wear light cotton dresses or skirts and blouses. When working on daily agricultural tasks, both men and women wear sandals or flip-flops, reserving regular shoes for trips to town or special occasions.

Urban men wear cotton slacks and shirts (often long-sleeved). Urban women wear light cotton dresses, although many also wear pants. Many businessmen will wear a *guayabera* (an embroidered dress shirt) as semi-formal wear instead of a tie and suit jacket. Suit coats are not worn during the hottest months of the year.

CUSTOMS AND COURTESIES

Greetings

When meeting another person for the first time, Nicaraguans smile, shake hands, and say either *Mucho gusto de conocerle* (Glad to meet you) or *¿Cómo está usted?* (How are you?). Inquiring about the health of family members demonstrates friendliness between acquaintances. Complete attention is given to the person being greeted. Common terms for greeting include *¡Buenos días!* (Good morning), *¡Buenas tardes!* (Good afternoon), and *¡Buenas noches!* (Good evening). A casual greeting, especially among the youth, is *¡Hola!* (Hi). Men greet each other with a hearty handshake, and close friends hug and pat each other on the back. Female friends usually greet with a kiss on the cheek and a gentle hug; however, rural women pat each other on the upper arm rather than hug. Those of higher social standing are greeted with titles, such as *Señor, Señora,* or *Señorita* (Mr., Mrs., or Miss) to show respect. One uses the titles *Don* and *Doña* with first names to indicate special respect, familiarity, or affection. For example, most Nicaraguans refer to President

Chamorro as *Doña Violeta*. Professional titles are also used before surnames.

Gestures

Nicaraguans use many gestures when speaking. To beckon, one waves all fingers with the palm facing down. One points by puckering the lips or extending the chin in the indicated direction. If a person is paying for something, he or she may rub one index finger repeatedly down the other, similar to the U.S. American gesture for shame. To indicate that someone has a lot of money or something is very expensive, a person separates the thumb and the forefinger as widely as possible, keeping the remaining three fingers closed.

Avoiding eye contact during conversation generally is not acceptable; however, some women may do so in deference to others. Offering a seat to pregnant women, the elderly, or women with children is common. Women may also offer to hold other people's children on their lap if the parents are standing. Upon entering a building, men remove their hats or caps. Raising one's voice and displaying affection in public generally are not acceptable.

Visiting

Nicaraguans are hospitable and enjoy visiting. In rural areas, people commonly (even daily) visit family and friends unannounced. Those in urban areas with access to telephones usually plan visits in advance. Relatives and friends who live in other areas often visit for weekends and holidays.

Due to the hot climate, hosts always offer their guests a cool drink. Water, juice, or natural beverages such as *pinol* (corn-based beverage) are most commonly served. Refusing a drink is considered a serious discourtesy. When one enters a home, it is important to greet everyone and wait for an invitation to sit. When visiting for a special purpose, guests first inquire about the health of the family before they discuss other matters. Good-byes may be drawn out and full of well-wishing. Visitors who arrive during mealtime are invited to join their hosts.

Guests tend to express admiration for their hosts rather than for material objects in the home. Dinner guests may take small gifts, such as flowers or candy, to the hosts. People also give gifts on special occasions, such as anniversaries, birthdays, and Catholic ceremonies.

Eating

Breakfast is usually eaten at 6:00 or 7:00 A.M., although people in rural areas may eat earlier during busy agricultural seasons. Lunch, the main meal of the day, is eaten at midday and is often followed by a *siesta* (afternoon rest). In rural areas, the siesta is taken from noon to 2:00 P.M., the hottest time of the day when work is difficult. Most people in urban areas eat lunch between noon and 2:00 P.M., with the siesta reduced to an hour break. Dinner is usually between 7:00 and 9:00 P.M.

Rural families eat lunch together; however, due to work and school schedules, many urban families do not. Most families make special efforts to eat together on weekends and holidays. In rural areas, people eat with a spoon or pick up their food with a tortilla. Sometimes the spoons are made from sections of a hard, dry gourd shell. In urban areas, people may eat with a tortilla or spoon but they also use knives and forks. They hold the fork in the left hand and the knife in the

right. Many fried foods are eaten with the hands. People keep both hands (not elbows) on or above the table. Hosts expect their guests to eat what is served. They may offer second helpings. One is expected to praise the quality of the meal.

LIFESTYLE

Family

The extended family is the basis of society and strongly influences an individual's life and decisions. Parents, children, aunts, uncles, and cousins commonly live together. Nearly all Nicaraguans aspire to have large families; both men and women gain social status by being a parent.

During the Sandinista period, women were given a greater role in society and the right to more actively participate in family matters. Service in the military was common for women under the Sandinista regime, and many became involved in civic affairs. About one-fourth of the labor force is female. Because a number of men died or were sent away during the civil war, many women became heads of families. While men are still seen as the authorities, and women generally defer to them, women control most household affairs. Rural homes are often made of straw and wood. More expensive rural homes and homes in urban areas are made of concrete. Patios and open areas are common. The redistribution of land seized by the Sandinista government remains a sensitive issue.

Nicaraguans have two family names. The last name is the mother's family name and the second-to-last name is the father's family name, which functions as the surname. Therefore, a person named José Muñoz Gómez would be called *Señor Muñoz*.

Dating and Marriage

A girl formally enters social life at age 15 and a large *fiesta* (party) is held in her honor. Thereafter, she is allowed to have a boyfriend and attend dances. Group dating is common among the youth. Clubs and social groups are also important.

Civil marriages are the most common, although those who can afford it also have a large church wedding. Most marry between the ages of 16 and 23. *Machismo*, the male attitude of proving one's manliness or superiority, remains strong in the country. Although marriage is a valued tradition, male infidelity, which is a part of *machismo*, is widely tolerated.

Diet

Obtaining a well-balanced meal is difficult for many people who cannot afford more than beans and rice. Among wealthier families, the main meal of the day generally consists of rice, beans, some kind of meat, and a salad or vegetable. This is served with tortillas and fruit juice. Most meals include beans and rice. Corn is an important ingredient in many foods. Typical dishes include tortillas, enchiladas, *nacatamales* (meat and vegetables, with spices), *mondongo* (tripe and beef knuckles), *vigorón* (vegetables with pork skins), and *baho* (meat, vegetables, and plantains). Tropical fruits are usually plentiful. Fried plantains are popular.

Recreation

Baseball is the national sport. Soccer, boxing, softball, basketball, and volleyball are also enjoyed. Nicaraguans of all ages love to dance, so most parties or large events include dancing. Salsa is the most popular music. Nicaraguan folk music features the marimba and the guitar. Going to the beach and participating in club activities are also popular.

Holidays

Public holidays include New Year's Day, Easter (Thursday–Sunday), Labor Day (1 May), Battle of San Jacinto (14 September), Independence Day (15 September), Gritería Day (7 December), Feast of the Immaculate Conception (8 December), and Christmas. Workers also receive a half-day vacation on Christmas Eve. Numerous holidays honoring local patron saints are the main annual events in towns and regions.

Commerce

Most merchants' shops are open from 8:00 A.M. to noon and from 1:00 to 6:00 P.M., Monday through Friday, and on Saturdays from 8:00 A.M. to noon. Government offices are generally open from 7:00 A.M. to 5:00 P.M., Monday through Friday. While some businesses close for the siesta, many in urban areas do not. In rural areas, business hours vary depending on the crops cultivated. Most people purchase basic supplies at open-air markets, although supermarkets are available in large cities.

SOCIETY

Government

The Republic of Nicaragua has 17 *departamentos* (provinces). The executive branch is composed of a president, vice president, and cabinet. The National Assembly (*Asamblea Nacional*) has 92 members. Legislators are directly elected to serve six-year terms. The next elections will be in November 1996. The voting age is 16. While more than 20 political parties are active in Nicaragua, many are joined in coalitions. For instance, the National Opposition Union (UNO) had ten parties when it came to power under Chamorro. The largest single party is the opposition Sandinista National Liberation Front. Dissident UNO parties also form a coalition. Allegiances can be fluid and destabilizing. If another broad-based coalition comes to power in 1996, instability could continue to be a problem.

Economy

Devastated by a decade of central planning under the Sandinistas, a civil war, and the U.S. trade embargo, the economy remains the country's greatest challenge. Since Chamorro's ambitious stabilization plan began in 1991, annual inflation has dropped from more than 750 percent to about 20 percent in 1994. Overall, however, expectations for change have greatly exceeded the government's ability to provide it. Economic growth was flat in 1992, dropping slightly in 1993. Underemployment is high (about 50 percent). Nicaragua's per capita foreign debt remains one of the highest in the world.

Still, Nicaragua has the potential for a much stronger economy, and current trends are encouraging. More than half of all state enterprises have been privatized. Unemployment is dropping, and the economy has received substantial amounts of foreign aid. Real gross domestic product per capita is $2,790, surpassing its 1960 level, which remained the highest for many years. About one-fifth of the population lives in poverty. These figures suggest that, while absolute poverty does not abound, the country as a whole is poor.

The economy relies on exporting agricultural commodities such as coffee, cotton, sugar, bananas, seafood, and meat. About 44 percent of the labor force is employed in agriculture. The currency is the gold *córdoba* (C$).

Transportation and Communication

Years of fighting and the poor economy damaged both the transportation and communications systems. Most roads are not paved or are in disrepair; many areas cannot be reached by car. In some cases, ox-cart trails are used to access rural regions. Buses provide service in cities. Postal, telegraph, and telephone services do not generally serve rural areas. The press is free and there are four newspapers.

Education

Schooling is mandatory and free between the ages of six and thirteen. Most children begin primary school, but only 36 percent complete it. Students have to pay for their own supplies, uniforms, tuition, and expenses, which often becomes too difficult for the poor. Those who complete primary training generally proceed to the secondary level. Nicaragua has five private and five state universities. The adult literacy rate is 65 percent.

Health

Health care is limited, particularly outside of Managua. Community volunteers have become active in promoting prevention and early detection of diseases. However, many people, particularly those in rural areas, do not get adequate care. The infant mortality rate is 50 per 1,000. Still, more than three-fourths of all infants are immunized and about the same number of women receive some prenatal care. Life expectancy ranges from 62 to 68 years. Access to safe water and sanitation is a problem in rural areas.

FOR THE TRAVELER

U.S. citizens do not need a visa for visits of fewer than 30 days, but a valid passport and proof of return passage are required. For longer visits, a visa is necessary and can be acquired from the embassy. Visas are valid for 30 days from the date issued. No vaccinations are required, but some may be advisable, depending on the nature and length of the trip. Although the civil war ended in 1990, travelers should exercise caution. Travel in remote areas, particularly at night, is discouraged. Land mines remain in some border regions, making off-road travel dangerous. U.S. citizens may want to contact the State Department at (202) 647–5225 for advisories.

Nicaragua is a beautiful country of large lakes, lovely mountains, and interesting people. Facilities are not well developed but are improving. For travel information, contact the Nicaragua Tourist Information Center, PO Box 140357, Miami FL 33114–0357; phone (305) 854–1544. You may also contact the Office of Tourism, Hotel Intercontinental, Managua, Nicaragua; or the Embassy of Nicaragua, 1627 New Hampshire Avenue NW, Washington, DC 20009; phone (202) 939–6531.

Kingdom of
Norway

Boundary representations not necessarily authoritative.

BACKGROUND

Land and Climate

Norway, one of the "three fingers" of Scandinavia, is just larger than New Mexico. It covers 125,181 square miles (324,220 square kilometers). Its coastline, indented with beautiful fjords, stretches more than 1,000 miles (1,600 kilometers) from the North Sea to the Arctic Ocean. *Norway* means "the northern way." In fact, the Arctic Circle crosses the country almost in its middle. Along the fjords on the western coast are numerous small islands. Norway is generally mountainous and has several glaciers. The mountains and high plateaus are interrupted by fertile valleys and small plains, but only about 3 percent of the country is suitable for cultivation.

Norway has many natural resources, including crude oil (in the North Sea), copper, nickel, zinc, lead, and timber. More than one-fourth of the land is forested. The North Atlantic Drift moderates the otherwise cold climate and allows for ice-free harbors and mildly warm summers. Rain is abundant on the west coast. In the interior, winters are colder and summers warmer than on the coast. Snow lasts for several months of the year. Above the Arctic Circle, the sun shines day and night for part of the summer and does not rise above the horizon for part of the winter. In the absence of the sun, the northern lights (*aurora borealis*) are visible for a period of time.

History

During the Age of the Vikings (800–1050), Vikings conquered many areas in Scandinavia and Europe and even settled briefly in parts of North America. For example, Leifur Eiríksson landed in present-day Canada. In Norway, Viking leader Harald the Fairhead became the first supreme ruler of a unified kingdom around 872. Christianity spread throughout the area by 1030. The country came under Danish domination from 1381 to 1814 before it was given to Sweden as a peace treaty provision to punish Denmark's alliance with Napoleon during the Napoleonic Wars. In reaction to being given to Sweden, Norway declared its independence and drafted a constitution. Still, the Swedish king was accepted as monarch and the two nations were unified. The union was dissolved by referendum in 1905 and a Danish prince (Carl) was chosen to be the constitutional monarch of an independent Kingdom of Norway. He took the name Haakon VII.

Norway was neutral in World War I, but Germany attacked in World War II (April 1940) and held Norway until its liberation in May 1945. During that time, the monarch was out of the country supporting the Allied effort against the Germans. The son of Haakon VII, Olav V, was king of Norway from 1957 to 1991. Upon his death, his son, Harald V, took the throne and is king today.

EUROPE

Norway's post-war period has been marked by political stability, economic progress, and development. The country has good relations with the United States. Norway is a member of the North Atlantic Treaty Organization (NATO) and the European Free Trade Area, but it is not a member of the European Union (EU).

The issue of joining the EU has been fairly sensitive in Norway ever since voters rejected membership in 1972. In 1990, a prime minister (Jan Syse) resigned over the debate. The opposition leader, Gro Harlem Brundtland, replaced him and served until elections in September 1993, when she was reelected prime minister for a four-year term. She and her party (Labor Party) risked her considerable popularity in 1994 to apply for membership in the EU and then to campaign to have voters approve the measure. In a 1994 referendum, held after neighbors Sweden and Finland voted in favor of joining the EU, voters rejected the application and Norway did not join the Union. Norwegians who voted against the Union expressed concerns that some autonomy may have to be sacrificed to EU leaders, which is not an acceptable option for most Norwegians. Further, people have enough confidence in Norway's resources and economy remaining strong without membership in the expanding EU.

THE PEOPLE

Population

Norway's population of 4.3 million is growing at only 0.4 percent annually, a rate similar to that of much of Europe. Norway is one of the most sparsely populated countries in the world. The population is predominantly of Nordic (Scandinavian) descent. There is also a small minority (20,000) of native Sami (pronounced SAY-me), who live mostly in the north. Also called Laplanders, their ancestors were the original inhabitants of northern Norway. Although Norway limits immigration, immigrant workers have become more common since the discovery of oil in the North Sea.

The Human Development Index (0.929) ranks Norway seventh out of 174 countries. An extensive social-welfare system affords people access to health care, education, and economic prosperity. Adjusted for women, the index (0.911) ranks Norway third out of 130 countries. Men and women enjoy equal access to opportunities for personal advancement.

Language

Norwegian, the official language, has two forms. *Bokmål*, or "book language" is used in most written works and is spoken by more than 80 percent of the people, especially those in urban areas. It is also the main language of instruction and broadcasting, although laws require that the other form, *Nynorsk*, be used in a certain percentage of schools and broadcasting media. *Nynorsk* was actually created in the 1800s as a combination of the many rural dialects then in existence. *Bokmål* is heavily influenced by Danish due to four hundred years of Danish rule. The Sami speak Sami (Lappish) but learn Norwegian in the schools as a second language. English is taught in the schools beginning at age 11, and it is spoken widely as a second language.

Religion

More than 85 percent of the population belongs to the state church, the Church of Norway, which is Evangelical Lutheran. Still, freedom of religion is guaranteed, and there are many other Christian churches are active in the country. Among them are the Pentecostals, Roman Catholics, and various Protestant groups. Most people attend church services only on special occasions or holidays.

General Attitudes

Tolerance, human kindness, and independence are important Norwegian ideals. Peace and progress are common themes in Norway, the country that sponsors the Nobel Peace Prize. Criticism of other peoples or systems is considered inappropriate. Norwegians take great pride in their individual and national independence. They are very patriotic and feel Norway has developed a superior social system with high standards. Indeed, social equality and a good standard of living are important values that have shaped post-World War II politics. Norwegians also love the outdoors and work hard to protect their environment.

Sincerity in friendship is important, but people show reserve in the expression of personal feelings. Neighbors, even in large cities, get along very well and usually consider each other close friends.

Personal Appearance

Dress generally follows conservative, European fashions and is influenced by the necessity to keep warm. Dressing well is important, and an unkempt appearance in public is considered inappropriate. Cleanliness is also stressed.

Traditional costumes (*bunad*), which vary according to region, are worn on special occasions, such as weddings and national and local holidays. They are often hand sewn and have elaborate embroidery. For women, these costumes usually consist of a white blouse (often embroidered), a jumper-type skirt, an apron, and a headdress. Men wear knee pants, shirts, and vests.

CUSTOMS AND COURTESIES

Greetings

Norwegians often take the initiative by introducing themselves to strangers. Natural courtesy is important in good relations. Shaking hands is the normal custom. Everyday acquaintances greet each other with a casual *Morn* (literally "Morning"), regardless of the time of day. The term is roughly equivalent to "Hi." *Hei* also means "Hi" and is as common as *Morn*. A slightly more formal greeting is *God dag* (Good day). Traditionally, only close friends addressed each other by first name, but the youth are increasingly using first names once they have been introduced. Older individuals continue to follow the custom of using titles with a family name. When being introduced for the first time, a person addresses the other by both first and last name.

Gestures

Norwegians keep hand gestures to a minimum during conversation. It is impolite to yawn without covering the mouth. It is common to offer a seat on public transportation to a woman or elderly person. Courtesy and good behavior are important in all cases.

Visiting

When visiting a home for the first time, one customarily brings a gift of flowers, sweets, or another small token of appreciation to the hosts. Guests wait to be invited in by the host, who traditionally helps them remove their coats as a gesture of hospitality. Guests also wait to sit down until they are invited to do so. Not everyone, of course, adheres to these rules of formal etiquette. It is considered poor taste to leave directly after dinner. Personal privacy is important; topics such as income and social status are avoided in casual conversation. It is considered rude for invited guests to refuse any refreshments the hosts offer. In the past, people visited unannounced, but now a call in advance is appreciated. Punctuality is important.

Eating

Guests do not start eating until everyone is seated and the host invites them to begin. Norwegians eat in the continental style, with the fork in the left hand and knife remaining in the right. It is impolite to leave food on the plate. At the end of a meal, whether in casual or formal situations, diners thank the person who prepared or is responsible for the meal. Indeed, children are taught to say *Takk for maten* (Thank you for the food) before leaving the table. Hands are kept above the table during the meal. In a restaurant, patrons summon the waiter with a raised hand. A service fee is usually included in the bill, but a small tip (perhaps 5–10 percent) is also customary.

LIFESTYLE

Family

The family unit is small but extremely important. Husbands and wives usually consider each other equal in authority. In fact, general equality for women is rather advanced. Women have a strong presence in politics (comprising one-third of Parliament) and make up 40 percent of the labor force. Their influence has helped Norway develop strong child care, educational, and family programs. Many people own their homes or condominiums. More than one-third also own or share a cabin in the mountains or by the sea. Spending time in these cottages is a favorite family activity. Although divorce was once uncommon, a dramatic increase has occurred over the last decade. Still, about half of all adults are married.

Dating and Marriage

Serious dating is discouraged among the youth, but group dating usually starts between the ages of 14 and 18. Dancing, participating in outdoor activities, and going to movies are favorite activities. It is not uncommon for couples to live together before or instead of marrying. Men usually marry around age 25; women are slightly younger.

Diet

Breakfast usually consists of open-face sandwiches and milk or coffee; lunch is often the same. Meat or fish, potatoes, vegetables, and a soup or dessert are generally prepared for the main meal (5:00 P.M.). A common meal is meatballs with potatoes and brown gravy, served with vegetables. Norwegians may also have a light evening snack. Norwegian specialities include fish balls in a sauce, smoked salmon, *lutefisk* (cod or coalfish, soaked in potash lye), *fårikål* (cabbage and mutton), *smalahode* (sheep's head), and a variety of other dishes. Ready-made or frozen foods are popular. Delis usually have ready-made fried fish, fish cakes, fish pudding, and meatballs.

Recreation

Most Norwegians are physically active. Nearly every Norwegian can ski and children learn at a very young age. A saying claims that Norwegians are born with skis on their feet. Norway is one of the world's centers for skiing, both Alpine (downhill) and Nordic (cross-country), and ice skating. The small city of Lillehammer was in the world spotlight in 1994 as the site of the Winter Olympics. Fishing is excellent and popular; trout, pike, and salmon abound in Norwegian waters. People enjoy soccer, swimming, and hiking during the summer months. Norway's national soccer team competed in the 1994 World Cup. Boating is popular when the frozen lakes and fjords thaw.

Sports are not connected to school activities, but each community has its own sports clubs for individual and team competition. Winning is not emphasized as much as participation. Most families are actively involved in these clubs. Many families also participate in cultural arts, either by performing themselves or by attending the theater, concerts, and other cultural events. Reading is a popular leisure activity.

Holidays

Official holidays include New Year's Day, Easter (Thursday–Monday), Labor Day (1 May), Constitution Day (17 May), and Christmas (24–26 December). The Norwegian flag is prominent for all holidays; it is even used to decorate Christmas trees. Constitution Day is celebrated much like the Fourth of July in the United States, with parades, flags, family gatherings, and the like. Families often take ski vacations during the Easter holiday. Christmas is the biggest celebration of the year. As in other countries, preparations begin well in advance. At 5:00 P.M. on Christmas Eve, bells ring and the holiday officially begins. Families gather to share a big meal and exchange gifts. Parties are common on Christmas Day and thereafter until the new year begins.

Commerce

The average workweek in Norway is about 37 hours, one of the shortest in the world. Office hours usually are from 8:00 A.M. to 4:00 P.M., Monday through Friday. Stores open from 9:00 or 10:00 A.M. to 4:00 or 5:00 P.M. In large towns, stores often stay open as late as 7:00 P.M. each Thursday. Shops close by 2:00 P.M. on Saturdays and are closed on Sunday.

SOCIETY

Government

Norway is a constitutional monarchy. The king has limited authority, except as head of the military and as a symbol of continuity and stability. Executive power is vested in the prime minister, who presides over the dominant party in the country's Parliament (*Storting*). The 165 members of Parliament are elected every four years. The *Storting* has an Upper Chamber (*Lagting*) and a Lower Chamber (*Odelsting*). The Labor, Center, and Conservative Parties are the largest in Parliament, but no party has a majority. Hence, the numerous smaller parties, which have substantial followings, can significantly influence political debate. All citizens may vote at age 18. Norway has 19 provinces (*fylker*).

Economy

Norway, which enjoys a strong economy, has one of the highest standards of living in the world. The decision to remain outside the EU has not weakened the economy, which grew nearly 4 percent in 1995. Unemployment (excluding those in job training programs) is 5 percent (about half the EU rate).

Real gross domestic product per capita is estimated at $18,580, which has tripled in the last generation. This figure indicates most people have access to a decent income. Highly developed social institutions are able to provide for general economic prosperity. The poorest 40 percent of households earn 20 percent of the nation's income.

The most important exports are petroleum products, natural gas, ships, and fish. Aluminum and some manufactured items, such as furniture, are also exported. Norway is a major producer of aluminum. Oil drilling, textiles, chemicals, and food processing are among the key industries. The government is attempting to further diversify the economy to reduce dependency on oil. Agriculture is important to the domestic economy, employing 6 percent of the labor force in livestock raising, fishing, and crop cultivation. The currency is the Norwegian *krone* (Kr).

Transportation and Communication

The transportation system is excellent. Trains, buses, and airplanes connect cities and towns. Most people own cars. Boats are used in some areas for transportation. The communications system is also highly developed and fully modern. Telephone and postal services are reliable.

Education

Schooling is free and compulsory for all children between the ages of seven and sixteen. The first six years constitute primary school, while the latter three are lower secondary school. Upper secondary school is open to anyone, although students usually are between the ages of 16 and 18. It includes both general education (preparation for higher education) and vocational training.

After secondary school, many people begin working. Others are admitted to a university or college, and a small number attend the folk high school, a boarding school for teaching liberal arts (after the Danish tradition). The literacy rate is nearly 100 percent. Universities are located in Oslo, Bergen, Tromsø, and Trondheim. There are a number of specialized colleges and institutes. Instruction is readily available to most citizens and basically free at all levels, including higher education. Space is limited at universities, however, and many students travel to other countries for their college education.

Health

In keeping with its commitment to social welfare, the government has an extensive system that provides not only health and hospital services to all but housing and work for needy Norwegians. There are very few private hospitals in Norway. Socialized medicine pays for all hospital charges, although small fees are charged for medicine and some procedures. Costs are shared between the central and local governments. The infant mortality rate is 6 per 1,000. Life expectancy ranges from 74 to 81 years.

FOR THE TRAVELER

While passports are required, U.S. citizens do not need visas for visits of up to three months' total time in Scandinavia—Denmark, Iceland, Finland, Norway, and Sweden. No vaccinations are required. Cruises along the fjords, hiking, skiing, and a variety of other vacation options are available in Norway. For more information, contact the Royal Norwegian Consulate/Information Service, 825 Third Avenue, 38th Floor, New York, NY 10022; or the Scandinavian Tourist Board, 655 Third Avenue, New York, NY 10017; phone (212) 949–2333. You may also wish to contact the Royal Norwegian Embassy, 2720 34th Street NW, Washington, DC 20008; phone (202) 333–6000.

Republic of
Panama

Boundary representations not necessarily authoritative.

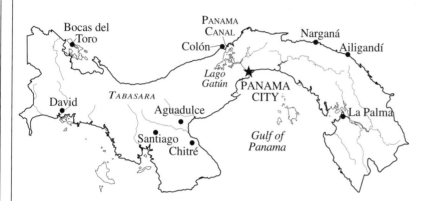

BACKGROUND

Land and Climate

Panama is a fairly rugged, mountainous country connecting Central and South America. Covering 30,193 square miles (78,200 square kilometers), Panama's total land area is just smaller than South Carolina. Volcanic activity has made the soil very fertile in some areas. About half the country is forested and 6 percent is suitable for cultivation. The Panama Canal, a man-made structure, runs through *Lago Gatún* (Lake Gatún) from Panama City to Colón, the country's two largest cities. They are home to most of the country's urban population. Areas outside the Canal Zone, which stretches between and includes the two cities, are collectively called *el interior* (the interior). The Tabasara Mountains (*Cordillera Central*) form a spine down the center of the western interior; there are also mountains in the eastern interior. Except for the higher elevations, the tropical climate is hot and humid. The average annual temperature is 80°F (27°C). In the mountains, the average is about 55°F (13°C).

History

The history of Panama has been greatly affected by its strategic location between the Atlantic and Pacific Oceans. Rodrigo de Bastidas, a Spanish explorer, visited Panama in 1501. Columbus claimed the area for Spain the next year. In the 16th and 17th centuries, Panama served as the route for shipping Incan treasures to Spain. In 1821, Spanish rule was overthrown, and Panama became a province of Colombia. During the 1880s, France attempted to build a canal across the narrow isthmus, but yellow fever claimed more than 20 thousand lives and the canal rights were sold to the United States.

On 3 November 1903, Panama declared its independence from Colombia and the United States sent troops to support the new Panamanian government. Construction of the Panama Canal began in 1907 under U.S. supervision. The canal was completed seven years later. It became an important passage for ships traveling from the Atlantic to the Pacific and vice versa. The United States controlled the canal and U.S. citizens worked in most managerial positions. In 1978, the U.S. Senate ratified a treaty signed by President Jimmy Carter concerning the permanent neutrality and operation of the canal after the year 1999. According to the treaty, Panama will assume control of canal operations and the United States will continue to guarantee its neutrality.

Omar Torrijos Herrera, commander of the national guard, seized control of Panama in 1968. He is credited with negotiating the canal treaty with the United States. Although he ruled as a dictator, most Panamanians now revere him as a national hero. He turned daily government powers over to a civilian administration in 1978 and allowed free, multiparty legislative elections in 1980. When he died in 1983, his defense minister, Manuel Antonio Noriega, became the strongest military leader in the country. Noriega soon consolidated power as head of the Panama Defense Forces.

Arturo Delvalle Henríquez, who became president in 1985, was ousted in 1988 for trying to fire Noriega, who had effectively suspended the constitution and civil rights in 1987. Noriega ruled under a state of emergency and controlled the national assembly. Although he allowed regularly scheduled elections to take place in May 1989, he refused to allow the newly elected president (who opposed Noriega) to take office. Noriega's rule became increasingly repressive in Panama, and relations with the United States worsened. When a 1989 coup attempt against Noriega failed, the United States responded to growing concerns regarding corruption, violence, and Noriega's threats against U.S. interests by sending troops to Panama in December 1989.

Panamanian troops loyal to Noriega were defeated and Noriega was eventually taken prisoner. When the elected government was installed, Noriega was extradited to the United States to stand trial for various drug-trafficking charges. He was convicted in 1992 and is serving a 40-year prison sentence.

Struggling to rebuild a nation with severe economic and social problems, President Guillermo Endara's government did not successfully address many issues or implement his desired constitutional changes. Strikes, crime, social unrest, poverty, and corruption hindered progress. Still, democracy prevailed under free elections in 1994 and Ernesto Pérez Balladares (known as *El Toro*) was elected president. Promising to end corruption and attack poverty, Balladares seeks to lower unemployment, attract foreign investment, modernize the economy, and reduce the government's size.

THE PEOPLE

Population

The population of Panama is about 2.68 million, growing annually at 1.9 percent. Next to Belize, Panama has the smallest population in Central America. *Mestizos*, people of mixed European and Indian heritage, comprise about 70 percent of Panama's citizens. Fourteen percent of the population is black, descendants of laborers from the Caribbean (mostly the West Indies) who came to work on the canal in the early 1900s. Ten percent of the people are white, having European ancestry, and the remaining people are members of various indigenous groups. These groups have their own rich cultural heritage and have often chosen not to integrate into Panamanian society. The capital, Panama City, has about 700,000 residents. Panama's Human Development Index (0.856) ranks it 49th out of 174 countries. Adjusted for women, the index (0.765) ranks Panama 41st out of 130 countries.

Language

Spanish is the official language of Panama. About 14 percent of the people speak English as a native tongue, and many others speak English as a second language. Many blacks speak Creole English. The indigenous peoples speak various languages, according to their ethnic background. Most prevalent are Cuna and Guaymí, both of which are spoken by more than 40 thousand people. Many Panamanians are bilingual.

Religion

About 85 percent of the population is Roman Catholic. Another 6 percent belongs to various other Christian organizations. There are small numbers of Muslims, Jews, Hindus and Baha'i in Panama. Even though the Catholic Church has great influence on the lives of the people, Panama has freedom of worship and separation of church and state. Many Catholics are critical of local ecclesiastical authorities but remain loyal to the pope.

General Attitudes

Although society is stratified in traditional social classes, Panamanians consider all people to be of worth. People should be treated with dignity and respect regardless of their class. This value for the individual is also evident in Panamanians' respect for personal strength and charisma. Tradition, family loyalty, stability, and wealth are all important values in Panamanian society. Panamanians generally characterize the ideal male as being very "masculine": a man of action, who is forceful, daring, and virile. But he is also polite. The ideal woman is well-bred, understanding, and feminine. People in the large urban areas are more cosmopolitan in their approach to these traditions.

Nationalism is strong in Panama. The motto of Panama is "For the benefit of the world." It is a reflection of the country's strategic position in the world and the service it provides to all nations. Most citizens, even interior *campesinos* (farmers), are well-informed on topics relating to national and international politics. Panamanians are also aware of their country's association with the United States. Many resent the relationship as unequal, but others appreciate its benefits. Panamanians also appreciate their Spanish heritage and, to a lesser extent, their indigenous roots.

Personal Appearance

Most male urban workers wear open-necked shirts called *camisillas*. Bankers and other executives wear dark suits and ties. Women dress in styles similar to those in the United States. Dress habits are informal, and sandals are common footwear. Panamanians, especially women, tend to pay careful attention to their public appearance. They rarely wear sloppy clothing and they admire a polished look. Traditional costumes are worn on special occasions. For women, this includes a *pollera*, a full-length dress with embroidery. For men, it is the *montuno*—baggy shorts and matching embroidered top—leather sandals (*cutarras*), and palm-fiber hats. Indigenous groups have their own styles of dress.

CUSTOMS AND COURTESIES

Greetings

When greeting, many women (and sometimes members of the opposite sex) give an *abrazo* (hug). That is, they clasp hands as in a handshake, lean forward, and press cheeks. Men shake hands with one another, often while patting the other on the shoulder. *Campesinos* usually only shake hands when greeting. Verbally, they may also "howl" a *gritando*, a personally styled "cry" used to express friendship, break the monotony of field work, and show joy at fiestas.

The most common verbal greetings include *¿Cómo está?* (How are you?), *¡Buenos!* (Good day!), *¿Qué tal?* (What's up?), *¿Qué hay de bueno?* (What's good?), *¿Cómo le ha ido?* (How's it been?), *¿Cómo le va?* (How's it going?), and *Hola* (Hi). Inquiring about the welfare of one's family members is polite after an initial greeting. Common terms for saying goodbye include *¡Hasta luego!* (See you later), *¡Que le vaya bien!* (May things go well for you), and in the cities, *Ciao* (Goodbye). *Adiós* is rarely used because it is considered fairly permanent.

In formal situations among the educated, it is very important to address people by educational title, such as *Maestro/a* (teacher), *Profesor/a* (professor), *Ingeniero/a* (person with a bachelor of science degree), or *Doctor/a* (doctor). The person's given name, not surname, is usually used with these titles. In written correspondence, the entire name is used. Other titles include *Señor* (Mr.), *Señora* (Mrs.), and *Señorita* (Miss). *Don* and *Doña* are used for respected or elderly men and women, respectively. Informally, nicknames are common and people often say one's given name or nickname as a greeting. Using someone's nickname is not polite unless the person is a close friend. People often address each other by terms of relationship: *hermano/a* (brother/sister), *amigo/a* (friend), *tio/a* (uncle/aunt), and so forth.

Gestures

People in the interior use nonverbal communication more often than those in urban areas. For example, they pucker their lips to point, to indicate "over there" or "time to go," or for many other uses. One might ask "What's up?" by shrugging with the palms facing up. "No" can be expressed by wagging the index finger from side to side. Drawing a circle with the finger in the air means one is coming right back. Wrinkling a nose can mean "I don't understand."

Politeness is important and chivalry common. Men offer their seats on public transportation to women or the elderly. Deference to elders in any situation is important. Personal space is generally small, and people sit or stand close when they converse. Eye contact is important. It is polite to cover the mouth when yawning.

Visiting

Panamanians enjoy hosting others in their homes. They are open, generous, and informal with their guests. Hosts customarily do not establish an ending time to a visit, as that might indicate to the guests that they are not as important as the hosts' schedule. It is polite for guests to allow their hosts to take care of them. That is, guests do not help with dishes, they take any offers of the best seat or food, and they graciously accept any good-bye gifts. When invited to dinner, guests usually do not take gifts to their hosts; this would imply the hosts are not expected to be thorough in providing hospitality. Rather than giving a gift, guests generally expect to return the favor of a dinner invitation.

Relatives and friends visit one another often. A visit is a compliment; it is expected of friends. Unannounced visitors are always welcome. In the interior, relatives see each other almost daily, depending on their relationship and how far they live from one another. Urban dwellers enjoy Sunday visits. All visitors are offered refreshments, such as a fruit drink and some crackers.

Sending (exchanging) gifts is common among friends in the interior, but gifts include items such as food or seedlings, not expensive items. The custom is a way of sharing one's good fortune with friends. It is not commonly practiced in the cities.

Eating

Urbanites generally eat three meals a day. Interior people often have a big breakfast early, a main meal at midday, and a small dinner around 5:00 P.M. *Campesino* families most often eat two meals: breakfast after 9:00 A.M. and then dinner around 6:00 P.M. They may have snacks before or during work. Hands are generally kept above the table during a meal. Conversation is light. The spoon is used most often in the interior.

Any guests present are served first, followed by the men, children, and the women and/or cooks. The cook or hostess usually prepares a plate for each person. Extra food might be put out for second helpings. Guests compliment the cook verbally and by finishing their food. Urbanites eat out often, but *campesinos* rarely do. Tips (5–10 percent) are usually given to urban servers.

LIFESTYLE

Family

In Panamanian families, the mother generally takes responsibility for the home. This traditional role is still quite admired and respected. Less than 30 percent of the labor force is composed of women. The father's responsibilities are usually outside the home, but he is still considered the undisputed leader of the family. As in other Latin American countries, the family is the basic unit of society. Due to the changing tempo of modern life, nuclear families are gaining prominence over the extended family. However, adult children expect to care for their aging parents, even if they do not live with them. In such cases, children are sure to send money or food, visit them, and arrange for their basic needs to be met. A large number of births take place out of wedlock, but many of these are within stable common-law marriages. Families in urban areas often live in rented apartments, while rural families may own a small home.

Dating and Marriage

Most girls begin group dating around age 14. Compared with girls of other Latin American countries, urban Panamanian girls experience a great degree of freedom. However, girls in the interior are often not allowed to date until much later and are subject to parental restrictions. Urban women usually marry in their early 20s; in the interior, women often marry by age 20. In most areas, rural and urban, boys have nearly complete freedom. Although rural boys have farm responsibilities, they have little supervision outside of school and have no domestic duties. When dating, couples enjoy going for walks, dancing, and watching movies. In the interior, common-law marriages are prevalent and are generally as well accepted and stable as legal marriages performed by the state. Couples desiring a church marriage must obtain a license; a registered religious official can then perform the marriage. Church weddings are common in urban areas.

Diet

In Panama, it is commonly said that one hasn't eaten if one hasn't had rice. Rice is served with nearly every meal, along with a source of protein (eggs, chicken, sardines, meat, fish, or beans). Corn and plantains are also staples. Fish is inexpensive and often made into a soup. Vegetables are usually eaten as part of the main dish or in a salad. Fruit is often eaten as a snack. *Chicha*, a popular drink, is made from fresh fruit, water, and sugar. Coffee is usually part of breakfast. Common dishes in the interior include *sancocho* (chicken soup), *guacho* (rice soup), *bollo* (corn mush that has been boiled in the husk), corn tortillas, and *guisado* (stewed meat with tomatoes and spices). *Arroz con pollo* (rice with chicken) is eaten on special occasions. Urban people eat traditional foods as well as a wider variety of international foods.

Recreation

In towns, many participate in team sports. Baseball is the most popular sport, while soccer, boxing, and basketball are also favorites. Panamanians enjoy attending horse races, cockfights, and the movies. The national lottery is popular. Socializing on the porch or visiting friends is an important leisure activity. Leisure time for rural women often revolves around domestic events; they may get together to make crafts or to socialize and make *bollo* when the new corn comes in.

Native peoples have a special talent for handicrafts (textiles, jewelry, baskets, ceramics, etc.).

Dramatic poetry readings are popular. Panamanians love to dance. Traditional Panamanian music, called *Típico,* is played by a band consisting of a singer and players with an accordion, a guitar, some percussion, and sometimes a violin. Lyrics usually pertain to love and life. *Típico* is more common in rural areas and is joined in cities by samba, jazz, salsa, and reggae. On the Caribbean coast, drumming and singing to an African beat are popular.

Holidays

Official holidays include New Year's Day (celebrated 1–2 January), Day of the Martyrs (9 January), Easter (Friday–Sunday), Independence from Colombia Day (3 November), the Uprising of Los Santos (11 November), Independence from Spain Day (28 November), Mother's Day (second Sunday in December), and Christmas. Each village or city holds celebrations to honor the local patron saint. *Carnaval* celebrations are held during the few days before Ash Wednesday (usually in February or March).

Commerce

The business day begins as early as 7:00 A.M. and ends by 4:00 P.M. Many stores stay open until 6:00 P.M. During holidays, they may remain open until 9:00 or 10:00 P.M. Most businesses are open Saturday until 6:00 P.M., with the exception of government offices and banks, which are closed. Urbanites shop at large grocery stores and open-air markets for most basics. *Campesinos* may shop daily for small amounts of items they need; they also collect from their harvests and exchange produce with friends and relatives. When necessary, they travel to shops and markets in larger interior towns.

SOCIETY

Government

Panama is a multiparty democracy divided into nine provinces. Its president is chief of state and head of government. The 67-seat National Assembly has several active parties; the Democratic Revolutionary Party (PRD), originally formed by Torrijos, is the governing party. All citizens are required by law to vote beginning at age 18. At the local level, communities elect a *junta local* to coordinate town events and functions.

Economy

Panama's potentially strong economy is slowly recovering from years of political instability, authoritarian rule, and U.S. economic sanctions (1988–90). After vital trade relations were restored with the United States, the economy grew an average of 7 percent annually in the early 1990s but dropped to about 4 percent in 1994. Panama faces high unemployment, a shortage of skilled labor, and structural problems. However, due to its key geographical position, Panama enjoys success in its strong banking industry, financial services, trade through the Colón Free Trade Zone, and tourism. Real gross domestic product per capita is $5,600, which has more than tripled in the last generation. One-fourth of Panamanians live in absolute poverty. These figures reflect a growing prosperity for the country but a widening gap between rich and poor. The middle class is still small.

Key exports include bananas, shrimp, coffee, sugar, and clothing. The Panama Canal, a major international trade route, provides vital foreign-exchange earnings. Tourism is another important sector. About 27 percent of the labor force is employed in agriculture-related industries. The official currency is the *balboa* (B), which consists mostly of coins. Bills are usually U.S. dollars, which are legal tender.

Transportation and Communication

The highway system is the hub of transportation in Panama. Roads are generally in good condition, especially in and around urban areas. The Inter-American Highway runs through Panama City. The capital is linked to Colón by the Trans-Isthmian Highway. Revenues from the national lottery help build and maintain roads. Domestic airlines provide service. Some transportation is available on shallow waterways. In cities, buses and *chivas* (minibuses) provide public transportation. Taxis are readily available. In the interior, people walk, use *chivas* or buses, or ride horses. The majority of the people do not own cars. Most telephones are owned by people living in urban areas. In the interior, centrally located public telephones are available. Communication facilities are well developed. A free press flourishes and there are many newspapers.

Education

Primary education is compulsory and free between the ages of seven and fifteen. Most school-aged children (72 percent) complete primary schooling and go on to more specialized secondary education. Rural families may have difficulty in sending children to secondary schools—usually located in larger towns—because they cannot afford to pay for daily transportation or room and board in the city. After completing the secondary level, a student may go on to one of several vocational schools or prepare to enter a university. Panama has a national university, established in 1935, as well as a Catholic university and other church-owned schools. The adult literacy rate is 90 percent.

Health

Panama's public health program is part of the national security system. It provides such services as free examinations, care for the needy, and intensified health education and sanitation programs. Most people have access to modern medical care of some kind, although the best facilities and personnel are located in Panama City and Colón. Some rural health centers are understaffed or poorly equipped. Malaria and yellow fever are active in the eastern areas near Colombia. The infant mortality rate is 16 per 1,000; life expectancy averages 75 years.

FOR THE TRAVELER

U.S. travelers need a passport or tourist card to enter Panama. A 30-day tourist card is issued through travel agencies or airlines. Vaccinations are recommended for some tropical diseases if one plans to leave main urban areas. Water is not always safe to drink, especially in the interior. For more information, contact the Embassy of Panama, 2862 McGill Terrace NW, Washington, DC 20008; phone (202) 483–1407.

Republic of
Paraguay

Boundary representations not necessarily authoritative.

BACKGROUND

Land and Climate

Paraguay is a landlocked country in central South America. Covering 157,046 square miles (406,570 square kilometers), it is slightly smaller than California. More than one-third of the country is forest or woodlands, although deforestation is a significant problem. About 20 percent of all territory is suitable for cultivation. There are no high elevations in the country and no real mountains. The *Río Paraguay* (Paraguay River) divides the country into two regions. To the northwest lies the arid, sparsely settled region known as the Gran Chaco or simply Chaco. Near the river, the Chaco is mostly wetlands. Southeast of the river is the fertile Paraná Plateau, where the population and agricultural centers are located. The plateau is subtropical and has a hot, humid, and rainy climate. Paraguay is south of the equator; seasonal changes are opposite those in the Northern Hemisphere. Summer is from September to June. The cooler rainy season is from June to September.

History

Spanish explorers came to Paraguay in 1524 and established Asunción in 1537. Colonial rule lasted until the 19th century. Paraguay peacefully gained independence in 1811, and José Gaspar Rodríguez Francia established the first in a long line of dictatorships. He closed the country to the outside world and ruled until 1840. In 1865, Francisco Solano López took Paraguay into the War of the Triple Alliance against Brazil, Argentina, and Uruguay. Ultimately (1870), the war was lost, along with 55,000 square miles (142,450 square kilometers) of territory and 500,000 lives. Foreign troops stayed until 1876, and Paraguay remained politically unstable for another generation.

In 1932, Paraguay waged a three-year Chaco War with Bolivia in a territorial dispute, but gaining two-thirds of the Chaco territory it claimed cost Paraguay a good portion of its male population and did not stabilize the nation. Various dictators and one elected president ruled until 1954, when General Alfredo Stroessner, commander of the army, took control of the Paraguayan government and established a long-term dictatorship. Although his tenure brought some economic development (mainly in the form of three hydroelectric dams), his government was responsible for human-rights violations, corruption, and oppression.

A coup in 1989 ousted Stroessner, who now lives in Brazil. Promising democratic reform, General Andrés Rodríguez Pedotti, who led the coup, was elected president. He restored civil rights, legalized political parties, and promised not to serve past 1993. Rodríguez was the first leader to successfully implement many democratic reforms. A new constitution was ratified in June 1992. Because of Rodríguez's administration, Paraguay has emerged from its isolation under decades of dictatorship to join in regional and international organizations. Juan Carlos Wasmosy, a civilian, was elected president in 1993. Wasmosy faced an attempted coup by army chief General Lino Oviedo in April 1996. However, popular pressure prevented a military takeover and strengthened Paraguay's commitment to democracy.

PEOPLE
Population
Paraguay's population is slightly more than 5.3 million and is growing annually at 2.7 percent. Paraguay is the most ethnically homogeneous country in South America, partially due to its many years of virtual isolation. Up to 95 percent of the population is *mestizo* (a mixture of descendants of Spanish and native Guaraní). Pure native Guaraní are few in number today; most live around Asunción or in northern Paraguay. Descendants of German and Italian immigrants have assimilated into *mestizo* society. Some Koreans, who are generally merchants, other Asians, and Arabs also reside in Paraguay, but they have not assimilated into Paraguayan culture. A small number of Mennonites, mostly around Filadelfia, maintain a distinct lifestyle based on their European agricultural heritage.

About half of all Paraguayans live in urban areas. Asunción has about 800,000 inhabitants. More than 40 percent of the population is under age 15. Paraguay's Human Development Index (0.723) ranks it 87th out of 174 countries. Opportunities for individual choice, provided by access to health care, education, and a decent standard of living, are not available to the entire population. Adjusted for women, the index (0.628) ranks Paraguay 63d out of 130 countries. Women earn a low percentage of the nation's income.

Language
Paraguay has two official languages, Spanish and Guaraní. Spanish is the language of government, urban commerce, and schooling, but Guaraní is the common language. In rural areas, some people speak only Guaraní, although most also speak or understand Spanish. Portuguese is spoken along the Brazilian border. Paraguay's Spanish is called *Castellano* (Castilian), not *Español*. Paraguayans mix many Guaraní words with Spanish, and many of their vocabulary words differ from those of other Spanish-speaking countries. They generally use the formal *vos* rather than the informal *tú* form of address.

Religion
About 90 percent of all Paraguayans are Roman Catholic, but most are tolerant of other religions. Catholic holidays play an important role in society. Women tend to be more religious than men. Various other Christian churches, both Protestant and other, also have members in Paraguay. The Mennonites practice their own religion. Many rural people also include a belief of mythical or mystical powers in their worship.

General Attitudes
Paraguayans are proud of being Paraguayan. They often define themselves by three aspects of their culture: speaking Guaraní, drinking *yerba* (herb) tea, and eating *mandioca* (cassava). Paraguayans say that Spanish is the language of the head, but Guaraní is the language of the heart. *Mandioca* is a staple food and is served at nearly every meal. Mate (MAH-tay) leaves are made into a mildly stimulating tea. Served cold, it is called *tereré*. Served hot, it is *mate*. *Yerba* tea has been part of the culture for hundreds of years.

Paraguay is a traditional society. Large families, property, beauty, virility, money, and status are valued. People are generally concerned with not having problems; that is, an ultimate desire is *tranquilidad* (tranquillity). Deviations from traditional mores and loud, disruptive behavior are not appreciated. Due to generations of isolation, wars with neighboring countries, and other factors, the *mestizo* population tends to look down on people with darker skin tones, including some foreigners, resident Asians, and dark-skinned or Black South Americans.

Paraguayans do not appreciate stereotypes about poverty and inferiority in developing countries; they are proud of their particular heritage. At the same time, they feel other countries take advantage of their nation. They do not appreciate people from the United States referring to themselves as "Americans." Paraguayans are South Americans. The preferred reference to residents of the United States is *norteamericano* or *norteamericana* (North American).

Personal Appearance
Western-style clothing is worn throughout Paraguay. Cleanliness is emphasized; even the poorest people have clean clothing and clean shoes. Adults do not wear shorts in public. Men generally do not wear sandals. Urban men wear slacks and a shirt for working, but suits and ties are less common because of the hot climate. Clothing is often lightweight; cotton is a popular fabric. Rural men wear work clothes and a hat when farming.

Women pay particular attention to their appearance, regardless of economic conditions. Styled hair, manicured nails, jewelry, and makeup are all important. Rural women nearly always wear dresses. Women in Asunción are especially fashionable. Society generally considers it important for women to be beautiful. The youth enjoy North American fashions.

CUSTOMS AND COURTESIES
Greetings
Spanish greetings, such as *¡Mucho gusto!* (Pleased to meet you), are often used with strangers or for formal situations. Acquaintances might use less formal Spanish, such as *¡Hola! ¿Cómo estás?* (Hi. How are you?), but friends and relatives more often use Guaraní greetings. The most common phrase is *¿Mba'eixapa?* (pronounced m-buy-ay-SHA-pah), which means "How are you?" The reply is almost always *¡Iporã!* (Just fine). In the countryside, it is friendly and polite to call out a greeting (*Adió*, holding out the "o") to a friend passing one's house.

Except in the workplace, men and women always shake hands when greeting, even if for the second or third time in a day. Friends greeting for the first time in a day (if at least one is a woman) will kiss each other on each cheek as well as shake hands. Rural women are more likely to pat the other's arm rather than kiss. When departing, most people repeat whatever gesture they used in greeting.

Urban men are respectfully addressed by the last name, often accompanied by *Don*. For women, *Doña* customarily accompanies the first name. Using a person's professional title also shows respect. Young people refer to each other by their first names. In rural areas, *campesinos* (farmers) often address one another by first name, preceded with *Ña* (for women) or *Karai* (for men). Paraguayans often greet a respected elder by holding their hands in prayer position and waiting for the elder to bless them.

Gestures

Perhaps the most common hand gesture is "thumbs up," which expresses anything positive or encouraging. A person uses the gesture when saying *¡Iporã!* or answering a question. Wagging a vertical index finger means "No" or "I don't think so." One beckons by waving all fingers of the hand with the palm facing out or down. Winking has romantic, even sexual, connotations; it is not used as a casual gesture.

Paraguayans are soft-spoken; they do not shout to get someone's attention. If making a "tssst tssst" sound does not work, a Paraguayan might whistle or run after the person. Paraguayan men usually give up their bus seats to older or pregnant women or women with babies. Seated bus passengers usually offer to hold packages or children for standing passengers. To make one's presence known at a home, one claps at the gate. It is impolite to enter the yard until invited.

Visiting

Paraguayans visit one another often. Unannounced visits are common and welcome. Paraguayans enjoy hosting friends and new acquaintances. Guests are usually offered refreshments. If the hosts are eating a meal or drinking *terere*, they will invite visitors to join in. Otherwise, guests might be offered a soft drink (in the city), coffee, juice, or water. Hosts offer *terere* to unannounced visitors only if they want them to stay a while. People often drink the tea from a common *guampa* (container, usually made of wood, cattle horns, or gourds) through a *bombilla* (metal straw). Powdered mate mixed with cold water produces *terere* (hot water produces *mate*, which is drunk less often). The host passes the *guampa* to one person, who drinks and returns the container to the host, who makes another portion for the next person. Participants enjoy this important social custom while relaxing and conversing.

Urban residents like to invite friends to their homes for a meal, while rural people generally extend invitations only for special occasions. Guests are not expected to be punctual; being late is accepted and more comfortable for all involved. Invited dinner guests might bring a gift of wine, beer, or a dessert. These guests are usually expected to stay after a meal for conversation and tea.

Eating

Mealtimes and eating habits vary according to region and family. Rural people often eat when they can; they don't necessarily sit down to a daily family meal. Farmers might eat lunch, for example, in their fields rather than go home. Urban families usually eat their main meal together.

When guests (not relatives) are invited, children might eat before the guests arrive or before they are served. Guests usually receive their plates of food fully served. They may take additional portions from serving dishes on the table. Not finishing one's food is considered an insult to the cook. Hosts usually insist their guests take second helpings. Proper etiquette is important in very formal situations, including not placing hands in the lap (they rest on the table edge) and waiting for the hosts to begin eating.

Few people, especially in rural areas, drink during the meal. They wait until they are done eating. At rural parties or celebrations, women eat after men do, or they eat at separate tables. The *asado* (barbecue) is a popular family gathering in many areas.

Street vendors sell a great deal of food on urban streets, and eating or drinking in public is common. A common custom is to share food or drink. In restaurants, one rarely buys a drink for oneself; one orders a large pitcher for all at the table. Additional rounds are ordered by other diners. When eating a snack or small meal, one offers the food to whomever is around. Declining the offer is not impolite. In restaurants, service is included in the bill and tips are not expected.

LIFESTYLE

Family

Society centers on the extended family. Three or four generations might live in one home or on one farm. Children are well behaved and polite. They generally show respect to their elders, and they expect to care for their aging parents when they themselves are adults. The father heads the family, with the wife taking care of the household. Most rural women, like the men, are involved in agriculture. Up to 40 percent of the urban labor force is female.

Rural families have few modern conveniences. They live in wooden or brick homes with dirt floors and grass or tin roofs. Urban homes are made of concrete with tile roofs. Nearly all homes in Asunción have running water and electricity.

Dating and Marriage

Most Paraguayan girls have a party at age 15 to celebrate becoming a *señorita*. They are then allowed to go to dances. In traditional homes, they are not allowed to date for another year or two. Young people get to know each other at community fiestas, large family gatherings, dances, and so forth. Customarily, a boy must have a girl's parents' permission to date her. Then he can only visit her on traditional visiting days (Tuesday, Thursday, Saturday, and Sunday). Later in a relationship, dating couples might be accompanied by a relative of the girl. Parents generally expect to approve of any marriage partners. For a marriage to be legal, the wedding must be performed civilly. In addition, couples may have a church wedding. Many couples enter into common-law relationships. Others have children together but do not live together.

Diet

Breakfast usually consists of *cocido* (mate, cooked sugar, milk) or coffee, bread and butter, and rolls or pastries. Lunch (the main meal) is eaten around midday, and dinner is often served after dark when work is finished. The most important staple foods include *mandioca*, *sopa Paraguaya* (cornbread baked with cheese, onions, and sometimes meat), *chipa* (hard cheese bread), *tortillas*, and *empanadas* (deep-fried meat or vegetable pockets). Small rural gardens provide *campesino* families with tomatoes, onions, carrots, garlic, squash, watermelon, cabbage, and other produce. Fruit is obtained from surrounding trees and bushes. Beef is very important to the adult diet. Paraguayans also eat chicken and pork dishes.

Recreation

Soccer is the most popular spectator sport, but volleyball is the most common participation sport. Urban men often play volleyball in the evenings. Many people enjoy tennis and basketball. Women generally do not play sports. Urban people might attend the theater, see movies, or enjoy other cultural events. The Paraguayan harp is world famous. Rural people relax by drinking *terere* and *mate* and visiting each other, as do urbanites. Latino polka music is quite popular in many areas. The youth enjoy music with a distinct beat (disco, rap, etc.).

Holidays

Paraguayans celebrate New Year's Day, Epiphany (6 January), *Carnaval* (a week of parades and parties in February), Heroes Day (1 March), *Semana Santa* (Holy Week before Easter), Labor Day (1 May), Independence Day (14–15 May), Mother's Day (15 May), the Chaco Armistice (12 June), *Día del Amistad* (Friendship Day, 30 July), Founding of Asunción City (celebrated with large parades, 15 August), Constitution Day (25 August), the Victory of Boqueron (29 September), Columbus Day (12 October), All Saints' Day (1 November), Virgin of Cacupe (8 December), and Christmas. *Semana Santa* is the most important holiday period and is a week for family gatherings.

Commerce

Urban business hours extend from 7:00 A.M. to noon and from 3:00 to 6:00 P.M. People in both urban and rural areas take a *siesta* during the three-hour break and eat their main meal of the day. Rural Paraguayans grow much of their own food; they purchase staples and other goods at small neighborhood stores, which are located in homes. Shopping must often be done on a daily basis due to the lack of refrigeration. Urban people purchase their food from markets or small stores.

SOCIETY

Government

Paraguay's young democracy, divided into 15 departments (provinces), is headed by an elected president. Legislators in the 45-seat Senate and 80-seat Chamber of Deputies are also elected. The voting age is 18; adults are required by law to vote until age 60. Paraguay's principal parties are the Colorado Party and the Authentic Radical Liberal Party.

Economy

Paraguay's economy is based on agriculture; most rural families grow cotton as their primary cash crop. The Mennonites grow soybeans. The country's other crops include sugarcane, corn, cassava, mate, and tobacco. Beef is an important export; cattle are raised on expansive ranches usually owned by nonresident foreigners. As the price of Paraguayan cotton has fallen, the government has sought ways to decrease dependence on the crop. However, little progress has been realized, and the economy is a major challenge for the new democratic system. Many rural families send one or more members to Argentina to work. Many farmers must keep their children out of school to help with crop production.

About one-fifth of all workers are employed by industry (meatpacking, textiles, light consumer goods, etc.). Contraband trade is a problem in Ciudad del Este. Inflation, foreign debt, and high unemployment are serious problems inhibiting economic progress. Deforestation has effectively ruined the potential for a sustainable timber industry. Land redistribution, foreign investment, and economic diversification are all necessary to improve conditions. Real gross domestic product per capita averages $3,390, which has more than doubled in the last generation. Forty percent of the population lives in poverty. Together these figures indicate that what the country does earn is held by a small wealthy class, and that economic opportunities are limited to urban residents. In an effort to strengthen regional economic activity, Paraguay joined the Mercosur trade bloc, which includes Brazil, Argentina, and Uruguay. The currency is the *guaraní* (G).

Transportation and Communication

While construction of paved highways has taken place in Paraguay, most roads are not paved. Many are impassable during heavy rains. Buses serve as the main form of public transportation in Asunción and throughout the country. Otherwise, rural people walk. Wealthier urban residents have cars. Taxis are available in Asunción. There are two television channels, one government owned and the other private. A private cable company services Asunción. Both AM and FM radio stations broadcast throughout the country. Most people do not have telephones, but public phones are available.

Education

Public education is provided free of charge, but students must buy uniforms and are asked to contribute to the school fund to help buy supplies. Facilities tend to be crowded. Instruction is usually in Spanish, which can be a hardship on rural children. Most children begin school, but fewer than 40 percent complete all six years of primary school. Less than one-third of eligible children attend secondary school. The school year runs from March to November. Opportunities for those who finish school are limited, and many either work in the fields or go to Argentina or other countries to find work. There are some vocational schools and other institutions of higher learning. The official literacy rate is 91 percent, but this does not reflect reality in rural areas.

Health

The health-care system includes hospitals and clinics in major towns. The smaller the town, the smaller the clinic. Rural health posts are staffed a few days a week by a nurse. Rural people use traditional herbs and cures to treat minor ailments. While Paraguayans value cleanliness, many unsanitary conditions (dirt floors, unprotected water sources, poor sewage systems, etc.) contribute to poor health. Malnutrition affects children. Severe dental problems afflict a majority of the population (especially in rural areas). The bite of the *vinchuga* bug can be deadly to rural dwellers who do not sleep under mosquito netting. The bug bites one's face at night, injecting a parasite that kills the person several years later. Paraguay's infant mortality rate is 25 per 1,000; life expectancy averages 70 years.

FOR THE TRAVELER

U.S. travelers need a valid passport to enter Paraguay, but a visa is not necessary for stays of up to three months. Some vaccinations may be necessary; check with your health-care provider. Water is not always safe to drink outside of Asunción. For travel information, contact the Paraguay Consulate, 18377 Beach Boulevard, Suite 212, Huntington Beach, CA 92648; phone (714) 848–3168. Paraguay's embassy is located at 2400 Massachusetts Avenue NW, Washington, DC 20008.

A *Culturgram* is a product of native commentary and original, expert analysis. Statistics are estimates and information is presented as a matter of opinion. While the editors strive for accuracy and detail, this document should not be considered strictly factual. It is a general introduction to culture, an initial step in building bridges of understanding between peoples. It may not apply to all peoples of the nation. You should therefore consult other sources for more information.

Republic of
Peru

Boundary representations not necessarily authoritative.

THE AMERICAS

BACKGROUND

Land and Climate

Almost the same size as Alaska, Peru is the third largest country in South America. It covers 496,223 square miles (1,285,220 square kilometers). Peru is divided into three distinct geographical regions: the narrow, dry coastal plain (*costa*) in the west; the high Andes Mountains (*sierra*), roughly in the center; and the tropical lowlands of the Amazon Basin (*selva*) to the east. The Andes rise to elevations of up to 22,000 feet (6,700 meters). The population is concentrated in the west. Because of the Andes and the Amazon Basin, more than half of the country is covered with various types of forests. Only about 3 percent of the land is suitable for farming. Earthquakes are common but usually mild, although they are potentially dangerous, such as those that struck in 1990 and killed several hundred people. Peru shares the famous Lake Titicaca, the highest navigable body of water in the world, with Bolivia. There is little rainfall along the coast, although the winter is foggy, humid, and cool. In Lima, the capital, the temperature is moderate year-round; it averages 65°F (18°C). Temperatures vary significantly between the rugged Andes and the eastern jungles.

History

Several of South America's most advanced cultures lived in pre-Columbian Peru. The great Incan Empire, which was unsurpassed in the art of stonecutting and also achieved a high degree of economic and political development, was the last of these groups. Incan and earlier Chimu ruins, notably at Cuzco, Chan Chan, and Machu Picchu, make Peru a favorite destination for archaeologists and tourists. In 1532, the Spanish invaded Peru under the leadership of Francisco Pizarro. They conquered the Incas the next year. The area soon became the richest and most powerful Spanish colony in South America because of its location and many mineral treasures.

Under the leadership of South American liberator José de San Martín, Peru declared independence from Spain in July 1821. With the help of Simón Bolívar, the Venezuelan general who liberated several other countries, the victory was complete by 1826. For a century, Peru worked to secure its territory and build its social institutions.

Although the 1933 constitution provided Peru with a president and legislature to be elected for six-year terms, military leaders and dictators dominated Peru until the 1960s. A free, multiparty election was held in 1963 and Fernando Belaúnde Terry was elected president. He was deposed in 1968 by a military junta that ruled for 12 years (a period called *la dictadura*). Belaúnde was reelected in 1980 when the military agreed to return control of the government to civilians. Troubles with the economy, which began during *la dictadura,* became worse under Belaúnde and were not resolved during Alán García's presidency (1985–90).

In 1980, the *Sendero Luminoso*, or Shining Path, began a decade of violent guerrilla warfare against the government. The Shining Path, a Maoist group determined to overthrow the government, and other terrorist organizations were responsible for some 18 thousand deaths during the 1980s. They held power in the Upper Huallaga Valley (several hours north of Lima) and were paid by drug traffickers for protection and the right to operate in the region. The drug traffickers sell locally grown coca leaf (the basis of cocaine) to Colombian drug cartels for eventual export. Many farmers would rather plant crops like coffee or cacao than plant coca.

Despite many problems, including terrorist attacks against the government, the country maintained democratic institutions and free elections. In June 1990, Alberto Fujimori, a son of Japanese immigrants, was elected president. He promised justice and ethics in government and vowed to overcome Peru's economic problems. However, Shining Path violence intensified and moved closer to Lima, and the economy struggled with Fujimori's austerity package.

Citing factors inhibiting Peru's progress, Fujimori suspended the constitution in April 1992 and dissolved congress. He took emergency powers and restricted civil liberties. His goal was to defeat the Shining Path and reform the government while proceeding with economic reforms. A new constitution was approved in a national referendum in October 1993. It enshrines principles of a free-market economy and a democratic system. National elections for the presidency and congress were held in 1995, with Fujimori winning by a large margin. His party also did well in the legislative elections.

Helping Fujimori to his victory was the 1992 capture of Shining Path leader Abimael Guzmán Reynoso. Guzmán was tried and sentenced to life in prison. Shining Path violence continues on a small scale, but the movement has effectively been shut down as a threat to Peruvian society. Fujimori can also credit success with economic reform for his popularity and electoral victory. In the longstanding border dispute with Ecuador, he has taken a strong stand. The two countries had fought in 1941 over territory, but the Rio de Janeiro Protocol (1942) supposedly ended the controversy. However, a remote stretch of border 48 miles (76 kilometers) long was never marked after the protocol was signed and became the subject of fighting in January 1995. Negotiations led to a cease-fire and demilitarization of the region, which diminished recent tensions. However, sporadic fighting still occurs, and the conflict is yet to be fully resolved.

THE PEOPLE

Population

The population of Peru is approximately 24.1 million and is growing at 1.8 percent annually. Population density is generally low, however, because of Peru's large land area. Peru's population is ethnically diverse. About 45 percent is Indian, descendants of the great Incan Empire. There are many ethnic and linguistic divisions among the Indian, some of whom are still fairly isolated in the Amazon jungle. Another 37 percent of the people are *mestizos* (mixed European and Indian heritage). Fifteen percent are of European descent (mostly Spanish), and the remaining 3 percent are composed of blacks (descendants of West African slaves), Japanese, Chinese, and other smaller groups. About half of the population is younger than age 20. Lima is the largest city, with more than six million residents. Seventy percent of all people live in urban areas.

Peru's Human Development Index (0.709) ranks it 93d out of 174 countries. Adjusted for women, the index (0.631) ranks Peru 62d out of 130 countries. These figures indicate that, although generally well educated, most people have only moderate access to adequate health care and a decent standard of living.

Language

Spanish and the Indian language, Quechua, are both officially recognized languages. Another Indian language, Aymara, is also spoken widely. Many Peruvians speak both Spanish and one Indian language. About 30 percent of the people speak no Spanish at all; they speak Quechua, Aymara, or another native language. Peruvians are taught English as a second language, and the more-educated can speak it well.

Religion

Until 1979, the Roman Catholic Church was the state church in Peru. Today, even though there is freedom of religion and all churches enjoy the same political status as the Catholic Church, most people are Roman Catholic and the church plays a significant role in their lives. Many Protestant and Evangelical churches also operate in the country. Many of the Indians who are Roman Catholic mix traditional indigenous beliefs with Christian values, sometimes calling their gods by Christian names.

General Attitudes

Peruvians are strong willed and nationalistic. They have been through many trials, politically and economically, but maintain a strong desire to endure and succeed. The people have a good sense of humor and are accommodating and eager to please. Still, they are also very sensitive about some things. Jokes about their lifestyle, especially those coming from foreigners, are offensive. Personal criticism, if necessary, is expected to be expressed in a positive manner. The Peruvian concept of time is more relaxed than in industrialized nations. Appointments and other meetings may not begin on time and Peruvians generally consider people to be more important than schedules. However, international visitors, to whom punctuality is more important, are expected to be on time for appointments.

Many native Indians, especially those who supported the Shining Path, feel they are discriminated against by Peru's *mestizo* and European populations. Indians are usually rural people, but even those who move to the city are not accepted. This has fueled great resentment among Indians and is one source of the country's social problems. But Indians now place hope in promises of increased investment coming from international organizations and the government. Urban residents, particularly in Lima, are turning their attention to economic progress. People are generally optimistic about the country's future, especially with the return of democracy, the near end of the Shining Path movement, and economic reforms.

Personal Appearance

Although people in Lima and other urban areas regularly wear Western-style clothing, rural *campesinos* (farmers) often wear traditional clothing related to their ethnic background. Their clothes are commonly made of handwoven fabrics.

CUSTOMS AND COURTESIES

Greetings

Both men and women shake hands when meeting and parting. Close friends often greet each other with a kiss on one cheek. Men may greet close friends with an *abrazo* (hug). An arm around the shoulder or a pat on the back is a polite way to greet youth. *¡Buenos días!* is a typical Spanish greeting. Friends are addressed by their first names, but elderly people and officials are referred to by their title (*Señor, Doctora,* etc.) and last names.

Gestures

One beckons a person by waving all of the fingers of one hand with the palm facing down. During conversation, people stand close to each other and constant eye contact is important. They also use hand gestures a great deal. When seated, men may place the ankle of one leg on the knee of the other, but this is inappropriate for women. On the other hand, women may cross their legs at the knee, but men do not.

Visiting

Peruvians enjoy visiting one another. Between friends and relatives, most visits are unannounced. In other cases, it is polite to make advance arrangements. Visitors are expected to feel at home and be comfortable. The traditional greeting *Está en su casa* (You are in your house) reflects Peruvian hospitality. Hosts always offer their guests drinks (water, juice, soda, etc.), but declining them is not impolite. Other refreshments might also be offered. In many areas, if guests visit around 5:30 P.M., they are invited to stay for *lonche*, which is a light breakfast-type meal eaten around 6:00 P.M. Hosts appreciate special acknowledgment of children in the home. It is polite to show concern for the health of the host's family and relatives. Gifts are not expected when one visits the home, but small gifts such as fruit or wine are welcome on any occasion. These would commonly be given by those invited to dinner.

Eating

A polite guest eats all of the food that is offered. Excuses for not eating something should be very tactful. Proper table manners are important. Peruvians use the continental style of eating, with the fork is the left hand and the knife remaining in the right. Both hands (but not elbows) are kept above the table at all times. Families enjoy having visitors eat with them. Casual conversation freely accompanies the meal. Reading at the table is rude. In a restaurant, one summons the waiter by waving. If service is included in the bill, a small tip is still given, and if service is not included, a tip is expected.

LIFESTYLE

Family

The family unit is important in Peru. Nuclear families have, on average, three children. The father is the undisputed head of the family, while the mother spends most of her time directing and performing household duties. Women occasionally work outside the home, a trend that is more evident in urban areas. About one-fourth of the labor force is female. Most families live in humble circumstances without many of the modern conveniences common in more industrialized nations.

Dating and Marriage

Some group dating occurs in the late teen years, but dating in couples is almost strictly reserved for courtship. The youth in urban areas enjoy dancing and other activities. Men usually marry in their late twenties, while women generally marry in their early twenties. People in rural areas often marry at a younger age. Common-law marriages are prevalent and widely accepted, except among the upper classes.

Diet

The main staples in the diet include rice, beans, fish, and a variety of tropical fruits. Soups are common. Corn, native to Peru, is the main staple among the Indians. *Seviche* (raw fish seasoned with lemon and vinegar) is popular on the coast. *Papa a la Huancaina* is a baked potato topped with sliced eggs and a sauce (such as hot chili). Potatoes, onions, and garlic are frequent ingredients for dishes in the highlands. Fresh vegetables are eaten in season. Most food is purchased on a daily basis, either in small corner stores (in cities) or large open-air markets. Bargaining is common in the markets.

Recreation

The most popular sport in Peru is soccer. Peruvians carefully follow World Cup competition, especially when their country's team is participating. Basketball, volleyball, and gymnastics are also favorites. Families enjoy picnics, and movies provide entertainment. Sunday is a favorite day for outings.

Music is important to most Peruvians. International music is popular, especially with the youth, but traditional music is also very popular. Two instruments that are often used to play traditional music are the *charango*, a small guitar of sorts, and the *antara*, an assortment of vertically placed flutes tied together.

Holidays

Many local holidays honor patron saints, celebrate the harvest, or provide recreation. National holidays include New Year's Day, Easter (Thursday–Sunday), Countryman's Day (24 June), St. Peter and St. Paul's Day (29 June), Independence Day (28 July), National Day (29 July), St. Rose of Lima Day (30 August), Navy Day (8 October), All Saints' Day (1 November), Immaculate Conception (8 December), and Christmas.

Commece

The average workweek in Peru is slightly more than 48 hours, one of the longest in the world. Businesses are open at least six days a week. Some small businesses close between 1:00 and 3:00 P.M. each day for a *siesta* (break), but this is not as common today as it once was. Many shops are open late into the evening. Business hours vary slightly according to the season, but generally they are between 8:00 A.M. and 5:00 P.M. Some government offices may close as early as 1:00 P.M.

SOCIETY

Government

Peru is a republic. It is divided into 24 departments (which are like states). The president holds executive power and serves a five-year term. The legislature consists of a Senate and a Chamber of Deputies. Members elected in 1995 will serve until 2000. All citizens older than age 18 may vote. The main political parties include Fujimori's Change 90–New Majority Party, the Popular Christian Party, and the Popular Action Party. Several other parties are also active.

Economy

In the early 1990s, the Peruvian economy faced severe strains. Inflation was high, output was low, and the standard of living was dropping. However, since the implementation of reforms, Peru's economy has stabilized and is growing again. Inflation (more than 2,600 percent in 1989) dropped to 15 percent in 1994. Boosted by foreign investment, the economy grew 12.9 percent (the world's highest) in 1994 and 7 percent in 1995. Foreign investment is creating jobs, tapping resources, and improving conditions in the poorest regions, and should increase with the return of democracy. Although the country remains poor, its potential for progress is high and people expect living conditions to improve substantially in the next few years.

Real gross domestic product per capita is $3,300, reflecting one of the first increases since the 1970s. Peru has many advantages that point to a bright future. Some factors include a commitment to a free-market economy, vast untapped resources, an educated workforce, and a fairly equal distribution of income. The greatest hindrance, beyond the threat of insurgency and rural poverty, is the drug trade. Peru is the world's largest producer of coca leaf, which is exported to other countries before it is made into cocaine.

Peru's natural resources include copper, silver, gold, oil, timber, fish, and iron ore. It has a relatively wide economic base, with a variety of industries it can depend on for growth. Wheat, potatoes, beans, rice, and coffee are important agricultural products. Agriculture accounts for 37 percent of all employment. Peru's fish catch is one of the largest in the world. The currency is the *nuevo sol* (S/.).

Transportation and Communication

Most people travel by bus in the cities, but in rural areas they travel on foot or with the help of animals. More and more Peruvians in urban areas have cars. Most roads are not paved. Train and air travel are available, but on a limited basis; some train routes are very scenic. The telecommunications system is fairly adequate for domestic and international use. Pay phones accept tokens that are purchased at newsstands. There are several daily newspapers.

Education

Public education is free and compulsory between ages seven and sixteen. Basic materials are lacking and facilities are inadequate. In the 1980s, Peru increased efforts to extend primary schools into remote areas. In some areas, the Shining Path controlled school facilities, so the government will have to work to reestablish control in these areas. Secondary education is also free in Peru. More than two-thirds of eligible children are enrolled in secondary schools. The average adult has completed at least six years of school, and more young people are staying in school. Peru has more than 30 universities, including the University of San Marcos in Lima, one of the oldest in South America. The adult literacy rate is about 87 percent and is higher among teenagers.

Health

Medical care is adequate in major cities but less so in other areas. Quality care is only available through expensive private clinics. Hospitals are often short on medicine and food, among other things. Many Peruvians are superstitious about health care and are reluctant to use medical facilities. They prefer to use home remedies made of herbs and roots before going to a doctor. Care in small towns is not reliable and not always available.

A 1991 cholera epidemic overwhelmed Peru, killing more than 1,200 people and causing about 200,000 to become ill. Nearly half of all school-age children suffer from malnutrition. Peru's infant mortality rate is 52 per 1,000. Life expectancy averages from 64 to 68 years.

FOR THE TRAVELER

Visas are not required of U.S. travelers for stays of up to 90 days, but a valid passport and proof of onward passage are required. Yellow fever vaccinations are recommended and even required in some cases. Water is usually not potable and should be boiled or treated before drinking. Avoid eating uncooked fish or vegetables, and carefully peel and wash all fruits before eating. If visiting rural areas, consider vaccinations against cholera, typhoid, hepatitis, and perhaps other diseases. Adjusting to the altitude in the highlands may take some time. For health advisories, call the U.S. Centers for Disease Control International Travelers' Hotline at (404) 332–4559.

Because of potential violence from insurgency groups and drug traffickers, the U.S. Department of State advises all tourists to be cautious. Even though major tourist areas have been largely unaffected, the potential for violence exists. Avoid "emergency zones" and always carry a passport. For recorded travel advisories, call (202) 647–5225. Peru has many attractions, including the archaeological sites mentioned earlier. For details on travel opportunities, contact the South American Explorers' Club, 126 Indian Creek Road, Ithaca, NY 14850; phone (800) 274–0568. You may also wish to contact the Embassy of Peru, 1700 Massachusetts Avenue NW, Washington, DC 20036; phone (202) 833–9860.

CULTURGRAM ™ '97

Republic of
Poland

Boundary representations not necessarily authoritative.

BACKGROUND

Land and Climate

The name *Polska* (Poland) means "land of fields." From the sky, Poland appears to be a vast, prairie-like expanse, flat except for the impressive mountains along the southern border: the Tatry (in the Western Carpathians) and the Sudety, which host the country's skiing and resort areas. Because of the plains, 48 percent of the total land area is suitable for cultivation. Poland's flat terrain has also made it vulnerable to territory-seeking armies throughout history, and its borders have changed several times. Covering 120,726 square miles (312,680 square kilometers), the total land area today is about the size of New Mexico. The climate is temperate, with mild summers. However, it is susceptible to extreme temperature variations within short periods of time. Winters are generally cold and precipitation is common throughout the year. The Poles say one must always carry an umbrella because the weather can change instantly. Poland has important natural resources, including coal, sulfur, silver, natural gas, copper, lead, and salt.

Poland's natural beauty is challenged by severe air and water pollution, as well as deforestation. The government is now recognizing the need to clean the environment to preserve future resources.

History

The Poles are descendants of a Slavic people that settled between the Oder and Vistula Rivers before the time of Christ. King Mieszko I adopted the Roman Catholic faith in A.D. 966.

In the late 14th century, Polish life and culture flourished under King Kasimir the Great. Poland combined with Lithuania in the late Middle Ages, creating a mighty empire that was a major power in Europe. An enlightened constitution in 1791, the second in the world, was patterned after the U.S. Constitution and gave freedom to the serfs. Due to political infighting among the ruling nobles, as well as other factors, the monarchy declined to the point that, in 1795, Poland was invaded and partitioned by Prussia, Austria, and Russia. For the next 125 years, Polish identity and culture were preserved by the Roman Catholic Church and Polish exiles.

Poland became a nation again in 1918, at the end of World War I. Unfortunately, political life was neither stable nor strong. The country did not have much of a chance to stabilize, as the German army invaded in 1939. Within days of the German invasion to the west, the Soviets invaded from the east and Poland was again partitioned. More than six million Poles died during World War II, including three million Polish Jews who died in the Holocaust. The Soviets were given administrative control over the regions liberated from German occupation when Germany was defeated. Elections were held, but by 1948 a Soviet-backed Communist government was in firm control and the country's political system came to be patterned after that in the Soviet Union, with some exceptions (such as land ownership and matters of religion).

In 1981, following a series of crippling strikes and the formation and activity of the Solidarity Labor Union, General Wojciech Jaruzelski declared martial law. The *Sejm*

(Parliament) outlawed Solidarity and its leaders were jailed. Martial law was lifted in 1983, and Lech Walesa, the leader of the still-outlawed Solidarity union, received the Nobel Peace Prize in recognition of his efforts to win freedom and a better standard of living for the Polish people.

In 1989, the government legalized Solidarity and implemented government changes. Many Solidarity members won parliamentary seats and Solidarity official Tadeusz Mazowiecki became prime minister. The government began a transition to a market economy to accompany its new democratic government. A bold economic program, referred to as "shock therapy," was instituted in 1990. It caused prices to rise sharply and immediately led to at least 10 percent unemployment.

Jaruzelski resigned to speed political reform, and voters elected Walesa president in late 1990. After nearly a year in power, Walesa came under increasing criticism for rising unemployment and economic recession. He eventually lost parliamentary support for his economic reforms. Former Communists gained control of Parliament in 1993 and have slowed the course of economic reform. In November 1995, former Communist official Aleksander Kwasniewski narrowly defeated Walesa in runoff presidential elections. Kwasniewski has pleged to pursue Poland's goals to join the European Union (EU) and the North Atlantic Treaty Organization (NATO). In January 1996, Jozef Olesky, newly elected prime minister, was forced to resign following allegations that he spied for Russia. He was replaced by Wlodzimierz Cimoszeswicz.

THE PEOPLE

Population

The population of Poland is 38.8 million and is growing at 0.4 percent annually. Urbanization is relatively high, with about 60 percent of the population living in cities. The country is also very homogeneous; 98 percent of the people are of Polish origin. The population also includes Ukrainians (0.6 percent) and Belarusians (0.5 percent), as well as Germans (1.3 percent) in Silesia, an area bordering Germany. Poland's Human Development Index (0.855) ranks it 51st out of 174 countries. Adjusted for women, the index (0.838) ranks Poland 22d out of 130 countries. Poland has yet to provide many citizens with desirable resources and opportunities needed to pursue personal and national goals.

Language

Polish is the official language. Smaller ethnic groups speak their own languages in addition to Polish. A Slavic tongue belonging to the Indo-European family of languages, Polish uses a modified Latin alphabet; a few unique characters look like Latin letters with accent markings but are distinct letters. Written Polish emerged in the 12th century but did not flourish until the 16th century when it began to overtake Latin, which was used by the ruling class. During partition periods, Polish was banned but was preserved by Poles around the world as a matter of patriotism. English and German are popular second languages.

Religion

The overwhelming majority of Poles belong to the Roman Catholic Church, which has had great influence in the country since Poland was catholicized in the tenth century. Approximately 75 percent of Poles consider themselves practicing Catholics, and another 15 percent belong to the church. Because the Catholic Church is a strong and unified entity, it has played an important political role in the past. The church in Poland historically has been nationalistic and patriotic, championing the cause of the people while under the Communist regime. The Catholic pope, John Paul II, is a native Pole.

Other churches represented in Poland include the Russian Orthodox, various Protestant faiths, and the Uniate faith (a combination of Russian Orthodox practices and loyalty to papal authority). The issue of Catholicism's influence in Poland is currently being debated. Some people prefer that laws and social customs remain secular, while others would like them to more fully reflect Catholic values.

General Attitudes

Polish people value self-reliance and individualism, although self-reliance is exercised on an extended-family level. They place great emphasis on the family and on education. Poles are generally outspoken, especially in private circles. They are straightforward and unaccustomed to cynicism. People value generosity and do not regard highly those who are not willing to share their time, resources, or power. Poles are proud of their cultural heritage and their ability to survive war, territory losses, and subordination to other nations. During periods of foreign domination, the Poles looked to their heritage as a great power in order to retain a belief they were not a conquered or subordinate people. Prior to World War II, the Polish noble class considered itself better than the occupying forces, which gave Poles the desire to maintain their culture and language.

Poland's new democracy and transition to a free market have tarnished some hopes. Many people express concern that they did not expect freedom to be so painful. Yet despite the fact that the poor were better off economically under communism, only a minority express a desire to return to the old system. They recognize the future has greater potential.

Personal Appearance

Poles generally dress conservatively, although a growing number favor European styles. Clothing is expensive, so some people make their own clothes. Businesspeople wear conservative suits or dresses. Women like to be well dressed in public. Older rural women continue to wear a scarf around their heads, full skirts, and thick stockings. Denim jeans are especially popular among the youth and in academic and artistic circles. Teenagers like sweatshirts with English slogans or emblems. Children are expected to be clean and well-groomed in school. They celebrate the first spring day or "truent day" outside, wearing funny and odd clothing.

CUSTOMS AND COURTESIES

Greetings

Adults usually shake hands upon meeting. When introducing a man, one uses *Pan* before the last name; for a woman, the term is *Pani*. One addresses a professional person by title and last name. The title is used alone in formal conversation or in business. Teenagers and children are called by their first names, but between adults, first names are used only by mutual consent. Friends greet each other with *Cześ ć,* a way of saying "Hi." A man might kiss the extended hand of an older or younger woman, but not the hand of a woman near his age. Both men and women greet close female friends by kissing both cheeks. Some common Polish greetings include *Dzien dobry* (Good day), *Dobry wieczór* (Good evening), and *Do widzenia* (Good-bye). *Dziekuje* (Thank you) often precedes an answer about how one is doing. When Poles sign their name, they sign their family name first and then their given name.

Visiting

Unannounced visits among friends and relatives are common. This is especially true in rural areas, where people are less likely to have telephones. Unarranged visits generally do not last more than a few hours. More formal, longer visits are arranged in advance. Poles often invite friends over for dinner or just for cake and tea, and they like to have formal parties on special occasions. Weekend visits may last until 6:00 A.M. in areas where buses do not run between 11:00 P.M. and 6:00 A.M.

For even a brief arranged visit, guests customarily give hosts a bottle of wine or vodka or an odd number of flowers (an even number is for sad occasions). They unwrap flowers before giving them to the hostess. Red roses express romantic feelings. White chrysanthemums are reserved for wakes or funerals.

Guests are nearly always offered tea or coffee; it is common to politely refuse at first and then accept when the hosts insist. Guests may be entertained at a *kawiarnia* (café), which offers pastries, coffee, and its own specialties. Such visits often last several hours. People more commonly entertain in the home, however, because going out is expensive.

Eating

Although schedules are changing with society, Poles generally eat breakfast between 6:30 and 8:00 A.M. Some urban people eat a second breakfast (e.g., a sandwich) around 10:00 A.M. Some families expect to gather for the main meal at 3:00 P.M. and enjoy the lighter evening meal between 6:00 and 8:30 P.M. Tea, coffee, and cocoa (for children) are common breakfast drinks. Poles also enjoy tea in the evening.

Poles eat in the continental style, with the fork in the left hand and the knife remaining in the right. They keep both hands (but not the elbows) above the table during the meal. One should not begin eating until everyone has been served and the host or head of the family has begun. Conversation during the meal is minimal, but it is polite to sit around the table just after eating to talk. It is impolite for guests not to finish their first helping. Taking seconds is appreciated, and not finishing that portion is acceptable.

In restaurants, one requests the bill from the waiter and pays at the table. Tips are generally expected. The host may toast a guest with vodka or wine, served between courses. It is appropriate for the guest to return the gesture later in the meal.

LIFESTYLE

Family

The average family has one or two children, although rural families often have three or four. The father, traditionally a dominant authority figure, demands obedience yet wants his children ultimately to be independent and have self-discipline.

In all households, children are given considerable responsibility from an early age. Because both parents usually work outside the home, children often fix their own breakfasts (school starts after work does) and go to school by themselves. Older children clean, sometimes cook, and often care for younger siblings. The economic situation of most families demands the equal involvement of both parents in raising the family and working outside the home, although women still bear most responsibility for homemaking. Women comprise nearly half of the labor force. The elderly often live with their adult children and provide child care for grandchildren.

Dating and Marriage

Young people who start working after the minimum required schooling marry earlier than those who continue their education. Women marry between ages 18 and 20; men begin marrying at age 21. Those who go to technical schools and universities usually marry after age 25. Parents of the couple often give financial assistance and allow the couple to live in their home for the first few years. This is necessary because housing is expensive and in short supply. Living together before marrying is discouraged.

Diet

While the early urban breakfast is often light, many rural people eat more substantial food (e.g., hot cereal). The main meal consists of soup, meat or fish, salad, and potatoes. Pastries or ice cream are eaten for a late-afternoon snack. Bread, dairy products, and canned fish are plentiful. Most foods are readily available. Some common dishes include *pierogi* (stuffed dumplings; stuffings vary), *uszka* (a kind of ravioli), *bigos* (sausage, mushrooms, pickled cabbage), braised pork and cabbage, poppy seed desserts, and cheesecake. People purchase bread several times a week, sometimes even daily. Only those who live far from a store eat bread that is more than two days old. Pork is more popular than beef. With the switch to a market economy, more food is available in greater variety, but prices are high and many families spend much of their income on food.

Recreation

Soccer is popular, but Poles also participate in track-and-field events, cycling, table tennis, skiing, basketball, volleyball, and various individual sports. Bridge is a favorite card game. Attending cultural events and visiting friends are common recreational activities. Poland has a rich heritage in music, art, dancing (e.g., the polka), and literature. Frédéric Chopin (1810–48) is Poland's best-known musician. His most popular pieces include the "Mazurek" and the "Polonais." Fame also extends to other areas, such as science (Copernicus and Marie Curie were Poles) and politics (King Jan III Sobieski broke the Ottoman siege of Vienna in 1683).

Holidays

Official holidays in Poland include New Year's Day, Easter (two days), Labor Day (1 May), Constitution Day (3 May), Corpus Christi (in May or June), All Saints' Day (1 November), Independence Day (11 November), and Christmas. Family graves are decorated on All Saints' Day. Adults generally celebrate their name day (the day assigned to the Catholic saint after whom a person is named) rather than their birthday.

Christmas is the most important holiday. On 6 December, children receive small gifts from St. Nicholas. On Christmas Eve, the family gathers when the first star is sighted for a large meatless meal that usually includes fresh fish, dishes featuring poppy seeds or mushrooms, a special compote, and other traditional foods. On the 26th, Poles visit and relax. Nativity scenes and caroling are popular throughout the season.

For Easter Saturday, people take a basket of specific foods (ham, eggs, sausages, pieces of bread, etc.) to church to be blessed; they eat the food Sunday after mass. Easter Monday is Wet Monday, a day for young people to squirt or dump water on each other. Local festivals, such as the Folk Art Fair in Kraków, and other celebrations are held throughout the year.

Commerce

Banks are generally open from 8:00 A.M. until 5:00 P.M., Monday through Friday, with hours varying on Saturday. Stores are generally open from 7:00 A.M. to 7:00 P.M., Monday through Saturday, although hours vary according to location and function. *Kiosks*, small newsstand shops that offer a variety of goods, are common in Poland's cities. Supermarkets in large cities carry fresh meat, produce, and other basic foods. In other areas, these goods are purchased in open-air markets and neighborhood stores. Bread is sold in grocery stores; bakeries sell pastries and other sweets.

SOCIETY

Government

Poland's president is head of state and the prime minister is head of government. The president is elected by the people, but he appoints the prime minister, who usually is the leader of the majority party or coalition in Parliament. A 1992 interim constitution is expected to be replaced by a more permanent document in the future. The country's Parliament, or National Assembly, has an upper house (100-seat Senate) and a lower house (460-seat Diet or *Sejm*). Poland's voting age is 18. There is no long-term trend indicating which of the many political parties is the strongest.

Economy

Poland continues to make progress in its transition toward a free-market economy. The period of hardships suffered by the people under the 1990 "shock therapy" plan has been followed by four years of increased economic growth. Economic reforms have softened, and the privatization of state-owned industries has been slow, but the country remains committed to becoming a successful free-market economy and joining the EU. Capitalizing on its natural resources and skilled labor may take some time, however, as inflation and unemployment remain high.

Led by a booming private sector, the economy grew by a strong 6 percent in 1995. Real gross domestic product per capita is $4,830. Most people earn enough for basic needs, but the gap between rich and poor is expanding quickly. This social problem contributes to political instability and general public distrust. In the past, wealth was associated with corruption, because only corrupt Communist officials had wealth.

Therefore, today's wealthy, no matter how honest, are viewed with suspicion.

About 25 percent of the labor force is engaged in agriculture, which has always remained in private hands despite Communist-era attempts at collectivization. Important products include grains, sugar beets, oilseed, potatoes, and pork, as well as dairy products. Poland has a strong industrial sector. Nearly half of all exports consist of machinery and equipment. Another 10 percent are manufactured items. Poland is a major producer of minerals and steel. The currency is the *zloty* (Zl).

Transportation and Communication

Public transportation is efficient and inexpensive. Most families do not have a car, but car ownership is on the rise. Most cities have streetcars and bus systems. On all trams, a few seats are clearly marked and reserved for the handicapped, the elderly, and women with small children. Travelers purchase tickets from *kiosks* and, on boarding, punch the tickets in machines mounted near the door. Railroads and airlines connect large cities. Most people have televisions and many have telephones. There are several daily newspapers.

Education

Poland's adult literacy rate is 99 percent. Education is free and mandatory for nine years, beginning with kindergarten. In eighth grade, students decide on the type of secondary school they wish to attend and take the appropriate entrance exams. Choices include four- and five-year technical and professional high schools, three-year vocational schools, or university prep schools. Entrance to a university is also determined by exam; about 5 percent of all applicants are accepted into the best schools. A university degree takes five to six years to complete. Two-thirds of dental and medical students are women.

Health

The government provides health care to all citizens. Facilities generally are accessible but are not up to Western standards. The poor economy has forced hospitals and other clinics to cut some services, to ask patients for donations, and to solicit help from family members in caring for patients. Private care in doctors' offices is better, but one must pay for it. The infant mortality rate is 12 per 1,000. Life expectancy averages 73 years.

FOR THE TRAVELER

U.S. travelers do not need a visa for stays of up to 90 days, but a valid passport is required. Poland is actively encouraging tourism and is improving facilities. Do not expect to use credit cards everywhere. Taking *zlotys* in or out of the country is prohibited. Travelers are warned that driving after dark is especially hazardous. Crime is on the rise against foreigners traveling by train, particularly on night and international trains and in stations in large cities. For more information, contact the Polish National Tourist Office, 275 Madison Avenue, New York, NY, 10016; phone (212) 338–9412. The Embassy of Poland is located at 2224 Wyoming Avenue NW, Washington, DC 20008; phone (202) 232–4517.

Printed on recycled paper

Portugal

(Portuguese Republic)

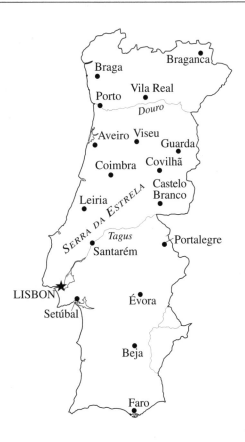

Boundary representations not necessarily authoritative.

BACKGROUND

Land and Climate

Portugal is situated on the west coast of the Iberian Peninsula, which it shares with Spain. The Portuguese Republic includes the mainland, the Azores and Madeira Islands (more than 600 miles or 950 kilometers off the Atlantic coast), and Macao (a small colony near Hong Kong). Covering 35,552 square miles (92,080 square kilometers), the total land area (not including Macao) is about the size of Indiana. Portugal is divided into two zones by the Tagus River, whose mouth is at Lisbon. In the north, the land is fairly mountainous (including the Estrela mountain range) and the climate is cool and rainy. The northwest experiences temperate winters and short summers while the northeast has long, cold winters with snow. South of the Tagus River, the terrain is less rugged, formed by hills and valleys, and the climate is warmer and more moderate. About one-third of the land is suitable for agriculture. Forty percent is forested.

History

Ancient Phoenicians, Carthaginians, and Greeks all built colonies on Portugal's coast. In 27 B.C., the Romans took control of the area and made it a province. After the Romans, the Visigoths ruled until they were defeated by the Moors. The Moors governed from the eighth century to the twelfth century. By 1140, Portugal was an independent nation under King Afonso Henriques. In the 14th and 15th centuries, Portuguese explorers claimed a huge overseas empire for Portugal. Phillip II of Spain ruled Portugal as Phillip I for a short time (1580–98) because Portugal's previous king had left no heirs and Phillip defeated other hopefuls. Phillip's sons also reigned in Portugal but lost control to the native nobility while Spain was at war with France. Portugal's monarchy was eventually overthrown (1910), and a republic was established.

However, political rivalries resulted in an unstable regime, and a military coup overthrew the democracy in 1926. From 1928 to 1968, António de Oliveira Salazar led an authoritarian dictatorship, denying the people basic civil rights. When he fell ill, Marcello Caetano succeeded him. Caetano tried to effect some reforms while maintaining the basic authoritarian government. In April 1974, a socialist military group, led by General Antonio de Spinola, took control of the government and vowed to restore democracy. In 1975, the junta held elections that led to the Third Republic. As politics shifted to the left, some industries were nationalized and some farmland collectivized.

Until 1985, the political situation remained somewhat unstable. In 1985 elections, however, voting patterns were more concrete and Mário Soares (a center-right candidate) was

EUROPE

chosen to lead Portugal. Under his leadership, and that of Prime Minister Aníbal Cavaco Silva, the government began privatization efforts, joined Portugal to the European Union (EU), and started a series of other reforms. Cavaco's popular leadership led to his reelection in 1991. However, the socialists returned to power in the October 1995 parliamentary elections and Antonio Guterres became prime minister. Not permitted to serve a third term as president, Soares stepped down in March 1996. He was replaced by socialist Jorge Sampaio, giving the socialists control of the presidency and Parliament.

THE PEOPLE

Population

Portugal has a population of slightly more than 10.5 million, which is growing at 0.3 percent annually. In the 1960s and 1970s, Portugal's population declined somewhat because many people emigrated. Today, migration takes place more within the country than from Portugal to other countries. Most Portuguese are of ethnic Mediterranean stock; there is not much ethnic diversity. During decolonization, Black Africans began migrating to Portugal, but they comprise less than 1 percent of the population. Unlike many industrialized countries, Portugal has a relatively small urban population. Nearly two-thirds of the people live in rural areas or small towns. Lisbon, the capital, is the largest city, with 950,000 people. Several smaller cities are located near Lisbon.

Portugal's Human Development Index (0.874) ranks it 36th out of 174 countries. Access to health care, education, and a decent standard of living affords the population many choices in their lives. Adjusted for women, the index (0.832) ranks Portugal 25th out of 130 countries.

Language

The official language is Portuguese. English, French, and German are taught in the schools and, therefore, are often understood by the Portuguese.

Religion

More than 95 percent of the population is Roman Catholic, and Catholic traditions have a strong influence on the lives of the people. Approximately 1 percent belongs to other Christian denominations, and some non-Christian religions are also practiced in Portugal. Freedom of religion is guaranteed. Portugal is much less secularized than other European countries.

General Attitudes

The Portuguese generally are traditional and conservative. They usually accept change and innovation only after careful consideration, and then quietly. People and relationships are more important than time, so punctuality is not always stressed. Being on time is considered impressive but not crucial, although more urban dwellers are finding it important. The Portuguese have an open, liberal society but place a greater emphasis on religious faith and moral values than do those in other European nations. People avidly discuss political issues (not parties). The Portuguese are proud of their cultural heritage, sense of nation, and economic progress. They are open and friendly to people of other nations. The Portuguese believe friendships should be strong and should last a lifetime.

Personal Appearance

The Portuguese generally are conservative in dress. Men wear suits to work, although sport jackets are also popular among some. Tattered clothing is improper. Leather dress shoes are worn for most occasions; tennis shoes are for recreation, not everyday wear. Clothing usually is ironed well; wrinkles are considered sloppy. People are careful to be well dressed in public. Some women, especially those in rural areas, may wear only black clothing after their husbands die. Each region of Portugal has a distinct costume that residents wear for festivals and special occasions. They are often elaborate and very colorful. For women, most costumes include scarves for the head and/or shoulders and skirts with aprons. Men's costumes usually include a hat, vest, and scarf.

CUSTOMS AND COURTESIES

Greetings

A warm, firm handshake is an appropriate greeting for anyone, although some Portuguese prefer lighter handshakes. Friends often hug. Relatives or close female friends often appear to kiss each cheek, beginning with the right. Actually, they "kiss the air" while brushing cheeks. Children are expected to kiss adults in the extended family when greeting them. Touching is a common part of greeting because it shows friendship. One uses first names for friends, youth, and children. Otherwise, one addresses an adult by title and surname. Sometimes the title is combined with the first name rather than the last, depending on personal preference and the relationship between the speakers. Some common terms used for greeting are *Bom dia* (Good day) and *Boa noite* (Good evening).

Gestures

Although the Portuguese are rather reserved, they use many physical gestures in conversation. It is impolite to point directly at a person with the index finger. To beckon, one waves all fingers with the palm facing up. Pinching the earlobe and shaking it gently while raising the eyebrows means something (a meal, for instance) is really good. Pulling down on the skin just below the eye with the index finger can mean "You are perceptive" or "You're kidding me." Spreading the fingers with palm down and rocking the hand means "more or less." Rubbing the thumb against the first two fingers with the palm facing up is a sign for money. Touching the tips of all fingers to the tip of the thumb with the palm facing up signifies fear or cowardice. It is a serious insult to make a "V" sign or "rabbit ears" behind someone's head, because it connotes a lack of morals.

Visiting

When visiting a family, guests wait outside the door until invited inside the home; likewise, guests do not let themselves out when leaving, but they let the hosts open the door. In urban areas, guests are more or less on time, but rural people are not as concerned with schedules. Because homemakers keep their homes very clean, guests are expected to wipe their feet before entering. Dirty shoes are removed entirely. It is polite to converse about a guest's family, positive aspects of Portugal, and personal interests. Guests usually avoid inquisitive personal questions. They often take small gifts to their hosts or send a thank-you note after a dinner engagement. Sincere compliments about the home and its decor are welcome. Guests are usually served refreshments and refusing them is impolite.

Most people socialize in the home, but business associates commonly go to a restaurant. People enjoy getting together at a café for casual conversation, sweets, and tea or coffee. Visiting relatives, especially those living in one's rural "homeland," is very popular. Urban people have strong roots to their hometowns or regions and try to visit as often as possible.

Eating

The Portuguese take time for conversation during the meal. To avoid seeming in a hurry, diners try to finish at the same time as others at the table. They eat in the continental style, with the fork in the left hand and the knife remaining in the right. When eating fish, one uses a special knife and fork, never a regular meat knife. Keeping the hands above the table at all times is important. Stretching, particularly at the table, is impolite and implies one is tired or bored with the company. One covers the mouth when using a toothpick. Unless enjoying ice cream cones, adults generally do not eat while walking in public.

A small breakfast is eaten around 8:00 A.M., a large lunch at about 1:00 P.M., and dinner is generally served between 8:00 and 9:00 P.M. The main meal of the day might consist of soup, two main dishes (meat or fish), vegetables, and more than one dessert. *Bica*, a strong espresso-type coffee, is often served after the meal. In some areas of the north, *bica* is called *cimbalino*.

In restaurants, one summons the waiter with a raised hand. The bill usually does not include a service charge, so a 15 percent tip is customary. People also tip for most personal services, from ushering to carrying luggage to driving a taxi.

LIFESTYLE
Family

The family is the core of Portuguese life and is strengthened by a clan spirit that extends to aunts, uncles, cousins, and beyond. Nuclear families tend to be small, averaging two children. Families in urban areas enjoy most modern conveniences and have a faster-paced lifestyle, while people living in rural areas still lead fairly simple lives. Their homes are small and many luxury items are too expensive to buy. Women often work outside the home in urban areas. More than one-third of the labor force is female.

Dating and Marriage

Dating habits in Portugal are similar to those currently prevailing in the rest of Europe, although they are more conservative in rural areas. Young people associate in groups first and later pair off in couples. Actually, going on a date signifies a serious relationship. Engagements are usually lengthy while the couple saves money for an apartment. Marriage ceremonies generally follow the Catholic tradition. It is not uncommon for young people to live together before getting married.

Diet

Staple foods in Portugal include fish, vegetables, and fruits. One national dish is *bacalhau* (dried cod), which is usually served with potatoes and green vegetables and sometimes garbanzo beans. *Bacalhau* is eaten often and can be prepared in a variety of ways, such as deep-fried with potatoes (called *pasteis de bacalhau*). The traditional Portuguese salad includes dark green lettuce, tomatoes, onions, vinegar, olive oil, and salt. Chicken is eaten throughout the country in many forms, such as *frango na pucara* (chicken in a pot) or *cabidela* (chicken with rice). Pork, partridge, quail, and rabbit are also typical meats in Portugal. Most parts of the pig are eaten in Portugal. A popular dish is *cozido à Portuguesa*, which contains potatoes, many vegetables, rice, and various meats. Olive oil is the favorite cooking oil, and garlic is a commonly used seasoning. Sweets are very popular, and Portugal has many pastry shops. Wine is inexpensive and consumed by adult family members with their meals.

Recreation

For recreation, families take walks, go to the park, have picnics, or go to the beach. Portugal's coast is beautiful, so its beaches are popular destinations. People often take short trips or visit relatives. Sitting outdoors or at a sidewalk café is popular. Going to movies is also common, as is going to night clubs or discos for dancing. A popular type of theater is the *revista*, which satirizes the government, international topics, or social issues. Soccer is by far the most popular sport. People also enjoy roller skating, hockey, and sailing. Portugal is known for its tradition with horses, and Portuguese bullfights incorporate the graceful movements of the horse and rider with the charges of the bull. At bullfights in Portugal, the bull is not killed as in other countries. A *forcado* must tackle the bull with his bare hands, but he is assisted by several others in the ring who distract the bull, hold on to its tail, and perform other functions. The bullfight is a favorite spectator sport; participants are amateurs, not professionals.

Holidays

National holidays in Portugal include New Year's Day, Easter (including Good Friday), Anniversary of the Revolution (25 April), Labor Day (1 May), Corpus Christi (in June), National Day of Portugal (10 June), Assumption (15 August), Proclamation of the Republic (5 October), All Saints' Day (1 November), Independence Day (1 December), Day of the Immaculate Conception (8 December), and Christmas. On

National Day, the poet Luis de Camóes is honored and the Portuguese communities scattered abroad are remembered. Throughout the year, local festivals honor patron saints or celebrate such events as the harvest.

Commerce

Business hours vary from place to place, but the traditional workday is from 9:00 A.M. to 1:00 P.M. and 3:00 to 7:00 P.M. Shopping centers are open later and do not close for lunch. Banks and government offices close around 4:00 P.M.

SOCIETY

Government

The Portuguese Republic is divided into eighteen districts and two autonomous regions (in addition to Macau, which will revert to Chinese control in 1999). Portugal's president is chief of state. The prime minister serves as head of government and is usually the leader of the legislature's dominant party or coalition of parties. Portugal's unicameral Assembly of the Republic has 230 members, all of whom are directly elected. All citizens older than age 18 can vote. The most influential political parties include the governing Portuguese Socialist Party and the opposition Social Democratic Party.

Economy

After joining the EU, Portugal experienced strong growth and rapid economic development until the recession of the early 1990s. Boosted by foreign investment and export growth, the economy showed definite signs of recovery in 1993 and 1994. However, long-term success remains tied to economic growth in the EU as a whole. Unemployment is 7 percent and inflation is 6 percent. Although development has favored urban areas over rural ones, the entire country has benefited from a more stable government and brighter prospects for its future. Portugal's future economic growth depends on the modernization of its markets, industry, workforce, and infrastructure in order to become competitive in the European market.

Real gross domestic product per capita is estimated at $9,850, which has more than tripled in the last generation. This figure indicates that, while Portugal lags behind its neighbors, economic prosperity is available to a growing number of people. Social institutions exist that can expand economic opportunities and improve conditions for the rising generation.

Twenty percent of the labor force is engaged in agriculture, but Portugal still must import much of its food. Its most important crops include grains, potatoes, olives, and grapes. Portugal exports cotton textiles, cork (from cork trees) and cork products, canned fish, wine, timber, and machinery. Tourism is an increasingly important source of income. The currency is the Portuguese *escudo* (Esc).

Transportation and Communication

Portugal has a good network of paved roads, but few roads are as modern as those in other EU countries. Driving is hazardous. Portuguese drivers have a reputation for driving too fast in wet conditions, passing cars around blind corners, and driving drunk. Traffic accidents are a leading cause of death and injury in Portugal. Buses and trains connect most areas. Lisbon has an efficient subway, and taxis are available in urban areas. Passengers need exact change to buy bus tickets from the driver. Train tickets must be purchased in advance, not from the conductor. The communications system is good. Portugal has more than 30 daily newspapers.

Education

Education begins at age seven and is compulsory through the ninth grade. Private schools and free public schools are available. After elementary school, students may attend three years of high school and two years of college preparation, or three to four years of vocational schooling that also incorporates some college preparatory courses. There are 18 universities in Portugal. The University of Coimbra, founded in the 13th century, is one of the oldest in Europe. The adult literacy rate is 86 percent. It improved through the 1980s but remains lower than most of western Europe because of a low average literacy rate in rural areas (50 percent).

Health

Health care is subsidized by the government. Public facilities are generally good and are improving. Private clinics are available for those who are able to pay more. The infant mortality rate is 9 per 1,000. Life expectancy ranges from 72 to 79 years.

FOR THE TRAVELER

A valid passport is necessary to visit Portugal, but a visa is not necessary for those staying fewer than 60 days. No vaccinations are required unless one is traveling to the islands or is coming from a yellow fever endemic zone. Water is safe for drinking. However, in rural areas one should exercise caution with drinking water during the dry season. Portugal is becoming a favorite tourist destination. For travel information, contact the Portuguese National Tourist Office, 590 Fifth Avenue, New York, NY 10036; phone (212) 354–4403. You may also contact the Embassy of Portugal, 2125 Kalorama Road NW, Washington, DC 20008; phone (202) 328–8610.

The Commonwealth of
Puerto Rico

Boundary representations not necessarily authoritative.

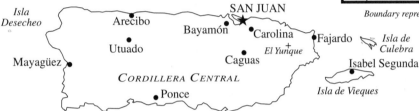

THE AMERICAS

BACKGROUND

Land and Climate

Puerto Rico is a Caribbean island located just east of the Dominican Republic. Covering 3,515 square miles (9,104 square kilometers), it is about the same size as Rhode Island and Delaware combined. Puerto Rico includes the islands of Culebra, Vieques, Desecheo, and Mona. The waters between *Isla Mona* (Mona Island) and the capital, San Juan, form a key shipping lane for vessels heading to the Panama Canal. San Juan also has one of the best natural ports in the Caribbean. The island of Puerto Rico is characterized by the *Cordillera Central* (a high central mountain range), a dry southern coast, fertile northern coastal plains, low eastern mountains, and El Yunque rain forest. Relatively little land (8 percent) is available for cultivation. The coastal plains are densely populated. Puerto Rico's climate is mildly tropical, with warm and sunny weather. Rain falls mainly between May and December; it is moderate in coastal regions and heavier in the mountains. Temperatures average 70°F to 80°F (21–27°C) year-round. The island is often hit by destructive hurricanes, such as Hurricane Hugo in 1989.

History

The indigenous Taino people were living on Puerto Rico when Columbus arrived in 1493 and named the island San Juan Bautista. He claimed the island for Spain, and colonizers began building settlements in 1508. Settlers imported African slaves beginning in 1513. The Taino were also enslaved; the men were soon annihilated, but the women remained. Slavery was abolished in 1873.

In 1897, Spain granted self-rule to Puerto Rico under the leadership of Luis Muñoz Rivera. In 1898, as part of the Spanish-American War, the United States invaded the island and conquered its Spanish defenders. Spain ceded the island to the United States that same year. In 1917, Puerto Rico officially became a U.S. territory and its people were granted citizenship. In 1946, Jesus Toribio Pinero was appointed by President Harry S. Truman as the first island-born governor. Two years later, Puerto Ricans directly elected a governor, Luis Muñoz Marin.

Puerto Rico became a commonwealth of the United States with its own constitution in July 1952. Opposition to commonwealth status has at times erupted into violence. In 1954, militants from Puerto Rico shot several congressmen in Washington, D.C., during a session of the House of Representatives. Since then, political groups have occasionally debated the island's status and its relationship with the United States.

Puerto Ricans today are divided by the issue of whether to request U.S. statehood or remain a commonwealth. A small group advocates full independence. A national referendum in November 1993 did not completely settle the issue, as the decision to remain a commonwealth passed by only a slim margin. Referendums in 1967 and 1981 approved the commonwealth status by a greater margin, so attitudes may be changing over time. It will probably be a number of years before another such referendum is held.

THE PEOPLE

Population

Puerto Rico's population of about 3.8 million grows at an average annual rate of less than 0.2 percent. This is due mainly to migration; growth rates rise when the U.S. economy is weak and people stay on the island. Growth rates fall when the U.S.

economy is strong and people emigrate to the mainland in search of work. More than 95 percent of the people are native Puerto Rican, with a mixed Spanish, African, and Taino heritage. San Juan is the largest city with a population of about 450,000. However, the largest Puerto Rican community, consisting of about one million people, is in New York City, the destination of most emigrants.

Language

Spanish and English share official status in Puerto Rico. For a short time in the early 1990s, Spanish was declared the only official language, but English has since regained equal status. Spanish is the language of school instruction and daily life. English is required as a second language in school and is used in business. Most people can speak English. The official status of either language often depends on the political climate surrounding Puerto Rico's relationship with the United States.

The close relationship Puerto Rico has with the United States and English has led people to mix many English words with spoken Spanish. Locally, people call this manner of speech *Spanglish*, and it is a comfortable, informal method of communication.

Religion

Roman Catholicism is the major Christian religion in Puerto Rico and claims about 85 percent of the population as members. Approximately 15 percent of the people belong to various Protestant and other Christian churches, and their numbers are growing. Although there is a separation of church and state, Catholic traditions and customs prevail among the people. Puerto Ricans consider themselves to be religious and often attribute their good fortunes to Deity.

General Attitudes

Puerto Ricans are sensitive people, quick to express sympathy and equally quick to resent a slight. They are gregarious and fond of *fiestas* (celebrations). They admire people who are intelligent, hardworking, dedicated, and humble. Puerto Ricans consider open criticism, aggressiveness, and greed offensive. Many believe a person's destiny is God's will, although individuals must also watch for opportunities.

Most Puerto Ricans value a good education, and a large number of students not only finish high school but also attend college or another institution of higher learning. To have a good education is considered a key to a better future. Being able to buy land for a home or business is a universal goal. National and regional pride are very strong. Having political influence is fairly desirable and individuals who have such power are admired.

The Puerto Rican concept of time is somewhat relaxed. People are considered more important than schedules. If a friend, relative, or business associate drops in unexpectedly, Puerto Ricans will stop everything they are doing to visit, even if it makes them late for other appointments. Business contacts are not made during lunchtime.

Personal Appearance

Puerto Ricans take great pride in what they wear in public. The youth favor popular North American fashions and also like a sporty look. Sloppy, overly casual, or revealing dress is considered inappropriate. Due to the climate, people prefer lightweight fabrics. Jeans are popular at all age levels for informal activities and outdoor work. Tennis shoes and sandals are the most commonly worn footwear. People living in interior towns may wear sweaters and jackets during winter months, as temperatures can be cool.

For most parties and social gatherings, formal clothing is expected, including suits with a shirt and tie for men, and dresses or skirts and blouses for women.

CUSTOMS AND COURTESIES

Greetings

People usually shake hands when greeting. Close friends often greet by grasping shoulders and kissing each other on the cheek. Women normally kiss women or men in this manner, but men do not greet other men this way. They may, however, embrace a good friend or relative after a long absence. People stand very close when talking, and females often touch each other with their hands. Moving away, even slightly, may be considered an insult.

Although Spanish is most common, both Spanish and English greetings are used. So one might hear *Good morning* or *¡Buenos días!*, *Good afternoon* or *¡Buenas tardes!*, *Good evening* or *¡Buenas noches!*, and *Hi* or *¡Hola!* When meeting someone for the first time, it is polite to say *How are you*? or *¿Cómo estás?* Young friends often begin a conversation with *¿Qué tal?*, a casual way to ask "How are you?" Which language speakers use depends on the situation (e.g., on the street, in a business meeting) and the relationship between the two people.

When addressing others in formal situations, one may use titles of respect or profession alone or in combination with a person's surname. These might include *Señor* (Mr.), *Señora* (Mrs. or Ms.), *Señorita* (Miss), *Doctor/a* (Dr.), *Director/a*, and so on. One respectfully addresses an older person by combining the title *Don* (for men) or *Doña* (for women) with the person's first name. Friends address each other by given name or nickname.

Most Puerto Ricans have two surnames in addition to one or two given names. The family name is the father's surname, but this appears as the second-to-last name, while the mother's surname comes last. So a person named Victor Arocho Ramos would be called *Señor Arocho*. Ramos would be his mother's surname. Women do not change their surnames when they get married.

Gestures

One beckons by waving all fingers with the palm down; beckoning people with the palm facing up is improper. Wiggling the nose can mean, "What's going on?" People often point with pursed or puckered lips. One should hand, rather than toss or throw, small items to another person. During conversation, Puerto Ricans might interrupt each other; this generally is not considered rude. Although peers will tease each other in informal situations, such joking is not appropriate in formal settings.

A person can get another's attention by saying, "Psssst." This is common and not rude, but if a man does it to a woman, she will likely ignore him. Men often smile and stare at women, but it is considered improper for a woman to smile indiscriminately at strangers. It is appropriate for a man to offer his seat to a woman on public transportation. On longer trips, people often share food and refusing such an offer is impolite.

Visiting

Visiting friends and relatives is considered a social obligation; people expect it as a basic courtesy. While inviting others to the home is not uncommon, most casual visits occur in the early evening without prior arrangement. Visits are relaxed and the entire family participates. Guests are treated to refreshments such as juice, soda, crackers, and cookies. If visitors arrive at mealtime, the hosts generally invite them to join the meal. In most cases, guests politely decline the offer a few times before finally accepting.

Unannounced visits are usually short (one or two hours), but planned activities can last longer. Friends and relatives invited for dinner are expected to stay after the meal to relax and enjoy conversation with the hosts. Invited guests are not expected to bring gifts, except on special occasions. If offered, gifts are opened in the presence of the giver. Guests often compliment the hosts on their home or family, but it is impolite (and even embarrassing) to highly praise individual objects or possessions.

Eating

Puerto Ricans eat three meals each day, and dinner is the main family meal. The eating atmosphere is relaxed and cordial. Diners keep both hands above the table and do not place them in the lap. No food should be left on the plate. Spoons and forks are the most commonly used utensils. Knives are used when appropriate. Some foods are eaten with the hands. Hosts might offer their guests second helpings, but guests may politely decline.

Food purchased at a street stand is normally eaten at or near the stand, but it is not uncommon for people to eat while walking in public. At a restaurant, leaving a 15 percent tip is customary when service is not included in the bill.

LIFESTYLE

Family

The Puerto Rican family is close-knit and supportive. Extended families usually do not share a household, but they often live in the same neighborhood or town. This facilitates frequent visits between relatives and allows grandparents to provide child care when both parents work. Adult unmarried children often remain at home until they get married. Families have an average of three children. Parents consider themselves responsible for their children throughout life and expect to give their adult children financial or emotional support if needed. Children show respect to their parents by taking care of them in their old age.

If parents emigrate to New York or elsewhere, they will take their children with them. Often, however, the husband will emigrate first and establish himself before his wife and children join him.

Dating and Marriage

Although the youth begin dating in groups, they move quickly to boyfriend-girlfriend relationships. Having a boyfriend or girlfriend is important, and dating begins at a fairly young age (12–13 years old). In rural areas, the relationship usually does not become serious until the boy has met the girl's parents. Dates may include going to the movies or on a picnic, dancing, or spending time at the beach. This early dating leads some Puerto Ricans to marry, either formally or in a common-law partnership, at an early age (16–17). Marriage at a young age is preferred to single motherhood for the majority of girls.

Civil weddings are the general rule, but whether a marriage is performed by a judge or in a church, a wedding is a time of great celebration and family gatherings. Families spend large amounts of money on decorations, food, and music, both traditional and modern.

Diet

Foods in Puerto Rico come from a variety of ethnic backgrounds, reflective of the people's mixed ancestry and colonial associations. Rice and beans is the most commonly eaten main meal. Other popular dishes include *arroz con pollo* (rice and chicken), *paella* (a spicy stew of rice, chicken, seafood, and vegetables), *arroz con gandules y pernil* (rice with roasted pig), and foods made with plantains. Plantains are a starchy banana-like fruit that must be cooked to be eaten. In addition to chicken and pork, beef is a favorite meat. Seafood (shrimp, octopus, clams, fish, etc.) and fruits (pineapples, bananas, mangoes, papayas, grapefruits, and oranges) are also common in the diet. Pasta and fast-foods are more popular with younger generations.

Packaged snack foods are as common as in the United States, but people also enjoy locally prepared snacks like *frituras* (foods fried in oil). Popular varieties of *frituras* include *alcapurrias* (plantains with meat) and *sorullos* (corn flour). The local flat bread typically eaten with meals, *pan sobao*, is made with water, shortening, and flour.

Recreation

Puerto Ricans' favorite sport is baseball, but they also enjoy basketball and volleyball. Cockfighting is popular among men. Families enjoy going to the beach or parks for picnics. In their leisure time, people may visit one another or watch television and videos.

The arts enjoy a wide following. Long before the United States took possession of Puerto Rico, a strong tradition of literature and music, as well as scholarship, had been established. Indeed, art and music are fostered in the home; nearly everyone can play a musical instrument, and a display of musical talent is usually expected at parties. *Salsa*, *plena*, *bomba*, and *danza puertorriqueña* are the most popular forms of music for dancing and singing. Puerto Rican films and other cultural arts are known throughout the world.

Holidays

Puerto Ricans celebrate New Year's Day as part of the Christmas season. The Day of the Three Kings (6 January) marks the end of the Christmas season and each child receives a gift. Puerto Rico celebrates both locally important holidays and U.S. national holidays. Holidays include the Birth of Eugenio Maria de Hostos (11 January), Martin Luther King Jr.'s Birthday (second Monday in January), Presidents' Day (third Monday in February), the Abolition of Slavery (22 March), Easter (including Good Friday), José de Diego's Birthday (third Monday in April), Memorial Day (last Monday in May), U.S. Independence Day (4 July), Luis Muñoz Rivera's Day (17 July), Constitution Day (25 July), José Celso Barbosa's Birthday (28 July), Labor Day (first Monday in

September), All Souls' Day (2 November), Discovery of Puerto Rico Day (19 November), Thanksgiving, and Christmas. One important part of the Christmas season is the *Parrandas*, a caroling tradition where groups of friends sing Christmas songs door-to-door. They expect food and drinks in return.

One of the most popular events is the Pablo Casals Festival in late May and early June. Also, every town honors its patron saint annually with several days of activities that include going to amusement parks, gambling, singing, dancing, and religious ceremonies. A beauty queen is selected for almost every activity. During February or March, *Carnaval* celebrations held before Lent (in the Catholic tradition) are most visible in Ponce, where "monsters" (called *vejigantes*) wearing papier-mâché masks with multiple horns roam the streets hitting people on the head with a dried pig's bladder. The masks are handmade and can be elaborate. The monsters are just one part of the lively celebrations in Ponce.

Commerce

Business hours generally run weekdays between 9:00 A.M. and 5:00 P.M., although there are variations. Stores and shops may stay open 24 hours, and many retail outlets are open on Saturday. Most close on Sunday. The same national retail chains found throughout the United States also have stores in Puerto Rico. U.S. companies doing business in Puerto Rico enjoy a tax-exempt status because federal taxes do not apply in a commonwealth.

SOCIETY

Government

The Commonwealth of Puerto Rico has 78 municipalities. Chief of state is the U.S. president, William (Bill) Clinton, but the head of government is a locally elected governor. Governor Pedro J. Rosselló was elected in 1992.

As commonwealth citizens, Puerto Ricans do not vote in U.S. national elections and do not pay federal income tax, but they do elect their own officials. They are subject to the draft and receive partial welfare benefits. They have no voting representation in the U.S. Congress and are restricted by federal controls in managing their territory. A locally elected resident high commissioner represents Puerto Rico in the U.S. House of Representatives. The high commissioner (Carlos Romero Barcelo) can introduce legislation, express opinions, and engage in dialogue on issues that relate to Puerto Rico, but he cannot vote.

Puerto Rico's Legislative Assembly is composed of a 29-seat Senate and a 53-seat House of Representatives. All citizens age 18 and older may vote. Elections are held on the same schedule as in the United States. The main political parties include the National Republican Party of Puerto Rico and the Popular Democratic Party. A few smaller parties also post candidates in elections but rarely have large followings.

Economy

Since World War II, industrialization and duty-free trade with the United States have transformed the once-poor island into a dynamic economy. The average gross national product per capita is $7,100. Annual economic growth is usually around 3 percent.

Only 3 percent of the population is engaged in agriculture; 14 percent works in the manufacturing sector. The government, services, and tourism provide most employment on the island. Unemployment is higher than in the United States, running more than 13 percent in 1995. Puerto Rico exports sugar, coffee, petroleum products, chemicals, pharmaceuticals, textiles, and electronic equipment. Drawbacks to industrialization include the fact that most food must be imported and is more expensive. But U.S. investment and labor laws have improved the standard of living for most people. The U.S. dollar (US$) is the official currency.

Transportation and Communication

Roads are generally in good condition, and most families have at least one car. Buses and taxis are available in large urban areas. *Públicos* serve most of the island. Up to six passengers fit in a *público*, which travels from a specified terminal to a fixed destination (with no stops in between). Air service operates domestically and internationally. Puerto Rico has numerous radio and television stations, as well as newspapers. Most people have telephones and they benefit from a modern communications network.

Education

Education is highly valued and the school system is continually improving. Primary and secondary schooling is the same as in the United States, with children beginning kindergarten at age five or six. A high school diploma, earned upon completion of the 12th grade, is necessary to get a good job or go to college. The drop-out rate is very low. Higher education is provided by several universities and colleges, including the University of Puerto Rico, with its nine campuses and 45,000 students. Other institutions include the Inter American University, Catholic University, Central University, World University, and Puerto Rico Junior College. The literacy rate among adults is 89 percent but is higher among the youth.

Health

A network of urban and rural health-care centers and two medical schools (one public and one private) serve Puerto Rico's medical needs. The system of health care is similar to that in the United States, although people are not always eligible for the same federal funds. The infant mortality rate is 13 per 1,000; life expectancy ranges from 71 to 80 years.

FOR THE TRAVELER

U.S. citizens do not need a visa or passport when traveling to Puerto Rico. However, identification is required and a passport is one acceptable form. Tap water is safe for drinking and no vaccinations are necessary. Puerto Rico is a favorite vacation destination because of the pleasant climate, fine beach resorts, and English-speaking population. For more information about travel opportunities, contact the Puerto Rico Government Tourism Company, 575 Fifth Avenue, 23d Floor, New York, NY 10017; phone (212) 599–6262. Offices are also located in Los Angeles, Miami, and Chicago.

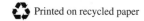

CULTURGRAM '97

Republic of
Romania

Boundary representations not necessarily authoritative.

BACKGROUND

Land and Climate

Covering 91,699 square miles (237,500 square kilometers), Romania is about the size of Oregon. Two mountain ranges dominate the central and northern regions. The Carpathians in the north run roughly north to southeast and the Transylvanian Alps run east to west in the center of the country. The famous Danube River, which begins in Germany and flows through several European countries, forms much of Romania's southern border. It runs north through a small portion of Romania's eastern territory and empties into the Black Sea. Low plains lie along the southern and eastern borders.

Romanian summers are warm and sunny; winters are cold and cloudy. The average temperature in July is 70°F (21°C); the average in January is 30°F (–1°C). Natural resources include crude oil, natural gas, coal, iron, and timber. More than 40 percent of the land is arable and 28 percent is forested. Romania faces severe pollution problems due to excessive industrialization in past decades and old technology. Many rivers, towns, and forests are contaminated, and the people suffer from respiratory diseases in some areas. The current government is seeking ways to address the problems, but it lacks the necessary funds, experience, and technology to make significant progress.

History

The ancestors of today's Romanians were Geto-Dacians, an Indo-European people. Between the sixth and fourth centuries B.C., the Dacians assimilated surrounding influences to form their own unique civilization. Around A.D. 100, the Romans conquered most of Dacia and made the area a province to supply grain, gold, and cattle to the empire. The province's natives soon adopted the Roman language and culture. The name *Romania* means "Land of the Romans." Between 200 and 1100, various barbarian tribes invaded the region. In the 14th century, Moldavia (to the east) and Wallachia (in the south) became independent principalities. In 1500, the principalities fell under Turkish control, but they were never an integral part of the Ottoman (Turkish) Empire. Several European wars led to exchanges of Romanian territory among various countries. Complete freedom from Turkish rule did not come until 1877, after Romania joined again with Moldavia and Wallachia.

Because of its part in the Allied alliance with France and England in World War I, Romania acquired Bessarabia (roughly present-day Moldova) from Russia and three provinces from the defeated Austro-Hungarian Empire. These acquisitions doubled the size of Romania but alienated it from its neighbors. Romania was occupied by Nazi Germany in 1940 and joined the German Army in attacking Soviet Russia in 1941. In 1944, however, King Michael arrested Romania's pro-Nazi dictator and Romania switched to the Allied side. Shortly thereafter, Russian troops occupied the country and Romania came under Soviet influence. The monarchy was abolished, King Michael went into exile (he still lives in Switzerland), and a Communist regime was established. Bessarabia was annexed by the Soviet Union as Moldavia. When that area became independent in 1991, ethnic Romanians on both sides initially favored reunification.

Such sentiment cooled in a few years with each side distrusting or otherwise disapproving of the other.

After 1965, when Nicolae Ceausescu came to power in Romania, the country broke with the Soviet Union to pursue an independent course. Communism remained strong and Ceausescu ruled with complete control over all aspects of local life. The extensive internal security system, *Securitate*, stifled dissent. Corruption and human-rights violations were common. The people suffered grinding poverty and brutality.

When democratic movements swept Europe in 1989, Ceausescu vowed nothing would change in Romania. However, large groups of demonstrators soon protested his regime. With the army supporting the people's revolution, the regime fell after several days of fighting. Ceausescu and his wife were executed and the National Salvation Front took control. Despite his close ties to the former regime, National Salvation Front leader, Ion Iliescu, won the election (May 1990). Iliescu's government restricted civil rights, but it granted Romanians freedom of speech, national elections, a new constitution, and plans for economic reform.

In 1991, civil unrest led to an interim government, which governed until September 1992 elections. Iliescu was reelected and sought to improve Romania's international image. Under the leadership of Prime Minister Nicolae Vacaroiu, Romania enjoyed increased agricultural harvests in 1994, higher industrial output, and some improvements. But undemocratic laws giving prominence to ethnic Romanians, as well as other nationalist activities, kept Romania from enjoying strong regional and European relations. In 1995, Iliescu announced plans to qualify for European Union membership by the year 2000. To do so, Romania will have to significantly alter certain social institutions, laws, and economic policies.

THE PEOPLE

Population

The population of Romania is about 23.2 million and currently is not growing. Ethnic Romanians comprise most of the population (84 percent). A significant Hungarian minority (8.9 percent) lives mostly in Transylvania. This group still identifies with Hungary and the Hungarian culture. They have been the subject of intense negotiations between the two countries. Hungary demands that Romania guarantee minorities their rights to education, language use, and expression, but the Romanian Parliament has been reluctant to do so.

The *Romi* (Gypsies) comprise about 8 percent of the population, although an exact count has never been made. This group tends to live separately from the Romanians and generally is not accepted by other ethnic groups. The *Romi* are poor, undereducated, and underemployed; they do not integrate into mainstream society and are often subject to discrimination throughout Europe.

Other minority groups include Germans, Ukrainians, Serbs, Croats, Russians, and Turks. The German population has declined because many have emigrated to Germany. Large numbers of other ethnic groups are also trying to leave Romania, but they are meeting increasing resistance in other countries. More than half of Romania's population lives in cities, largely because of forced urbanization under Ceausescu. Forty percent of the population is younger than age 25.

Language

The official language is Romanian, a Latin-based language in the same family as Spanish, French, Italian, and Portuguese. Young people may also speak English, German, or Italian. French is a common second language among older people. The Germans and Hungarians speak their native ethnic tongues. The *Romi* speak Romany.

Religion

Nearly all Romanians are Christian. About 70 percent belong to the Romanian Orthodox Church. Six percent of the people (mostly Hungarians) are Roman Catholic and 3 percent are Uniate (Greek Catholic). Other Christian religions, Islam, and Judaism are also practiced. During the Ceausescu regime, religious organizations were carefully regulated, but now people are free to practice religion as they wish. Devotion to religion is especially strong in rural areas. About 15 percent of the population claims no religious affiliation.

General Attitudes

The Romanian people seem confused and divided about their future. Having emerged from the authoritarian regime of the Ceausescu era (1965–89), but still not possessing the economic and political freedoms they thought would be theirs, they worry that the future is no longer bright. Many people, especially in large urban areas, continue to distrust the government and would like to see greater democracy. These people favor a country where many opinions (political, religious, and social) can be expressed and appreciated. They seek to change traditional Romanian society to make it more similar to other European societies. Other people would like to see economic reform but not necessarily a change in government or traditional society; they would be more prone to accept a single political party and a single approach to social order.

These conflicting attitudes about the future of the nation have led to violence, instability, and the rise of dangerous tensions between ethnic groups. The resulting instability has allowed for the rapid expansion of organized crime and for extremist groups to gain political prominence. Economic troubles have led to greater poverty and disillusionment. Indeed, living standards in 1995 were lower than in 1988. Resolving such wide differences is one of the greatest tasks facing the nation today. Unfortunately, most people have to deal with the more urgent concern of feeding and housing their families.

Personal Appearance

Romanians attach importance to their appearance, although clothing worn in rural areas is often less fashionable. People generally dress conservatively in public. Women wear skirts and dresses. Slacks usually are worn only by younger women and girls. Female office workers may also wear tailored suits. Businessmen wear conservative suits. The youth prize denim jeans, T-shirts, short jackets, and other Western-style clothing. People do not commonly wear hats, but in rural areas older women wear scarves. The elderly generally wear dark, conservative colors.

Colorful folk costumes may be worn on Sundays, at festivals, or on special occasions. Gypsy women wear long, colorful skirts. Family members mourning the death of a loved one may remain in black from six weeks to a year.

CUSTOMS AND COURTESIES

Greetings

Women greet each other with a kiss on each cheek or a handshake. Men shake hands with others. A man usually waits for a woman to extend her hand first. When greeting, women often use the phrase *Bună* (Good), while men say *Salut* (Salutation). In cities, a man might greet a woman by kissing her hand. Even if he does not, he may say *Sărut-măna* (Kiss your hand) as a sign of reverence. Young people also use this greeting with their parents or elders. In rural areas, everyone is greeted individually; people also greet strangers and expect their greeting to be returned.

The most common verbal greeting is *Bună Ziua* (Good day). *Bună dimineata* (Good morning) and *Bună seara* (Good evening) are also used. Only close friends and relatives greet each other by first name. However, adults normally address young people by their first name. When applicable, people use professional titles ("Doctor," "Professor," etc.) before surnames.

Gestures

Yawning without covering the mouth is impolite. When one sneezes, others often say *Sanatate* (Good health) or *Noroc* (Bless you). *Noroc* is also used at parties to mean "Cheers." Making eye contact during conversation is a sign of honesty. It is impolite for men to keep their hands in their pockets when speaking to women, officials, older people, or a large audience. People also avoid chewing gum during conversation and do not cross their legs in mixed company. Friends often hold hands or walk arm in arm. On public transportation, men generally offer their seat to a woman. Gentlemen remove their hats before entering buildings, except stores.

Visiting

Romanians like to receive and pay visits, which usually are arranged in advance. People often gather for birthdays, anniversaries, holidays, or just to socialize. Hosts generally offer their guests a drink—coffee, tea, brandy, or a popular regional wine— and perhaps other refreshments. It is polite for dinner guests to bring an odd number of flowers (three or more) or a small gift for the hostess. Guests avoid giving red roses (a sign of romantic affection) or an even number of flowers (often associated with funerals). Gifts usually are opened immediately and admired. Guests typically ask the hosts for permission before smoking.

Eating

Lunch traditionally is the main meal of the day; however, due to work and school schedules, many families can only eat lunch together on Saturday and Sunday. Supper is similar to lunch, but the servings are somewhat smaller. Romanians eat in the continental style, with the fork in the left hand and the knife remaining in the right. They keep both hands (not elbows) above the table during a meal. The hostess indicates when the meal will begin and when it will end. Toasting is usually a part of formal and informal lunches and dinners.

LIFESTYLE

Family

The family has always been important to Romanians, and the father maintains a dominant role. Urban families tend to be smaller than rural families because of a shortage of housing and the high cost of living. Most women work outside the home, but they are also responsible for the upkeep of the home and the children. Men generally are not involved in household chores. Grandparents often live with the family.

A private farm includes a two- or three-bedroom home, a garden and orchard, and small farm buildings. Ceausescu attempted to destroy these farmsteads—and, with them, rural individualism—by tearing down homes and forcing people to move into large housing blocks. The apartments had no running water, bathrooms, or heat, and strictly enforced regulations limited the amount of electricity each apartment could use. These buildings are bitterly resented in rural areas, and some have called for their destruction. A housing shortage prevents that from happening at this time. While forced urbanization and limits on electricity use are no longer practiced, improvements in living standards have not yet developed because of a poor economy. Many families, urban and rural, lack proper housing and most go without modern conveniences.

Dating and Marriage

Boys and girls usually begin to socialize in high school. Popular activities include going to movies, parties, sporting events, and school dances and taking walks.

Most adults expect to marry and have a family in spite of economic difficulties. In urban areas, men usually marry between ages 23 and 25; women marry at about age 22. People in villages still marry at a young age. Local and ethnic customs regarding courtship and marriage vary by region. People in rural areas enjoy engagement ceremonies in which the groom's family brings the engagement and wedding rings to the bride's family. Both families celebrate the event with dinner, singing, and dancing. Before the wedding ceremony, the groom may carry a pine tree on the way to the bride's house as a sign of long life. Most weddings involve church ceremonies. Godparents are expected to take an active part in wedding activities.

Diet

Romanian food is characterized by distinctive ethnic specialties including *mititei* (grilled meatballs), *patricieni* (grilled sausage), *mamaliga* (cornmeal mush served like mashed potatoes), and *sarmale* (minced meat with rice, rolled in pickled cabbage leaves). Breakfast usually consists of eggs, cheese, rolls or other breads, and coffee. Lunch begins with soup, followed by meat, potatoes, and a vegetable. Most people eat bread with every meal. Wine or beer is usually served as well. A special plum brandy called *tzuica* is also popular. Pastries are popular for dessert. Although food is now more readily available, people cannot easily afford the higher prices.

Recreation

Romanians enjoy sports, particularly soccer. Romania's national soccer team competed in the 1994 World Cup. *Oina*, a kind of baseball, is a traditional sport. Romanian athletes have done well in international competitions, especially in gymnastics, weightlifting, and tennis. Leisure activities include meeting with friends or family, watching television, taking walks, reading, or going to the theater. Many enjoy folk shows, with music and dancing.

Holidays

With the fall of Ceausescu, people now openly celebrate Christmas, Easter, and other religious holidays. Romania's national day (1 December) commemorates the union of the kingdom of Romania and three smaller territories in 1918. Other national holidays include the New Year (1–2 January) and Labor Day (1–2 May).

Commerce

Factory workers usually begin their day at 7:00 A.M. and work until 3:00 or 5:00 P.M., depending on the institution. Most factories close on Saturday and Sunday. Government offices are open from 8:00 A.M. to 4:00 P.M., while banking offices are open from 9:00 A.M. to noon and 2:00 to 4:00 P.M. A few stores may close around lunchtime but remain open later in the evening. General department stores are open all day. Except for restaurants, coffee stops, and some private shops, most businesses are closed on Sunday. Depending on their seniority, workers enjoy two- to four-week vacations.

SOCIETY

Government

Romania's new constitution established it as a republic in 1991. The president is head of state but also has broader powers. Romania's prime minister is head of government. Parliament has a 143-seat Senate and a 341-seat House of Deputies. The voting age is 18. National elections were scheduled for November 1996. The most powerful political parties are the Party of Social Democracy in Romania and the Democratic Convention. Several other parties hold blocks of seats in Parliament and are relied on for passing legislation.

Economy

Before World War II, Romania was an agricultural nation. However, postwar policy led to rapid industrialization. Industry came to account for more than 60 percent of the gross national product, while agriculture fell to less than 10 percent. During the 1980s, in an attempt to reduce the foreign debt, Ceausescu diverted large portions of the domestic agricultural crop to exports. While the plan succeeded in decreasing the debt, it also caused food rationing and lowered the standard of living. The plan was halted in 1989. Today, food is plentiful but expensive, often consuming up to 70 percent of a family's monthly income.

The most important exports are machinery and equipment, natural gas and oil products, consumer goods, and foods. During the 1980s, Romania increased trade with Western Europe to increase earnings. Trade continues, but economic progress is lagging behind other nations. A 1991 law that returns farmland to the families who owned it before communism is designed to encourage private ownership and enterprise in the agricultural sector. Unfortunately, land transfer has been very slow. Even if it were quicker, most farmers lack credit or capital and, therefore, could not buy equipment, seeds, or fertilizers. Thus, the collective farm system remains.

High inflation, unemployment, political instability, and the slow pace of structural reform have hampered economic progress and kept foreign investment at a minimum. A few foreign companies have been attracted by tax incentives, skilled workers, and Romania's extensive industrial complex. Romania's Human Development Index (0.703) ranks it 98th out of 174 countries. Real gross domestic product per capita is estimated at $2,840. These figures indicate that most people struggle but are able to meet basic needs. Although the country is industrialized, it ranks below many developing nations in its ability to create economic opportunities for the people. Romania's currency is the *leu* (L).

Transportation and Communication

Public transportation in the cities is reasonably efficient and inexpensive. Boarding passes for buses are obtained from ticket booths and magazine stands. The train network links major cities, but many trains are poorly maintained and lack heat in the winter. In rural areas, travel by bicycle and horse- or donkey-drawn carts (called *leiterwagons*) is still common. Few people own cars. In urban areas, many people have telephones; communications systems are limited in some rural areas. The press is free to print what it wishes.

Education

Education is compulsory and free between the ages of six and sixteen. Students then seek employment, enter vocational training, or prepare for a university education. Most students complete some education beyond the required ten years. University entrance was determined in the past by loyalty to the Communist Party and good performance in school. Loyalty to the party is no longer required, and university students are among the most vocal supporters of political change. The literacy rate is 95 percent.

Health

Many important health problems face the people of Romania. Due to a practice of giving newborn babies blood transfusions if they appeared anemic, many children contracted AIDS from contaminated needles and blood. Romania has large concentrations of AIDS-infected children. Many women also have the disease (whereas it affects mostly men in other countries). Hepatitis B is another danger. Illnesses associated with heavy pollution are common. Health facilities are often poorly equipped and understaffed. Large groups of orphaned children do not receive necessary attention or care. With the help of Western nations, the government is trying to address these problems. The infant mortality rate is 19 per 1,000. Life expectancy averages 69 to 75 years.

FOR THE TRAVELER

U.S. travelers must have a valid passport to enter Romania and a visa to stay more than 30 days. Visas can be obtained at the border or applied for at the embassy. No vaccinations are required, but some may be advisable depending on the itinerary. Credit card use is limited but increasing. Areas isolated by mountains offer a look at a culture that has not changed for decades. For travel information, contact the Romanian National Tourist Office, 342 Madison Avenue, Second Floor, Suite 210, New York, NY 10173; phone (212) 697–6971. The Embassy of Romania is located at 1607 23d Street NW, Washington, DC 20008; phone (202) 232–4747.

A *Culturgram* is a product of native commentary and original, expert analysis. Statistics are estimates and information is presented as a matter of opinion. While the editors strive for accuracy and detail, this document should not be considered strictly factual. It is a general introduction to culture, an initial step in building bridges of understanding between peoples. It may not apply to all peoples of the nation. You should therefore consult other sources for more information.

CULTURGRAM '97

Russia
(Russian Federation)

Boundary representations not necessarily authoritative.

BACKGROUND

Land and Climate

Russia is the largest country in the world. At 6,592,734 square miles (17,075,200 square kilometers), it is nearly twice the size of the United States. Russia is bounded by the Arctic Ocean in the north, by the Pacific Ocean in the east, and in the south and west by many countries. Four of the world's largest rivers (Lena, Ob, Volga, and Yenisey) and the world's deepest freshwater lake (Baikal) are in Russia. Most of the country's territory consists of great plains, but there is a large tundra in the extreme north and much of western Russia is covered by forests. Parts of eastern Russia are desert. The low Ural Mountains divide Russia in two parts: the smaller European and the larger Asian regions. The climate is generally dry and continental, with long, subzero winters and short, temperate summers.

History

Slavic peoples settled in eastern Europe during the early Christian era. In 988, they were converted to Christianity by Prince Vladimir. At the beginning of the 13th century, the area was conquered by the Mongols, who dominated the Slavs for 240 years. The Slavs defeated the Mongols in 1480 and regained their sovereignty. In 1547, Ivan the Terrible (1533–84) was the first Russian ruler crowned Czar of Russia. He expanded Russia's territory, as did Peter the Great (1682–1724) and Catherine the Great (1762–96). The empire reached from Warsaw in the west to Vladivostok in the east. In 1812, Russian troops defeated France's Napoleon, and Russia took its place as one of the most powerful states on earth.

When Czar Nicholas II abdicated because of popular unrest during World War I, Vladimir Lenin, head of the Bolshevik Party, led the 1917 revolt that brought down the provisional government and put the Communists in power. Lenin disbanded the legislature and banned all other political parties. A civil war between Lenin's Red Army and the White Army lasted until 1921, with Lenin victorious.

In 1922, the Bolsheviks formed the Union of Soviet Socialist Republics (USSR) and forcibly incorporated Armenia, Azerbaijan, Georgia, Ukraine, and Belarus into the union. During Lenin's rule, which ended with his death in 1924, many died as a result of his radical restructuring of society. Lenin was followed by Joseph Stalin, a dictator who forced industrialization and collective agriculture on the people. Millions died in labor camps and from starvation. Germany invaded the Soviet Union in 1941, and World War II (the "Great Patriotic War") eventually took more than 25 million Soviet lives.

Nikita Khrushchev, who took over after Stalin's death in 1953, declared he would build real communism within 20 years, but his reforms and policy of détente with the West were opposed by hard-liners and he was replaced by Leonid Brezhnev in 1964. Until his 1982 death, Brezhnev orchestrated the expansion of Soviet influence in the developing world, and he ordered the invasion of Afghanistan.

In 1986, soon after Mikhail Gorbachev came to power, he started *perestroika* and attempted to reform government by introducing *glasnost* (openness) and freedom of speech. Many of his reforms failed, exposing in the process inherent weaknesses in the Soviet system. The union quickly unraveled in

1991 after many republics declared independence. Russia's Boris Yeltsin moved to introduce his own reforms.

In 1993, after months of political battles with legislators, Yeltsin dissolved Parliament and called for elections. Parliament instead voted to impeach Yeltsin and his opponents seized the White House (parliament building) in an effort to overthrow the government. Following street riots, the showdown turned violent and militants were forced from the building by tank fire. Even with Yeltsin victorious in that crisis, an anti-Yeltsin ultranationalist party emerged far stronger than expected in new parliamentary elections. On the other hand, voters approved a new constitution supported by Yeltsin. At the same time, a violent civil war with separatists in the Chechnya region tarnished Yeltsin's image and caused international concern. Despite alternate efforts at peace and at crushing the rebellion, Russia remains unable to solve the Chechnya problem. The war continued well into 1996. In March 1996, Russia and Belarus formed a political union, closely linking their societies but stopping short of an actual merger.

Questions about Yeltsin's leadership, health, and economic policies allowed Communists and other factions to present a strong challenge to him in the 1996 national elections. By allying with former enemies after the first round of balloting, Yeltsin was able to claim a substantial victory in 1996 to become Russia's first freely elected president. Communists had a strong showing and will therefore have a voice in Yeltsin's government.

THE PEOPLE

Population

The population of Russia is about 149.6 million and is growing annually at only 0.2 percent. There are some 120 different ethnic groups, but most are small. Ethnic Russians form 82 percent of the entire population. Other groups include Tartars (4 percent), Ukrainians (3 percent), Chuvashes (1 percent), Belarusians (less than 1 percent), Udmurts, Kazakhs, and others. The capital and largest city is Moscow, with a population of more than 10 million. Other large cities (one to three million residents each) include St. Petersburg, Novosibirsk, Nizhniy Novgorod, Yekaterinburg, Saratov, and Samara. Most Russians still live in rural areas, but young people are moving to the cities. Russia's Human Development Index (0.849) ranks it 52d out of 174 countries. Social institutions exist that could provide people with opportunities for personal success, but they do not yet function well enough for many people to take advantage of them. Gaps between rich and poor, skilled and unskilled, and healthy and ill are widening and threatening Russia's development.

Language

Russian is the official language, and it was also the main language of the Soviet Union. Russian uses the Cyrillic alphabet, which consists of 33 letters, many of them unlike any letter in the Roman (Latin) alphabet. Non-Russians also speak their own languages. For example, Tartars speak Tartar, Chuvashes speak Chuvash, and Udmurts speak Udmurt. These individual languages are only taught at schools in the republic (state) of Russia where the ethnic group is prominent. Non-Russians speak Russian in addition to their native language.

They often consider Russian a second language and do not speak it on a daily basis. For their part, ethnic Russians are not required to study other local languages. Foreign language courses are growing in popularity, with English, French, German, and Spanish being the most common.

Religion

The Russian Orthodox Church is the dominant religion. After the October Revolution (1917), the Communists separated the church from the state (which were previously tightly bonded) and discouraged all religious worship. Many churches were forced to close under Lenin and Stalin. Mikhail Gorbachev was the first Soviet leader to change official policy and tolerate—even support—religion. Yeltsin also embraced the church, which is regaining its influence. Churches other than the Russian Orthodox are scarce in rural areas, but nearly every major religion and many Christian churches have members in cities. Islam is practiced in some southern regions.

General Attitudes

In Russia's long history of totalitarianism, its inhabitants have had few opportunities to make their own decisions, whether ruled by a Czar or the Communist Party. Personal initiative, personal responsibility, and the desire to work independently were suppressed by the state, and one was expected to conform to official opinion and behavior.

In the current climate, Russians are searching for new social values. The resulting confusion and chaos have led some to wonder whether the old ways weren't better—as evidenced in the Communists' strength during 1996 elections. Many Russians are not happy with their rapidly changing society, characterized by high prices, increasingly violent and rampant crime, unemployment, and a reduced quality of life. Some feel unprepared to pay such a high price for future economic benefits. Others, especially the younger generations, are eagerly taking advantage of the open environment. Indeed, Russians are learning the value of discussion and compromise, personal creativity, and risk-taking. This long-term process carries hard lessons such as financial loss, political polarization, economic instability, and social disruption.

Friendship is extremely important in Russia. Russians are warm and open to, as well as trusting of, their friends. They rely on their network of friends in hard times and will go to great lengths to help friends whenever possible.

Although intensely proud of "Mother Russia" and its achievements, Russians are basically pessimistic and usually do not express much hope for a better life in the future (except among the youth). Even generally happy and optimistic Russians might not show their true feelings in public but rather express frustration with everyday life. A general feeling in Russia is that the "soul" of Russia is different from that of other countries, that development cannot take the same course as it has in Europe, for example. Russians often believe they must find a different path that takes into account their unique historical heritage and social structure. In general, Russians desire to be remembered not for the negative aspects of the Soviet period and its aftermath but for Russian contributions to world literature, art, science, technology, and medicine.

Personal Appearance

Russian clothing styles are the same as in Europe but not as sophisticated. Jeans are popular among most age groups, except older women. In winter, people wear *chapkas* or *ushanki* (fur hats). Shorts are becoming popular among the younger generation; young women like short skirts. The older generation dresses conservatively.

CUSTOMS AND COURTESIES

Greetings

When meeting, Russians shake hands firmly and might say *Zdravstvuyte* (pronounced sdrav-STVUH-teh, it means "Hello"), *Dobry dien* (Good day), or *Privet* (a casual "Hello"). Some women prefer not to shake hands, but it is impolite for a man not to offer his hand. Friends and family may kiss on the cheek. The question *Kak dela?* (How are you?) is taken literally; Russians answer in detail and at length. Asking the question without waiting for a full response is rude. *Kak dela?* is not used as a formal greeting. Titles such as *Gospodin* (Mr.) and *Gospozha* (Mrs.) were not used under the Communists, but they are being revived. In addressing an older or respected person, one uses the given name and a patronymic (the possessive of the father's first name), but surnames are preferred in formal greetings. It is considered inappropriate for a younger person or subordinate to address an elder or superior in a casual manner.

Gestures

Pointing with the index finger is improper but commonly practiced. It is impolite to talk (especially to an older person) with one's hands in the pockets or arms folded across the chest. To count, a Russian bends (closes) the fingers rather than opens them.

Visiting

Russians like to visit and have guests. Sitting around the kitchen table and talking for hours is a favorite pastime. One usually removes shoes when entering a home. Hosts generally offer refreshments, but guests may decline them. Friends and family may visit anytime without prior arrangement. They make themselves at home and usually can expect to be welcomed for any length of time. Visits with new acquaintances are more formal and require prior notice.

Giving gifts is a strong tradition in Russia, and almost every event (birthdays, weddings, holidays, etc.) is accompanied by presents. For casual visits, it is common (but not required) for guests to bring a simple gift (flowers, food, or vodka) to their hosts. The object given is less important than the friendship expressed by the act. Flowers are given in odd numbers; even numbers are for funerals. If a bottle of vodka (which means "little water") is opened, custom dictates it be emptied by those present.

Eating

Eating with the fork in the left hand and the knife in the right is standard, but many people use only a fork. People keep the hands above the table and not in the lap. Most Russians like to eat a large breakfast whenever possible. Soup is common for lunch or dinner. Traditionally, a popular feature of any meal is *zakuski* (appetizers). There are many different kinds of *zakuski*; eating too many may spoil an appetite. Russians put more food than they can eat on the table and leave some on the plate to indicate there is abundance (whether true or not) in the house. Guests who leave food on the plate indicate they have eaten well.

Russians generally do not go to lunch in cafés or restaurants because the few that exist are fairly expensive. Instead, people eat at workplace cafeterias or bring food from home.

LIFESTYLE

Family

The family is the basic social unit in Russia, and most people expect to marry and have children. The average urban couple has one child, but rural families are larger. Because housing is difficult to obtain, young couples often live with their parents for some time. It is the normal practice to support children financially until they reach adulthood. The father is considered the head of the family. Both husband and wife usually work, but women are also responsible for housekeeping. Men rarely share in household duties. Child care is available, but few families can afford it. When the elderly live with their children, they often provide child care and do the shopping.

Urban apartments are small and it is common for a family of three or more to live in one room. A typical apartment has one room, a kitchen, and a bathroom. Rural homes are small but larger than apartments. While they have more room, they often lack running water.

Dating and Marriage

When young people date, they usually go to movies or for a walk in a city park. Sometimes they go to bars or cafés, but this is presently too expensive for many people. Instead, the youth like to have parties in their apartments when their parents are not home. Many couples live together before or instead of marrying. There is a new trend to be married in a church first and then to have an official civil ceremony in a "wedding palace," the only place people could get married before 1991.

Diet

Although food is plentiful, many products are expensive or available only in hard-currency markets. For the common person, this means fruits and vegetables are difficult to come by. Hence, menus consist mainly of bread, meat, dairy products, and potatoes. To improve the diet, a growing number of people in urban areas are growing vegetable gardens on plots near the city. People on fixed and limited incomes (mainly the elderly) eat more bread than anything else. Common Russian foods include *borsch* (cabbage soup with beets), *pirozhki* (a stuffed roll), *golubzi* (stuffed cabbage leaves baked with tomato sauce and eaten with sour cream), and *shi* (soup with sour cabbage). *Borsch* is still one of the most popular foods in the country. Its ingredients (potatoes, cabbages, carrots, beets, and onions) almost complete the list of vegetables used in everyday life. Pork, sausage, chicken, and cheeses are popular, but they are often very expensive. Russians prefer tea to coffee. Mineral water, juice, and soda are readily available at high prices. Russians drink far more vodka than wine.

Recreation

Russians have little leisure time because of the hours they devote to getting food, working extra jobs, or taking care of their households. Urban Russians spend their spare time at their *dachas* (country cottages), if they have them, relaxing and growing fruits and vegetables for the winter. There are relatively few nightclubs, and entertainment usually ends by

11:00 P.M. Even Moscow is essentially dark and quiet after that hour.

The country's favorite sport is soccer. Russia's national soccer team competed in the 1994 World Cup. Winter sports such as ice skating, hockey, and cross-country skiing, are particularly popular in Russia. Watching television is the most common way to spend extra time. Gathering mushrooms is a favorite summer activity. Russia has a grand and abiding heritage in cultural arts. The people highly appreciate theaters and movies, but these are available only in big cities. Rural people can watch movies at *dvorets kultury* (palaces of culture), which serve as community recreation centers.

Holidays

New Year's Day is the most popular holiday in Russia. Almost everyone decorates fir trees and has parties to celebrate the new year. Grandfather Frost leaves presents for children to find on New Year's Day. Christmas is on 7 January, according to the Julian calendar used by the Russian Orthodox Church. Women's Day is 8 March. Solidarity Day (1 May, also known as May Day) is a day for parades. Before 1991, people were required to attend; now they attend voluntarily and the nature of the celebrations has changed dramatically. Victory Day (9 May) commemorates the end of World War II and is deeply important to the older generation. Easter and Christmas observances, long interrupted by communism, regained their prominence in 1990.

Commerce

The business week is 40 hours, with Saturdays and Sundays off. Offices generally are open from 9:00 A.M. to 6:00 P.M. They close at lunchtime (1:00 P.M.). Prices in state stores are not negotiable, but prices are flexible on the streets, where an increasing number of items are sold. Capitalism is booming in Russia and a new generation of entrepreneurs is beginning to thrive. Numerous small businesses and joint ventures with foreign firms are finding success, and employees are buying state-run factories and working to make them profitable.

Under communism, there were no incentives for bureaucrats to perform well or even be nice to clients, so the usual answer to any question was "No." This practice is still found in society, but "no" is no longer final. One must simply bargain and be persistent to get what one wants. Russians prefer having social interaction before discussing business. Trying to do business on the phone without seeing the prospective business partner is ineffective. One often spends a lot of time in meetings before even a small deal can succeed.

SOCIETY

Government

Russia is a federation of 21 autonomous republics. The 1993 constitution provides for a president (Boris Yeltsin) as head of state and a prime minister (Viktor Chernomyrdin) as head of government. The president is strong and has power to dissolve Parliament, set foreign policy, and appoint the prime minister. The Federal Assembly has two houses, a 176-seat Federation Council and the 450-seat State Duma. The Constitutional Court is Russia's highest. The voting age is

18. An array of political parties are represented in the *Duma*. The actual party names are less important than their alliances. Communists form the largest block, but not a majority, and nationalists and liberals form other substantial voting blocks.

Economy

Russia's natural resources give it great potential for economic growth and development. Natural gas, coal, gold, oil, diamonds, copper, silver, and lead are all abundant. Heavy industry dominates the economy, although the agricultural sector is potentially strong. Russia's economy is weak and unstable. Liberal reforms designed to attract foreign investment and privatize the economy led to higher unemployment, high inflation (about 100 percent), and lower production. Organized crime and corruption weigh heavily on the economy's ability to perform well. Real gross domestic product per capita is $6,140 and falling, as poverty increases as fast as wealth. The currency is the *ruble* (R).

Transportation and Communication

Most people use public transportation. Major cities have subways, trolleys, and buses. Taxis are expensive and hard to find, but unofficial taxis are increasingly common. Domestic air travel is not always reliable. Railroads are extensive, but service is poor. The telephone system is old and inadequate. The press is free, active, and constantly changing.

Education

Education is free and compulsory between ages six and seventeen. In 1994, new curriculum guidelines were introduced to encourage choice and innovation over previous approaches to teaching, but many public schools are unable or unwilling to implement the reforms due to lack of money and clear local leadership. Students attend primary, middle, and high school. They specialize in their last two years, and several electives are available. Private schools provide high-quality education to children of the wealthy and influential. Education is highly valued, and Russia's literacy rate is 99 percent. More than five hundred universities, medical schools, and technical academies are found throughout the country.

Health

Medical care is free, but the quality of service is poor. Doctors are highly trained and qualified but lack modern equipment and medicine to adequately treat their patients. Private clinics provide better care but are expensive. The infant mortality rate is 26 per 1,000. Life expectancy ranges from 64 to 74 years. Common major diseases are alcoholism, cancer, diabetes, and heart ailments. Diptheria, dysentery, and other intestinal maladies are spreading.

FOR THE TRAVELER

U.S. travelers are required to have a valid visa and passport to enter Russia. Vaccinations are not required, but some may be recommended. While drinking water is generally safe, bottled water is recommended. There are many opportunities to experience the Russian culture through travel; contact your travel professional for more information. You may also wish to contact the Consular Section of the Russian Embassy, 1825 Phelps Place NW, Washington, DC 20008.

A *Culturgram* is a product of native commentary and original, expert analysis. Statistics are estimates and information is presented as a matter of opinion. While the editors strive for accuracy and detail, this document should not be considered strictly factual. It is a general introduction to culture, an initial step in building bridges of understanding between peoples. It may not apply to all peoples of the nation. You should therefore consult other sources for more information.

CULTURGRAM™ '97

Federation of
Saint Kitts and Nevis

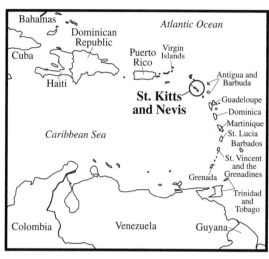

Boundary representations not necessarily authoritative.

BACKGROUND

Land and Climate

Saint Kitts—also called Saint Christopher—and Nevis are leeward islands in the Caribbean Archipelago about 200 miles southeast of Puerto Rico. The two are separated by a channel called The Narrows that is only two miles wide at its narrowest point. St. Kitts is 68 square miles (176 square kilometers) in size, while Nevis is 36 square miles (93 square kilometers). A mountainous central ridge extends throughout the length of St. Kitts. Its highest peak, Mount Liamuiga, rises to 3,792 feet (1,102 meters). On Nevis, Nevis Peak rises to 3,232 feet (939 meters). Both mountains are long-dormant volcanoes, but there is some evidence of volcanic activity in the form of fumaroles and hot sulfur springs.

Below 1,000 feet, St. Kitts is a patchwork of cultivated fields, mostly sugarcane. Above these fields, slopes are covered with tropical rain forests. The peninsula has a number of salt ponds and is quite different from the rest of the island. Nevis is rockier and has clay soils. It is covered with a higher concentration of natural vegetation. Cultivation is limited to small vegetable and fruit farms. The most valuable natural resources include the islands' beauty, tranquillity, and unspoiled natural environment. The climate is dry and tropical, with temperatures ranging from 82°F (28°C) in December to 91°F (33°C) in July and August. The rainy season runs from July to December, while January to June is generally drier. Hurricanes are possible between July and November.

Nevis's shoreline is ringed by coconut palms. The island is home to goats and donkeys. Deer roam St. Kitts, and West African green vervet monkeys live on both islands. Booby Island boasts a large pelican and seagull population.

History

Prior to the arrival of Christopher Columbus, St. Kitts and Nevis were inhabited by Caribs who had migrated from South America. They called St. Kitts *Liamuiga* (Fertile Island) and Nevis *Oualie* (meaning unknown). Columbus discovered St. Kitts and Nevis on his second Caribbean voyage in 1493. St. Kitts was eventually named San Cristóbal and Nevis was named Santa María de las Nieves (Our Lady of the Snows) because of the cloud cluster lying on Nevis Peak. San Cristóbal (Saint Christopher) was later shortened to St. Kitts by its English colonists while Nieves became Nevis.

Sir Thomas Warner colonized St. Kitts (1624) and Nevis (1628). French settlers arrived in 1626 and St. Kitts was partitioned by formal treaty. Despite initial friendly relations with the Carib people and their King Tegreman, the British and French massacred or expelled most Caribs; many leapt from a sea cliff to their deaths.

The English and French coexisted peacefully until war broke out between Britain and France in 1666. The 1713 Treaty of Utrecht ceded the island entirely to the British. Today, the only trace of a French presence remains in historical sites and names (such as the capital, Basseterre).

Sugar production, begun in the 1650s, propelled the islands to 18th century prosperity. Irish indentured servants, Dutch refugees, and Spanish and Portuguese Jews from Brazil all found their way to the islands. From 1675 to 1730, Nevis was also the headquarters of the African slave trade in the Leeward Islands. The African population eventually outnumbered Europeans ten to one.

The 19th century saw the decline of the sugar industry and the 1833 emancipation of the slaves. A subsequent economic downturn was felt acutely by the African population. Many inhabitants emigrated to Western Hemisphere; some of those who remained protested conditions by rioting.

Riots in 1935 were followed by social and political change, including the establishment of trade unions, representative government, and universal adult suffrage (1952). The Crown Colony of St. Kitts-Nevis-Anguilla joined the short-lived West Indies Federation in 1958. In 1967, the three islands were given the status of Associated Statehood, making them responsible for their internal affairs. Anguilla left the union and eventually reverted to colonial status (1982). Robert Bradshaw, leader of the Labour Party, dominated the national political scene from the 1950s until 1980.

St. Kitts and Nevis have not always enjoyed harmonious relations, but with independence in 1983 they made their association more permanent. That occurred under the leadership of Prime Minister Kennedy Simmonds, whose People's Action Movement (PAM) was in power from 1980 to 1995. Elections in 1995 led to a Labour Party victory and a new prime minister, Denzil Douglas, being installed.

PEOPLE

Population

The current population of 41,000 is down from 42,000 in 1989. St. Kitts is home to 72 percent of the total population. One-fourth lives in Basseterre. The country's Human Development Index (0.873) ranks it 37th out of 174 nations. This reflects the people's expanding access to resources such as education, health care, and a decent income.

Most inhabitants are of African descent, but a small percentage is European, Lebanese, or East Indian. A large number of St. Kitts and Nevis nationals live in North America, Britain, and other Caribbean nations. Ties between these emigrants and the nation remain strong. On Nevis, many European and North American expatriates own vacation homes.

Language

English is the official language, although people use a local dialect for daily informal communication. A combination of English and African words and syntax, the dialect is spoken most heavily in rural areas. It is appreciated for its colorful expressions, folk wisdom, proverbs, and riddles.

Religion

Nearly all people on the islands are Christian. The traditionally dominant churches—Anglican, Methodist, Moravian—are being challenged in prominence by a growing number of Pentecostal, Seventh-Day Adventist, and other Christian congregations. A small number of Rastafarians and Baha'is also live on the islands.

Religious beliefs and values have a noticeable influence on daily life. Not only do people regularly attend church services but they (especially women) also participate in other church-sponsored activities. Most children are exposed to religious teachings while growing up. Major family events such as weddings, christenings, and burials are usually observed in a church.

General Attitudes

People in St. Kitts and Nevis are sociable, outgoing, and friendly, both among themselves and toward strangers. They are flexible about time and are seldom in such a hurry that they cannot extend a greeting or engage in a conversation with someone. Like members of most small communities, they take a keen interest in one another's affairs, and rumors and gossip are common.

People respect their social institutions, including the law. Therefore, most disputes are settled through litigation. People place considerable emphasis on personal loyalties in politics, as well as on personal relationships with lawyers, priests, doctors, and business and community leaders. They expect equality in social interaction.

Traditionally, people in Nevis are known for their thrift and for valuing land and livestock. In St. Kitts, and generally in urban areas, greater importance is placed on material possessions such as an impressive home or a car. Residents of both islands value financial security and a good education, the traditional route to social mobility.

Personal Appearance

Except when engaged in jobs like farming or fishing that require old clothes or overalls, people are meticulous about their appearance. Women are particularly fashion conscious and they like jewelry. They also pay great attention to the grooming of their hair and that of their children.

Women usually wear dresses or skirts to work, reserving shorts and trousers for casual occasions. Swimsuits are worn only on the beach. Clothes are made of brightly colored, lightweight fabrics. People like colorful T-shirts, embroidered or tie-dyed Caribbean designs, or the latest North American fashions. The latter are popular with the youth. Children generally wear uniforms to school. Men may wear suits on formal occasions but prefer to work in light *shirt-jacs* and trousers. Jeans, shorts, and T-shirts are casual wear.

CUSTOMS AND COURTESIES

Greetings

It is important to greet people with *Good morning*, *Good afternoon*, or *Good night*. Other more informal greetings are *Howdy*, *How you do?* or *Hey, wha' happ'nin'?* When leaving, one might say *Goodbye*, *See you*, or *Take care then till next time*. Older or rural people may still say *See you soon, D.V.* (*Deus Volunte*, or God willing).

Remembering people's names is crucial. One addresses older people, those in important positions, or people one does not know well as *Mr.*, *Mrs.*, or *Miss* with their surname or, less formally, their initial (e.g., *Mr. B*). Older women may be addressed familiarly as *Auntie*, *Mother*, or *Mama* (e.g., *Mother Saunders*, *Mama Liz*). Informally, one may also be addressed as *Darlin'*, *Me dear*, or *Sweetheart*. Many people have nicknames and are seldom called by their original names. Children are expected to address older people as *Mr.*, *Mrs.*, or *Miss* or as *Auntie* or *Uncle*.

People often touch hands or arms when meeting. A man may put his arm around a woman's shoulder or hold her hand in a friendly meeting. Hugging is more prevalent than kissing, particularly when people meet old friends and children. Handshakes are normally used in formal introductions.

Gestures

As in the rest of the Caribbean, individuals "talk with their hands," indeed with the whole body. Speaking is accompanied by a variety of hand and arm movements, and the livelier the discussion, the more gestures there are. Women may put their hands on their hips when arguing or as a sign of defiance or aggression. Coming up very close to someone during an altercation is also considered aggressive. People shrug their shoulders to indicate uncertainty. They may pucker their mouths, toss their heads, and make a sideways motion with the thumb and hand when humorously mocking someone or indicating real derision. Individuals may purse their lips and make a sound by sucking air through their teeth (known as "sucking the teeth") to indicate disgust or anger.

Men and younger people are expected to give up public transport seats or offer help to the elderly, pregnant women, and people with young children. Chewing gum during conversation or eating in the street is not well regarded.

Visiting

People in St. Kitts and Nevis tend to entertain formally for family celebrations like weddings, christenings, or birthday parties or during festive seasons like Christmas. On such occasions, there is a lot of food and drink, music, and perhaps dancing. Gifts are not expected, but for an evening party a guest might bring a bottle of something to drink.

Generally, people "drop in" or "drop by" unannounced for short visits. Hospitality is important; visitors are always welcomed and usually offered a cool drink and possibly a slice of cake. On weekends, friends socialize on the verandah or in the garden. When expatriates return to the islands, they spend time visiting family members and old friends.

Eating

The average family normally eats three meals a day. Breakfasts are hurried and usually consist of a hot drink, eggs, cereal, or a sandwich. In rural areas where people have been working in the fields for several hours, breakfast may be later and heavier. The main family meal used to be at midday. Increasingly, due to work and school schedules, lunch consists of a snack, and the family eats a substantial cooked meal together in the evening. This meal, preceded by grace, is usually eaten around the table, but entertaining is often buffet style. People eat out much more today than they did 15 years ago. Many go to restaurants and snack bars for lunch.

LIFESTYLE

Family

The extended family structure is still a feature of life on the islands, but with socioeconomic changes it is gradually being eroded. Families are close-knit. Many households are headed by women who are raising their children, grandchildren, or children of parents who work abroad. Elderly relatives may also live in the home.

Middle-class people are most likely to get married and, at least initially, have a typical nuclear family. Common-law marriages are widespread among lower-income groups, and the children enjoy the same rights under the law as do children of formally married couples. Men are encouraged to have contact with their children and are legally required to support them financially, even if they have not married the mother. It is not unusual for an individual, male or female, to have children by two or more partners. Women prize motherhood, while men judge their machismo by both their prowess with women and the fathering of children.

In general, women have the greatest responsibility for raising children. They may also be the sole or most consistent breadwinners for the household. Most women work outside the home, traditionally as farmers, domestics, nurses, teachers, or in commercial and administrative jobs. More recently, many have found employment in the light-manufacturing sector or are self-employed in micro-enterprises.

Grown children are committed to improving their parents' lives by upgrading the family home and contributing to the family income, particularly if they migrate abroad. Unless they work some distance away, young unmarried people, particularly young women, continue to live with their parents.

Dating and Marriage

Young people go out together, although the activities of teenage girls tend to be supervised and controlled by parents. Boys and girls meet at school and church functions, at parties, on the beach, during festive occasions, at sporting events, or at a few spots where they simply "hang out."

Older couples may spend a lot of time together, especially on weekends. People generally marry between the ages of 20 and 35. Most weddings are performed in a church. They can be quite elaborate social events with many guests.

Diet

Probably the best-known traditional dishes in St. Kitts and Nevis are salt fish and dumplings (salted, dried codfish prepared as a stew with dumplings—a Good Friday staple), chicken and rice *pelau* with red beans or pigeon peas, and *goatwater*, a spicy stew made from goat, breadfruit, and dumplings. Other dishes include *souse* (prepared from pickled pigs' trotters, cucumbers, and hot peppers) and *black pudding* made from pigs' blood, rice, and herbal stuffing.

People eat a lot of chicken and fish, both dried and fresh. Pork and mutton are also popular. Peas, beans, and lentils are an important source of protein in the national diet. Bread is eaten for breakfast and snacks, while cooked staple carbohydrates include rice, breadfruit, yams, cooked cornmeal (usually eaten with steamed fish and okra), dumplings (or the fried version, *johnny cakes*), and macaroni.

Vegetables generally are cooked, although people do eat lettuce and cucumbers or a coleslaw salad. Cabbage, carrots, eggplants, and sweet potatoes are also common. Local fruits include mangoes, sugar apples, soursops, pawpaws, plantains, golden apples, tomatoes, and guavas. The latter are turned into a guava jelly or a sweet known as *guava cheese*.

At breakfast, people generally drink tea, coffee, cocoa (cocoa tea), or herbal teas (*bush tea*). Otherwise, they prefer cold drinks. Lunch and dinner are served with locally made lemonade, ginger beer, or drinks made from such fruits as tamarinds or passion fruit. The most popular Christmas drink is sorrel, which is made from the petals of a sorrel plant.

Recreation

Popular team sports include cricket, *football* (soccer), and basketball for men; *netball* for women; and volleyball for both. Cricket and *netball* are national sports. Nevis prides itself on being the Caribbean territory that, relative to its population size, has produced the highest number of cricketers for the West Indies cricket team. Tennis is growing in popularity.

People also go to beaches or organize picnics or hikes. Men get together in bars or elsewhere to talk, drink, and play dominoes or cards. Women meet in their homes, at church-related social activities, or at various leisure spots. People may also belong to community service clubs. Many are engaged in the development of local music, drama, or folklore. Some, especially young people, seek out night spots and enjoy themselves at dances. Watching cable television is a favorite leisure activity. People travel frequently throughout the Eastern Caribbean to visit family and to shop. The United States, Canada, and Britain are favorite holiday destinations.

Holidays

National holidays include New Year's Day (1 January) and National Carnival Day (2 January), Good Friday and Easter Monday, Labor Day (first Monday in May), Whitmonday (seven weeks after Easter Monday), Emancipation Day (first Monday in August), and Culturama Day—an annual August festival on Nevis. Independence Day is 19 September. The Christmas season includes Christmas Day and Boxing Day (26 December) and is a time for family gatherings, gift giving, and related activities. The carnival season runs for a week after the 26th and includes street dancing, costumed bands, calypso competitions, beauty contests, and beach parties.

Commerce

Stores generally open at 8:00 or 8:30 A.M. and close at 4:00 or 5:00 P.M. Smaller stores may close for lunch at noon. Many are closed on Thursday afternoon but are otherwise open Monday through Saturday. Supermarkets and small corner grocery stores may remain open later in the evening. Each island has public markets for vegetables, fruits, meat, and fish. The main market days are Thursday, Friday, and Saturday, but some vendors sell their goods every weekday. Most banks are open from 9:00 A.M. to 3:00 P.M., Monday through Thursday, and a bit later on Friday afternoon. Banks and government offices are closed on Saturday, except for the National Bank, which is open in the morning.

SOCIETY

Government

St. Kitts and Nevis are a parliamentary democracy with a federal constitution. The central government is based on St. Kitts. Nevis has a local government responsible for island administration. The National Assembly has eleven elected members—eight from St. Kitts and three from Nevis. In addition, two senators are appointed by the ruling party and one by the opposition. St. Kitts and Nevis are members of the Commonwealth and the British Queen is technically head of state. She is represented by a governor general. The voting age is 18; elections are held at least every five years.

Economy

Agriculture, tourism, and manufacturing are the most important sectors of the islands' economy. Sugar is the principal export, but the recent diversification of agriculture improved domestic self-sufficiency and provided links with the tourist industry. Tourism is becoming important both in terms of foreign-exchange earnings and employment. Manufacturing concentrates on textiles, data processing, electronic assembly, and computer software development.

More than 20 percent of the labor force is employed in agriculture, another 20 percent in manufacturing, and 13 percent in tourism. The government also employs one-fifth of the workforce. In 1994, the economy's real growth rate was 4 percent. Real gross domestic product per capita is $5,398. The currency is the East Caribbean dollar (EC$).

Transportation and Communication

Cars and buses are the primary forms of transport in St. Kitts and Nevis. Private buses operate routes between main towns and rural areas. There are 190 miles of road, including the newly built Kennedy Simmonds Highway that opened the southeast peninsula of St. Kitts to general development.

A government ferry operates five days a week between islands. Many private boats also ply the waters with freight and passengers or for fishing and sight-seeing. St. Kitts has an international airport and Nevis is expanding its airport to increase carrying capacity.

Most people have at least one radio, and 70 percent have access to television. More than half of all households have a telephone. Two national newspapers, *The Democrat* and the *Labour Spokesman*, are owned by the major political parties. Regional newspapers from neighboring islands are also available. One government and one private television station broadcast to the nation. Cable television is also available.

Education

The education system consists of preschool, primary, secondary, and some postsecondary facilities. Education is free and accessible to all. Children are required to attend school between the ages of five and sixteen. The literacy rate is approaching 99 percent. A majority of children who enroll in school finish the primary level. About two-thirds of enrolled children pass to the secondary level. The drop-out rate is higher among boys. Students who complete their secondary education can obtain vocational and technical education in the country. They may also attend a teacher-training program or study other subjects. For a university degree, students study at the University of West Indies in Jamaica, Barbados, or Trinidad or go elsewhere abroad.

Health

Four hospitals and 17 clinics comprise the national health-care system. There are fewer than 50 doctors. Health care is subsidized by the government, especially for lower-income groups. The government is also upgrading facility equipment and staff training to improve care. Hospitals in Jamaica, Barbados, and Guadeloupe take patients whose needs cannot be met on St. Kitts or Nevis. The nation has an excellent child immunization program. The infant mortality rate is 19 per 1,000; life expectancy is about 67 years.

FOR THE TRAVELER

U.S. travelers need proof of citizenship (a passport is best) and a return ticket to enter the country. Visas are not necessary. The islands offer a range of activities for the tourist. For information, contact the Chancery of St. Kitts and Nevis, 3216 New Mexico Avenue NW, Washington DC 20016; phone (202) 686–2636.

Saint Lucia

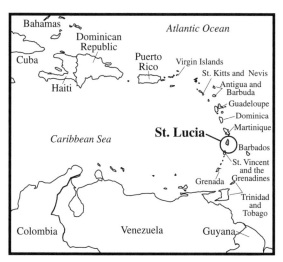

Boundary representations not necessarily authoritative.

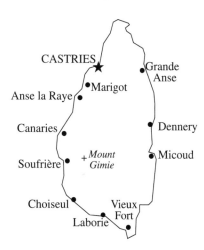

BACKGROUND

Land and Climate

Saint Lucia, often called "The Helen of the West Indies" for its beauty, lies about 1,300 miles (2,100 kilometers) southeast of Florida. It covers 236 square miles (610 square kilometers) and is about three times as large as Washington, D.C. On its west is the Caribbean Sea, while on the east is the Atlantic Ocean.

St. Lucia is a volcanic island with a subtropical climate. As such, it is mountainous and has a lush interior rain forest. The town of Soufrière is near the island's volcanic center. Both black and white sand beaches are found on the island.

Both of St. Lucia's seasons (wet and dry) tend to be warm, with June to August being the hottest months. The rainy season extends from June to October; as much as 160 inches of rain can fall. Constant trade winds moderate the temperatures year-round. The average highs are 80° to 90°F (26–32°C).

History

St. Lucia was originally inhabited by Arawak Indians. By A.D. 800, they were conquered by Carib Indians. Christopher Columbus is said to have "discovered" St. Lucia in the 1500s, but that event is now discounted. The first English settlers came in 1605 and the French arrived in 1651. Eight years later, the two groups began fighting over land ownership. Hostilities endured for 150 years and St. Lucia changed hands between the powers 13 times. The Caribs were eliminated and African slaves were imported to work on plantations. St. Lucia was finally ceded to the British in 1814 when France lost the Napoleonic Wars.

St. Lucia remained a British colony until 1967, when the West Indies Act extended self-rule over internal affairs. Full independence came in 1979, although St. Lucia remains a member of the Commonwealth.

John Compton's United Workers Party (UWP) prevailed in internal affairs from 1964 until independence, when the opposition St. Lucia Labour Party (SLP) managed to take office. By 1981, public discontent with the SLP led its leaders to resign, and John Compton became prime minister. The UWP dominated from then into the 1990s, partly because the SLP split into two parties.

PEOPLE

Population

St. Lucia's population of 156,000 is growing annually at 1 percent. The majority of the people (90 percent) descend from African slaves. Five percent are of mixed heritage. St. Lucians of East Indian descent (3 percent) live mostly in rural areas; their ancestors came as indentured laborers after slavery was abolished. Many urban merchants are of Syrian origin, and a small number of people with European heritage also live in St. Lucia. Castries, the capital, is home to nearly 40 percent of the population.

St. Lucia's Human Development Index (0.732) ranks it 84th out of 174 nations. Although most people have access to education and health care, economic opportunities are limited.

Language

English is the official language. It is used in school instruction, government, and business. While most people speak English, some rural St. Lucians are not fluent. Patois, an oral language developed during French colonial rule, is the primary tongue for most rural and many urban residents. As such, it is the daily language of communication between St. Lucians, except among the upper class. Urban residents often mix Patois and English in conversation. There is a movement to preserve Patois and develop a written form that could be taught in school.

Religion

Religion plays an important role in the lives of most St. Lucians. Business meetings, meals, the school day, and other events open with prayer. Most community activities are church sponsored or related. Roman Catholicism is practiced by about 80 percent of the population. Most other St. Lucians are Christians of other denominations, including Seventh-Day Adventist (6.5 percent), Pentecostal (3), and Anglican (2.4).

General Attitudes

St. Lucians view themselves as friendly and accepting of others. They tend to be "laid-back" and make fun of others' perceived pretensions. St. Lucians can be confrontational at times, quickly engaging in an argument or even a fight. But just as harsh words are easily spoken, tempers cool readily and conflicts are soon forgotten. Long-term confrontations are avoided because of local gossip.

While St. Lucians admire punctuality, they feel the pace of life should not be governed by the clock. Hence, on "Lucian time" everything starts late and no one expects otherwise. People do not like to schedule rigid appointments due to the belief that events occur by the grace of God.

Among St. Lucians, racial and class divisions cause some tension. Prejudices are verbally expressed but rarely rise to a level of hatred or violence. The concept of coexistence prevails, and the country enjoys overall unity. St. Lucian men express traditional West Indian male dominance over women through macho acts or sexually oriented language. Professional or otherwise economically independent St. Lucian women are becoming less tolerant of this attitude and increasingly are seeking partnerships based on equality and respect. St. Lucian women with fewer opportunities in life try to ignore the macho attitude or resign themselves to accepting it as part of life.

Personal Appearance

St. Lucians try to dress neatly in unwrinkled, modest clothing. Bathing suits, short skirts, and other revealing clothing is not appropriate away from resort areas. Children must be properly dressed for church and social functions.

Attire indicates social status and occupation. Many banks, hotels, and schools have uniforms for their employees. Professional women might wear a skirt and blouse to work. Men often wear a *shirt-jac*: a pleated, square-cut shirt with pockets and light embroidery. The youth prefer U.S. American fashions, especially jeans, denim shirts, shorts, and skirts. Young urban men sometimes wear gold necklaces with medallions. Men might also let their pinkie fingernails grow long.

Some people wear the national costume for cultural events. Men have black trousers, a white shirt, and a cummerbund. Women wear a red-and-orange-checked skirt with a white frill underskirt, a white blouse with a triangle of checked fabric over one shoulder, and a fabric hat that is tied differently depending on one's marital status.

CUSTOMS AND COURTESIES

Greetings

Greeting strangers, acquaintances, and friends is important. Formal greetings include *Good morning*, *Good afternoon*, and *Good night*. Such a phrase is expected when one enters a place of business or boards a "transport." Between people passing on the street, a nod or short greeting (*Alright, Morning, Afternoon, Evening*) is acceptable. Greetings between friends are less formal. In Patois, *Sa ka fet?* (What's happening?) is appropriate. In English, an enthusiastic *Alright?* may be exchanged. Among friends, men might "high five," "jam" (lightly touch closed fists), or shake hands vigorously; women pat each other on the shoulder or brush a hand against the other's upper arm.

Nicknames are ubiquitous. In many cases, St. Lucians are referred to by nicknames almost exclusively, and one might not even know an acquaintance's given name. Daily radio obituaries list both the given name and nickname of an individual. Nicknames are derived from one's physical appearance, given name, characteristics, or an experience. For example, *Sparks* means intelligent and knowledgeable and may be a nickname for a highly educated man.

Adults often address children as *ish mwe* (my child) or *ti ma mai* (my little one). Out of respect, younger people call older ones *auntie*, *uncle*, *mummy*, or *daddy*—even if not related. When titles (*Mr.*, *Miss*, etc.) are used, they are often combined with the given name. Married, divorced, or widowed women may be called by *Mrs.* or *Mistress* plus their husband's given name or nickname.

Gestures

St. Lucians use their faces and hands to express emotions when conversing. Clapping hands to show excitement or while laughing is common. Bending over while laughing is also common. People often nod to show agreement or shake their heads to show disapproval during conversation. Discussions may be punctuated with "eh-eh," which can mean disapproval, concern, or disbelief. People sometimes express extreme irritation by sucking air through closed teeth (known as *choopsing*). While St. Lucians will point to indicate direction, they say "pssst" to get another's attention.

Visiting

St. Lucians visit friends and relatives often and unannounced. Visits are rarely the result of a formal invitation. People never seem too busy to stop at a friend's home. When one drops by, it is customary to first call out a greeting from outside the home. The residents may come out and engage in leisurely conversation. The visitors may or may not be invited inside for a drink or snack. The closer the people are, the more likely the invitation will be extended. Guests remove shoes when they enter the home.

Arranged visits occur most often on weekends. One may be invited to a *fete* (party) or on an excursion to another part of the island. For a *fete*, it is acceptable but not required for guests to bring a beverage or food item to share. Evening parties start late and continue into the early morning hours. If a meal is served, it might be as late as 11:00 P.M.

Eating

St. Lucians usually rise early to begin work or chores before the hottest part of the day (11:00 A.M.–3:00 P.M.). Therefore, they may eat breakfast very early (before 7:00 A.M.). Breakfast usually is light, consisting of locally baked bread and butter. It may be accompanied by a hot drink, such as *tea* (green tea), coffee, or *cocoa tea* (Ovaltine).

Lunch (referred to as *dinner* or *the food*) is usually the main meal. Most St. Lucians begin preparing it in the morning before work. They return home at midday to enjoy the meal, which consists of rice, meat or fish, *peas* (any legume—including lentils, red beans, pigeon peas, etc.), *ground provisions* (foods grown in the ground, such as sweet potatoes or other root vegetables), and locally grown fruit (breadfruit, plantains, and bananas). Unripe bananas might be boiled and put in salads. For people unable to return home for *the food*, the main meal is supper. Otherwise, supper consists of bread and butter, fried fish or tinned meat, sometimes cheese, and tea.

On Sundays, people eat a large meal in the early afternoon. It consists of meat or chicken, rice, *peas*, macaroni and cheese, and perhaps a *ground provision*. For special occasions, a goat or sheep may be roasted or stewed.

The spoon is often the only utensil used for lunch and supper. Certain foods (fruit, bread, chicken, etc.) are eaten with one's hands. Children might eat separately before adults, especially when guests are present. To show appreciation for a meal, guests accept offers of second helpings.

LIFESTYLE

Family

Families tend to be large and include more than two generations. Grandparents and other members of the extended family might help raise children and do household chores. St. Lucia has many single-parent families. Except among the elite and well educated, it is not uncommon to have a female head of household and several generations with no adult men. St. Lucian women might have children with different partners throughout their lives. Men often date even when married; many consider it macho to father babies by different *baby mothers*. Even as a woman's partners change, her children remain with her and are raised together with half siblings. If the mother cannot care for a child, another relative or even a friend might raise it. Few men provide financial support for their children, but St. Lucian society is increasingly pressing fathers to take more responsibility for their offspring.

Adult children usually remain home until they get married. If they remain in their parent's home after marrying or having children, they are expected to help maintain the household. While some apartments are found in Castries, most families have their own homes. Private ownership is high (more than 70 percent). The property on which the home sits may have been in the family for several generations. Urban houses are made of concrete and may be built on stilts to avoid flooding. Rural houses are commonly built of brightly painted wood planks. Both styles have corrugated tin roofs. Around a home, families often plant a small garden with tropical flowers and *ground provisions*. Houses are small and simple, decorated with locally made wrought iron or wooden furnishings, as well as curtains and other accessories made from imported fabric.

Dating and Marriage

Most St. Lucians date individuals they know from their community. Relationships may also develop through school or church attendance and activities. Men prefer to date several women simultaneously, but more women are demanding monogamous relationships.

While marriage and monogamy are considered important, St. Lucians often do not get married or commit to one partner. Instead, they may live together in common-law arrangements that do not involve legal ceremonies. More dedicated couples marry after they have built a house, begun to raise a family, or have just lived together for a number of years. Common-law marriages are increasingly being recognized by the legal system for the purpose of child support and other family matters.

Diet

Rice, *ground provisions*, and *peas* are staples. Beef and chicken are both imported and raised locally. Certain fish (red snapper, dolphin, and tuna) are expensive and considered delicacies. Conch, goat, and sheep are eaten for special occasions. Cabbage, tomatoes, peppers, and onions are used in small quantities to garnish a dish. Seasonal fruits include tamarinds, oranges, limes, guavas, mangoes, passion fruit, papaya, and golden apples; they are often used for making juice. Mangoes are peeled and eaten whole. Ginger tea is made with fresh ground ginger, sugar, and boiling water. Herbal teas are made from local plants for medicinal purposes. *Coconut water*, drunk from green or immature coconut shells, is available year-round.

Urban residents (in Castries and Vieux Fort) eat more imported foods (like canned fruit juice, frozen chicken, cheese, and canned or powdered milk). They are also more likely to eat in restaurants. Rural people rely on produce grown in their gardens, fruit they pick from local trees, or livestock they raise themselves. Locally caught fish is available near coastal villages. A common rural meal is the "one-pot" stew that is cooked on an outdoor coal pot.

Recreation

Soccer (*football*) is St. Lucia's most popular sport, closely followed by cricket. Community leagues provide organized competition, but teams may also play against squads from other West Indian nations. Men listen to broadcasts of cricket matches in other nations or World Wrestling Federation events. St. Lucians love to play dominoes for pleasure or for gambling. The rich join bridge clubs.

Carnival provides St. Lucians with a chance to dance, sing, and participate in calypso talent contests. Many people compete for the title of Calypso King and Queen; everyone follows the event closely. Winners are featured in many Carnival events and hold the titles for one year. Several weeks of preparation precede the calypso contests and *Jouvert*, a street parade that begins at sunrise with bands and costumed marchers. Spectators often join the parade.

In addition to calypso, St. Lucians enjoy other types of music, such as *soca*, reggae, U.S. American country, and *cadance* (a lively dancing music from the French Antilles). Quadrille dancing is also popular.

There are no movie theaters. People watch movies on VCRs and enjoy U.S. American television shows. St. Lucians go to the local beach for a barbecue or *fete*. Beach parties are usually impressive, with plenty of food served to casually dressed guests. The primary purpose of these events is to socialize and eat, not to swim or play beach sports.

Holidays

Christmas is the primary religious holiday. The Christmas season begins 13 December, which is also National Day (previously called Discovery Day for Christopher Columbus). The

Christmas Eve midnight mass is widely attended. Special festivities begin after mass and continue into Christmas Day. On Boxing Day (26 December), St. Lucians like to relax and visit. Visitors may come throughout the holiday season, and people save for months to fix up their homes and have special foods to serve their many guests. Visits continue through New Year's. On New Year's Eve (*Old Year's Night*), friends and relatives toast the coming year at each home they visit.

Independence Day (22 February) marks independence from Britain. At Easter, the emphasis is on family and religion. Labour Day is 1 May. Emancipation Day (first Monday in August) commemorates the end of slavery. Thanksgiving is held on the first Monday in October. Local festivals, such as Creole Day (usually 31 October), are held in various communities throughout the year.

Commerce

Weekday office hours are 8:00 A.M. to 4:00 P.M.; banks close an hour earlier. Stores keep the same basic hours but are also open on Saturday until 12:30 P.M. Some local mini-markets or small malls have extended evening hours. Castries has an open-air produce market that stays open until the food is sold or until dusk. Most stores close on Sunday.

SOCIETY

Government

St. Lucia is a parliamentary democracy recognizing Britain's Queen Elizabeth II as head of state. She is officially represented by a governor general, currently Sir Stanislus James. Prime Minister Compton is head of government. He and Parliament's 17 members are directly elected for five-year terms. All citizens are required to vote beginning at age 18. The next elections are in 1997.

Economy

St. Lucia's economy historically has been based on agricultural production for trade with Britain. Bananas are the most important export, but the export of winter vegetables and organically grown produce is expanding. Because trends within the European Union are expected to adversely affect St. Lucia's trading position with Britain, the island has sought since 1990 to develop its tourism industry. New hotels and the supporting infrastructure have been built along the beaches surrounding Castries, Soufrière, and Vieux Fort to attract U.S. American, Canadian, and European tourists.

Real gross domestic product per capita is $3,026. A significant gap separates the rich from the poor. St. Lucia does not have the resources to be self-sufficient and must import foods, fuel, and manufactured goods. Unemployment and underemployment are serious problems. Many people go overseas in search of work. Remittances from these workers provide vital income for St. Lucia. Light manufacturing is mostly controlled by foreign firms. The East Caribbean dollar (EC$), used throughout the West Indies, is St. Lucia's currency.

Transportation and Communication

St. Lucia's main paved road runs the perimeter of the island. Several miles of it were constructed around Vieux Fort in World War II by U.S. military units wanting easy access to their airport, now Hewanorra International. All towns and villages are connected to the main road. Urban streets are mostly paved, but rural and other roads are not. Certain remote areas cannot be reached by road.

On paved roads, the most popular form of travel is the *transport*. These private minivans run regular routes. They leave from a central location when full and pick up/drop off passengers along the way. They often have a name or slogan painted on them; fares depend on where passengers board and exit. Many St. Lucians also own cars, and it is common for drivers to stop and offer pedestrians a ride.

St. Lucians without phones have access to public phones. Radio and television broadcasts reach most people. Radio is the main source of news; people are well-informed on local and regional matters.

Education

Education, based on the British system, is compulsory for children ages five to fifteen. Uniforms are required. About 80 percent of all eligible children attend school, and the literacy rate is 78 percent. Children are sometimes taken out of school to work on family banana farms.

At age 11, students take the Common Entrance exam to determine where they will go to secondary school. Those who finish secondary school can take the Caribbean Examination Council (CXC) exam to enter the Sir Arthur Lewis Community College. To graduate from there, students must take the British "A" level exam in one or more chosen disciplines (arts, science, general studies, teacher education, nursing, technical education, or management studies). To complete a full college degree, students must transfer to the University of West Indies in Jamaica, Barbados, or Trinidad. Some students gain an education abroad. St. Lucia is proud to have produced two Nobel laureates: Sir Arthur Lewis (Economics, 1979) and Derek Walcott (Literature, 1992).

Health

St. Lucia is striving to provide health care to all citizens. Free or low-cost care is available at public clinics and urban hospitals. Rural clinics are staffed by nurses who often live there full-time; doctors visit weekly. Private doctors serve those who can afford them. The infant mortality rate is 18 per 1,000; life expectancy averages 70 years.

FOR THE TRAVELER

U.S. citizens need a valid passport or proof of citizenship (birth certificate and photo ID) to enter St. Lucia. Adventurous visitors can travel windy roads, explore remote regions, and go scuba diving or mountain climbing. It is important to be polite but firm when turning away beach vendors. Tourists are expected to behave as guests and respect St. Lucian modesty. For travel information, contact the Embassy of St. Lucia, 3216 New Mexico Avenue NW, Washington, DC 20016; phone (202) 364–6792; or the St. Lucia Tourist Board, 820 Second Avenue, Suite 900E, New York, NY 10017; (800) 456–3984.

Shetland Islands

Orkney Islands

OUTER HEBRIDES

NORTH WEST HIGHLANDS

Inverness

GRAMPIAN MOUNTAINS

• Aberdeen

INNER HEBRIDES

Perth • Dundee

Stirling • • St. Andrews
Firth of Forth

Glasgow • Edinburgh

Firth of Clyde

SOUTHERN UPLANDS

Scotland

(United Kingdom)

Shetland Islands

SCOTLAND

Norway

NORTHERN IRELAND

United Kingdom

Denmark

Ireland

North Sea

ENGLAND

WALES

LONDON ★

Netherlands

English Channel

Germany

Belgium

Luxembourg

Atlantic Ocean

France

Liechtenstein

Switzerland

Boundary representations not necessarily authoritative.

BACKGROUND

Land and Climate

Located north of England on the island of Great Britain, Scotland covers 29,909 square miles (77,464 square kilometers) and is about the same size as South Carolina. Scotland's famous Highlands, which include the Grampian Mountains and the North West Highlands, are in the north. Upland wilderness areas surround the central urban valley, which is often referred to as the "Central Belt of Scotland." Mineral wealth has made this region the wealthiest and most populated area.

Throughout the country, rugged mountains, green valleys (glens), deep blue lakes (lochs), and offshore islands provide beautiful scenery. The climate is generally temperate and wet, although it differs from east to west. The west coast and island areas experience high winds and heavy rainfall and have large areas of marsh and peat bogs. The east, with its fertile agricultural land, is colder, drier, and less windy. Summer temperatures average 60°F to 70°F (15–21°C), while daytime winter temperatures usually remain above freezing.

History

The Scots are descendants of Celtic peoples. Scotland is named after the colony of Scots who came from Ireland in the sixth century and united with the original inhabitants (Picts) in the ninth century. The Scots fought for many years against Vikings from the north and English from the south. Finally, King James VI—son of Mary, Queen of Scots (Mary Stuart)—came to the English throne as King James I of England and united both countries under one monarch in 1603.

Since that time, the histories of Scotland and England have interwined. In 1707, the Scottish and English Parliaments were united by the Act of Union, which founded the constitutional monarchy of the Kingdom of Great Britain. The kingdom became known as the United Kingdom (UK) in 1801 when Ireland was joined to the union. Scotland shared England's industrial revolution, the great British Empire that spanned the globe, and the trials of the world wars. Despite its close ties with England and its function in the kingdom, Scotland has remained a distinct political and cultural entity. Actually, local histories of the individual cities and towns tell far more about the people of Scotland than does the political history of the UK.

A budding nationalist movement that reemerged in the 1970s has gained momentum in the 1990s. Although about 30 percent of the population favors outright independence from the UK, a greater number wants Scotland to have more control of its own economy and politics. Overall, 80 percent of Scots want a change. The most popular proposal is to avert actual independence by creating a Scottish parliament within the UK that has limited tax-raising powers.

EUROPE

THE PEOPLE

Population

Most of Scotland's 5.2 million people live in crowded urban areas; only about 350,000 people live in the rugged Highland and island regions. Although most residents are of Scottish origin, several small minority groups have immigrated from England, Ireland, India, Pakistan, and Hong Kong and live in larger cities. English settlers make up a substantial part of the population in some rural areas. Scots account for less than 10 percent of the total population of the UK which also includes England, Wales, and Northern Ireland.

The UK's Human Development Index (0.916) ranks it 18th out of 174 countries. Good access to health care, education, and economic prosperity affords people opportunities and choices in their lives. Adjusted for women, the index (0.862) ranks the UK 13th out of 130 countries.

Language

English is the official language; however Gaelic (a Celtic language and Scotland's original tongue) and Scots (an English dialect spoken for centures in the lowlands) are also spoken. Highlanders speak English with a soft, melodic accent, while urban dwellers may have a strong local accent. Gaelic is spoken by about 70,000 people, particularly those living on the Outer Hebrides and in parts of Glasgow. Although Gaelic is the primary language in some areas, people also speak English; shop and street signs are in Gaelic and English. Learning Gaelic has become a popular pastime in many areas. Scots is spoken in Aberdeen and some rural areas.

Everyday conversation includes many terms derived from Gaelic and Scots. For example, the word for dull is *dreich*. A *brae* is a hill; a *bairn* is a baby. Scots also use certain English idioms unique to their culture. *Aye* means "yes." Visitors should be aware that several American English words have different meanings in Scotland.

Religion

The Church of Scotland (or Presbyterian Church) is the official church, but people may worship as they choose. While the Church of Scotland has the most members (about 750,000), Roman Catholics, Baptists, Congregationalists, Episcopalians, Methodists, and other groups are represented. Some younger Scots are more secular and, therefore, less interested in religion or less influenced by religious traditions.

General Attitudes

Scots are proud of their heritage. They have a strong sense of their national identity that is expressed in their view of politics and through their traditional culture. Scots are offended by those who refer to Scots as English. They see Scotland as the most independent nation within the UK and will often emphasize its differences. When asked of their nationality, most English will respond "British," while Scots universally identify themselves as "Scottish."

Scots are known for their courtesy and their reserve with acquaintances. Often critical and very independent, the Scottish character has been described as a "combination of realism and reckless sentiment," including rashness, moodiness, and the ability to relentlessly persevere. Honesty, integrity, and generosity are valued. Loyalty to family and friends, the ability to work hard, and a sense of humor are also highly regarded. Scots share a more socialist mindset than other members of the UK. This is reflected in their strong support of left-of-center political parties.

Divisions between the working class and the middle class are present, although they are somewhat less apparent than in England. Education and employment goals usually vary between classes. Attitudes also differ between regions. Those on the west coast have a more relaxed view toward life than their eastern counterparts. They are perceived as softer in character and less ambitious. People living on the east coast are considered hardworking, quiet, reticent, and single-minded.

Personal Appearance

Popular European fashions are worn in Scotland. However, climate also influences the choice of clothing. Woolen sweaters are popular during the cooler months. Lighter fabrics are more common in the summer.

Scottish men often wear the traditional tartan kilt on formal occasions, particularly for weddings. The kilt is a heavy pleated tartan skirt worn only by men and accessorized with several traditional items. Tartan patterns (or plaids) originated in the Highlands and gradually became associated with local surnames. Native Scots seldom wear other tartan garments, although women may wear tartan skirts.

CUSTOMS AND COURTESIES

Greetings

Scots usually shake hands when meeting people for the first time. However, handshakes are used less often than in other European countries and are generally light and nonaggressive. Scots do not stand close to each other when greeting or speaking. Hugging is reserved for people they know well.

Scots can be somewhat formal, yet friendly, in their greetings. In formal situations, one might say *Good morning/afternoon, Mr./Mrs. . . . How do you do?* In less formal situations, *Hi, Hello,* or *How are you today?* are used. Among friends in the northeast, *Fit like?* replaces *How are you?* The Gaelic equivalent is *Ciamar a tha thu* (pronounced KEE-MIR A HA OO). People often use the phrase *Cheers* when leaving. To say good-bye (particularly from a distance), one may lift the hand up to the height of the head while walking away.

Nicknames are used between boys at school and between husbands and wives. People are referred to as *laddie* (male) or *lassie* (female). The terms *wifey* (female), *mum* (mom), and "chap" may also be used.

Gestures

Scots generally do not use their hands when speaking. A pat on the shoulder may be acceptable when people know each other and want to express appreciation or agreement. Shouting in public in rude. Forming a "V" with the index and middle fingers and the palm facing inward is vulgar and should be avoided. It is polite to offer the elderly seats on buses and trains.

Visiting

Scots, particularly those in the Highland areas, take pride in their hospitality. Visits to the home are usually prearranged. Only close friends and family drop by unannounced. The custom of enjoying *afternoon tea* around 3:00 P.M. on a daily basis is no longer common. However, friends may be invited to drop by on weekends for an *afternoon tea*. During these short visits, hosts serve a drink and cake or *biscuits* (cookies). Invitations for *tea* in the evening include a formal meal, although most Scots refer to this as *dinner*. Scots are open and candid in conversation and have a keen but subtle sense of humor. Religion, salary, and (less often) politics are topics to be avoided. When invited to a home, one customarily brings a small gift, such as flowers, chocolates, or a bottle of wine. Guests usually give their gift to the hosts when they arrive.

Outside of the home, most social interaction takes place in *pubs* (public houses). People go to *pubs* not only for drinks but also for meals and socializing. It is quite common for entire families to go to a *pub*.

Eating

Proper table etiquette is important and admired. Scots use the continental style of eating, with the fork in the left hand and the knife remaining in the right. Asking for and accepting second servings is appropriate. A person indicates that he or she is finished eating by placing the fork and knife together on the plate. Breakfast is usually cereal (sometimes porridge), coffee or tea, and toast. Lunch is a light meal often consisting of sandwiches, soup, and a drink. Dinner is the main meal of the day and is served in the evening. In restaurants, a common tip is about 10 percent. People do not leave tips in *pubs*.

LIFESTYLE

Family

In urban areas, families are small and tend to keep to themselves. Although relatives visit each other often, families remain separate from each other. The elderly prefer to stay in their own homes and remain independent as long as possible, rather than live with their married children. About half of all families live in rented homes or apartments (*flats*). All Scots value home ownership. While the husband is regarded as the head of the home among older couples, younger couples are more likely to make decisions jointly. A majority of women now work outside of the home and this proportion continues to increase. Women still have a greater share of household responsibilities, although this is changing among younger couples.

Early Highland families were loyal to their clan, but contemporary clans are largely irrelevant to national Scots. Clans were originally tribal groups that defended Highland areas until the clan system was destroyed in the early 19th century. Although clans have existed in some form since then, the family has had greater significance. Each clan is still headed by a chieftain who is mainly symbolic. Family associations linked to clans are primarily popular with U.S. Americans of Scottish descent.

Dating and Marriage

Dating in Scotland is different than in the United States. Relationships are formed within a social circle, not as separate couples. Then, rather than dating many different people, Scots date one person at a time. Popular dating activities include going to discos, the cinema, or *pubs*. People also enjoy going to a *ceilidh*, a dance featuring traditional Scottish music. Living together before or instead of marrying is becoming more common, although it is not always accepted. People usually marry in their mid- to late 20s, but some marry later.

Diet

While daily meals usually are not elaborate in Scotland, many Scottish dishes can be complex and exquisite. The normal diet includes *mince* (ground meat) and *tatties* (potatoes), *fish suppers* (fish and chips seasoned with salt and vinegar), stews, beef, lamb, *neeps* (boiled turnips), and simple vegetables. *Haggis* is a national dish. It is made from ground sheep entrails that are mixed with oats and spices, tied in a sheep's stomach, and cooked. *Stovies* (roast beef, onions, and potatoes) are also popular. Scots enjoy sweet desserts. Typical desserts, known as *puddings,* include *crumbles* (fruit pies), ice cream, and trifle. Beer and Scottish whisky are common drinks.

Recreation

The most popular organized sport is *football* (soccer), followed by rugby. Basketball, volleyball, and badminton are played in the high schools. The Scots invented golf in the 1500s; it is still one of their favorite games. Scotland's golf courses are spread over the rolling, green countryside and are considered some of the world's best. The Highland Games, which resemble track meets, are held in the late summer. Popular winter sports include curling and skiing. Curling involves two teams of four players that slide granite stones over ice to reach a target. *Shinty*, a Celtic sport similar to hockey, is popular in the Highlands.

The Highland bagpipe was used throughout Scotland's history as an instrument to inspire warriors. It is used today mostly for ceremonial and sporting occasions, although bagpipe music is enjoyed by many. Television, videos, and movies (films) are favorite leisure activities. Social drinking is common, and there are many lounges and *pubs*.

Arts festivals, such as Glasgow's Mayfest and the Edinburgh International Festival (one of the largest in the world), are popular. Scotland has produced many of Britain's most talented people, including poet Robert Burns and James Watt, inventor of the steam engine.

Holidays

Scotland celebrates many UK holidays. Official holidays include New Year's Day, Easter, Christmas, and Boxing Day (26 December). New Year's Eve is known as *Hogmanay* and is the biggest holiday of the year. Virtually everything closes down for Christmas, including restaurants and shops. Boxing Day comes from the old British tradition of giving small boxed gifts to service workers the day after Christmas; it is now a day for visiting and relaxing. Banquets called *Burns Suppers* honor Robert Burns on his birthday (25 January). *Haggis* is always served at these suppers. Other holidays include May Day, celebrated 1 May or the first Monday in May; the Queen's Birthday, celebrated the last Monday of May; and Remembrance Day, held the Sunday closest to 11 November. Scots also enjoy local holidays such as a Monday spring holiday and autumn holiday.

Commerce

Businesses are open generally from 9:00 A.M. to 5:30 P.M., Monday through Friday. Government offices close between 1:00 and 2:00 P.M. and stay open until 5:30 P.M. Each town has a local half-day during the week when most shops close for the afternoon. Glasgow and Edinburgh are the main centers of business, and major stores often remain open until 8:00 P.M. at least one night a week. Some large stores open on Sunday.

SOCIETY

Government

The UK's constitutional monarchy, with Queen Elizabeth II as head of state, is a parliamentary system. The House of Lords (with noblemen, life appointees, and Church of England bishops) has limited legislative power, although it is the highest judicial body in the land. Laws are passed in the 651-seat House of Commons, whose members are elected by the people. Scotland has 72 seats in the House of Commons. The leader of the majority party (currently the Conservative Party) is appointed by the queen as prime minister. The prime minister (currently John Major) selects a cabinet and runs the government. Elections, which were last held in 1992, are held at least every five years, but they may be held sooner if called by the prime minister.

Scotland maintains its own legal system, related to but different from that of England. Police forces are organized regionally. Several other departments are not directly controlled from London. Scotland's two-tier local government system was replaced by a unitary authority on 1 April 1996.

Economy

Many Scots are employed in technology, fishing, manufacturing, forestry, tourism, and textiles. Whisky is also an important industry. Several newer industries, such as chemicals, have taken hold in Scotland. Agriculture is intensive and efficient. Potatoes, vegetables, and grains are among the most important agricultural products. The discovery of oil in the North Sea has brought economic growth to the area. Scotland has many fine ports from which the UK conducts trade. The currency is the pound sterling (£). Scotland also issues its own bank notes.

Real gross domestic product per capita is $16,340, which has more than doubled in the last generation. These figures indicate most people have access to a decent income, although there is a larger gap between the wealthy and the poor than in some other European countries. Likewise, the UK's middle class is not as prosperous as its counterpart in other developed nations.

Transportation and Communication

Scotland is linked by international and domestic air services. Railway also connects most parts of the country, except in the northwest. Most roads are paved and most people own cars. Following the British tradition, traffic moves on the left side of the road. Buses and taxis are common in the cities. The public transportation system is excellent. Telecommunications are well advanced, with international fiber-optic cable links and satellite systems. There are a number of daily newspapers and nearly every home has a television.

Education

Education is free and compulsory from ages six to sixteen, although most Scots begin school a bit earlier. Scotland has its own education system. The examinations given at the completion of secondary schools are not the same as in England. Both *state* (public) schools and private schools are available in Scotland. Private schools receive some state funding and are subject to some control. There are various vocational schools, as well as 13 universities. University education is free. The universities of St. Andrews, Glasgow, and Aberdeen were founded in the 1400s. The adult literacy rate is 99 percent.

Health

The UK's National Health Service provides, on the basis of taxation, free medical treatment and many other social services. Individuals pay only for prescriptions and some dental services. Medical facilities are advanced and life expectancy (74–80 years) is similar to that in the United States. Scotland has a high rate of lung cancer and heart disease. Infant mortality is 7 per 1,000.

FOR THE TRAVELER

While a valid passport is necessary, a visa is not required of U.S. citizens visiting the UK. Victorian architecture, cultural events, castles, beautiful countryside, and more await visitors. For information, contact the Scottish Tourist Board, 23 Ravelston Terrace, Edinburgh EH4 3EU, United Kingdom. Ask your travel agent about information available through the S.C.O.T.S. program. You may also contact the British Tourist Authority, 551 Fifth Avenue, 7th Floor, New York, NY 10176; phone (800) 462–2748; or the British Information Service, 845 Third Avenue, New York, NY 10022; phone (212) 752–5747. The Embassy of the United Kingdom is located at 3100 Massachusetts Avenue NW, Washington, DC 20008; phone (202) 462–1340.

Printed on recycled paper

CULTURGRAM '97

Serbia and Montenegro

Boundary representations not necessarily authoritative.

BACKGROUND

Land and Climate

Serbia and Montenegro together cover 39,435 square miles (102,136 square kilometers)—about the same area as Kentucky. Serbia accounts for 34,136 square miles; Montenegro, 5,299. Several major rivers flow through this region, including the Danube, Sava, Tisa, Morava, and Drina. Vojvodina (in the north) is part of the Danubian plain and contains fertile agricultural land. The North Albanian Alps (*Prokletije*) and Sar Mountains are in the southwest, and the Balkan Mountains are in the east. Montenegro (literally "black mountain") is mostly mountainous and consists of the Zeta Valley, Dinaric Alps, and Skadarsko Lake (shared with Albania). Montenegro also has a coastline on the Adriatic Sea that includes the picturesque Bay of Kotor and Saint Stefan Island.

The climate is central continental, with Montenegro experiencing more severe weather and colder temperatures than Serbia. Serbian winters are cold, averaging 32°F (0°C) in January; summers are hot, averaging 75°F (23°C) in July. Central Serbia is susceptible to strong winds (*kosava*) that pick up speed on the plain of Vojvodina. Belgrade is the federal capital as well as Serbia's capital. Podgorica (Titograd until 1992) is Montenegro's capital.

History

Slavic peoples settled on the Balkan Peninsula in the seventh century and for several generations were organized by clans rather than in a united state. In the 11th century, Serbs united and consolidated territory that eventually became the empire of Tzar Dusan. Montenegro was incorporated in the 12th century. In 1346, Tzar Dusan's rule included Albania, Epirus, and northern Greece. Serbian power began to decline

with the Battle of Kosovo (1389), when Serbs were defeated by the Turks. For the next five hundred years, Serbians were ruled by the Turkish Ottoman Empire and consider the era one of bondage. Montenegro remained independent.

Serbia rebelled under the leadership of Karageorge (1804) and Obrenovic (1815), both of whom formed ruling dynasties. Serbia achieved full independence in 1878. Other Balkan Slavs had been subjugated to both the Turkish and Austro-Hungarian Empires, and Serbia determined to rid the Balkans of these forces. In the first Balkan War (1912), it defeated Turkey with the help of neighboring nations. The second Balkan War (1913) brought victory over the previously allied Bulgarians. In 1914, a Bosnian Serb assassinated Austrian Archduke Francis Ferdinand in the effort to liberate Serbs in Bosnia. Austria declared war, regional alliances formed, and the conflict quickly became World War I. The Austro-Hungarian Empire lost in the war and was broken into several new states. At that time, Serbia led the move to unite Slavs under one government, becoming the principal power in the Kingdom of Serbs, Croats, and Slovenes in 1918. The name was changed to the Kingdom of Yugoslavia in 1929.

When Germany invaded Yugoslavia in 1941, Croatian leaders sided with the Fascists against Serbia. At the same time, a bloody civil war was being waged in Yugoslavia between Communists and monarchists. Fighting on both fronts, many Serbs lost their lives in battle and at the hands of fellow Slavs. Thousands of civilian Jews, Gypsies, and Serbs were killed in Croatian concentration camps, a fact not easily forgotten by Serbs who later (1990) came under Croatian domination.

The civil war ended when World War II did, and the Communist partisan fighters emerged victorious. They formed,

EUROPE

under the leadership of Josip Broz ("Tito"), a federal socialist state. Its politics were more liberal and economics more progressive than other socialist countries.

Tito died in 1980 and the various ethnic groups began to bicker among themselves. As the federation weakened, a deepening economic crisis led Croatia and Slovenia to demand secession in 1990. Slovenia's independence proceeded smoothly, but Croatia's was resisted by resident Serbs who wanted to remain united with Serbia. A war ensued (1991) in which the Yugoslav Army helped Croatia's Serbs gain control of Croatia's Krajina region (which Croatia regained in 1995). Serbia also supported Serbs in Bosnia-Herzegovina in their war against Muslims and Croats but withdrew its support when Bosnian Serb leaders would not cooperate with international negotiators. With Serbia's crucial support, peace efforts finally bore fruit for Bosnia in the form of the 1996 Dayton Peace Accord.

In 1992, Serbia and Montenegro declared themselves the Federal Republic of Yugoslavia, but they were not recognized as such by the international community. People in Serbia and Montenegro consider themselves citizens of Yugoslavia. However, territorial disputes and other issues make it difficult for Serbs and Montenegrins to receive the recognition they claim.

PEOPLE

Population

Serbia's 10.4 million people are joined by Montenegro's 667,000 in a population that is growing by about 0.5 percent per year. Most Serbians are urban dwellers, while Montenegrians tend to be more rural. Similarities between the two groups are great and differences are found mostly in historical experience. Until after World War II, Montenegrians were counted as Serbs in the census.

In Serbia, most people (66 percent) are ethnic Serbs. Ethnic Albanians (17 percent) dominate in Kosovo, which has been the site of serious ethnic tension and violence between Serbs and Albanians. The latter only settled in large numbers in the region in the past 50 years. Albanians seek some form of autonomy or guaranteed equal rights. A few advocate independence; most oppose Serbian rule. Hungarians (4 percent) are concentrated in Vojvodina. Serbia is also home to smaller numbers of Romanians, Croats, Ruthenes, Turks, and Slovaks.

In Montenegro, most people (62 percent) are ethnic Montenegrian, but there are also Slavic Muslims (12.5 percent), Serbs (9.2 percent), Albanians (6.2 percent), and Croats (1 percent).

Language

The principal language is Serbian, a Slavic tongue virtually identical to Croatian. In fact, before 1990, the language of Yugoslavia was Serbo-Croatian. Serbian can be written in both Cyrillic and Latin scripts. Cyrillic is the official and more popular script, but school children are required to learn both. In 1974, Albanians and Hungarians won the right to use their language in local government, media, and education.

Religion

Serbs and Montenegrins are Serbian Orthodox Christians. The Serbian Orthodox Church was formed in 1221 by St. Sava and is similar to the Greek and Russian Orthodox Churches in practice and doctrine. It has strong ties to these churches but distinguishes itself from them in some respects. For example, it teaches that each family is protected by a specific patron saint. On each saint's day, relevant families prepare large amounts of food for anyone who enters their homes. It is a ritual to serve these guests a spoonful of *zito*, a mush made of wheat, sugar, and nuts.

The Serbian church follows the Julian calendar, which is 13 days behind the Gregorian calendar. Patriarch Pavle is the current head of the church.

Religion was neglected during the Communist period, but activity has surged since 1990, as evidenced by growing numbers of baptisms and religious wedding ceremonies. Religious freedom allows for the current proliferation of Muslim mosques and Catholic churches. Other Christian denominations are small, as is the Jewish community.

General Attitudes

Serbs consider themselves principally to be a heroic and proud people. Likewise, Montenegrins value their heroic traits above all else. Based on a history of resisting Turks, Austrians, and Germans, Serbs view themselves as liberators. Both Serbs and Montenegrins are warrior peoples that honor the memory of military conquests. The Battle of Kosovo has been ingrained in the national consciousness as the time that the Christian Serbs tragically and heroically chose death at the hands of the Muslim Turks rather than surrender.

Serbs are openly emotional and are not a very private people. They share their lives with extended family, neighbors, and friends. The tend to be pessimistic and sometimes fatalistic about events that surround them. They value family, country, and honesty. Serbs also have a sense of humor that allows them to laugh at their own faults.

Montenegrins, while sharing many Serbian traits, tend to be more traditional and patriarchal. Men still dominate society and women are considered subordinates.

Personal Appearance

People are concerned with their public appearance and take care to look well dressed and groomed. Most dress in Western clothing, except in a few rural areas where older people wear *nosnje*. This traditional attire varies by region but tends to include long skirts and cotton shirts for women; men wear wide pants, vests over their shirts, and *opanke* (leather shoes with upturned toes).

In urban areas, older men wear hats. Women often dye their hair (gray hair is seldom seen); red and auburn shades are popular among younger women. Western running shoes are popular throughout the country.

CUSTOMS AND COURTESIES

Greetings

When people are introduced, they shake hands and say their last name, followed by *Drago mi je* (I am pleased). If people already know each other, they shake hands or kiss (often three times on alternating cheeks) and say *Zdravo* (Hello) or *Dobar dan* (Good day). In greeting an older person, a younger one must rise. Men always rise when greeting women.

Adults are addressed by professional ("Dr.," "Professor") or conventional titles and their last names. *Gospodin* (Mr.), *Gospodja* (Mrs.), and *Komshija* (neighbor) have reemerged to replace "comrade" as conventional titles. *Tetka* (auntie) and *Chika* (uncle) are reserved for older people who are not family but for whom "Mr." and "Mrs." are too formal. People never refer to others, except close friends and family, by their first names. Likewise, they use *vi* ("you" formal) to address others, especially initially. Moving from *vi* to *ti* ("you" informal) must be initiated by the older person or, if two people are the same age, by the female.

Gestures

Serbs do not use hand gestures much when speaking. It is impolite to stretch, yawn, or crack one's knuckles in public. It is also impolite to point with the index finger or eat in the streets. Smoking in public used to be rude, but it is increasingly evident in both urban and rural areas. Eye contact is valued, especially when people are raising glasses in a toast prior to drinking.

Visiting

People spend a lot of time visiting and entertaining. Sitting for hours over cigarettes and a cup of coffee or some *rakija* (alcoholic drink usually made from plums) is common. The length of visits reflects a leisurely pace of life. Most visiting is on an informal, unannounced basis; people simply drop in. Sometimes people prearrange socializing but usually not far in advance. Guests often bring gifts such as flowers or a box of chocolates; if one is visiting for the first time, a gift is nearly obligatory. Flowers are given in odd numbers, as even numbers are reserved for funerals. Guests bring relatively expensive gifts when visiting on special occasions.

Eating

Since the workday begins at 7:00 A.M., people wait until 10:00 A.M. for their breakfast (*dorucak*), which can be a substantial meal. The main meal of the day is *rucak*, eaten after work around 4:00 P.M. This is a heavy meal that includes soup and a meat dish. Given the size of the meal, it tends to be followed by a nap. Dinner is a light snack.

Guests invited to dinner are served *meze* (an antipasto of cheese, sausages, etc.) before the meal. When entertaining, it is important to offer more food than can be eaten; this is a sign of wealth and hospitality. Hosts offer food to guests consistently during the meal, and guests customarily decline several times before accepting. The host or hostess often places more food on the guests' plates despite protests. As times change, people are declining only once or twice before accepting; further protests are taken seriously by a growing number of hosts. Guests are expected to finish all food on their plates. Meals are times for conversation and social interaction.

LIFESTYLE

Family

The family is highly valued; nearly everyone expects to marry and have children. Divorce and remarriage are common. Rural families tend to have more children than urban ones. The father is the head and backbone of the family; in rural areas, male children are valued more highly than females.

Rural households include three generations. Upon marriage, a couple moves in with the groom's parents. Due to a housing shortage, urban couples might also live with parents (more often the bride's) for a while, but this is seen more as an economic necessity than a desirable tradition.

Throughout the country, both husband and wife usually work outside the home. Children are cared for primarily by grandparents or other relatives and, less commonly, in child-care facilities.

Dating and Marriage

When dating, young people tend to go out with one steady partner. They go for walks, to cafés and parties, and to each other's homes. Wedding ceremonies tend to be civil, but religious ones are on the rise. Rural weddings are more elaborate than urban ones; they include several days of drinking, dancing, and eating that often force the family into debt. The bride's family usually pays most wedding expenses, except in less traditional urban areas where costs are more evenly split. Rural brides often have a dowry (home furnishings or cash), and they usually are given a piece of jewelry by the groom's family. Among Albanians, the groom's family pays a bride-price to the woman's family and the bride has no dowry.

Diet

The cuisine is influenced by Turkish, Austrian, Hungarian, and Greek cultures. The most common foods include *pasulj* (beans), *sarma* (cabbage leaves stuffed with minced meat and rice), *rostilj* (grilled meats), *cevapcici* (small, elongated minced meatballs eaten with chopped onions), and *punjenje paprike* (stuffed peppers). Roasted pork or lamb, served with potatoes, is favored on special occasions. Montenegrins are known for their smoked meats. Coastal Montenegrins eat more seafood.

Typical cheeses include *kajmak* (consisting of the accumulated skim of boiled milk) and *sjenicki sir* (a hard cheese often crumbled on *sopska*, a Greek-like salad). Locally grown produce includes cabbage, lettuce, tomatoes, potatoes, carrots, apples, pears, watermelons, strawberries, and others. Bread (usually white) is eaten with each meal and wine is served at the main meal. People also drink coffee and juices; they drink tea more during illness.

Recreation

Visiting and talking is the favorite leisure activity, but people also enjoy watching television. In small towns, residents walk the main streets in the evening. Music is popular throughout the country, but folk music (*narodna muzika*) is especially favored in rural areas. People perform folk dances such as the *kolo*, consisting of small movements by dancers sometimes linked in a long line. The *gusle*, a small, traditional stringed instrument, is played throughout the country. Urban cultural events are relatively inexpensive and well attended.

Soccer is the most popular sport, followed by basketball, volleyball, swimming, and skiing. Sports are stressed in school, so young people tend to be more enthusiastic about them. Some people enjoy boating on lakes and rivers.

Holidays

Celebrated holidays have changed since 1990, with religious holidays becoming more popular. Orthodox Christmas is 7 January and New Year's is 14 January. Western New Year (1 January) is also celebrated. On Women's Day (8 March), women are honored in the home and at work. Easter is in the spring. Workers' Day (1 May) is a major holiday for all. *Vidovdan* (28 June) commemorates the Battle of Kosovo. Four times throughout the year, Orthodox Serbs mark *Zadushnice* (a day to honor the dead). One such day is in early November soon after Catholics and Protestants have their day (1 November) to visit the graves of family and friends.

Commerce

Public offices are open from 7:00 A.M. to 3:00 P.M. Private businesses and kiosks tend to have more flexible and longer hours. Food shops and large department stores remain open until 8:00 P.M. Some urban *dragstors* (drugstores) that sell basic foods are open 24 hours. Outdoor food markets open around 6:00 A.M. and close in the early afternoon so the vendors can return to their villages.

SOCIETY

Government

Before 1990, Serbia was a republic that incorporated two autonomous provinces, Kosovo and Vojvodina. Since the breakup of Yugoslavia, those regions have been reincorporated into Serbia (as they were before 1974). While this move met little resistance in Vojvodina, the Albanian autonomy movement is still very active in Kosovo.

The president of the Federal Republic of Yugoslavia is Zoran Lilic. The president of Serbia is the more influential Slobodan Milosevic. His counterpart in Montenegro is Momir Bulatovic. The federal assembly consists of a Chamber of Republics and a Chamber of Citizens. The former has 40 seats split equally between Serbs and Montenegrians. The Chamber of Citizens has 138 members. Serbia's dominant political party is the Socialist Party of Serbia (SPS); in opposition stand the Serbian Radical Party and the Democratic Renewal Party, among others. Montenegro's dominant Democratic Socialist Party is allied to the SPS. Active opposition parties are few in Montenegro. The voting age is 18.

Economy

Before 1990, Yugoslavia's economy was based on market socialism characterized by social ownership (as opposed to Soviet-style public ownership), in which enterprises were controlled by their workers through a complex system of committees and councils.

The economy is in chaos because, first, the government proceeded to dismantle the old system after 1990, divide its assets, set up new institutions, and reform the economy to be more capitalistic. Second, external trade was blocked and foreign assets frozen until 1996 due to international sanctions. Third, significant funds were spent in supplying Serbs in warring areas. And finally, Serbia has borne the burden of housing some 850,000 refugees from both Bosnia and Croatia. These factors combined to suffocate the economy and precipitate hyperinflation (3 million percent in 1993).

Food rationing was not uncommon in 1993 and 1994, and the standard of living plummeted to developing-nation levels. Inflation was brought under control in 1994 with the introduction of the new *dinar* (YD) currency, and the lifting of sanctions has improved the country's long-term prospects.

But recovery will take some time and will be hampered by a "brain drain" of skilled labor.

Serbia produces fruit, vegetables, wheat, corn, oats, and livestock. Natural resources include lead, zinc, copper, and lignite. Manufacturing plants are located in Serbia, while Montenegro has aluminum and steel factories. Montenegro also has tourism, shipping, and agricultural potential.

Transportation and Communication

A well-developed public transportation system serves most of the population. Private cars are popular but expensive to operate due to high fuel costs (most gasoline is smuggled in). Air travel connects major cities, as does rail and bus service. Rural areas are reached by bus and private vehicles. Roads are mostly paved.

Most of the country's newspapers and magazines receive government support, but private printing presses are slowly becoming established. In addition to the state television and radio stations, some private stations have begun to broadcast. People also have access to satellite television.

Education

Free schooling begins at age seven with eight mandatory years at the basic (*osnovna*) level. Optional middle school (*srednja* or *skola*) includes grades nine through twelve. Graduates can then go to a two-year technical college, called *visa skola* (higher school), or to a university. Entrance to the four universities is determined by examination. Ethnic minorities have the right to education in their language: Albanians, Hungarians, Ruthenes, Slovaks, and Turks have schools through high school. The one Albanian-language university has been closed due to secessionist activity. Literacy is 90 percent.

Health

An extensive national health system covers the rural and urban population. Private practice was legalized in 1990, but most people cannot afford the growing number of private doctors, dentists, and nurses. Public hospitals suffer supply and equipment shortages, and the country has suffered from a deterioration of health standards. With food shortages prior to 1996, the average caloric intake of children dropped from 3,200 to 2,100. The infant mortality rate is 21 per 1,000 in Serbia (11 per 1,000 in Montenegro). Life expectancy averages 80 years in Montenegro and 73 years in Serbia.

FOR THE TRAVELER

Since it does not have full diplomatic relations with Serbia and Montenegro, the United States does not recommend travel to the country. U.S. citizens who do visit must have a valid passport and visa. Credit cards are not accepted, but Western currencies (especially the German *mark*) are. Popular tourist spots include Novi Sad and Belgrade, especially Skadarlija Street and the Fort of Kalemegdan (where the Danube and Sava Rivers intersect). Orthodox monasteries featuring religious art are in Sopocani, Gracanica, Pec, and Mileseva. Montenegro's old mountain town of Cetinje is worth a visit, as is the remarkably beautiful coast. The embassy of the former Socialist Federal Republic of Yugoslavia is located at 2410 California Street NW, Washington DC 20008.

A *Culturgram* is a product of native commentary and original, expert analysis. Statistics are estimates and information is presented as a matter of opinion. While the editors strive for accuracy and detail, this document should not be considered strictly factual. It is a general introduction to culture, an initial step in building bridges of understanding between peoples. It may not apply to all peoples of the nation. You should therefore consult other sources for more information.

Slovakia

(Slovak Republic)

Boundary representations not necessarily authoritative.

BACKGROUND

Land and Climate

The Slovak Republic is a landlocked country situated in the heart of central Europe. Covering 18,859 square miles (48,845 square kilometers), it is about the size of West Virginia; it is mountainous, with the Carpathian and Tatry ranges being most prominent. The highest peak is Gerlach at 8,707 feet (2,857 meters). Mountain ridges have inhibited travel at times, preserving Slovakia's variety of dialects and customs. The country's fertile south is part of the Great Hungarian Plain. Slovakia is rich in natural resources such as timber, copper, zinc, mercury, limestone, and iron ore. With a continental climate, summers are hot (especially in southern lowlands) and winters are cold and snowy (especially in northern highlands). Corn, oats, wheat, and potatoes are the most abundant crops. Forests cover much of the central region. Bratislava is the capital.

History

Slavic peoples first settled in the area during the fifth century. In 863, they founded a loose confederation that became the Great Moravian Empire. Its brief history ended in 907 with the invasion of nomadic Magyars (today called Hungarians) and the area came under Hungarian rule. In 1526, Hungary became subject to Austrian Hapsburg rule. Upon its defeat in World War I (1918), the Austro-Hungarian Empire disintegrated. Slovaks joined with Czechs under the leadership of Thomas Masaryk and Milan Rastislav Štefánik in founding the First Czecho-Slovak Republic (the hyphen was dropped in 1920).

Czechoslovakia became the most democratic of the Hapsburg successor states, although some Slovaks wished for more autonomy within the union. In 1938, the country was not able to withstand Hitler's foreign policy machinations. Even as Germany was annexing Czech lands, Slovakia declared independence in March 1939 and allied with Germany throughout World War II. The move still stirs controversy today. Central and eastern Slovaks staged a revolt in 1944 that was quickly crushed. Upon Germany's defeat, the Soviet Union's Red Army helped install a new unitary Czechoslovak government.

After 1948, Communists seized control of the government, all major institutions, and significant property. Slovaks suffered under forced Stalinization and persecution in the 1950s. During the 1960s, the reform-minded Slovak Communist Alexander Dubček led a movement to create "socialism with a human face." Censorship was relaxed and a spirit of revival and hope swept the country. The experiment met with an abrupt end when Soviet-led Warsaw Pact troops crushed the movement in August 1968. Within two years, nearly all reforms were abolished except that Slovakia was granted the status of a republic and allowed more regional government offices.

During the 1970s, Gustav Husák's regime attempted to satisfy citizens by making consumer goods more available, but ruthless repression of political dissent continued. Economic stagnation and Mikhail Gorbachev's changes in the Soviet Union laid the foundations for the fall of communism in 1989. Censorship and travel restrictions were lifted, and

EUROPE

the iron curtain collapsed. All of this happened without one person being killed, so the events have been called the "Velvet" or "Gentle" Revolution.

The burst of emotions that accompanied the revolution soon gave way to the sobering realities of rebuilding democracy. Nationalism reemerged as a major issue. In 1990, Slovaks began pressing for a greater voice in their own affairs. Disagreements over the amount of autonomy for Slovakia and the pace of economic reform led to victory for Slovak nationalists in 1992 elections. When the newly elected Czech and Slovak national governments could not agree about the division of federal powers, Czech Prime Minister Václav Klaus and Slovak Prime Minister Vladimír Mečiar decided to split the state peacefully and fairly.

After Slovakia became independent in 1993, Mečiar continued some reforms, but his confrontational style of leadership produced political instability. Parliament removed him from office in 1994 and selected an interim prime minister until elections in September 1994. No party gained a majority through those elections, and Mečiar's Movement for a Democratic Slovakia (HZDS) eventually formed a coalition government, with Mečiar as prime minister. Slovakia applied for European membership in 1995 but faces regional territorial disputes. Political instability remains a problem.

THE PEOPLE

Population

About 5.4 million people live in the Slovak Republic, and more than 80 percent of them are Slovaks. Hungarians (Magyars) constitute the largest minority (10.8 percent) and most of them live in southern Slovakia. The Romany (Gypsy) ethnic group officially accounts for a documented 1.5 percent of the population, but this figure may actually be as high as 9 or 10 percent. The Romany are nomadic and difficult to count, and many listed themselves as Slovaks in the 1992 census. The Romany are not well integrated into mainstream society, especially in rural areas, and they have been struggling against discrimination in many countries.

Smaller ethnic groups that are more integrated in society include Czechs (1 percent), Carpatho-Rusyns (Ruthenians), Ukrainians, Germans, Poles, Moravians, and others. About half of all people live in towns with more than 10 thousand inhabitants.

Slovakia's Human Development Index (0.872) ranks it 40th out of 174 nations. The country provides its people adequate access to health care, education, and a decent standard of living. Adjusted for women, the index ranks (0.855) Slovakia 16th out of 130 countries, indicating that women earn a comparable share of the income.

Language

Slovaks speak Slovak, a tongue in the Slavic language group that includes Czech, Polish, Russian, and other languages. Slovak uses a Latin script. Literary Slovak is used in official capacities, but numerous dialects exist in various regions. Hungarian is the second most commonly spoken language, especially in the south. Although a 1995 law made Slovak the only offical language, Hungarians still want their language to have official status. The Romany speak Romany, an unwritten tongue with Indo-Aryan roots, and Slovak.

German is widely understood, while English is the language of choice to study in school. Russian was required before 1989. Other languages are also offered.

Religion

Freedom of worship is guaranteed in Slovakia and many people have deep religious convictions. Of the total population, 60.4 percent is Roman Catholic, followed by Evangelical Lutheran (6.2), and Greek Catholic (3.4). Smaller groups include the Calvinist Reformed (1.6 percent), Eastern Orthodox (0.7), Baptist, and others. Nearly 10 percent of the population is atheist, while the rest either belongs to various smaller groups or has no religious affiliation.

General Attitudes

Slovakia is going through a difficult transition that is a natural part of newly acquired statehood. Some people are extremely sensitive about topics related to independence. People are especially interested in the way foreigners view them, and they are anxious to foster a positive image abroad.

Although Slovakia has industrialized, particularly since 1948, a romantic attachment to peasant ideals and the countryside remains in the hearts of many Slovaks. Poetry, literature, song, and dance glamorize those rural roots. Slovaks are proud of their rich cultural heritage, as well as famous Americans with Slovak roots: pop artist Andy Warhol, whose parents are from Miková; astronaut Eugene Černan; radio inventor Joseph Murgáš; and parachute inventor Štefan Banič.

Slovaks are usually outgoing and value good humor and hard work. They are also generous, especially in the countryside, and will go out of their way to help a stranger. Education, modesty, and honesty are admired. Those who are self-confident or aggressive are often thought to be "too" self-confident or "too" aggressive. Entrepreneurs are considered to be "price gougers" and greedy, especially in rural areas. This attitude is changing in urban areas as economic change progresses.

Personal Appearance

Clothing in urban areas is fashionable, while older, rural people remain more conservative. Most Slovaks are very concerned with their appearance. Professional women dress up for work; businessmen wear suits. Women and girls may wear dresses and skirts or casual attire, depending on the occasion. Jeans and T-shirts are quite popular, and short pants are increasingly common in the summer. Villagers might wear traditional folk costumes for special occasions.

CUSTOMS AND COURTESIES

Greetings

Shaking hands is the most common form of greeting, but one does not cross over another handshake to shake hands in a group. A man usually waits for a woman to extend her hand. Upon parting, men will often hug women or kiss them on both cheeks (sometimes not really touching) and firmly shake hands with men.

Formal titles carry a particular significance. People are addressed as *Pán* (Mr.) or *Pani* (Mrs.), followed by any professional title (doctor, engineer, professor), or the surname, or both. First names are used upon mutual consent, among friends, and among the youth. More formal greetings include *Dobrý deň* (Good day) or *Vel'mi ma teši* (Pleased to meet you). "Good-bye" is *Do videnia*. More casual terms are *Ahoj* (Hi), *Čiao*, and *Servus* (both mean "Hello" or "Good-bye"). Some older villagers still use the traditional *S Bohom* (God be with you). "Thank you" is expressed with *Ďakujem*. The use of *Prosím* (Please) is considered polite before making any requests and for saying "You're welcome."

Gestures

Hand gestures are frequently used to emphasize speech. To wish luck, instead of crossing fingers, Slovaks "hold thumbs." That is, they fold the thumb in and close the fingers on it. Yawning in public is considered improper, and chewing gum is not acceptable during polite social interaction. Smiling is courteous.

Visiting

Impromptu visits are common, but only between close friends and family members. Invited guests, especially those coming from a distance, receive a warm welcome. An invitation to dinner is usually in a home rather than a restaurant. Guests remove hats and shoes in a home; hosts often provide slippers. Visitors wait for hosts to invite them to be seated. Invited guests often present the hosts with a gift of flowers, wine, liquor, or something else. Flowers are fresh, unwrapped, and given in odd numbers (three, five, or seven). Even numbers and dried flowers are for funerals; red roses imply romantic intentions. Visitors should not overly admire anything in the home, as the item will be given to them, even if it is a prized heirloom.

Guests are usually offered refreshments. Rural Slovaks might serve friends or relatives *slanina* (home-smoked bacon) and bread, as well as a drink. Typical is homemade *slivovica* (plum liquor), but beer, coffee, tea, and other drinks may also be offered. Urban hosts tend to serve chips, nuts, and wine rather than homemade refreshments. On special occasions, a tray of ham, cheese, eggs, vegetables, and sweets may be offered. Out of courtesy, guests often politely decline offers before eventually accepting them. Refusing refreshments all together is impolite, but one may decline liquor or another specific item without offending. An empty cup or glass will be refilled, so guests should leave a little bit of drink when they are finished.

If guests wish to wash up before a meal, they knock on the bathroom door before entering. All doors in a home are typically closed, even if no one is in the room. Homes often have water closets (toilets) separate from the bathroom.

Slovaks typically accompany their departing guests outside and then wave to them until they are out of sight. Guests may turn often and return the wave.

Eating

Slovaks eat in the continental style, holding the fork in the left hand and the knife in the right. They eat three meals each day. Breakfast consists of bread and rolls, sliced meat or sausage, and cheese. Soup is commonly served with the main meal at midday, which also consists of meat, dumplings or potatoes, and a vegetable. Slovaks eat a lighter meal of cold cuts, cheese, and bread in the evening. Mid-morning and mid-afternoon snacks are common. Families usually eat together on weekends but not as often on weekdays. Before eating, the head of the home says *Dobrú chuť* (equivalent of *Bon appétit*), and others at the table respond with the same. Diners keep both hands above the table but do not rest elbows on the table. They keep napkins on the table, not in the lap. A plate of baked goods is often served before or after the meal.

When guests are present, women typically serve the meal but do not eat at the table. Often, only the guests are fed. Slovak guests wait to be offered second helpings, but it is greatly appreciated if a foreigner asks for seconds. Conversation usually occurs after the meal. Toasting with *Na zdravie* (To your health) is common on both formal and informal occasions.

Restaurants do not provide water unless requested. Commonly ordered drinks include beer, wine, soft drinks, and mineral water. Slovaks consider milk a drink for children. A small cup of Turkish coffee frequently completes the meal. Tipping is accepted at most sit-down restaurants; it is added to the bill, not left on the table.

LIFESTYLE

Family

Typical Slovak families have two or three children. The state used to provide families with free medical care, schooling, and social security, but budget cuts have resulted in charges for some services. Paid maternity leave for mothers, a cash allowance for each birth, and child-care facilities are still provided. While most women hold jobs outside the home and comprise 47 percent of the labor force, they usually are also responsible for the home and children. However, some men are beginning to share in household duties.

Most urban families live in small, modest apartments built during the Communist era. Rural inhabitants continue to reside in single-family homes that provide a more pleasant environment.

Dating and Marriage

Popular dating activities include dancing and going to the movies or theater. Festivals are also popular. Men marry between the ages of 23 and 26, and women marry about three years earlier. Most Slovak weddings involve church ceremonies, and brides are often paraded around the village in a traditional procession. The reception afterward lasts until morning, sometimes longer. Inflation has made celebrations lasting several days too expensive for many families. The groom carries his bride over the threshold of their new home. Due to a housing shortage, new couples must often live with parents until an apartment is available.

Diet

Among the most popular Slovak foods are *rezeň* (breaded steak) and potatoes, as well as other kinds of meat served with potatoes, rice, dumplings, or pasta and sauce. Slovakia also has a variety of sweet dishes served as a main course (such as prune dumplings). The national dish is *bryndzové halušky* (small dumplings with processed sheep cheese), but it is not eaten often in the home. Fresh-baked bread and soup are considered staples at the dinner table. Dairy products such as milk, cheese, and butter are widely available. Fresh fruits (apples, plums, and grapes) are abundant and eaten in season. Bananas and oranges are popular for holidays and throughout the year. Potatoes, cabbage, and carrots are the most frequently eaten vegetables. Popular desserts include *koláč* (nut or poppy seed rolls) and *torta* (cake).

Recreation

Soccer, ice hockey, skiing, and tennis are the most popular sports in Slovakia. Other forms of recreation include movie-going, hiking, camping, swimming, and attending local festivals, cultural events, or art exhibits.

Slovaks take special pride in their folk music. They sing with marked enthusiasm at gatherings, and knowing folk songs is considered part of being Slovak. Slovaks have a saying: *Kde Slovák, tam spev* (Wherever there is a Slovak, there is a song). Folk art is also appreciated and is often given to foreign visitors as a gift. It is mostly available in special stores, as few people carry on the old traditions of embroidery and wood carving. Many Slovaks spend weekends or vacations in the beautiful Tatry Mountains, at health spas, or in the countryside. More Slovaks are beginning to tour other parts of Europe.

Holidays

Holidays include St. Sylvester's Day (New Year's Eve), New Year's Day (also Independence Day), Easter, and Cyril and Methodius Day (5 July), which honors the two saints who introduced Christianity to the region and who developed the Cyrillic alphabet used with many Slavic languages. Slovak National Uprising Day (29 August) commemorates the 1944 rebellion against the Nazis. Constitution Day is 1 September. Christmas is the most celebrated holiday. Children receive gifts of candy, fruit, and nuts on St. Nicholas Day (6 December). In eastern Slovakia, Christmas Eve supper is called *Vilija* and includes mushroom soup, fish, peas, prunes, and pastries. Following the meal, people decorate the tree and exchange gifts. Slovaks celebrate Christmas Day with family gatherings featuring ham or poultry, baked goods, and drinking. Church attendance is also traditional.

Birthdays are celebrated more often with family, whereas name days are occasions for parties among friends or colleagues. The name day usually is more important, involving gifts and flowers. People celebrate it on the day commemorating the saint who shares their name.

Commerce

Some grocers open before 8:00 A.M. Most other businesses and government offices open at 8:00 A.M. and close by 3:00 or 4:00 P.M. Shops are open until at least 6:00 P.M. weekdays and 2:00 P.M. Saturdays. Except for a few restaurants and stores, nearly all businesses close on Sunday. Small urban shops and most rural businesses close for lunch. Many people grow their own fruits and vegetables in addition to buying them from markets. Even most urban residents have gardens in the countryside.

Employees typically receive four weeks of vacation each year. Retirement occurs between ages 53 and 60. Friendly social relationships are important between business associates. Foreign business representatives should also have an interest in Slovak culture and accept any offered hospitality.

SOCIETY

Government

Slovakia's president, Michal Kováč, is head of state. The prime minister is head of government. The Slovak National Council has 150 elected members. The voting age is 18. Slovakia has four departments (regions) and several smaller districts. Court judges are chosen by the National Council.

Economy

Slovakia has proceeded at a slower pace than the Czech Republic with market reforms. Prime Minister Mečiar continues to hold up the pace of privatization, and many large firms remain in state control. Many of these industries built under Communist rule are inefficient and environmentally unsound. Military-related industries still in operation have the capacity, but not yet the capital, to switch to civilian products. Steel, chemical, textile, cement, and glass factories produce goods and semifinished products that could be globally competitive once the political climate stabilizes.

High unemployment (nearly 15 percent) and inflation hinder progress, but the low level of foreign investment is seen as a more significant problem. Real gross domestic product per capita is $6,690. Slovaks generally enjoy a good standard of living. The currency is the Slovak crown or *koruna* (Sk).

Transportation and Communication

Although Slovak families usually have a car, extremely high fuel prices discourage regular use. Instead, public transportation by bus, streetcar, and train is common. Main roads are paved, but there are only a few good superhighways. More are being planned. Railroads link major cities.

Slovakia's press expanded rapidly with the freedom introduced in 1989. More than 120 newspapers, as well as numerous magazines, are published. There are several television and radio stations. People with satellite dishes can access international programming.

Education

Education, which is free at public institutions, begins at age six and is compulsory for ten years. Education and research have a high priority, and the literacy rate is 99 percent. Although public universities charge no tuition, admission is limited and highly competitive. The oldest of Slovakia's 13 universities is Comenius University in Bratislava. Those who do not attend college can obtain work skills through vocational schools.

Health

Slovakia's national health-care system, anchored by state-run hospitals, is undergoing change. Nearly all people have access to physicians, and medical advances have lowered the infant mortality rate to 10 per 1,000. Life expectancy averages 71 years. Health spas service patients from around the world. Pollution poses serious health hazards in both rural and urban environments. Funds are lacking to clean the water and air and to restore decimated forests.

FOR THE TRAVELER

If staying fewer than 30 days, U.S. travelers need only a passport to visit Slovakia. For additional information, consult the Embassy of the Slovak Republic, 2201 Wisconsin Avenue NW, Suite 250 , Washington, DC 20007; phone (202) 965–5164.

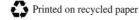

CULTURGRAM ™ '97

Republic of
Slovenia

Boundary representations not necessarily authoritative.

BACKGROUND

Land and Climate

Slovenia covers 7,896 square miles (20,451 square kilometers) and is slightly smaller than Massachusetts. The Julian and Kamnik Alps, the Adriatic seacoast, and rolling gentle plains give the country a diversity of climates from alpine to continental to Mediterranean. Dynamic geographic formations include some six thousand limestone caves, natural bridges, sinkholes, springs, waterfalls, and thermal springs. Half of Slovenia is forested and supports rich animal and plant life. Wildflowers adorn the fields, hills, and mountains. The Slovene national flower, the red carnation, is a traditional folk motif that appears in many different forms, as does the leaf symbol for the national tree, the linden. The highest peak, Mount Triglav (9,396 feet or 2,864 meters) in the Julian Alps, is portrayed on Slovenia's national flag. The three major rivers are the Sava, Drava, and Soča. The alpine lakes of Bled and Bohinj are well-known, as is the disappearing Lake Cerknica in southern Slovenia. The average temperature in January is 35–39°F (2–4°C) and in July 68–75°F (20–24°C).

History

Slovenia was inhabited by ancient Illyrians and Celts, followed by Greeks and Romans. Slavs, including Slovenes, began settling the Balkans in the sixth century A.D. The Slovenes enjoyed brief independence in the state of Carantania from 620 until it recognized Bavarian supremacy in 745. The Carantanian constitution was one model referenced by Thomas Jefferson in preparing the U.S. Constitution. The Bavarian state submitted to the Franks in 788 and eventually (963) became part of the Holy Roman Empire. Slovene territory later fell under Hapsburg domination.

During the Bavarian period, Slovenes began to accept Christianity. It was later more fully embraced when Cyril, Methodius, and others taught the faith in Slavic languages. In addition to continuing pressures of Germanization, the Slovenes suffered terribly from Turkish raids in the 15th and 16th centuries. Peasant uprisings against feudal masters began at the end of the 15th century and lasted almost 250 years.

For a short time (1809–13), much of Slovenia was under French rule as the province of Illyria. This furthered the rise of nationalism and the use of the Slovene language. The Hapsburgs regained control of Slovene territory, but the spirit of a national consciousness continued to grow. The enlightenment of 1830 to 1848 further promoted the development of Slovene language and literature. At the beginning of the 20th century, hopes for a South Slav state that would include Slovenia under a Viennese crown were never realized, and Slovenia continued as part of the Austro-Hungarian Empire until it collapsed at the end of World War I. Slovenia then joined the Kingdom of Serbs, Croats, and Slovenes (renamed Yugoslavia in 1929) under a Serbian monarch. Italy and Germany occupied Slovenia during World War II. Some Slovenes allied themselves with Fascist forces, but others joined partisan (Communist) fighters to resist the Germans and wage a civil war for control of the region. The partisans were helped to victory by Allied forces. After World War II, Slovenia became one of the six republics of the Socialist Federal Republic of Yugoslavia, a Communist state ruled by partisan leader Josef Broz Tito.

When democracy began sweeping through Eastern Europe, the Slovenes voted for self-determination and proclaimed independence in 1991. This move prompted an attack by the Yugoslav Army. A ten-day war in the summer of 1991 was resolved peacefully, and the last Yugoslav soldier left Slovenia in October 1991. In 1992, Slovenes elected Milan Kučan to be president. Together with other leaders, he worked to stabilize society and build the economy.

PEOPLE

Population

Slovenia's population of two million is growing anually at 0.2 percent. Most people are native Slovenes, except for small Hungarian and Italian minorities. Other nationalities living in Slovenia are Croats (3 percent), Serbs (1 percent), Muslims, Montenegrins, and Albanians. The capital, Ljubljana, has 340,000 residents. It was first inhabited some five thousand years ago. In Roman times, it was a major settlement called Emona.

Between the 1880s and 1920s, more than 75,000 Slovenes migrated to the United States. Later immigrants went to Canada, South America, Australia, and western Europe.

Language

Slovene, the official language, is a Slavic language. It uses the dual, a special language construction referring to two persons or things. Like Croatian, Slovene uses Roman letters but excludes *q*, *w*, *x*, and *y* and incorporates the letters *š* (sh), *č* (ch), and *ž* (zh). The oldest preserved documents written in Slovene, the Freising Fragments, date to A.D. 1000. The first book was printed in Slovene by Primož Trubar in 1550. In 1584, Adam Bohorič produced a grammar book. Starting around 1774, elementary school students were taught in their native language. Despite pressures to Germanize, Slovene became widely used in all spheres of life. Many Slovenes speak English, followed by German, Italian, French, Croatian, and Serbian. Hungarian and Italian have official status for use in border areas.

Religion

Slovenes are predominantly Roman Catholic. A few are Protestant. Serbs tend to be Orthodox Christian. Muslims and Jews also have small congregations in Slovenia. Many buildings neglected under communism are being restored to their former glory. In the countryside, small churches dot the mountaintops, and small shrines (*kapelica*) are found along roadways.

General Attitudes

Slovenes are proud of their country and heritage. They are reserved initially but are warm in relationships with family and friends. In conversation, people maintain a certain distance from each other, even if they are longtime acquaintances. Slovenes do not admire people when they are late, untruthful, rude, boastful, unreliable, aggressive, fearful of change, pessimistic, or xenophobic.

When they receive a compliment, Slovenes smile and say, "I invite you for a drink," meaning they gracefully accept the compliment. Motherhood is greatly respected and children are cherished. People treat pets with affection and kindness.

Slovenes are industrious and hardworking. They may spend their free time working in the garden or building their own homes over a span of several years. A clean, neat, and attractive home and garden are important. People's respect for the land is reflected in relatively clean streets and parks and well-tended rural fields. Many city dwellers have a small plot of arable land where they plant vegetables, fruits, and flowers. Homegrown foods are regarded as a precious commodity. People often place flowers on sunny windowsills to grow throughout the year, especially in the countryside.

Personal Appearance

It is important to be well-groomed, clean, and neat in public. Contemporary European styles are popular. People wear furs in the winter to protect against the cold. A traditional fur hat (*polhovka*), made from the skins of the dormouse, is worn in southern regions. People's daily dress reflects their occupations. Village women working in their homes and on the land wear work dresses covered with a full-length apron. When visiting, they may wear a dress and sweater or skirt and blouse. Men wear coveralls or heavy trousers with a blue coat and heavy boots during the day. Young people usually attend secondary school in the cities and live there in dormitories during the week, so they become acquainted with the dress of the city youth.

In cities, men wear suits or sport coats and slacks with a shirt and tie to work. Urban women wear suits, dresses, slacks, jackets, and other cosmopolitan fashions. Urban youth wear blue jeans and adopt fashions from abroad.

CUSTOMS AND COURTESIES

Greetings

Upon meeting, people smile, shake hands, and greet each other with *Kako se imate?* (How are you?). Informally, the term is *Kako se imaš?* Some people kiss on both cheeks when greeting. Hello is expressed with *živijo* or *zdravo*. *Dobro jutro* (Good morning), *Dober dan* (Good day), *Dober večer* (Good evening), or *Lahko noč* (Good night) are also common. Some Slovenes bow their heads slightly when shaking hands. If the hand is soiled, they will bow slightly and greet the person verbally while offering an apology for not using the hand. Urban residents rarely greet strangers on the street. In the countryside, people look at strangers directly and may offer a greeting.

Women are addressed as *Gospa* (Madam) or *Gospodična* (Miss), and men as *Gospod* (Sir). The use of titles shows respect. Only close friends use first names, usually after many years of acquaintance. This formality is also reflected in the Slovene use of the formal pronoun for "you" (*vi*). Only relatives and close friends use the informal *ti*. Likewise, verb forms can be more formal. The youth usually do not observe these formalities. When parting or exiting a room or an elevator, people customarily say *Na svidenja* (Good-bye) or *Adijo* (Adieu) even if they do not know the others present.

Gestures

Hand movements emphasize conversation. Hand-holding and other displays of affection usually are seen only among young people. Two girls or women, especially older ladies, may walk along the street arm in arm. When conversing with another person, one stands straight and does not place the hands in the pockets. It is customary to adhere to good manners, i.e., hold the door for other persons, avoid chewing gum in public and during conversation, cover the mouth when coughing, and avoid conversation with food in the mouth. Slovenes remove their hats when they reach their destination and prepare to sit down.

Visiting

Family and friends enjoy visiting each other. They usually call ahead, as spontaneous visits are not frequent. It is also common to invite friends to one's home. Visiting is more common on Sundays and holidays but also occurs during the week. Invited guests take a bouquet of flowers to the hostess, a bottle of wine to the host, or a small gift for the children. Hosts offer guests refreshments such as coffee, juice, cookies, or pastries. Visitors take care not to stay for a long period of time. Shortly after the meal, once coffee is served, guests take their leave. Hosts will accompany guests to the door and sometimes to the street or car if appropriate.

Many Slovenes remove their shoes in the home and wear slippers. Thus, it is impolite for guests to pass a home's entryway without first offering to remove their shoes.

Slovenes enjoy eating at local inns called *gostilne*, where the atmosphere is warm and the food is well prepared. They also enjoy meeting acquaintances at indoor or outdoor cafés for coffee or a drink.

Eating

Slovenes traditionally eat in the continental style, with the fork in the left hand and the knife in the right. Daily meals usually include *zajtrk* (breakfast) early in the morning, *malica* (mid-morning snack), *kosilo* (main meal) in the mid-afternoon or after work, and *večerja* (light supper) in the evening. Families usually eat the main meal together. These patterns are changing in the face of modern lifestyle factors such as more women in the workforce, greater access to convenient and fresh foods, and improved cooking facilities.

When drinking together, all persons raise the glass and toast each other with *Na zdravje* (To your health) or *Živijo* (Long live). A customary toast of wine precedes a meal when guests are present. After serving the food, the host nods and offers all present the wish *Dober tek* (the equivalent of *Bon apétite*). Members of the group then offer each other the same greeting. Diners follow the host's lead to begin eating. Guests are always served first and are later offered additional food and drink. Glasses and plates are continually refilled.

LIFESTYLE

Family

Family size and living arrangements are changing. The average family has one or two children, but couples might also choose to remain childless. Ten years ago, it was not unusual for two or three generations to live in the same household. Now young couples move out on their own. However, family ties remain strong. Both parents work outside the home and share child raising and housework. Most urban people live in apartments, while small private homes are common in rural areas. City dwellers may own a small weekend house in the country to which they retreat on weekends and holidays.

Dating and Marriage

Dating takes place throughout the teenage years. Young people attend movies and fairs, dance, visit museums and other historical places, visit friends, gather in groups in cafés, enjoy outdoor sports, travel, walk in the hills or the town, and people watch from some vantage points. A large number of young people live in the Ljubljana area, attending high school or university.

Marriages usually occur after schooling is completed. Civil ceremonies and church weddings are common. There are more church weddings now than in the past, even in the cities. Rural weddings are elaborate and incorporate more of the old customs. For instance, a bridal carriage bedecked with flowers may transport the bride and her party to the ceremony. In the *šrange* custom, the bride is detained by young men in her village until the groom ransoms her. Old castles, such as Castle Snežnik near Kožarišče in the Notranjska region, are now being used as wedding sites.

Diet

Slovene cuisine has been influenced by Austrian, Italian, South Slavic, and Hungarian kitchens and is therefore a mix of tastes and textures. However, a typical main meal includes meat (beef or chicken) and potato soup with thin egg noodles, green salad, and apple, cherry, or cheese strudel with coffee.

Pork, veal, chicken, and turkey are commonly served. Organ meats also appear often on the dinner table. No matter the season, Slovenes serve a daily lettuce-and-herb salad with vinegar-and-oil dressing. Potatoes, onions, cabbage, celery, carrots, bananas, apples, and walnuts round out the dietary staples. The forests provide a variety of mushrooms, berries, and nuts.

People traditionally produce homemade wine, fruit brandies, sauerkraut, pickled foods, sausages, dried fruits, canned fruits and vegetables, and fruit juices. Households now have better access to fresh fruits and vegetables, frozen foods, and seasonal specialties.

A hearty fall meal may consist of blood sausage, braised potatoes, pickled turnips, and dark bread; *jota*, a hearty soup of kidney beans, sauerkraut, and bacon; or *kurja obara*, chicken stew with buckwheat groats. On New Year's Day, roasted pork and sauerkraut brings good luck. Slovenes celebrate spring with a salad of dandelion greens or *motovilec* (a green called "corn salad" in English).

Slovenes enjoy sweets, pastries, cakes, and chocolate candy. *Potica* is a traditional nut roll served during Christmas and Easter. Slovenes also drink a variety of coffees. In the past, they drank tea only as a medicinal remedy but now accept it as an alternative to coffee. Many people still grow herbs used to make teas for treating a variety of maladies. Wine, beer, and mineral water are all produced locally.

Recreation

Slovenes of all ages enjoy sports and outdoor activities. The major winter sport is skiing. Popular team sports include hockey, basketball, volleyball, and soccer. A walk along city streets, through the parks, or in the hills is a daily regimen considered essential for health. Bicycling is a popular means of transportation as well as exercise. Hiking is a very popular recreational activity. In the country, a *veselica* (summer picnic) may be sponsored by a firemen's group or other local groups. A revered pastime is picking berries, mushrooms, and nuts in the forests. During July or August, families usually vacation in the mountains, at a health spa, at a family farm adapted for tourism, by the seaside, or in another country.

The arts are well developed, and many Slovenes attend the theater, opera, concerts, art exhibits, and museums. Slovenes enjoy poetry and literature. Movies are especially popular. People like to listen to folk music, sing in choirs, and play the national instruments: the button box accordion and the zither.

Holidays

Official holidays are New Year's Days (1–2 January), National Culture Day (8 February), Day of Uprising against the Nazi Occupation (27 April), Labor Days (1–2 May), National Day (25 June, for independence in 1991), Reformation Day (31 October), and Independence Day (26 December, for the 1990 plebiscite to form an independent state). Easter, Assumption Day (15 August), All Souls' Day (1 November), and Christmas Day (25 December) are also holidays.

Slovenes celebrate seasonal events such as the harvest and grape-picking days. Farmers celebrate *Koline* by sharing newly butchered pork and special sausages with neighbors. *Pust* is the Slovene equivalent of Mardi Gras. The eve of a holiday is also celebrated. The name for such evenings is suffixed with *-ovanje*: *Silvestrovanje* (New Year's Eve), *Miklavžovanje* (St. Nicholas Eve), *Kurentovanje* (the evening before *Pust* when the *Kurent*, demon figure, appears to chase away the winter), *Kresovanje* (Midsummer's Night Eve), and so on.

Commerce

Offices are open from 8:00 A.M. to 4:00 P.M. and shops from 8:00 A.M. to 7:00 P.M. during the week and sometimes on Saturday until noon. Kiosks and private shops are open longer in the evenings, on weekends, and on holidays. Ljubljana's large farmers' market is open weekdays and Saturdays. Other towns also have smaller open markets. Slovenia is in the process of privatizing state grocery stores, and many new private businesses are being established.

SOCIETY

Government

Slovenia is a democratic republic. All citizens age 18 and older have the right to vote for members of the National Assembly and for the president, who is head of state. Parliament is a 90-member National Assembly. One seat each is reserved for an elected representative of the Italian and Hungarian minorities.

The president, elected for a five-year term, appoints the prime minister with approval of Parliament. President Milan Kučan, former Prime Minister Lojze Peterle, and Prime Minister Janez Drnovšek have guided the country toward economic and political stability. Several major political parties are represented in Parliament, but the largest are the Liberal Democrats of Slovenia, Slovene Christian Democrats, and Associated List of Social Democrats.

Slovenia is a member of the United Nations and the Council of Europe, as well as many other international organizations. It is negotiating with the European Union (EU) for an association agreement.

Economy

Slovenia has worked diligently to create a strong market economy. Success is evident in the gross domestic product (GDP) per capita of $9,270 in 1995. GDP growth for that year was 4 percent. Inflation was 8.5 percent, down from 93 percent in 1992. Unemployment is about 12 percent. All workers belong to a union that negotiates labor contracts with the Chamber of Economy (representing employers) and the government. The EU receives nearly 70 percent of Slovene exports. In June 1996, Slovenia and the EU signed an important association agreement, taking a significant step toward full membership. Key economic sectors include manufacturing and mining. Slovenia's monetary unit is the *tolar* (SIT).

Transportation and Communication

Public rail, bus, and highway systems are well developed and linked with other European cities. Many persons own cars but may prefer public transportation in cities where parking is a problem. Adria Airways is the national airline. The port of Koper provides full cargo services for central Europe. Slovenia enjoys a free and active press with six daily newspapers and a large variety of periodicals. One state-owned television/radio enterprise and several private television and radio stations operate throughout the country.

Education

Children begin primary school at age six and must attend for at least eight years. Thereafter, they may attend gymnasium (an academic high school that prepares students for university) or a vocational school to learn a trade or crafts. After the eighth grade, students must pass the *matura* exam to get a workbook. Without it, one cannot get a job. Maribor and Ljubljana each have a university, with the larger one in Ljubljana (founded in 1919). The adult literacy rate is nearly 100 percent.

Health

Slovenia continues to have the best medical facilities of all the former Yugoslav republics. Its network of public health centers, hospitals, and pharmacies were gradually developed in the Austro-Hungarian period and maintained in the Yugoslav years. The quality of care has kept pace with that in western Europe.

Legislation in 1992 provided that physicians and other health workers may work in public or private practices. Health-care facilities and pharmacies may also operate under private ownership. All Slovenes have basic health insurance. Workers and employers contribute to a fund, and the unemployed are covered by public money. People may purchase additional insurance to cover services not provided in the basic package. The infant mortality rate is 8 per 1,000. Life expectancy ranges between 71 and 79 years.

FOR THE TRAVELER

U.S. citizens need a valid passport to enter Slovenia, but a visa is not needed for stays of up to three months. Credit cards are widely accepted and automated teller machines are located in major cities. Interesting sites include Lake Bled, Ljubljana, the Postojna Caves (among the world's largest), and the well-preserved Castle Snežnik. English is spoken in most tourist areas, and police officers speak several languages. For travel information, contact the Embassy of the Republic of Slovenia, 1525 New Hampshire Avenue NW, Washington, DC 20036; phone (202) 667–5363.

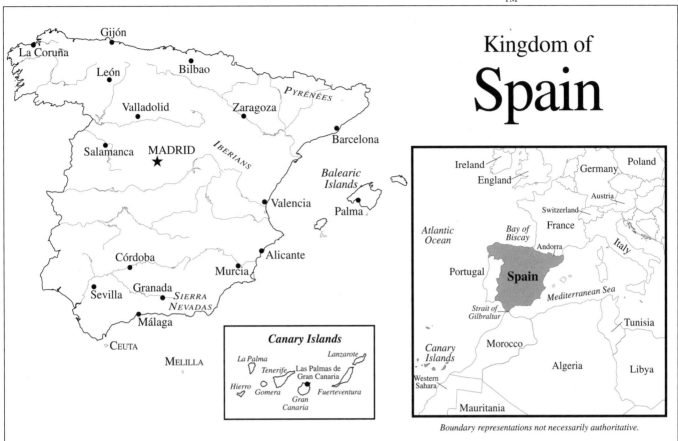

Kingdom of
Spain

Boundary representations not necessarily authoritative.

BACKGROUND

Land and Climate

Spain occupies the majority of the Iberian Peninsula in Europe. Covering 194,884 square miles (504,750 square kilometers), it is nearly as large as Nevada and Utah combined. Much of central Spain is a high plateau, surrounded by low coastal plains. The famous Pyrénées Mountains are in the north. Other important mountain ranges include the Iberians in the central part of the country and the Sierra Nevadas in the south. The northern coasts enjoy a moderate climate with some rainfall year-round. The southern and eastern coasts have a more Mediterranean climate, with long, dry summers and mild winters. Spain has many natural resources, including coal, iron ore, uranium, mercury, gypsum, zinc, copper, potash, and others. About 30 percent of the land is forested. Spain also includes various islands. The Canary Islands, in the Atlantic off the Moroccan coast, are a popular tourist retreat. Also included in Spain's territory are the Balearic Islands, Ceuta, and Melilla (both on the northern coast of Morocco).

History

Civilization on the Iberian Peninsula has been recorded as far back as 2000 B.C. Various peoples migrated over the centuries to populate the area. Rome began to exercise its influence around 218 B.C. and controlled the entire peninsula by the time of Christ. In the centuries after the Roman Empire fell, Spain was first ruled by the Visigoths, Germanic tribes who invaded in the fifth century, and then by the Muslim Moors, who invaded from North Africa in 711. Christians began to fight the Muslim Empire and finally defeated the Moorish king. Two kingdoms emerged in 1479; they united by 1492.

During the 16th century, Spain was one of the largest and most powerful empires in the world. Its territories in the Americas were extensive and wealthy. Spain was a monarchy during its colonial period. One of its most famous rulers was Philip II (1556–98), who was a staunch supporter of the Roman Catholic Church and fought many wars in the name of destroying Protestantism. Several Spanish territories in Europe were lost during the War of the Spanish Succession (1701–14). Spain was involved in the Napoleonic wars that ended in 1814. By 1850, Spain had lost most of its overseas possessions. Spain then lost a war (along with the Philippines and other territory) to the United States in 1898.

King Alfonso XIII abdicated his throne in 1931 when the people called for a republic. Unfortunately, civil war erupted in 1936 between the Nationalists (led by Francisco Franco) and the Republicans. After a brutal war, Franco's forces were victorious in 1939. Franco assumed complete control of the government and ruled as a dictator until 1975. In 1969, Franco named Juan Carlos de Borbón y Borbón as his eventual successor. When Franco died in 1975, Juan Carlos restored the monarchy and became King Juan Carlos I. He also instituted a democractic constitutional monarchy; he remains popular today for those actions. Elections were held in 1977, and the political system was reformed to protect human rights.

The Socialist Democrats, who took power in 1977, continued in office through the 1980s but had to form a coalition government when they lost their parlimentary majority in 1990. Although a member of the North Atlantic Treaty Organization (NATO), Spain threatened at one time to withdraw from the alliance. Relations with Europe and the United States improved in the late 1980s. Violent terrorist attacks by Basque separatists (ETA) have caused problems for the government, but Spain is cooperating with France in addressing the issue. The ETA seeks autonomy but is considered an antidemocratic organization by most people in Spain.

Domestic political and economic problems in 1992 did not dampen enthusiasm for what the Spanish called the "Year of Spain" because of the Summer Olympics, the World's Fair, and the five hundredth anniversary of Columbus's voyage to the Americas. The troubles did lead Prime Minister Felipe González to call for elections a few months ahead of schedule. In June 1993, voters chose to return him to office for another term by a narrow margin.

By 1994, a political crisis was evident and threatened to bring down the government. Many sources called for the prime minister's resignation for not cracking down on high-level corruption. Several government ministers and officials resigned; some were arrested. González lost a majority in Parliament during the summer of 1995 and new elections were called more than a year early. In the March 1996 elections, conservative José María Aznar, leader of the Popular Party, defeated González, ending 13 years of socialist rule. Lacking a majority, Aznar was unable to form a government. He became prime minister and formed a coalition government only after garnering support from Catalan nationalists and other groups, who favor greater regional self-rule.

THE PEOPLE

Population

The population of Spain is 39.4 million and is growing annually at 0.27 percent. This figure includes the population of islands that are part of Spain. The Spanish are a composite of Mediterranean and Nordic ancestry but are considered a homogeneous ethnic group. A small portion of the population is composed of immigrants from Latin American nations, other European countries, Africa, and Asia. More than three-fourths of the population lives in urban areas. Madrid, the capital, has the largest population with 3.6 million people. Barcelona is the next largest urban area with 1.8 million (3 million including suburbs).

Spain's Human Development Index (0.930) ranks it ninth out of 174 nations. Access to education, health care, and economic prosperity affords most of the population opportunities and choices in their lives. Adjusted for women, the index (0.795) ranks Spain 34th out of 130 countries, indicating that, compared to their European neighbors, Spanish women earn a smaller share of their nation's income.

Language

Spain has four official languages. Castilian Spanish is the main language of business and government. The other official languages include Catalan (spoken by 17 percent of the population), Galician (7 percent), and Basque (2 percent). In Catalan areas (mostly in the northeast corner, down the coast to Valencia, and on the Balearic Islands) nearly everyone speaks Catalan; many do not speak Castilian. The same is true for speakers of other languages. Galician is spoken in the northwest and Basque is spoken in the north. English can be heard in tourist centers, and many Spaniards know some French. Because Barcelona is in Catalonia, Catalan was an official language of the 1992 Summer Olympics (with Spanish, English, and French).

Religion

Spain historically is a Roman Catholic nation; 99 percent of the people are baptized members. All aspects of Spanish life are influenced by deep-rooted Catholic traditions. Freedom of religion was granted in the 1970s, opening the way for Spaniards to join other churches. One percent of the population is involved with other (mostly Christian) religious groups. Participation in these smaller groups (such as attendance at worship services) is proportionally much higher than in the Catholic Church. Some Muslims and Jews also reside in Spain.

General Attitudes

The Spanish are generally friendly, helpful, and individualistic. They enjoy conversation and giving advice. The Spanish often consider it their duty to correct "errors" as they see them in others. Along with their spirit of individualism comes a strong sense of personal pride. Spanish people feel it important to project an impression of affluence and social position. Appearance is extremely important. Regional pride and devotion are strong and increasingly expressed.

Personal Appearance

The Spanish are concerned with dress. Style and quality of clothing are important indicators of a person's status and respectability. Men usually dress conservatively, avoiding flashy or bright colors. Women like to be stylish, and children are dressed as nicely as possible. Colorful regional costumes are sometimes worn for festivities.

CUSTOMS AND COURTESIES

Greetings

Men usually greet each other with a handshake. Good friends often add a pat on the back and, if they have not seen each other for some time, an *abrazo* (hug). Women too shake hands when greeting others, and close female friends also kiss each other on the cheek. When parting, women give each other a slight embrace and kiss on the cheek. Typical greetings include *¡Buenos días!* (Good day), *¡Buenas noches!* (Good evening), and the more casual *¡Hola!* (Hi). One may also ask *¿Cómo estás?* (How are you?) of friends or *¿Cómo está?* for new acquaintances. Other local greetings are also used according to the primary language of the region.

People may address professionals or older persons by family name and title, such as *Señor* (Mr.), *Señora* (Mrs.), and *Señorita* (Miss). In some areas, the titles *Don* and *Doña* are used with the first name to show special respect. Close friends and young people call each other by first name.

Visiting

When invited to someone's home, a person often declines at first because the invitation may be only a polite courtesy. If the host insists, then one may accept the invitation. Guests invited to a home usually expect to stay from one to two hours. It is polite for guests to take or send flowers, especially if they are invited to dinner or if someone is ill. On special occasions, hosts might give gifts to guests, who open the gifts immediately in the hosts' presence. Hosts usually serve refreshments.

Eating

For a formal dinner, the host or hostess indicates the seating arrangements. Women and older people are seated first. Compliments on the meal are welcome. Spaniards eat in the continental style, with the fork in the left hand and the knife remaining in the right. The knife is used to push food onto the fork; one never pushes food onto the fork with the fingers or other food. Upon finishing the meal, one places the knife and fork side by side on the plate. Leaving them crossed or on opposite sides of the plate indicates one wishes to eat more.

During the meal, people always keep their hands (but not elbows) above the table. If a person enters a home or room when others are eating, he or she will be invited to join in eating. The invitation usually is extended out of courtesy, and the person generally refuses politely, saying *¡Que aproveche!* (Enjoy your meal!). It is considered bad manners for adults to eat while walking down the street.

In restaurants, one summons the waiter by raising a hand. The bill, which is paid to the waiter, usually includes a service charge, although it is also customary to leave a small tip. Compliments or friendly remarks to waiters or other workers are generally appreciated.

LIFESTYLE

Family

The family is important in Spain. Divorce rates are low. The average family has two children. The father is traditionally the undisputed head of the home. Generally the wife is responsible for caring for the house and children, although many women living in urban areas also work outside the home. About one-third of the labor force is female. Grandparents, aunts, uncles, and cousins commonly maintain close relations with the nuclear family. Men are expected to be strong and masculine, while women are expected to be understanding and feminine. These attitudes are changing in urban areas but still play a key role among rural peoples. In such cases, men enjoy more social freedom than do women.

Dating and Marriage

The youth usually begin dating in groups around age 14. Couples begin dating at about age 18. In some areas, couples only date if they plan to marry; otherwise, group activities prevail. Rather than call on a girl at her home, a boy often meets a girl at a prearranged site. Couples normally are engaged for a long time while they work and save money to pay for an apartment. Potential spouses usually must be approved by parents. The average marriage age for men is 27, while women marry between 20 and 24.

Diet

Typical Spanish food includes fresh vegetables, meat, eggs, chicken, and fish. Most fried foods are cooked in olive oil. Breakfast is generally a light meal of coffee or hot chocolate, bread and jam, or sometimes *churros* (a batter made of flour and butter, deep-fried, and sprinkled with sugar). A substantial meal is eaten at about 2:00 P.M., usually including soup, salad, a dish consisting of some kind of fish, a main dish, and fresh fruit. Adults usually drink wine with their meals and children drink mineral water or soft drinks. There is always plenty of bread (French style). At 5:00 or 6:00 P.M., Spaniards eat a snack (*merienda*), usually a sandwich (*bocadillo*) or sweet bread or crackers, with tea or hot milk. Dinner is usually at 9:00 or 10:00 P.M. and is not as large as the midday meal. Common dinner foods include soup and a *tortilla española* (omelet with potatoes and onions). Each region also has it own specialities, including seafoods, ham and pork sausages, lamb stew, roasted meats, *gazpacho* (cold vegetable soup), *paella* (rice with fish, seafood, and/or meat), *Arros negre* (rice with calamar ink), *Cocido* (Castilian soup), and a wide variety of other foods.

Recreation

The main spectator sport is soccer. When important teams play, local bars are crowded with fans watching the matches on television. Many also watch from their homes. During the World Cup competition, the entire country is involved. Spain participated in the 1994 World Cup competition. Bullfighting, a popular attraction, is considered more an art than a sport. Spaniards interested in participating in sports (tennis, basketball, swimming, and others) join private clubs. Team sports are not part of school programs. Hunting, skiing, and fishing are popular activities in certain areas of Spain. Many Spaniards enjoy going to movies, watching television, or going for walks. *Tertulias* are popular intimate social groups that meet together regularly in cafés to discuss ideas, events, and politics. Men play dominoes, cards, or other games in bars.

Music and dance have always played an important part in the lives of Spaniards. The guitar is the favorite instrument for traditional music. Each region has its own folk dance, music, and dress. Many types of modern music and dance are also enjoyed in Spain. The Spanish greatly appreciate the performing arts and are proud of their international achievements. Famous opera tenors Placido Domingo and José Carreras are both Spaniards. Other cultural arts are also important in Spain, which boasts such masters of painting as Velázquez, Goya, Picasso, and others.

Holidays

Festivals (*fiestas*) play a major role in Spanish life. People eagerly await and plan them well in advance. Each city and region has its own special *fiesta*, often in honor of a patron saint. Associated activities include processions, fireworks, bullfights, amusement attractions, dancing, and wearing regional costumes. Official national holidays include New Year's Day, Feast of San José (19 March), Holy Week and Easter, Labor Day (1 May), Corpus Christi, the King's Birthday (24 June), Santiago Day (25 June), National Day (12 October), All Saints' Day (1 November), Constitution Day (6 December), Immaculate Conception (8 December), and Christmas. Christmas gifts are not opened until the Day of the Three Kings or Wise Men on 6 January.

Commerce

Businesses are traditionally open six days a week from about 9:00 A.M. to 1:30 P.M. and from 5:00 to 8:00 P.M. Banks are open from 9:00 A.M. to 2:00 P.M. The midday break traditionally allowed families to be together for the main meal and a *siesta* (a time for relaxing). This practice is disappearing, however, and families might not eat the midday meal together. Children often eat at school. Businesses are increasingly staying open all day or having a shorter meal break. *Siesta* is no longer common in urban areas. Because of the high cost of living, many men have two jobs. Boys older than age 14 and girls older than age 16 sometimes work during the day and attend high school at night. Their wages often supplement the family income. People typically vacation for three to four weeks in July or August. Those living in central Spain go to the beaches or mountains to escape the heat. Business usually is not conducted during these months because so many people are away.

SOCIETY

Government

Spain is a parliamentary monarchy. King Juan Carlos I is Spain's chief of state, but the prime minister is head of government. Spain's bicameral legislature (*Cortes Generales*) consists of a 255-seat Senate and a 350-seat Congress of Deputies, the latter having the greater power. The voting age is 18. The primary political parties are the Spanish Socialist Workers Party and the Popular Party.

Spain is divided into 17 autonomous communities (regions). Each region has its own rights, elected officials, and justice system. The constitution recognizes the Catalan, Galician, and Basque nationalities as having distinct historic and cultural heritages.

Economy

Although Spain was traditionally one of the poorest countries in western Europe, conditions improved substantially after it joined the European Union in 1986. Real gross national product per capita is $13,400, which has more than doubled in the last generation. This figure indicates that economic opportunities are now available to the majority of the population. Most people earn a decent income. However, unemployment, which was more than 22 percent in 1995, represents a major problem for the economy and has prevented

it from fully recovering from the economic recession of the early 1990s. Many modern economic institutions are already well suited for European markets, but political turmoil has complicated the establishment of economic policies needed for European integration. Inflation remains low and growth is stable.

Although industry is vital to the economy and employs 35 percent of the labor force, the services sector (including tourism) employs 55 percent. Agriculture is less important to the economy than it was a generation ago but still employs 10 percent of the labor force. Agricultural products include grains, citrus and other fruits, vegetables, and wine grapes. The country exports some food as well as live animals. Spain is a world leader in the production of wine. Tourism is increasingly important to economic development, especially in coastal regions. Tourists enjoy visiting Spain for its climate, and it is a popular destination for many other Europeans. The currency is the *peseta* (Pta).

Transportation and Communication

Efficient air and rail service is available throughout the country. Trains connect most cities. Private bus companies serve rural areas. Buses are also common in large cities. Madrid and Barcelona have subway systems. Taxis are normally available. The telecommunications system is generally modern and good for domestic and international use. Dozens of radio and television stations serve the country.

Education

School is compulsory between the ages of six and fourteen. Many schools are operated by the Roman Catholic Church or by private organizations. Middle- and higher-income families spend a good share of their incomes on private education. Spain's literacy rate is 98 percent. While many young people quit school and begin work at age 14, an increasing number are finishing high school and continuing their education in vocational schools. Others prepare for a university education.

Health

The Spanish enjoy a good system of medical care that is coordinated by the government. The infant mortality rate is 7 per 1,000. Life expectancy ranges from 75 to 81 years.

FOR THE TRAVELER

Although a passport is necessary for travel to Spain, a visa is not required of U.S. visitors staying up to three months. Spain has a well-developed tourist industry. For more information on travel opportunities, contact the Tourist Office of Spain, 666 Fifth Avenue, 35th Floor, New York, NY 10022; phone (212) 265–8822; or 8383 Wilshire Boulevard, Suite 956, Los Angeles, CA 90211; phone (213) 658–7188. You may also wish to contact the Embassy of Spain, 2375 Pennsylvania Avenue NW, Washington, DC 20037; phone (202) 452–0100.

Kingdom of
Sweden

Boundary representations not necessarily authoritative.

BACKGROUND
Land and Climate

Sweden, one of the "three fingers" of Scandinavia, is just larger than the state of California. It covers 173,731 square miles (449,964 square kilometers). From the northern tip to the southern tip is about 1,000 miles (1,600 kilometers). Thousands of tiny islands line the coast. Mountains form much of the northwest, but most of Sweden is relatively flat with some rolling hills. Many rivers flow from the mountains through the forests and into the Baltic Sea. Sweden is dotted with lakes, which, with the rivers, provide ample water for the country. More than half of Sweden is forested. North of the Arctic Circle, winters are long and relatively cold while summers are short and pleasant. But summer's "midnight sun" makes the days long. Although Sweden is located far to the north, most of the country has a temperate climate, moderated by the warm Gulf Stream. Important natural resources include timber, silver, zinc, lead, iron ore, copper, and the country's potential for hydroelectric power from its many waterways.

History

Sweden has been inhabited for nearly five thousand years and is the home of the Gothic peoples who battled the Roman Empire. In the ninth century, Rurik, a semilegendary chief of the Swedes, is said to have founded Russia. Christianity was introduced in the 11th century and adopted by the monarchy. Queen Margrethe I of Denmark united Denmark, Norway, and Sweden in the Union of Kalmar in 1397.

Sweden remained fairly autonomous and even had its own Parliament in 1435. It became an independent kingdom in 1523, with Gustaf I Vasa as ruler. The kingdom fought wars with Denmark and Russia in the 16th and 17th centuries, and by the 17th century, Sweden was one of the Great Powers of Europe. It acquired Norway in 1814 through the Napoleonic Wars. Swedish power declined in the 19th century. Finland was an integral part of Sweden until 1809, when it briefly became an archdukedom of Russia. Norway became independent in 1905. The Frenchman Jean Baptiste Bernadotte was elected Sweden's crown prince in 1810 and became king in 1818 as Karl XIV Johan. His dynasty continues today.

During the 20th century, neutrality and nonalignment were cornerstones of Sweden's foreign policy, keeping it out of both world wars and allowing it to transform its rather poor society into a prosperous social welfare state. The Social Democratic Party dominated politics and led every government until 1976, when its rule was interrupted until 1982. With the end of the Cold War, and in view of European integration, Sweden joined the European Union (EU) in 1995.

Sweden prides itself on being a peaceful, egalitarian society in which crime has been relatively low. That image was shaken in 1986 when Prime Minister Olof Palme was assassinated on the streets of Stockholm after attending a movie. Unfortunately, crime has since been on the rise. Palme was succeeded by Ingvar Carlsson of the Social Democratic Party. Faced with a declining economy, Carlsson introduced an austerity package in 1990. When it was rejected, he resigned and formed a new minority government, which he led until elections in 1991. After the elections, Carl Bildt of the Moderate Party formed a coalition government. His administration concentrated on economic challenges and negotiated Sweden's entry to the EU.

In 1994 elections, Bildt's party was defeated and Ingvar Carlsson returned to power as prime minister. Carlsson retired from the party leadership in November 1995 and was replaced by his finance minister, Goeran Persson. A fiscal conservative, Persson seeks to continue his tough austerity measures while protecting essential welfare benefits.

THE PEOPLE

Population

Sweden has a population of 8.8 million and an annual growth rate of 0.5 percent. At least 85 percent of the people are ethnic Swede. Finns compose about 5 percent of the population; most of them are immigrants from Finland, but some are native to northern Sweden. A small indigenous minority (up to 20,000 people), the Sami (pronounced SAY-me), live in the north. Traditionally, they herded reindeer for a living. While some continue that occupation, most are involved in other fields. The Sami are known to some as *Lapps*, but this is a derogatory term and therefore not used in Sweden. Since the 1960s, many immigrants have added to Sweden's population. Today there are many foreign-born or first-generation immigrants from Yugoslavia, Greece, Turkey, and some Latin American countries, among others. Immigrants from other Scandinavian nations, such as Denmark, Finland, and Norway, also live in Sweden.

Sweden's Human Development Index (0.929) ranks it tenth out of 174 countries. An extensive social welfare system provides for most of the people's needs and affords them many choices in their lives. Adjusted for women, the index (0.919) ranks Sweden first out of 130 countries. Men and women enjoy equal access to opportunities for personal advancement.

Language

Swedes speak Swedish—a Germanic language related to Danish, Norwegian, and Icelandic. Swedish emerged as a distinct language around the tenth century. The Sami speak their own language and the Finnish minority speaks Finnish. Most new immigrants continue to speak their native tongue in the home. Many people speak English, which is also taught in the schools.

Religion

Sweden, like most of Europe, is a highly secular society. Freedom of religion is guaranteed by the constitution. Most Swedes (about 86 percent) are members of the Evangelical Lutheran Church but rarely attend church services. The Lutheran Church is supported by the state; however, plans to largely separate church and state began in 1995. Membership is growing in other religious organizations. Most of these are various other Christian churches, such as the Roman Catholic faith, which has a following of about 1 percent of the population. Other groups, such as Muslims and Jews, are also expanding, primarily due to the immigrant population.

General Attitudes

Swedes are somewhat more reserved than people in the United States, although that does not make them less friendly. They are proud of their nation, as well as their regions and towns. Visitors who recognize this pride are careful not to praise another area over the one being visited. Swedes value modesty and material security.

Roughly since World War II, Sweden has built one of the most egalitarian societies in the world and has managed to develop a strong capitalist economy. Swedes can rely on a generous social welfare system to provide health, education, and retirement benefits. While public sentiment in the early 1990s led to some cuts in the system, most people oppose deep changes in what are called cradle-to-grave benefits.

With the exception of the Nobel Peace Prize, which Norway sponsors, Sweden awards the Nobel Prizes each year. These prizes are given to significant contributors in the areas of chemistry, literature, medicine, and physics. Alfred Bernhard Nobel (1833–96), the inventor of dynamite and a wealthy businessman, was born in Sweden.

Personal Appearance

General European fashions are common in Sweden. However, because of the country's cooler climate, Swedes wear warm clothing more often than other Europeans. People generally dress conservatively; it is important to be neat and clean in public. Swedes may not "dress up" as much as people in other countries when they go out. They prefer to avoid glamorous clothing but are still very fashionable. Like other Scandinavian countries, Sweden has traditional costumes that are worn on special occasions.

CUSTOMS AND COURTESIES

Greetings

Swedes commonly shake hands upon meeting. From a distance, one may nod the head or raise the hand to greet another person. People usually address each other by first name; they use titles only in very formal situations. More formal greetings include *God dag* (Good day) or *God morgon* (Good morning). Most people, however, are more casual and say *Hej* (pronounced HEY, meaning "Hi"). One answers the phone with *Hallå* ("Hello") and clearly identifies oneself. "Goodbye" is *Adjö* or, more casually, *Hej då*.

Gestures

Eye contact is important during conversation. Swedes avoid excessive hand gestures when speaking. Chewing gum, yawning, or having one's hands in the pockets when speaking to another person is considered impolite. Although in the past people seldom embraced in public or put their arm around another's shoulder, the population in general is becoming more casual and such displays of friendship are increasing.

Visiting

Swedes enjoy visiting one another, but they do not often visit without prior arrangement. Hosts usually offer guests coffee or something else to drink. It is popular to invite friends over for an evening meal. People most often entertain in the home, although going out is becoming more popular. Still, one does not usually invite someone to a restaurant instead of the home. Dinner guests should arrive on time because the meal is usually served first. If the weather is bad, guests are expected to change shoes (they bring an "indoor" pair) when entering the home. They bring an odd number of flowers or a box of chocolates as a gift to the hosts. Sweets for the children are appropriate if the parents approve. Guests unwrap flowers before giving them to the hostess. If they do not give a gift, guests usually send a thank-you card later in the mail. It is also customary to thank the host or hostess for their hospitality the next time a guest sees them.

It is impolite to "eat and run." Swedes expect guests to stay for coffee and conversation, even as late as 11:00 P.M. Conversation, ranging over a wide variety of topics, is a popular pastime. When leaving, guests say good-bye before they put on their coats.

Eating

Swedes eat a light breakfast around 7:00 A.M. and might have a coffee or tea break at mid-morning. The main meal (*middag*) was traditionally eaten at midday. This is still the case in most rural areas, but urban residents eat only a light lunch at noon and then have their main meal around 6:00 P.M. Swedes eat in the continental style, with the fork in the left hand and the knife remaining in the right. A dinner knife is not used as a butter knife, since separate butter knives are usually provided. Diners keep hands, not elbows, above the table during the meal. When finished eating, a person places the utensils side by side on the plate. Leaving any food on the plate is impolite. Guests usually wait for the hosts to offer second helpings. Declining is not impolite, but guests may take more if they desire. Food is placed in serving dishes on the table, so if they are empty there is usually no more food and asking for more would be impolite.

For some occasions, the host makes a welcome speech at the beginning of the meal. The host then makes a toast (*skål*) and all dinner guests taste the wine. The guest of honor makes a speech during the dessert, elaborating on the meal and the charm of the hostess. Each guest personally thanks the host directly after the meal.

LIFESTYLE

Family

As in many countries, the structure of the family in Sweden has changed over the years. Extended family relationships are maintained through gatherings and holiday visits. The nuclear family is the basic social unit, and it is usually strong and close-knit. Most families have only one or two children. Many women work outside the home; they comprise nearly half of the labor force. Young children are cared for during working hours at day-care centers. Adult children are expected to be independent. Elderly individuals generally rely on the social system or themselves for their care and support.

Many urban families live in apartments, but most people in smaller towns and rural areas have single-family dwellings. Sweden is known for its red wooden houses built in the 18th and 19th centuries that still dot the countryside.

Dating and Marriage

Although serious dating is reserved for older teens, Swedes start to date very early. They enjoy going to movies, eating out, having parties, and dancing. Many people choose to live together rather than get married, or they live together for several years before marrying. Often, a couple marries when they have a child. Divorce and single-parent homes are on the rise. Unmarried couples who live together have nearly the same rights and obligations as married couples. That is, cohabitation is nearly the same as marriage under the law.

Diet

The Swedish diet, as with other parts of society, has changed over the years. Health concerns have affected eating patterns in much the same way they have in other industrialized countries. Once heavy in meat, fish, and cheese, the diet now includes many fresh vegetables and fruits. Common foods include potatoes (eaten a few times a week), cheeses of many types, seafoods, and other fresh foods. For breakfast, one might eat *fil* (a kind of yogurt), *knäckebröd* (crisp bread) with margarine, and coffee. Open-face sandwiches (*smörgåsar*) are also popular. Some favorite main-meal dishes include *Köttbullar med kokt potatis, brun sås och lingonsylt* (meatballs with brown sauce, boiled potatoes and lingonberry jam); *Stekt falukorv med senap och potatis* (fried slices of thick German sausage with mustard and boiled or fried potatoes); and *grillad lax med spenat, citron och potatis eller ris* (grilled slices of salmon with spinach, slices of lemon, and potatoes or rice).

The *smörgåsbord* is a lavish buffet eaten on special occasions or at parties. It is not an everyday meal. A *smörgåsbord* includes warm and cold dishes, meat, fish, and desserts. Many families have a special type of *smörgåsbord* on Christmas Eve.

Recreation

Swedes are sports enthusiasts. Popular sports include soccer, skiing, tennis, golf, swimming, ice hockey, bandy, and orienteering races (using a map and compass to cross an area). Sweden's national soccer team competed in the 1994 World Cup. Bandy is a game related to hockey and believed to be its prototype. Skating and other winter sports are common. Even more popular than sports are activities such as hiking, fishing, and bird-watching. The Swedes love nature and spend as much time as possible outdoors. For many, the ideal is owning a summer cottage for weekends and vacations. Sweden's mountains and fells are popular destinations. Favorite leisure activities also include reading, attending cultural events such as the theater or concerts, and watching movies and television. Most people have a great interest in music, whether modern or traditional. Singing in choirs is by far Sweden's most popular hobby, with 1.5 million participants.

Holidays

Sweden's national holidays include New Year's Day, May Day (1 May), and National Day (6 June). There are, of course, many other holidays, often associated with the season or a religious event. In late June, usually around the 24th, when the summer days are much longer than the nights, *Midsommar* (Midsummer) celebrations are held, including dancing around the maypole and having picnics. At *Påsk* (Easter), children dress up like old witches with brooms and go door-to-door (among friends and neighbors only) to collect candy. Colored Easter eggs are also common at this time.

In contrast to *Midsommar* celebrations, *Lucia* coincides with the longest night of the year. On the morning of 13 December, a girl in the family assumes the role of St. Lucia (the "light queen") and dresses in white with a crown of candles in her hair. She sings the family a special song and serves them coffee and *lussekatter* (Lucia cats), a type of roll. This often marks the beginning of *Jul* (Christmas) celebrations. The climax is Christmas Eve, when a family *smörgåsbord* is accompanied by gift giving. The *Jultomte*, which was once a Christmas gnome who lived under the house, is now the Swedish Santa Claus who brings gifts to the door for the children. A Christmas tree is placed in the house only a few days before Christmas Eve. Christmas Day is spent relaxing, while 26 December is for visiting family and friends.

Commerce

Business hours generally run from 9:00 A.M. to 5:00 P.M., with some variations. For example, many businesses (but not shops) close by 4:00 P.M. in the summer. Banks usually close at 3:00 P.M. People buy their food and other goods from supermarkets and department stores, as well as smaller neighborhood shops. Open-air markets operate in some places; they usually only sell fresh produce.

Swedes enjoy one of the shortest workweeks in the industrialized world. They receive at least five weeks of vacation each year and other benefits. Some benefits were recently cut to reverse a trend toward lower productivity and absenteeism.

SOCIETY

Government

Sweden is a constitutional monarchy. King Carl XVI Gustaf, a descendant of the Bernadotte Dynasty, has ruled since 1973. His duties are mostly ceremonial. The head of government is the prime minister. Members of the 349-seat Parliament (*Riksdag*) are elected for three-year terms. The voting age is 18. Municipal councils handle local affairs. Immigrants must reside in the country three years before they can vote in local elections. Citizenship is required to vote in national elections. The next elections are in 1997.

Economy

Sweden has one of the most prosperous economies in the world. It is highly industrialized, has a modern distribution system, and boasts a skilled and educated labor force. About 5 percent of the workforce is engaged in agriculture, while 22 percent labors in mining and manufacturing. Sweden is a major producer of automobiles (such as Volvo and Saab) and exports machinery and steel products. Timber exports (mostly pulp for paper products) are also important.

The economy usually grows by about 2 percent per year. Unemployment remains a challenge; nearly 9 percent of the population was without work in 1995, while an additional 5 percent participated in government retraining programs. Real gross domestic product per capita is $18,320; however, the cost of living is also high. An income tax funds the country's extensive welfare system. When the tax rate peaked at 70 percent in 1989, society began calling for private alternatives and other changes. Taxes were lowered in 1991 to 51 percent, and several cuts were made to encourage greater productivity and reduce overall cost. Future challenges facing the government include stimulating growth, being globally competitive, and preserving key elements of the social welfare system.

Sweden's membership in the EU is expected to provide greater opportunities for trade and economic growth. The nation's currency is the Swedish *krona* (SKr).

Transportation and Communication

In Sweden, only one in four households does not own a car. Although private cars provide important transportation, public transport is well developed and frequently used. Trains, buses, subways, and streetcars are common. There are three international airports. Most roads are paved and in good condition. The telecommunications system is excellent and highly developed. Numerous newspapers and radio stations serve the country. The Swedish Broadcasting Corporation, which used to have a legal monopoly on television broadcasting, is now facing competition from other broadcasters. Cable and satellite television are available.

Education

Illiteracy is virtually unknown in Sweden. The Swedish government spends more money per pupil than most other countries. The public school system is a comprehensive nine-year program that children begin at age seven. All education is free and one free hot meal is provided each day. Immigrant children have the right to some instruction in their native language. When compulsory education ends at age 16, students have several choices. About one-fifth start working. The others choose between a three-year high school (with a focus in either the social or natural sciences) and a three-year vocational school. There are more than 30 institutions of higher learning. Tuition is free and loans are available for living costs. There is also an extensive adult education program.

Health

All Swedes are covered by national health insurance. The government pays nearly all fees incurred for medical care. At least 85 percent of day-care costs are also covered. Dental fees are shared by the individual. While basic health care is readily available, elective surgery must often wait several months before being approved. In response to public demand, private health-care options are now more widely available, as are private child-care facilities. The government pays an ill person's wages for an extended period. Parents share a total of 12 months' leave when a child is born. The infant mortality rate is one of the lowest in the world at 6 per 1,000. Swedes can expect to live between 75 and 81 years.

FOR THE TRAVELER

While passports are required, U.S. citizens do not need visas for visits of up to three months' total time in Scandinavia (Denmark, Iceland, Finland, Norway, and Sweden). No vaccinations are needed. Warm clothing is advised for winter months. Sweden offers a number of vacation opportunities, from outdoor recreation to resorts and beautiful scenery. The tourist industry is well developed, and plenty of printed material is available to assist the traveler. For more information, contact the Swedish Travel and Tourist Council, 655 Third Avenue, New York, NY 10017; phone (212) 949–2333. You may also wish to contact the Embassy of Sweden, 1501 M Street NW, Washington, DC 20005; phone (202) 467–2600.

Printed on recycled paper

Switzerland

(Swiss Confederation)

Boundary representations not necessarily authoritative.

E
U
R
O
P
E

BACKGROUND

Land and Climate

Covering 15,942 square miles (41,290 square kilometers), Switzerland is just smaller than Denmark or slightly more than twice as large as New Jersey. The country is landlocked and shares borders with France, Germany, Austria, and Italy. Switzerland is sometimes called the "roof of Europe" because of its towering Alps. When people from other countries wish to describe scenic beauty, they often use Switzerland as a standard. It is truly one of the most beautiful places on earth.

The Alps cover more than half of the country, running east to west. The Jura Mountains (running north to south in the west) cover another 10 percent of the territory. Green valleys are interspersed throughout the mountains. Swiss waters drain into five key European rivers: the Rhine, Rhône, Po, Adige, and Danube. The highest mountain peaks include Monte Rosa at 15,209 feet (4,635 meters) and the Matterhorn at 14,691 feet (4,478 meters). The climate varies according to elevation and region but is generally temperate. Winters can be long and snowy, while summers are mild.

History

The Celtic tribes that occupied the area of present-day Switzerland were part of the Roman Empire for five centuries. Later, Burgundian tribes settled in the west and Alemannians in the east; both were Germanic tribes, but they developed along different lines. During most of the Middle Ages, Switzerland was part of the Holy Roman Empire.

The founding of the Swiss Confederation took place on 1 August 1291, when the mountain cantons of Uri, Schwyz, and Unterwalden began a revolt against Austrian Habsburg control by signing the Perpetual Covenant of 1291. Through a series of military victories, Swiss soldiers gained a reputation for their fighting prowess. The confederation later grew more powerful by adding other cantons (Luzern, Zürich, Bern). After withstanding the turmoil and war of the 16th and early 17th centuries, Switzerland received official recognition as an independent nation in the 1648 Treaty of Westphalia.

In 1815, because of a brief invasion by Napoleon, Switzerland became permanently neutral. Early in the 19th century, the Swiss proclaimed the Helvetic Republic—*Helvetia*—and Switzerland became a centralized nation-state. In 1848, it adopted a constitution, making it a federal state. In 1874, direct democracy by the people became an integral part of the constitution. During the 19th century, Switzerland became industrialized and urbanized. While other neutral European nations fell to attacking armies during World Wars I and II, Switzerland, aided by natural geography, remained neutral and was not invaded.

As part of its neutrality, the Swiss Federation is not presently a member of the United Nations (it has observer status), the North Atlantic Treaty Organization (NATO), or the European Union (EU). Still, it has solid relations with many nations. In August 1991, the Swiss celebrated their 700th anniversary as a confederation. The anniversary gave the Swiss cause to honor their nation as one of the world's oldest democracies.

THE PEOPLE

Population

The population of Switzerland is about seven million and is growing at 0.6 percent annually. Switzerland is made up of a variety of ethnic groups. In the east and central cantons, Germans dominate and account for 65 percent of the total population. The French are located mostly in the west and comprise 18 percent of the population. In parts of the south, most people are of Italian descent and make up 10 percent of the total. One percent of the population has Romansch ancestry. Currently living in Switzerland are many peoples (6 percent of the population) from different lands: the former Yugoslavia, Spain, Greece, Italy, some Middle Eastern nations, and a variety of others. Most of them are guest workers and do not have Swiss citizenship.

Switzerland's Human Development Index (0.925) ranks it 13th out of 174 nations. The country affords its people a high standard of living and excellent access to health care, education, and economic opportunities. Adjusted for women, the index (0.852) ranks Switzerland 19th out of 130 countries. This figure reflects an income gap between men and women.

Language

Four official languages are spoken in Switzerland: German, French, Italian, and Romansch. Each canton has the right to declare which language it will use. All street signs are in that language only. In the schools, all the languages are available for study, but the language of instruction is that of the canton. Most Swiss can understand at least one of the other official languages of the confederation, and many speak English, which is also offered in the schools. Although French and Italian are basically spoken as written, there is a difference between written German (standard German) and what is spoken every day by the German Swiss. Their dialect (*Schweizerdeutsch*) is rather unique and difficult for other German-speaking peoples to understand. Protection of minority languages and relations between the different language groups continue to be important political issues the confederation must address.

Religion

Close to half of the people are Roman Catholic and the other half belong to various other Christian churches, mostly Protestant. There is a small Jewish minority (0.3 percent of the population). Switzerland is a secular society and participation in religion is often reserved for special events and holidays. Switzerland was the center of the Zwingli and Calvin Protestant Reformations of the 16th century and has produced important modern theologians. Swiss Protestant churches are locally controlled and democratic. Both Catholic and Protestant churches have generally worked toward greater harmony. As elsewhere in Europe, religion has greater influence in rural areas than in the cities.

General Attitudes

The Swiss have a high regard for nature and beauty, and they are proud of their efforts to protect the environment. Their attitudes have been influenced by the majestic mountains and beautiful lakes found throughout Switzerland. The Swiss also value hard work, sobriety, thrift, and independence. They prize tolerance, punctuality, and a sense of responsibility. A favorite saying claims that if people are late, they are either not wearing Swiss watches or are not riding Swiss trains.

The Swiss are proud of their political and social system, which is unique in Europe. One of its key elements is the federal system that unites different groups into one country. The motto is "Unity, yes; uniformity, no." Each canton is highly autonomous, but all citizens participate in national civic affairs. For example, every physically fit male serves in the Swiss Army. They train on occasion and keep their gun and uniform at home—always ready to form a militia to defend the country. There are only a few professional officers; most serve part-time. While this structure has been recently challenged, it remains intact. The Swiss are politically neutral and sponsor the International Red Cross.

Switzerland's self-confidence has been affected by changes in Europe, social problems, and a debate over immigration. When certain elements of society supported joining the EU's European Economic Area, voters rejected the proposal through a national referendum in 1992. Many feel this will isolate Switzerland from the future course of Europe's economy. In another referendum, voters also banned heavy truck traffic from its roads, effectively causing large transportation problems for other European nations. For the future, the Swiss may have to redefine their role in Europe and determine how best to adapt their grassroots form of democracy to the 21st century. This is a challenging task to face because of intense national pride in the Swiss way of life.

Personal Appearance

The Swiss place a high value on cleanliness, neatness, and orderliness. People dress conservatively and well. Overly casual or grubby attire in public is frowned upon. The Swiss wear modern European fashions but also have traditional costumes that are worn on special occasions.

CUSTOMS AND COURTESIES

Greetings

A handshake is appropriate for men and women. Waving to someone across the street is also acceptable. When entering an elevator or a store, most Swiss exchange simple greetings, even with strangers. Because the Swiss Confederation is a multilingual society, actual verbal greetings vary. They also vary according to the time of day and the situation. It is most polite to address others by their title and surname. The youth use first names, but adults generally reserve first names for close friends and family members. While the Swiss appreciate foreign visitors who speak (or try to speak) the language of the area they are in, most also understand English greetings.

Gestures

Chewing gum or cleaning one's fingernails in public is not appropriate. Talking to an older person with one's hands in the pockets is disrespectful. Legs are crossed with one knee over the other and are not placed on a desk, chair, or table. Pointing the index finger to one's own head to indicate a person is crazy may be considered a serious insult by some.

Visiting

The Swiss are hospitable to guests and expect courtesy in return. Visits are generally arranged in advance. It is polite for guests to wipe their feet before entering the home. Visitors often bring candy or flowers to the hosts, especially if visiting for the first time. Flowers are generally presented in odd numbers and are unwrapped before being given to the hosts. Red roses are only given to signify romantic love. When one leaves a home, it is customary to shake hands with all members of the family or group.

Eating

In the home, a family waits to begin eating until one of the parents begins. The Swiss use the continental style of eating, with the fork in the left hand and the knife remaining in the right. Soft foods, such as potatoes, are cut with a fork, not a knife. Cutting such foods with a knife implies they are improperly cooked. The best compliment one can give is to take additional helpings. Asking for salt or pepper is often considered an insult because it implies the food is improperly spiced. When finished eating, a person places the utensils side by side on the plate. If they are placed another way, it may mean the person wants to eat more. During a meal, hands (not elbows) are always kept above the table. In restaurants, service charges are usually included in the bill, which is paid at the table.

LIFESTYLE

Family

The nuclear family is the most important social unit in Swiss society. Families are generally small, with only one or two children. The man is traditionally the head of the household. Family privacy is very important. Women often work outside the home, although to a lesser extent than in many other European countries. About 37 percent of the workforce is female. Parliamentary representation among women is also lower than elsewhere in Europe. Only in 1971 did women receive the right to vote in national elections and in most cantons. By 1990, only the Appenzell canton of Inner-Rhoden continued to deny women the right to vote on local issues.

Dating and Marriage

Young people often socialize in groups as early as age 14; they begin dating a few years later. The legal age for marriage is 18 for women and 20 for men. Most adults marry in their mid- to late twenties. Many couples prefer to live together for several years before or instead of marrying. It is often important to finish one's education or to become financially established before getting married.

Diet

With so many ethnic backgrounds in the country, the Swiss diet is diverse. There are numerous regional specialties, including various sausages, leek soup, rich cheeses, fish, special wines, and pork. Breakfast is usually light and might include various types of fresh breads, cheeses, and coffee. The main meal of the day is traditionally at midday and usually consists of a main dish with meat and some form of potatoes or pasta and salad. A light dinner is served between 6:00 and 7:00 P.M.; it often consists of open-faced sandwiches. In major urban areas, the trend is to have the main meal in the evening.

Recreation

The Swiss enjoy vacationing, either within their own country or abroad. They love nature and the outdoors and enjoy hiking, skiing, and other such activities. Mountain climbing is a favorite for some. Soccer and cycling are the most popular sports. Switzerland competed in the 1994 World Cup. A small number of Swiss also enjoy traditional games unique to Switzerland. For example, a type of wrestling (*Schwinger*) is popular in some areas. It is similar to Graeco-Roman wrestling but does not have weight classifications. The Swiss enjoy taking walks, watching movies, and attending cultural events.

Holidays

The most important holidays in Switzerland include New Year's Day, Easter (Friday–Monday), Labor Day (1 May), Ascension, Whitsunday and Whitmonday, National Day (1 August), Federal Day of Prayers (a thanksgiving holiday in mid-September), and Christmas. Christmas is the biggest celebration of the year. Gifts are exchanged on Christmas Eve, when the family gathers for a large meal. The family relaxes on Christmas Day and visits friends on 26 December. New Year's Eve is a time for parties and fireworks.

Commerce

In general, business hours are from 8:00 A.M. to noon and from 2:00 to 6:00 P.M., Monday through Friday, although large stores do not close at midday. Some stores remain open later in the evening on certain nights, and hours vary between the different cantons.

SOCIETY

Government

Switzerland is a highly decentralized federal state with most political power residing in the 26 cantons, as well as local communities. Constitutional amendments can be initiated by a "popular initiative," and virtually all important legislation is subject to popular referendums. Each community has its own constitution and laws but is under the supervision of the canton. Each canton also has its own constitution and control over such things as school systems, police, welfare, and local issues. At these two levels, decisions are made by the people.

At the federal level, democracy becomes more representative. The Federal Assembly has two houses, one with representatives of the people (200-seat National Council) and one with representatives of the cantons (46-seat Council of States). The members are directly elected to four-year terms. Members elected to both bodies in 1995 face reelection in 1999. Several political parties have legislative representation, including the Free Democratic Party, Social Democratic Party, Christian Democratic People's Party, and Swiss People's Party.

A Federal Council constitutes the executive branch; it has seven members elected to a four-year term by the Federal Assembly. Each year, the council selects one council member to serves as its president. That person is then technically the president of Switzerland for a calendar year because that is the highest office in the land. A vice president is also chosen for a year. The federal government is responsible for foreign policy and matters affecting all cantons.

Economy

Despite a lack of natural resources, Switzerland has one of the strongest economies in the world. Its people enjoy a high real gross national product per capita ($22,580), second only to the United States. This figure reflects an economy with high standards of performance and a strong middle class. Poverty is nearly nonexistent. The economy grew 2 percent in 1994, ending a three-year recession. Unemployment is about 5 percent, while inflation remains low. Still, the Swiss people's refusal to join the EU (against the advice of Swiss business and political leaders) may eventually lead to slightly lower living standards in the future.

Switzerland is known as the banking and finance capital of the world. Its finance industry has fueled economic success. Tourism is a vital and driving force in the economy; industrial production is equally important. The Swiss not only produce fine watches and cheeses, but also machinery, chemicals, textiles, and various precision instruments. They are known for their excellent quality and craftsmanship. Switzerland donates money to various development projects around the world. The currency is the Swiss *franc* (SFr).

Education

Education is the responsibility of the individual cantons. Although there are differences between the systems, similarities can be found. Education is free and compulsory for eight or nine years, usually ending at age 16. There are three basic levels: primary, secondary, and high school (*gymnasia*). The high schools provide preparation for a university education. Many students choose to enter a vocational school after their secondary education. There are a number of private schools in addition to the state schools. Seven cantonal universities, two federal institutes of technology, a college of education, and a university for economic and social sciences serve more than 70 thousand students. Many students also travel abroad for advanced training. Switzerland spends a slightly lower percentage of its income on education and has a lower enrollment rate than many other industrialized countries. The adult literacy rate is 99 percent.

Transportation and Communication

Due to Switzerland's small land area and high population density, the country has a very well-developed public transportation system. Buses, streetcars, and trains form the backbone of the transportation network. Still, most families have cars, and private transport is common. Like the transportation network, communication facilities are excellent and completely modern. Numerous television and radio stations broadcast throughout the country, and daily newspapers are available everywhere.

Health

Both private and public hospitals exist. Medical facilities offer efficient care and personnel are well trained. While the government provides for such things as old-age benefits and social welfare, it does not have a uniform system of health insurance. Each canton has different laws regarding insurance, but most people must purchase private insurance. The infant mortality rate is 6 per 1,000. Life expectancy ranges from 75 to 82 years.

FOR THE TRAVELER

U.S. travelers do not need visas for stays of up to three months, but a valid passport is required. No vaccinations are necessary. Switzerland is a popular tourist destination and offers a wide variety of attractions and activities. The Swiss National Tourist Office produces a number of brochures for tourists, provides discount tickets for public transportation, and has ideas for travel itineraries. They have three offices in the United States: 222 North Sepulveda Boulevard, Suite 1570, El Segundo, CA 90245; phone (310) 640–8900; 150 North Michigan Avenue, Suite 2930, Chicago, IL 60601; phone (312) 630–5840; and 608 Fifth Avenue, Swiss Center, New York, NY 10020; phone (212) 757–5944. You may also wish to contact the Embassy of Switzerland, 2900 Cathedral Avenue NW, Washington, DC 20008; phone (202) 745–7900, or one of several consulates.

CULTURGRAM '97 ™

Republic of
Turkey

Boundary representations not necessarily authoritative.

BACKGROUND

Land and Climate

Turkey is located at the juncture where Europe meets Asia, forming a bridge and a link to each continent. Covering 301,382 square miles (780,580 square kilometers), Turkey is about the size of Texas. The western portion is called Thrace, while the eastern portion is known as Anatolia or Asia Minor. Several countries, as well as the Aegean, Mediterranean, and Black Seas, border the country. Anatolia is a plateau that becomes more mountainous to the east. Mountains are also found along the Black Sea. Both the Euphrates and Tigris Rivers flow through Turkey. The coastal regions are generally low. Winters can be very cold in some portions of the country, although they are mild along the coasts. Summers are pleasant but can be hot in some areas.

History

Modern Turkey is the most recent in a series of important states and empires that have inhabited the Anatolian peninsula since the beginning of history. The oldest known site of human urban habitation is located in central Turkey at Chatalhuyuk (6500 B.C.). The great Hittite Empire (3000–2000 B.C.), which dominated much of the Middle East, was centered east of Ankara. Ancient Troy, the scene of much of Homer's *Iliad*, was located near the Dardanelles. Alexander the Great captured Anatolia in the fourth century B.C., and the Romans followed three centuries later, establishing important cities, such as Ephesus and Antioch, as major provincial capitals.

In A.D. 330, the Roman Emperor Constantine founded the city of Constantinople, which later became the center of the Byzantine Empire. This great state dominated eastern Europe for one thousand years. The Muslim Seljuk Turks entered Asia Minor in the 11th century and began the long process of Islamization and Turkization. In 1453, the successors of the Seljuks, the Ottoman Turks, captured Constantinople and went on to create a vast empire, stretching beyond the bounds of the Byzantine Empire into the Balkans, the Middle East, and North Africa. The Ottoman Empire survived until World War I when it allied itself with the Central Powers. With the defeat of the Central Powers, the empire was dismembered.

In 1923, out of the ruins of the Ottoman Empire, General Mustafa Kemal (known as Atatürk) fashioned the Republic of Turkey. Under Atatürk, the nation was reformed from an Islamic empire to a secular state with an Islamic majority. Although most of Turkey is in Asia, it has always had important European ties. In 1952, Turkey joined the North Atlantic Treaty Organization (NATO) and provided land for a U.S. military base.

Over the next three decades, the country went through various cycles of political turmoil. In the late 1970s, serious economic problems and political upheaval, which nurtured widespread domestic terrorism, so paralyzed the government that the military seized control in 1980. The military restored stability, called for elections in 1983, and withdrew from power after the elections. The military commander responsible for these actions, Kenan Evran, was elected president. His prime minister, Turgut Özal, became the dominant political figure in the 1980s.

In 1989, Özal was elected by Parliament to be president for a seven-year term. Parliamentary elections in 1991 brought Özal's rival to power as prime minister. Suleyman Demirel had been prime minister before and was twice (1971 and 1980) ousted in coups. When Özal suddenly died in 1993, Demirel was elected by Parliament as the new president. Mrs. Tansu Ciller was chosen to replace Demirel and became Turkey's first female prime minister. Ciller's government was immediately faced with economic challenges and the ongoing insurgency by Kurdish rebels. A cease-fire declared in 1993 did not hold and violence only worsened. In 1995, Turkish troops swept into Northern Iraq to wipe out rebel bases from which Kurds had staged terrorist attacks. Some Kurdish leaders offered to end the fighting in exchange for more cultural rights, but rebels connected with the Marxist Kurdish Workers Party (PKK) prefer to fight and have expressed a desire to establish an independent Kurdish state.

PKK terrorist attacks and government retaliations against Kurds, a rise in Islamic conservatism, and economic difficulties combined to give the Islamic leader Necmettin Erbakan's Welfare Party (RP) a slim victory in December 1995 parliamentary elections. When the RP was unable to form a government, Ciller joined with a former rival to create a center-right coalition. When infighting caused that government to fall a few months later, Erbakan was given an opportunity to form a viable coalition. In June 1996, Erbakan worked out an arrangement in which he is to alternate with Ciller as prime minister, with each serving for one year at a time.

THE PEOPLE
Population
Turkey has 63.4 million inhabitants, a population that is growing at 2 percent annually. Ankara, the capital, has more than 3.5 million people. Istanbul (ten million), once called Constantinople, was the center of the Byzantine Empire. It is still the industrial, commercial, and intellectual center of the country. About 80 percent of the people are Turkish, 17 percent are Kurdish, and 3 percent belong to a variety of smaller groups. Kurds live mostly in the southeast. As in most cultures, urbanization has increased over the years, and 64 percent of Turkey's population now lives in urban areas. Turkey's Human Development Index (0.792) ranks it 66th out of 174 nations. Adjusted for women, the index (0.744) ranks Turkey 45th out of 130 countries. These figures indicate Turkey has done reasonably well in providing most citizens with the potential to live well and participate in society.

Language
Turkish, the official language, is related to the Uralic-Altaic languages spoken across Asia (from Finland to Manchuria). Arabic script was used during the Ottoman Empire period, but a Latin-based alphabet has been used since 1928. Most of the Kurdish minority speaks Kurdish. However, Kurdish was banned for many years and some people forgot how to use it. Bans on its use in education and domestic broadcasting are still in effect, but Kurdish can be used in some publications and public speaking. Arabic is also spoken. English is an increasingly popular second or third language.

Religion
Although 98 percent of Turkey's population is Sunni Muslim, the government makes it clear that Turkey is a secular state with complete freedom of religion. Islam's status as the state religion was abolished in 1923. Still, Islam maintains an important influence on society. This became even more significant when the Welfare Party nearly took national power through elections in 1995. The party still controls some city governments and its influence is seen in an increased observance of Islamic dress and other behavioral codes.

Muslims believe in one God, *Allah*, and that his will was revealed to the prophet Muhammad through the angel Gabriel. These revelations were recorded in the *Qur'an* (Koran), the holy book of Islam. Muslims accept many Judeo-Christian prophets but proclaim that Muhammed was the last and greatest. Throughout life, they strive to live the five pillars of Islam: professing Allah's name and Muhammad's role as prophet; fasting during the holy month of *Ramazan*; giving aid to the poor; making a pilgrimmage to Makkah, Saudi Arabia; and praying daily at five specific times.

General Attitudes
Turkey is often described as a bridge between East and West. Due to centuries of interaction with Europe and Asia, Turks have incorporated features from both areas into their lifestyle and thinking. At the same time, they are patriotic and have developed a unique society. The people are proud of the achievements of their modern state as well as the accomplishments of their ancestors, who ruled great empires. Turks consider their society to be progressive, Europe-leaning, and strongly influential in the region. They often feel misunderstood by European and other Western nations because of the often publicized Kurdish rebellion. Turkey is known in the United States, Turks believe, mostly for its past and the terrorist violence; Turks emphasize another side of the country, one that is modern and ethnically diverse but tolerant and democratic.

Individually, Turks prize a good sense of humor; it is considered a sign of intelligence. Group orientation is valued over personal assertiveness or aggression, and honesty and cleverness are admirable qualities. People value a good education, secure employment, social status, and an honorable heritage.

Personal Appearance
Western-style clothing is most common. European fashions are especially popular among the youth. Some Muslim women may wear a turban (scarf) to cover their hair. Some traditional costumes are still worn in rural areas or for special occasions. The design of a costume's headdress and the type of material used signify a person's social status.

CUSTOMS AND COURTESIES
Greetings
When greeting friends or strangers, one shakes hands and says *Nasilsiniz* (How are you?) or *Merhaba* (Hello). A typical response to *Nasilsiniz* is *Iyiyim, teshekur ederim* (Fine, thank you). Greetings among friends are followed by polite inquiries about one's health, family, and work. Among close friends of the same (or sometimes the opposite) gender, Turks clasp hands and kiss on both cheeks when greeting. To show respect to an older person, their hands may be kissed and touched to the greeter's forehead. The youth often greet each other with *Selam* (Salute). Someone entering a room, office, or teahouse might say *Günaydin* (Good morning) or *Iyi günler* (Have a nice day). When parting, it is customary to wish for blessings from *Allah* (*Allahaısmarladık*) and respond agreeably (*Güle güle*).

Upon joining a small group, one greets each person in the group individually. When addressing others formally, one uses professional titles. Otherwise, the title *Hanım* is used for women and *Bey* for men among peers or with younger persons. These follow the given name: *Leyla Hanım* or *Ismail Bey*. With older people, one uses *Abla* for women (*Fatma Abla*) or *Aabey* for men (*Ahmet Aabey*). These terms mean "sister" and "brother." If there is a great age difference, one uses *Teyze* (aunt) and *Amca* (uncle) after the first name.

Urban people generally do not greet strangers when passing on the street; rural people are more likely to greet strangers.

Gestures

Turks generally use their hands a great deal during conversation, forming gestures that add meaning and emphasis.

Social courtesies are valued in Turkey. One does not put feet on a desk or table, point the sole of the foot toward another person, smoke without asking permission, or cross the legs while in the presence of an older or superior person. It is not proper for adults to eat or smoke on the street. Public displays of affection are not acceptable. To some more traditional people, it is an insult to pass an item with the left hand. "No" can be expressed by either shaking the head or lifting it up once quickly.

Visiting

Turks enjoy visiting one another in their homes, and hospitality is an integral part of the culture. Friends, relatives, and neighbors visit often. In large cities, people call ahead, but this is not practical in smaller villages, where unexpected visits occur more frequently. As hospitality is customary, guests are always invited in and offered refreshments. This usually involves something to drink (tea, coffee, soda) and sometimes to eat (crackers and cookies). It is impolite to decline these refreshments. Many Turks remove their shoes when entering a home and replace them with slippers. Guests are expected to do the same at homes where this custom is followed. Visitors are expected to bring a pleasant presence to the home; bad news or accounts of problems are saved for other occasions and locations. It is not polite to ask personal questions of hosts. First-time visitors to a home may bring a small gift, such as candy, fruit, or flowers. Turks work hard to make their guests feel comfortable. For example, even if the hosts do not think smoking is appropriate, they may allow visitors to smoke in their homes.

Eating

Breakfast is usually eaten around 7:00 A.M., or earlier in rural areas. Lunch is at midday and dinner is around 7:00 P.M. Dinner is the main meal and the family generally expects to sit down together for this meal.

Eating habits vary with the region and the food being eaten. Turks generally observe the continental style of eating, with the fork in the left hand and the knife remaining in the right. Some foods are eaten with the hand. To begin or end a meal, one might say *Afiyet Olsun* (May what you eat bring you well-being). One may compliment the cook on the meal by saying *Elinize saglik* (roughly, Bless your hand). Meals can be lavish, and Turks are quite proud of their rich cuisine. Types of restaurants range from those offering fast-food to international cuisine, but the most common is the Turkish kebab restaurant. Some restaurants include a service charge in the bill (about 10 percent), in which case a 5 percent tip is customary. If no service charge is included, a 15 percent tip should be given.

LIFESTYLE

Family

The primary social unit in Turkey is the family. In rural areas, traditional, patriarchal values prevail. An individual is loyal to and dependent upon the family. The Turkish household often consists of an extended family: a mother and father, their unmarried children, and, in some cases, married sons with their families. The married sons remain until they are financially independent. In urban areas, nuclear families are the standard and traditional authority structures are less pronounced. It is uncommon for a person to live alone, mostly for economic reasons. Polygamy, as permitted by Islamic law, was abolished in 1930. Women gained the right to vote in 1927 and the right to divorce in 1934 when civil marriage contracts were introduced. Urban women frequently work outside the home. Thirty-three percent of the labor force is female.

Dating and Marriage

Except perhaps at universities or in large urban areas, dating in the Western sense is not common. Young people associate more in groups. In the cities, this association is generally open and casual. In rural areas, chaperones are common. Rural families are heavily involved in deciding who a person will marry, but the choice is generally the couple's in urban areas. It is against the law for women to marry before age 15 and men before age 17. In the cities, many wait to marry until they have completed their education and sometimes military service. Hence, the average age for marriage is 22 for women and 25 for men. Most Turks expect to marry and have children.

Traditional wedding celebrations last three days and are still practiced by some in rural areas. Urban couples often follow more European traditions when marrying. Traditional festivities begin with the *Kına Gecesi* (henna evening), an event only for women. They decorate the hands and fingers of the bride with henna leaf dye and dance and sing. On the second day, both sets of parents serve lunch and dinner to their guests. On the third day, the bride is taken to the groom's home on a horse after folk dances are performed. This tradition is increasingly rare because of the time and expense involved.

Diet

Turkish cuisine is among the finest in the world. Lamb and rice are served with many meals. Seafood is more abundant along the coast. The famous *kahve* (Turkish coffee), a thick brew served in very small cups, is served with nearly every meal. Breakfast is usually light, consisting of tea, white cheese, bread, butter, marmalade or honey, and olives. The main meal of the day is eaten in the evening and may consist of several courses. Turkish cuisine is famous for many things, among them the *meze*, a tray or table of hors d'oeuvres, including stuffed grape leaves, salads, shrimp, and a variety of other items. There are also many unique Turkish soups. Shish kebabs (chunks of lamb on a skewer) are a favorite, as are vegetables prepared in olive oil. Rice *pilav* is common. Turkish desserts are famously sweet, including *baklava* (syrup-dipped pastry) and *muhallebi* (milk pudding). The most popular drink next to coffee is *raki*, a drink made of fermented grapes (not a wine).

Recreation

The most popular sport for both spectators and participants is soccer, which was introduced by the British in the 19th century. Volleyball, basketball, cycling, grease wrestling, traditional wrestling, swimming, and a variety of other sports are also enjoyed. Picnics are common family activities. August is the month for most vacations. During their leisure time, urban residents may watch television, eat out, visit others, or attend movies. Women often do volunteer work. Rural women visit one another in their homes or watch television. Men throughout the country gather at teahouses (like cafés) to socialize. When at home, they also watch television. Folk dancing and other cultural arts are popular.

Holidays

The ninth month of the Muslim lunar calendar is *Ramazan*, during which practicing Muslims fast from dawn to dusk. At the end of *Ramazan* is a three-day holiday called *Seker Bayrami* (sugar holiday), during which sweets are eaten to celebrate the end of the fast. A second Muslim holiday is *Kurban Bayrami* (sacrifice holiday), which marks the season of pilgrimage to Makkah. It also commemorates Abraham's willingness to sacrifice his son. An animal is usually sacrificed and the meat distributed to the poor. Other official holidays include New Year's Day, National Sovereignty Day (23 April, also Children's Day), Atatürk's Memorial Day and Youth Day (19 May), Victory Day (30 August), and Republic Day (29 October).

Commerce

Businesses are generally open from 9:00 A.M. to 5:00 P.M., Monday through Friday. Some are open for a half day on Saturday. Most people buy fresh produce at open-air markets but get other goods from supermarkets (in large cities) or neighborhood shops.

SOCIETY

Government

Turkey is a parliamentary democracy composed of 73 provinces. The president is head of state; the prime minister is head of government. The Grand National Assembly (Parliament) has 550 members. In addition to the Welfare Party, major parties include Ciller's True Path Party and the Motherland Party. The voting age is 21.

Economy

Agriculture is the traditional backbone of the economy, once providing the bulk of all exports. Today, it still employs half of the labor force and accounts for one-fifth of all exports. Chief agricultural products include cotton, tobacco, fruit, cereals, nuts, and opium for medicine. Manufacturing employs 15 percent of the labor force but accounts for nearly 60 percent of all exports. Its success is therefore vital to the economy. Mining and tourism are also important. Turkey enjoyed solid growth until about 1993, when mismanagement and other problems sent inflation above 100 percent and led to economic decline for 1994 and 1995. Industrial production slipped, and many factories laid off workers or cut output. The government implemented reform measures to address

the problems. A high number of migrants, especially in Istanbul, has increased unemployment and strained urban infrastructure. Real gross domestic product per capita is $5,230, which has tripled since 1960. Income distribution is unequal: urban residents enjoy far higher incomes than rural people or migrants. The currency is the Turkish *lira* (£T).

Transportation and Communication

Around major urban areas, the roads are paved and in good condition. In rural areas, infrastructure is generally adequate but not always well maintained. Taxis, buses, streetcars, and *dolmus* (shared taxis) provide public transportation. The railroad is used for travel between cities, as are the airways. Turkey is connected with other countries by international air links. The overall communications system is fairly good, with several television and radio stations broadcasting throughout the country. The press is free and active. Telephone service is best in urban areas.

Education

Primary and secondary education is free and coeducational. Primary schooling lasts five years and secondary education lasts three. Additional years are possible to about age 17. Nearly all children complete the primary level, and about half go on to the secondary level. A foreign language is required. Exams determine university entrance. There are more than 25 universities in Turkey, the oldest of which was founded at Istanbul in 1453. Some 250 specialized colleges and institutions offer vocational and other training. Adult literacy averages 81 percent. It is higher among men and urban residents.

Health

The government provides basic health care, but it is not sufficient to meet the country's needs. Urban facilities are generally modern and adequate, but rural facilities are not as well equipped. Besides public health care, institutions such as the military, state-owned enterprises, etc., provide care to their personnel. Reform measures have been introduced to address the most serious problems, including a relatively high infant mortality rate (46 per 1,000) attributed to poor education about child care and the lack of family planning. The government seeks to reduce the figure to fewer than 30 by the year 2000 through improved child immunizations, prenatal care, education, and other programs. Life expectancy averages 72 years.

FOR THE TRAVELER

U.S. citizens need a valid passport and visa to enter Turkey. For tourist visits of less than three months, a visa can be obtained at the border. Bottled water is recommended. Fruits and vegetables should be cleaned and peeled before eating. Air pollution in the winter, particularly in Ankara, can be hazardous to those suffering from respiratory ailments. A number of interesting sites are worth visiting. For information regarding travel opportunities, contact the Turkish Tourist Office, 821 United Nations Plaza, New York, NY 10017. You may also wish to contact the Turkish Embassy's Tourist Office, 1717 Massachusetts Avenue NW, Suite 306, Washington, DC 20036; phone (202) 429–9844.

CULTURGRAM™ '97

Ukraine

Boundary representations not necessarily authoritative.

BACKGROUND

Land and Climate

Ukraine, located in southeastern Europe, covers 233,089 square miles (603,700 square kilometers) and is slightly smaller than Texas. It is dominated by large plains (steppes) with fertile soil covering more than half of the area. One-third of the world's black soils are in Ukraine, giving it great potential as a food producer. Forests cover some 13 percent of the territory, chiefly in the Carpathian Mountains on the western border. The Crimean Peninsula extends into the Black Sea, with its northeastern coast on the Sea of Azov and its southern coast marked by the Crimean Mountains. Major rivers flowing through Ukraine include the Dnipro, Dnister, Donets, Dunai (Danube), and Buh. Europe's largest wetland (Prypiat Marshes) is located in a forested northern basin of the Dnipro and Prypiat Rivers. Ukraine has cold winters and cool summers, except in the Crimea, where a Mediterranean climate prevails.

History

Ukraine has been continuously inhabited since about 1500 B.C., but the Slavic ancestors of today's Ukrainians did not begin to settle the region until the seventh century A.D. In the eighth and ninth centuries, seven Slavic tribes merged under the leadership of a Norse tribe (Varangians) to form the state of Kievan Rus'. A prominent early leader, Volodymyr I (ruled 980–1015), converted to Christianity and established close ties with the Byzantine (Eastern Orthodox) Church. Kievan Rus' weakened in the 12th and 13th centuries to the point that Mongol invasions in 1220 and 1240

destroyed the state. Despite some independent principalities, the Ukrainians were without unity and autonomy for many centuries. The Mongols held the east even as expansionist Poland and Lithuania controlled the west. The Mongols were eventually forced out, and by the mid-1500s Poland and Lithuania (which had merged) controlled most Ukrainian lands. The Poles introduced Western Christianity, which clashed with the traditional Eastern Christianity of the people and embittered them against their rulers.

Rebellion soon followed, most notably from a group of militants called Cossacks. They functioned with autonomy because of their military capacity and soon challenged Poland and, by extension, the Roman Catholic Church. The Cossacks waged a national liberation war (1648–54) under the leadership of Cossack Bohdan Khmelnytsky. A Cossack state was carved out of the east (the west remained with Poland), and it prospered for a century. During the reign of Russia's Catherine the Great, Russia defeated the Cossacks (1775) and took control of the east. It gained control over the west that same year by partitioning Poland. Ukraine became a Russian province and so remained until the monarchy fell in 1917.

Ukraine declared independence but was occupied by Germany in World War I and then forcibly incorporated into the Soviet Union (USSR) in 1922. Communist repression was greatest under Stalin, who collectivized farms and thereby caused a famine that took seven million lives. Dissidents were executed and the Ukrainian language was banned.

Independence became increasingly desirable even as the USSR added territory (Crimea) to Ukraine and developed its industry to further integrate it into the Soviet system. The language ban was lifted and repression eased after Stalin's death. Disaster struck the republic in 1986 with the meltdown of a nuclear reactor at Chornobyl (north of Kyiv). Radioactive fallout from the accident killed many Ukrainians, ruined the surrounding land, and affected much of Eastern Europe. In 1996, Ukraine announced it will eventually replace remaining Chornobyl reactors.

Hopes for independence strengthened as the Soviet Empire weakened, and local elections in 1990 paved the way for official independence in August 1991. Leonid Kravchuk became the first president. Regional issues such as a dispute with Russia over control of the former Soviet Black Sea fleet, Ukraine's possession of nuclear weapons, and demands in Crimea for autonomy somewhat hindered progress on economic and social fronts. But Ukraine did attract some foreign investment and aid. Elections in 1994 brought Leonid Kuchma to office as president, a post he strengthened in 1995 when Parliament granted him greater authority to control the course of reform. Declining living standards led Kuchma to slow economic liberalization for several months, but he reinstated reform programs in 1996 to obtain vital International Monetary Fund loans.

PEOPLE

Population

The population of Ukraine, 51.8 million, is growing annually at 0.04 percent. Ethnic Ukrainians comprise 73 percent of the population, while Russians account for 22 percent. In Crimea, Russians make up two-thirds of the population and have voiced a desire to be more closely associated with Russia. Smaller groups in Ukraine include the Tatars, Poles, Germans, Hungarians, Romanians, and Greeks. Tatars live in Crimea but lack citizenship rights. They were expelled in 1944 for working with German occupation forces and returned in smaller numbers only in 1989. More than seven million ethnic Ukrainians also reside in western Europe, North America, and other areas. Two-thirds of all people live in urban areas. Kyiv, the capital, is the largest and oldest city; its population is more than 2.5 million. Other major cities include Kharkiv, Odesa, L'viv, and Dnipropetrovsk.

Ukraine's Human Develoment Index (0.842) ranks it 54th out of 174 nations, meaning people have some degree of access to resources that would enable them to pursue personal goals.

Language

Ukrainian is a Slavic language written in the Cyrillic alphabet of 33 letters. It is the official and most commonly spoken language. During the Soviet period, Russian was also official and was the language of instruction in secondary schools and universities. Russian is no longer as prominent, but it is the primary language of ethnic Russians. Minorities also speak their languages, including Polish, Hungarian, and Romanian. More than half of the population is bilingual. New language laws guarantee ethnic minorities the right to use their native language for public and judicial business.

Religion

Christianity is the dominant religion of Ukraine, represented by Orthodox (Russian and Ukrainian), Greek Catholic (Uniate), and Roman Catholic Churches. The Ukrainian Orthodox Church split in 1992 from its parent Orthodox church in Russia; it has no official status. Catholicism is found only in the west. Communism led many people to abandon their beliefs. As a whole, however, Ukrainians maintained their religious heritage. When religious freedom was allowed in the late 1980s, Christianity began to revive. This intensified with independence, and today Christians also include small but growing groups of Protestants and other denominations. Jews now represent only 1 percent of the population, but their numbers were much higher prior to World War II. Ukraine is home to many sacred Jewish sites.

General Attitudes

Ukrainians consider themselves a merry people, prone to singing and dancing. They appreciate openness and wit, as well as humor. Individualism is also valued, although it was somewhat muted during the Soviet era. Friendships play an important role for most Ukrainians, and neighbors are generally supportive of each other.

Nationalism is a strong tendency in most people, given the long struggle for independence. Pride in the national heritage and appreciation for resisters of oppression serve as a basis for Ukrainian patriotism. Ukrainian culture was preserved through folk songs and legends, which are now highly treasured. Ukrainians also appreciate traditional art, including embroidered clothing and tapestries. The country is known worldwide for the delicate art of Easter egg painting (*pysanka*), an art still practiced with great skill today.

Despite people's general optimism, Ukrainian society is in great transition. Those accustomed to Soviet work patterns are learning the meaning and value of private enterprise, individual labor, and personal initiative. At the same time, Ukranians have been faced with economic hardships and other problems that challenge their positive outlook on life.

Personal Appearance

Urban fashions are similar to those in other European countries. Men wear suits, ties, and hats. Women wear pantsuits, dresses, and skirts. Clothing is often imported and quite expensive, but many women have sewing machines and make clothes for their family. They also knit sweaters, hats, and scarves for the winter. Taste and tidiness are important; it is improper to wear wrinkled or soiled clothes.

Rural fashions lag behind urban ones, with more traditional styles dominating. Likewise, the older generation is more conservative; elderly women usually wear dresses and cover their heads with scarves.

On special occasions, like weddings, festivals, and religious holidays, people wear the national outfit, *vyshyvankas*—shirts embroidered in patterns that have not changed for centuries.

CUSTOMS AND COURTESIES

Greetings

When meeting informally, men and women usually wave the hand and give a verbal greeting like *Pryvit* (Hi) or *Dobryj den'* (Good day). *Dobryj den'* is also appropriate in formal situations, in which case people often shake hands. Men wait for women to extend their hand first. In official situations, people address each other by professional title or *Pan* (Mr.), *Pani* (Mrs.), *Panna* (Miss), or *Panove* (Sirs or Gentlemen).

Relatives and close friends often hug and kiss cheeks when greeting. They address each other by first name. A respectful form of address is using the first name followed by the patronymic, which is the father's given name and a gender-specific (for son or daughter) suffix.

Gestures

Ukrainians use hand and body gestures only moderately in daily conversation. It is important to establish eye contact a few times (but not constantly) during a conversation. People express approval by giving "thumbs up." Pointing with the index finger is considered uncultured, but some people do it anyway. To speak to a superior (teacher, boss, official, or senior) with one's hands in the pockets or arms folded across the chest is viewed as disrespectful and cause for reprimand. Chewing gum is similarly improper.

Women expect some chivalry from men. It is rude for a man not to open a door for a woman. Men commonly help women carry heavy items or at least offer to do so.

Visiting

Because of the Ukrainian tradition of hospitality, both expected and unexpected guests are welcome. Still, visits arranged in advance are preferred whenever possible. Friends, neighbors, and relatives often visit just to socialize. In these cases, hosts always offer guests tea or coffee and some refreshments. Dinner guests are offered a meal that is more than abundant and are expected to stay for a while afterwards. They commonly present their hosts with flowers, cake, or a bottle of liquor or with candy or toys for the children.

Guests remove footwear when they enter a home. They do not sit on the floor or put their feet on furniture. It is polite to stand when a woman enters the room.

Eating

People eat a light *snidanok* (breakfast) in the morning before leaving for school or work. The main meal, eaten in mid-afternoon, is called *obid*. It consists of two main courses, the first being some kind of soup, the second containing meat or fish. Working people usually bring food from home or go to canteens (cafés) for *obid*. The third meal, *vechera*, is eaten at 6:00 or 7:00 P.M. and is usually the time when family members eat together. People generally eat out only on special occasions.

When eating, Ukrainians usually keep hands (not elbows) on the table. Placing them in one's lap is improper. The fork is held in the left hand and the knife in the right. Leaving food on the plate is considered wasteful. Guests honor hosts when they ask for or accept second helpings.

LIFESTYLE

Family

The family unit is important in Ukraine and extended family ties are valued. The average family has two children and is led by the father. Both parents usually work outside the home. Child care is expensive and in short supply. Many elderly parents live with their adult children, and they often assume responsibility for daily child care. Women perform all household chores.

The elderly are treated with love and respect. It is a common practice for parents to support children until they reach adulthood and even after they are married. In turn, children expect to care for aging parents when it becomes necessary. When parents live in the country and adult children in the city, the latter may send their children to live with the grandparents for several weeks during the summer.

The usual home for urban families is a small one- or two-bedroom apartment. Most affordable apartments are leased from the government; renting from a private owner is expensive. Few people own their apartments. Suburban families have most modern conveniences (electricity, gas, and water), but rural people have much simpler houses.

Dating and Marriage

Young people meet at discos and concerts, in school and at work, as well as through friends. When dating, they usually visit friends, go to bars or movies, or dance at discos. From April to October, they spend a lot of time in parks, engaging in a variety of outdoor activities. Young couples usually marry in their early twenties. A marriage is legal only if performed in a "Wedding Palace," but most couples today also have a religious ceremony.

Urban wedding parties are fancy but do not involve much tradition. On the other hand, rural weddings are big events that usually last for three days. Such weddings resemble a combination of a grand party and a performance, since many people are responsible for performing traditional acts. For example, at some point the bride must be "stolen." The successful thieves "demand" a ransom for her return.

Diet

Vegetables, breads, dairy products, and starchy foods are basic staples. Ukraine is one of the few areas in Europe where corn-on-the-cob is eaten. The most popular Ukrainian dishes are made of cereal grains and flour pastes. Common grains include buckwheat, oats, and millet. Rice is imported. Popular dishes include *varenyky* (dumplings), *holubtsi* (cabbage leaves stuffed with ground meat and rice), and *kasha* (cooked or baked cereal). *Kasha* is served with either meat or poultry. Pork and beef are the favorite meats. Chicken Kyiv is known worldwide. Soup is essential. *Borsch,* the most popular soup, usually contains cabbage, beets, potatoes, and carrots; meat is optional. It can be served hot or cold, with or without sour cream, and there are several varieties according to locality and season.

Ukrainians enjoy such seasonal fruits as apples, pears, plums, strawberries, and melons. If available, fresh produce is very expensive in the winter, so in summer and autumn people make numerous preserves for the winter months.

Recreation

On weekends, young people enjoy leaving the city and camping on a riverbank or in the woods. Mountain climbing, hiking, and skiing are popular activities. In the summer, people enjoy swimming, volleyball, soccer, and table tennis. Fishing and soccer are especially popular with men. Watching television or visiting friends is a typical leisure activity.

Urban people with *dachas* (country houses) spend much time there tending a garden, making preserves, and relaxing. People without *dachas* often have a small plot of land near the city on which to grow a garden.

Theaters and musical concerts are available in cities. Rural people get together on weekends to play music, sing, and dance. Traditional instruments still played in Ukraine include the *sopilka* (flute), *volynka* (horn pipe), and *bandura* (stringed instrument); the *bandura* is the national instrument of Ukraine. Literature is important to Ukrainians and most read avidly.

Holidays

Celebrated on 25 December by Catholics and on 7 January by Orthodox Christians, Christmas is the most popular holiday. During the Christmas season, which also includes New Year's, people decorate fir trees and have parties. Children enjoy *koliadki*, when they go door-to-door and receive candy and cookies in exchange for songs and jokes. National holidays include International Women's Day (8 March), Solidarity Day (1 May), Victory Day (9 May), and Independence Day (24 August). An old holiday (Soviet Army Day, 23 February) is unofficially celebrated as a sort of Men's Day. On Women's Day, women receive flowers and gifts, household help from husbands, and a day off from work. Special attention is paid to mothers, and girls are congratulated as future women. Victory Day marks the end of World War II and is extremely important for most families.

Religious holidays are regaining prominence. Ukrainians observe most of these by visiting, having parties, and sometimes exchanging presents.

Commerce

Offices are open weekdays from 8:00 or 9:00 A.M., closed for an hour lunch break around 2:00 P.M., and open again until 5:00 or 6:00 P.M. Stores and services are open an hour earlier and two hours later. A banking system has not yet fully developed.

Prices are fixed in stores, but people bargain in the markets. Small street boutiques offer imported goods not often available in stores. The old business structure is just now being replaced by a capitalist market, and the transitional period has produced some inconsistencies and difficulties for entrepreneurs. The younger generation is more business oriented than those who were used to the Communist system.

SOCIETY

Government

Ukraine is a parliamentary democracy led by a strong executive president. Parliament (*Verkhovna Rada*) has 450 directly elected members. A large number of political parties are represented. The prime minister, Yevgeny Marchuk, was appointed in June 1995. All citizens may vote at age 18.

Economy

Ukraine was the Soviet Union's "bread basket" because it produced more than one-fourth of the USSR's agriculture. The potential for agriculture to be the basis of Ukraine's growing economy exists, but it cannot be tapped without significant reform. The government is privatizing farms as the first vital step, but farms must be modernized and laborers must adjust to wage work. Large coal and iron deposits contributed to the development of a large industrial base that produced goods for many other republics. In fact, Ukraine was the second (behind Russia) most productive Soviet republic. But industry also requires materials from outside Ukraine, and these can be purchased only with hard (convertible) currencies that are in short supply. The country also has a large defense industry (space and nuclear) that must be converted into consumer-oriented firms before it can be useful.

Political uncertainties in the early 1990s hindered economic growth, but future prospects are strong. Real gross domestic product per capita is $5,010. Most people can meet basic needs. Inflation fell to less than 25 percent in 1996. The *kupon* is a transitional currency eventually to be replaced by the *hryven'*.

Transportation and Communication

Urban public transportation is efficient. Street cars, buses, and trolleys are the main means of transport, but major cities also have subways. Most families do not own cars. Roads are extensive but often in poor repair. Fuel is expensive. This makes taxis expensive and not always easy to find. Unofficial "taxis" often pick up people who ask for a ride.

Rural people get around on bicycles; buses or trains take them to nearby towns. The railroad network is developed, although trains are in need of modernization. Air Ukraine is the domestic airline. Telephone and postal services are currently inadequate for a modern economy, but they will receive attention as general conditions improve. The press is free and active, but the government currently owns all radio and television stations.

Education

Education is highly valued in Ukraine and the literacy rate is more than 95 percent. Children begin attending elementary school at age six and must attend until age fourteen, when they finish middle school. At this point, they have several options: go to high school and prepare to enter a university, work in the day and attend evening school, train at schools specializing in certain careers, or enter job-training programs. Universities are located in major cities. Entrance exams are required by all institutions of higher education.

Health

Medical care is free but service is poor. Facilities often experience basic supply shortages, and hospitals lack modern equipment and procedures necessary to give patients adequate care. Pollution levels are high and tap water is not safe to drink. Cancer and other problems stemming from the Chornobyl nuclear accident continue to afflict a large portion of the population. Ukraine's infant mortality rate is 20 per 1,000; life expectancy is about 70 years.

FOR THE TRAVELER

To enter Ukraine, U.S. citizens must have a valid passport and obtain a visa in advance. A visa applicant must show a letter of invitation from someone in Ukraine or a voucher from a tour company. Travelers staying more than three working days must register with local authorities, either through a hotel, business, or their private host. Only cash is accepted at most places. For more information, contact the Embassy of Ukraine, 3350 M Street NW, Washington, DC 20007; phone (202) 333–7507. Tourist information may also be obtained from Inturyst-Ukraine, Vulytsya Hospitalna 12, Kyiv, Ukraine.

Printed on recycled paper

CULTURGRAM '97

United States of America

ALASKA

Anchorage

HAWAII

Honolulu

Boundary representations not necessarily authoritative.

Seattle
Portland
CANADA
Minneapolis
Detroit
Boston
San Francisco
Salt Lake City
Chicago
New York
Philadelphia
Pacific Ocean
Las Vegas
Denver
Kansas City
St. Louis
WASHINGTON, D.C.
Los Angeles
Phoenix
Nashville
San Diego
Dallas
Atlanta
Atlantic Ocean
Houston
MEXICO
New Orleans
Gulf of Mexico
Miami

BACKGROUND

Land and Climate

The United States covers the central portion of North America and includes Alaska and Hawaii. Covering 3,618,765 square miles (9,372,610 square kilometers), it is the fourth largest country in the world. Because of its size and location, the United States experiences many different climates and has a variety of geographical features. Large mountains, vast deserts, wide canyons, extensive coasts, subtropical forests, wetlands, rolling hills, prairies, frozen tundra, and more features can be found. Beyond the beaches and mountains of California, the Rocky Mountains in the west give way to a vast central plain, which merges with the rolling hills and low mountains of the east. Hawaii's rugged, volcanic topography is lush and green year round. Alaska has towering mountains, broad valleys, glaciers, and a varied landscape. Climates throughout the country are as varied as the terrain. Natural resources include coal, copper, lead, uranium, bauxite, gold, phosphate, iron, mercury, nickel, silver, petroleum, natural gas, timber, and much more. Natural disasters, such as floods, hurricanes, tornadoes, earthquakes, and severe winter storms, impact various regions.

History

North America's history before Europeans arrived is incomplete, but the original inhabitants had advanced civilizations. From the 17th century on, Native Americans were displaced by European settlers who had come for riches, territory, and a "new world." British colonies (the thirteen colonies) were established on the east coast of North America. The American Revolution of 1776 led to independence from Britain and a loose confederation of states. The Constitution of 1787 established the basic form of government as it exists today. Explorers and pioneers headed west and settled large areas of land. The United States acquired territory from France, Mexico, Russia, and Spain throughout the '19th century, expanding its borders from the Atlantic Ocean to the Pacific.

In 1861, civil war broke out between Union states in the north and Confederate states in the south over issues of slavery, secession, and economic differences. Union forces, under President Abraham Lincoln, defeated the Confederates in 1865 and reunited the country.

American troops were only involved in the last year of World War I, but the United States was a major combatant in World War II and emerged as the strongest economic and military power in the world. It became a major donor of financial aid and technological assistance to developing countries and spread American values and ideals throughout the world (which were not always welcome). In the 1970s, after the U.S. defeat in Vietnam, American prominence declined. This trend seemed to reverse toward the beginning of the 1990s. Americans consider their country a guardian of democracy and freedom, as well as a promoter of peace. Although U.S. leadership has not always been in the best interest of all parties involved, it was pivotal in the 1991 Gulf War. It is currently vital to the ongoing Middle East peace process, peace efforts among former Yugoslav republics, democratization in

Haiti and other lands, and in international free-trade negotiations. The United States is an active member of the the United Nations and a key donor of international aid. It has always had free elections to determine its leadership.

THE PEOPLE

Population

The population of the United States (about 264 million) is the third largest in the world, following China and India. Eighty-two percent of America's population is white, which includes people of European, Middle Eastern, and Hispanic origins. Other racial groups include African Americans (12 percent), Asians (3 percent), and Native Americans (1 percent). Hispanics, who can be of any race, comprise 9 percent of the total population. *Hispanic* is an artificial term not always accepted by members of that diverse group. Most Hispanics (or Latinos) prefer to be called by their country of origin (e.g., Mexican American). The term *Hispanic* is only used here to identify a group that consists of many peoples otherwise too diverse to list. Indeed, all designated minority groups are represented by many smaller groups with origins in nearly every country around the world. Primarily due to immigration, Asians are the fastest-growing minority.

Although members of any ethnic group can be found anywhere in the country, the mixture is not the same in every region. For example, California's population is only 57 percent white, while New Hampshire's is 98 percent. Hispanics reside mostly in the west and southwest, while African Americans live mostly in the east and southeast. More than 60 percent of the people in Hawaii are Asians. Whites commonly live in rural and suburban areas, while minorities tend to live in large urban areas. Nearly 80 percent of all Americans live in metropolitan areas. *American* is the term most often used to describe a citizen or product of the United States, even outside of the country.

The United States's Human Development Index (0.937) ranks it second out of 174 countries. Most Americans enjoy access to education, adequate health care, and economic prosperity that is needed to make choices in their lives. Adjusted for women, the index (0.901) ranks the United States fifth out of 130 countries.

Language

English is the predominant language of the United States and is spoken by most citizens. The English spoken in the United States is referred to in other English-speaking nations as *American English*. It is characterized by spelling and pronunciation variations from *British English*, as well as unique idioms. Spoken English is very flexible, while written communication is more formal and standardized. Many first-, second-, or even third-generation immigrants also speak their native tongue. In fact, one in seven Americans speaks a language other than English in the home. Spanish is spoken in many Hispanic communities. Native Americans speak a variety of Amerindian languages.

Religion

Although the United States has never had an official state church, about 95 percent of the population professes some religious beliefs. Most Americans (80–85 percent) are Christians. Early European settlers were primarily Christian, and the Constitution and Bill of Rights are based, in part, on Christian values and principles. However, the Constitution dictates that church and state remain separate. There are scores of different Christian churches throughout the country. About 24 percent of the population is Roman Catholic. Baptists, Methodists, and Lutherans are the largest Protestant groups; more than half of all Americans belong to these or other Protestant organizations. Other Christian denominations account for another 3 to 5 percent of the total. Between 40 and 50 percent of Christians attend religious services weekly. Jews (2 percent), Muslims, Buddhists, and other non-Christians also have substantial memberships in the United States. About 10 to 15 percent of Americans have no religious affiliation but may still have spiritual faith or convictions. Religion is generally a personal matter for Americans, but those with an active interest in it often discuss their beliefs with others.

General Attitudes

Americans are frank and outspoken. They openly voice their opinions and share their views on a variety of subjects. In general, they appreciate people who are candid. There are few subjects that an American will not discuss. Of course, there are exceptions, and religious values may keep some from discussing certain issues. Those who are not close friends avoid extremely personal questions. Americans value innovation, industry, and integrity. They enjoy a good sense of humor, including sarcasm. Americans have the ability to laugh at themselves as well as at others. They are proud of their country. Even though they may criticize the government, most are patriotic and believe the United States is one of the greatest countries in the world. Americans strongly value their freedom and independence, both as a nation and as individuals. Individualism, as opposed to conformity, is often cited as an American characteristic. Even when working as a team, Americans usually think in terms of several distinct individuals blending their efforts rather than a group working as one unit.

Personal Appearance

Although fashion trends affect general clothing patterns, Americans usually feel free to wear whatever they please. Some use clothing to make a social or personal statement. Americans emphasize cleanliness but may purposely wear tattered clothing or casual attire in public. Dressing "down" (casually) is a trend in the workplace; still, suits for men and pantsuits, dresses, or skirts for women are standard attire in many offices. Formal clothing is worn for certain social occasions. Appearance, in general, is important to the individual American.

CUSTOMS AND COURTESIES

Greetings

Both men and women usually smile and shake hands when greeting. The American handshake is often firm. Good friends and family members may embrace when they meet, especially after a long absence. In casual situations, people may wave instead of shaking hands. Friends also often wave to each other at a distance. Americans may greet strangers on the street by saying *Hello* or *Good morning*, although they may pass without any greeting. Among the youth, verbal greetings or various hand-slapping gestures (such as the "high five") are common. Except in formal situations, people who are acquainted address one another by given name. Combining a title (*Mrs.*, *Dr.*, *Miss*, for example) with a family name shows respect. When greeting someone for the first time, Americans commonly say *Nice to meet you* or *How do you do?* A simple *Hello* or *Hi* is also common. There are regional variations, such as *Aloha* in Hawaii or *Howdy* in parts of the west. Friends often greet each other with *How are you?* and respond *Fine, thanks.* Americans do not really expect any further answer to the question.

Gestures

When conversing, Americans generally stand about two feet away from each other. However, they may spontaneously touch one another on the arm or shoulder during conversation. Members of the opposite sex may hold hands or show affection in public. To point, a person extends the index finger. One beckons by waving all fingers (or the index finger) with the palm facing up. Direct eye contact is not necessary for the duration of a conversation, but moments of eye contact are essential to ensure one's sincerity. When sitting, Americans are casual. They may prop their feet on chairs, place the ankle of one leg on the knee of the other, cross legs at the knee, or sit with legs spread apart. Poor posture is not appropriate but is not uncommon. People often hand items to one another with one hand and may even toss something to a friend.

Visiting

Although Americans are informal, they are generally conscious of time. Appointments are expected to begin promptly. Guests invited to a home for dinner should arrive on time because the meal is often served first. Hospitality takes many forms: a formal dinner served on fine dishes, an outdoor barbecue with paper plates, or a leisurely visit with no refreshments. Most events are casual. Guests are expected to feel comfortable, sit where they like, and enjoy themselves. Guests are not expected to bring gifts, but a small token such as wine, flowers, or a handicraft might be appreciated. Among close friends, dinner guests may be asked to bring a food item to serve with the meal. Americans enjoy socializing; they gather in small and large groups for nearly any occasion, and they enjoy talking, watching television or a movie, eating, and relaxing together.

Eating

Eating styles and habits vary between people of different backgrounds, but Americans generally eat with a fork in the hand with which they write. They use a knife for cutting and spreading. Otherwise they lay it on the plate. When a knife is used for cutting, the fork is switched to the other hand. Bread is often used to push food onto the fork. People eat some foods, such as french fries, fried chicken, hamburgers, pizza, and tacos, with the hands. They generally place napkins in the lap. Resting elbows on the table is usually considered impolite. Dessert, coffee, or other after-dinner refreshments are frequently served away from the dining table. Guests are expected to stay for a while after the meal to visit with the hosts. In restaurants, the bill usually does not include a service charge; leaving a tip of at least 15 percent is customary.

LIFESTYLE

Family

The American family is the basic unit of society, but it has been changing. A generation ago, the average family consisted of a mother, father, and two or more children. The nuclear family often maintained important ties to members of the extended family. Today, the *traditional* American family consists of a mother, father, and one or two children, but this only accounts for about one-fourth of all households. *Nontraditional* family structures are more common, including families with a single parent (30 percent) and unmarried couples with or without children. One of every four children is born out of wedlock. Children may live with or be cared for by grandparents, especially if the parent is young and not married. More than half of all households have no children. A "household" can be comprised of a single person.

Nearly half of all working Americans are women. In homes where both the husband and wife work, men are expected to share household duties. Men also play an important role in raising children. With both parents working, the use of and need for day-care facilities is increasing. This is especially true for single-parent families. Elderly individuals who cannot care for themselves live in retirement communities or other institutions; many live with their adult children. Otherwise, the elderly live in their own homes and comprise a rapidly expanding segment of the population. More than half of all young, unmarried adults (ages 18–24) live with their parents. The American family is mobile. Many people move from one region of the country to another for education, employment, or a change in living conditions.

Dating and Marriage

Dating is a social pastime in the United States. Youth may begin dating in couples as early as age 13, although group activities are more common at that age. More serious dating begins around age 15. Going to movies, dancing, having picnics, participating in sports, or eating out are all popular activities. Casual sexual relationships are common. Many couples choose to live together before or instead of marrying. Still, marriage is the most preferred living arrangement. Weddings can be either lavish or simple, depending on the region and one's religious affiliation. The age for marriage averages 26 for men and 24 for women.

Diet

It is difficult to name a national dish. The abundance of fast-food restaurants in the United States seems to indicate that the national foods are hamburgers, french fries, pizza, and chicken. While these foods are popular among most segments of the population, they reflect a busy lifestyle as much as preference. Americans eat beef, pork, chicken, and other fowl in fairly large quantities, although eating habits have changed with health concerns. Fresh vegetables and fruits are available year-round. Americans consume large amounts of candy, ice cream, and other sweets. Most Americans will readily try any food, and the culture easily adapts to new tastes.

Recreation

Baseball, basketball, and American football are the most popular spectator and participation sports. Public schools provide team sports for the youth. Professional sports are an important part of the culture. Americans also enjoy soccer, cycling, racquetball, handball, tennis, swimming, golf, bowling, jogging, and aerobic exercising. Leisure activities include watching television, going to movies, picnicking, attending music concerts, and traveling.

Holidays

Each state has its own public holidays and each city may have celebrations. National public holidays include New Year's Day, Martin Luther King Jr.'s Birthday (third Monday in January), Presidents' Day (third Monday in February), Memorial Day (last Monday in May), Independence Day (4 July), Labor Day (first Monday in September), Columbus Day (second Monday in October), Veterans' Day (11 November), Thanksgiving (fourth Thursday in November), and Christmas. Although they are not holidays, other observances include Groundhog Day (2 February), Valentine's Day (14 February), St. Patrick's Day (17 March), Easter, Mother's Day (second Sunday in May), Father's Day (third Sunday in June), Flag Day (14 June), and Halloween (31 October).

Commerce

Business office hours usually extend from 8:00 or 9:00 A.M. to 5:00 or 6:00 P.M. However, retail and grocery stores often remain open until 9:00 P.M. and many are open twenty-four hours a day, seven days a week. Suburban Americans shop for groceries and other goods in supermarkets, large enclosed *malls* with department and specialty stores, smaller open-air *strip malls* that feature specialty shops, and chain discount stores. Urban residents shop in many of the same stores but might also buy goods at small, neighborhood shops that are part of large office or apartment buildings.

SOCIETY

Government

The United States is a democratic federal republic. Individual states hold sovereignty over their territory and have rights that are not reserved by the federal government. Each state has its own legislature for enacting local laws. The federal government has a president elected by an electoral college of delegates chosen to represent the vote of the people in each state. Presidential elections will be held in November 1996. The bicameral legislature (Congress) has two houses: the 435-seat House of Representatives, whose members serve two-year terms, and the 100-seat Senate, whose members serve six-year terms. There is a separate judicial branch. The voting age is 18. Due to the two-party political system, Congress is dominated by the Republican and Democratic Parties. Smaller parties are active throughout the country and a few have seats in the legislature, but most act as pressure groups rather than viable political parties.

Economy

The United States has the largest, most diverse, and technically advanced economy in the world. Economic growth is strong. Real gross domestic product per capita is $23,760, the highest in the world. This indicates that the average American has greater buying power than people in other countries. However, while American society as a whole is prosperous, there is a widening gap between the wealthy and the poor, and even between those who earn a comfortable income and those who struggle to meet basic needs.

The country's economic strength is based on diversified industrial and services sectors, investments abroad, the dollar as a major world currency, a demand-driven consumer society, and exports. The services sector employs more people than manufacturing, but industry is still the most vital part of the economy. The United States exports capital goods, cars, consumer goods, food, and machinery. It also exports pop culture (movies, music, television programming, fashion trends, and more), which can fuel demand for American goods. The United States is a key world financial center, and its economic fortunes affect global markets and international economic growth. The currency is the U.S. dollar ($).

Transportation and Communication

The United States has an extensive network of paved highways, and the private car is the chief form of transportation. In large cities, urban mass-transit systems are common. In many areas, however, public transportation systems are not well developed. Many people travel by air, and the United States has the largest number of private airline companies in the world. Train travel is limited to short commuter distances and relatively few cross-country routes. However, goods frequently are transported by train. The communications network is extensive and modern. Most people have a telephone. There are literally thousands of radio and television stations in operation throughout the country; most are privately owned. Freedom of the press is guaranteed. Although newspapers are available everywhere, only about half of all Americans read one every day. Others watch television for news.

Education

Each state is responsible for its educational system. Education is free and compulsory for ages five through sixteen. Most students complete their high school education with grade 12 (at age 17 or 18). Many enter the labor force at that age or seek vocational and technical training. Others enter a university or junior college to pursue higher education degrees. The literacy rate is 99 percent, although functional illiteracy is a problem for many adults.

Health

The health problems facing Americans are different than those in some other countries in that a sedentary lifestyle and risky physical behavior are the two greatest causes of adult health problems. Most people must have private insurance to receive medical care without paying very high prices. The health network is extensive and modern, except in some rural areas. The United States is the only industrialized country in the world without a national (public) health-care system. Each state has its own regulations regarding health care, and there are some national standards as well. Public and private reform movements are changing how health care is provided and paid for. The United States is a world leader in medical research and training. The infant mortality rate is 8 per 1,000. Life expectancy ranges from 73 to 80 years.

FOR THE TRAVELER

While many Americans enjoy traveling to other countries, most vacation in the United States. Tourism is important to many local economies. For information on places to explore, contact local travel agencies or state travel bureaus.

Printed on recycled paper

Oriental Republic of

Uruguay

Boundary representations not necessarily authoritative.

THE AMERICAS

BACKGROUND

Land and Climate

Uruguay covers 68,039 square miles (176,220 square kilometers) and is about the same size as Washington state. Bordered by the Atlantic Ocean, Río de la Plata, and two rivers (Uruguay and Cuareim), the country is nearly enclosed by water. Rolling, lowland plains covered with prairie grass extend across most (about 78 percent) of the country. These plains provide excellent pastures for stock raising and agriculture. Forests and hills dominate the northeast region of Los Cerros. Uruguay's coastline has several fine beaches. Free of many natural disasters, the land has remained relatively unchanged over time, providing a constant and stable environment. The climate is temperate and the seasons are opposite those in North America. June is the coolest month, with temperatures averaging above freezing; January is the warmest month, with Fahrenheit temperatures in the 80s.

History

Originally, Uruguay was home to a group of small native Indian tribes called the Charúas. Spanish explorers first came to the area in 1516. Their first settlement was in 1624 at Soriano. The Portuguese had a presence in the area from 1680 to about 1726, when the Spanish drove them out and pursued colonization. Nearly all of the indigenous population was conquered, killed, or driven out.

A war of independence began in 1811 in conjunction with a general uprising throughout South America. After five years of fighting, Uruguay was unsuccessful in breaking from Spanish rule, despite the efforts of José Gervasio Artigas, leader of the revolt. Although he failed, he is considered the "Father of Uruguay." His efforts inspired another uprising in 1825, when a group of patriots known as the "Thirty-three Immortals" declared Uruguay an independent republic.

At the time, Uruguay was dominated by the Portuguese from Brazil. Spanish rule had effectively ended in 1820 when the Portuguese invaded. The country gained freedom from Brazil in 1828, when full independence was granted. Civil war (1839–51) and war with Paraguay (1865–70) were followed by dictatorship. The first president (José Batlle y Ordóñez) was finally elected in 1903. Ordóñez served two terms, then changed the constitution to allow himself to govern until 1929.

Uruguay was the first South American country to give women the right to vote and among the first to legalize divorce (1905). It was also the first to recognize the rights of trade unions. Through the first part of the 20th century, liberal governments applied socialist principles to the political and economic systems.

In 1970, terrorist violence and unrest due to severe economic problems led President Juan M. Bordaberry to ban all political activities in an attempt to restore control. A military coup in 1973 ousted him from power. Thirteen years of brutal military rule followed, during which thousands were detained and tortured. Elections were held in 1980 to decide whether the military should retain control of the government. When the vote went against the military, the military nullified the results and appointed General Gregorio Alvarez president in 1981.

Reforms during Alvarez's tenure, such as the re-legalization of trade unions, paved the way for general elections in 1984. The military stepped down when the elected president, Julio Maria Sanguinetti, took office in 1985. Basic human rights were restored. To avoid clashes with the military, the new government granted amnesty to personnel suspected of human-rights violations. Elections in 1989 marked the first democratic transfer of power from one elected government to another since 1971. Luis Alberto Lacalle Herrera was elected president. Lacalle encouraged market-oriented solutions to Uruguay's economic troubles, but his plan was not overly popular with the public. His successes in regional co-operation, export expansion, and economic reform were countered by a 1992 referendum that overturned important privatization measures. Lacalle did not run for reelection due to a constitutional ban on consecutive presidential terms. In the 1994 elections, his party (the Blancos) was defeated by Sanguinetti, who returned to office as president for another five-year term.

THE PEOPLE

Population

Uruguay has a population of 3.22 million. Unlike most other nations in South America, it has a low annual growth rate of less than 1 percent. More than 85 percent of the people live in urban areas. People of European descent, mostly Spanish and Italian, account for 88 percent of the total population, a figure also dissimilar to other South American countries, where *mestizos*, people of mixed native Indian and Spanish ancestry, are usually the majority ethnic group. In Uruguay, *mestizos* comprise only 8 percent of the population. Four percent of the people are black (descendants of slaves who were imported by the Spanish). Montevideo (MOAN-tay-vee-DAY-oh) is the capital and largest city, with about 1.5 million people. It is the country's financial, political, and cultural center.

Uruguay's Human Development Index (0.881) ranks it 32d out of 174 countries. People enjoy good access to education, health care, and a decent standard of living. Adjusted for women, the index (0.802) ranks Uruguay 32d out of 130 countries, the highest among South American countries.

Language

Spanish is the official language of Uruguay and is spoken by nearly the entire population. People in nothern border towns often speak *Brazilero* (a mixture of Spanish and Portuguese). Uruguayans speak with a fairly heavy accent quite different from that heard in other Spanish-speaking countries. Most notable is the Uruguayan "sh" pronunciation of *y* and *ll*. For instance, *yo* (I) is pronounced more like "show" than "yoh." Italian and other languages are spoken by small minorities.

Religion

Uruguay is perhaps the most secular of Latin American countries. Although 65 percent of the population belongs to the Roman Catholic Church, less than half regularly attends services. There is no official religion, and church and state are strictly separated. Religious freedom is guaranteed. About 2 percent of the population is Protestant and roughly the same percentage is Jewish. The rest, about 30 percent, belongs to various other Christian churches or non-Christian organizations or professes no religion at all.

General Attitudes

Uruguayans have retained a European bias in their culture and often view themselves as one of the more culturally advanced countries in South America. They are also proud of their country's cultural traditions, such as the *gaucho* (a cowboy-like figure), which is regarded as a symbol of the country's rugged independence. People are conservative in nature and often distrustful of change. They are generally pessimistic, opinionated, and individualistic, but they do not like aggressiveness.

Punctuality is not as important as it is in some other countries. Arriving later than a scheduled time is not improper. However, the more formal a meeting, the more important it is to be on time. Uruguayans are extremely proud of their country, but they are also aware of its problems. They do not appreciate individuals who praise other countries over Uruguay—not because they do not appreciate other countries but because they do not want to be treated as inferior.

The immediate family is close knit and devoted to each other, but community involvement is limited. Uruguayans value education highly and parents will often go to great lengths to make sure their children have good schooling. The elderly are respected and adult children often take care of aging parents.

Personal Appearance

Conservative, well-tailored clothing is the general rule. Subdued colors (blue, brown, and gray) are pervasive. Fashion generally indicates a person's social status. Although women do not wear much makeup or jewelry, they wear dresses more often than U.S. women do. European fashions are common. Businessmen wear conservative suits.

CUSTOMS AND COURTESIES

Greetings

Men usually greet others with a warm, firm handshake. Women (and sometimes men) appear to kiss one cheek when greeting each other. Actually, they brush cheeks and "kiss the air." Men only use an *abrazo* (hearty hug) with family or close friends. Verbal greetings depend on the time of day or situation. *¡Hola!* (Hi) or *¿Cómo andas?* (How's it going?) are common casual greetings. Especially popular in the morning is *¡Buen día!* (Good day).

People generally do not greet strangers when passing on the street, particularly in cities. It might be misunderstood by the other person if one were to extend a greeting or even a smile. Rural people are more open and more likely to greet passing strangers with *¡Ciao!* (Good-bye). They use *¡Ciao!* because they are passing (not stopping) and therefore saying good-bye more than hello.

One greets all individuals in a small group when one arrives at a social function. Group greetings and farewells are considered impolite. In general, people address each other by an appropriate title and surname. For example, *Señor* (Mr.), *Señora* (Mrs.), or *Señorita* (Miss) are used with the family name. Only close friends and family members address each other by given name.

Gestures

To beckon, one snaps the fingers or makes a "ch-ch" sound. The "ch-ch" sound is used for many things, such as getting someone's attention or having a bus stop. People use hand gestures often in conversation. One avoids hiding the hands or fidgeting with them when conversing because such actions can convey unintended messages. Forming a zero with the index finger and thumb is extremely rude. Brushing the back of the hand under the chin means "I don't know." Raising one's shoulders quickly can mean "What's up?"

People do not sit on tables or ledges or rest their feet on objects in a room. They avoid yawning in public because it usually indicates that one is sleepy, bored, or not enjoying the company. On public transportation, it is polite for a man to offer his seat to a woman.

Visiting

Visiting between friends and relatives is important, but busy schedules make this increasingly difficult. On some occasions, visits are arranged in advance. Invited guests are not expected to take gifts to their hosts, but flowers or chocolates are considered a nice gesture. Hosts always offer their guests refreshments (usually soft drinks, tea, coffee, etc.). It is impolite to visit unannounced during regular mealtimes. People in rural areas often visit in the late afternoon or early evening.

Many Uruguayans, particularly men, appreciate having friends come by to socialize and share a round of *mate* (pronounced MAH-tay). *Mate* is a strong, bitter herb tea that is drunk from a gourd through a silver straw (*bombilla*) that has a screen at the bottom. The gourd is filled almost to the brim with *mate* and is repeatedly filled with hot water for each person to finish and pass on to the next. Holding on too long to a passed *mate* is impolite. Men like to share *mate* when discussing sports, politics, or family matters. Sharing *mate* has become a cultural ritual for many.

Eating

Uruguayans eat in the continental style, with the fork in the left hand and the knife remaining in the right. During the meal, they keep the hands (not elbows) above the table rather than in the lap. People often wipe their plates clean with bread as they finish eating. Taking second helpings indicates one likes the food. When finished, one places the utensils side by side on the plate. Dinner guests remain at the table until all have finished eating. Using a toothpick in public or reading a newspaper at the family table is impolite.

Although habits in urban areas are changing to accommodate schedules, Uruguayans traditionally eat a light breakfast of coffee and bread. They have their main meal at midday. When possible, workers go home for this meal. Supper is lighter and later in the evening (9:00 or 10:00 P.M.). Children usually have a snack when they get home from school, and adults may snack around 5:00 P.M.

LIFESTYLE

Family

Strong ties traditionally unite the family. Although extended families do not live together, they play a significant role in the social lives of Uruguayans. The father presides in the home and plays an important role as patriarch. This patriarchal order is still predominant, but the role of women is increasing in significance. A large percentage of women work or study outside the home. Uruguay has more professional women than men; however, men are still expected to earn the better salary. Many couples today share family responsibilities more evenly. The average family has two children and nuclear families are the norm. Nannies or family members often care for children while the mother is at work.

Due to housing shortages, children remain at home until they marry, regardless of their age. Young university students from the interior (rural areas) may stay with relatives in Montevideo while attending college.

A small number of wealthy families generally control politics and the economy. Most families live in more humble circumstances, although few are without basic modern conveniences. Most families rent their home or apartment because of the difficulty and cost involved in financing a home purchase.

Dating and Marriage

Dating customs are similar to those in the United States, although young people usually date only one person at a time. Some rural families have retained traditional European customs in which the young man asks the parents' permission to date the young woman for the first time. He must also request her hand before getting engaged. Young people enjoy dancing, eating out, going to the beach, and watching movies.

Men and women usually marry in their mid- to late-twenties. Both families play a large role in preparing for the wedding and often associate closely after their children are married. The marriage reception usually includes a formal, catered party, from which the couple generally leaves early.

Diet

Uruguay produces most of its own food. Wide varieties of meats, fish, vegetables, and fruits are available. Wheat and rice are the principal grains. Beef is consumed in some form almost daily. Families often eat roasts and stews, served with potatoes and carrots. Meat pies are popular menu items. Traditional dishes include *asado* (grilled beef), *chivito* (steak and egg with cheese and mayonnaise), *milanesa* (fried breaded steak), and *guiso* (ground beef with rice, onion, egg, etc.). Homemade pasta is also common.

Recreation

Fútbol (soccer) is the national sport. Uruguayans closely follow the country's national team in World Cup competitions. Basketball, volleyball, swimming, and other water sports are also popular. Young urbanites like rowing. Middle- and upper-class families are increasingly playing *paddle*, which is a game similar to tennis but played on a smaller court. The ball can be played off the wall or court and is hit by a small racquet with a wooden face that has holes. *Asados* (barbecues) are popular social events. People also enjoy watching movies or television and attending cultural events. Going to the beach is very popular, especially during summer (January) vacations.

Holidays

The most important holidays are New Year's Day; Carnival; Easter (including Holy Thursday and Good Friday); the Landing of the 33 Patriots (19 April), honoring those who fought for independence in 1825; Labor Day (1 May); Constitution Day (18 July); Independence Day (25 August); Christmas Eve; and Christmas. Most Catholics have celebrations to honor local patron saints, and some celebrate name days. Christmas Eve and New Year's Eve are celebrated with large family parties and midnight fireworks.

Commerce

Business hours are from 9:00 A.M. to 7:00 P.M., Monday through Friday. Businesses in interior towns often close for a *siesta* at midday; a *siesta* may last two to four hours depending on the season (longer in summer). Government hours vary between the seasons, running primarily in the morning during the summer and in the afternoon and evening during the winter.

SOCIETY

Government

Uruguay is a democratic republic divided into 19 departments (like states or provinces). The executive branch is headed by the president and vice president. The legislature, called the *Asamblea General* (General Assembly), has two houses: a 30-seat Chamber of Senators and a 99-seat Chamber of Representatives. Beginning at age 18, all citizens are required to return to their place of birth to vote. Uruguay's major political parties include the National (Blanco) Party, Colorado Party, and Broad Front Coalition. A few smaller parties also have legislative representation.

Economy

Uruguay's greatest natural resource is its fertile land. More than 80 percent of the land is used for agriculture and livestock production. Agriculture employs about 20 percent of the labor force. Uruguay is a world leader in the production of cattle and wool. Other products include wheat, rice, corn, and sorghum. The industrial sector is tied to agriculture as well, with the chief industries being meat processing, wool and hides, footwear, leather apparel, and fish processing.

The economy suffered several setbacks in the 1980s due to depressed world prices and uncertain political conditions. Under Lacalle, Uruguay's economy improved, with the annual economic growth rate at more than 7 percent in 1992. However, inflation remained high and poor labor relations resulted in long and frequent strikes. Growth in 1994 was about 4 percent. Since 1995, Uruguay has been a member MERCOSUR, the southern cone common market. The country's currency is the new Uruguayan *peso* (N$Ur).

Real gross domestic product per capita is $6,070, which has improved substantially in the last generation. Personal incomes are modest for most people, but they are sufficient to meet basic and other needs. Members of the rising generation can expect better economic conditions because existing social institutions are able to empower them to take advantage of employment opportunities.

Transportation and Communication

Buses are the primary form of public transportation. Many Uruguayans also travel in private automobiles. Taxis are readily available in the cities. Roads are generally good around major urban areas but are less developed in rural areas. Key highways are paved and well maintained. Uruguay has international airway links. The communications system is moderately developed; the best facilities are in Montevideo. Phone rates are relatively expensive and private lines can be hard to get. The country has a national radio relay system and a number of radio and television stations. Newspapers enjoy wide circulation.

Education

Uruguay has one of the highest literacy rates in South America at 97 percent. Primary schooling is compulsory for nine years. Afterwards, student may choose to enter a government-subsidized *liceo* (secondary school) or receive technical training at a vocational school. The government provides education free of charge through postgraduate studies. This enables Uruguay to boast a very large percentage of professionals (lawyers and doctors, for example). Uruguay has a rich national tradition in the arts and literature. The University of Montevideo, founded in 1849, and the Catholic University have fine reputations throughout South America.

Health

Health care is free and available to all citizens. Uruguay has good health standards, and modern facilities are available in Montevideo. Health and other social programs are highly valued. Private health organizations also provide care for those who can afford it. Sanitation is good. The infant mortality rate is 16 per 1,000. Life expectancy is between 71 and 77 years.

FOR THE TRAVELER

U.S. travelers need a valid passport but do not need a visa for stays lasting less than three months. No vaccinations are required. Uruguay is known for its fine beach resorts and pleasant climate. For more information, contact a travel agent or write to the Consulate of Uruguay, Tourism Office, 1077 Ponce De Leon Boulevard, Suite B, Coral Gables, FL 33134; phone (305) 443–9764. You may also wish to contact the Embassy of Uruguay, 1918 F Street NW, Washington, DC 20006; phone (202) 331–1313.

CULTURGRAM '97

Republic of
Venezuela

Boundary representations not necessarily authoritative.

BACKGROUND

Land and Climate

Venezuela is a tropical land located in the northern part of South America. Covering 352,143 square miles (912,050 square kilometers), it is slightly larger than Texas and Oklahoma combined. The country is roughly divided into four geographical zones: west, central, east, and south. The Andes Mountains dominate the west, where Pico Bolívar rises 16,427 feet (5,007 meters) above sea level. The central zone includes the northern coast and Venezuela's largest cities. To the east of the Orinoco River is a large plain (*llano*). The south is dominated by high plateaus and jungle. Angel Falls, the highest waterfall in the world at 3,212 feet (979 meters), displays its beauty in the southeast. Venezuela's tropical climate is moderated at higher altitudes. The rainy season is from May to November. Temperatures average between 70°F and 85°F (21–25°C), but the mountains can experience cool temperatures, and some Andean peaks are snowcapped year-round.

In 1991, the government created a reserve in the far south for the country's 14,000 Yanomami Indians. Covering 32,000 square miles (almost 83,000 square kilometers), the area is off-limits to farmers, miners, and all non-Yanomami settlers.

History

Before the arrival of Columbus, Venezuela was inhabited by a number of indigenous groups, including the Caracas, Arawaks, and Cumanagatos. Columbus discovered the area in 1498. The Spanish soon began conquering offshore islands and coastal regions. They named the area Venezuela ("little Venice") because the coastal homes were built on stilts, reminding them of Venice. Caracas, the capital, was founded in 1527. The Spanish Crown, which claimed the territory, controlled Venezuela through the 18th century. After various failed revolts, a congress formed and declared independence in 1811. This began a ten-year struggle to achieve the desired freedoms. Finally, in 1821, the forces of Simón Bolívar were victorious at the Battle of Carabobo, and a republic was established. The republic (Greater Colombia) contained Venezuela, Ecuador, and Colombia. It dissolved in 1830 and Venezuela became independent.

Venezuela experienced instability and dictatorships for many years. The 20th century began under a dictator (Cipriano Castro). He was deposed by his vice president, Juan Vicente Gómez, who ruled as a brutal dictator until 1935. More political instability and military coups followed.

A freely elected president came to power in 1958, and democratic elections have been held since. For a time, Venezuela was the most stable South American country and was also one of the wealthiest in the region. Its oil reserves are the largest in the world outside of the Persian Gulf area, and it benefited from high oil prices in the 1970s and 1980s. Carlos Andrés Pérez, who took office as president in 1989, introduced a controversial economic austerity plan to address the plummeting price of oil and rising foreign debt. Riots were put down by the military, and Pérez continued to introduce economic reforms. The reforms boosted gross domestic product and produced growth, but the wealth was concentrated in the hands of a few. Poverty, inflation, and unemployment increased, and violent opposition soon rose to challenge Pérez. He was nearly overthrown by two coups in 1992. In 1993, he was impeached for misusing government security funds. His 28-month prison sentence ends in the fall of 1996.

December 1993 elections brought a former president, Rafael Caldera, to office. He promised to slow privatization that had begun under Peréz, to end corruption, and to stabilize the economy. His task remains daunting, as the country is still politically unstable and Caldera's government does not have a majority in Congress. Price and other market controls implemented in 1994 were designed to stabilize the economy but have eliminated many aspects of a free-market system. Under pressure, Caldera recently announced an economic stabilization plan that reverses his interventionist policies and liberates price controls.

THE PEOPLE

Population

Venezuela has a population of 21 million, which is growing at 2.1 percent annually. More than 90 percent of the people live in urban areas. Caracas has 3.3 million inhabitants. The majority of the population (67 percent) is *mestizo* (mixed Indian and Spanish heritage). In coastal regions, many people (21 percent) are either of European descent (mostly Italian or Spanish) or *mulattos* (mixed European and black). About 10 percent of the population is black and 2 percent is native Amerindian.

Venezuela's Human Development Index (0.859), which ranks it 47th out of 174 countries, has fallen slightly in the last few years. Access to health care, education, and a decent standard of living is somewhat limited among the general population, in spite of the country's economic prosperity. If long-term political stability can be achieved, existing social institutions are in a position to help people realize better economic conditions in the future. Adjusted for women, the index (0.765) ranks Venezuela 40th out of 130 countries.

Language

Spanish is the official language and is spoken by all but the most remote Amerindians. These indigenous groups speak a variety of native languages. There is a great deal of Portuguese influence in Venezuela, so it is not uncommon to hear Portuguese spoken along with Spanish, especially in Caracas. The Spanish spoken in Venezuela differs from that in other Latin American countries. For example, a papaya is called a *lechosa*. The word *papaya* is vulgar in Venezuela. In addition, while a banana may be called a *plátano*, it is also called a *cambur*. English is a required second language in the schools.

Religion

Religious freedom is guaranteed by the constitution. Most people (90 percent) are Roman Catholic. Protestant and other Christian faiths are becoming more prevalent. Venezuelans are somewhat less religious than other Latin Americans. Rural people tend to be more devoted to their faith than urban residents.

General Attitudes

Venezuela is the most urbanized country in South America. Because it is a cosmopolitan nation, changes and improvements occur often in all phases of life. It is not uncommon to see the old and new side by side, whether it be transportation, housing, or entertainment. Venezuelans tend to be spontaneous in their expressions. They feel that the joy of an event or the needs of an individual are more important than the demands of a time schedule. Therefore, they may be late for appointments, and scheduled events may last longer than expected. Venezuelans have a good sense of humor.

Venezuelans also feel great pride in their country. The South American liberator, Simón Bolívar, was Venezuelan. While he is honored in many other nations, he is a national treasure to Venezuela. Most cities have a *Plaza Bolívar* that occupies a block near the city center. It is rude to behave disrespectfully in that plaza or to refer negatively to Bolívar.

Personal Appearance

Venezuelans are quite fashion conscious; urban people wear the latest European styles. In all areas, it is important to look one's best in public. Being neat, clean, and properly groomed is stressed at all levels of society. In the summer, cotton clothing is the most common and comfortable. Shorts and swimwear are worn only in urban recreation areas and at the beach. Native peoples may wear European or traditional dress, or a combination of both, depending on how much contact they maintain with *mestizo* society.

CUSTOMS AND COURTESIES

Greetings

Men greet close friends with an *abrazo* (a full embrace, while patting each other on the back), while women greet with an *abrazo* and a kiss on the cheek. Usually a man and a woman exchange an *abrazo* only if they are close friends or relatives. A handshake is common among acquaintances and strangers. During conversation, people stand much closer than in the United States. Backing away is improper. Some common greetings include *¡Buenos días!* (Good morning), *¡Buenas tardes!* (Good afternoon), and *¡Buenas noches!* (Good evening). The youth generally use the more casual *¡Hola!* (Hi). In addition, greetings often include polite inquiries about a person's health.

Gestures

It is courteous to maintain continual eye contact during conversation. When sitting, a person does not slouch or prop the feet up on any object. Pointing with the index finger can be considered rude; motioning with the entire hand is more polite.

Visiting

When visitors arrive at a home, a business, or the office of a government official, they are often served *un cafecito* (a black, thick coffee) in a very small cup. This is a symbol of hospitality and a way of extending friendship. Polite discussion usually precedes any business matters. Venezuelans generally only invite close friends to their homes, but they will often invite business contacts and other visitors to dine at a restaurant. Venezuelans are hospitable and careful to provide for their guests. In the home, hosts may offer guests refreshments in addition to coffee.

While hosts do not expect gifts from visitors, gifts are appropriate gestures of friendship. A woman appreciates flowers, especially an orchid, the national flower. Men enjoy useful items for the home or office. It is also customary for service personnel, such as garbage collectors or postal carriers, to present a calling card requesting a *regalo* (gift) in the form of money at Christmastime. Failure to respond to this request may result in the discontinuance of service. The expediting of needed services or supplies sometimes requires a tip in advance.

Eating

Out of respect for parents, seats at the head and foot of the dinner table are usually reserved for the mother and father of a family. Invited guests take seats at the table's sides. Venezuelans use various eating styles. Some follow the continental style, with the fork in the left hand and the knife remaining in the right. Others use the style more common in the United States, with the fork in the right hand, unless the knife is picked up to cut something. In this case, the tips of utensils not in current use are rested on the edge of the plate; the handles rest on the table. When a person is finished, he or she places the utensils together at the center of the plate. It is inappropriate for adults to eat on the street. In restaurants, the bill usually includes a service charge, but patrons are expected to leave a small additional tip.

LIFESTYLE

Family

Family ties are strong and most families are close-knit. However, about half of all births in Venezuela are out of wedlock or in common-law marriages. The father dominates in the home, but the responsibility for raising the children and managing the household rests with the mother. An increasing number of women also work outside the home, especially in Caracas. In all, women comprise about one-fifth of the labor force. If members of a family are affluent, they customarily share their wealth with less-fortunate relatives.

Diet

Much of the Venezuelan diet consists of hot foods, casseroles, meat pies, stews, and pasta dishes. One favorite is the *arepa*, a deep-fried thick pancake made from white corn flour and sometimes filled with butter, meat, and cheese. Corn is the basis of many dishes. *Punta-trasera* is a favorite tender steak. Rice is common. *Pabellón criollo* consists of black beans, rice, shredded meat, and plantains. In most cities, open-air markets provide a large variety of tropical fruits and fresh vegetables. Hot chocolate is almost as popular as coffee.

Recreation

The most popular spectator sport in Venezuela is baseball. Venezuelans also enjoy horse racing, bullfighting, and soccer. They participate in fishing, hunting, swimming, tennis, basketball, and golf. Private recreational clubs are expensive and generally are enjoyed only by the wealthy. For entertainment, Venezuelans like to go dancing, to movies, or to cultural events. In rural areas, local festivals provide recreation.

Holidays

Official public holidays include New Year's Day, *Carnaval* (two days before Ash Wednesday), Ash Wednesday, Easter (including Holy Thursday and Good Friday), Declaration of Independence Day (19 April), May Day (1 May), Battle of Carabobo (24 June), Independence Day (5 July), Simón Bolívar's Birthday (24 July), Public Officials' Day (first Monday in September), Columbus Day (12 October), Christmas Eve, Christmas, and New Year's Eve. During *Carnaval*, water fights, parades, dancing in the streets, and other activities are popular. Flowers are important in Venezuelan celebrations. During each holiday, statues of Simón Bolívar, the father of Venezuela, are decorated with colorful wreaths.

Commerce

Business hours generally extend from 8:00 A.M. to 6:00 P.M. (with a one- or two-hour break), Monday through Friday. Government offices maintain similar hours, with regional variations. Urban dwellers purchase basic goods from larger stores and shopping centers, while rural residents rely on local markets, small specialized retail shops, and their own labor for these basics.

SOCIETY

Government

Venezuela is a republic, headed by a president that serves a five-year term. He is the chief of state and head of government. He governs with a Council of Ministers. The Congress of the Republic has two houses, a 52-seat Senate and a 201-seat Chamber of Deputies. The next national elections are in 1998. The voting age is 18. Several political parties are active in Congress, but the largest number of seats are held by the Democratic Action Party (AD), Social Christian Party (COPEI), and Radical Cause Party (Causa R). The president's party, National Convergence, is a minority party in Congress. Venezuela is divided into 21 states, one federal dependency, one federal district, and one territory.

Economy

Venezuela's most important natural resource, petroleum, is the cornerstone of the economy. It accounts for 70 percent of all export earnings. Oil revenues have allowed the country to develop a modern infrastructure. However, oil has also made Venezuela subject to market fluctuations. When the price of oil drops, the entire economy suffers. Therefore, the government stresses economic diversification. The country also exports some minerals and other raw materials. Agriculture employs 6 percent of the population and produces grains, sugar, fruits, coffee, and rice.

After taking office in 1994, Caldera reversed the austerity measures of his predecessor. Implementing strict price and exchange controls, he cut many free-market initiatives and nearly stopped the privatization of state enterprises. In 1994, the economy shrank 3 percent. Adding to concerns about economic stability, several major banks went bankrupt at the end of the year, which led to a severe currency devaluation of the *bolívar* (Bs). Since the currency devaluation, inflation has risen to more than 70 percent. Unemployment is 12 percent

Real gross domestic product per capita is $8,520. Although this figure has doubled in the last generation, it reflects Venezuela's oil wealth that eludes a signficant proportion of the population. The standard of living of most Venezuelans is falling; about 40 percent of the population now lives in poverty. The gap between rich and poor continues to widen and is a factor in the country's violence. Political corruption and the loss of foreign capital remain serious problems for the economy.

Transportation and Communication

Domestic transportation is handled by private cars, buses, taxis, or the domestic airline. *Por puesto* is a popular system of taxi-like automobiles that travel a regular route throughout the city, picking up and letting off passengers at any point. The cost is less than a taxi but more than a bus. Highways are excellent in Venezuela, but driving is often hazardous. Because Venezuela assembles U.S. and other foreign vehicles, many people are able to buy cars. Railroads generally are not used for passenger travel. The communications system is modern and expanding. Private phones are expensive, but public phones are readily available. Several radio and television stations broadcast in Venezuela.

Education

Elementary education is compulsory from ages seven to fourteen. All education, including university level, is free in government-financed institutions. The government has taken great strides in improving the literacy rate, which is currently 90 percent. About three-fourths of all students complete primary school, and most of those children go on to secondary school. But about two-thirds of the overall school-aged population does not attend a secondary school. After secondary school, students may choose from a variety of vocational schools or prepare to enter institutions of higher learning.

Health

Good medical facilities can be found in urban areas, but the best are private and very expensive for the average citizen. Rural facilities lack staff, equipment, and supplies. Only about two-thirds of all infants are immunized against childhood diseases, but the government is trying to improve its performance in this area. The infant mortality rate is 27 per 1,000. Life expectancy ranges from 71 to 78 years. Malaria is active in some rural areas, and cholera has affected some people.

FOR THE TRAVELER

A visa and a valid passport are necessary for U.S. travelers staying more than 60 days. A tourist card issued by an airline is adequate for stays of up to 60 days. All travelers pay a departure tax at the airport. No vaccinations are required, but malaria suppressants are recommended for travel to certain areas. For updated recorded health advisories, call the U.S. Centers for Disease Control International Travelers' Hotline: (404) 332–4559. Bottled water is safest to drink.

There are some beautiful sights in Venezuela, as well as numerous cosmopolitan resorts. For travel information, contact the nearest consulate office. Consulates are located in New York, San Francisco, Miami, Boston, Chicago, and Houston. The Embassy of Venezuela is located at 1099 30th Street NW, Washington, DC 20007; phone (202) 342–2214.

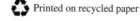 Printed on recycled paper

CULTURGRAM '97™

Wales

(United Kingdom)

Boundary representations not necessarily authoritative.

BACKGROUND

Land and Climate

Wales, situated in the west of Britain, has an area of 8,019 square miles (20,769 square kilometers); it is slightly larger than New Jersey. It is a mostly mountainous nation, bordered by England to the east. The Irish (or Celtic) Sea is to the west; Wales is bounded on three sides by water. The climate is mild and wet, and the landscape is generally green. This makes the land, especially in the countryside, very picturesque. The highest mountain is Snowdon (3,560 feet or 1,085 meters). Valleys just north of Cardiff tend to be densely populated. Wales has three national parks. In 1996, a 70,000 ton oil spill damaged more than 120 miles (190 kilometers) of coastline in Pem-brokeshire Coast National Park (southwestern Wales). Efforts to save fish and wildlife continue.

History

The Welsh are descendants of the Britons, who were already on the island of Britain when the Romans first arrived in the first century B.C. After the Roman withdrawal in the fifth century A.D., Britain was invaded by Saxons who remained in the southeast. The Saxons gradually absorbed the British population and then extended their dominion over what later became England. The Welsh, under their native princes, preserved their independence in the western part of the island until long after the Norman Conquest of England in 1066,

even though William the Conqueror proclaimed himself Lord of Wales in 1071. The Welsh eventually were defeated in the 13th century when Llywelyn ap Gruffydd, known to the Welsh as the "Last Prince," was killed by the English under King Edward I in 1282. In 1301, King Edward named his heir the Prince of Wales, and that title has, since then, been given to the oldest son of the British monarch (England's Prince Charles is the Prince of Wales).

The national hero of the Welsh, Owain Glyndwr, rose against the English in 1400 but without success. Wales was formally incorporated with England by the Act of Union in 1536; this gave Welshmen the same rights as Englishmen, but it outlawed the Welsh language (which survived anyway). The Welsh were early converts to Protestantism, but they broke away from England's established church, leading to the development of separate religious traditions for the Welsh. Scotland joined the Union in 1707 and Ireland in 1801, after which the Union was called the United Kingdom of Great Britain and Ireland. Only Northern Ireland is included today; most of Ireland became independent in 1921.

With the creation of the University of Wales toward the end of the 19th century (by which time Wales had become an industrial nation) there was a renaissance in Welsh culture that has continued to the present. Indeed, since 1950 there has been a growth in Welsh nationalism and in calls for greater

EUROPE

Welsh autonomy. Still, when a 1979 referendum gave the Welsh the chance to have limited self-government, the people chose to maintain their existing ties with England. The Welsh are well represented in British politics; in the 1992 parliamentary elections, Welshman Neil Kinnock (then leader of the Labour Party) was a candidate for prime minister.

THE PEOPLE

Population

The population of Wales is about 2.9 million. About half live in the industrial urban areas of the south—mainly in Cardiff, the capital city, and its hinterland, including the valleys to the north. The rest of Wales is sparsely populated, people living mostly in small towns and villages. The majority are ethnic Welsh, but many English people have recently settled in Wales, especially along the northern coast. There are also people of Irish descent, mainly in the industrial valleys, as well as other ethnic groups. Immigrants from former British colonies are found mostly in Cardiff and large towns such as Newport and Swansea. Wales has suffered from emigration, many of its people having left in search of work. It is not known exactly how many Welsh people live in England.

The Human Development Index (0.916) ranks the United Kingdom (UK) 18th out of 174 nations. Good access to health care, education, and economic prosperity affords people opportunities and choices in their lives. Adjusted for women, the index (0.862) ranks the UK 13th out of 130 countries.

Language

English is spoken nearly everywhere in Wales and has official status. Welsh, a Celtic language related to Breton, Irish, and Scottish Gaelic, is also spoken by about 20 percent of the population. The heartlands of the Welsh language are in the north (Gwynedd) and west (Dyfed). There are also many Welsh-speakers in Cardiff and other areas. Welsh has a degree of official status throughout Wales and can be seen, for example, on road signs and public buildings. The language is used extensively in cultural affairs. Several organizations encourage its use, and a number of magazines and books are published in Welsh. A movement of young people, *Cymdeithas yr Iaith Gymraeg* (Welsh Language Society), campaigns for official status for the language in such areas as law, education, and local government. The Welsh name for Wales is *Cymru* (the land of compatriots); *Wales* is the English name for "the land of the foreigners."

Religion

Wales is basically a secular society. The sister organization to the Church of England (Anglican Church) is the Church in Wales; it has its own archbishop. Most Welsh people are of Christian Protestant (nonconformist) stock, which means they are affiliated through faith or family tradition to the Presbyterian Church of Wales (Calvinistic Methodists), Welsh Baptist Union, Methodist Church (Wesleyans), Union of Welsh Independents (Congregationalists), or Church in Wales. Other Christian denominations are also represented in Wales.

General Attitudes

The Welsh regard themselves as a nation and a people who are different from the English, although many still think of themselves as British as well. They are, after all, descendants of the original Britons who first inhabited the island of Britain. They have a reputation for being warmhearted, gregarious, articulate, and democratic. They are also emotional, inquisitive, quick-tempered, and individualistic. Local pride is well developed; every Welsh person feels a strong attachment to a particular place. Some differences can be observed between northerners and southerners, but they have much more in common. Most Welsh belong to the working class or have working-class origins, but there is also a middle class. Few belong to an upper class. Traditionally, the Welsh have a keen interest in genealogy and a respect for education. Famous Welsh people include David Lloyd George (former prime minister of Great Britain), Dylan Thomas (poet), Richard Burton and Anthony Hopkins (actors), and Tom Jones (singer).

Personal Appearance

There is not much difference between fashions in Wales and those in the rest of Britain, although some clothes are made from Welsh materials. The national costume is seen only on ceremonial occasions. On Sundays, people tend to dress in their best clothes—suits for men and more expensive dresses for women. It usually is possible to distinguish, say, a farmer from an office worker by the style of their clothes. High fashion is seen only in the larger towns. Men wear dinner jackets only on very formal occasions; the expectation of formal dress is usually indicated on invitation cards.

CUSTOMS AND COURTESIES

Greetings

The Welsh are known for their friendliness and hospitality. With strangers, they shake hands on first being introduced but not thereafter unless they have not seen them for some time. A firm handshake is better than a limp one. The Welsh use first names soon after meeting. When meeting for the first time, they say *How d'you do?* or *Pleased to meet you* or even *How are you?*, but not *Hi!* Good friends, especially the youth, greet each other with *Hello* and *Hi*. Women who are close friends may embrace, kissing each other once lightly on the cheek; men may also kiss women this way. Women remain seated when being introduced and shaking hands, while men stand up. Introductions usually begin with *This is . . .* or *I'd like you to meet . . .* or *Have you met . . . ?* or, more formally, *May I introduce . . . ?* If practical, it is polite to introduce each person in the company and to shake hands with them. Children and teenagers are introduced and usually will shake hands. Gentlemen stand when a woman or unknown man enters the room and sit down only after the other person is seated.

Gestures

It is impolite to keep one's hands in one's pockets during conversation, and money should not be rattled in pockets.

Crossing the arms during conversation is acceptable. Legs may be crossed at the knees, but the ankle of one leg should not be placed on the knee of the other. Feet must be kept off all furniture. Maintaining eye contact during conversation is important. Yawns, coughs, burps, and sneezes are covered with the hand. A gentleman gives up his seat on a train or bus to a lady. Women do not put on makeup in public. The Welsh avoid pointing at others and touching others (on the arm, knee, or shoulder), unless they are well acquainted. Whispering is considered impolite. Chewing gum is generally thought unsophisticated, as are public nose picking, nail cutting, and head scratching.

Visiting

The Welsh enjoy good company. They like visiting friends and neighbors in their homes, often without an invitation, for a chat and a cup of tea. It is customary to always offer guests refreshments. Friends who have traveled a long distance are offered a meal. Otherwise, lunch or dinner is usually by invitation. At more formal meals, old friends often bring a bottle of wine and sometimes a delicacy. Strangers on their first visit are not expected to bring a gift, although the hostess will appreciate flowers. It is considered impolite to arrive for a meal more than a half hour late. Sherry is usually served before lunch or dinner; wine is served with the meal, unless the hosts abstain from alcohol.

After the meal, guests are invited to sit in a comfortable place, perhaps to have a cup of coffee. Only friends offer to help with clearing the table or washing the dishes. Guests invited to lunch usually stay for the afternoon. Dinner guests often stay until about 11:00 P.M., except on weekends when they may stay later. It is considered good manners to call the hosts within a day or two after the meal to thank them for their hospitality, or more formally, to write a note, especially after visits of a few days.

Eating

People eat breakfast (toast, marmalade, cereal, bacon and eggs, sausages, and coffee) between 7:00 and 9:00 A.M. and a bit later on weekends. Many eat a lighter breakfast of cereal, toast, and tea or coffee. Lunch (meat or fish, with vegetables) is at about 1:00 P.M. *Tea* (a cup of tea and cakes, or bread and butter with jam) is between 4:00 and 5:00 P.M. Dinner (meat, vegetables, and dessert) is at 7:00 or 8:00 P.M. In Wales, lunch is often called *dinner* and dinner is known as *supper*. *Tea* can be a substantial meal. Guests are sometimes invited for coffee at about 11:00 A.M. Lunch on Sunday tends to be an important meal.

At meals, the food is placed in dishes on the table and guests are asked to help themselves, or else the hostess serves it. The Welsh eat with the knife in the right hand and the fork in the left; they do not use the fork as a scoop or put the knife in the mouth. People do not use fingers to pick up food, except among friends. The napkin is placed on the lap; elbows are not placed on the table. Guests are expected to talk at the table and to share the conversation with the persons sitting next to them. The hostess likes to be complimented on the meal, and second helpings show an appreciation for the food. In restaurants, at the end of a meal, the waiter brings the bill to the table on request, and the host pays the bill either to the waiter or the cashier. Tips of 5 to 10 percent are given to the waiter.

LIFESTYLE

Family

The Welsh usually live in houses rather than *flats* (apartments), which are common only in the cities. Houses may be detached or semidetached, as in suburban areas, or in terraces, as in the industrial valleys. Families usually are closely knit. The nominal head of the household is the father, but the mother plays an equally important role in all family affairs. Many women work outside the home after their children have grown up. Elderly grandparents sometimes live with the family. Unmarried children live at home or move into their own apartment. Single-parent families are becoming more common. The average family has two or three children.

The main family celebrations occur at Christmas and Easter or for birthdays and weddings. There are special celebrations for a person's 18th birthday, when he or she comes of age, is eligible to vote, and gains other legal rights.

Dating and Marriage

Dating usually begins by the age of 15 or 16. Young people enjoy discos, clubs, movies, and parties. They also spend a lot of time in each other's homes. Marriage is legal at 16, but most marry in their mid-twenties. Many young people live together before or instead of marrying. While most couples remain married for life, the divorce rate is on the rise.

Diet

Traditional Welsh dishes include *cawl* (a soup), *bara lawr* (laver bread), *bara brith* (currant cake), and Welsh pancakes, but the Welsh also eat a variety of foods common throughout Europe. The Welsh enjoy all kinds of food, from fish-and-chips to Chinese and Indian cooking to the cuisine of France and Italy. Beer, wine, and other alcoholic drinks are sold in *pubs*. Snacks, tea, coffee, and sandwiches are available in cafés. At home, the Welsh drink water, lemonade, fruit juice, or beer with meals. They drink wine on special occasions or when entertaining guests. After the main course, there is a dessert, sometimes called a *sweet* or *pudding*. It is customary to serve bread and butter with canned fruit.

Recreation

The national sport in Wales is rugby, also known as rugby football. The national stadium is the Cardiff Arms Park. Soccer (or football) and cricket are also popular, among other sports. Most people enjoy watching television or listening to the radio. Most large towns have movie theaters and arts centers. The National *Eisteddfod* (an arts festival and social gathering) is held every year during the first week of August, alternately in the north and south of Wales. The festival is conducted in Welsh. There is also an annual week-long

Eisteddfod for youth. The Welsh like to sing in choirs and enjoy singing in public places (sporting events, *pubs*, etc.). *Pubs* are popular places for socializing.

Holidays

Wales has the same national holidays as England, including New Year's Day, Good Friday (before Easter Sunday), May Day (1 May), the spring and summer bank holidays, Christmas, and Boxing Day. Boxing Day comes from the tradition of giving small, boxed gifts to service people. It is now a day for relaxing and visiting friends. St. David's Day (1 March), named for the nation's patron saint, is not an official holiday but is celebrated with dinners, concerts, and special programs. On St. David's Day, people wear a leek or daffodil (the national emblem) on their clothing.

Commerce

Factory hours are from 8:00 A.M. to 4:30 P.M. and office hours are from 9:00 A.M. to 5:00 P.M. Some people work on Saturday morning. Some shops close for a half day during the week. Offices and smaller shops close for an hour at lunchtime. Supermarkets are open until 8:00 or even 10:00 P.M. Banks are open between 9:30 A.M. and 3:30 P.M. Stores are closed on Sunday because of a law (in England and Wales) banning Sunday trade, but many businesses are trying to have the law changed. Small towns have market days for vendors to sell items from outdoor booths.

SOCIETY

Government

Eight counties, governed by their own councils, make up what is known officially as the Principality of Wales. The Welsh tend to elect Labour Party parliamentary representatives because of Labour's traditional support for greater self-rule in Wales. Britain's constitutional monarchy, with Queen Elizabeth II as head of state, has two houses in Parliament. The 1,200-member House of Lords (with noblemen, life appointees, and Church of England bishops) has little legislative power. Laws are passed by the 651-seat House of Commons, whose members are elected by the people. Wales has 38 seats in the House of Commons. The leader of the majority party (currently the Conservative Party) is appointed by the queen as prime minister (currently John Major). Elections are held at least every five years but can be called sooner. The next elections must be held by May 1997.

Economy

The heavy industries of Wales (steel and coal) are increasingly being replaced by light industries, agriculture, business, and service industries. Unemployment in Wales is usually higher than in England. Income usually is a bit lower. Real gross domestic product per capita is $17,160, which has more than doubled in a generation. This figure indicates that most people have access to a decent income, although there is a larger gap between the wealthy and the poor than in other European countries. Likewise, the middle class is not as prosperous as its counterpart in other European nations. The currency is the pound sterling (£).

Transportation and Communication

While all parts of Wales are accessible by road, some roads are difficult to travel because of mountainous terrain. Because Wales has many small towns that generally lack extensive public transportation, private cars are the main form of transport. Ferries regularly go from Wales to Ireland, and an international airport is located near Cardiff. Cardiff is two hours away (by rail) from London. Many homes have telephones. Television and radio are controlled by the British Broadcasting Corporation (BBC) Wales and one independent company. Channel S4C operates in Welsh. Postal service is reliable.

Education

The education system is connected to that of England. Welsh is taught as a subject, and English is the official language of instruction. However, some schools are teaching classes in Welsh. Schooling is free and compulsory between ages five and sixteen. At age 16, students take the General Certificate of Secondary Education exam. Some spend two more years in school and then take the Advanced Level exams, which basically are used as entrance exams by universities. The University of Wales has campuses in five cities. An Open University offers correspondence and broadcast courses. There are several colleges of education. The Polytechnic of Wales is changing its name to the University of Glamorgan. Many Welsh students attend universities in England. The literacy rate is 99 percent.

Health

Standards of health are comparable to those in England, although industrial illnesses still exist. Wales participates in Britain's National Health Service, under which free medical care is provided on the basis of taxation. There is a small charge for prescriptions and dental treatment. Infant mortality is 7 per 1,000. Life expectancy ranges from 74 to 80 years.

FOR THE TRAVELER

The U.S. visitor to Wales needs a passport but not a visa. No vaccinations are required. Tap water is safe to drink. Many parts of Wales are worth visiting. For suggestions and lodging information, contact the British Tourist Authority, 551 Fifth Avenue, Seventh Floor, New York, NY 10176; phone (800) 462–2748; or the Wales Tourist Board, Brunel House, 2 Fitzalan Road, Cardiff CF2 1UY, United Kingdom. You may also wish to contact the British Information Service, 845 Third Avenue, New York, NY 10022; phone (212) 752–5747. The Embassy of the United Kingdom is located at 3100 Massachusetts Avenue NW, Washington, DC 20008; phone (202) 462–1340.
